80/-

PEASANTS, POLITICS,
and ECONOMIC CHANGE
in YUGOSLAVIA

PEASANTS, POLITICS,
and ECONOMIC CHANGE
in YUGOSLAVIA

By

JOZO TOMASEVICH

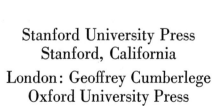

Stanford University Press
Stanford, California

London: Geoffrey Cumberlege
Oxford University Press

1955

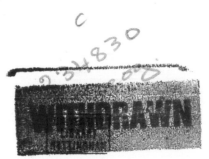

STANFORD UNIVERSITY PRESS, STANFORD, CALIFORNIA

Published in Great Britain and India by Geoffrey Cumberlege,
Oxford University Press, London and Bombay

The Baker and Taylor Company, Hillside, New Jersey
Henry M. Snyder & Company, Inc., 440 Fourth Avenue, New York 16
W. S. Hall & Company, 510 Madison Avenue, New York 22

FOREWORD

AMERICAN life has long been greatly enriched by the contributions of foreign-born citizens to our arts, sciences, and literature. These have broadened and deepened American understanding of many countries from which the newcomers have sprung. Here is a notable example in the social sciences.

This illuminating volume needs no advance endorsement from one who is an almost total stranger to most of the field that it cultivates so fully. But long, deep friendship for the author has impelled me to honor his request that I write a brief Foreword to the book, which I am proud to have watched grow from small beginnings into a *magnum opus*.

The subject is highly complex, and the basic materials are scattered and far from complete or trustworthy. Only mastery of several languages, great industry and pains, and extreme patience born of love of two peoples have enabled the writing of a story that is surprisingly comprehensive and in good perspective. One can see not only the trees but the forest. And different readers will find particular chapters especially appealing to their diverse interests.

The unique position of Yugoslavia today, as the only Communist country with which the United States not only coexists but co-operates, heightens the value of the work. By skillfully tracing the complicated history of its many segments up to 1918, and by detailed analyses of the structure and functioning of Yugoslavia's interwar state, economy, and society, the author has laid strong foundations for interpreting developments since World War II. Now, as heretofore, the "legacy of the past" is "difficult to erase."

In a period in which the problems of underdeveloped countries engage wide interest and international concern, it is especially advantageous to have so extensive an account of a European country struggling to overcome its heritage of backwardness. Notwithstanding the very limited success of the first regime of the ostensibly unified state, "Yugoslavia of the interwar period was a great improvement over the political conditions under which the South Slav nations lived until 1918." And along with the low state of agriculture and industry, and the persistence of poverty, illiteracy, agricultural overpopulation, malnutrition, and ill health, it is impressive to be shown various evidences of social progress.

After thoroughgoing disruption during World War II, can this progress be resumed and accelerated under the postwar regime? This question presses for answer. And it is a tribute to the present work that many readers will find it hard to restrain their impatience to read its sequel.

JOSEPH S. DAVIS
Director Emeritus

FOOD RESEARCH INSTITUTE
STANFORD UNIVERSITY

ACKNOWLEDGMENTS

IN THE COURSE of writing this book I have received help from many people and institutions. I wish to express my thanks, first of all, to Dr. Joseph S. Davis, Director Emeritus, Food Research Institute, Stanford University, for the reading of an early draft, and for his encouragement and steady interest in the progress of this work. I owe him more than can be expressed by words. I also thank Dr. Merrill K. Bennett, Director, Food Research Institute, for his friendly interest and support, and for the financial assistance by the Institute which made the publication of this study possible. I gratefully acknowledge the grants-in-aid from the Rockefeller Foundation and the Food Research Institute which enabled me to carry out part of the research.

In securing source material I was greatly helped by the staff of the Hoover Institute and Library, Stanford University, and of the Library of the University of California, Berkeley; by several relatives in Yugoslavia; and by a number of friends in this country and Yugoslavia. To all my warmest thanks.

Dr. A. W. Ford of San Francisco and Dr. Mirko Lamer of Washington, D.C., read most of the manuscript. Dr. Helen C. Farnsworth and Dr. V. P. Timoshenko, both of the Food Research Institute, read chapters 22–25 and 17–19, respectively. Mrs. Sandra C. Howell, University of California, Berkeley, read chapter 25, and Dr. L. E. Gibson, my colleague at San Francisco State College, read chapter 14. It is a pleasure to thank them for the comments and suggestions they made and to express my appreciation to Mr. P. Stanley King for preparation of the maps.

J. T.

NEW YORK CITY
March 22, 1955

CONTENTS

MAPS

PEASANTS, POLITICS,
and ECONOMIC CHANGE
in YUGOSLAVIA

CHAPTER 1

INTRODUCTION

YUGOSLAVIA of the interwar period was established at the end of World
War I. It was partly a result of internal political forces within the various areas which in 1918 were consolidated into the new state that aspired to and worked for the liberation and unification of the South Slav
peoples.[1] To a greater extent Yugoslavia was the result of the general
political and social forces at work in Europe, which culminated in the
conflagration of World War I, and resulted among other things in the
collapse of several empires and in the disintegration of the two multinational empires—the Habsburg and the Ottoman empires—which for
centuries controlled or strongly influenced the destinies of the nations
of the Danube Basin and the Balkans. Yugoslavia rose on the ruins of
these two empires. Throughout the interwar period the new state remained quite unsettled in regard to internal political matters, and its
conditions in regard to foreign political and economic relations were
also beset with great difficulties.

The new state included, as Map 1 shows, seven different areas which
on the eve of World War I formed either sovereign states or parts of
the Austro-Hungarian Monarchy. The sovereign states were Serbia
and Montenegro. As a result of the Balkan Wars of 1912 and 1913,
both of these states were greatly enlarged at the expense of the Ottoman
Empire. Serbia acquired a part of Macedonia, the so-called Old Serbia,
and a part of the Sandjak of Novi Pazar, while Montenegro obtained the
other part of the Sandjak of Novi Pazar and some territory near Lake
Scutari. Areas formerly belonging to Austria-Hungary were the following: (1) Croatia-Slavonia, which was a separate unit within the Hungarian half of the Dual Monarchy, enjoying a limited degree of autonomy. (2) Vojvodina, consisting of a part of Baranja, Bačka, and the
western parts of the Banat, which up to 1918 formed an integral part of
Hungary. Two additional small areas in the northernmost part of the
new state around the Mura River, called Medjumurje and Prekomurje,
were also parts of Hungary. The former was in 1918 included with

---

[1] The term South Slavs includes also Bulgarians, but throughout this study the
terms South Slavs and Yugoslavs refer only to those South Slav peoples living within
Yugoslavia since 1918.

MAP 1

TERRITORIAL FORMATION
OF YUGOSLAVIA
1913-1919

Kingdoms of Serbia & Montenegro before 1913

Acquired from Bulgaria in 1919

P.-Prekomurje M.-Medjumurje

Croatia-Slavonia and the latter with Slovenia. (3) Slovenia, not a historical province as such, included during the interwar period the territory of the former Austrian Crown land of Carniola, a considerable section of Styria, and a small section of Carinthia. All this territory belonged up to 1918 to the Austrian half of the Dual Monarchy. (4) Dalmatia, also a province within the Austrian half of the Dual Monarchy. (5) Bosnia and Herzegovina, which from 1878 to 1918 formed a special Austro-Hungarian condominium, administered by the common Austro-Hungarian Ministry of Finance.

As originally conceived, the objective of this study was to investigate the development of the Yugoslav peasantry and agriculture during the interwar period alone. It soon became clear, however, that proper understanding of that period on the part of the readers with little or no background in the history of the South Slav peoples would be impossible without an exhaustive introduction covering their development in the pre-1918 years. It should be said at the outset that although the South

Slav lands included in Yugoslavia in 1918 are peopled by closely related nations, never before 1918 had they been united into one state. In
the course of their previous existence these nations and/or some of the
specific areas were under the influence of various political powers and
socioeconomic forces and developed different political and socioeconomic institutions and by 1918 reached various levels of political,
economic, and cultural development. All these differences were carried
over into the new state and gave it an extremely heterogeneous character. Thus to make it possible to view the conditions and developments
during the interwar period in a meaningful historical perspective, it was
necessary to present a review of the pre-1918 history of the various
South Slav areas.

The study as finally completed consists of three separate parts:
Part One deals with the development of the South Slav nations or of
specific areas prior to World War I as well as with certain developments which were common to all these peoples during the century preceding World War I; Part Two deals with the short but eventful period
of World War I which resulted in the formation of Yugoslavia; and
Part Three deals with the development of Yugoslav peasantry and agriculture during the interwar period.

Part One is divided into two subparts. Chapters 2 to 5 describe the
specific developments in the various South Slav nations and/or territories prior to 1914. The reading of these chapters will show the extraordinary variety of political and socioeconomic conditions under
which these peoples lived from the time of their settlement in the
Balkans in the early Middle Ages to World War I. A large portion of
space in these chapters is devoted to the problems of land tenure and
factors causing its changes, while most of the other aspects of the social
and economic history of these areas has been covered very briefly. There
is no doubt, however, that during the Middle Ages and in fact in the
South Slav lands until the present time, the problem of land tenure and
its effects on agricultural production and the distribution of income in
agriculture represented the most important socioeconomic problem of
these lands. It was agriculture which was the source of livelihood for
the overwhelming majority of their population. Actually there was no
other choice because the social and economic history of the South Slav
peoples, with the exception of the history of land tenure, is as yet very
little examined. To present properly the social and economic history of
these peoples it would be necessary to cover not only the history of the
medieval South Slav states and partly the history of Byzantium, Hungary, and Venice, which affected profoundly the life of the South Slav

peoples for many centuries, but also many aspects of the history of the Habsburg and the Ottoman empires, which between them fully controlled almost all of the South Slav areas for four or five centuries preceding World War I. This is a task requiring a great deal of preparatory work to open and utilize the vast amounts of source material relating to the social and economic history of the South Slav peoples which is reportedly available in various Yugoslav, Turkish, and other archives and institutions. This undertaking can be satisfactorily accomplished only by co-operation of experts from various fields of social sciences, and will undoubtedly take a long time before it is successfully completed. It seems that a considerable number of Yugoslav social and economic historians are now engaged in that effort, and various products of their labors will be mentioned in the course of this study.[2]

Since the economic history of the South Slav peoples is as yet only slightly investigated, we made no attempt to establish a scheme of periodization of the economic history of the South Slav lands. The course of economic development of the various areas differed so much that it probably will be impossible ever to establish a common scheme applicable to all these areas. The periodization of the history of the South Slav peoples by the interwar political historians was orientated purely by political factors.[3]

Chapters 6 to 9 deal with some general developments which were common to all South Slav areas during the century preceding World War I, although these developments had different intensity and were

[2] For a review of the problems of Yugoslav social and economic history, with special reference to problems which were little investigated or completely ignored, see Josef Žontar, "Hauptprobleme der jugoslavischen Sozial- und Wirtschaftsgeschichte," *Vierteljahrschrift für Sozial- und Wirtschaftsgeschichte*, XXVII, 347–73. The only general economic history of the South Slav lands is the study by Nikola Vučo, *Privredna istorija naroda FNRJ* (Economic History of the Peoples of the Federal People's Republic of Yugoslavia). It was written as a textbook from the Marxian point of view, and shows all the earmarks of a rush job and of a dogmatic approach to the economic history of the South Slav peoples. Books and articles dealing with the economic history of specific areas and with specific topics will be referred to as we move along.

Complete identification of all works referred to in this study may be found in the Bibliography, pp. 703–26. For the convenience of readers unfamiliar with the South Slavic languages, all titles of books in these languages are translated and follow the original titles in parentheses. The titles of articles published in Yugoslav serials and periodicals are given only in translation. When official publications contain both the Serbo-Croatian and the French text, as was the case with the general statistical annual, the foreign trade statistics, and agricultural statistics, only the French title is quoted.

[3] Milko Kos, Ferdo Šišić, and Stanoje Stanojević, "Periodization of Yugoslav History," *Jugoslovenski istoriski časopis*, I, 313–35. In fact, the authors do not present a general, common periodization of Yugoslav history, but separate periodizations of the Slovenian, Croatian, and Serbian histories, respectively.

variously timed in different areas. Among these common developments were the rise of the bureaucratic state and the rise of nationalism,
the rapid growth of population, the changes in the structure of agricultural production, the spread of market and money economy and the
growth of the capitalist forms of enterprise, the growth of communications and industry, the changes in the peasant family in the direction
of greater psychological and economic individualization, and so forth.
In Chapter 10 we review the size-structure of farm units in various
South Slav areas around the turn of this century and in Chapter 11
we give a short recapitulation of these developments during the preceding century.

The discussion in Part Two, or Chapter 12, dealing with World
War I does not need any additional explanation. Chronologically this
period forms the bridge between the events covered in Part One and
those in Part Three. More important is, however, the fact that World
War I gave birth to the new Yugoslav state and thus to the whole range
of problems covered in Part Three.

Part Three represents the bulk of the study. In it we endeavor to
give a rather complete picture of the conditions and of the development
of the Yugoslav peasantry and agriculture during the interwar period.
As throughout the centuries prior to World War I, so during the interwar period, political factors and changes affected profoundly the life
and welfare of the peasantry of Yugoslavia. Thus, in addition to out-
lining the political framework under which the Yugoslav peoples lived
during the interwar period (Chapter 13), we pay considerable attention
to political factors also in the discussion of many other topics, primarily
in connection with the agrarian reform, agricultural credit, taxation,
and the like.

Chapter 14 deals with the natural resources base of Yugoslav agriculture. It shows great differences in the endowment of various areas
with land resources and their quality. Chapters 15 to 17 discuss the
growth and problems of population in agriculture, with special emphasis on the problem of agricultural overpopulation, which was by far
the most important and most difficult socioeconomic problem in Yugoslavia during the interwar period. Chapters 18 to 20 discuss the general
topic of land tenure during the interwar period in Yugoslavia, with
special emphasis on the problems of agrarian reform following World
War I and the size-structure of farms. Chapter 21 is devoted to the discussion of the organization of production factors in Yugoslav agriculture and the state of agricultural technology. Special stress is put on the
lack of balance in the combination of land, capital, and labor at the

disposal of most farm units and of the agriculture as a whole and the resulting underemployment of manpower and often also of capital resources.

Chapters 22 and 23 discuss the crop and livestock production. Chapter 24 discusses the problem of food utilization in Yugoslavia during the period 1934–38 and the problem of nutrition. Thereupon follows a discussion of health conditions in rural areas in Chapter 25. Chapter 26 deals with the relationship between agriculture and the market. Finally, Chapter 27 presents the problem of agricultural credit and Chapter 28 the problem of agriculture and taxation.

During the past 150 years the South Slav peoples have been going through a series of revolutionary changes in their political, social, and economic life. The character and the course of these changes up to the beginning of World War II we have woven into the general presentation of the various aspects of the social and economic life of the Yugoslav peasantry. The speed of political and socioeconomic change has been greatly intensified during the past ten years under the Communist regime. The objectives and methods of this change differ greatly from those which were characteristic of the development prior to 1940, but the conditions of the Yugoslav peasantry since 1940 are outside of the frame of reference of this study.

CHAPTER 2

SERBIA

THE SERBS, presently the most numerous of the South Slav peoples, settled in the central Balkans during the sixth and the early seventh centuries. There exists some difference of opinion in regard to the question of whether the Serbs came to the Balkans from their trans-Carpathian homeland in one or in two separate migrations, but this problem was much less discussed in regard to the Serbs than the Croats. The exact nature of the migration of the South Slavs into the Balkans still remains an open issue among historians.[1]

The territories settled by the Serbs were under the control of Byzantium. For several centuries the Serbs lived in their new land in tribal formations and loose tribal associations recognizing Byzantine authority. In this period the basic territorial and political units among the Serbs, as among the Croats, were the *župe*. The chiefs of the *župe*, coming from the leading clans and families of the tribe, were known as *župani*. While in the beginning of their life in the Balkans the members of the tribes might have been on a rather equal political and economic footing, the leading families from which the chiefs were recruited soon developed into hereditary ruling tribal nobility.

[1] For a general review of the problem of the arrival of the South Slavs into the Balkans and of the early stages of their life in the new homeland, see Bogo Grafenauer *et al.* (eds.), *Istorija naroda Jugoslavije* (History of the Peoples of Yugoslavia), I, 63–130. This history, which covers the developments of the South Slav peoples from their arrival in the Balkans to the beginning of the sixteenth century, represents the most ambitious attempt to give a history of all South Slav peoples. As a product of the new Yugoslav scholarship, it is written from the official, Marxist point of view. While it represents a corrective against the almost exclusively political treatment of the history of the South Slavs by earlier writers, which often had a romantic and chauvinist flavor, the authors of this new history occasionally strained their arguments to the breaking point in order to fit their scheme of historical interpretation. Each part of the study contains valuable bibliographical data. The authors also repeatedly point out issues which are still matters of controversy among Yugoslav historians. With regard to the specific problem of migrations of Serbs and Croats into the Balkans, see the writings referred to in footnote 1, Ch. 3.

THE FORMATION OF THE SERBIAN MEDIEVAL STATES

When some of the *župani* succeeded in establishing their control over the neighboring *župe* and concentrated in their hands the power over several tribes and a wider area, the tribal phase began slowly to give way to the development of rudimentary state forms among the Serbs. This process thus took the form of territorial expansion and conquest, whether achieved by the forces of the victorious tribal chiefs alone or with outside military help. The emerging rulers were dependent both on the outside protectors and to a certain extent also on the subjugated chiefs of other tribes. They shared with the latter some of their political authority and left to them part of the lands and prerogatives that they already had or granted them such lands and prerogatives in exchange for their loyalty and military support. Thus the former tribal structure gave way not only to rudimentary state forms but also to the beginnings of the feudalization of the social structure.

One factor which acquired great importance for all South Slavs soon after their arrival in the Balkans and remained a basic force in their life ever since was Christianity. The South Slavs accepted Christianity during the eighth and ninth centuries. It came to them from Byzantium, Rome, and in the case of the Slovenes partly from the German lands. After the separation of the Roman and the Eastern churches, the Serbs remained firmly within the orbit of the Eastern Church while the Croats and Slovenes were kept in the orbit of the Roman Catholic Church. From the last quarter of the fourteenth century Islam became the third leading religious force in the Balkans.

In addition to the various external forces that affected their development, these Serbian tribes and their *župa* organizations had from the beginning a power within their own midst to contend with. That was the remainders of the semi-Romanized Illyrian population and of the so-called Danubian Romanic population or Vlakhs, both of which, however, we include under the common name of Vlakhs. During the Roman rule the Vlakhs represented the bulk of population in those parts of the Balkans which were later taken by the Serbs. In order to avoid being completely submerged during the *Völkerwanderungen*, including the Slavic migrations, the Vlakhs withdrew partly into the mountainous areas and partly to the Dalmatian coastal towns and islands. Those who withdrew to the mountainous areas pursued a nomadic or quasi-nomadic pastoral type of economy. Their basic political organization was the pastoral village or *katun*, which continued under the new conditions to carry on the social and political functions of the Vlakh population. As they lived in the same territory with the Slavic population and recognized their authority, a certain mutual influencing of the Vlakh and the South Slav population took place, which continued for many centuries.

The first Serbian states were formed around the middle of the ninth century.[2] There were two geographic areas in which separate early Serbian states developed: the area of the present-day Montenegro and some surrounding territory in which the state of Dioclea (Duklja) arose and the area of present southwestern Serbia where the early state of Rascia (Raška) emerged. Being nearer to the coast and to some Byzantine strongholds in the Adriatic, Dioclea was under strong Byzantine influences in both political and socioeconomic matters. Rascia, on the contrary, being located in the center of the Balkans and occupying a rugged mountainous area quite isolated geographically, was under considerably weaker Byzantine influence, whether this influence came from the Adriatic coast or from across the Morava River in the east.

Like the Croatian state in the western Balkans, so the early Serbian states were established as vassal states recognizing foreign authority. Serbian states had to recognize Byzantine authority most of the time, but at some intervals their territory was under Bulgarian influence. Needless to say, as soon as the power of these foreign states declined or their attention was fully occupied elsewhere, and their grip on the Serbian vassal states relaxed, the latter tried to reduce as much as possible their dependence on the foreign protecting power. With the exception of short intervals Byzantine authority over the Serbian states was quite effective until close to the end of the twelfth century.

In 1168 Byzantium reorganized its hold over the Serbian lands by dividing the whole area among several sons of one of the Serbian *župani* and established them all as its vassals. Soon thereafter the attention of Byzantium was engaged in Asia Minor, and one of these vassals, Stevan Nemanja, began to extend his influence over the territory of his brothers, removed one of them altogether, and proclaimed himself as the great *župan*. His tendency to expand his rule brought him repeatedly into conflict and wars with Byzantium and his brothers, but in the end he succeeded in consolidating his position as the ruler of all of Serbia and by 1190 virtually liberated Serbia from any dependence on Byzantium. One of the important achievements of Nemanja was that he conquered

---

[2] For the medieval history of Serbia, see among the new studies Bogo Grafenauer *et al.* (eds.), *op cit.*, pp. 229–55, 328–514, and Anto Babić, *Istorija naroda Jugoslavije* (History of the Peoples of Yugoslavia), pp. 79–88, 115–22. The basic work on the history of medieval Serbia, still unsurpassed, is Konstantin Jireček, *Istorija Srba* (History of the Serbs), four volumes, translated from the German by Jovan Radonić. See also Vladimir Ćorović, *Istorija Jugoslavije* (History of Yugoslavia), pp. 89–202.

the state of Dioclea and established effective union between that area and Rascia, the latter becoming the center of the later medieval Serbian state and the base for its further expansion. This expansion took place in practically all directions in the course of the following century and a half: toward the Sava and Danube rivers in the north, toward the east across the Morava River, northward along the Adriatic coast, and, above all, toward the Vardar River Valley and the Aegean. Nemanja was the founder of the Nemanid dynasty which ruled Serbia until the 1360's, extended its frontiers, and brought it to such political and cultural greatness that in the middle of the fourteenth century Serbia aspired to become the heir of the Byzantine Empire.

Another achievement of Nemanja was the successful suppression of the Bogomil heresy which originated in, and came to Rascia from, Macedonia. As will be shown in Chapter 4 Bogomilism played an all-important role in the Bosnian medieval state.

With the expansion and consolidation of the Serbian state under Nemanja the development of the feudal system in Serbia advanced, primarily by taking over or imitating Byzantine feudal forms and institutions. It was also at this time that the Serbian rulers began the practice of building and richly endowing monasteries and churches in Serbia. This practice was continued by the other Nemanids and made the church into a fundamental economic and political factor in the state.

Nemanja's immediate successors continued his work of territorial expansion and political consolidation of the Serbian state.[3] An exceedingly important development in regard to the political consolidation of the state, which has had great political and cultural consequences for the Serbian people ever since, was that Nemanja's sons (Stevan and the monk Rastko, the latter St. Sava of the Serbian Church) succeeded in 1219 in obtaining permission from the Patriarch of Nicaea to establish an independent Serbian archbishopric, which was the foundation of the Serbian national church. As the church was formerly under the strong influence of the Greek clergy, its independence meant a curtailment of Greek cultural and political influence in the country and closer co-operation of the Serbian state with its own church. This act also helped to eliminate almost completely the influence of the Roman Catholic Church in Serbia.

During the thirteenth and the first half of the fourteenth centuries Serbia expanded under various rulers from the Nemanid dynasty, primarily in the direction of Macedonia and the Aegean. The more it ex-

[3] Bogo Grafenauer *et al.* (eds.), *op. cit.*, map facing p. 344.

panded into the Greco-Byzantine areas the greater became the Byzantine political and land-tenure influences. The principal way in which the new areas were ruled was by distributing most of the land to the Serbian feudatories, although a certain number of Byzantine feudatories continued in possession of their estates. But also the more the state expanded the more varied and stronger became certain centrifugal tendencies of the big feudatories in various areas. Undoubtedly, this was the chief political weakness of the Serbian medieval state and was one of the important reasons of its later downfall.

FEUDALISM AT THE PEAK OF SERBIAN MEDIEVAL POWER

In the middle of the fourteenth century Serbia was the most powerful state in the Balkans. In this, its golden era, Serbia's political, social, and economic organization was marked by a mixture of predominantly Byzantine with some Western European feudal forms, retaining also much of the native Serbian customs and institutions. Its political and social structure at that time is best illustrated by the famous Code of Tsar Stevan Dušan (1331–55) which was promulgated at the State Council in 1349 and amended in 1354.[4] The nature of the Serbian medieval feudal order is clearly indicated also in many preserved grant charters—*chrysobulls*—the earliest dating from the beginning of the thirteenth century, by which the Serbian rulers donated huge land estates and granted many privileges to churches and monasteries, as was common practice in Byzantium and in Western Europe at that time. It is interesting to note, however, that no royal grant charters of feudal estates to temporal feudatories are preserved.

At this stage in medieval Serbia, the ruler owned all of the land in the country, that is, he exercised eminent domain over it, but the bulk of it was given to various churches and monasteries and to the temporal feudatories either in full ownership or *baština*, or only for usufruct as

---

[4] For an English translation of the Code with notes and commentaries by Malcolm Burr, see *The Slavonic and East European Review* (London), XXVIII, No. 70 (November 1949), 198–217, and No. 71 (April 1950), 516–39. From Burr's commentary one sees many parallels between the Code of Stevan Dušan and the Western European and British institutions of that period. Not all legal rules in operation in medieval Serbia were codified, however. According both to Stojan Novaković, who issued and commented upon the Code of Tsar Dušan in 1898, and to Teodor Taranovsky, *Istorija srpskog prava u Nemanjićkoj državi* (History of Serbian Law in the Nemanid State), the traditional legal customs were so well known and part of the institutional fabric that there was no need to codify them in their entirety. For a detailed study of the land-tenure conditions in medieval Serbia on the basis of various grant charters to the monasteries and on the basis of the Dušan Code see Stojan Novaković, *Selo* (The Village), and Milan Wlainatz, *Die agrarrechtlichen Verhältnisse des mittelalterlichen Serbiens.*

pronoia. Thus, in actual ownership all lands belonged either to the ruler, to the Church, or to the temporal feudatories. As will be shown presently, various types of dependent subjects were settled on these lands. As a general rule, the relation of the individual to the landownership determined his position in the political and social structure of the country.[5]

In addition to having the right of eminent domain over all land in the country, the ruler was a large landowner. He had his own serfs and other dependent people, and his estates were managed by special administrators. The ruler's economic power was enhanced by the exclusive privilege of ownership of such natural resources as minerals, and the right to mint money and to collect custom duties. Moreover, the ruler obtained a tax from the feudatories as a token of their vassalage. The personal treasury of the ruler and the treasury of the state as such were one and the same.

The second feudal power in the state was the Church—the Serbian Eastern Orthodox Church—which thus had a tremendous political and economic power. Church lands were in the form of *baštine* or full, heritable property, freely disposable. The Church obtained its estates primarily by grants from the ruler and to a small extent by grants from other owners of *baštine*, and these grants could not be withdrawn either by the ruler or by other grantors under any circumstances. Church estates were exempt from all taxes and labor services, including the general transport service, as well as from the duty of supplying the ruler with the feudal levy. The Church lords had full judicial power over their serfs, while this right of the temporal feudatories was somewhat limited. The only obligations of the Church arising from obtaining these land grants were to supply transport needs for the ruler when he himself traveled and to feed the poor. The Church properties centered mostly around monasteries, endowments of the Serbian rulers, which are the only material witnesses of the Serbian medieval greatness still in existence. There was only one limitation imposed on the monasteries—they could not have more than 50 monks for each 1,000 settlers on monastic estates. The political purpose of richly endowing

---

[5] Teodor Taranovsky, *op. cit.*, I, 133–36; III, 11–13. This is as good a place as any to say that at no place in this study do we attempt to give a general definition of the terms feudalism and serfdom, although we repeatedly use them. This omission was made on purpose, because the real meaning and content of these institutions varied greatly among various areas and in various periods of time. It is therefore necessary to keep in mind the specific character of these institutions as here described for various areas and their changes in the course of time. It is especially important to remember the great differences between the various systems of feudalism originating in Europe and the relationship between landlords and serfs under that system and the Ottoman feudalism and its way of regulating that relationship.

the Church and of granting it great political privileges was to ensure its moral and political support for the ruler. Thus the Church served as a counterbalance to the powerful temporal feudatories who, as in other countries, were willing to obtain from the ruler all grants and privileges that he was able and willing to give, but at the same time tried to be as little dependent on him as possible.

The third group of landowners were the temporal feudatories, who were divided into the high and the lower nobility and the *pronoia* holders, a distinction clearly indicated by the size and nature of their estates and the offices they held in the state. Some of these nobles were heirs of the old tribal nobility, others were created by the grants of land and titles from the ruler.

Feudal lands in Serbia were of two categories: the heritable estates or *baštine*, corresponding to the alod in Western Europe, and the *pronoia*, corresponding to the military fief or feud in Western Europe. In the first case the grantee became full owner of the land and was able to dispose of it freely. *Baštine* were heritable both in the male and female line to the third cousin. Not even the ruler could take such grants back or even buy them without the consent of the owner. Of course, if the grantee were to commit treason or failed to keep up the obligations stipulated in the grant charters or having the force of traditional custom, his lands reverted again to the ruler. The *pronoia*—which came to Serbia from Byzantium—is mentioned in Serbia for the first time around 1300. After the conquest of Byzantine territories in Macedonia it became widespread in all parts of the Serbian state.[6] In the case of *pronoia* the ruler remained the owner of the land, the grantee obtaining only the usufruct. He could neither sell, convey, nor bequeath the land, nor donate it to the Church. And such fiefs could be withdrawn by the ruler at any time, which, in fact, was done only when the grantee failed to live up to his obligations. While the *pronoias* were not explicitly heritable, according to Serbian practice some of them were heritable and were held by the same families for a long time. Another development in regard to the *pronoia* in Serbia was that some monasteries, unlike those in Byzantium, had their own *pronoia* holders whose function was to defend the monastic properties.[7]

[6] On Byzantine feudalism see: Georg Ostrogorsky, "Agrarian Conditions in the Byzantine Empire in the Middle Ages," in J. H. Clapham and Eileen Power (eds.), *The Cambridge Economic History of Europe*, I, 194–223; Georg Ostrogorsky, *Istorija Vizantije* (History of Byzantium) (translation from the German), *passim*; Georg Ostrogorsky, *Pronija—prilog istoriji feudalizma u Vizantiji i u južnoslovenskim zemljama* (*Pronoia*—A Contribution to the History of Feudalism in Byzantium and the South Slav Lands).

[7] Georg Ostrogorsky, *Pronija*, p. 130.

The grants of land to the feudatories, both those in the form of *baštine* and those in the form of *pronoias*, represented a remuneration for services already performed for the ruler and for the obligation of continuous military service. The Serbian feudatories—as those elsewhere—were obliged to go to war and to supply additional warriors at their expense depending on the size of their land grants. From the point of view of the ruler the assurance and maintenance of the feudal levy was the primary objective of the whole feudal system. The Code of Tsar Dušan did not, however, specify the number of warriors that each feudatory was obliged to supply, but simply said "according to law," meaning actually according to the traditional customs. Feudatories whose fiefs were located at the frontiers of the state had the double duty of protecting the frontiers against foreign armies and against foreign plunder bands.

The *baština* or alod land proprietors were free from all obligations of *corvée* and all tithes to the ruler in exchange for their military obligation.[8] They were, however, obliged to supply transport services for the needs of the ruler, to the *corvée* for building of fortresses, and to the policing of roads. Furthermore, they were obligated for the payment of a tax—the *soće*—to the ruler as a sign of their vassalage. The ruler also had the right to decree new taxes and new labor services. Needless to say, the feudatories were only the "collectors" of these services and taxes for the ruler, all of these burdens being actually borne by the serfs and other dependent population. The *pronoia* holders had the same obligations to the ruler as the holders of the alod grants. The institution of subvassalage was known and the subvassalage of lower nobility on big estates belonging both to the temporal feudatories and to the monasteries was practiced.

Feudal estates belonging both to temporal feudatories and to the monasteries—especially the large estates—were often composed of lands in different parts of the country and were usually exploited in two ways. A part of the land was managed directly by the landlord or his administrators. This part of his estate was worked essentially by his serfs obliged to render *corvée*, but to some extent also by other types of dependents of the feudatory. Another part of the estate was in the hands of the serfs, who, in addition to the just mentioned *corvée* obligation, had to pay a tax in money or produce to the feudal lord. It is not known what portions of land belonging to the feudatories were worked in these two different manners at various periods of time. But as in other parts of Europe where similar conditions existed, that varied from time to

---

[8] Teodor Taranovsky, *op. cit.*, I, 22–27.

time and on various estates, depending on specific conditions. Economically, however, the two portions of the feudatory's land formed one unit. Since big feudal lords and monasteries also had artisans and slaves among their subjects, such estates were essentially self-sufficient economic units, practicing to a considerable degree a division of labor in their production organization. Having some surpluses of various commodities produced on their estates and lacking other commodities that they could not produce, both the estates of the temporal feudatories and those of the monasteries participated to a considerable extent in market economy. They sold primarily agricultural products such as grains, wine, and olive oil, as well as livestock and livestock products, and bought such products as salt, textiles, leather products, and various utensils and tools.

The feudal superstructure in medieval Serbia rested on several classes of working people, neither politically nor economically free and known under the general name of commoners or *sebri*. The main group among the commoners in the mid-fourteenth century were the serfs or *meropi*. They were the chief source of labor power on all *baštine* and *pronoias* and according to law were "tied to the land." As such, the serfs were included with all grants and other transfers of land. The obligations of the serfs on the estates of the king, monasteries, and the temporal feudatories differed somewhat in extent; in the best position were the serfs on monastic estates. The serfs were tied to the land in a hereditary manner, but as long as the serfs worked the land on which they were settled they could not be evicted. Of course, eviction would not have served the interests of the feudal lords, because only land with serfs on it was productive and only by having serfs was the feudatory able to command their labor for work on those parts of his estates which he himself managed. Moreover, the inability of the feudatory to evict his serfs was probably a survival from the earlier rural organization when the peasants were free and were full owners of their land. Whether the peasants were subjected forcefully by the feudatories or surrendered voluntarily in order to enhance their security even at the price of complete dependence, the rule that the serf holds the land in a hereditary fashion was of extraordinary importance to him. This custom exercised, and has continued to exercise ever since that time, a powerful influence on the psychology of the Serbian and of the South Slav peasants in general. In the spirit of Serbian custom, which had essentially the nature of generally acceptable law, the peasants considered the land they worked as their own *baština*, that is, full, heritable, property, subject only to feudal obligations. Thus, in actual life there were in medieval Serbia two types of *baštine*: the absolutley free *baštine* of the feudatories and monasteries, and subordinated *baštine*, that is the properties of the serfs, subject to feudal obligations toward the feudal lords.[9] Both in medieval Serbia and in later centuries, customary law and statutory law distinguished between the *baština*, the land that the peasant family inherited from its forefathers, and the land that was bought or was brought into the family as dowry. Actually this distinction is observed practically in all South Slav lands to the present day. This is an interesting distinction, because it is primarily the *baština* that the peasant considers as his sacred property and as a part of his body and soul.

According to Article 68 of the Dušan Code, the serf was obliged to render two days of *corvée* each week to the feudal lord, one day annually of hay cutting and one day of work in the vineyards. He was also obliged to pay a tax amounting to one gold perper (worth about 6 to 10 gold francs in the fourteenth century), which could be paid either in money or in grain. While it is not clear how these taxes were assessed, it appears that they were set by families or households. Moreover, the serf was obligated for special work services or *bedba* to the feudal lord for pressing jobs, such as plowing, harvesting, and work in the vineyards. This work obligation was also of a general nature but not strictly fixed. There was finally the *corvée* for special public purposes away from home, or *zgon*, which seems to have been a heavy and greatly resented obligation in medieval Serbia. Transport service of the serfs was also a heavy obligation. Furthermore, certain serfs on the estates of the ruler and the temporal feudatories were obligated for military service with their landlords. The above obligations should be taken as a general approximation of the existing conditions, because both prior to the enactment of the Dušan Code and thereafter, there were considerable variations in the obligations of the serfs on various types of estates.[10]

Since the serfs were the chief source of labor in the feudal society and since they also possessed most of the tools for agricultural work, the assurance of their obedience was one of the basic concerns of the state administration, equally important to the ruler, to the Church, and to the temporal feudatories. The Code is therefore replete with provisions protecting the hold of the landlords over the serfs and of one class of landlords against abuses on the part of the other in respect to the serfs. That the serfs did not take their dismal situation without opposition becomes obvious from Article 69 of the Code, which states: "Commoners have

9 Stojan Novaković, *op. cit.*, pp. 155–57.
10 *Ibid.*, pp. 215–25; Milan Wlainatz, *op. cit.*, pp. 206–59.

no council . . ." and proceeds to specify the cruel penalties if they should assemble and act contrary to the provisions of the law. According to Article 139, the serfs of the temporal feudatories and those on royal estates had the right to sue their landlords in the imperial courts for illegal exactions in work and tithes. It is not known, however, when this right of the serfs was actually introduced in the Serbian feudal system or how effective it was.

The second group of dependent people in medieval Serbia were the *sokalnici*, who were primarily engaged as cooks, helpers, servants, and artisans on feudal estates. They also worked small plots of land for their sustenance. Their position seems to have been somewhat worse than that of the serfs. Special rules obtained in regard to lower clergy living in villages, but they also had to make a living by raising crops on land provided by the feudatories.

The third group of dependent people were the slaves, or *otroci*. They were the chattels of their owner and were employed both in household work and in agriculture. But, as in other countries of Southeastern Europe, this social category was declining fast during the Middle Ages and in the South Slav lands disappeared completely by the fourteenth or fifteenth century.

A special social and racial group in medieval Serbia—at that time apparently still quite numerous—were the Vlakhs. They were separately treated by the Dušan Code. The Vlakhs lived in pastoral villages or *katuni* and pursued a nomadic or quasi-nomadic life. This group of people and their social organizations were largely absorbed by the medieval South Slav feudal states, but at that time they still retained their group individuality. In medieval Serbia the Vlakhs were subject to the payment of a grazing tax in kind, to tithes from their flocks, to labor services as shepherds, and especially to the transport services to the landlord on whose lands their flocks grazed. A part of the Vlakhs rendered a special military service connected with the upkeep of the horses of the ruler and the feudatories in times of peace and during military operations, which was later maintained under the Turks (see footnote 27, p. 29). The position of the Vlakhs was apparently somewhat easier economically than that of the serfs. The Dušan Code prohibited intermarriage between the Serbs and the Vlakhs.

Furthermore, there were in the Serbian society some remnants of free peasants, peasants who owned fully and absolutely their *baština*, having no obligation toward any feudal lord or monastery, but having to render to the ruler specified taxes, *corvée* for public purposes, as well as military service. Owing to the fact that they lacked protection of a temporal feudatory or monastery, their position seems to have been exceptionally difficult. They therefore often submitted voluntarily to a feudal lord or a monastery and let themselves be impressed into serfdom in order to better their lot. The importance of this group seems to have been very small in the fourteenth century because the Dušan Code failed even to mention them separately.

The authority of the central government and thus the stability of the state in medieval Serbia depended primarily on the personality of the ruler. Centrifugal forces manifested by the leading feudatories in various areas made the state exceedingly vulnerable whenever weaklings were at its helm. There were defections among powerful feudatories even under Dušan the strongest of the Serbian rulers. Serbian medieval history showed therefore a great number of crises owing to this inherent weakness of the feudal state. As pointed out earlier, these centrifugal forces became stronger as the state expanded into non-Serbian areas in Macedonia and Epirus. The absence of strict rules regarding succession contributed to the instability of the state as struggles among the various pretenders to the throne were a normal occurrence. But here, too, the divergent interests of various powerful feudatories played an important role. Moreover, a social order like feudalism based on systematic exploitation and oppression of the mass of population by a small caste of feudatories was also weak because of the dissatisfaction of the population at large. Thus, while Serbia under Dušan expanded by leaps and bounds and was the most powerful state in the Balkans, it disintegrated upon his death into a series of areas, ruled by powerful feudatories minding exclusively their personal and regional interests, without even a semblance of central rule.[11] It was in such conditions that Serbia was called upon to defend itself against the upcoming militaristic power of the Osmanli Turks.

Economic life[12] in medieval Serbia, like that in other medieval South Slav states and areas, was based on agriculture and animal husbandry. The primary crops were wheat, barley, and oats. Cultivation of flax and hemp was widespread. From repeated references in preserved documents to vineyards, it seems that the production of wine was important, especially in the coastal areas and in Macedonia. The cultivation of olives in coastal areas was also widespread. All of these crops were actually cultivated during classical antiquity in the whole area around the Mediterranean. Livestock raising was of basic importance not only among the Vlakhs in the mountains, but also among the Serbian

---

[11] Bogo Grafenauer *et al.* (eds.), *op. cit.*, pp. 407–44 and map following p. 416; A. A. Vasiliev, *History of the Byzantine Empire, 324–1453*, pp. 609–24.

[12] Konstantin Jireček, *op. cit.*, III, 170–258.

population. Sheep, cattle, and horses were the chief types of livestock raised. The raising of bees was also widespread, resulting from the high demand for wax for church use and household lighting and for honey, which was partly used for the preparation of a fermented drink.

As already mentioned, large feudal and monastic estates produced considerable amounts of commodities for the market and were buyers of other commodities. All preserved records indicate that internal trade in medieval Serbia, as well as export and import trade, was of considerable proportions. The bulk of foreign trade was in the hands of the merchants from Dubrovnik and Venice. Both of them, but especially the former, had strong merchant colonies in all larger Serbian towns and managed trade by caravan over well-established routes. In addition to agricultural and livestock products, medieval Serbia exported large quantities of metals from its rich silver, lead, and copper mines. In fact, some of the mining towns in medieval Serbia were the centers of trade and of foreign merchant colonies. Mining activity was financed primarily by capital supplied by the merchants from Dubrovnik and Venice. The ruler obtained a share of the proceeds. Skilled workers were the miners from Saxony who came to Serbia from the Carpathian mining districts. They were given considerable concessions by the ruler in order to further mining activity. The metals were transported by caravan to the coastal towns in Dalmatia and thence across the Adriatic Sea to the West.[13] Preserved records testify to a considerable development of many handicrafts in medieval Serbia, but most of the handicraft activity was carried on by the *sokalnici* within the large estates of the ruler, the temporal feudatories, and the monasteries. A part of the trade was carried on by barter, but the circulation of various foreign coins and the coining of silver money by many Serbian rulers, as well as the payment of taxes and tithes in money, indicate that money economy was well advanced. Political and economic advance of the country was accompanied also by big strides in the field of culture and art, which is shown primarily by architecture and art in the Serbian medieval monasteries.

The ensuing Turkish rule put a stop to this development, and national survival rather than political, economic, and cultural advance was the main task of the Serbian people.

---

[13] Some of these mines had already been worked during Roman times. After the Turkish conquest of Serbia, mining activity continued for some time but then almost completely stopped. During the interwar period many of these mines were reopened, mostly by British-owned companies. These mines were nationalized after World War II; they continue to be worked, and the export of nonferrous metals plays an important role in the Yugoslav export trade.

TURKISH CONQUEST OF SERBIA AND INTRODUCTION OF THE TURKISH SYSTEM OF LAND TENURE

Less than a score of years after the Serbian medieval state reached its apogee and after the warrior people of Osmanli Turks established themselves for the first time in the Balkans (1354), Serbia, already disrupted and greatly weakened, received the first staggering blow at their hands in the Battle of Maritsa River in 1371. The defeat of the Serbs shortly after in the Battle of Kosovo Field in 1389[14] virtually destroyed the Serbian medieval state. By 1459 even its last vestige, the vassal despotate of Smederevo (Semendria) was eliminated. Shortly thereafter the other neighboring states or provinces fell. Bosnia was crushed in 1463, Herzegovina in 1482, Montenegro in 1499. Gradually the Turks conquered most of the Dalmatian mainland and parts of southwestern Croatia. Spilling over the Sava and Danube rivers they conquered most of Slavonia and Hungary during the 1520's and 1530's. They remained in the latter two groups of territories until 1699 or 1718, respectively.[15]

With the elimination of the Serbian medieval state its domestic feudal class also disappeared, mostly by extermination, but partly also by emigration into Hungary and toward the West, to some extent by falling into lower social strata, renouncing the worldly life and going into monasteries, and to a small extent by accepting Islam.

It is essential for our study to set down some of the characteristics of the Ottoman state organization and especially of its system of land tenure,[16] because the Ottoman Empire affected for centuries the political, cultural, and economic developments, and especially the land tenure, in most South Slav lands. In Serbia, as in other countries conquered by the Turks in which relatively few natives accepted Islam, the Turks controlled the communication lines, towns, strategic points, and the border areas. The Christian population was excluded from political activity in the state, but it was left mostly in peace, especially in the earlier

[14] This battle and defeat inspired the most famous ballads in the Serbian folk poetry and, through them, had a peculiar hold on the mind of the Serbian people up to the present time.

[15] For the growth and decline of the Ottoman-controlled territory in Southeastern Europe from the fourteenth to the twentieth centuries, see Harry W. Hazard, *Atlas of Islamic History* (Princeton, 1951), pp. 21–33.

[16] The material in this regard is voluminous, but only two items in English are listed. Albert H. Lybyer, *The Government of the Ottoman Empire in the Time of Suleiman the Magnificent*, pp. 45–61 and *passim*: H. A. R. Gibb and Harold Bowen, *Islamic Society and the West*, I, 39–199, 235–75. An earlier standard work, Josef von Hammer, *Des osmanischen Reiches Staatsverfassung und Staatsverwaltung* (two volumes, Vienna, 1815), was, unfortunately, not available to this writer for consultation.

phases of the Turkish rule, free to preserve its religious beliefs and church organization,[17] to continue or develop its local political and social institutions, and to engage in its economic activity. All this was allowed and proceeded within the limits set up by the conqueror, subject only to the payment of prescribed taxes, tithes, and the rendering of a relatively small amount of *corvée* for public purposes and for the feudal lords. Until the times of great reforms (*Tanzimat*) during the nineteenth century, the state paid little or no attention to the promotion of economic activity. "The idea of labor for the public welfare or of effort toward progress was not present" in the system of Turkish government. "Change came, not by conscious striving toward betterment, but by growth, development, and decay, the effects of which were adjusted when it became necessary."[18] As long as the Empire existed, namely, until the end of World War I, it showed little genuine economic and social progress.

The whole military system of the Ottoman Empire, and closely bound up with it the administrative and taxation organization of the country, followed the principles of a plunder economy. The Empire was often at war. It appears that proper functioning of its whole political, military, and economic organization was predicated on continued expansion—the Empire was feeding upon victory. Its whole political and economic system began to decay after its advance into Central Europe was stopped, and the decay was greatly intensified after it began to lose territory toward the end of the seventeenth century.

Owing to the fact that the Ottoman Empire was an agglomeration of many areas and peoples in different relationships to the Sultan, and that whenever advantageous to the Turks they maintained or modified various institutions that they found in areas which they conquered, the rights and obligations of various areas and groups of people toward the Sultan were different. All of these factors were also reflected in the organization of land tenure and taxation in various parts of the Empire. Albert H. Lybyer classified all land in the central portion of the Ottoman Empire into tithe lands, tribute lands, and state lands.[19] A Turkish legal authority whose treatise on the Turkish feudal organization in the seventeenth century, dating from 1653,[20] was discovered in the 1930's by

[17] Ladislas Hadrovics, *Le peuple serbe et son église sous la domination turque,* pp. 44 ff.

[18] A. H. Lybyer, *op. cit.,* pp. 193–94.

[19] *Ibid.,* pp. 31–32.

[20] Hamid Hadžibegić, "A Treatise by Ali Čauš of Sofia About the Timar Organization in the Seventeenth Century," *Glasnik Zemaljskog muzeja u Bosni i Hercegovini,* New Series, II (Sarajevo, 1947), 139–205. This publication has changed its name several times—now called *Glasnik Zemaljskog muzeja u Sarajevu*—but we quote it throughout under the above, original name.

Yugoslav students of Ottoman history, divided all areas of the Ottoman Empire with respect to administration and land tenure into two main groups: provinces in which the government collected taxes and tithes directly, paid the armed forces and other government servants, and took the surplus of revenue as their contribution to the general cost of government; and provinces with military fiefs. Land in the former provinces belonged to the categories of tithe and tribute lands, and here there were no military fiefs. Most of the land in Asia Minor and all the land in the European Turkish domain were, however, according to all writers, in the second category, i.e., state land, and the bulk of it was distributed in the form of military fiefs to the feudal cavalry (spahis) and to holders of various offices.

In the spirit of the *Sheri* law based on the Koran, all land in territories conquered from the infidels was considered God's land. The Sultan as the head of the state was considered the owner of all that land and exercised over it the right of eminent domain. All issues pertaining to land and the rights and obligations of the population of an area toward the feudal lords and toward the state were regulated by various *kanuns* or laws, which, however, had to be in agreement with the *Sheri* law. Of the state land used for agricultural purposes there were four main categories:

1. The *mulk* land, which the Sultan granted in full ownership to individuals, who thereby were free to sell it, divide it, or dispose of it as they pleased, subject only to paying taxes to the ruler. In the European areas such grants were made only to the Turkish settlers in Macedonia and Thrace, to Mohammedanized peasants in Bosnia and Herzegovina, and apparently also to some Christian peasants in Bosnia.[21] These land grants were called *čiftliks* when granted to the Mohammedan peasants, and according to the quality of soil they varied between 60 and 150 *donums*.[22] These were peasant farms which could be cultivated with one team of oxen and were sufficient to assure the livelihood of a single family. This type of *čiftliks* was legal, but with the exception of areas with large Mohammendan peasant population they were quite insignificant in importance in comparison with the *čiftliks* which developed illegally in more recent times through the degeneration of the Turkish feudal order. Whenever *čiftliks* are mentioned in the following pages,

[21] Branislav Djurdjev, "The *Kanun-name* for Bosnia of 1530," *ibid.*, New Series, III, 189–200.

[22] A *donum* varies in size. Usually it is 1,600 square arshins, or one-twelfth to one-fifteenth of a hectare. In Bosnia in more recent times it had been set at 1,000 square meters or one-tenth of a hectare.

we have in mind the latter type. Real estate in cities and towns, and houses and a plot of land around the house of one *donum* in rural areas, were also in the category of *mulk* property. Needless to say, *mulk* lands were open to seizure on behalf of the Sultan until the middle of the nineteenth century.

It is interesting to point out that the disposition of the peasant farms in the form of *čiftliks*, in spite of the fact that they were *mulk* land, was somewhat limited. This limitation had two basic objectives: on the one hand, the state wanted to preserve these peasant farms as a source of tax revenue; on the other, the state wanted to preserve the land in the hands of small peasants and to prevent the accumulation of land in few hands. It was further thought that the peasants were tenants on the ruler's land and that their *čiftliks* could be taken away if they were not worked.[23]

2. The *wakf* lands, often very large in extent, were religious and charitable endowments either granted by the Sultan or bequeathed by the owners of *mulk* land. Once declared *wakf*, a fact attested by a special document, neither status nor the purpose of such endowments could be changed. A portion of the former Serbian monastic estates were declared *wakf*. These lands were free from all taxes and could not be mortgaged. Each *wakf* was administered by a special administrator subject to the supervision of a judge (*khadi*). The purpose of the *wakfs* was to finance various religious, educational, and public welfare institutions and activities, and with their revenue mosques, schools, public libraries, hospitals, bridges, poor houses, bath houses, and the like were built and supported. This was a very important function because no other public welfare institutions or provisions for public buildings, except those serving military and administrative purposes, existed in the Empire.[24] It often happened also that the owners of *mulk* land transferred their land to the *wakf* for a nominal price, reserving the right of usufruct for the family in a heritable fashion, thus creating a sort of family fideicommissum. This was obviously done not only for reasons of security—that is, to prevent usurpation of such land by powerful feudatories and officials—but also to ensure a subsistence for the family and to prevent squandering by some of its members. Much of the land and buildings owned and administered by the *wakf* was mismanaged

[23] Omer Lutfi Barkan, "*Čiftlik*," Serbo-Croatian translation by Hamid Hadžibegić of an article published in the Turkish edition of *The Encyclopaedia of Islam* in 1945, *Godišnjak Istoriskog društva Bosne i Hercegovine*, II, 287–98, esp. 290–91.

[24] Vladislav Skarić, "The Influence of Turkish Rule on Social Life," *Knjiga o Balkanu* (Book on the Balkans), II, 139. Regarding these endowments see also W. Heffening, "*Wakf*," *The Encyclopaedia of Islam*, IV, 1096–1103.

and some writers think that the institution of the *wakf* was partly to blame for the economic and agricultural decadence of the Ottoman Empire.

3. A third, small part of the state land was kept by the Sultan himself as his personal estates. They were administered by special officials and the revenue went into the Sultan's coffers.

4. The bulk of the state lands in Asia Minor and in European Turkey was distributed in the form of military fiefs to various officeholders and to the feudal cavalry or spahis. The organization of the military fiefs, their nature, and their evolution since the middle of the fifteenth century form the most important and most interesting problem of Ottoman feudalism. As originally established, this system of military fiefs was to support the feudal levy and to serve as a principal source of tax revenue.

Two other types of land were of some importance for agricultural purposes: the *metruke* and the *mevat* lands. The former were lands used for public purposes or for common needs of the villagers, such as grazing land or for timber and woodcutting. The *mevat*, on the other hand, were lands at some distance from inhabited places, which were not occupied. These lands could be freely cleared and occupied with the permission of local officials, and after three years of utilization the squatter was able to obtain for it a deed of usufruct, the land becoming subject to feudal obligations and taxes.

THE ORGANIZATION OF MILITARY FIEFS

The military and the administrative organization of the Ottoman Empire when it was at the zenith of its power—that is, during the reign of Suleiman the Magnificent (1520–66)—was one and the same thing. This remained so formally to a large extent until the period of great reforms (*Tanzimat*) during the first half of the nineteenth century, when the army and government administration were reorganized along the European patterns. It was, however, during the sixteenth century that the classical forms of Turkish feudalism were developed, and it was these forms which in later centuries degenerated and gave way to new features in the land-tenure system in the European areas of the Turkish Empire.

At the time of Suleiman the Magnificent the standing armed forces of the Ottoman Empire were composed of two chief components, the Janissaries and the spahis of the Porte, with certain other smaller armed corps.[25] These were the only armed forces which were paid out of the

[25] A. H. Lybyer, *op. cit.*, pp. 90–113; H. A. R. Gibb and Harold Bowen, *op. cit.*, pp. 39–71.

Sultan's treasury. The Janissaries, or the "new troops," were originally recruited from boys obtained by the Sultan by gift, capture, purchase in the slave market, or from tribute or levy in blood. Blood levy was drawn from the healthiest and most gifted boys from about 10 to 20 years of age among the Christian population (last time undertaken in Serbia in 1638). After Mohammedanization and thorough schooling and indoctrination these boys became members of the military elite. They were slaves of the Sultan and composed with him what Lybyer and most writers after him called the Ruling Institution, which ran the state. The interpretation of the Moslem laws and the education of the members of the Ruling Institution were in the hands of the *ulema*, whose members were recruited from Moslem families. The mercenary troops formed perhaps half of all armed forces. They were kept primarily in Istanbul but considerable contingents were kept in other parts of the Empire. It is important to stress that, in the classical period of this rule, the members of the Ruling Institution could not marry and that children of Moslems were ineligible to enter its ranks. The intention was to eliminate nepotism and to force the members of the Ruling Institution to devote all their energies and thoughts to the state.

On the other hand, there was the feudal spahis.[26] They obtained military fiefs, or, more precisely, a part of income from such fiefs, regularly a tenth, but occasionally more, of gross production, and various other payments from the peasants settled on these fiefs. The largest fiefs were called *khasses* and yielded an income of above 100,000 aspers annually, followed by the ziamets with an annual income from 20,000 to 99,999 aspers, and timars with an annual income up to 19,999 aspers. The *khasses* were granted, as a rule, only to various high officeholders, or, rather, they went as salary with high offices, while the two smaller types of fiefs were granted to individual feudatories as such. Each fief was composed of one or a number of *kiličs* or sabres, a *kilič* amounting to between 3,000 and 6,000 aspers and being identical with the income which was capable of supporting and supplying one warrior of the feudal levy. Thus the income assigned to each fief strictly determined how many *kiličs* or warriors each fief had to supply. In each district the spahis were organized as a territorial army with their special fief-holding officers as heads. In the case of war they drew together and formed the feudal levy. Only a part of the feudal levy went to war, while the other part, according to prevailing conditions, remained at home to maintain law and order, protect the borders, collect the tithes, send supplies to

---

[26] In addition to the already quoted literature, see in regard to the military fiefs especially J. Deny, "Timar," *The Encyclopaedia of Islam*, IV, 767–76, and J. Deny, "Ziamet," *ibid.*, pp. 1221–22.

the levy in the field, and carry other duties. As long as the Empire was expanding, some Christians were among the spahis, but after the end of the seventeenth century when the Empire began to crumble, Christian spahis became very rare.

Military fiefs above a certain size were obtained only by a decree from the Sultan, while the smaller ones were distributed by the district spahi chieftains (beglerbegs), again with a special decree. The holders of the ziamets (*zaims*) and timars (timariots) obtained the fiefs not in a heritable or even lifelong fashion; the land remained the Sultan's and the spahis could not in any way dispose of it. They were simply beneficiaries of a part of the income from the timars and ziamets as long as they satisfactorily performed their duties. The spahis could be deposed instantaneously. But actually these fiefs belonged to the same family for generations, though upon the death of the father one of the sons had to apply anew for the fief and pay certain taxes to have it confirmed. Thus the position of the spahis was totally different from the holders of the alod lands in the West, but similar to that of the holders of military fiefs in Central and Western Europe and to the holders of the *pronoias* in Byzantium and medieval Serbia. The spahi did not have the function of a judge over the settlers on his fief. Originally the spahis had to live in the territory of their fief, and they could not farm out the collection of tithes, but both of these limitations were later dropped.

Owing to the fact that the fiefs were the economic basis of the feudal cavalry, and the fact that the settlers on these fiefs were the chief sources of taxes, a special administration of the fief lands was maintained in the Imperial Treasury listing their location, their income, the exact number of serf families, the number of tax heads, etc. Each district also had its own special administration listing all of the fiefs in its territory and their particulars. All changes regarding the holding of these fiefs were registered with the administrations of fief lands.

With the exception of a few offices which carried *khasses* with them, there were no other fiefs of this category in the South Slav lands at any time. Even the number of ziamets was relatively low. The overwhelming number of all fiefs not only in the South Slav lands but elsewhere was of the timar type. Actually this type of fief was so predominant that the whole Turkish feudal system is often referred to as the timar system. At the beginning of the nineteenth century there were in Serbia about 900 spahis, almost exclusively timar holders.

In addition to *khasses*, ziamets, and timars, there were several other types of military fiefs, but with the exception of the hereditary captainships in Bosnia and Herzegovina (see p. 98) they were of no importance in the South Slav lands. Moreover, some Turkish officials were granted the right to collect certain types of taxes or other income (*mukatas*) which took the place of a salary or of an addition to a salary. In the South Slav lands there were certain auxiliary troop formations composed of Christians, which in consideration of special duties enjoyed various tax exemptions and other privileges. The most important among these formations appear to have been the *voynuks*.[27]

Timars and ziamets in the earlier times usually consisted of two separate portions: (1) the so-called *hassa* land or an amount of land that was given to the spahi individually, which he was free either to work himself or to lease to the surrounding peasants, and (2) the land on which were settled the Christian serfs or *reaya* (including some Moslems), who held the *tasarruf* or the right of usufruct of that land and were obliged to render to the spahi the prescribed tithe in produce and pay various other tithes and dues. The right of usufruct was confirmed by a title deed or *tapu* which was issued by the spahi for a fee. The peasants held the land in a heritable fashion, though rules of inheritance differed from area to area and over periods of time. As long as the peasants worked the land the spahi could not evict them from their farms. Nor was that in the latter's interest, either personally as a participant in the income from these farms or as a protector of the Sultan's interests. But the law

---

[27] The non-Moslem population in the Ottoman Empire was not allowed, generally, to bear arms and therefore did not go to war, but paid a special military exemption tax instead. (However, since the 1820's, as a part of the program of great reforms [*Tanzimat*] the problem of equal rights of the non-Moslems, including military service, have been a matter of discussion.) But there were numerous exceptions in earlier times in addition to the service of a few Christian spahis already mentioned. Thus various Vlakh groups in the Balkans served as special, auxiliary troops called *martolosis*. Another auxiliary group recruited from among the Vlakhs was the *voynuks*. Their obligation in peacetime was to care for the horses of the Sultan and of various high government officials for about four months annually. In war they carried special arms, provided forage and tended the horses, and served also as a part of the scouting troops. These Vlakhs performed similar duties in the medieval Serbian and Bulgarian states and the institution was taken over by the Turks. In the course of the seventeenth and eighteenth centuries the *voynuks* were absorbed by Turkish feudalism, though some remainders persisted in Bulgaria until the nineteenth century. Special Christian troops called *derbendjis* served as watchmen and leaders of caravans in mountain passes. In all these cases the occupation seems to have been hereditary in the families or villages and these groups were freed from all obligations and taxes on their *baštine*, with special rules regulating the inheritance of these properties. Christian headmen in the villages were also freed from such taxes because they served as immediate collectors of the Sultan's taxes and as contact men between Turkish officialdom and the Christian *reaya*. For the position of all these groups in the scheme of Turkish feudalism in the Balkans, see Branislav Djurdjev, "Investigations of the *Voynuks*, with Special Reference to the Development of Turkish Feudalism and the Question of the Bosnian *Agalik*," *Glasnik Zemaljskog muzeja u Bosni i Hercegovini*, New Series, II, 75–137; Branislav Djurdjev," The *Kanunname* of Požega District of 1545," *ibid.*, I, 129–38, esp. 136–37.

and the spahi insisted that the land be worked, because only if worked was it able to fulfill its function. If the land was not worked for three years (in some periods for one year) the spahi was entitled to take it away from the peasant who held it and to give it to another peasant who was willing to work it. The peasants were free to move away from their farms, but in that case they lost the right of usufruct on their farms. But this freedom of movement was discouraged and often prohibited. The peasant could sell or bequeath the land by a simple recording with the spahi as the *tapu* officer and by paying of a transfer fee. Thus, according to traditional customs, just as formerly under the domestic feudal medieval lords, the peasants in the South Slav lands under the regime of timars and ziamets considered that the land they worked was their full, heritable property, their *baština*, subject only to feudal obligations. In fact, it was not a fully free property, but rather a type of conditionally free, heritable property or subsidiary *baština*.

The obligations of the Christian *reaya* or serfs settled on the military fiefs consisted of the payment of various tithes to the spahi, rendering a small amount of *corvée* for the spahi, payment of taxes to the Sultan and to the local government, and rendering an amount of *corvée* for public purposes. These obligations were set down in imperial laws (*kanuns*) for the various districts (sandjaks). They varied considerably from district to district, as well as over periods of time.[28] The *kanun-names* (collection of laws) did not contain any general principles of land tenure and taxation, but rather, they were specific rules pertaining to these matters in individual districts. Four characteristics, however, were common to all these decrees: all produce was subject to tithes and taxes either in kind or in money; traffic in all products was subject to indirect taxation; traditional usages with regard to rates of tithes and taxes were repeatedly stressed, though increases in the existing levies and introduction of new ones were constant; the decrees were replete with admonitions and penalties for infraction of the laws on the part of the officials collecting various levies, indicating that abuses in assessment and collection of these levies were a common occurrence.

The basic right of the spahi was to collect a portion of the crops from the *reaya* on his fief. His share in crops was regularly one-tenth, but in some areas and at various times it was as high as one-fourth of the gross product. The transformation of the tithe in kind into a tithe in money,

---

[28] For examples of detailed *kanun-names* for individual districts (sandjaks), see Branislav Djurdjev, "The *Kanun-name* of Požega District of 1545," *op. cit.*; Branislav Djurdjev, "The *Kanun-name* of Bosnia of 1530," *op. cit.*; Hamid Hadžibegić, "The *Kanun-name* for Bosnia of 1565," *ibid.*, pp. 201–22; Nedim Filipović, "A *Kanun-name* of the Zvornik District," *ibid.*, pp. 223–34.

if not allowed by law, was prohibited. The *reaya* also paid a small tithe in money to the spahi, the so-called *ispence*, and several other special taxes. *Corvée* obligations of the serfs were, as a rule, much smaller than those prevailing in medieval South Slav states or in Central European states. The serfs were obliged to build the house for the spahi, to transport the tithe collection to his residence, and to render a few days of *corvée* on his *hassa* land if that land was not leased to the tenants but worked directly by the spahi. When leased to the tenants, the latter usually paid the spahi as rent one-fourth of the gross product.[29] The rights and obligations of the *reaya* on various types of fiefs and on the *wakf* lands in the same area and at the same time were approximately the same. The *reaya* also paid a head tax or *cizya* (referred to also as *harač*) and several other taxes to the Sultan and local government.

To give one example of the obligations of the *reaya* in terms of tithes and taxes to the government: In the 1820's, when Serbia already had a degree of autonomy, the obligations of the *reaya* to the spahis consisted of the tenth of the grain crop; of a small head tax on every married man and a smaller head tax on unmarried men; special taxes on orchards, vineyards, and beehives; a special tax on pigs for the utilization of acorns; a special tax on water mills, kettles for distilling brandy, and on kilns. Except for the tenths from grains and beehives, other obligations were paid in money. Furthermore, there was a tax on the occasion of the marriage of a girl and a special tax after the death of the head of a family. Often all obligations toward the spahis were paid in a lump sum of money. Inasmuch as the spahis at that time were not allowed to live in villages, they or their representatives came to the villages only at the time of the harvest to collect the tenth. The products had to be delivered to the residence of the spahis at the peasants' expense. The spahis then sold a part of their collection.

The taxes for the Sultan were set in a lump sum by the Pasha of the Belgrade Pashalik in agreement with the headmen of the Serbian local government (*nahije*) on the basis of the number of taxable persons (tax heads). Taxes for the needs of the local government would then be added as a surtax on the main tax. The headmen, in turn, apportioned the tax load among the lower units of local government (*knežine*). The *knežina* headmen divided the burden among their constituents and collected the tax. The tax proceeds were then delivered to the Pasha. It was a set policy of the Turkish regime that there be little contact between

[29] Branislav Djurdjev, "A Contribution to the Problem of the Development and Nature of the Timar Organization in Turkish Feudalism," *Godišnjak Istoriskog društva Bosne i Hercegovine*, I, 101–67, esp. 154.

the Turkish officials and the *reaya*, a principle of indirect rule both practical and quite successful. The Sultan's taxes at that time consisted of a
head tax (*harač, cizya*, or tribute) imposed on all male non-Moslems
between the ages of 7 and 80 and a tax on sheep and goats. Customs
duties and a number of excise taxes were collected directly by the Turkish officials or were farmed out by them. There was also a host of various
indirect taxes on goods entering trade. Moreover, there was an assortment of labor services for public needs, for the needs of various Turkish
officials, and for native headmen.[30]

The ziamet and timar system as here outlined was the basic feature
of the Turkish feudal order as it evolved after Turkish conquest of the
Balkans and reached its zenith and ideal codification in the times of
Suleiman the Magnificent. It was brought about by a resurgence in the
power of the central government vis-à-vis the feudal and regional magnates and adjusted to the specific conditions of an empire expanding by
continuing conquest of new territory. Ottoman feudalism as characterized by the ziamets and timars developed basically out of the feudalism
of the Seldjukian Turks, but was greatly influenced by the feudal forms
of Byzantium and later also by the feudal forms which were found in the
conquered Balkan Slavic states.

The main characteristic of the Turkish feudal system as developed
during the sixteenth century, and also during the following centuries,
was that the chief reliance was put on rent in kind, while both the tithes
in money and *corvée* obligations were of subsidiary importance. Because of this and the fact that the military fiefs were in principle not
heritable and were often small, the manorial type of economy could not
develop as long as the system of timars and ziamets worked. As long as
the Ottoman central government was strong and its top officials able
and willing to enforce the laws on the spahis, the Janissaries, and other
officials in the capital and in the provinces, the Turkish feudal order as
developed during the sixteenth century worked well. But such conditions did not endure for long, and in future centuries that system completely degenerated.

DEGENERATION OF THE TURKISH FEUDAL ORDER

The feudal system based on the ziamets and timars was conceived
and organized in a manner to make the spahis tend to the business of
the state rather than their personal interest. The nonheritable nature of
the fiefs and the legal regulation of the spahi's rights in regard to the
tithes were the strongest features of the system from the point of view

---

[30] M. Gavrilović, *Miloš Obrenović* (Miloš Obrenović), II, 361–440.

of the central government, and also most satisfactory from the point of view of the *reaya*. But this system did not protect enough the personal and family interest of the spahis and thus it was tenable only as long as it was enforceable. Quite naturally, the *zaims* and timariots coveted the opportunity to make their fiefs heritable and to have greater latitude in the exploitation of the *reaya*. There lies the reason for their striving to transform the ziamets and timars into a free and heritable type of estate. In fact this tendency did not originate with the spahis, but rather with the top officials in Istanbul, who also wanted to increase their revenue and to make at least a part of their fiefs heritable property free of any obligations toward the Sultan and from any legal limitations regarding the rights and obligations of the peasants settled on these properties. The fact that a great number of offices were bought and that the collection of various tithes, taxes, and other revenues was farmed out contributed also to the tendency of the people who bought the offices and the rights to collect the revenues to acquire a more permanent hold on landed properties. This striving of Ottoman officialdom, the spahis, and tax farmers to acquire heritable land holdings similar to the alod lands in Western Europe and to increase their revenue from these holdings, on the one hand, and the general decay and corruption of the Turkish government, on the other, were the basic causes of the degeneration of the Turkish feudal system in the course of the seventeenth, eighteenth, and nineteenth centuries.

A powerful factor working for the degeneration of the Turkish feudal system was the fact that from the middle of the sixteenth century the Empire's growth was practically stopped, removing thus the opportunities for plunder of new areas and for the formation of new military fiefs, causing generally great difficulties in a state which thrived on continued expansion. This became even more so after the Empire began to lose territory following great defeats toward the end of the seventeenth century and at the beginning of the eighteenth. As a result of these defeats great numbers of spahis, Janissaries, and Turkish officials were thrown out of Hungary, Croatia-Slavonia, and Dalmatia. Many of them settled in Bosnia, Serbia, and Macedonia and tried to make a living partly by obtaining new fiefs and partly by usurping the established ones. Moreover, the increase in the number of descendants of the spahis led to the division of the existing timars and ziamets, which became small and insufficient to assure the living of the spahi and his family, thus inducing him to look for an increase in his income and economic security.

In order to claim the timars or ziamets or other land as their full heritable property, free of any obligations toward the ruler and free of any rights of the *reaya* to the usufruct on that land, these lands were transformed into *čiftliks*, but *čiftliks* as a type of feudal estates characteristic of the phase of degenerated Turkish feudalism. (In Bosnia two different types of these estates were developed, but for this see Chapter 4.) The person claiming ownership of such a *čiftlik* was called *čiftlik-sahibia*, and the peasants settled on such *čiftliks* were called *čifčije* or kmetovi. The formation of the *čiftliks* took place either by the changed position of the former spahi or by a third person injecting himself forcefully between the spahi and the *reaya*, in both cases claiming the right of full heritable ownership of the *čiftlik* without the peasant having the usufruct of the land, and claiming a share of its production. The *čiftliks* were formed by taking away forcefully from the *reaya* the *tapu* to the land they tilled, by forced "sales" or forging of the *tapus*, the enlargement of the *hassa* land of the spahis, the occupation of unoccupied or deserted lands and settling them by *čifčije*. The relationship between the spahi and the *reaya* was a relationship of public law fully regulated by law and fixed mutual rights and obligations, including the heritable right of the *reaya* to the usufruct of their farms if they worked them. The relationship between the *čiftlik-sahibia* and the *čifčija* was a private relationship, a form of tenancy, but tenancy which did not result from free choice, but rather from a situation in which the landlord had the force in his hands and used it freely—while the peasants were in a hopeless position lacking protection. The formation of the *čiftliks* and their existence were never legally regulated, but they were tolerated by the government to such an extent that they completely replaced the timars and ziamets as the chief feature of Turkish feudalism in the course of the eighteenth and nineteenth centuries. In part, the *čiftliks* were worked as large agricultural estates, in part, the land was held by a great number of peasants in small farm units, obliged to render a part of the production to the landlord. Needless to say, as long as the institution of spahis existed, the peasants also had to render the tenth and other obligations to the spahis. Furthermore, they were subject to various taxes and obligations as before.

Formation of the *čiftliks* was anathema to the peasants, who resisted it as much as possible. Abuses in the formation of *čiftliks* developed gradually into the basic cause of peasant unrest in the South Slav lands under the Turks and was also the immediate cause for the beginning of the First Revolt in Serbia in 1804. Two things were especially resented by the peasantry: (1) the *čiftlik-sahibias* claimed the land as their full, heritable property, which they could freely dispose of. They thus considered themselves free to evict the peasants whenever they refused to accept the imposed conditions of tenancy. This fact militated against the traditional view of the Yugoslav peasantry that their farms were their full, heritable *baštine*, albeit subject to feudal obligations toward the feudal lord. As long as the timars and ziamets were in existence this was true. With the appearance of the *čiftliks*, the peasants were actually dispossessed, the *čiftlik-sahibia* claiming the full, heritable ownership of the land, while the peasant had no rights to it. (2) Rents on the *čiftliks* were always much higher than the tithes paid to the spahis. Usually the share of the *čiftlik* owner was between one-fourth and one-half of the gross product. Thus the formation of the *čiftliks* meant two things for the Yugoslav peasants: lowering of their political and social status and increased exploitation and reduced economic security. (For further discussion of the problem of *čiftliks* see Chapter 4 and Chapter 5, section on Macedonia.)

TURKISH RULE AND SERBIAN MIGRATIONS

The peasantry of Serbia and other South Slav lands did not take the abuses by the Turkish regime passively. These abuses increased as the Ottoman central rule decayed and after the Empire began to lose territory, and so did the variety of people's reactions to these abuses. The favored technique of avoiding Turkish oppression, before the wars of liberation at the beginning of the nineteenth century, was migration. Two migration processes have to be distinguished. On the one hand, the South Slav population partially withdrew from the plains and areas along the main communication lines, where Turkish control was most effective, into the mountainous areas where it was absent or ephemeral. Thus was repeated a stratagem used centuries earlier by the Vlakhs in defense against the pre-Slav and South Slav invaders of the Balkans. There were also practically no Serbs or other Christian South Slavs in the towns as long as the Turkish rule lasted. The withdrawal of large segments of population into the mountainous areas meant a structural change in the economy of these areas. The relative importance of crop agriculture decreased and that of animal husbandry increased. This change of habitat and occupation had deep consequences for the development of peasant culture and institutions of the South Slavs and particularly of the Serbs (see pp. 192–97).

On the other hand, there was a constant stream of migration from the Yugoslav areas south of the Sava-Danube rivers into the Habsburg Monarchy lasting several centuries. These migrations were prompted not only by Turkish oppression, but also by the overpopulation of the mountainous areas in the Balkans, as the increasing population soon outstripped the capacity of the pastoral economy of this area to support it.[31] The greatest single move out of Serbia into Hungary in 1691, known as the "Great Migration," involved about 30,000 people, and strengthened the already large Serbian population in that country. The Habsburg Empire welcomed these refugees and settled most of them in the depopulated or underpopulated areas which were organized as a Military Frontier along the border of the Ottoman Empire (see pp. 74–81 and 135).

In addition to these voluntary migrations there were also migrations forced by the Turks: transplanting of populations of whole regions for security and other political reasons and abduction of prisoners caught in military operations and plunder raids.

Needless to say, one of the ways of resisting Turkish terror was through armed resistance of individuals and small groups. But in such instances it is often hard to say where legitimate armed resistance in defense of people stops and brigandage begins. At any rate this type of resistance caught the imagination of the people and its praise is perpetuated in folk epic poems.

As will be shown later, migrations continued on a large scale also after the liberation of Serbia as a result of special policies followed by Prince Miloš. The foremost Serbian ethnographer, T. R. Djordjević, said the following about the effects of all these migrations for various areas of Serbia:

Because of migrations whole areas became deserted or underpopulated, which after a shorter or longer period of time again became settled either by the return of former settlers or by people from totally different regions, or both. This is the reason that in many areas changes occurred in the language, economy, way of life, customs, clothing, and so on.[32]

It might be pointed out that the population mixture in most areas of Yugoslavia, especially those inhabited by Serbs and Croats, goes back to these population shifts during the Turkish rule or is a consequence of systematic colonizing of areas, e.g., Vojvodina and Slavonia, which were left underpopulated after the Turkish withdrawal, by settlers of different nationalities. In the course of centuries under the pressure of the Turks (and to a certain extent of the Albanians) from the south, the whole body of the South Slav nations was shifted toward the north. Two factors contributed greatly to the ability and willingness of the Yugoslav

[31] Jovan Cvijić, *Balkansko poluostrvo i južnoslovenske zemlje* (The Balkan Peninsula and the South Slav Lands), pp. 194–203.
[32] Tihomir R. Djordjević, *Iz Srbije Kneza Miloša—Stanovništvo, Naselja* (The Serbia of Prince Miloš—Population, Settlements), p. 7.

peoples to migrate en masse both within and without the territory of the Ottoman Empire. First, animal husbandry rather than crop agriculture was their chief source of livelihood and made them quite mobile, and second, owing to sparse population large stretches of land were available for settlement.

For the sake of completeness it should be noted, however, that migrations across the frontiers did not always take place out of the Ottoman Empire. As a result of the Turkish defeat in the Austro-Turkish war of 1715 and the following Treaty of Požarevac (Passarowitz) of 1718, a large section of Serbia was occupied by Austria and held until 1739. The harshness of the Austrian rule and especially Jesuit attempts to convert the people to Roman Catholicism led many Serbs to seek refuge in Turkish territory. These "inverse" migrations also continued later, especially after the liberation of Serbia.[33]

THE GRADUAL LIBERATION OF SERBIA FROM TURKISH RULE

Forceful creation of *čiftliks* in Serbia at the turn of the nineteenth century, where previously they were exceptional, and contemporaneous widespread Janissary terror supplied the spark for the First Revolt in Serbia in 1804 under the leadership of Djordje Petrović.[34] In the begin-

---

[33] Jovan Cvijić, *Balkansko poluostrvo i južnoslovenske zemlje*, pp. 181–82.

[34] Djordje Petrović (Kara or Black Djordje, from which the family name Karadjordjević was later derived) and Miloš Obrenović were also the founders of the two dynasties which alternated at the helm of Serbia until 1903, when the last of the Obrenovićes was liquidated. The Karadjordjevićes ruled Serbia and later Yugoslavia until 1941 or 1945 when the republic was proclaimed. The imprint of Miloš, who ruled from 1817 to 1839 and again from 1859 to 1860, on Serbian life and institutions was greater and more lasting than that of any other ruler of the two dynasties. Both he and Kara Djordje rose from peasant families. While Miloš, who also participated as a village headman in the First Revolt under Kara Djordje, seems not to have been as outstanding a military leader as the latter, his strength was in his great capacities as a politician, diplomat, administrator, and businessman. After the successful Second Revolt he was elected in 1817 a hereditary prince by the National Assembly, a fact formally recognized by the Sultan in 1830. He did much more for Serbia, and for himself personally, by astute diplomacy than could have been done by force, though he never hesitated from using force when necessary. He used his political office to promote his financial interests and became one of the richest men in the Balkans. He became tax farmer general, the administrator of the salt monopoly, and collector of customs revenues for the Sultan in Serbia; he became the greatest pig trader and practically held a monopoly of pig exports, the chief export commodity of the country; he became a huge landowner both at home and in neighboring Rumania. In a fashion he established the Serbian tradition of both a strong and sinister hand of the government and of large-scale corruption in public affairs, both of which became characteristic marks of Serbian political life and have endured up to the present time. Much of Prince Miloš' political success has to be ascribed, however, to the fact that by that time the Turkish administration in Serbia was in a truly delapidated state and that its garrisons there were small and poorly organized and commanded. In the early reign of Prince Miloš Serbia had something like 500,000

ning this revolt was avowedly not directed against the Sultan, but rather, with the support of the spahis whose interests were also affected, against the Turkish troublemakers, who started usurping rights and properties in contravention of the Ottoman laws, international agreements (Peace of Sistova of 1791), and the rights of the *reaya* and the spahis. Soon, however, with great successes to its credit, it became a revolt against the Turkish rule as such and resulted in freeing all of the Belgrade Pashalik. Independence thus won was maintained by force of arms, but owing to the changed international situation which freed the Turks from other military worries, it was crushed in 1813. The ensuing Turkish terror led in 1815 to the Second Revolt, this time under Miloš Obrenović,[34] who succeeded in wresting a status of partial independence for Serbia and its later recognition by the Porte. This marks the beginning of the modern Serbian state.[35] Its political status evolved gradually from an outright Turkish province in 1815, through various phases of increasing independence (small Turkish garrisons were kept in Serbia until 1867 and it paid a tribute to the Sultan until 1878) to a sovereign principality in 1878, and a kingdom in 1882. Its territory increased greatly in 1833 and again in 1878. With the victories in the two Balkan Wars in 1912–13 it acquired Macedonia and a part of the Sandjak of Novi Pazar from the Ottoman Empire (Map 1, p. 4).

THE AGRARIAN REFORM OF PRINCE MILOŠ

The basic fact in connection with Serbian developments in agrarian affairs during the nineteenth century was that the issue of landownership was solved in accordance with the principle "The land belongs to those who till it." Considering the ideas and customs of the Serbian peasantry with regard to landownership, formed and observed through centuries, it could hardly have been otherwise. But there is also little doubt that this course of events was greatly helped by the political wisdom and strong hand of Prince Miloš.

---

people. The Turkish population numbered about 15,000 to 20,000 civilians and about 2,000 to 3,000 troops. M. Gavrilović, *op. cit.*, II, 253–57. Since bribing was an essential cog in the whole fabric of the Turkish state administration and politics, Miloš as an extremely wealthy and shrewd man also used that weapon to full advantage. For a general interpretation of the Obrenović rulers as men and as statesmen, see Slobodan Jovanović, *Vlada Aleksandra Obrenovića* (The Reign of Alexander Obrenović) (Collected Works), XII, 383–435.

[35] One of the factors in securing Serbia's partial independence early in the nineteenth century was the support of Russia, which proclaimed itself in 1774 (Peace of Kuchuk Kainardji) as a protector of all Christian Orthodox population under Ottoman rule. The Russo-Turkish Treaty of 1812 put the name of new Serbia for the first time into the modern diplomatic annals. Needless to say, the objective of Russia was to use the Balkan nations as pawns in its diplomatic and armed warfare against the Porte.

The economic aim of the Serbian peasantry during the wars of liberation—and at that time Serbian peasantry was synonymous with the Serbian nation—was to prevent the establishment of the *čiftliks* and to get rid of all obligations toward the spahis and the Sultan, namely, the establishment of a free Serbia with peasants owning their land fully. It is quite understandable that they were also against any policy which would have substituted domestic feudal lords for Turkish ones. There were such tendencies among some leaders of the wars of liberation who were mostly wealthier peasants and livestock traders. But Miloš chose to depend for his rule on the masses of free peasants whom he thoroughly knew and, as an astute politician, was able to sway masterfully, rather than on a few potential feudal lords. A democratic land policy was thus in the interest both of the peasantry and Prince Miloš and his dynasty.[36]

No *čiftliks* were allowed in Serbia after 1815, and the dissolution of the Turkish feudal order based on the timars and ziamets proceeded in an ideally simple fashion. From 1815 to 1833, when this feudal system was abolished in Serbia, the spahis were forced to observe strictly the laws specifying their rights toward the peasants. With the Hatti-Sherif of 1833 the peasants became full owners of their land not only in fact but also in law. No indemnity for the rights of the spahis on these lands was paid by the Serbian peasants. Serbia continued, however, to pay a tribute to the Sultan until 1878, and it included not only a settlement for the *cizya* or *harač*—the head tax imposed on the Christian population— but also all other obligations of Serbia, including nominally the obligations to the spahis. These payments came out of the general tax revenue of the state. Of course, the peasants continued to pay the tithe, which now was a regular state tax. Only such liquidation of the feudal order could correspond to the spirit of the Serbian peasants. But this solution was conditioned also by the fact that at that time there was a great deal of free land in Serbia, that the new state lacked written laws, and that the strict notions of legality and sanctity of private property had still to be formed. Furthermore, the differentiation of the Serbian society at that time was little advanced. There was no domestic class which would have insisted on "orderly," "legal" procedures, thus protecting its existing or potential interests. The reform was truly national and revolutionary. It was at the expense of the Turks alone and was profitable to all Serbs.

It was a different story when, in 1878, according to the decisions of the Berlin Congress, Serbia incorporated some new territories in the

[36] Slobodan Jovanović, "Prince Miloš and the Peasant Problem," *Sociološki pregled*, I, 24–25.

southeast and was obliged to indemnify Turkish landlords whose properties were expropriated. The indemnities were set by mixed commissions by capitalizing the annual income of the landlords for a period of
years. According to a special law of February 1880, the former Serbian
serfs, now freed from feudal bondage, had to repay these indemnities.
Since the Serbian government took upon itself to settle accounts with
the Turkish government, the peasants were obliged to repay the Serbian
state by annuities. Serbia even obtained a special foreign loan to help
finance these payments to Turkey and took mortgages on the properties
of the peasants to ensure payment of their annuities. The passage of
the law of 1880, especially with its provision for the payment of indemnities, was defended on the basis of the general principle that the formerly existing system was a legal one and that established rights can
be taken away only by proper indemnification. The fact that this was
an international obligation played an important role. But the overwhelming majority of the peasants never paid either the principal or
the interest due on these annuities, in spite of the state mortgages on
their land.[37] Thus, as far as the peasants were concerned, this new agrarian reform was similar to the earlier one.

The agrarian problem in Serbia after liberation did not consist only
in the breaking up of feudal bondage. As a consequence of wars, Turkish terror, and shifts in population, the country was largely depopulated.
Great expanses of land were uncultivated or in forests. One of the first
tasks that Prince Miloš undertook immediately after 1817 was to attract
new settlers into Serbia. He generously offered free land to the new
settlers, treated them on equal terms with the old-established population,
and granted to them temporary exemption from taxes, which, in fact,
had to be borne by other villagers. As security of life and property was
greatly enhanced, the influx of population into Serbia was heavy. Second, he allowed all peasants to acquire new land by taking unoccupied
agricultural land or by the clearing of forests. Much of the village common and of the former church and *wakf* land passed into private hands
at this time, as these lands were not properly delimited. The ensuing
general scramble for land resulted, naturally, in considerable inequities
in land distribution. Prince Miloš himself, his lieutenants, and the
wealthier and more powerful peasants availed themselves of the force of

---

[37] Ž. Živanović, *Politička istorija Srbije u drugoj polovini devetnaestog veka* (Politi-
cal History of Serbia During the Second Half of the Nineteenth Century), II, 52–54;
Milorad Nedeljković, *Istorija srpskih državnih dugova* (History of Serbian Public
Debts), pp. 94–96, 113.

their positions or wealth in the enclosure of choice land.[38] But, on the other hand, in 1820 Prince Miloš ordered his officials in the villages to take away land from those who had too much and were not able to work it and to give it to those who had not enough land and were eager to cultivate more.[39] This affected neither him nor his lieutenants, as they forced the peasants in the surrounding villages to *corvée* on their lands, and thus were able to work all their land. *Corvée* on the properties of various village headmen he later abolished under pressure from the peasants, but continued the practice of forced labor for his own properties.

Prince Miloš gained many enemies through the introduction of a considerable measure of law and order, often with drastic means, the increase in taxes to finance the newly developing state administration, the abolition of village self-government (*knežina*), and replacing of elected village headmen by appointed government officials, the exacting of *corvée* for his private needs, for the village headmen, and for public works, and lack of observance of property and trading rights of his subjects. Several abortive revolts took place before he was finally deposed in 1839, to be recalled to the throne in 1859, shortly before his death in 1860. Many of his contemporaries and later students of Prince Miloš severely criticized his rule. If one remembers the situation existing at the time Miloš ruled, the conditions which preceded his advent to power, and the notions about the relationship between the individual and the state in Serbia at that time, the pattern of his rule becomes quite understandable. As far as his peasant policy was concerned, one has to agree with the leading Serbian social scientist of recent decades, Slobodan Jovanović, when he said:

Miloš' peasant policy suffered from a certain contradiction: on the one hand, Miloš made the peasant an independent owner of his land; on the other, he tried to keep him under a despotic rule which gave the peasant neither full legal security nor real economic freedom. . . . In short, there existed free peasant land property, but not a free peasantry.[40]

The achievement of a peasant freehold was the cornerstone of the political and economic emancipation of the Serbian peasantry. But while it

[38] Slobodan Jovanović, *Ustavobranitelji i njihova vlada* (The Defenders of the Constitution and Their Rule) (Collected Works), V, 14.

[39] Stojan Novaković, *op. cit.*, p. 190; Jelenko Petrović, *Okućje ili zaštita zemljoradničkog minimuma* (The Protected Minimum Homestead), pp. 66–77; quoted hereafter as Petrović, *Okućje*.

[40] Slobodan Jovanović, "Prince Miloš and the Peasant Problem," p. 26.

strove to ensure and enlarge this basic achievement both in the economic and in the political fields, most of its aims remained only a dream during the following century and a quarter.

THE INSTITUTION OF THE PROTECTED MINIMUM HOMESTEAD

The agrarian reform undertaken by Prince Miloš which made practically every peasant family an owner of a small or medium-size farm did not mean that all of them were to keep their farms. The inroads of a money and credit economy, the breaking up of the large peasant family or zadruga and of the traditional (patriarchal) ways of life and economy, freer traffic in farm real estate, the increasing economic differentiation in the village, speculative trade ventures by peasants, and occasional disorderly living and gambling—all characteristics of a society in the process of transition from a rather static, patriarchal, and collectivist way of life to a more dynamic individualistic one—led to indebtedness on the part of many peasants. As interest rates were exorbitantly high, indebtedness grew easily into overindebtedness. This threatened not only to cause misery in individual families, but to create large numbers of landless rural proletariat and the amassing of land property in few hands. To prevent this, and thus to secure the economic achievements of the wars of liberation, Prince Miloš decreed in 1836 that the house, a certain amount of agricultural land with two oxen and a cow, deemed necessary as a minimum to provide lodging and food for the peasant family, could not be sold or foreclosed for the payment of debts.[41] This was the beginning of the protected minimum homestead or *okuće* institution in Serbia, an institution of great political and economic importance.[42] The decree also covered the houses of urban families.

With the promulgation of the law of 1839 regulating the various land-tenure problems which arose after the formal elimination of the feudal bondage in 1833, and with the passage of the Civil Code of 1844, the peasant's ownership of land was legally fully assured and protected, even against abuses on the part of the ruler. With the passage of the legislation of 1836 and 1839, the administrators of Serbia thought that in addition to obtaining his political freedom, the Serbian peasant had solved also the problem of economic security, and that a society had

[41] Petrović, *Okuće*, pp. 87–90.

[42] The institution of a protected minimum peasant homestead did not originate in Serbia. Prince Miloš, many of whose administrators and advisers were Serbs from Austria and Hungary, copied and partly modified this institution as developed in the Military Frontier in Croatia-Slavonia and in Banat (see pp. 77–79).

evolved in which everybody was a land proprietor and thus economically safeguarded. With these tasks considered accomplished, the peasant was left to shift for himself. Certain attempts to teach the Serbian peasant rational methods of agricultural work, undertaken in the early 1850's, proved failures (see p. 462).

In the second quarter of the nineteenth century two groups and social powers—the bureaucracy and the usurers—developed in Serbia from the womb of the peasantry itself. These, of course, were also emanations of the penetration of new social and economic forms into Serbia. The Serbian peasant raged and fought against them in the following decades but without avail.[43] The bureaucracy with its paternalistic attitude toward the people assumed the role of tutor over the peasantry and introduced, in the words of Slobodan Jovanović, a regime of "administrative despotism." It introduced, enforced, and worshiped laws and the principles of legality for their own sake without any regard to how they agreed either with the legal philosophy or the economic needs of the people. Thus, in the Serbian Civil Code of 1844 and in the Civil Procedure Act of 1853, both conceived in the spirit of Roman law, individualism, and laissez faire, no provisions were made for protection of peasant property in the sense of the minimum protected homestead. On the other hand, changes in the economic structure of Serbian society following the gradual penetration of a money and market economy greatly stimulated usurious practices. In the 1850's the issue of peasant debts became the chief economic and political problem of the country. The situation became much worse with the economic crisis which followed the Crimean War. There arose a popular cry across the land that political freedom in a peasant society in which peasants do not own their

---

[43] The literature on the role of bureaucracy and its development as well as on usury in Serbia in the nineteenth century is quite voluminous. The earliest systematic social and political critic of these two social groups in Serbia writing in the early 1870's was Svetozar Marković (1846–75), the father of socialism in Serbia as well as the intellectual father of the People's Radical party. See Svetozar Marković, *Celokupna dela—Srbija na istoku* (Collected Works—Serbia in the Orient), VI, 91–125; Slobodan Jovanović, *Ustavobranitelji i njihova vlada*, pp. 44–74, 110–83; Slobodan Jovanović, *Političke i pravne rasprave* (Political and Legal Studies) (Collected Works), II, 59–298; Jovan Skerlić, *Svetozar Marković, njegov život, rad i ideje* (Svetozar Marković, His Life, Work, and Ideas), *passim*. For a Marxian interpretation of Svetozar Marković, see Veselin Masleša, *Svetozar Marković* (Svetozar Marković), pp. 11–84.

Except in the case of Svetozar Marković, Socialist ideas played a negligible role in the discussion of the agrarian problems in the South Slav lands prior to 1918. The same was largely true also of the interwar period. For the whole problem of Socialist and Communist treatment of the problem of peasantry and peasant farming in Eastern and Southeastern Europe from Marx to the present time see David Mitrany, *Marx Against the Peasant*.

land is only a sham and that after freeing himself from the Turkish spahis the Serbian peasant was about to fall into bondage to another type of spahis, the usurers, "who would take not only the tenth, but the whole [property]." The return of Prince Miloš to the throne in 1859 was partly related to the hopes of the peasantry that he would solve the problem of peasant overindebtedness.

As a result of widespread unrest among the peasants due to the problem of debts and usury during the 1850's, an amendment to the Civil Procedure Act in 1860 introduced protection from foreclosure of a certain amount of peasant working implements and draft animals, to which the following year the protection of "two days of plowing" or roughly one hectare of land was added.[44]

That was not enough. The problem of usury persisted and became worse. In 1873 the protected minimum homestead legislation was completely overhauled and codified in the famous Section 4(a) of Article 471 of the Civil Procedure Act, which remained on the law books of Serbia to the end of World War II. This amendment provided that the following peasant property should be protected from foreclosure for private debts: (a) his house, stables, and the lot around the house up to one "day of plowing" or 5,760 square meters; (b) a minimum of cropland, vineyards, orchards, or forest, together with the unharvested crops, amounting to five "days of plowing" or, together with the plot around the house, 3.45 hectares or 8.5 acres for every tax head in the household;[45] (c) two oxen (or two buffaloes, or two draft horses), one cow with calf up to one year (or a mare with foal, or buffalo cow with calf), ten sheep, five goats, and five pigs; (d) one plow, one cart, one hoe, one ax, one pick, and one scythe; (e) enough food for the family and enough feed for the livestock until the new harvest.[46]

But in addition to the enlarged protected minimum of land and the increased quantity and assortment of movable property, the new amendment introduced a totally new provision. It prohibited the peasant from selling his protected minimum of land and from using it as collateral for credit, except when he changed his occupation—by officially, though not necessarily actually becoming a merchant or "speculator" and thus losing the protection accorded to him by law. In this new formulation

---

[44] Petrović, *Okućje*, p. 92.

[45] The definition of the tax head caused great difficulties to the authorities who administered and enforced this law. The protected minimum of land rose with the increase of tax heads in the household, but other provisions remained the same. The minimum of 8.5 acres of land would be applicable to a family consisting of a husband and wife, or a husband, wife, and several small children.

[46] Petrović, *Okućje*, pp. 237–38.

the law was directed against both the usurers and the carelessness of the peasant himself, because he desired credit primarily for financing of his consumption or for speculative trade ventures, rather than for improvements on his farm directed toward an increase in production. The law tried to ensure that, if possible, all Serbian peasants should own and keep a minimum of land. In a broader sense the legislator wanted to achieve what in the 1840's was thought to be already established, namely, a minimum of economic security based on landownership as appropriate for a country of peasants. While the provisions of 1860 and 1861, according to some interpreters, were designed to "prevent the indebted peasant from starving, the legislation of 1873 had the purpose of preventing him from becoming a pauper." It is interesting, however, that the legislation of 1873 did not prohibit the division of peasant farms into units smaller than the protected minimum homestead. Thus another wide avenue toward pauperization of the village—the excessive division of farm property—remained open.[47]

The protected minimum-homestead legislation had its determined defenders as well as its determined adversaries. There is no doubt that it had reduced, if not completely destroyed, the capacity of the peasant to use legitimate sources of credit and thus reduced his chances of advancement through improving his production. The peasant was also relentlessly driven into the hands of loan sharks who conspired with him to outwit the law. Jelenko Petrović, the best Serbian authority on the history of this institution, gives not less than 14 different ways by which the law was evaded.[48] And, above all, the state itself violated the idea if not the letter of the law as it continued with the foreclosures of peasant property for overdue taxes without regard to any minimum area. But the trend toward a complete statutory protection of a minimum homestead was not to stop until a somewhat reduced minimum of peasant property was protected against all foreclosures including those for taxes, which protection was introduced in 1899 and amended in 1907. An amendment to the Direct Tax Act passed in 1899 provided that the state could not foreclose for taxes the house in which the peasant lived, together with 2,000 square meters of land around the house. To this was added a pair of draft animals by legislation of 1907.[49] It appears, however, that the state did not scrupulously observe the letter of the law in this regard.

[47] Živojin M. Perić, "The Institution of the Protected Minimum Homestead with Regard to Division in the Serbian Law," *Ekonomist*, July–August, 1939, pp. 304–12.

[48] Petrović, *Okućje*, pp. 278–84.

[49] *Ibid.*, pp. 115–35.

OTHER MEASURES FOR PROTECTION OF THE PEASANTS

Serbian authorities tried to protect the peasant in other ways too. The Commercial Act of 1860 prohibited the peasants from issuing and signing bills of exchange, a provision that was to continue in force until 1929. Moreover, Prince Miloš' decrees and the Village Commercial Stores Act of 1870 and 1891, which remained in force in Serbia until 1934, hindered the opening of commercial stores in rural areas and, so far as they allowed them, prohibited them from selling such commodities as coffee and sugar, tea, manufactured woolens, silk, and the finer types of cooking utensils. This measure was intended to reduce the opportunity of the peasants to buy such goods, to keep him attached to the traditional patterns of consumption, and also to reduce his opportunity to go into debt. But the law also safeguarded the trading monopoly for the city.[50]

The purpose of all these measures was to safeguard the Serbian peasant from the dangers that a money and market economy represented to his ownership of land and his old-established patriarchal economic order by telling him, as a true ward of the state: "Thou shalt not . . . !" But he did take credit from the usurers as this was the only source. He did issue bills of exchange even if he had to sign them as a "merchant and speculator"; he did buy more manufactured goods; he continued unnecessary feasting; and he did gamble occasionally. Such is human nature.

In addition to these measures for the safeguarding of peasant property, little else was done by the Serbian state for its peasantry and agriculture. The problem of agricultural credit remained a subject of political discussion for a century, but achievements in this field were meager indeed. This attitude toward agriculture persisted in spite of the fact that the peasant was the political and economic pillar of the state, that he carried on his shoulders the burden of the wars of liberation, railroad building and road construction, military strengthening, the organization of public administration, all consequences of the economic warfare with Austria-Hungary, and, through tariff protection, even the burden of some industrialization.

The general effect of this static approach to the problem of peasant economy was to give the land to the peasant and then to tie him to it. Serbian agriculture could not advance. It remained technically primitive. The peasant remained ignorant, in poverty, an object of abuse by

[50] Mijo Mirković, *Održanje seljačkog posjeda* (The Preservation of Peasant Property), p. 113; L. M. Kostić, "The Village and the Law," in Miloslav Stojadinović (ed.), *Naše selo* (Our Village), pp. 250–54.

those in power. However, the process of differentiation in the property structure in Serbian agriculture could be neither avoided nor stopped. The process of change in an underdeveloped economy exposed to the forces of capitalism was a much more powerful force than the resisting strength of either the traditional economic order or the government's measures of protection and pious admonitions. The worsening of the land-population ratio as a result of the increasing population led to an excessive subdivision of peasant property and to making Serbia a country of predominantly dwarf and small peasants. Moreover, in one way or another land property was slipping out of the peasant's hands. Already the census of 1897 showed that over 11 percent of all rural families were landless (see Table 6, p. 206). In spite of its obvious shortcomings and its utter failure to solve the problem of economic security for the Serbian peasant, the homestead institution had such a psychological hold on the peasants and politicians that it was established in some other parts of Yugoslavia after 1918 (see Chapter 20).

In its production aspects the agriculture of the country changed greatly during the nineteenth century. Formerly it was based essentially on animal husbandry, which necessitated the import of cereals. With the establishment of a greater degree of law and order, the country became more and more populated and crop agriculture and fruit production developed. At the beginning of the twentieth century, as ever since, Serbian agriculture had three basic components: production of grains, primarily wheat and corn; production of livestock, especially pigs and cattle; and production of fruits, primarily prunes. As we shall see later, it was predominantly a subsistence type of agriculture.

THE PEASANTRY AND POLITICS IN SERBIA PRIOR TO 1914

Ever since Serbia acquired a degree of independence in 1817 it has gone through a great many political convulsions, many of them colored by dynastic and constitutional issues. The fight between the principles of despotism—be it personal, bureaucratic, or party-political—and democratic forces permeated its whole political life. As already stated, the peasantry was always incensed against the bureaucrats and their cohorts. This found expression in the great political upheaval of the peasantry organized in the People's Radical party, which from the early 1880's to 1929 was the most important party-political force in Serbia and later in Yugoslavia.[51] But this party, fathered and organized by

[51] For the nature and development of political parties in Serbia, one finds a wealth of material in the writings of Slobodan Jovanović, those which were quoted above and many others. Of the newer works, see Jaša M. Prodanović, *Istorija političkih stranaka i struja u Srbiji* (History of Political Parties and Movements in Serbia).

people schooled in socialism of a Russian brand, especially that of Chernyshevsky, which started as the representative of the peasant interests, proved to be heedless of these interests as soon as it tasted the fruits of power. In time it became the standard-bearer of corruption, though it continued to keep a powerful hold on the Serbian peasantry. With the lack of trained personnel, insufficient financial resources, and the preoccupation of bureaucracy and of politicians with purely political issues and abuse of power, there was little talent, means, or time left to work on economic and, especially, agricultural improvements in Serbia. Thus, while Serbia, especially between 1903 and 1914, had the reputation of being a political and economic peasant democracy, it was always governed by the few in the interest of the few. But all political forces had to pay lip service to peasant interests; the saying was, "It is possible to rule against, but not without, the peasants." In spite of all that has been said above, political independence and lack of feudal forms made Serbia attractive as an example to other South Slav nationalities which were under foreign rule, and it played an important role in the liberation and unification of all South Slav nations.

CHAPTER 3

CROATIA-SLAVONIA

THE WAY in which the Croats settled in the territory presently occupied by them is still a debatable issue among historians. For a long time the view was generally held—and this view still continues to be held by many—that the Croats came from their trans-Carpathian homeland and settled in the western Balkans together with the other South Slavs, namely, during the sixth and the early seventh centuries, and in one migration. Around the turn of this century, and especially during the past thirty years a new theory has arisen which maintains that there were really two Slavic migrations into the western Balkans. The main bloc of the Slavic population came with the Avars, who were their masters, and settled in these areas, followed shortly thereafter by a small Slavic group, the Croats, who imposed their rule on the earlier Slavic settlers. The Croats led the struggle against and overthrew the Avar rule, and merged with the older Slavic population into one people referred to since the middle of the ninth century as the Croats. The difference in these views stems exclusively from the varying interpretations of the references to the Croats found in the work *De administrando imperio* by the Byzantine emperor Constantine Porphyrogenitus (913–959).[1]

---

[1] For a general review of Croatian history from the earliest times to the union with Hungary in 1102, see Bogo Grafenauer *et al.* (eds.), *Istorija naroda Jugoslavije* (History of the Peoples of Yugoslavia), I, 167–228, which also includes detailed bibliographical data. For a brief general review see Anto Babić, *Istorija naroda Jugoslavije* (History of the Peoples of Yugoslavia), pp. 44–57. In addition to older authors representing the view of a single Slavic migration into the Balkans such as Franjo Rački, the most important recent writer, and with Rački the foremost historian of the Croatian medieval state, is Ferdo Šišić (same as Ferdinand von Šišić). See his *Geschichte der Kroaten*, pp. 49–60 and *passim*; and *Povijest Hrvata u vrijeme narodnih vladara* (History of the Croats in the Period of Domestic Rulers), pp. 236–65 and *passim*. The second view is represented, among the historians in the South Slav lands, by Vjekoslav Klaić, "Croatian Tribes from the Twelfth to the Sixteenth Centuries," Yugoslav Academy of Science and Art, *Rad*, CXXX, 1–85, and especially by Ljudmil Hauptmann in his several studies. Of these the most important are: Ljudmil Hauptmann, "The Arrival of the Croats," Yugoslav Academy of Science and Art, *Zbornik kralja Tomislava* (Symposium of King Tomislav), pp. 86–127; Ljudmil Hauptmann, "The Migrations of the Croats and Serbs," *Jugoslovenski istoriski časopis*, III, 30–61; Ljudmil Hauptmann, "The Origin of the Croatian Nobility," Yugoslav Academy of Science and Art, *Rad*, CCLXXIII, 79–112. See also Bogo Grafenauer, "Some Problems Regarding the Settlement of the South Slavs in the Balkans," *Zgodovinski časopis*, IV, 23–126; Bogo Grafenauer, "A Contribution to

THE MEDIEVAL CROATIAN STATE UNDER DOMESTIC RULERS

Like the other South Slav peoples, the Croats—whether they came to the western Balkans in one or in two migrations—continued to live for several centuries in their new home in loose tribal associations recognizing foreign authority, primarily Byzantine. Even after the formation of the Croatian state in the ninth century and after it had reached considerable size and acquired considerable power—becoming a kingdom in 925—it was necessary most of the time to recognize foreign authority. This was unavoidable because in comparison with either Byzantium in the East or the Franks in the West the Croats were small and weak.[2]

Before proceeding any further it is important to make clear that the center of the Croatian medieval state in the beginning, and as long as it was under the rulers from domestic dynasties, was located in the central and northern areas of the present-day province of Dalmatia and the adjoining parts of Bosnia and Croatia, thus taking most of the old Roman province of Dalmatia. This—the so-called Dalmatian Croatia—was the cradle and the center of the Croatian state until the beginning of the twelfth century and the union with Hungary (1102). North of these areas, primarily between the Gvozd Mountain (southwest of the Kupa River) in the south and the Drava River in the north, was Pannonian Croatia, which played at that time a subordinate role. But after the union with Hungary, its role increased greatly, and gradually it became the center of Croatian political life.

The basic unit of the political organization of the Croats during the tribal period was the *župa* or *županija*, that is, the area of one tribe, in which the tribal chiefs or *župani*, recruited from the leading clans, exercised the ruling function. The *župe* continued to be the basic administrative units also in the medieval Croatian state, but with the growth of the authority of the central government, the *župani* became royal officials rather than tribal chiefs. While there exist considerable differences of opinion regarding the origin and development of the Croatian medieval state,[3] it stands to reason that the early Croatian state developed on the

---

the Critic of the Report of Constantine Porphyrogenitus on the Arrival of the Croats," *Historijski zbornik*, V, 1–56, esp. 53. For the problem of the origin and migrations of the Croats and Serbs see also Francis Dvornik, *The Making of Central and Eastern Europe*, pp. 268–304.

[2] In addition to the above works, all of which touch also on the problem of Croatian recognition of foreign authority, see especially Antun Dabinović, "The Relationship of the Croats to the Byzantine Empire from the Point of View of Public Law," Yugoslav Academy of Science and Art, *Rad*, CCLXX, 49–148.

[3] In addition to the controversial issue of one as against two migrations of the Croats, two additional questions referring to the early medieval Croatian state have produced

basis of or out of the tribal organization, when a single chief and his tribe imposed their will over other tribes and their leaders, whether by their own power or with the help of outside factors. This development was inevitable for two reasons: first, to establish a stronger and more permanent order over a wider territory, resulting in greater political and economic power of the victorious chiefs, and second, in order to strengthen the defensive power of the area against undesired outside interference.

In the phase of tribal organization, arable land in the *župe* was held as private property by individual clans and families (of which a part were apparently zadrugas or joint families). Forests and grazing lands were mostly held as tribal common. Disposition and utilization of the land were regulated by custom. How far the economic and social differentiation between the leaders and the members of the tribes advanced by the time rudimentary forms of state organization began to be formed is impossible to say, but the latter fact undoubtedly advanced the process of that differentiation. It is also not known what part of the socioeconomic institutions of the Croats in their early stages of life in the Balkans was their own, brought from the trans-Carpathian homeland, and what part they found already in use in their new home and gradually adapted to their own needs.

As soon, however, as the actual state which included many tribes took a more definite shape, part of the land in all tribes, especially their chief fortified centers and lands around them, became the property or at least fell under the control of the head of the state. Without the control of these foci of military and economic power, no ruler could hope to maintain for any length of time effective dominion over these tribes. Thereafter, by granting these lands and titles which went with them to persons and families in his trust, the ruler did two things: first, he was building up a group of powerful nobles whose power came directly from

considerable controversy and attracted much attention from the historians. These issues are the origin of the Croatian medieval state and the nature of the Croatian medieval nobility. To a certain extent all these questions are closely connected. Regarding these matters see especially: Franjo Rački, "The Internal Conditions in Croatia Before the Twelfth Century." Yugoslav Academy of Science and Art, *Rad*, LXX, LXXIX, XCI, XCIX, CV, CXV, and CXVI; Ferdo Šišić, *Geschichte der Kroaten*, p. 46 and *passim*; Mihajlo Lanović, "The Constitutional Law of the Croatian State Under Domestic Rulers," Yugoslav Academy of Science and Art, *Rad*, CCLXV, 167–242, esp. 190; Vjekoslav Klaić, *op. cit., passim*; Ljudmil Hauptmann, "The Origin of the Croatian Nobility," esp. pp. 110–12. In recent years Soviet writers have also become interested in the problem of the formation of Slavic states in the Balkans. See in this regard Alexander Vucinich, "The Soviet Theory of Social Development in the Early Middle Ages," *Speculum*, XXVI, 243–54.

the ruler or was markedly increased by the ruler and thus strengthened his own power, and second, he was reducing both the political and the economic power of the old, purely tribal nobility and of the political and economic system that it represented. Besides granting properties and privileges to persons in his trust, the ruler was granting properties and privileges also to the Catholic Church, with the idea of gaining the Church's support for the promotion of his political objectives. On the other hand, the Church was eager to support any ruler willing to further its own objectives. These objectives under the conditions existing in Croatia during the period of domestic rulers were the following: recognition by the Croats of the supreme authority of the Pope as against that of the patriarch of Constantinople, suppression of the Slavic liturgy and of that part of the Croatian clergy who were supporting it, and in the eleventh century virtual vassality of some Croatian rulers to the Pope. Thus the feudal organization in the medieval Croatian state developed slowly and gradually under the domestic dynasties from the ninth to the beginning of the twelfth century, through the advancing political and economic differentiation between the tribal leaders and the common members of the tribes whereby the latter became economically dependent on the former, and through the granting of estates, offices, and privileges by the ruler to individuals and families in his trust and to the Catholic Church.

In the Croatian medieval state under domestic rulers there were, according to Rački, the following types of land property: the land of the ruler, spread over various parts of the state and administered by the representatives of the ruler (this apparently was the main source of royal revenue); lands of the Catholic Church and its monasteries, which were granted to them by the ruler, various nobles, and other persons, or which were occasionally bought by the Church; lands belonging to the townships; lands belonging to the tribal nobility; and lands belonging to free individuals.[4]

It appears that throughout the existence of the Croatian state under the domestic rulers the main source of labor on these various properties, with the exception of those belonging to free peasants, were the slaves who were the chattel of their owners. The slaves were born as such, bought, or acquired for nonpayment of debts.[5] From the eleventh cen-

[4] Franjo Rački, "The Internal Conditions in Croatia Before the Twelfth Century. Pt. V: Property and Economic Relations," Yugoslav Academy of Science and Art, *Rad*, CV, 202–38, esp. 209–12.

[5] Viktor Novak and Petar Skok, *Supetarski kartular* (Cartulary of St. Peter), pp. 77–115. This cartulary refers to an endowment with land property and other inventory of the Monastery of St. Peter near Split in Dalmatia by a noble around 1080. The

tury onward the number of slaves fell and their place was taken by serfs as the chief source of labor on landed estates. How exactly this process advanced, what the conditions were under which the serfs lived, and what their obligations were toward the landlord in the old Croatian state are not known.[6]

In Croatia as in Serbia there was a considerable nomadic and semi-nomadic Vlakh population in the interior of the country, which in later centuries was absorbed by the feudal order and racially completely assimilated by the Slavic population. Moreover, the Dalmatian towns were populated primarily by a Romanic population which was of the same origin as the aforementioned Vlakhs.

The basis of economic life in medieval Croatian was crop agriculture and animal husbandry. From preserved records one sees that barley, oats, and wheat were produced and that in the coastal areas of Dalmatia the cultivation of grapevines and olives was very important. The chief types of livestock raised were apparently sheep and cattle. In addition to agricultural products and livestock, slaves seem to have been an important object of trade up to the beginning of the twelfth century. A portion of trade was accomplished by barter, but part was carried on with money, since Byzantine and other foreign coins were in circulation.

As stated above, the chief portion of royal revenue was apparently derived from royal estates. The nobles, the Church, the townships, and the free peasants who owned land were obliged to pay a land tax to the ruler. Many of the nobles and churches, however, were freed from this obligation. In exchange for this privilege the nobles were undoubtedly obligated to be loyal to the ruler and to go to war at his call. The Church tithe was also paid.[7]

Among the most important factors which affected the destinies of the Croatian medieval state were the following: reliance of the Croatian rulers on foreign protectors (Byzantium, the Franks, and in the eleventh century also the Pope); in religion, the issue of the Slavic liturgy and the greater influence in this regard of the clergy of Croatian origin, as against the Latin liturgy and the greater influence of the coastal towns, their clergy, and thus of the Pope; and finally, the development of

cartulary itself was written around 1105. It is interesting to note that the monastery was conceived to serve as a center for promoting Latin liturgy and the reforms coming from the West and for the suppressing of the Slavic liturgy and domestic forces supporting it.

[6] *Ibid., passim*; Antun Dabinović, *op. cit.*, pp. 96–119; Miho Barada, *Hrvatski vlasteoski feudalizam po Vinodolskom zakonu* (Croatian Feudalism According to the Vinodol Law), pp. 30–32.

[7] Ferdo Šišić, *Geschichte der Kroaten*, pp. 384–407; Mihajlo Lanović, *op. cit.*, CCLXVI, 1–10.

various offices related directly to the ruler, and the growth of their political and economic power at the expense of the tribal chiefs. While these
issues were constantly present in the Croatian state, they became critical
in the second half of the eleventh century (after the final break between
the Roman and the Greek churches in 1054). In the 1070's and 1080's
these issues came to a breaking point under King Zvonimir, a virtual
vassal of the Pope, a ruler who depended for his support almost exclusively upon the coastal towns and the high clergy, and who through
other reforms wanted to reduce the power of the old tribal nobility.
Zvonimir was assassinated at a general assembly of the nobles in 1089,
while advocating the sending of Croatian troops abroad at the request of
the Pope, and another king was elected. This precipitated the offer of
the Croatian crown by the followers of Zvonimir, with papal support, to
the Hungarian king. The ensuing war led to the defeat of the Croats, in
which their last ruler from the domestic dynasties lost his life. The following stalemate between the Croatian nobility and the Hungarian king
was solved in 1102 when the representatives of the so-called "twelve
tribes," the high Croatian nobility, reached an agreement (*Pacta con-
venta*) with the Hungarian king whereby he acquired the Croatian
crown. This political marriage lasted for over 800 years, until 1918.

UNION WITH HUNGARY AND THE INTRODUCTION OF
DONATIONAL FEUDALISM

The chief concern of the Croatian nobility in the agreement with
the Hungarian king was to ensure for themselves the properties and
privileges, including the land tax exemptions, that they had formerly
enjoyed. As obligation they pledged loyalty to the king and, in the case
of war, armed forces at their own expense to the frontiers of Croatia and
at the expense of the king beyond these frontiers. The other basic factor
for the Croatian nobility resulting from the union with Hungary was
increased general security of the country and thus of their own possessions and rights. The properties and all rights of the former Croatian
kings were now acquired by the Hungarian king. He also acquired, in
the sense of feudal law, supreme ownership over all land in Croatia
which was not owned by various tribes, institutions (e.g., the Church),
or individuals. The king now apparently owned more land than the
Croatian tribes themselves. The possession of these lands gave him a
powerful lever for the promotion of his own policies and interests in
Croatia, as he was able to make land grants to churches and to nobles in
his trust.

From the Hungarian point of view, the union with Croatia, a smaller and weaker link in the union, was advantageous for several reasons. Hungary strengthened its military position through acquisition of additional population and territory; it secured a foothold in the western Balkans, thus opening the way for extending its influence in the central parts of the Balkans, e.g., in Bosnia; it received increased standing with the Pope, whose exponent in the Danube Basin it was; and, above all, it gained access to the Adriatic Sea. This latter point was extremely important both from the political and economic points of view, but it brought Hungary into collision with Byzantium and Venice, making for several wars and great complications with the latter during the Fourth Crusade.

Croatia was strong enough, however, to assure for itself a separate administration under the new rule, with its *banus* (a Croatian institution from the times of the rulers of domestic dynasties) as the chief executive in the name of the common Hungaro-Croatian king, and from the thirteenth century also its own separate diet (Sabor). Undoubtedly, it was the strength of the Croatian nobility which assured this standing for Croatia. Of course, the actual content of the Croatian autonomy, and even its forms, differed in various periods of time and under various rulers.

The union with Hungary had a decisive influence on further political and economic developments in Croatia. It would be folly, however, even to attempt to sketch the extremely involved history of Hungaro-Croatian relations as they unfolded in the following centuries.[8] A few general remarks must suffice. The first Hungarian dynasty which ruled Croatia was the House of Árpád, which remained in power until its extinction in 1301. It was succeeded by a branch of the House of Anjou. Later, rulers from other dynasties wore the Hungarian crown and thus were also Croatian kings. Finally, in 1526 the Croatian nobles, after the Turkish victory over the Hungarians at Mohács and the virtual dismemberment of the Hungarian state, elected Ferdinand of Austria as their king. Soon thereafter the Magyars also recognized the Habsburgs as their kings, and the latter ruled Hungary and Croatia until 1918.

Undoubtedly, Hungarian influence on Croatian affairs was much more profound prior to 1526 than at any time since then, for various reasons: the Turkish victories weakened the Magyars greatly; a large portion of Croatian free territory was organized as a Military Frontier

[8] For the period from 1102 to 1526 see Bogo Grafenauer *et al.* (eds.), *op. cit.*, pp. 613–744, Vjekoslav Klaić, *op. cit.*; Ferdo Šišić, *Povijest Hrvata za kraljeva iz doma Arpadovića (1102–1301)* (History of the Croats During the Reign of the Árpád Dynasty, 1102–1301), Pt. I (1102–1205).

and subjected directly to the authority of the Austrian emperor; fundamental changes in the distribution of power and feudal properties in
Croatia after the liquidation of the Zrinski and Frankopan families in
1671 and after the liberation of Slavonia from the Turks were directed
by Austria; the granting of *urbars* during the eighteenth century was
carried out by Austria; and many of the changes which took place during
the nineteenth century were influenced more by Vienna than by Budapest.

From the point of view of internal politics and economic organization, the basic consequence of the union with Hungary was the advance
of feudalism in Croatia and its development along new patterns. Under
the new conditions feudalism in Croatia became more and more influenced by and adjusted to the Hungarian donational type of feudalism.
Under this system the king, by granting a donation to a person, was
granting to him both the title of a noble—if he did not have one before—
and the land and other rights that went with it. That means that thereafter not only the members of the old Croatian nobility, who were
the primary beneficiaries of the grants from old Croatian kings, but also
other people, primarily Hungarian nobles and other members of the
following of the Hungarian king, could obtain feudal estates in Croatia.
In Pannonian Croatia, and especially in the territory between the Sava
and Drava rivers,[9] the donational type of feudalism almost completely
supplanted feudalism based on tribal foundations by the end of the
twelfth century. Here Hungarian penetration of the Croatian body
politic, especially in eastern and central parts of Slavonia, was most
thorough, so that the leading feudal families in Slavonia became almost
exclusively families of Hungarian origin. Moreover, in this area large
latifundia were developed, through royal grants and other means, similar to those owned by the magnates in Hungary proper.

In the Croatian areas south of the Gvozd Mountain, in which tribal
formations were much stronger than in Slavonia, the normal procedure
for the Hungarian kings from the House of Árpád was to grant, or, more
precisely, to confirm, to the leading Croatian noble families as their
feudal donations the lands that they held as tribal nobles. That is the

---

[9] During the Middle Ages Slavonia referred essentially to Pannonian Croatia, that
is, areas between the Drava River in the north and the Gvozd Mountain in the south.
For some time around the sixteenth century Slavonia indicated only the area between
the Drava and Sava rivers. From the middle of the eighteenth century Slavonia denotes
only the eastern part of that area. On the other hand, the name Croatia in the narrower
sense of the word was applied to a territory steadily moving northward. Thus the territory of the present province of Dalmatia was completely excluded from Croatia, while
the western portion of old Slavonia from the Gvozd Mountain to the Drava River was
included under Croatia.

way in which a number of famous Croatian noble families held whole areas as their hereditary donations.

The basic legal difference between the Western European and the Hungarian donational type of feudalism lay in the fact that the donational feudatories were not vassals of the king, but together with the king they were members of the Holy Crown of St. Stephen, as the incarnation of the Hungarian state. The Church and the free cities were also participants in this unique community. The basis of all free land possession was in the Holy Crown. Those who held such land, which could be distributed only by the duly crowned king (to a limited extent also by the viceroy and the Croatian *banus*), were thereby in a direct relation to the Crown and thus participated in the formation and execution of state power as state organs. Thus the nobility considered itself a partner, with the king, in the state. The grants were made as full property, but without infringements on the rights of third persons, which the grantee could freely dispose of, in a heritable form (normally inheritance was limited to the male line), and free from all obligations toward the king except loyalty and military obligation. On the extinction of the grantee's family, depending on the conditions of inheritance stipulated in the donational charter, the land reverted to the Crown, as did land taken away from grantees because of treason. Treasonable acts were defined in a broad manner so that the withdrawal of donations was quite common. Of course, certain land grants were already subject to certain specific regulations and conditions when granted.[10] Most important in this regard was the fact that on certain land grants serfs were already settled and these serfs were held to obligations toward the feudal lord, in which, however, both the ruler and the Church participated. These were the lands which in Croatian legal terminology were known as urbarial lands, as against the alod lands which were not settled with serfs. In regard to the serfs, the feudal lord acquired full jurisdiction as the organ of the state.

Generally speaking, the system of donational feudalism favored large feudatories, and since in Hungary, as in other countries, they showed strong tendencies toward independence from the king, the Hungarian kings tried often to curb the power of the magnates. Thus there was a constant struggle between the king and the magnates. Sometimes the small feudatories were able to force large concessions from the Crown which, in turn, used them against the magnates. On other occasions

[10] Mihajlo Lanović, *Zapadno-evropski feudalizam i ugarsko-hrvatski donacionalni sustav* (Western European Feudalism and the Hungaro-Croatian Donational System), pp. 64–104.

various types of freemen, such as the troops in royal fortresses (*jobagiones castri*), were raised to the level of full nobility in order to provide more balance among the various groups of feudatories and between the feudatories and the king. But above all it was the concept of the Holy Crown of St. Stephen as the incarnation of the state that helped the Hungarian kings to preserve the unity of the state and some balance among the various types of feudatories.

Internal administration and taxation in Croatia were also reorganized under Hungarian rule. In place of the former *županije* as the units of tribal and governmental organization came the Hungarian organization of *comitates*, which is of purely feudal origin. In Croatia the original name of *županije* for *comitates* was maintained, but gradually the units were transformed into regional organizations of feudatories with their own diet and administrative apparatus of local government. The *comitates* remained the bulwark of political power of the feudatories until 1848, since it was through the *comitates* that the administration of the country was carried out and the laws of the central government were applied. The Croatian nobles south of the Gvozd Mountain continued to be freed from the land tax. In Slavonia, however, a general land tax, originally paid in marten skins, was revised soon after 1102, and thereafter it was paid in money. From this tax a tithe went to the Church, while two-thirds of the remainder were taken by the king and one-third by the feudatory. Many feudatories, however, were freed from paying the king's share and received the whole proceeds of the tax. The manner of payment and the nature of this tax changed greatly in later centuries. It is still mentioned in the seventeenth century, but only as an obligation of the serfs to the landlord, payable in kind.[11] As time went on, the number of taxes increased, practically all of them payable exclusively by the serfs. In addition to the state tax or regular contribution, they paid the Church tithe,[12] a special *comitate* tax, and various obligations to the feudal lord, of which more will be said later.[13] On the other hand, the alod lands of the feudatories paid only the special contribution. For some time a basic source of state income was the profit from the coining

[11] Vjekoslav Klaić, "*Marturina*—The Slavonian Tax in the Middle Ages," Yugoslav Academy of Science and Art, *Rad*, CLVII, 114–213, esp. 158 and 212–13.

[12] The most complete study of the character and development of the Church tithe in the Croatian lands is to be found in an article by Heinrich Felix Schmid, "Die Grundzüge und Grundlagen der Entwicklung des kirchlichen Zehnrechts auf kroatischem Boden während des Mittelalters," Grga Novak (ed.), *Zbornik naučnih radova posvećen Ferdi Šišiću* (*Mélanges Šišić*), pp. 423–54, esp. 444–50.

[13] Vjekoslav Klaić, "*Marturina* . . . ," *passim*; Josip Bösendorfer, *Agrarni odnosi u Slavoniji* (Agrarian Relations in Slavonia), p. 55.

of money, which later was replaced by a regular tax. Customs duty was also paid on commodities entering trade channels.

The Roman Catholic Church continued to be a most important factor in the whole feudal structure of Croatia-Slavonia after 1102, as it was during the rule of the domestic dynasties. The bishopric of Zagreb, which was established by Hungary soon after the union with Croatia, obviously as an instrument of Hungarian policy in the newly acquired lands, soon became one of the biggest feudatories in Croatia. The bishop of Zagreb often filled the position of the *banus* of Croatia.

The cities also began to play a larger role in the political life of Croatia-Slavonia. Free cities enjoying royal charters were also participants in the Holy Crown, and, as such, were owners of considerable areas of land and state organs in their territories. Furthermore, their economic importance grew as a consequence of the increase in the volume of trade and the development of handicrafts.

The social structure of Croatia during the period of advanced feudalism was quite complex and by no means static. In the main, the nobility was divided into magnates, including archbishops and bishops, and the lower nobility; that is, feudatories with large estates and performing high offices in the state and Church, and the lower nobility who had smaller estates and thus held lower state offices. Lower dignitaries of the Church corresponded to the lower nobility. Furthermore, there were nobles who had no serfs, owning only their own farms which they worked themselves. These nobles came from former troops in royal fortresses and in some cases they originated from tribal nobility. The serfs were the basic labor force in the country, and they had different names, depending on whose land they were working. Those on the estates of the temporal feudatories were called serfs or kmetovi and those on the Church properties were called praedialists. But their obligations were essentially the same. During the twelfth and thirteenth centuries there were still many slaves in the Croatian lands, but they were mostly employed in various workshops on feudal estates and as house servants. The category of slaves gradually disappeared. Furthermore, there were free peasants who were not in a position of dependence on any feudal lord, but who, naturally, were obliged to pay taxes to the ruler. Their numbers were decreasing. Furthermore, there were free citizens or burghers in towns, who were mostly organized into guilds, depending on their occupation. Most of the towns had special charters and were administered on the basis of their statutes as separate units.[14]

---

[14] Josip Bösendorfer, *ibid.*, pp. 37–62.

ALOD LANDS AND URBARIAL LANDS

The lands held by the feudatories in Croatia-Slavonia for many centuries prior to the abolition of serfdom in 1848 were divided into two basic categories: the alod lands and the urbarial lands. Alod lands were held by the feudal lords as their unlimited property, whether they received such land in the form of grants from the ruler directly or acquired it through inheritance, purchase, dowry, or the like. These lands were mostly managed by themselves or through their administrators. In such cases they were worked by *corvée* labor of their serfs settled on the urbarial land; or they kept on their alod lands regular tenants who paid rent in money or in kind, or both, as agreed by a written or parole contract or as defined by general custom. The tenants on the alod lands were not subjects of the landlord in the same sense as the serfs. The owners of alod lands were free from any duties to the state save the duty of going to war and loyalty to the Crown. The owner of such land could freely sell it, divide it, bequeath it, or mortgage it. A basic point with regard to the alod land was that it was not subject to any taxes (except temporarily certain special contributions) to the ruler or any tithe to the Church. Such lands were granted by the ruler to deserving individuals or families, and, as a rule, they were inheritable in the male line alone, although occasionally in both male and female lines. If a grantee's family died out, such lands reverted to the state and were free for new grants. Such land grants could be lost only for treason, when the property reverted to the Crown. In regard to the management of such properties there was at times a tendency to let a larger portion, or all of such land, be worked by the tenants; at other times more of such land was managed directly by the owner. Undoubtedly this depended on the amount of urbarial land that such a feudatory had, on the nature of the obligation of his serfs and thus on the amount of free labor that he was entitled to, and also on the level of rents paid by the tenants.

Urbarial lands were also obtained through grants from the ruler, inherited, bought, or obtained through dowry, but they remained encumbered by the rights of serfs to live on such land. Serfs rendered various obligations to the feudal lord, the Crown, and the Church. Such land could be disposed of freely by the feudatory, but it remained urbarial land, and the serfs could not be evicted (as a rule) from the land. In addition to the taxes to the central government and the tithe to the Church, the basic and major obligations of the serfs were toward the feudal lord. The nature and extent of these obligations changed greatly over time and differed very much from area to area. All serfs were, however, under complete jurisdiction of the feudal lord, who in his person, represented all state organs. Basic rules regarding the obligations of the serfs were stipulated in various laws of the central government (the Hungarian state), for example, in regard to the tithe in produce, the amount of tax in money, and the mobility of the serfs. Much of the time the serfs were "tied to the land" and could not leave the landlord without his consent. They could not marry or change their occupation without his consent. But, on the other hand, only under very specific and limited circumstances could the landlord evict the serf. When a serf died without male successors, his widow and daughters were given an indemnity and the urbarial land reverted to the feudal lord, but such land could not be transformed into alod land and had to be settled by another serf.

The grants of urbarial land, just as those of alod land, were of a permanent nature and inheritable. The feudatory's basic obligation for such a grant was again military duty and the duty of loyalty. Upon the extinction of the grantee's family or following treasonable activity, these grants reverted to the Crown.

While the basic rules about the obligations of the serfs settled on urbarial land were regulated by the laws of the central government, many details remained to be regulated by other means. In earlier stages, local custom and parole agreements between the feudatory and the serfs regulated in detail the obligations of the serfs. Royal grant charters also often contained data on the obligations of the serfs. From about the thirteenth to the middle of the eighteenth century one of the principal ways in which these rules were specified was by issuing of the *urbars*.[15] These were documents issued by individual feudatories (including churches), containing details on the number of serfs on their estates, their holdings of land, and their obligations. There were many such *urbars* pertaining to major feudal estates in Croatia-Slavonia. The collection of *urbars* assembled by Radoslav Lopašić,[16] containing only those written in the Croatian language (many were written in Latin and Ger-

---

[15] The origin of the medieval *urbars*, known in some areas as *libri censuales*, polyptychs, or simply as charters, is not clearly established. Josef Šusta in his study, "Zur Geschichte und Kritik der Urbarialaufzeichnungen," Study No. 8, *Sitzungsberichte der philosophisch-historischen Classe der kaiserlichen Akademie der Wissenschaften*, CXXXVIII, 8–10, thinks that they have developed from government tax rolls or cadasters of Roman times. This view is opposed by Charles H. Taylor, "Note on the Origin of the Polyptychs," in *Mélanges d'histoire offerts à Henri Pirenne*, II, 475–81, who, however, does not present a theory of his own on the origin of the *urbars*. The question of origin of the *urbars* is of no interest to us. What is important is the fact that the *urbars* represent a basic primary source of data on agricultural and social conditions of the Middle Ages.

[16] Radoslav Lopašić, *Urbari na hrvatskom jeziku* (*Urbars* in Croatian Language), Yugoslav Academy of Science and Art, *Monumenta historico-juridica Slavorum meridionalium*, V.

man) from the thirteenth to the seventeenth centuries, shows great differences in the obligations of the serfs on various feudal estates, in
various villages belonging to the same estate, and especially in various
periods of time. The obligations were always stated in terms of one
complete homestead (generally speaking, of an amount of land sufficient for the livelihood of a single family), and for its halves
and even fourths. Generally, the serfs were obligated for one or two
days of *corvée* per week, to transport services, and occasionally to military duty. They were obliged to pay one or two general taxes in cash
and a series of special taxes, to render tithes in produce ranging from
one-tenth to as high as one-fourth of the gross product, and to special
donations in kind on festive days. Furthermore, they paid the Church
tithe. It is generally agreed that the obligations of the serfs were smaller
during the Middle Ages than from the sixteenth century onward, but it
is impossible for us to enter here into this problem.[17]

Two other points have to be mentioned when talking about the alod
and urbarial lands and the *urbars*. First, all reform work with regard
to land tenure during the eighteenth century and in 1848 referred exclusively to the urbarial lands and left the alod lands of the feudatories
aside; second, laws of the central government issued during the eighteenth century regulating land tenure were also called *urbars*. These
problems, however, are discussed in later sections.

Instead of the *urbars*, certain large feudal estates had special laws
regulating in considerable detail the relations between the feudal lords
and the clergy, on the one hand, and the serfs, burghers, and other people
living in the territory of these estates, on the other. The most important
of these laws was the famous Vinodol Law of 1288 pertaining to the
Vinodol area on the upper Adriatic coast.[18]

Furthermore, several Croatian rural communities had a special
standing in regard to their government and social organization, going
back to the Middle Ages. Thus neither the free commune of Poljica
near Split in Dalmatia nor the noble communes in the neighborhood of
Zagreb in Croatia, of which the most interesting was that of Turopolje,

[17] Josip Bösendorfer, *Agrarni odnosi u Slavoniji, passim*; Nada Klaić, "Regarding
Some Problems of Feudal Organization in Medieval Slavonia," *Historijski zbornik*, IV,
107–31.

[18] Marko Kostrenčić, "The Vinodol Law," Yugoslav Academy of Science and Art,
Rad, CCXXVII, 110–226, esp. 121–26; Marko Kostrenčić, "The Vinodol Law," *Historijski zbornik*, II, 131–52. The second article by Professor Kostrenčić was prompted by
a study by the Soviet historian, B. D. Grekov, *Vinodolskii statut ob obshchestvenom i politicheskom stroye Vinodola*. Grekov read into the Vinodol Law a much greater politico-
sociological meaning than it deserves and even considered Vinodol as a miniature state
(p. 5). Miho Barada, *op. cit.*

were subject to the rule of any feudatory. These communities had special statutes (constitutions) which governed their political life and the social and economic relations among the inhabitants.[19]

SOME EFFECTS OF THE BORDER POSITION ON CROATIA-SLAVONIA

Among factors which profoundly affected the political and economic developments of Croatia-Slavonia since the Middle Ages was the fact that it served as a border area of the Hungarian and later of the Austro-Hungarian state. This meant among other things that wars were often fought in and over its territory, that the Hungarians and later the Austrians distributed much of the Croatian land to their own, more trusted feudatories at the expense of the Croatian aristocracy, and that in these areas economic advance was slow.

The border position of Croatia-Slavonia had especially important effects from the middle of the fifteenth to the middle of the eighteenth century in connection with the Turkish conquests. The first great Croatian defeat at Turkish hands took place in 1493 at Krbava Field, in which apparently the flower of the Croatian nobility was lost. The Turks conquered the bulk of Slavonia and of Croatia south of the Gvozd Mountain during the 1520's and 1530's,[20] but they engaged repeatedly in sorties and plunder raids, and were a constant military threat. The Turks remained in most of these areas until the Peace of Karlovci in 1699 and in some of them until the Peace of Požarevac in 1718. As important for the Croatian political and economic developments as these Turkish conquests and the threatening Turkish proximity was the fact that both the Croatians and the Hungarians had to look to the neighboring Habsburgs for support against the Turks. Thus from 1526 until 1918 the destiny of the Croats was closely connected not only with Hungary but also with Austria.

In areas they conquered the Turks introduced their feudal system based on military fiefs of the timar and ziamet type, but it is not necessary to discuss this system any further here (see Chapter 2).[21]

Turkish conquest caused large-scale migrations northward, both of Croatian feudatories and of peasants from conquered areas. Many of

[19] Djuro Ljubić, "Leagues and Fraternities in the Old Croatian Law and Their Relation to the Statute of Poljica," Yugoslav Academy of Science and Art, *Rad*, CCXL, 1–104, esp. 72–86 and 103.

[20] Bogo Grafenauer *et al.* (eds.), map facing p. 680.

[21] See, however, Branislav Djurdjev, "The *kanun-name* of Požega Sandjak of 1545," *Glasnik Zemaljskog muzeja u Bosni i Hercegovini*, I (New Series), 129–38; Branislav Djurdjev, "The *kanun-name* of the Sandjak of Srijem of 1588/89," *ibid.*, IV–V, 269–84.

these feudatories, especially the small ones who did not have any estates in the civil parts of Croatia-Slavonia, became administrators on the estates of the big feudatories and the Church in the civil territory, and some of them emigrated into the free areas of Hungary to the north. The peasants who moved into the free areas were settled partly on the feudal estates in the civil areas of the country, partly in the growing Military Frontier as peasant soldiers. A small part emigrated toward free areas of Hungary and into Slovene and Austrian lands. The movement of the feudatories and serfs into the civil parts of Croatia-Slavonia tended to worsen the position of the serfs in these areas. The difficulties of the serfs were greatly increased also because new levies for financing wars with the Turks, for building fortifications and caserns in the Military Frontier, and for maintenance of troops in these areas were introduced and were primarily borne by them. On the other hand, the productive capacity of the land was not increasing. Turkish plunder raids often laid the land waste and resulted in the taking of large numbers of people into captivity. All these factors prevented the country's economy from advancing and resulted in a general economic stagnation.

Another factor of considerable political import to the present day was the fact that Turkish rule led to the migration into the territory of Croatia-Slavonia of large numbers of people from Turkish-occupied areas south of the Sava-Danube line. Some of these people settled in Slavonia and other areas held by the Turks, but many more were settled in the Croatian areas within the Habsburg Empire. Most of these immigrants were of the Eastern Orthodox denomination and were settled in the Military Frontier. They form the basis for the large Serbian population which is now living in Croatia.

Throughout the centuries of struggle between the Habsburg and the Ottoman empires much of the territory of Croatia-Slavonia was fought over repeatedly. It was in this territory and in Hungary that the Habsburgs gradually organized the Military Frontier (see pp. 74–81), essentially with manpower composed of Croats and Serbs commanded by German officers, and defended the German lands and Central Europe against the Turks.

When the Turks were driven out of Croatia-Slavonia, the formerly Turkish-held areas remained largely depopulated. The succeeding colonization of Slavonia partly by population from other Croatian areas, partly by refugees from the Ottoman Empire, and partly by peasants from German lands, and the sale or distribution of land to nobles and military dignitaries of non-Croat origin resulted in great changes in racial composition and in the land tenure of Slavonia.

During the centuries of Croatian existence within the Hungarian or Austro-Hungarian state and the struggle with the Turks, the Croatian national nobility was largely eliminated. What remained was made impotent. From the fifteenth century onward little is heard of most of the old aristocracy from the "twelve tribes." But prior to that date and until well into the seventeenth century a few of these families, such as Šubić (later known as Zrinski), developed temporarily into powerful feudal families controlling large areas and holding important positions, even that of *banus* in a hereditary manner. In the course of time the lands and the position of the old Croatian aristocracy were taken over by the Hungarian (especially in Slavonia) and later especially by the German (Austrian) feudal families or nobles from many other lands who were in the service of the Habsburgs.[22] This especially refers to large feudatories. The Croatian nobility suffered a heavy blow in 1671 with the beheading by the Austrians of the chiefs of the two leading Croatian noble families of that time (Counts Zrinski and Frankopan) for their plans to free Croatia from the Habsburgs. Their properties in civil Croatia—and they owned a large portion of it—were confiscated and distributed among or sold at nominal prices to nobles and servants of the Crown who were almost exclusively of non-Croatian origin. Thus, since the last quarter of the seventeenth century the overwhelming portion of large feudal estates in Croatia-Slavonia belonged to the feudatories of non-Croatian origin and to the Catholic Church.

The association of Croatia with Hungary in 1102 was basically dictated by the wish of the Croatian tribal nobility to protect their interests against the spreading power of their kings, and through them of high court and church dignitaries. The election of Ferdinand of Habsburg for their king in December of 1526 was directly related to their need for protection against the invading Turk and came shortly after the Turkish defeat of the Hungarians at Mohács and the almost complete collapse of the Hungarian state. The virtually total submission of Croatia to Hungary in 1790 was directly related to the wish of the Croatian nobility to protect their interests against the policy of centralization and Germanization carried on by Maria Theresa and Joseph II, and against the revolutionary ideas spreading from France in the wake of the French Revolution. With the exception of some interludes, of which the de-

[22] For the extraordinary mixture of the Austrian, and to a much smaller extent, the Hungarian, nobility in the eighteenth century, see chapters on Austria by H. G. Schenk and on Hungary by C. A. Macartney in A. Goodwin (ed.), *The European Nobility in the Eighteenth Century*, pp. 102–17 and 118–35, respectively. An indication of the prevalence of foreign nobility in the South Slav lands can be gauged also from information on the owners of large estates affected by the agrarian reform after World War I (see p. 336).

struction of the families of Counts Zrinski and Frankopan in 1671 was one, this arrangement between Croatia and Hungary and/or Austria worked fairly well for the interests of the ruling class of Croatia—its nobility. In their specific geographic and political position in Europe, there was hardly any other way open to them but to co-operate with a strong neighbor. Moreover, their numerical weakness and their difficult location gave them little latitude for bargaining. Owing to this, the Croats insisted throughout their coexistence with Hungary and Austria on the inviolability of "Croatian state rights," and on the strength of this argument they obtained occasionally meager concessions. The most important consequence of the idea of "Croatian state rights" was that it helped to preserve the individuality of the Croatian territory and later of the Croatian nation as such.

The relationships between Hungary and Croatia became greatly strained after 1790, went through a critical phase in 1848–49 involving the two nations in war, and did not improve much after the Hungaro-Croatian Compromise of 1868. The basic reason for this situation was the policy of attempted Magyarization of all non-Magyars in the lands of the Crown of St. Stephen and the complete supremacy of the Magyars, or the "state nation," in the affairs of the state. The root of this Magyar policy is to be found basically in the spirit of Magyar nationalism and in what the Magyars considered as their historic mission in the Danube Basin. But it was also the spirit of nationalism among the subject nations that frustrated completely the achievement of Magyar aims.

PEASANT REBELLIONS IN CROATIA-SLAVONIA

The border position of Croatia-Slavonia, the fact that a large part of its territory was in Turkish hands and another large part was organized as a Military Frontier, and the large shifts in population were the external factors leading to increased pressure upon and greater economic exploitation of the serfs in civil Croatia. But oppression and exploitation of the serfs were intensified also by the internal developments within feudalism itself. In the course of time the needs of the feudal class began to increase and be more varied, more of the serfs' obligations became expressed in money, population increased, military technology advanced and became more expensive, the feudal class started to appreciate the advantages not only of the accumulation of landed property but also of durable consumer goods and money, and the large feudal estates began to pay more attention to the management of their lands and to sell more of their products. The serfs as the main category of producers in the feudal system had to carry on their shoulders the main burden of this whole development.

While latent opposition on the part of the serfs—and as time went on practically all peasants became serfs—against the feudal class was continuous, it became stronger and more open as feudalism developed and became more oppressive. Thus, like serfs in most other parts of Europe, the serfs of Croatia-Slavonia rebelled repeatedly against their masters.

The first revolts against the feudal lords which took place in Croatian lands were those of the subvassals and serfs on the estates of the bishop of Zagreb, primarily against the payment of the Church tithe, during the period 1326 to 1340.[23] But these were actually not peasant rebellions in the true sense of the word, because they were led by the subvassals whose specific rights and obligations, rather than those of the serfs, were involved. Peace was restored primarily by the removal of the recalcitrant subvassals from their lands and the enforcement of the obligations of the serfs. The rebellions of the townspeople against the town aristocracy in the Dalmatian city of Split in 1389 and on the Dalmatian island of Hvar between 1510 and 1514 were also not true peasant rebellions, but rather upheavals of the underprivileged groups in these localities against the privileged town aristocracy.[24]

The most notable and the most typical Croatian (and Slovenian) peasant rebellion took place in 1573 under the leadership of Matija Gubec. This rebellion was planned on a large scale, but remained only of local character, although it spread over the northwestern areas of Croatia and the neighboring areas inhabited by the Slovenes. The slogan of the rebellion was "For the Old Rights" (*za stare pravice*). This slogan is met very often where conflicts between the peasantry and the feudal lords appear. The content of the "old rights" cannot often be defined. What they generally denoted was the earlier, the traditional, and for the serfs more favorable, burden of obligations and their specific rights toward the feudal lord, to which the peasantry tenaciously clung, especially in times when the feudatories tried to increase their obligations and reduce their rights. The leaders of the Croatian peasant rebellion of 1573 planned to free the peasants from serfdom and to establish a peasant government in Zagreb responsible directly to the

[23] Ivan K. Tkalčić, "Resistance to the Church Tithe and Rebellion Against It in the Diocese of Zagreb in the Fourteenth Century," Yugoslav Academy of Science and Art, *Rad*, XLIX, 165–230; Ferdo Čulinović, *Seljačke bune u Hrvatskoj* (Peasant Rebellions in Croatia), pp. 43–49.

[24] Ferdo Čulinović, *op. cit.*, pp. 49–55.

Emperor, in whom the peasants believed as a protector against the rapacious feudatories. They also advocated equality among classes and payment of taxes and military service by all classes.[25]

The rebellion of 1573 was crushed with sword and fire within two weeks. At least 6,000 peasants were reported killed and many villages reduced to ashes.[26] This rebellion and the following ones in Slavonia were destined to failure because all decisive political, economic, and military factors at that time were in the hands of the feudal class, which in the suppression of peasant revolts showed a remarkable unity. Moreover, the Church, which itself was a leading holder of feudal estates, acted always in unison with the temporal lords when it came to the suppression of peasant rebellions. In spite of the complete failure of the 1573 rebellion and the savage punishment of its leaders and the serfs in general, the memory of that rebellion and of its leader, Matija Gubec,[27] remained a powerful factor in the psychological make-up of the Croatian peasantry and inspired it to maintain its opposition against the feudal order and its clamor for the "old rights." The fear of possible emergence of a new Gubec haunted the Croatian feudal class until the abolition of serfdom in 1848. In fact, it could be safely said that Matija Gubec was much more important as a legend than as a historical figure. As in Hungary after the crushing of the peasant rebellion of 1514, the position of the serfs in Croatia after 1573 was worsened.

In spite of the failure of the Gubec rebellion, the serfs continued to rebel in Croatia-Slavonia until the abolition of serfdom in 1848.[28] These rebellions were especially numerous in Slavonia during the eighteenth century, but they took place also in civil Croatia. Rebellions took place also among the peasant soldiery in the Military Frontier. Since these peasants were not serfs, but rather holders of military fiefs in the form of family farms, their rebellions were usually caused by actual or threatened curtailment of their special privileges and thus were different from the rebellions of the serfs against their feudal lords.

[25] Milan Durman, *Hrvatska seljačka buna 1573* (The Croatian Peasant Rebellion of 1573) ; Ante Fiamengo, "The Peasant Rebellion of 1573," *Djelo*, I, 94–103; Ferdo Čulinović, *op cit.*, pp. 56–71.

[26] Vjekoslav Klaić, *Povjest Hrvata* (History of the Croats), III, 300–301.

[27] Matija Gubec was accused also of having been proclaimed the "king of the peasants." After his capture, he was sentenced to death and executed, apparently in a manner similar to that accorded to the leader of the Hungarian peasant rebellion of 1514, George Dózsa. Gubec's flesh was first torn with hot irons; he was then crowned with a glowing iron crown and finally quartered.

[28] Josip Predavec, *Selo i seljaci* (The Village and the Peasants), pp. 148–85; Rudolf Bićanić, "The Liberation of the Serfs in Croatia in 1848," *Djelo*, I, 190–200; Ferdo Čulinović, *op. cit.*, pp. 71–148.

INTERVENTION OF THE CENTRAL GOVERNMENT IN
FEUDAL RELATIONSHIPS

During the seventeenth and eighteenth centuries the feudal order in the Habsburg Empire was subjected to growing pressures. First, there was the oppression of the peasantry, with constant passive resistance and periodic rebellions hindering improvements in agricultural production. Second, the increasing commodity production for the market brought about by the growth of the early capitalist forms affected unfavorably the production within the feudal sector, although many feudal estates increased their agricultural production for the market, promoted handicrafts within the estates, and engaged in commercial operations. Third, political ideas based on the principles of natural law and rationalism coming from Western Europe began to demolish the ideological and political tenets of the feudal regime in Central Europe. The trend toward political and social emancipation of urban and rural masses proved irresistible. Fourth, the growth of the modern state with its large standing army and advanced military technology and spreading bureaucracy collided with the feudal system and made it obsolete both as the carrier of local administration and even more so as a system of military organization. The existence of a large and well-functioning Military Frontier along the Ottoman border directly under the imperial administration, with a socioeconomic organization which was considerably better for the peasantry than the feudal system in the civil parts of the country, acted also as a disrupting factor on the feudal order in Croatia-Slavonia and Hungary. Fifth, enlarged powers, a growing body of functions of the central government, and many wars required a much larger tax revenue for the state. This was obtainable only by a radical reform of the tax system whereby a part of the tax burden was to be carried by the feudal class. Finally, the mercantilist policies of the central government in regard to the stimulation of trade, transportation, and manufacturing activity, and its increasing concern for the welfare of the serfs ran against the whole philosophy and tradition of feudalism.

These political and economic changes made relaxation of feudal bondage inevitable. Under the circumstances existing in the Habsburg Empire, the reforms could come only from above, that is, from the Crown as the promoter of the power of the central government and the representative of the general interest. Before we take a closer look at the land-tenure reforms undertaken during the eighteenth and nineteenth centuries, it is necessary to point out that in the territory of Croatia-Slavonia at that time three different land-tenure systems can be distinguished: those of civil Croatia, of civil Slavonia, and of the

Military Frontier. The latter will be discussed in the following section. In civil Croatia many nobles of Croatian nationality were still in existence. Large estates were held, however, only by the Catholic Church, by the feudal lords of foreign blood, and by a few domestic feudal families. A large number of the nobles actually had no serfs. Civil Slavonia developed during the eighteenth century along completely different lines from civil Croatia. After the expulsion of the Turks from Slavonia and southern Hungary, the newly conquered land was proclaimed the patrimony of the ruler and subjected to direct imperial administration. Until 1745 Slavonia was administered by a dual military-civilian administration and it was during that period that its new land-tenure system was developed. A small part of land in Slavonia was returned to the feudal families which owned these lands before the Turkish era. Some land was distributed to colonists brought in from the German lands, who were settled as free peasants but in much smaller numbers than in Bačka and Banat. Some land was granted to various religious orders and monasteries. A considerable portion of land was sold at nominal prices to various nobles, merchants, bankers, and government officials; some land was granted to the civilian and military dignitaries to reward them for their services to the Habsburgs; and some land remained in the hands of the military administration. The bulk of the serfs in Slavonia was the settlers who moved into the province during the eighteenth century, mostly from the various Turkish-occupied areas south of the Sava River. But some came also from the Military Frontier and other areas. Through this land policy, the medieval system of latifundia was re-established in Slavonia, although now the latifundia were in the hands of other proprietors. The difference in the structure of the feudal order between civil Croatia and Slavonia can be seen by a comparison of the numbers of nobles in the two areas. While the territory of these areas was nearly equal, the census of 1785 showed that there were in the three *comitates* of civil Croatia a total of 9,459 male nobles while in the three *comitates* of civil Slavonia there were only 314 male nobles.[29]

The first attempt at intervention of the central government into the relations between the feudal lords and the serfs took place with the issue of the Robot-Patent of 1680. It attempted only to regulate the *corvée* obligations of the serfs, but remained without practical effect. Much more regulatory was the *urbar* for Slavonia, issued by Emperor Charles VI in 1737 following the widespread peasant revolts in that

[29] Fran Vrbanić, "One Hundred Years of the Development of Population in Croatia and Slavonia," Yugoslav Academy of Science and Art, *Rad*, CXL, 32–33.

province against the abuses of the feudatories.[30] This *urbar* enumerated both the obligations of the serfs that were considered legal at that time and the rights of the feudatories. By inserting various prohibitions it also indicated the types of abuses practiced by the landlords.[31]

Enforcement of the *urbar* of 1737 had to be carried out through the *comitates*, whose administration was completely in the hands of the feudatories. Its application was therefore successfully sabotaged. But the promulgation of that *urbar* was the first important step in putting the central government into a position of arbiter between the landlords and the serfs, from which it could hardly withdraw, and it did somewhat raise the hopes of the serfs and granted them what they began to call their "new rights."

The *urbar* of 1737 proved ineffective. The abuses of the feudatories, and, therefore, the unrest of the peasants continued. New steps in the direction of alleviating the burdens of the serfs and of regulating the serf-landlord relationship were needed. The reign of the two enlightened absolutist Habsburg rulers, Maria Theresa (1740–80) and her son Joseph II (1780–90), and their legislation mark the beginning of the final stages of feudalism in the Habsburg Empire. They were also strong champions of a policy of Germanization and centralization. But they did pay a great deal of attention to the promotion of the general welfare, and their policies with regard to the problem of feudal bondage were important components of their reform work. First of all, Maria Theresa abolished as of 1745 the dual administration in Slavonia, leaving only a civilian administration, with part of the territory going to the Military Frontier. In 1756, following a peasant rebellion in the western parts of Slavonia in 1755, she issued the *urbar* for Slavonia, which came fully into effect in 1762.[32] This *urbar* was divided into two parts, the first regulating the obligations of the serfs and the second regulating various administrative and judicial matters. A full homestead was defined according to the quality of soil as 24, 32, or 40 yokes of land. The basic obligations of the serfs in Slavonia were the payment

[30] For the history of the intervention of the central government into the Slavonian serf-landlord relations during the eighteenth century, see Josip Bösendorfer, "How It Came to the Slavonian *Urbar* of 1756," Yugoslav Academy of Science and Art, *Rad*, CCXL, 220–56; *ibid.*, CCXLII, 1–92.

[31] *Ibid.*, CCXL, 241–44; Josip Bösendorfer, *Agrarni odnosi u Slavoniji* (Agrarian Relations in Slavonia), pp. 193–98.

[32] Josip Bösendorfer, *op. cit.*, CCXLII, 52–64; Josip Bösendorfer, *Agrarni odnosi u Slavoniji*, pp. 111–58, 198–205. By far the most complete collection of government laws and regulations regarding the intervention of the central government in the serf-landlord relations in Croatia-Slavonia is to be found in Milivoj Vežić, *Urbar hrvatsko-slavonski* (The Croato-Slavonian *Urbar*).

of a tithe of three florins and the rendering of 24 days of *corvée* with a team of draft animals, or 48 days of manual *corvée*, per homestead. *Corvée* with a team of draft animals and manual *corvée* could, under certain circumstances, be paid in money, with a standard wage of 20 kreutzers for the former and 10 kreutzers for the latter per day. If the landlord needed additional labor, he paid the serfs a standard wage (24 and 12 kreutzers per day, respectively). *Corvée* for public works remained. The serfs delivered one thirty-second of their wine production to the landlord, if their vineyards were not part of the urbarial land. There was no tithe in produce in Slavonia, except from newly cleared land (after three years of free use), when it amounted to one-tenth of all produce. Keeping taverns and butcher shops remained an exclusive privilege of the feudal lords, as did the rights of fishing and hunting. Agricultural workers without land, but owning a house, paid a tithe of one florin annually and rendered 12 days of manual *corvée*. New settlers were subject to the provisions of the *urbar*. The serfs were obliged to give a special donation to the feudal lord when he went to the state diet. Rural police had to be maintained at the expense of the landlords. The *urbar* contained also various provisions on woodcutting and hauling, clearance of land, and pasture utilization. Most of the serfs were subject to the judicial jurisdiction of the feudal lords. Landlords were able to punish the serfs by imposition of various fees, beatings, and irons, and sometimes even capital punishment. The Church tithe continued to be paid. In addition, of course, the serfs were obliged to pay various state and local taxes. These taxes were collected by the feudal lords, thus giving them additional opportunity for abuse.[33]

Neither the feudal lords nor the serfs were satisfied with the *urbar* of 1756, and some of its provisions were sabotaged by the landlords. But with some amendments it remained the basis of the feudal order in Slavonia until 1848.

In 1755 Maria Theresa issued a temporary and in 1780 a definite *urbar* for civil Croatia which was more detailed than that for Slavonia and considerably harder for the serfs. According to the *urbar* of 1780, a full homestead in Croatia amounted to between 14 and 24 yokes of arable land and 6 to 8 yokes of meadows, depending on the quality of soil. The *corvée* amounted to 52 days annually with a team of draft animals or 104 days of manual work per full homestead, of which 45½ days had to be actually rendered, while the remainder could be paid in money. Serfs with smaller farms had to render proportionately

[33] Josip Bösendorfer, *op. cit.*, CCXLII, 6–7; Josip Bösendorfer, *Agrarni odnosi u Slavoniji*, pp. 63–66.

smaller amounts of *corvée*. The tithe in money in Croatia was only one florin per homestead, but the serfs in Croatia, unlike those in Slavonia, had to deliver to the landlord a tithe in produce—a ninth of all crops, wine, and livestock. There was also a special tax on houses. If the landlord and serf agreed, both *corvée* and the tithe in produce could be paid in money. Furthermore, the serfs were obliged to render to the landlords a couple of capons, a couple of chickens, a dozen eggs, and a quantity of butter per full homestead annually. They were also obliged to render transportation services to the landlord. Other provisions were identical with those in the *urbar* for Slavonia.

Both in Slavonia and in Croatia the serfs could individually leave their landlord if they had fulfilled all their obligations toward him and were duly released. Migration of groups of serfs or of whole villages was not allowed. All these factors reduced the actual freedom of movement to a minimum. Both in Slavonia and Croatia the property of a serf who died without male progeny reverted to the feudal lord, after certain indemnities were provided for the widow and female progeny. But on the urbarial land thus obtained, the landlord had to settle another serf.[34]

Joseph II continued the reform work of his mother and intensified the policies of centralization and Germanization. With the law on religious tolerance he reduced considerably the power of the Roman Catholic Church in the Empire, and with the decrees of 1782 and 1783 he prohibited the activity of many religious orders, confiscated their estates, and allotted the income of these properties to a state fund for religious and educational purposes. The law of 1785 proclaimed the serfs personally free. They were able to move freely, to marry without the permission of the feudal lord, were free to go to school or take up training in handicrafts, and were free to dispose of their movable property. But they did not become the owners of the land they tilled, they became tenants. As a follower of the physiocratic ideas, Joseph II embarked on a radical tax reform which at the same time was to be a reform of the landlord-serf relationship. To prepare this reform a general census was undertaken. A decree in 1789 abolished the *corvée* obligation of the serfs and ruled that 70 percent of the gross income from the urbarial land was necessary for maintenance of the serf's family. Of the remaining 30 percent, roughly 18 percent was the over-all share of the landlord and roughly 12 percent was to be paid by the tenants as land tax to the state. Moreover, the landlords had to pay a

[34] Josip Bösendorfer, *Agrarni odnosi u Slavoniji*, pp. 111–58; Milivoj Vežić, *op. cit.*, pp. 105–45; Josip Predavec, *Selo i seljaci* (The Village and the Peasants), pp. 196–202.

land tax on income from their alodial lands, thus far free from taxes.

The political and social reforms of Maria Theresa and particularly of Joseph II aroused the strong opposition of the feudal class. Their policies of centralization and Germanization greatly strengthened the opposition of the feudal class of Hungary and Croatia-Slavonia because the protection of their feudal interests could be represented as the defense of prerogatives of their respective nations. The central government was actually unable to enforce many of the reforms, because the feudal class was still strong. Most of the reforms of Joseph II, including the tax reform and those regarding the serfs, were therefore repealed shortly before his death in 1790, while others remained only on paper. Nevertheless, a considerable easing of the position of the serfs was achieved during the years 1740 to 1790.[35]

The victory of Reaction stopped all reform work, and the old regime continued in effect essentially as before. Some further easing in the situation of the serfs came by the law of 1836, and in 1840 optional freeing of the serfs was allowed if the serfs and landlords agreed on liberation and the amount of indemnity. But the serfs refused to take advantage of that measure. The internal decay of the feudal order was already so well advanced and the external pressures upon it so strong that only a decisive push was needed to topple it. This came in the revolutionary year 1848.

THE AGRARIAN INSTITUTIONS OF THE CROATO-SLAVONIAN MILITARY FRONTIER

The third system of land tenure in the territory of Croatia-Slavonia, lasting until 1873, was the one prevailing in the Military Frontier, comprising during the nineteenth century slightly over one-half of the whole territory and somewhat less than 40 percent of the population of the land.[36] The development of the military organization and of the

[35] Josip Bösendorfer, *Agrarni odnosi u Slavoniji*, pp. 93–96; Ferdo Šišić, *Pregled povijesti hrvatskoga naroda* (A Survey of the History of the Croatian People), pp. 222–29.

[36] The literature on the Military Frontier is voluminous. Of the earlier works, three basic studies are those by Carl Bernhard Hietzinger, *Statistik der Militärgränze des österreichischen Kaiserthums* (two parts in three volumes, Vienna, 1817 to 1823), the official history by Fr. Vaniček, *Specialgeschichte der Militärgrenze* (four volumes, Vienna, 1875), and J. H. Schwicker, *Geschichte der österreichischen Militärgrenze* (Vienna, 1883), all of which this writer, unfortunately, was not able to consult. Among the most recent works is a study by Rupert von Schumacher, *Des Reiches Hofzaun*. References to this work pertain to the fourth edition of 1943. In Serbo-Croatian see Fran Vrbanić, "Economic Conditions of the Croato-Slavonian Military Frontier During the Nineteenth Century," Yugoslav Academy of Science and Art, *Rad*, CXLIV, 40–131, and Fran Vrbanić, "One Hundred Years of the Development . . . ," *ibid.*, CXL, 117–58. Re-

socioeconomic constitution of the Frontier was a gradual process which began in the first half of the sixteenth century. The Frontier became a separate territory in 1578 and continued as such, though varying in size, until its abolition. The Military Frontier or the Confine (Map 2)

MAP 2

was a belt of territory, a *cordon sanitaire*, along the border, with the Ottoman Empire extending from the upper Adriatic due north and then east and northeast up to the northern end of the Moldavian Carpathians. During the eighteenth and nineteenth centuries the Frontier was divided into the Croato-Slavonian and the Banat frontiers, and the Transylvanian Frontier further northeast (the latter not shown in Map 2). Each Frontier was divided into territorial military units— generalates, regiments, battalions, and companies—and was governed exclusively by military authorities responsible directly to the Austrian Emperor.

The organization of the Frontier began in the early 1520's, and after the selection of Ferdinand of Habsburg as Croatian king in 1526 its area steadily grew. The first century and a half of the existence of the Frontier falls in the time of Ottoman conquests in Central Europe. The immediate purpose of the Frontier was to organize a better defense of the Habsburg Empire against the Turks, both in times of war and

garding the Serbs from the Ottoman Empire who fled to the Military Frontier and settled there, see Aleksa Ivić, *Migracije Srba u Hrvatsku tokom 16, 17 i 18 stoleća* (Migrations of Serbs into Croatia in the Course of the 16th, 17th, and 18th Centuries), and Aleksa Ivić, *Migracije Srba u Slavoniju tokom 16, 17 i 18 stoleća* (Migrations of Serbs into Slavonia in the Course of the 16th, 17th, and 18th Centuries). See also Josip Bösendorfer, *Agrarni odnosi u Slavoniji*, pp. 72–78.

against their plunder raids, to control the border for the defense against pest, and later to carry on trade between the Habsburg and the Ottoman empires. But in time the Frontier acquired a larger meaning within the Habsburg Empire as an extremely cheap source of reliable and excellent military manpower. During most of the existence of the Frontier practically all males in the Frontier from 16 to 60 years of age were members of military contingents subject to call at any time. Thus its broader aim was defined as follows: ". . . the Frontiersmen should be trained soldiers, usable against any enemy, always ready for call, and costing no money in times of peace."[37] The burden in blood which the Frontier was called upon to bear is best indicated by the fact that during the Napoleonic Wars it lost over 100,000 men, or every ninth inhabitant.[38] As late as 1860, when the Frontier was in its last stages of existence, it gave one soldier for every nine inhabitants while the remainder of the Habsburg Empire gave one soldier for every 142 inhabitants.[39] Moreover, by securing the border in the southeast, one of the Frontier's purposes was to assure a free hand to the Habsburgs in other parts of Europe.

The Frontier was settled partly by the peasantry who were there prior to Turkish times, partly by the refugee Serbs and Croats from the Ottoman Empire, who were systematically attracted to settle in the Frontier, partly by peasants from civil Croatia and Slavonia, and to a very small extent by settlers from other parts of the Habsburg Empire, and their respective descendants. Relatively the largest segment of the Frontiersmen was the refugees from the Ottoman Empire and their descendants, and, of these, a majority were of the Eastern Orthodox faith. But while more than 80 percent of the total Frontier population consisted of Croats and Serbs, the officers of the Frontier troops consisted mostly of Germans, although some Croats and Serbs rose also to high positions in the Frontier.[40]

From the earliest history of the Frontier its inhabitants enjoyed special privileges as a counterpart of their permanent military obligation. Chief among these privileges was possession of small farms as military fiefs, together with personal freedom with allegiance to the Emperor directly, at a time when serfdom and subservience to feudal lords were the general rule in the surrounding areas; freedom of re-

[37] Quoted in Fran Vrbanić, "Economic Conditions of the Croato-Slavonian Military Frontier During the Nineteenth Century," p. 47.

[38] Rupert von Schumacher, *op. cit.*, p. 252.

[39] Rudolf Horvat, *Najnovije doba hrvatske povijesti* (The Latest Period of Croatian History), p. 173.

[40] Rupert von Schumacher, *op. cit.*, pp. 202–43 and *passim*.

ligion; freedom of taxation until the middle of the eighteenth century; and freedom to select local headmen, in some areas up to the middle of the eighteenth century. Moreover, in the earlier stages of the Frontier the Frontiersmen had the right to their war booty. The Frontiersmen were extremely jealous of their privileges, and on many occasions when these privileges were threatened they took up arms to defend them.[41]

The institution of military frontiers in which land is granted to settlers on condition of permanent military service originated apparently in the Roman Empire in the first half of the third century, when the defense of the *limes* was based on the frontier settlers, or *milites limitanei*. This institution was maintained in the Byzantine Empire and was greatly extended and improved during the seventh century. In fact, the great strength and resilience of the Byzantine Empire from the seventh to the beginning of the eleventh century was ascribed by some Byzantinologists to its financial and economic power based on small farms of free peasantry and military power based on professional peasant soldiers (*stratiotes*).[42] This military defense device was used by many other powers in the Middle Ages, notably the German states. The Military Frontier organized by Austria along the Turkish border was, however, one of the best-organized institutions of its kind in modern times. Owing to its efficacy, from a military point of view, and its low cost, it was copied more or less fully and successfully by the Turks in the form of captainships in Bosnia and Herzegovina, by Venice in the Dalmatian areas acquired from Turkey around the end of the seventeenth century (see pp. 98 and 116), and by Russia in the form of military colonies which existed from 1810 to 1857.[43] From the point of view of this study the importance of the Frontier consists first, in the fact that it formed the framework of socioeconomic development of a large portion of the people of Croatia-Slavonia for over 300 years, and, second, that its agrarian institutions had a direct influence on the development of the institution of the protected minimum homestead in Serbia during the nineteenth century and thus also on the maintenance and spread of that institution in Yugoslavia in the interwar period, of which more will be said in Chapter 20.

An important advance in the formal organization of the Frontier

[41] *Ibid.*, pp. 149–66; Ferdo Čulinović, *op. cit.*, pp. 78–119.
[42] Georg Ostrogorsky, *Pronija—Prilog istoriji feudalizma u Vizantiji i u južnoslovenskim zemljana* (*Pronoia*—A Contribution to the History of Feudalism in Byzantium and in the South Slav Lands), pp. 5–10.
[43] Anatole G. Mazour, *The First Russian Revolution 1825*, pp. 37–45.

was made in 1630, when the Frontier was taken from the jurisdiction of the Croatian *banus* and the rules pertaining to duties and privileges of the Frontiersmen were codified in the form of statutes. This was followed by other regulations which gradually improved and unified the organization of the Frontier and transformed it into a society dedicated exclusively to military service, in which all economic activities were directed only to enable the Frontier to perform its military functions. A general reorganization was undertaken by Maria Theresa, who issued the "Militar Gränitz-Rechte" in 1754. After the issue of this basic law, permanent settlers in the Frontier could be only peasant soldiers, the inhabitants of the towns who were also members of the Frontier soldiery, the clergy, and the officers and military administrators. The family farms of the peasant soldiers were proclaimed the property of the ruler and were granted to the Frontiersmen as heritable military fiefs as long as the Frontier family was able to respond to its basic duty, i.e., to supply and maintain one or more soldiers. The rules regarding disposition of the land and the inheritance system were so ordered that land could be owned only by peasant soldiers and to a very limited extent by other people who were allowed to reside permanently in the Frontier. The grant of land was the soldier's permanent pay. Officers were not allowed to own land in the Frontier territory because they obtained regular salaries. All people who were not serving the military purpose of the Frontier had to leave.

Even more complete was the basic law of 1807, which was issued after many years of study, at a time when the Habsburg Monarchy was under strong pressure from Napoleonic France and it was necessary to secure more thoroughly the borders in the southeast and to enable the Frontier to carry the great drain of manpower. The law of 1807 retained the basic idea that Frontier homesteads were military fiefs granted for all time to the Frontier family, provided it could respond to its military obligations. The size of full homesteads differed somewhat in various regiments. The settlers had also grazing and woodcutting rights in the pastures and in the large forest domain belonging to the state. Only Frontiersmen (*graničari*) had the right to own land fully within the Frontier, while other classes of people, e.g., artisans and merchants in towns, were either completely excluded from landownership or owned land under strict limitations, both with regard to amount and freedom of disposition. Thus neither Frontiersmen nor other people could accumulate land in the Frontier beyond a very limited extent. In addition to military service, the Frontiersmen were obliged to pay a small land tax as well as other taxes if engaged in other than agricultural occupations, and they had to render a certain amount of *corvée* for general needs of the state and for the needs of their respective communities.

The farm land of a Frontier family consisted of two parts: (*a*) a homestead consisting in some regiments of 18 yokes of arable land and 6 yokes of meadows and in others of 24 yokes of arable land and 10 yokes of meadows, and (*b*) the surplus of land, namely, the land that a Frontier family may have had over and beyond the homestead. In some cases the farm consisted of one full homestead, in others of three-quarters, a half, or even a quarter of the homestead. Dividing these farms below a certain minimum size considered sufficient for the maintenance of one family and the support of one soldier was prohibited. Generally, though the law did provide some exceptions, the homestead could not be sold, leased, mortgaged, or foreclosed.

As some traffic in land was necessary and unavoidable to give a certain degree of elasticity to the system of land tenure, all families, even those with incomplete homesteads, had a portion of their land declared surplus, and could dispose of it freely within the general provisions of the law. In cases where families were unable to work their land, owing to labor shortages caused by absence of men in military service or sickness, the military authorities ordered the neighbors to help without pay. Shifting of land from one use to another had to be approved by the proper authorities.

As the social basis of this militarily organized rural society, the Austrian authorities adopted the zadruga, the joint family, which was very widespread among the Croats and Serbs, and of which more will be said in Chapter 9. The zadruga as a large family with collective ownership of land and strong internal discipline was easier to control, and above all it could stand better than the single family the frightful drain on manpower both in time of war and in time of peace for the internal needs of the military establishment (frontier watch duty, chasing of robber and smuggler bands, and *corvée*).[44]

The tremendous drain on the manpower of the Frontier and military regulation of the economy, often without real understanding of the needs of the people, resulted in a harsh and economically rather static life in the area. Still, as long as serfdom existed elsewhere in the Habsburg Empire, the position of the Frontiersmen was considerably better than that of the serfs in civil Croatia and civil Slavonia. While the

[44] Fran Vrbanić, "Economic Conditions of the Croato-Slavonian Military Frontier During the Nineteenth Century," pp. 50–52; Rupert von Schumacher, *op. cit.*, pp. 167–201.

feudatories in these two areas constantly clamored for the reincorporation of the Frontier into the civil administration of the province, the serfs in the civil portions of the land were in favor of the extension of the Frontier. The former hoped thereby to reacquire some of their lost estates and to eliminate the alluring psychological influence of the Frontier on the serfs, while the serfs were in favor of the extension of the Frontier because that would free them from subservience to the feudal lords.

The last basic reorganization of the Military Frontier took place in 1850. The farms (military fiefs) on which Frontier families were settled were now proclaimed full and permanent property of the Frontier family. The inheritance system was changed so that the last surviving member of a Frontier family could bequeath his land by testament, while formerly it was added to the farms of needy local Frontiersmen or reverted to the state for settlement by families which could furnish men for military duty. Division of the zadrugas was allowed if the majority of the zadruga members agreed, while formerly the agreement of all members was required. *Corvée* for public purposes was abolished. Former limitations on the transfer of Frontiersmen into other professions were removed, granting them freedom of occupational mobility. These and many other changes in the constitution of the Frontier were a sign of the times. Two basic sets of factors caused the decadence of the Frontier, and these forces became stronger as the nineteenth century advanced. First, the frontier toward Turkey was pushed into the middle of the Balkan Peninsula and Turkey lost its earlier military significance, thus removing much of the military *raison d'être* for the continuation of the Frontier. Second, the advance of political and social ideas, especially those of nationalism and democracy, made the maintenance of the Frontier politically impossible. Its military organization precluded the introduction of modern political institutions, and the maintenance of its contingents represented a danger to the development and maintenance of democratic institutions in the whole Dual Monarchy, which was clearly shown in 1848 when Frontier troops were used to fight democratic revolutionaries all over the Empire. Moreover, the advance of capitalism in the Dual Monarchy could not be stopped at the borders of the Frontier, which was clearly attempted in its earlier constitutions.[45]

After the demilitarization of the Frontier in 1873 and especially after its reunification with other parts of Croatia-Slavonia in 1881, its

---

[45] Rupert von Schumacher, *op. cit.*, pp. 269–88.

administrative and legal system was adapted to that of the civil parts of the land. One of the agrarian institutions developed at the time of the demilitarization of the Frontier, the so-called "property commune," i.e., communal properties of grazing lands and especially of forests, survived until 1947. It developed in the following way: After the demilitarization of the Frontier the forests and grazing lands, totaling 1,245,000 cadastral yokes in which Frontiersmen had grazing and wood-cutting rights, were separated into two parts. One part amounting to 493,000 cadastral yokes was taken over by the government. In it the peasants lost the rights of woodcutting and grazing. The other part, amounting to 752,000 cadastral yokes, was consolidated into the property communes and made the full property, albeit collective, of the respective communities.[46] Since most of the Frontier in Slavonia and parts of it in Croatia had many forests, these property communes were often very rich. A similar institution existed in the civil portions of the land under the name of "land associations," but of this more will be said below. There was an important difference between the two, however. The rights in the land associations could be sold and the associations could be divided, neither of which could be done in regard to the property communes. Both property communes and land associations were nationalized by a special law of the republican government of the People's Republic of Croatia of April 15, 1947.[47]

FRENCH OCCUPATION OF THE SOUTH SLAV LANDS, 1806–13

A factor of great importance for political and social development in the South Slav nations during the nineteenth century was the ideas proclaimed by the French Revolution of 1789, though their influences were felt considerably later. The advance of these ideas was much helped by the short but eventful rule of the French in the South Slav areas. French troops occupied Dalmatia, including the Republic of Dubrovnik (Ragusa) in 1806. In 1809 by the Peace of Schönbrunn France also obtained parts of the Croatian Military Frontier and of civil Croatia, all of Istria and Trieste, and most of the areas inhabited by the Slovenes. All of this territory and a large portion of Carinthia were then consolidated into the Illyrian Provinces and made part of the French Empire.

From the French point of view the establishment of the Illyrian

---

[46] Stanoje Stanojević (ed.), *Narodna enciklopedija srpsko-hrvatsko-slovenačka* (National Encyclopedia of the Serbs, Croats, and Slovenes), II, 36–37.

[47] Ivo Krbek, "The Nationalization of Land Associations and Property Communes," Yugoslav Academy of Science and Art, *Rad*, CCLXX, 41–66.

Provinces had several purposes. Militarily, it was supposed to consolidate French rule in Italy, to outflank Austria from the south, and to establish direct territorial contact with the Ottoman Empire. Economically, the main objectives of the provinces were, first, to complete the Continental blockade against British trade with the European mainland, especially through Trieste, and, second, to establish an overland route for the Franco-Levantine trade.[48]

While French rule lasted only a few years, it was very eventful because the French not only preached but also practiced revolutionary principles. First of all, the French established an efficient system of administration and separated the administrative from the judicial agencies of the government. They developed a good system of schools where before there were only few or none. They introduced national languages both into the government and into schools and started to publish the first paper in the national language. This innovation later contributed greatly to the cultural and political renaissance of the South Slav nations. All people were declared equal before the law, thus eliminating at one stroke the previously existing medieval stratification of society. Former serfs were proclaimed full owners of the land they tilled, and former owners of the land were promised an indemnity. The tithe was maintained but transformed into a state tax; it continued to be paid in kind. *Corvée* for the landlords was abolished outright without any indemnity. The tithe for the Church was abolished and its former receivers promised indemnity. Code Napoléon took the place of a variety of statutory laws and customs dealing with civil matters. Land reclamation work was undertaken in many areas, cisterns for potable water were built, systematic measures for the improvement of agricultural techniques were undertaken, handicrafts and trade were promoted, strict decrees against usury were proclaimed, and various public health measures were instituted. Furthermore, the French built or improved a whole network of roads.

A considerable portion of this impressive reform work remained on paper, because at that time the French were almost constantly at war and their rule was all too short for many of the political and social reforms to take deeper roots. It is interesting to note, however, that considerable differences of opinion exist among Yugoslav scholars in their appraisal of the French rule in the Illyrian Provinces. Some historians were of the opinion that Dalmatia, for example, had not ex-

[48] Melitta Pivec-Stelè, *La vie économique des Provinces Illyriennes (1809–1813)*, pp. 10–27.

perienced such prosperity since Roman times,[49] while others thought that
the French left Dalmatia economically in ruins.[50] But in the most complete work on the economic conditions in the Illyrian Provinces during
French rule, it was pointed out that the effects of that rule differed considerably in regard to various branches of the economy and in various
areas, as well as at various times.[51]

Needless to say, the victory of Reaction after the collapse of the
Napoleonic regime swept away all these liberal measures and programs.
But the ideas of the French Revolution and the reforms undertaken by
the French in the Illyrian Provinces gave to the Croats and Slovenes
in the cultural, political, and social fields an impetus which was not
lost and bore fruit in later decades.

ABOLITION OF SERFDOM IN 1848

The French Revolution of 1789 and the Napoleonic regime had a
great influence on the emergence or strengthening of cultural and political nationalism and the emergence of democratic ideas in the South Slav
lands, as elsewhere in Continental Europe. But it was the Paris revolution of February 1848 that caused a general liberal revolutionary
wave in Europe and played a direct hand in the abolition of serfdom
in the Habsburg Monarchy, including Croatia-Slavonia. Long before
1848, however, feudalism in Croatia-Slavonia was in the process of
decline and disintegration. Politically, the most important reason for
the disintegration of feudalism was the advance of liberal political
ideas which militated against the medieval stratification of society
comprising the privileged few, on the one hand, and the great mass of
underprivileged people deprived of all political rights, on the other.

Economically, the most important cause of the disintegration of
feudalism was the advance of the dynamic system of capitalism, with
all that this implied for the economic and social life: growth of market
and money economy, growth of the urban economic sector and manufacturing production, rise of the bourgeoisie, strengthening of the centralistic and bureaucratic state, etc. Owing to these political and
socioeconomic changes, the feudal class of the Habsburg Empire, including that of Croatia-Slavonia, became less and less capable of coping
with the political and economic developments of the eighteenth and

[49] Ferdo Šišić, *Pregled povijesti hrvatskoga naroda*, pp. 268–79.
[50] Grga Novak, *Prošlost Dalmacije* (Dalmatia's Past), Pt. 2, pp. 293–315.
[51] Melitta Pivec-Stelè, *op. cit.*, pp. 333–44. For a general appraisal of the French
rule in the Illyrian Provinces see also Hermann Wendel, *Der Kampf der Südslawen um
Freiheit und Einheit*, pp. 113–39.

nineteenth centuries. Another difficulty facing the feudal class of Croatia-Slavonia, in particular, was that toward the middle of the nineteenth century almost half of the nobles (the lower and peasant nobility) had no serfs and economically were not in a much better position than the serfs.[52] This economic differentiation among the nobles produced also political tensions, so that the feudal class itself was divided both economically and politically.

It is interesting to note that by the middle of the nineteenth century there existed great differences also in the size of farms held by the serfs in various areas of civil Croatia-Slavonia. Rudolf Bićanić's study of 10,468 serf households, settled on 6,450 homesteads on 113 feudal estates, and accounting for about one-fifth of all serf homesteads in 1847, showed that in the *comitate* of Zagreb in Croatia roughly one third of the serfs held one full homestead and more land, accounting for about 55 percent of the homesteads included in this survey. On the other hand, in the *comitate* of Srijem in Slavonia, where the latifundia system prevailed and strong capitalist elements were already at play in agriculture, only 1.1 percent of the serfs held farms of one full homestead and more land, accounting for only 3.7 percent of the homesteads included. In Slavonia the number of serfs with dwarf farms and of landless agricultural workers was already large. In spite of being serfs, some of the peasants in Croatia-Slavonia were quite wealthy and engaged in trade with livestock and in usury.[53]

The truly revolutionary and democratic temper of the Croatian population in 1848 is best shown in the so-called "popular demands" formulated by the popular assemblies in various parts of civil Croatia-Slavonia and in the Military Frontier, in the "popular demands" formulated by the assembly convened in Zagreb on March 25, 1848, and in the June–July, 1848, sessions of the Croatian Diet (Sabor). The immediate cause which led to this revolutionary situation in Croatia-Slavonia was the liberal revolution in Vienna in March 1848 and the forcing through of a constitution by the Hungarian Diet in April 1848.[54]

One of the early acts of the Hungarian Diet sitting in Pressburg after the proclamation of the Constitution was the abolition of serfdom. As the Croatians were not willing to accept the decision of that Diet, it

[52] Rudolf Bićanić, "The Liberation of the Serfs in Croatia in 1848," p. 191.

[53] *Ibid.*, p. 196.

[54] Vaso Bogdanov, *Društvene i političke borbe u Hrvatskoj 1848/49* (Social and Political Struggles in Croatia in 1848/49), pp. 101–242; Jaroslav Šidak, "Revolution of 1848–49," *Historijski zbornik*, I, 25–41; Rudolf Bićanić, "Industrial Revolution in Croatia and the Year 1848," *ibid.*, pp. 67–101.

was claimed that the Croatian Diet had to pass a similar law. But the decision of the Hungarian Diet became known among the peasants in Croatia, and the serfs accepted its decision. The liberation of the serfs in Croatia-Slavonia was formally confirmed by the proclamation of the newly appointed *banus* of Croatia, General Jelačić, on April 25, 1848, but the laws to that effect were passed by the Croatian Diet during its sessions the following June and July. The serfs refused to render *corvée*, tithes, and other obligations to the landlords and the Church from the time of the unofficial announcement of their liberation, and they rebelled in some areas where landlords tried to force them to old obligations, so the official proclamation and the passing of the necessary laws by the Diet were only the recognition of an accomplished fact. Speedy formalization of the new situation was designed to a large extent to forestall more radical developments, which were a distinct possibility.[55]

The basic principles of the new legislation were that the obligations of the serfs based on the *urbars* in regard to *corvée*, tithes, Church tithe, and various minor obligations to the feudal lords were abolished, that the former serfs were proclaimed completely free, that they become full owners of the land they had tilled as serfs, and that the feudal lords and organizations which owned urbarial lands were to be fully indemnified for their lost rights and rents. The full ownership rights of the feudal lords in their alodial lands were not affected in the least by the reform. The property of the feudal lords and Church property became subject to general taxation.

While the main act of the liberation of the serfs was carried out in 1848, the completion of the reform in its legal, administrative, and financial aspects took almost 30 years. Most of this was carried out during the neoabsolutist era of the 1850's without participation of those political factors which played an important role during 1848–49.[56]

The main issue for the feudatories of Croatia-Slavonia in 1848 was not the saving of feudalism, for the great majority among them were convinced that it could not be saved, but the amount of indemnity to be received for the lost rents and rights. As a rule, the landlords obtained

[55] Vaso Bogdanov, *op. cit.*, pp. 105–13, 227–42; Aleksije Jelačić, *Seljački pokret u Hrvatskoj i Slavoniji god. 1848–49* (Peasant Movement in Croatia-Slavonia in 1848–49) ; Josip Predavec, *op. cit.*, pp. 203–12.

[56] The most complete collection of documents pertaining to the liberation of the serfs in 1848 and the settlement of various administrative, legal, and financial matters connected with that agrarian reform is to be found in Milivoj Vežić, *Urbar hrvatsko-slavonski*, pp. 353–588. See also Josip Bösendorfer, *Agrarni odnosi u Slavoniji*, pp. 178–92.

indemnities amounting to the annual rents from their properties or other rights capitalized for 20 years. The former serfs paid these indemnities over a period of 20 years, together with the land tax. The grazing lands and forests in which the serfs had the rights of grazing their herds and of woodcutting were divided (segregated) between the landlords and the serfs. The portion of these lands that was given to the landlords became their full property. The portion which fell to the former serfs, however, was not divided into individual plots and assigned to individual peasant households, but rather was consolidated into the so-called land associations, belonging to each commune as mass partnership property. The land shares in these associations could be sold and associations could be divided, but only according to the rules of special laws governing the ownership rights, inheritance, transfer, and management of the land belonging to these associations. As mentioned earlier, this special regime pertaining to land associations and to the property communes in the territory of the former Military Frontier continued in operation until 1947, when these properties were nationalized (see p. 81).

The abolition of serfdom created problems of adjustment for both the erstwhile feudatories and the serfs. A considerable number of the former were not able to make the adjustment to new conditions, which required a radical change in their psychology and a modernization of their estates if they had any alod lands. Some were uprooted, especially those with small and badly managed properties and those who tried to live beyond their means. Other nobles made the transition successfully, the more so as their alod lands, which often were managed as large agricultural units, were not touched by the agrarian reform of 1848. Of course, they depended now exclusively on hired labor, which, however, was plentiful and cheap. Many of these estates included large hectarages of arable land and large tracts of grazing land, and especially of forests. In time some of these estates established plants for processing of agricultural raw materials, modern livestock farms, fish farms, and lumber mills. Some were run by trained agricultural managers. Thus a large number of former feudatories successfully transformed their former alod estates, increased by the grazing and forest lands that they obtained through segregation after 1848, into efficient capitalist agricultural enterprises. But many large estates continued to be run inefficiently. Some of the large estates developed anew as capitalist enterprises in agriculture, but the overwhelming number of large estates in the whole northern territory of the later state of Yugoslavia were of feudal origin.

The adjustment of the former serfs to the new conditions was easily achieved. Not all of the serfs profited in the same manner from the agrarian reform of 1848. The former serfs with larger properties profited most from the reform. The serfs with smaller holdings now had more time to devote to the land they tilled, and especially much more time to work for wages either in agriculture or outside. Soon after 1848, peasant farming in Croatia-Slavonia came under a triple pressure, caused by a growing money and market economy powerfully stimulated by the development of communications and larger production, a large increase in the peasant population, and the inclusion of the agriculture of Croatia-Slavonia in the nexus of international economy, creating thus the problem of competition in agricultural products on an international scale. Naturally, the first and third factors also affected agriculture on the large estates, many of which were in a better position to cope with those problems than the peasant farmers.

While the liberation of the serfs in 1848 did not solve all the problems of the Croatian peasantry, it represented the fulfillment of the centuries-old yearnings of the peasant people for personal liberty, ownership of the land they tilled, freedom from obligations toward the feudal lord and the Church, and freedom of action to improve their economic position.

One of the consequences of the abolition of serfdom in 1848 of considerable import for the peasantry of Croatia-Slavonia was the speeding up of the process of dissolution of the zadrugas. The many causes of that process during the second half of the nineteenth century are treated fully in Chapter 9. What has to be stressed here is the fact that the division of the zadrugas on a large scale was impossible as long as the feudal order existed, because the division of the serf's farm required permission of the feudal lord. As it was generally believed that a larger family was a better source of *corvée* labor, such divisions were not in the interest of the feudal lord and thus, as a rule, were not allowed. The abolition of serfdom and the introduction of the Civil Code in Croatia in 1853 gave full freedom to the peasants to divide the zadrugas. As many other forces were favoring their division, a general trend of zadruga dissolution appeared.

The dissolution of the zadrugas proceeded in Croatia-Slavonia without check until 1889, when the Law on the zadrugas was passed, which prohibited their division if the resulting peasant farms were to be below a certain minimum in size (*najmanja izmjera*). This minimum varied from region to region. In the densely populated areas it had to be at least three or four yokes of land (one yoke equals 0.5755 hectare) per family of six members, while in less populated areas it amounted to six or eight yokes per family of six. No zadruga could be divided without the majority approval of its adult members, and the property of the new households resulting from the division of the zadruga had to be registered in the land property records as the property of the family collective; that is, the new families remained zadrugas. For the property of the divided zadrugas to be registered as individual property of the father of the family or of any other member or members of the new family, the consent of all adult members was required. But the prohibition of the Law of 1889 against dividing zadrugas if the resulting farms would be smaller than the legally defined minimum was circumvented by many peasants by resorting to secret division. The basic purpose of this law, and of its amendment of 1902, was to prevent the pauperization and proletarization of the peasantry. Thus, in spirit, it was similar to the protected minimum homestead legislation in pre-1912 Serbia.

POLITICAL DEVELOPMENTS IN CROATIA-SLAVONIA, 1860–1918

Political life in Croatia-Slavonia during the second half of the nineteenth century and up to the end of World War I was conditioned by its constitutional position within the Austro-Hungarian Monarchy. After a short democratic interlude in 1848–49, a period of neoabsolutism directed from Vienna was imposed on the Habsburg Empire, lasting until 1860. The defeat of Austria in the war with Prussia in 1866 and the internal pressure for constitutional reform led in 1867 to the Austro-Hungarian Compromise, establishing dualism, which regulated the relationships between the Austrian and the Hungarian halves of the Habsburg Monarchy until 1918. In 1868 the Hungaro-Croatian Compromise was concluded, granting Croatia a semiautonomous position within the Hungarian half of the Empire. Croatia continued to have its own diet (Sabor), but its chief executive, the *banus*, was appointed by the king at the suggestion of the Hungarian government and was not responsible to the Sabor. Croatia was independent in matters of internal administration, education, and judiciary, and certain economic matters, while all other affairs were common with Hungary. Hungarian political, economic, and cultural encroachments on Croatia-Slavonia even after the Compromise were a source of intermittent conflict, which ended in 1918 with the complete dissolution of this long-enduring and, for the last 130 years for the Croats, decidedly unfavorable political marriage.

The upheavals of 1848–49 broke the political monopoly of the feudal class in Croatia-Slavonia, though both the former feudal class and the Catholic Church continued to wield some, but steadily declining, political power in the following decades. Since the middle class was very small in Croatia-Slavonia, and because of the political tradition in the Habsburg Empire and the fact that both in Austria and in Hungary the former feudatories continued to wield great power, the middle class could not inherit the political position held formerly by the feudal class. Instead, bureaucracy, which was strong even before 1848, became together with the armed forces the most important political factor in the country.

Political parties began to be organized in a formal sense in Croatia-Slavonia in 1841, partly under the influence of the developments in Hungary and partly as a consequence of the cultural and political renaissance in Croatia-Slavonia itself.[57] The first was a party of conservatives organized by the nobility and dedicated to the preservation of the existing political and social order and close co-operation with Hungary. In one form or another a conservative, pro-Hungarian party existed until 1918. Also in 1841 a liberal popular party, led and composed mostly of intelligentsia, was launched, and was the political emanation of the cultural and literary Illyrian movement, which reached politically its first flowering in 1848–49. Early in the 1860's an ultra-nationalist Croatian party was formed which professed to be against Austria and Hungary and for a completely independent Croatia on the basis of "Croatian state rights."

The basic political problem in Croatia from the 1860's until 1918 was whether to co-operate or not, and how to co-operate with Austria and Hungary (after 1868 especially with Hungary). While the representatives of the Croatian political parties, especially those in opposition, were often very vocal, both their influence and that of the parties supporting the existing situation were of limited significance. This was especially true from 1883 until 1903 when Croatia was under virtual dictatorship of its *banus*, a Hungarian noble. With the growing urban population, with growing political education and experience, the Croatian bourgeois parties advanced in stature, and at least some of them learned the advantages of political co-operation against a divisive policy which was favored from Budapest. Thus, in the decade before World War I the political parties in Croatia-Slavonia showed some real strength and even in the opposition began to wield some

[57] Josip Horvat, *Stranke kod Hrvata i njihova ideologija* (Political Parties in Croatia and Their Ideology), pp. 25 ff.; Vaso Bogdanov, "The Beginnings of Party-Political Life in Croatia," *Hrvatsko kolo*, Nos. 1–2, 1951, pp. 112–33.

influence. But these political parties were almost exclusively the representatives of the urban population and intelligentsia.

The mass of the Croatian population, the peasantry, which formed over 80 percent of the total population, remained, however, essentially in political bondage until World War I. This population was virtually disfranchised by setting up a very high tax payment qualification for the right to vote. In a population of roughly 2.5 million people in 1906, there were only 45,381 persons who had the right to vote.[58] A revision of the election laws brought this number to about 190,000 in 1910. Furthermore, it was thought at that time that a good goulash and a liter of wine on the morning of election day could buy the vote of any peasant.

A new factor in Croatian political life appeared in 1905 with the launching of the Croatian Peasant party by the brothers Antun and Stjepan Radić. The significance of this political party lay in the fact that it resolutely and persistently strove for, and finally achieved after World War I, the political education and mobilization of the politically passive peasantry, which was slighted by the bourgeois parties. The political mobilization of the peasant masses was a partial fulfillment of the principles of democracy in a peasant country. The Croatian Peasant party acquired only a small following before 1914, but the educational and organizational drives of the Radić brothers in pre-1914 years, the collapse of the "old system" during World War I, and the breakthrough of the ideas of democracy and national self-determination into the lands of the dissolved Dual Monarchy enabled it to develop immediately after World War I into the greatest party, and, soon thereafter, into a practically single-party political force among the Croats (see pp. 254–60).

[58] Rudolf Horvat, *op. cit.*, p. 292.

CHAPTER 4

BOSNIA AND HERZEGOVINA

BOSNIA was the last of the large medieval South Slav states to lose its independence. The original cradle of the state was in the central sector of the present-day province of Bosnia, and its independent statehood began in the second half of the twelfth century. But throughout its existence it had intermittently to recognize foreign suzerainty, especially Hungarian. In the process of its growth it acquired lands from both Serbia to the east and southeast and from Croatia to the west and northwest. Thus large segments of Serbs and Croats were for the first time under a single state roof. With its mixed population, Bosnia has continued to the present time to be a kind of buffer and an object of contention between these two nations. In spite of its large territory, the Bosnian medieval state showed two fundamental weaknesses. First, centrifugal propensities of the leading feudal families, especially those in eastern Bosnia and in Herzegovina, were exceedingly strong. Second, the state lacked a unified church that could serve it as a powerful support, in contrast to the Serbian medieval state or many medieval Catholic states. On the contrary, throughout its whole existence it was torn by religious dissentions which weakened the state internally and led to continuous struggles with the Roman Catholic Church and with the neighboring countries.[1]

CHARACTERISTICS OF THE BOSNIAN MEDIEVAL FEUDALISM

Medieval Bosnia was a typical feudal state. The standing of a feudal lord was obtained with the grant of a feudal estate or "noble land" (*plemenita zemlja*) from the ruler. These grants occasionally included whole areas and important fortified towns. But such a grant had most of the time to be approved by all other nobles. This fact, together with their right to elect the king, indicated the great power that their assemblies (*rusag, stanak*) exercised in the state. These grants were of the alod type, and the grantees were free to dispose of them in any way they

[1] For a general history of Bosnia and Herzegovina see Vladimir Ćorović, *Historija Bosne* (History of Bosnia), I, and Bogo Grafenauer et al. (eds.), *Istorija naroda Jugoslavije* (History of the Peoples of Yugoslavia), I, 515–76. Herzegovina acquired a certain degree of independence in the middle of the fifteenth century and has since maintained its special individuality.

saw fit. The grants were distributed by the ruler in recognition of various services rendered to him by the nobles. While in many grant charters the military obligation of the grantee was stated, others did not mention this obligation, which, however, was self-evident. All charters are based on mutual loyalty between the grantor and the grantee, just as was the practice in Western and Central Europe.[2] The grant could be withdrawn only for high treason. According to the size of their estates, the nobles were divided into the higher and lower nobility. No documents were preserved which would indicate the existence of military fiefs in medieval Bosnia, that is, grants of land in exchange for military obligation, which, however, could be withdrawn by the ruler at will or after the death of the grantee. Furthermore, under the influence of the Bogomil sect, which was opposed to landownership by churches, there were no large feudal estates in the hands of monasteries and churches in medieval Bosnia,[3] as was the case in Serbia and to a lesser degree in Croatia. Both of these factors show that the medieval Bosnian feudal system was not influenced by the Byzantine feudal system, in which both the military fief (*pronoia*) and the monastic estate played an important role.

There is almost no original information on the actual conditions of serfs (*ljudi*, kmetovi) in medieval Bosnia. The lack of data on the obligations of the serfs led some authors to state that serfs in medieval Bosnia were obliged to deliver to their feudal lord usually one-half or one-third of the gross product of the land they worked, that they were not "tied to the land" and were not obliged to render *corvée* to the feudal lord. They concluded that the position of the serfs in Bosnia was considerably better than that of the serfs in the Serbian medieval state.[4] This line of reasoning has been challenged recently as untenable, and attempts are being made to prove that the conditions of the Bosnian serfs were similar to those in the neighboring states. This proof is sought on the basis of information pertaining to the neighboring areas,

---

[2] Aleksandar Solovjev, "Grant Charters Issued by the Bosnian Rulers," *Istorisko-pravni zbornik*, I, 79–105, esp. 91–102.

[3] *Ibid.*, pp. 80, 96.

[4] The chief authority for this view is Ćiro Truhelka, who was connected for many years with the Provincial Museum of Bosnia and Herzegovina. Cf. Ćiro Truhelka, "The Historical Foundations of the Agrarian Problem in Bosnia," *Glasnik Zemaljskog muzeja u Bosni i Hercegovini*, XXVII, 109–218. From this source this view spread to a large portion of pre-World War II writings on the history of agricultural relations in Bosnia and Herzegovina. See, for example, Otto von Frangeš, *Die sozialökonomische Struktur der jugoslawischen Landwirtschaft*, p. 136; Vaso Čubrilović, "The Origin of Moslem Nobility in Bosnia and Herzegovina," *Jugoslovenski istoriski časopis*, I, 368–403, esp. 382–83.

or to areas which were once under Bosnian rule but were transferred to other states (parts of the territory of the Republic of Dubrovnik, certain areas in Serbia). According to this view, in addition to obligations in kind, which probably had varied greatly from area to area and even among various estates, the Bosnian serfs were obliged to render *corvée* to their feudal lord and were "tied to the land."[5] While this view seems quite plausible, it is only a conjecture, not based on unimpeachable Bosnian documents.

As in many other countries, the serf relationship was often established by agreement between a free peasant who wanted to increase his security and a feudal lord who was able to provide it. In addition to the serfs, there were in medieval Bosnia also free peasants, some purely nomadic and quasi-nomadic peoples (Vlakhs), and finally, up to the end of the fifteenth century, some slaves.

BOGOMILISM

One of the basic marks of the medieval Bosnian state was the existence within its territory of a sect of Gnostic and Neo-Manichaean character, known as Bogomils, Patarini, Bosnian Christians, or the Bosnian Church, whose members were considered heretics and were fought with determination by both the Roman Catholic and the Eastern Orthodox churches. The true nature and significance of the Bosnian Church have been a matter of debate in Yugoslav historiography for over 80 years. The debate is still continuing.[6] It seems beyond doubt,

[5] Vojislav Bogićević, "The Abolition of *Corvée* and the Introduction of the *Trećina* in 1848," *Istorisko-pravni zbornik*, III–IV, 181–99; Vojislav Spaić, "The Land Property System in Medieval Bosnia," *ibid.*, I, 107–15.

[6] Božidar Petranović, *Bogomili. Crkva bosanska i krstjani* (The Bogomils. The Bosnian Church and the Bosnian Christians); Franjo Rački, "The Bogomils and Patarini," Yugoslav Academy of Science and Art, *Rad*, VII, 84–179; VIII, 121–87; X, 160–263. Of newer studies the most important are Jaroslav Šidak, "The Problem of the 'Bosnian Church' in our Historiography from Petranović to Glušac," Yugoslav Academy of Science and Art, *Rad*, CCLIX, 37–182; Vaso Glušac, *Istina o bogomilima* (The Truth About the Bogomils); Aleksandar Solovjev, "The Disappearance of Bogomilism and the Islamization of Bosnia," *Godišnjak Istoriskog društva Bosne i Hercegovine*, I, 42–79; Dragutin Kniewald, "The Veracity of the Latin Sources Regarding the Bosnian Christians," Yugoslav Academy of Science and Art, *Rad*, CCLXX, 115–276. According to Kniewald (p. 269), "The Bosnian Christians were a Neo-Manichaean sect, related and similar to the Cathari, Patarini, and the Albigenses in the West, and to the Bogomils in the East. It appears that they originated from the Bulgarian Bogomils, and that together with the latter they influenced the Neo-Manichaean sects in the West."
One of the most important studies on Bogomilism in English is Dmitri Obolensky, *The Bogomils*. Obolensky concentrates his attention on Bogomilism in Bulgaria and Macedonia, dealing with the sect in Russia, Serbia, and Bosnia only in an appendix. But he pointed out that in no other country did this faith have such repercussions as in Bosnia (p. 285).

however, that this Church emerged as a protest against the too great worldliness and power-seeking of both the Roman Catholic and the Eastern Orthodox churches, and against their interferences directly, and through their exponents such as the Hungaro-Croatian kings and Serbia, in Bosnian affairs.[7] This Church was, therefore, what in modern times would be characterized as a nationalist and democratic movement which found many adherents in a country in which Christianity and the two great churches were not yet fully consolidated.[8] The sect had undoubtedly many social-revolutionary features up to the last century of its existence, when it tied itself completely with the feudal class.

While the sect penetrated into the ruling groups of the state, including its rulers, its loose hierarchical organization, pacifism, and lack of worldliness prevented it from serving as a politically constructive bulwark of the state. On the contrary, the spreading of the sect involved Bosnia in continuous struggles with the Catholic Church and in wars with Hungary and to a lesser extent in controversies with the Serbian Orthodox Church and Serbia. In this regard Hungary acted both as an agent of Rome and on its own account in order to further its influence in the Balkan area. But both the Bosnian State and the Bosnian Church withstood all these religious, political, and armed attacks for almost three centuries, although at times both the Church and the State had to make concessions to the Catholic Church and to Hungary. The result was different, however, when they were matched with the Turks and Islam.

The special significance of the Bosnian Church from the point of view of this study lay not only in its influence on the nature of feudalism and thus on the land tenure in medieval Bosnia, but especially in the influence of that Church on the attitude of its members toward the Turkish rule and Islam after the conquest of Bosnia, which materi-

---

[7] The idea that the Bogomils (including here not only Bosnian but also Macedonian and Bulgarian Bogomils) were ideological precursors of the Reformation and Protestanism has been stated many times. Cf., for example, Robert Munro, *Rambles and Studies in Bosnia-Herzegovina and Dalmatia*, p. 389. More recently an Austrian writer called them even the precursors of Bolshevism. Cf. Josef Leo Seifert, "Von Bogomil über Hus zu Lenin," *Zeitschrift für Völkerpsychologie und Soziologie*, III, 129–58.

[8] Vladimir Ćorović, *op. cit.*, pp. 175–89; Ferdo Šišić, *Povijest Hrvata za kraljeva iz doma Arpadovića (1102–1301)* (History of the Croats During the Reign of the Árpád Dynasty, 1102–1301), Pt. I (1102–1205), pp. 128–58. It is interesting to note that the Popes used against the Bosnian Church both the Dominican Order, established in 1215, and especially the order of the Franciscan Friars, established in 1291. These orders served in Bosnia both as missionaries and as inquisitors. From then until 1945 the Franciscan Order played a prominent political and cultural role in Bosnia and Herzegovina.

ally influenced later developments in that province with regard to land tenure.

TURKISH CONQUEST OF BOSNIA AND HERZEGOVINA

Bosnian and Turkish arms met for the first time in the Battle of Kosovo Field in 1389, in which some Bosnian and Croatian troops supported the Serbs. Soon thereafter the Turks penetrated deep into Bosnia, subdued some important regions to the northeast and in the center, and began systematic softening and cajoling of the feudal class and of the serfs. It was at that time that the Bosnian population, and in particular the members of the Bosnian Church, began to embrace Islam.

The central government of the Bosnian state could assert its will against the feudal lords only during short intervals. The tenuous internal cohesion within the state began to diminish rapidly after the advance of the powerful Turk from the southeast, and the Bosnian state was no match for the new conquerors. Thus, after being politically and economically weakened through internal struggles and external pressures, the Bosnian state was easily crushed in 1463. Its king and a great number of leading feudal lords were exterminated, and their sons taken into captivity and Mohammedanized, while other feudal families fled abroad. The last remainders of Herzegovina fell in 1482.

However, some of the Bosnian nobles accepted Islam immediately after the conquest of Bosnia, as did a large number of the serfs, and people continued to do so in the following centuries. The important point to remember is that these converts to Islam were primarily former members of the Bosnian Church.[9] This conversion is explainable from both religious and socioeconomic motives. The members of the Bosnian Church were opposed and persecuted by both the Catholic and the Eastern Orthodox churches; many of them were forcefully converted to Catholicism and their leaders exiled in the closing years of the Bosnian state. Acceptance of Islam on their part is therefore easily understandable. Moreover, if they were feudal lords, the conversion to Islam served as a means of preserving some of their former property and power. If they were serfs, conversion to Islam made them, as a rule, free peasants.

The modern Moslem population of Bosnia and Herzegovina[10] con-

[9] Aleksandar Solovjev, "The Disappearance of Bogomilism and the Islamization of Bosnia," *op. cit.*, p. 53.

[10] According to the census of 1931, 31 percent of the population of Bosnia and Herzegovina was Moslem.

sists essentially of descendents of those people who in large numbers accepted Islam after the Turkish conquest. Of course, as long as these provinces were within the Ottoman Empire, some influx of Moslems from other parts of the Empire took place. That was especially true during the last two decades of the seventeenth century, after the Turks lost Hungary, Slavonia, and those sections of Croatia and Dalmatia which they held.

After the conquest the Turks established in Bosnia and Herzegovina the same system of land tenure that they introduced in other parts of the Balkans, except that here large segments of the local population accepted Islam, which, in turn, affected their position toward the state and thus their position on the land. The former serfs who accepted Islam obtained family farms or *čiftliks*, free of any feudal obligation. The land which remained in the hands of the Christians was divided among the various officeholders and feudal cavalry—the spahis—in the form of military fiefs, whose holders were entitled to a portion of income from that land. The Christian *reaya* kept this land as their *baština*, namely, heritable property subject to feudal obligations toward the spahi and government taxes, provided they worked the land. Some of the former Bosnian feudal lords after accepting Islam became either spahis or other government officials, and succeeded in preserving some of their properties. The Turkish feudal system as developed during the fifteenth and sixteenth centuries in its pure form was described in more detail in Chapter 2. Here we propose to discuss only the ways in which Turkish feudalism deteriorated in Bosnia and Herzegovina after the central government lost effective control over the internal administration of these and other provinces, the forms which this feudalism took, and its development up to 1918.

THE NATURE OF NINETEENTH-CENTURY BOSNIAN FEUDALISM

In addition to the above-mentioned difference of opinion among historians on the nature and extent of the obligations of the serfs in medieval Bosnia, there existed also a difference of opinion on the origin of the nineteenth-century Bosnian Moslem nobility. Both of these factors bore directly on the issue of the origin and nature of nineteenth-century Bosnian feudalism. The fact that a great number of Bosnian nobles accepted Islam after the Turkish conquest, that many Moslem Bosnians rose to high positions in the Ottoman Empire, that some medieval noble families have survived to the present time, and, finally, that the land-tenure system in these provinces in the nineteenth century showed various features which were thought to be very similar to the

Bosnian medieval land tenure, led some historians to believe that there was a straight, unbroken continuity between both the medieval and the nineteenth-century Bosnian nobility and between the medieval and the nineteenth-century systems of land tenure. It was argued that the former feudal lords, by becoming Moslems, safeguarded their properties and actually remained hereditary holders of their estates and in addition became Turkish spahis or other officials; and that the obligations of the former serfs, if they did not accept Islam, continued to be what they had been in the Middle Ages.[11] This view was often fostered by the Bosnian feudal lords themselves during the nineteenth century in defense of their feudal prerogatives. The acceptance of these two propositions meant that both the Bosnian nobility and the Bosnian feudal order as they existed in the first half of the nineteenth century were institutions reaching back to the times of the Bosnian kingdom and thus were consecrated by long tradition and customs of the land.

Both of these propositions have been challenged and proved false. According to Vaso Čubrilović of the University of Belgrade, there was no unbroken continuity between the Bosnian medieval nobility and that of the nineteenth century, just as there was no unbroken continuity between the medieval and the nineteenth-century land-tenure systems of Bosnia and Herzegovina. Both the nineteenth-century Bosnian nobility and the land tenure were results of specific developments in the period of the decline of the Ottoman Empire. This view is now generally accepted.[12]

While it was true that many members of the Bosnian medieval nobility accepted Islam, and some families have continued to exist to the present time, the Bosnian nobility of the ninteenth century was actually of a very mixed background. The higher nobility, or begs, several hundred strong, consisted to a small extent of the heirs of the medieval noble families, but the great majority was of more recent origin and was recruited from high military dignitaries and some spahis, partly

[11] This view was presented by Eduard Eichler, *Das Justizwesen Bosniens und der Herzegowina*, pp. 43–44. But its chief advocate was Ćiro Truhelka in the above-mentioned study, "The Historical Foundations of the Agrarian Problem in Bosnia," published in 1915, from which it found entry into practically all literature published during the interwar period. Cf. Otto von Frangeš, *op. cit.*, pp. 135–50; Milan Ivšić, *Les problèmes agraires en Yougoslavie*, pp. 87–92; Mirko Kosić, *Osnovi ekonomne politike* (Principles of Economic Policy), p. 202.

[12] Vaso Čubrilović, *op. cit.*, pp. 368–403; Vladislav Skarić, "The Formation and Development of Serfdom in Bosnia and Herzegovina," *Pregled*, XIII, 481–89; Jaroslav Šidak, "Bosnia Under Turkish Rule," *Encyclopaedia Croatica*, III, 151–54; Branislav Djurdjev, "Investigations of the *Voynuks*, with Special Reference to the Development of Turkish Feudalism and the Question of the Bosnian *Agalik*," *Glasnik Zemaljskog muzeja u Bosni i Hercegovini*, New Series, II, 75–137, esp. 125–33.

of Bosnian, partly of other South Slavic, and partly of Turkish origin. The lower Moslem nobility, or agas, several thousand in number, were recruited from the spahis, part of whom were heirs of the Bosnian medieval nobility, and especially from among the Janissaries, of whom large numbers lived in Bosnia and Herzegovina during the seventeenth and eighteenth centuries.[13]

As mentioned earlier, the Turks introduced into Bosnia after its conquest the system of military fiefs consisting of *khasses*, which went with a few high offices, and ziamets and timars, which were granted to individuals who thereby became a part of the feudal cavalry, or spahis, and were obliged to give military service at the call of the Sultan. The ziamets and the timars were not unconditionally hereditary, though many were kept by the same families for a long time. These fiefs actually represented the right of the spahis to a share of the income from the *reaya* settled on the ziamets and the timars, usually a tenth (though occasionally more) and various other fees. Furthermore, the Turks established in Bosnia and Herzegovina the so-called *kapudanliks* (captainships, *kapetanije*), or hereditary military fiefs charged with the protection of the frontiers and of the important points in the lines of communications, whose heads or captains enjoyed regular salaries and income from land grants. There were 39 such fiefs in Bosnia and Herzegovina. They were essentially an imitation of the Military Frontier in Croatia-Slavonia. The captains acquired great political strength during the eighteenth century.[14]

All the rights to revenue on the part of the spahis and thus the obligations of the *reaya* on the military fiefs were regulated by law, though great differences existed among various areas in this respect, and the peasants could not be removed from the land as long as they worked it. Their right to land use, or *tasarruf*, affirmed by a *tapu*, was heritable.

As long as the Ottoman central government was able and willing to supervise and to impose the existing laws pertaining to military fiefs,

---

[13] According to Evliya Chelebi, a Turkish traveler and writer, in Bosnia in 1660 there were 3,761 spahis, of whom only 144 were holding ziamets (*zaims*). In 1711 a partial census of the Bosnian fief holders who were present at the battlefield on the Prut River in southern Russia showed that there were present 198 *zaims* and 1,371 timariots. Since Skarić thought that at that time usually about one half of the spahis went to war at the call of the Sultan and the other half remained at home to maintain order and to supply those in the field, he believed that the figures quoted by Chelebi and by the census of 1711 essentially agreed, except that the latter showed relatively more *zaims*. Vladislav Skarić, "The Census of the Bosnian Spahis of 1123 (1711)," *Glasnik Zemaljskog muzeja u Bosni i Hercegovini*, XLII, 1–99, esp. 8–10.

[14] Hamdija Kreševljaković, "Captainships and Captains in Bosnia and Herzegovina," *Godišnjak Istoriskog društva Bosne i Hercegovine*, II, 89–141.

the system operated quite satisfactorily. From repeated government pronouncements one sees, however, that there existed strong tendencies to abuse or disobey the laws on the part of fief holders. One of the basic proclivities of the government officials, the various types of the military, and the tax farmers was to acquire landed estates of a hereditary nature, free of military obligation, which would increase their economic security and well-being and grant them greater latitude in exploiting the *reaya*. This opportunity came on a large scale only after the Empire began to crumble and its governmental fabric to decay, that is, from about the beginning of the seventeenth century. Thus a process of deterioration and transformation of the fief system was engendered which thoroughly changed the nature of the Turkish feudal system. In Bosnia and Herzegovina this process was facilitated by some specific factors: great distance from the capital, Bosnia's character as a borderland in which there were many powerful hereditary frontier fief holders (captains), large numbers of domestic spahis and Janissaries, settlement in Bosnia of many spahis and Janissaries chased out of Hungary, Slavonia, and Dalmatia at the end of the seventeenth century, reduction in the size of the timars and ziamets, depopulation of whole areas due to transfer of populations, pestilences, and war operations, and colonization of these areas by new settlers.

Both begs and agas acquired landed property in the period of the declining Ottoman central rule by a number of various methods: enlargement of the *hassa* land that was included in their military fiefs, outright seizure of the land which the peasants had the right of use, change-over of the fiefs into private property, appropriation of lands on which they had bought the right of tax or tithe collection, purchase of land from the peasants under duress, and appropriation of deserted land and its settlement by new tenants. Most of these methods of land acquisition were illegal, but for the lack of enforcement of the original laws they continued for centuries. In this process the erstwhile system of military fiefs disintegrated, and in the course of the eighteenth century the spahis lost almost completely their former military significance.

In Bosnia and Herzegovina gradually two types of landed estates developed through the degeneration of the earlier feudal system. The first type was the *agaliks*, which was the Bosnian version of the *čiftliks* (see pp. 32–35), though with a certain difference. On these lands the *reaya* had formerly the *tasarruf*, or the right of utilization. In the process of *agalik* formation these lands were claimed as their full, hereditary properties by the begs and the agas who assumed the role of *čiftlik-sahibias*. But while in Serbia the *čiftliks* were exceptional, and in Macedonia the *čifčije* were completely robbed of any rights to the land, the *reaya* in Bosnia maintained on the *agaliks* certain rights of utilization. As we shall see later, in the 1850's these rights became guaranteed by law as the serf-rights or *kmetoprava*. Whether the *agalik* was formed by the changed role of the former spahi, or by a third person interposing himself as *čiftlik-sahibia* between the *reaya* and the spahi, economic obligations of the peasant in tithes and *corvée* increased, his personal security declined, and his personal independence deteriorated. The *reaya* resented the formation of *agaliks* in these provinces as much as the peasants in Serbia and Macedonia resented the formation of *čiftliks*, because here too the peasant considered the land he worked his hereditary, full property, though under obligation to the feudal lord for the traditional tithe, be it a tenth, a ninth, or even a larger share of the crop. With the formation of *agaliks*, all these obligations rose, as this was the chief purpose of the change. Moreover, in most areas, the introduction of *agaliks* led to the imposition anew or to the increase in the existing *corvée* obligations of the serfs.

The other type of lands in the hands of the nobles was the *begliks*. These lands were always considered full property of the landlords and developed either from the enlargement of the *hassa* lands of the spahis, by occupation of unoccupied or deserted lands, or from *agalik* lands on which the *reaya* gave up or were forced to give up their rights, either from force or, after 1859, by the decision of the authorities. Thus the *reaya* had no rights on such lands, and their owners were free either to work them themselves, which they did with the smaller *begliks*, or to give them to the tenants under conditions stricter than those on the *agaliks*, as the matter was completely one of agreement between landlord and tenants, or the *beglučari*. As far as the *beglik* lands were managed directly by their owners or hired managers, their serfs from the *agalik* lands were obliged in almost all areas of Bosnia and Herzegovina to render *corvée* for the *beglik* owner. This free labor was another reason for the tendency of the begs and agas to increase their *begliks*, although it was necessary to maintain a balance between the two types of estates in order to assure a sufficient amount of free labor for the landlord.

The census of the Bosnian spahis of 1711 (see footnote 13, p. 98) showed that most of the Bosnian military fiefs were already small at that time. During the ensuing century they became even smaller, and this fact contributed to the formation of the *agaliks* and to the greater exploitation of the peasants. Only the begs, and some of the agas, controlled large tracts of land.

The Bosnian feudal system of the first half of the nineteenth century was thus developed through an almost complete degeneration of the former system of ziamets and timars. It was an outgrowth of the use of political and economic force on the part of the landlords in contradiction of the original spirit of the laws which controlled the feudal lord and protected the peasants if they fulfilled their obligations. The agrarian issue in Bosnia and Herzegovina at that time centered around three chief questions: the continuous formation and existence of the *agaliks,* the *corvée* on the *begliks,*[15] and the system of tax farming, which imposed great burdens and caused great abuses of the peasants while at the same time the landlords were paying no taxes. Owing to this system of land tenure and to the abusive character of the Bosnian landlords, agrarian unrest became a perennial problem. In the course of the nineteenth century it became greatly complicated by political and diplomatic factors. As will be presently shown, the feudal land-tenure system was partly reorganized in the 1840's and 1850's, but its final solution took place only after World War I.

OTTOMAN REFORMS OF THE NINETEENTH CENTURY AND BOSNIA

The awakening of the subject nationalities, the pressure from the Great Powers, and, above all, the conviction among a growing number of Turkish statesmen that the Empire could survive only if its whole military, political, and social life was reorganized and brought as close as possible to the institutions of Western Europe led Turkey to embark in the second quarter of the ninteenth century upon a program of reforms. The *Tanzimat,*[16] or program of reforms, was initiated with the dissolution of the Janissaries and of the spahis in 1826 and the beginning of the reorganization of the army patterned on the European model. Reforms of the political institutions and administrative organization of the Empire were actually started with the Hatti-Sherif of Gulhané (imperial edict) of 1839. Principles announced in that edict were reiterated by the Hatti-Humayoun of 1856. In 1864 a special law on the reorganization of vilayets or regional government was passed. In 1876 the Ottoman Constitution was proclaimed. Moreover, a great number of various codes and decrees were promulgated to put into operation the basic principles proclaimed in the edicts of 1839 and 1856, e.g., the Law of 1858, regulating the principles of land property, and the introduction of the civil code through a series of special laws proclaimed between 1868 and 1876. However, many of these reforms

[15] *Beglik* or *begluk* meant in Bosnia also *corvée* for the landlord.
[16] Ed. Engelhardt, *La Turquie et le Tanzimat.*

remained on paper because the central government either did not know how or was unable or unwilling to enforce them. From the point of view of European diplomacy these reforms were of great importance because they tended to ameliorate somewhat the conditions in the Empire, and thus prolong its life and delay the problem of division of the territory of the Empire among the European powers.

The application of all these reforms in Bosnia was fought stubbornly by the Bosnian Moslem nobles. The Bosnian nobles of the nineteenth century represented politically and psychologically a very interesting caste "entirely immune from all western influences, but also profoundly hostile to all idea of interference from Constantinople."[17] They were accustomed to unlimited rule. Traditionally, they were known as valiant soldiers. But they shunned work, were oblivious to the importance of economic progress,[18] lived by exploiting and abusing the great mass of Christian peasants, and showed a great predilection for epicurean living. As a body, they were marked by an extraordinary degree of conservatism and fanaticism. Most of them were of South Slav blood and spoke only Serbo-Croatian, but they called themselves Turks. They hated and opposed all representatives of the Porte in Bosnia and the interference of the central government in their affairs. This became especially pronounced when the Porte tried to introduce various political and social reforms in Bosnia. As a rule it succeeded in doing so only after repeated armed interventions, and the Bosnian oligarchs never accepted these reforms wholeheartedly.

The bloodiest conflict with the Porte occurred in 1831, following the dissolution of the Janissaries and the spahis by Sultan Mahmud II

[17] R. W. Seton-Watson, *The Role of Bosnia in International Politics (1875-1914)*, reprint from the *Proceedings of the British Academy*, XVII, 7.

[18] There was, however, one notable exception among these men. That was Ali Pasha Rizvanbegović, the Pasha of Herzegovina from 1833 to 1851, when Herzegovina, because it sided in 1830 and 1831 with the Porte against the Bosnian nobles, was made a special pashalik. Fully aware of the importance of economic progress, Ali Pasha preached the gospel of work and coined the famous slogan, still often heard in Herzegovina: "There shall hammers pound or rifles clang," which meant that Herzegovina in times of war should fight and in times of peace should build. Especially important was his work in land reclamation and in the furthering of the cultivation of rice, olives, potatoes, corn, silk cocoons, subtropical fruits, the renewal of vineyards, and beekeeping. He even tried to attract foreign capital to exploit the forests of his land. He never shrank from using force in order to make his subjects work and follow his orders. He was represented in the folk poetry as a ruthless landlord who forced his serfs to *corvée* much beyond the measure which was considered legal, but this should not blind us to his great stature in other respects. He was an efficient administrator and seems to have been conscious of the importance of better education. But he became a symbol of independence from the Porte and lost his life in 1851 in the process of Omer Pasha Latas' suppressing of the recalcitrant Bosnian and Herzegovinan nobles. Kasim Gujić, "Ali Pasha Rizvanbegović," *Nova Evropa*, XXIX, 244-53.

in 1826 and the attempt of the Porte to reorganize the army in Bosnia. This revolt, which was co-ordinated with a similar revolt in Albania, was crushed[19] and the army partly reorganized in the following years. Especially important in this regard was the abolition of the hereditary captainships in 1835, because these were the backbone of the military strength of the Bosnian oligarchs.

The Bosnian nobles opposed equally strongly the reforms introduced by the liberal Hatti-Sherif of Gulhané in 1839, which guaranteed personal and property security, and equality with regard to taxation, to all Ottoman citizens without regard to religion. This edict disavowed also the practice of tax farming.[20] The principle of equality of the Ottoman non-Moslem subjects with the Moslems was truly revolutionary, as it was at variance with the Koran and with the whole philosophy, tradition, and practice of Turkish government.

The implementation of the Hatti-Sherif of Gulhané in Bosnia was gradual. It was of specific importance for the future land tenure in that province.[21] While the spahis were dissolved in 1826 as feudal levy, they continued to collect the tithe from the *reaya* as well as various fees. This right was taken from them formally in 1840, granting them life pensions as indemnity. Actually, they continued to collect the tithe until 1851. But the threatened curtailment of the rights of the Moslem landlords induced them to speed up and complete the transformation of the former timars and ziamets into *agaliks* and *begliks* and to increase the obligations of their serfs in terms of tithes and *corvée*. This development increased the dissatisfaction and resistance of the serfs against the landlords. Thus the central government had to deal not only with an unruly and recalcitrant caste of feudatories who were bent on the protection of their economic and political privileges, but was also forced to take into account the situation of the Christian serfs. The latter was the more important as the Christian serfs were appealing to foreign governments, especially to the Austrian government, to intercede with the Porte on their behalf.

[19] Carl Ritter von Sax, *Geschichte des Machtverfalls der Türkei*, pp. 245–47.

[20] Tax farming was temporarily suspended in 1840 but was reintroduced in 1841 and remained in practice in Bosnia until the end of Turkish rule. As the tax farmers tried always to extract from the taxpayers the maximum possible contribution and, to achieve this, used force profusely, tax farming was one of the important reasons for dissatisfaction of the Christian population in Bosnia and Herzegovina.

[21] The period of *Tanzimat* as it affected Bosnia and Herzegovina, with special reference to its implications for land tenure and the position of the Christian serfs, is covered in great detail in Vasilj Popović, *Agrarno pitanje u Bosni i turski neredi za vreme reformnog režima Abdul-Medžida (1839–1861)* (Agrarian Question in Bosnia and Turkish Disorders During the Period of the Reform Rule of Abdul-Medjid, 1839–1861). See also Ed. Engelhardt, *op. cit.*, I, 90–93, and *passim*.

A certain amelioration in the relationship between the Moslem landlords and Christian serfs was attempted by the Bosnian provincial government in 1843 and again in 1847, without avail. But an important step in this regard was the reform undertaken in 1848 by Tahir Pasha, the new head of the Bosnian administration, a great believer in the principles of *Tanzimat* and in the prerogatives of the central government. This reform consisted essentially of two things: (*a*) The obligation of the serfs to deliver one-third (*tretina* or *trećina*) of the gross product of grains and one-half of hay (after the tenth had been taken for the tax) to the landlord, which at that time was the prevailing custom only in central Bosnia, was extended to the whole province. In some counties where peasants delivered one-fourth or even one-half of the gross product to the landlord, this custom was maintained. (*b*) In all areas the obligation of *corvée* was abolished. *Corvée* was especially heavy—two or three days per week—in northern Bosnia, but the share of the landlord in these areas was usually only one-tenth or one-ninth of the gross product (after the tenth for the tax). Moreover, in most areas the landlord was obliged to provide housing for his serfs. And in some areas the landlord also provided seed and draft animals. All these different systems of obligations were now largely unified. The principal objective of the Tahir Pasha's reform was to abolish the *corvée*, which was most resented by the Christian population. But in order to make it acceptable to the Moslem landlords, he increased the tithe in many areas. The main objection of the serfs to the reform was that while they were forced to pay one-third of the gross product to the landlords, which in many areas meant an increase in the tithe, many landlords continued to force them to render *corvée*.[22]

The reform of 1848 was thus opposed by both landlords and serfs. In 1849 and 1850 new rebellions of the Moslem landlords took place. In 1850 and early 1851 the forces of the central government crushed the rebels, a process in which some were killed and hundreds lost their properties and were exiled or jailed. Thereafter, the Bosnian Moslem nobles never regained their former power and resilience. At the same time the reform of the army was completed, and the collection of the tenth taken away from the former spahis. Ironically enough, it was a Croatian renegade, Omer Pasha Latas, who accomplished this harsh task. The curbing of the Bosnian feudal lords was necessary to ensure power for the bureaucracy of the central government, to carry out the modernization of the army, and to modernize and increase the taxes.

The dissatisfaction among the Bosnian Christian population rose not only because their economic situation was becoming worse, owing

[22] Vasilj Popović, *op cit.*, pp. 67–97; Vojislav Bogićević, *op. cit.*, pp. 194–99.

to the unbridled behavior of the Moslem landlords, but also because of the fact that the ideas of political liberty and abolition of social bondage found their way also into the Bosnian village. The tendencies of rebellion were strengthened by the fact that serfdom was abolished in Serbia in 1817 (formally only in 1833) and, by 1848, also in Croatia-Slavonia. But the nature of these internal Bosnian struggles was extremely complex, as it involved economic, social, political, and religious matters, since the landlords were exclusively Moslem and the serfs were almost exclusively Christian (Serbian Orthodox and Roman Catholic). By the middle of the nineteenth century Bosnian political and agrarian questions acquired great significance in international politics, and practically all the European Great Powers had some influence on their future development.

New reforms followed after the Crimean War. They were based on the Hatti-Humayoun of 1856, which reiterated the principles announced in the Hatti-Sherif of Gulhané of 1839. Thus a special law of 1858 classified the various types of land in the Ottoman Empire into the following categories: *mulk* (private property), *miri* (state land), *mefkufe* (*wakf* or religious endowments), *metruke* (the common), and *mevat* (unoccupied land far from inhabited places). This division of land categories was partly maintained in Bosnia until 1945. Moreover, this law increased greatly the rights of disposition of the holders of various types of land.

As political and agrarian unrest continued in Bosnia and Herzegovina and the agrarian problem was one of the basic causes of that unrest, the Porte approached anew the issue of Bosnian land tenure by calling the representatives of the landlords and of the serfs to Istanbul. The result of this effort was the Safer decree of 1859.[23] This decree was represented as a codification of the existing popular customs regarding the obligations and rights of the serfs and the rights of the landlords, but in fact it was a codification of the rules introduced in 1848 by Tahir Pasha. And these rules reflected only partly popular customs. The Safer decree proclaimed that the begs and agas were the owners of the *agaliks*, and the serfs on them were proclaimed tenants. But there were certain qualifications. The rights of the serfs had to be attested by a special contract, contract duration had to be limited, and the tithe, called *hak*, was strictly regulated and amounted to one-fourth to one-half, but mostly one-third of the gross product after the tenth for the tax had been subtracted. All these stipulations had to be recorded in special public records. Furthermore, the landlord was obliged to pro-

---

[23] For the full text of this important document see Vasilj Popović, *op. cit.*, pp. 316–23.

vide housing for his serfs and to help with the repair of that housing. While the serf was free to leave his landlord, the latter could evict the serf for nonpayment of the tithe and unsatisfactory working of the land, but only on the basis of a decision of government authorities. Thus, according to the Safer decree the nobles were not unlimited owners of the *agalik* lands, since the serfs were guaranteed certain rights to the land if they fulfilled specific obligations. These rights of the serfs became known as serf rights or *kmetoprava*. As no such limitations encumbered the *beglik* lands, there was a tendency on the part of the landlords to transform the *agalik* lands into *beglik* lands. The Safer decree of 1859 gave them the right to do so under certain circumstances, and they took advantage of this possibility until 1918.

The Safer decree did not touch the *beglik* lands, which were considered full, unlimited, hereditary property of their owners, whether these lands were worked by their owners directly or by tenants. In the latter case, this was considered a private contract between landlord and tenant rather than a feudal relationship, and thus a matter of private rather than of public law. But the bulk of the *beglik* lands was undoubtedly of feudal origin.

The basic significance of the Safer decree was in the fact that the *agalik* lands were proclaimed almost the full property of the landlords, while in the situation of the serfs no material change took place, though they were proclaimed tenants and acquired a certain degree of protection for their serf rights. Second, this decree opened a way for legal transformation of the *agalik* lands into *beglik* lands. And, finally, it regulated the land tenure in Bosnia and Herzegovina until 1918 and affected the procedure of the post-1918 agrarian reform in these provinces. The reform of 1859 had the multiple purpose of pacifying the Moslem nobles, of assuaging somewhat the situation of the serfs, and of furthering peace and order in the provinces in order to postpone the intervention of the Great Powers, which, after the Crimean War, had assumed virtual protection of the Christians in the Ottoman Balkan possessions and half-independent principalities. But the new land-tenure regime created in Bosnia and Herzegovina during the 1840's and 1850's remained an anachronism full of political and social dynamite. This was the more so as it existed within a reactionary, abusive, and decrepit political regime. Peasant unrest continued. The final Turkish act on land tenure in Bosnia and Herzegovina was the Law of February 1876 on the optional freeing of the serfs.[24] According to this law, the

---

[24] Karl Grünberg, *Die Agrarverfassung und das Grundentlastungsproblem in Bosnien und der Herzegowina*, pp. 39–40. An excellent review of the situation of the

serf could free himself with the consent of the landlord and after paying an indemnity agreed upon with the latter.

OCCUPATION BY AUSTRIA-HUNGARY IN 1878

The largest and best-organized revolt of the Christians of Bosnia and Herzegovina against Turkish rule began in 1875, and became more complicated as Montenegro and Serbia declared war on Turkey. Both of them coveted the provinces and the rebels advocated union with them. Somewhat later there followed a war between Russia and Turkey. Meanwhile Austria-Hungary, vitally interested in the Bosnian issue, reached an agreement with Russia providing for the occupation of the provinces by the Dual Monarchy in exchange for its neutrality in the Russo-Turkish War. Bosnia and Herzegovina became openly an object of diplomatic trading among the European Great Powers. The Russo-Turkish War led to a Turkish defeat and to the conclusion of the Peace of San Stefano. It provided, among other things favoring Russia, for the autonomy of Bosnia and Herzegovina. The European Great Powers refused to accept this sweeping Russian diplomatic victory, and the Berlin Congress was convened in 1878 in order to take a hand in the division of spoils taken from the Ottoman Empire.

In presenting its case for the occupation of Bosnia and Herzegovina at the Berlin Congress and on some previous occasions, Austro-Hungary also used the argument that the agrarian question was the chief source of disorders in the provinces, that the Porte should solve it, but that it was so complicated that only "a strong and impartial government could solve it."[25] Thus it was clearly implied that this was the Austro-Hungarian intention, if they obtained the right to occupy the provinces.

Article XXV of the Berlin Treaty of 1878 provided that "the provinces of Bosnia and Herzegovina will be occupied and administered by Austria-Hungary." It further provided for Austria-Hungary to main-

---

Christian population in Bosnia and Herzegovina in the concluding years of the Turkish rule is given by Vojislav Bogićević, "The Situation of the *Reaya* in Bosnia and Herzegovina on the Eve of the Revolt of 1875–1878," *Godišnjak Istoriskog društva Bosne i Hercegovine*, II, 143–84.

[25] A passage from the statement of the Austro-Hungarian Foreign Minister, Count Julius Andrássy, at the Berlin Congress ran as follows: "[La Sublime Porte] devrait mettre en oeuvre le règlement de la question agraire, source principale des secousses périodiques qui ont agité ces contrées, problème hérissé d'obstacles au milieu d'une population déchirée par les haines religieuses et les rancunes sociales, problème qu'un pouvoir fort et impartial seul peut résoudre dans un pays où toute la propriété foncière se trouve dans les mains des Musulmans, pendant que les Chrétiens laboureurs ou fermiers forment la majorité des habitants." Great Britain, *British and Foreign State Papers, 1877–1878* (London, 1885), LXIX, 949.

tain garrisons in the Sandjak of Novi Pazar (which was a part of the Turkish province of Bosnia) in order to protect military and commercial communication lines and "to maintain the new political order" created by the Berlin Congress. After the necessary arrangements with Turkey, Austria-Hungary proceeded with the occupation of the provinces. This was resisted with arms by the intrepid Bosnian Moslems, though without avail, and was greatly resented by the Serbian Orthodox population, but was greeted favorably by the Roman Catholics (the strength of these denominations in 1879 was 39, 43, and 18 percent, respectively). Article XXV contains, however, no obligation for the occupying power with regard to the agrarian question.[26]

AUSTRIA-HUNGARY UPHOLDS THE EXISTING FEUDAL ORDER

At the time of Austro-Hungarian occupation there were in Bosnia and Herzegovina about 85,000 families of kmetovi or serfs, of which 60,000 families were Serbian Orthodox, 23,000 families Roman Catholic, and a few thousand Moslem, lorded over by about 6,000 to 7,000 Moslem begs and agas. About 77,000 free peasant families were almost exclusively Moslem.[27] Instead of solving the agrarian question, as its diplomats implied, before they obtained Bosnia and Herzegovina, the Austro-Hungarian government pursued throughout its rule in these provinces a policy of maintaining the land-tenure system it found on the day of occupation. The Austro-Hungarian authorities gave the force of law to the Safer decree of 1859, which amounted to a policy of favoring the Moslem landlord class at the expense of the Christian serfs. They also supported optional freeing of the serfs on the basis of the Turkish Law of 1876, with full indemnity for the landlord to be paid by the serf. In the period between 1879 and 1911 a total of 28,481 serf families bought themselves out of serfdom. The optional freeing was speeded up following the promulgation of a special law in 1911. In the following two years another 13,078 families freed themselves. But at the beginning of 1914 there were still in the two provinces 93,368

[26] While Great Britain had a hand in the Bosnian politics of that time and its representatives at the Berlin Congress made the motion for Austro-Hungarian occupation of Bosnia and Herzegovina, its statesmen were indifferent to many issues facing the Bosnian population and were opposed to a more fundamental solution of the Bosnian problem. According to R. W. Seton-Watson (*op. cit.*, pp. 16–17), "He [Disraeli] and Lord Derby, it is strange to note, opposed anything like full autonomy for Bosnia-Herzegovina, and even the more modest reforms urged by Count Andrássy upon the Turks [in 1875]—and this, not on the merits of the case, but simply because they saw an analogy between the details of land reform in Bosnia and the demands put forward in Ireland and were afraid to create a precedent."

[27] Milan Ivšić, *op. cit.*, pp. 231–42.

serf families working approximately one-third of all arable land.[28] There were also several thousand families partly serf, partly freeholders. Furthermore, there were many thousands of peasant families working on the *beglik* lands as tenants.

A piece of legislation which helped the serfs materially was the simplification of the tenth (tax) and the tithe (*hak*) collections introduced in 1906. Austria-Hungary declared all pasture and forest lands state property if individuals or organizations—e.g., the *wakf*—were not able to prove their ownership rights to them. It planned to regulate by a special law the area and the use of pasture and forest commons (the *mera* and the *baltalik* lands), but World War I intervened.

And that was all that Austria-Hungary did on land tenure during its rule in the provinces. The solution of the agrarian question was little advanced indeed during these 40 years. Meanwhile it continued to be the basic hindrance not only to a real political settlement in these provinces, but also a barrier to agricultural progress, since it robbed the serfs of all incentive to work more and thereby better their land and increase their production.

While Austria-Hungary did not disturb the land-tenure system existing in Bosnia and Herzegovina at the time of occupation, it undertook a program of modernization of the provinces. It introduced an efficient system of administration and security. It engaged in building railroads and roads, developing mining, coal, iron, and chemical industries, and in tapping the rich timber resources of the area. Railroads were financed by public loans, obtained partly outside of the Dual Monarchy, and industrial development was carried on by foreign entrepreneurs and capital imported from Austria, Hungary, and Western Europe. Railroads and roads were built, however, more according to military than economic criteria. A large part of other building effort went into caserns, fortresses, and the like. A consideable portion of this building effort was accomplished by forced labor (*corvée*). But from the point of view of the Austro-Hungarian policy this military development of the provinces was understandable because the provinces were primarily considered a steppingstone for the expansionist drive toward Salonika, a great aim of Habsburg imperialism for almost 200 years.

Austria-Hungary established in Bosnia and Herzegovina a system of agricultural credit, relatively well adapted to the needs of the small and dwarf peasants. It undertook considerable research and planning on the zoning of crop and fruit production and livestock raising, on

[28] *Ibid.*, p. 238.

reforestation of the karstic areas, and water supply for rural population, and put some of these plans into operation. Use of modern agricultural implements and of better methods in agricultural work was furthered.[29] It was years after the establishment of the new Yugoslav state before the real value of many of these measures had been fully appreciated, but by that time many of their effects, or potential effects, were lost. Of course, the utterly conservative and suspicious Bosnian peasant met these modernization measures and programs with great doubts and made the work of the occupying authorities in this respect much more difficult. The first aim of more than half of all peasants, the serfs, was freedom from feudal bondage, and this requirement was not met.

With regard to production, the pre-1914 agriculture of Bosnia and Herzegovina was similar to that of Serbia. Grains, livestock, and, in the northeast, prunes were the chief sources of livelihood. Technically, it was on a somewhat lower level than Serbian agriculture. As incentives for higher and better production were absent, and as the peasants had small and dwarf farms almost exclusively, agriculture showed a typical subsistence character with insignificant surpluses for the market. The land-tenure system led to the anomaly that the provinces had to import cereals while large stretches of land were under fallow year in, year out. In spite of the feudal order and large ownership units of specific types, there were practically no large estates under single management in Bosnia and Herzegovina. The land was worked by a multitude of serfs and tenants in separate dwarf and small farms.

THE AGRARIAN AND NATIONAL QUESTIONS CLOSELY CONNECTED

From the beginning of the nineteenth century until the end of World War I the national and the agrarian issues in Bosnia and Herzegovina were closely interwoven. The existence of the feudal order, whose representatives were Moslem begs and agas, diversity of religious affiliations and political orientations of feudal lords and serfs, foreign occupation, which suppressed national aspirations of the majority of the population, and opposing economic interests of various groups were responsible for a pronounced revolutionary mood in these provinces for decades preceding World War I.[30] When political parties

[29] Austria-Hungary, Gemeinsames Finanzministerium, *Bericht über die Verwaltung von Bosnien und der Herzegowina, 1906*, pp. 239–96. This report contains a detailed review of the Austro-Hungarian policies in Bosnia and Herzegovina between 1878 and 1906.
[30] For a succinct presentation of the problem of Bosnia and Herzegovina under the Austro-Hungarian rule, see Oscar Jászi, *The Dissolution of the Habsburg Monarchy*, pp. 411–14.

began to be formed, they were organized along religious lines. While the Serbian Orthodox (Serbs) looked for cultural and political leadership to Belgrade, the Roman Catholics (Croats) had their eyes on Zagreb. The Moslems had their own political organizations, and while some of them identified themselves as Croats and others as Serbs, most of them lived in the afterglow of their old glory, considering more important their religious than their national affiliation. As their political leadership continued to be held primarily by members of old feudal families, the protection of their feudal interests colored their whole political activity.

Between 1875 and 1878, and again in 1908 and in 1914, Bosnia and Herzegovina played a role in international affairs out of all proportion to their size or economic importance. The annexation of the provinces by Austria-Hungary in 1908,[31] in contravention of the stipulations of the Treaty of Berlin of 1878 (as a compensation to Turkey it withdrew the garrisons from the Sandjak of Novi Pazar), produced one of the European crises introducing, as it were, the series of diplomatic crises culminating in World War I. It was the assassination of the Austrian crown prince, Archduke Francis Ferdinand, in Sarajevo, the capital of Bosnia and Herzegovina, in June 1914 which served as the igniting spark of that war. The revolutionary youths who killed the Archduke explained their feat as an act of opposition to both foreign oppression and to the feudal order, and their aim as both national and social liberation.

[31] Bernadotte E. Schmitt, *The Annexation of Bosnia, 1908–1909;* Momtchilo Nintchitch, *La crise bosniaque, 1908, et les puissances européennes,* 2 vols.; Arthur J. May, *The Hapsburg Monarchy, 1867–1914,* pp. 405–24.

CHAPTER 5

THE FRINGE PROVINCES: DALMATIA,
MACEDONIA, MONTENEGRO, SLOVENIA, VOJVODINA

THIS CHAPTER contains sketches of the historical developments in the remaining five provinces included in Yugoslavia in 1918. Their political and agrarian past is as different as one can find in that part of a world of unending variety. In the case of Macedonia and Vojvodina, little specific source material pertaining to the area included in Yugoslavia is available up to 1914, because they were not separate administrative units. There are, however, considerable similarities in the development of Vojvodina with that of Croatia-Slavonia, particularly Slavonia. Macedonia and the other areas which were under Turkish rule until 1913 developed along lines similar to Bosnia and Herzegovina until 1878. The developments in Montenegro were unique. Slovenia and Dalmatia also developed along different lines.

There is one factor, however, which is characteristic of the development in all these areas in comparison with the development in the three areas already discussed. All of them are fringe areas of the territory inhabited by the South Slavs. Because of that, they were either much longer and/or under a much stronger foreign political, cultural, and economic influence, or, owing to specific geographic factors such as those affecting Montenegro, they were almost completely isolated from outside influences. Although the following remarks about the five provinces are extremely brief, it is hoped that the specific influences under which they developed will become clear.

DALMATIA

Dalmatia was one of the provinces which in 1918 belonged to the Austrian half of the Dual Monarchy. Its population of 646,000 in 1910 consisted of 78 percent Croats, 18 percent Serbs, 3 percent Italians (exclusively in towns), and about 1 percent of other nationalities. For political reasons, the unification of Dalmatia with Croatia-Slavonia was prevented in the Dual Monarchy, although such union was advocated by the nationalist politicians and desired by the majority of the people of the province. Throughout the nineteenth century Austria used, among other things, the small Italian minority, officials recruited from that minority, and the Italian language as tools for ruling the province of Dalmatia.

Dalmatia in its entirety was assigned to Austria by the Vienna Congress in 1814–15. During the Middle Ages and prior to 1814 parts of Dalmatia had been under the rule of various powers, and for varying lengths of time: Byzantium, the Frankish Empire, Croatia, the Normans from Southern Italy, Hungary, Serbia, Bosnia, the Republic of Dubrovnik (Ragusa), Venice, the Ottoman Empire, and for a short while France. The shifts in rulers of the province led, naturally, to many changes in the political, social, and economic institutions, and thus also in the system of land tenure and in economic conditions generally.

Political and economic institutions and conditions in coastal towns and on the islands differed greatly from those in the interior of the country. Prior to, in the course of, and following the settlement of the South Slavs in the Balkans, a part of the Vlakhs withdrew from the interior to the coastal towns and islands, and the rest withdrew to the more isolated mountainous areas. Even after the South Slav population became the dominant factor in these towns, their Romanic character remained quite pronounced for many centuries. Most of these towns were governed as independent communes enjoying special privileges. They regulated their economic and social affairs basically by the rules of Roman law.

The paucity of land resources in Dalmatia forced the population of coastal towns early in their development to look for their livelihood in trading with the interior of the Balkan Peninsula, with Venice, with various towns on the Italian Peninsula, and later with Asia Minor and other areas in the Mediterranean. To engage successfully in trade across the seas, these towns developed their shipping, and in time their strength grew in capital resources, manpower, daring, and commercial ingenuity. Trade led to the development of various handicrafts for the processing of domestic and imported raw materials, which were then exported as finished products. Chief among the handicrafts were those connected with the production of textiles.

Undoubtedly the most important among these Dalmatian commercial towns was Dubrovnik (Ragusa), the center of the tiny Republic of Dubrovnik. Although squeezed between the Eastern and the Western worlds and between Islam and Christianity, this small republic from the middle of the fourteenth to the beginning of the nineteenth centuries succeeded in preserving by infinite diplomatic skill its precarious independence and liberty. Throughout that time it recognized the formal suzerainty of the Sultan and paid him annual tribute. But in ex-

change for that, it enjoyed great trading privileges throughout the Ottoman Empire, including for some time the monopoly of trade in salt,
the chief export article and one of the chief sources of wealth of
Dubrovnik. In fact, for many centuries Dubrovnik and its skillful and
resourceful merchants were the primary economic link between much
of the Balkan Peninsula and the West across the Adriatic. Other important trading towns of the Dalmatian coast were Kotor in the south,
Trogir and Split in central Dalmatia, and Zadar in the north. From
the beginning of the fifteenth century all these towns were constantly
under the Venetian rule until the end of the eighteenth century. Needless to say, a considerable portion of the Balkan trade was directly in
the hands of the Venetians.

The chief articles that the Dalmatian towns, and especially Dubrovnik, sold in the Balkans were salt, woolens, glass, leather products, gun-
powder, spices, gold and silver products, while the chief products that
they bought in the Balkans were grain, livestock, raw wool, skins, furs,
and, above all, gold, silver, copper, and lead. Mining in Serbia and
Bosnia before and after the Turkish conquest was greatly furthered by
the merchants from Dubrovnik and their organization, which enabled
the transport of these metals to the coast and their export across the
Adriatic.[1]

---

[1] The literature on the medieval development of the Dalmatian towns is quite voluminous. On the general background of these towns see Viktor Novak, "The Slavonic-
Latin Symbiosis in Dalmatia During the Middle Ages," *The Slavonic and East European
Review*, XXXII (London, December 1953), 1–28. Regarding the institutions and
economy of the city and Republic of Dubrovnik (Ragusa) see Lujo Vojnović, *Dubrovnik i Osmansko carstvo* (Dubrovnik and the Ottoman Empire), pp. 67–128, a work
referring primarily to developments between the sixteenth and the eighteenth centuries,
and generally not reliable; Dragan Roller, *Dubrovački zanati u XV. i XVI. stoljeću*
(Dubrovnik's Handicrafts in the Fifteenth and Sixteenth Centuries); Ivan Božić,
Dubrovnik i Turska u XIV i XV veku (Dubrovnik and Turkey in the Fourteenth and
Fifteenth Centuries); Bogo Grafenauer *et al.* (eds.), *Istorija naroda Jugoslavije* (History
of the Peoples of Yugoslavia), I, 577–612; Fernand Braudel, *La Méditerranée et le Monde
méditerranéen à l'époque de Philippe II, passim*; Ivan Božić, "Economic and Social
Development of Dubrovnik in the Fourteenth and Fifteenth Centuries," *Istoriski glasnik*,
No. 1 (1949), pp. 21–61. A study of the economic conditions in the town of Trogir,
based on recently published documents, is Mijo Mirković, "Economic Relations in Trogir
in the Thirteenth Century," *Historijski zbornik*, IV, 21–54. Scattered information on
the economy of the Dalmatian towns in the Middle Ages is supplied also by Konstantin
Jireček, *Istorija Srba* (History of the Serbs), translation from the German by Jovan
Radonić, III, 99–258. On the other hand, information on the economic and social conditions in Dalmatia during the nineteenth century, with the exception of matters pertaining to land tenure, is scanty and for the most part has to be looked for in general
histories of Dalmatia. Two general and recent reviews of the history of Dalmatia are
to be found in the article "Dalmatia" in *Encyclopaedia Croatica*, IV, 438–95, and in
Grga Novak, *Prošlost Dalmacije* (Dalmatia's Past).

In spite of the concentration on shipping, trade, and handicrafts, agriculture and animal husbandry were important branches of the economy of the Dalmatian towns. Naturally, most of it was carried on in the immediate vicinity. This activity supplied important articles of trade, such as wine, grains, livestock, and livestock products. Since most of the land was in the hands of the leading families of the towns who had also the necessary capital to finance agricultural operations, various types of land tenure developed, based either on sharecropping or payment of rents in money. "Sharecropping" was developed also in animal husbandry. The important point to stress is that in Dalmatian areas under Venice, instead of serfdom, they used the land-tenure system of colonate.

Partly by conquest, partly by purchase (1409), Venice became gradually the ruler of all Dalmatian cities on the coast, with the exception of Dubrovnik, which it held from 1205 to 1358 and which in time became its chief trade competitor in the Balkans and in the whole Adriatic area. Venice utilized the eastern Adriatic coast for trading, both with these cities themselves and through them with the interior of the Balkans. But the primary purpose of the Venetian rule over the eastern Adriatic coast was to protect its trade and communication lines in the Adriatic from hostile powers and piracy. On the other hand, the Croatian (later Hungaro-Croatian) kings and some powerful Croatian feudal families, as well as the Serbian and Bosnian kings, and during the sixteenth and seventeenth centuries the Turks, tried to establish and maintain their rule on the eastern Adriatic coast, since access to the sea and control of sea lanes was always an attribute of political power and a great economic asset. All of them succeeded in holding some territory for a time, but nobody was more successful in this than Venice. Much like Croatia-Slavonia in regard to the Turks, Dalmatia also served as a border area over which the Croats and Venetians, and later the Croats, Venetians, and Turks, struggled for centuries.

As long as the interior and coastal areas along the Adriatic were under the rule of Croatian, Serbian, or Bosnian kings or feudal magnates, the feudal system that prevailed in these states was in existence also in these Dalmatian areas.[2] In some parts, e.g., in the free commune of Poljica near Split, certain remnants of the institutions of the tribal system were maintained for a long time. Churches and monasteries

[2] As the first Croatian medieval state had its origin and for a long time continued to have its center in present central Dalmatia, much of the discussion of the Croatian medieval institutions and conditions presented in Chapter 3 (pp. 49–59) refers actually to the territory nowadays called Dalmatia.

were important political and economic factors and holders of large estates both in the coastal towns and in the interior.

After the conquest of the Dalmatian mainland by the Turks, completed by 1537, the Turks established in these parts their feudal system based on the military fiefs of the timar and ziamet type. This feudal order remained in existence until the Turks were forced out of Dalmatia at the turn of the eighteenth century.

Following the liberation of the Dalmatian mainland from the Turks in the period 1684–1714, Venice obtained through the peace treaty of Karlovci (1699) and the peace treaty of Požarevac (1718) practically all that it conquered in Dalmatia. Thus it more than doubled its territory on the eastern coast of the Adriatic. It kept all these areas until its downfall in 1797 at the hands of Napoleon. In the newly acquired areas Venice established a land-tenure system combining features of large military fiefs and of peasant soldiery, forming thus a Military Frontier. Large estates were distributed to some leaders and peasant farms to those peasants who participated in the wars against the Turks. The land tenure in these areas was then regulated by a special law (Lex Grimani) of 1756. The state maintained the supreme ownership of the land, granting to recipients only the usufruct against payment of the tenth to the state. The beneficiaries were prohibited from selling, dividing, or mortgaging the land, and it was inheritable only in the male line. But it was possible to give the land so obtained in tenancy (colonate). As a rule, large land grants were so worked. The tenant paid the tenth and usually one-third of the product to the original recipient of the land grant. The Lex Grimani regulated many other matters pertaining to agriculture and animal husbandry and tried to further a diversification of agricultural production. It was generally agreed that it was an excellent law, but it was not enforced, and its general effect was small.[3]

From the collapse of Venice in 1797 to 1805 Dalmatia was for the first time under Austrian rule. The French entered Dalmatia in 1806. As described in Chapter 3, their rule in the South Slav lands, which lasted only until 1813, was eventful while they were in possession of the territory. Moreover, political, cultural, and social ideas which sprouted from the French Revolution and from their rule had considerable consequences for the later development of the South Slavs. They occupied the Republic of Dubrovnik in 1806 and abolished it in

[3] Grga Novak, *op cit.*, Pt. 2, pp. 241–42; regarding the organization of the Dalmatian Military Frontier under the Venetians, see also *Encyclopaedia Croatica*, IV, 494–95.

1808. The whole of Dalmatia formed a part of the Illyrian Provinces between 1809 and 1813 and partook of all political and social reforms undertaken by the French (see pp. 81–83).

At the beginning of the nineteenth century a part of the agricultural land in Dalmatia was worked by the land proprietors themselves. There were, however, two other basic types of land tenure: the colonate system in all areas which up to 1797 were under Venice, and the system of serfdom and sharecropping on a fifty-fifty basis in the territory of the Republic of Dubrovnik. Moreover, there were in central and northern Dalmatia about half a dozen large feudal estates which were organized according to the principles of neither the colonate nor serfdom as it existed in the Republic of Dubrovnik.

The origins of the colonate system are to be found in the times of the Roman Empire. It represented a type of land tenure which was widespread in all areas around the Mediterranean. It was based on a written contract, or upon a parol contract well defined by custom, between the landlord and the *colonus*. The *colonus* was formally free and entered the contract in formal equality with the landlord. Local customs exercised a profound influence on the nature and extent of the obligations of the *colonus* so that the conditions of land tenancy under the colonate showed great differences from locality to locality. The conditions varied with regard to various crops, the sharing of the same crops, the duration of the contract, the selling of the land and the selling of the rights of the *colonus*, and with regard to the inheritance of the rights of the *colonus*. The landowner's share amounted, as a rule, to between two-thirds and one-fourth of the gross product. The tenant could not begin harvesting without the permission and supervision of the landlord and he had to deliver the landlord's share to his home. If the tenant was evicted from the land—and that was usually possible only after the expiration of the contract—he was entitled to an indemnity for all improvements he carried out on the land, including the value of the grapevines and trees. In many cases the tenant paid a fixed amount of money as rent; in others he was obliged to deliver to the landowner a share of the crop and to render certain additional donations and labor services. The landowner usually owned the housing facilities in which the *colonus* lived, and this was taken into account in the sharing of the crop. Some of the taxes were paid by the landowner, others by the *colonus*.

The Republic of Dubrovnik had at the begining of the nineteenth century a system of serfdom which was exceedingly oppressive for the serfs or kmetovi, though it had also a sharecropping system in which the

usual division of the crop between the tenant and the landlord was on
an equal basis. As far as the first system was concerned, the nobility
of Dubrovnik owned the land and the rural housing facilities. The serfs
could not own any land. They were obliged to deliver to the landlord
usually one-third of the crop, but as a counterservice for the use of the
housing facilities they had to render to the landlord a certain amount of
corvée. The amount of *corvée* was not fixed and this proved to be a
source of great abuses. In 1800 it was fixed by law at 90 working days
annually. Moreover, the serfs were obliged to give the landowner special "gifts" in meat, eggs, and fruit on the occasion of festive days.[4]

After Dalmatia was taken over by Austria in 1813, the existing land-
tenure relationships continued. The colonate system continued to be
treated as a matter of private law and remained so until the Yugoslav
agrarian reform after World War I. The serfdom (*kmetstvo*) and the
sharecropping system in the former territory of the Republic of Dubrovnik were declared matters of public law, and with certain relaxations
this system continued to exist until 1878, when it was abolished. The
system of land tenure which existed in this area between 1878 and 1918
was similar to the colonate system in other parts of Dalmatia. According to the census of 1902, of the total of 83,455 farm units in Dalmatia
only 47,881 units, or 57.4 percent, were exploited exclusively by the
owners while the remainder was worked in some form of tenancy, mostly
in colonate.

Although agricultural production in some parts of Dalmatia was
very labor-intensive, especially in the coastal areas where cultivation
of the grapevine prevails, the system of land tenure in existence until
1919 proved to be a hindrance to agricultural progress. The kmet and
the *colonus* lacked the incentive for greater productivity because the
landlord was the primary beneficiary of any increase in productivity.
The landlords also insisted on the cultivation of crops in which they
could exercise easy control over production, such as grapevines, olives,
and in the interior areas grains. This was also one of the reasons which
precluded greater crop diversification, e.g., larger cultivation of forage
crops for more intensive animal husbandry, or larger cultivation of
vegetables.

When comparing the economic role of Dalmatia from the beginning
of the nineteenth century onward with its role during the preceding centuries, one basic change has to be stressed. Prior to the nineteenth cen-

---

[4] For more details on the history of land tenure in Dalmatia, see Milan Ivšić, *Les
problèmes agraires en Yougoslavie*, pp. 272–98, and A. Decaris, *Die Agrarfrage Dalmatiens*, pp. 48–70.

tury Dalmatia was the door through which the bulk of trade of the central Balkan areas with the West was carried on. Its merchants derived great advantages from that trade. From the beginning of the nineteenth century, and especially after the Balkans became relatively well connected by roads, railroads, and river shipping with the large Central European markets, practically all of the trade emanating from the northern and central Balkan areas, both in regard to exports and imports, was channeled into these newly enlarged trade routes, and was carried on by Central European merchants. This affected the Dalmatian economy profoundly and, so to speak, meant the completion of a long trend of falling commercial importance of the Dalmatian coast and its once prosperous towns.

Two factors played an important role in the over-all economic conditions of Dalmatia during the second half of the nineteenth century. While its shipping industry during the 1850's (largely in connection with the Crimean War) and 1860's was exceedingly prosperous, Dalmatia's shipping owners failed to make a successful shift from sailing to steamships. In the 1870's Dalmatian shipping entered a long period of depression, from which it never fully recovered. Certain diseases which affected the grapevine in Italy and later the ravages of phylloxera in France led in the 1870's and 1880's to a large expansion of vineyards in Dalmatia and large exports of wine from Dalmatia. But this was only a temporary prosperity, because the vineyards in Western Europe were renewed, and in the 1890's phylloxera invaded Dalmatia, destroying almost completely this branch of agriculture. While the vineyards were later renewed on the American grapevine basis, Dalmatian wine production never reached the level of the 1880's.

Dalmatia suffered from overpopulation for many decades, and this fact explains partly the severity of land-tenure conditions prior to 1919. A part of the working population looked for a livelihood in fishing, in the merchant marine, and above all in emigration overseas. As long as the latter was possible, it was the most important safety valve for population pressure. For decades emigrant's remittances played a very important role in the national income of Dalmatia.

MACEDONIA

The territory acquired by Serbia from the Ottoman Empire after the Balkan Wars of 1912 and 1913—39,474 square kilometers with about 1,660,000 people—consisted of the Yugoslav portion of Macedonia proper in the south, the area known as Old Serbia, located between Macedonia and the pre-1912 Serbia to the north, and a part of the

Sandjak of Novi Pazar in the west (most of the latter two areas have formed since 1945 the autonomous region of Kosovo-Metohija within the People's Republic of Serbia). In the official Serbian and Yugoslav parlance of the interwar period all these parts were known as Southern Serbia. Yugoslav Macedonia as well as those parts of Macedonia which now belong to Bulgaria and to Greece were under Ottoman rule for nearly 530 years.[5] Being in the center of the Balkan Peninsula and controlling the strategic Vardar River Valley, Macedonia, in addition to the Straits, was perhaps the most important area of European Turkey, especially during the nineteenth century. Salonika was the principal economic center of this whole area, but its commercial intercourse with the hinterland was greatly intensified after the building of railroads in the 1870's, which connected the port city with the interior.[6] The division of Macedonia among Bulgaria, Greece, and Serbia in 1913 required also considerable economic readjustments of these various portions to their new political and economic frameworks.[7]

In addition to the Macedonians (called by some writers Macedo-Slavs), Yugoslav Macedonia had a large Albanian and Turkish, and some Greek population, as well as remainders of some populations of the pre-South Slav era in the Balkans, such as the nomadic or seminomadic Vlakhs. A Macedonian nation is now a fact, but its development is of rather recent date.[8] During the half century preceding the Balkan Wars of 1912 and 1913, when the end of Turkish rule in Macedonia was known to be only a matter of time, Macedonian land and population were claimed by each of the three neighbors, namely,

[5] For the Macedonian history in the pre-Turkish era, which was closely related to the Bulgarian and Serbian medieval history, see Bogo Grafenauer *et al.* (eds.), *op. cit.*, pp. 261–302, 328–444.

[6] Milan Čemerikić, "Trade, Handicrafts, Industry, and Credit Establishments from 1875 to 1937," in Aleksa Jovanović (ed.), *Spomenica dvadesetpetogodišnjice oslobodjenja Južne Srbije, 1912–1937* (Jubilee Record of the Liberation of Southern Serbia, 1912–1937), pp. 685–732. With regard to the role of Salonika in the developments in Macedonia, as interpreted from the contemporary Macedonian Communist point of view, see also D. Zografski *et al.*, *Egejska Makedonija vo našata istorija* (Aegean Macedonia and Our History), pp. 3–169.

[7] A very interesting and, to this writer, the only known attempt at treating the Macedonian economy as a whole during the 1920's, that is, within a territory defined by the author as Macedonia and cutting across the international boundaries as established after the Balkan Wars and World War I, is to be found in D. Iaranoff, *La Macédoine économique.*

[8] H. R. Wilkinson, "Jugoslav Macedonia in Transition," *Geographical Journal*, CXVIII, Pt. 4, 389–405; H. R. Wilkinson, *Maps and Politics: A Review of the Ethnographic Cartography of Macedonia.*

the Serbs, the Bulgarians, and the Greeks.[9] But after achieving control over part of Macedonia in 1913, each one of these neighbors abused portions of the people of Macedonia.

The social and agricultural structure of Yugoslav Macedonia at the time of the Turkish invasion, when it was the center of the Serbian medieval state, was described in Chapter 2. In addition to the Turkish soldiers and some administrators, who took possession of the towns, strategic points, lines of communication, and the spahis who obtained agricultural land of the Christian *reaya* as military fiefs, considerable numbers of Turkish peasants came to Macedonia from Asia Minor and settled there in the early stages of Turkish rule. This was never the case in other South Slav lands which later came under Turkish rule. These settlers were given heritable family farms or *čiftliks* with an area of 10 to 15 hectares, depending on the quality of soil.[10] Thus this type of small *čiftliks*, which was legally allowed, was common here, just as in Thrace, from the beginning of Turkish rule. But this type of hereditary farms of Moslem peasants should not be confused with the large-sized *čiftliks* which developed during the seventeenth, eighteenth, and nineteenth centuries through a degeneration of the Turkish feudal system. This second type of *čiftlik*—discussed already in Chapter 2— became the dominant feature of the agricultural organization in the flat areas of Macedonia, and remained in force in the Yugoslav parts of Macedonia formally until 1913 and actually until 1918. Many of these *čiftliks* were owned by absentee landlords living in Istanbul and Salonika. Some were administered as large agricultural enterprises. In other cases an individual village or a group of villages formed a *čiftlik* and all their inhabitants were obliged to render specified obligations to the *čiftlik* owner.[11] So far as *čiftliks* were administered by hired managers, the latter were paid at the expense of the tenants. The Macedonian *čifčije*, the tenants on the *čiftliks*, were the most exploited and

---

[9] Carnegie Endowment for International Peace, *Enquête dans les Balkans*, pp. 1–53; L. Schultze Jena, *Makedonien*, pp. 32–40, 150 ff.; H. R. Wilkinson, *Maps and Politics*, *passim*.

[10] Omer Lutfi Barkan, "*Čiftlik*," Serbo-Croatian translation by Hamid Hadžibegić of an article published in the Turkish edition of the *Encyclopaedia of Islam* in 1945, *Godišnjak Istoriskog društva Bosne i Hercegovine*, II, 287–98.

[11] One of the latest and very thorough studies on the problem of *čiftliks*, with special emphasis on their more recent evolution but from the point of view of cultural geography, is to be found in Richard Busch-Zantner, *Agrarverfassung, Gesellschaft und Siedlung in Südosteuropa*, pp. 84–104. For the concept of the *čiftlik* as a type of agricultural estate during the more recent phases of the Turkish feudal system, see especially pp. 81–84.

the worst treated among all of the Balkan peasants during the nineteenth century.

In more recent times two main types of tenants were working on the *čiftliks* in Yugoslav Macedonia: (*a*) The *čifčije*, corresponding largely to the kmetovi of Bosnia and Herzegovina, were in most cases actually if not formally in a long-term dependent relationship to the landlord. They were obliged to deliver from one-third to one-half of their produce to the landlord and were obliged to render various labor services to the landlord and to local authorities. They sometimes owned their own houses, draft animals, tools, and a small plot of land, but often the housing was provided by the landlord in the *čiftlik* village,[12] and sometimes also draft animals, tools, and seed. The owning of a pair of oxen for draft was normally a basic requirement for a peasant family to obtain or maintain the position of a *čifčija*. (*b*) Regular tenants, or *ćesimlije*, paid a fixed rent in money, produce, or both. In addition, there were individual agricultural workers, or *momci*, who contracted mostly by the year and were paid in money or produce and usually given a small plot of land whose produce belonged to them exclusively.[13]

Needless to say, there existed great differences in the landlord-tenant relationship in various parts of Macedonia. This is quite natural, as the relationship was not one of public law, but formally rather one of "free" agreement between the two. It varied according to geographic area, the crops grown, the arrangements with regard to housing, draft animals, and seed, the type of management of the *čiftliks*, the prevailing political conditions, and the ability of the peasant to find another landlord with more satisfactory conditions and greater security, and of the landlord to find other *čifčije*. The settlement on the *čiftliks* was by far the least satisfactory form of peasant dependence under Turkish rule. In the sharing of the crop in Macedonia, when the tenant provided everything except land and housing, most often the following

[12] The *čiftlik* system led in Macedonia to the development of a special type of village —the *čiftlik* village. It was a compact, square or rectangular structure consisting of a large building for the *čiftlik* owner, a separate building for the manager of the *čiftlik*, the necessary stables, a shack for implements, storage for produce, and a large number of housing units (either separate or under one roof) for the tenants. This type of building made the supervision of work and sharing of crops with the tenants quite easy. Very often the *čiftlik* village gave the impression of a fort. Jovan Cvijić, *La Péninsule Balkanique*, pp. 222–23; L. Schultze Jena, *op cit.*, pp. 140–50; R. Busch-Zantner, *op. cit.*, pp. 104–18.

[13] Müller, "Die Landwirtschaft in der europäischen Türkei," in Germany, Reichsamt des Innern, *Berichte über Handel und Industrie*, XIX, Pt. 13 (Berlin, June 21, 1913), 701–35; Jevto Dedijer, *Nova Srbija* (New Serbia), pp. 161–62, 236; Janko Vukičević, "Agriculture," in Aleksa Jovanović (ed.), *op. cit.*, pp. 523–31.

procedure was applied: from the total crop that was assembled in the yard of the *čiftlik* village, one-tenth and, in more recent times, even one-eighth would be taken as the state tax; then the necessary seed would be subtracted. From the remainder one-half would be taken by the *čiftlik-sahibia* and the other by the *čiftčija*. As, however, the collection of the tax was regularly farmed out and the payment of the *čiftlik* manager had also to be borne by the tenants, the tenant who formally worked on a fifty-fifty basis usually obtained only one-third of the produce.[14] In the case of crops requiring more preparatory or processing work, e.g., hemp, the tenant's share was larger.

The *čiftčija* was not "tied to the land." But owing to his low share of the gross product and the fact that he needed credit, both to feed his family part of the year and to buy draft animals and tools, he often came into a debtor relationship with the landlord. As he was unable to leave the landlord before paying his debts, and he was not in a position to do that, his freedom to move was very limited. In other cases *čiftčije* often moved from one landlord to another in search of better conditions. They could be evicted by the landlord at any time. In addition to the difference in the sharing of the crop, the unlimited freedom of the landlord to evict his *čiftčija* was the main difference which separated the latter from the Bosnian kmet. Essentially, however, the *čiftčija* was a tenant in name and a serf in fact.

Free peasants had their farms mostly on mountain slopes and in the mountain areas. As a rule these farms were of dwarf or small size. Only in the last few decades of Turkish rule did more free peasants acquire land in the plains by buying it from the *čiftlik* owners. There were also some groups of population in the mountain areas which were still of a quasi-nomadic character. Both of these groups, of course, were subject to the paying of the tenth or the eighth as well as to the paying of other state taxes.

The paucity of land resources in many areas of Macedonia forced many peasants into temporary emigration. These were the famous *pečalbari*, mostly masons, who up to the close of the nineteenth century ranged over the whole of the Ottoman Empire in search of work, and later came also to the United States. As a rule the peasants from the mountainous areas went much more into *pečalba* than those from the flat sections of the country where the hold of the *čiftlik* system was much stronger. *Pečalba*, commonly, is a type of temporary emigration with regular trips home every year or every third year.

---

[14] Müller, *op. cit.*, pp. 710–11; L. Schultze Jena, *op. cit.*, pp. 50–52.

Because of its Continental climate with Mediterranean climatic influences, Macedonia grew some specialty crops, in addition to grains, wheat, barley, corn, and rye. These were tobacco, poppies for the production of opium, cotton, rice, red pepper, hemp, and a variety of oilseeds. It also grew mulberry trees, which served for the cultivation of silk cocoons. Because of the great expanses of mountain pastures—forests in Macedonia have been largely destroyed, partly by men and partly by goats—livestock, especially cattle, sheep, and goats, were and still are one of the main pillars of the Macedonian economy. In most communities in mountainous areas people were pursuing a predominantly pastoral economy based on periodic transhumance.

Lack of political order and security, especially from the 1870's onward, with widespread terror and counterterror, and the policy of "plunder economy" pursued by the Turkish ruling class, made of Macedonia a region of backwardness, poverty, and insecurity.[15] The harshness of the *čiftlik* system was such that some areas of Macedonia became relatively depopulated. According to official Turkish data, only 8.26 percent of the total area of European Turkey was under crops in the fiscal year 1907/8. Some *čiftliks* had to be abandoned for lack of labor and some were only partly cultivated.[16] Moreover, a certain number of *čiftliks* passed into the hands of Christians and Jews from the cities and some were subdivided and sold to the peasants. It appears that a considerable portion of emigrants' remittances was used for the buying of land.

Turkish political and social reforms undertaken before 1870 (discussed in the preceding chapter), as well as some reforms undertaken during the ensuing 40 years, were supposed to apply also to Macedonia (of course with the exception of the Safer decree, which applied only to Bosnia and Herzegovina). But it is one thing to proclaim the laws and another to enforce them. In fact, all these reform laws remained without practical effect in Macedonia as they could not be enforced, and the local chieftains and officials continued their willful and abusive practices. As a consequence, little if any improvement in the status of the Christian peasantry was noticeable. On the other hand, the activity of the irredentist groups, mostly of a guerrilla character, grew steadily and in turn provoked stronger repressive actions on the part of the Turks. This was

[15] H. N. Brailsford, *Macedonia*, pp. 1–58 and *passim*; Sreten V. Vukosavljević, "The Development of Certain Forms of Feudal Order During the Eighteenth and Nineteenth Centuries," *Letopis Matice Srpske*, January-February, 1946, pp. 100–109.

[16] Müller, *op. cit.*, pp. 714–15; R. Busch-Zantner, *op. cit.*, pp. 124–34, considers not only the *čiftlik* system but a whole series of factors which contributed to the emigration from and economic decline of Macedonia.

especially true after 1893 when the so-called Internal Macedonian Revolutionary Organization (IMRO) was established with a far-reaching political program. Furthermore, various other political or armed groups, with pro-Bulgarian, pro-Serbian, or pro-Greek sentiments, were active in Macedonia.[17] This situation continued until the Balkan Wars of 1912–13, which ended Ottoman rule in Macedonia and led to the splitting of the province among Serbia, Bulgaria, and Greece.[18] At the same time the Sandjak of Novi Pazar was split between Serbia and Montenegro.

Pre-1912 Serbia had barely started to incorporate the newly acquired regions—a process noted for graft and abuse of native population—and to recuperate slowly from the economic effects of the two Balkan Wars when World War I broke out. A considerable number of Turkish landlords and peasants, as well as members of other nationalities—Macedonians, Greeks, and Albanians—left Macedonia during the Balkan Wars and immediately thereafter, as did others after World War I (see p. 155). Yugoslav Macedonia entered World War I as a part of Serbia, and actually almost in the same social and economic conditions in which it was found when wrested from Ottoman rule.

The abolition of the *čifčija* relationship, which materially was very near to serfdom, was promised in the Serbian Royal Proclamation of October 5, 1912, which was issued together with the declaration of war (First Balkan War) on the Ottoman Empire. Serbia was also very much interested in colonizing Macedonia in order to increase the strength of the Serbian element in the province and in order to further economic development of the area. The colonists were to be granted free land. A Decree of February 20, 1914, prescribed the rules of the colonization program. But World War I came before any agrarian reform or colonizing work could be started in Macedonia by the Serbian administration.[19] Both were undertaken only after 1918 (see Chapter 18).

[17] For an interpretation of this period from the Serbian point of view, see Aleksa Jovanović, "The Guerrilla Movement in Southern Serbia During the Turkish Rule," in Aleksa Jovanović (ed.), *op. cit.*, pp. 271–307; the Bulgarian view, on the other hand, can be seen from Draganof, *La Macédoine et les Réformes*; see also Wayne S. Vucinich, *Serbia Between East and West*, pp. 24–30.

[18] The course of the First Balkan War with its military and political interpretation from the Serbian point of view is presented in St. Stanojević, *Srpsko-turski rat 1912 godine* (The Serbo-Turkish War of 1912) ; for a detailed and detached analysis of the Balkan Wars, see Ernst C. Helmreich, *The Diplomacy of the Balkan Wars, 1912–1913*.

[19] *Zbornik uredaba za novooslobodjene i prisajedinjene oblasti* (A Collection of Decrees for the Newly Liberated and Annexed Areas), pp. 107–15.

MONTENEGRO

Montenegro was the second sovereign state which in 1918 became part of the new state of Yugoslavia. The Turks conquered Montenegro in 1499. But as they controlled only the plains, the lines of communication, and the towns, the population of a part of the forbidding mountain territory remained outside their grip. Being extremely poor, and not strategically located, Montenegro was not of sufficient importance to the Turks to warrant the trouble of complete conquest. The Montenegrins[20] pride themselves, however, on having resisted the Turks for 500 years and for never having been fully subdued. Their full independence was formally recognized by the Ottoman Empire only at the Berlin Congress in 1878.

For centuries Montenegro was a loose association of tribes ruled nominally by a bishop prince. It obtained a rudimentary state organization during the first half of the nineteenth century. This organization was considerably strengthened and improved during the 1850's when Montenegro ceased to be a theocratic (or as some writers prefer to call it aristocratic) state organization (1851). In 1878, by the decision of the Berlin Congress, and following the successful wars with Turkey between 1876 and 1878, the territory of Montenegro was enlarged by about 70 percent and its population almost doubled. The agricultural resources of the land were greatly increased, as the newly incorporated areas contained some fertile plains and river valleys. Moreover, the new area had several towns in which trade and handicrafts were practiced. With the new population Montenegro obtained some skilled craftsmen and merchants, skills which it dismally lacked, as only the professions of warrior and herdsman were considered to be worthy of a male Montenegrin.

From the Berlin Congress to World War I, Montenegro made considerable advances in its state administration, in the development of schools, building of roads, and advancement of agriculture.[21] After the Balkan Wars of 1912 and 1913, Montenegro acquired a part of the Sandjak of Novi Pazar and a strip of territory in the neighborhood of Lake Scutari. Sections of this territory were very fertile. Montenegro's

[20] The question whether the Montenegrins form a separate nation or whether they are a part of the Serbian nation is still open in the minds of many social scientists. Considering the fact that the Montenegrins have had a different political past than the Serbs and that many of them think of themselves as being members of a separate nation, this writer is of the opinion that there exists a separate Montenegrin nation.

[21] Jagoš Jovanović, *Stvaranje crnogorske države i razvoj crnogorske nacionalnosti* (The Formation of the Montenegrin State and the Development of the Montenegrin Nationality), pp. 340–46.

territory was increased from 9,080 to about 15,000 square kilometers, and its population, which in 1912 was estimated at 220,000, rose to about 350,000.[22]

The territory now known as Montenegro was called Dioclea (Duklja) in the Middle Ages, and prior to the middle of the twelfth century it had its own state organization. After the ascendancy of Racia as the center of the Serbian medieval state during the second half of the twelfth century, Dioclea lost much of its significance and became part of the Nemanid state. The evolving feudal order of the Serbian medieval state, which had many characteristics of the Byzantine and some characteristics of the Western European feudalism, was at that time prevalent also in the Dioclean territory. It was after Serbian defeat in 1389 that independent developments again took place in the latter territory under domestic leadership. Because of the forbidding landscape, the utter poverty in arable land and other resources, its isolation from the lines of communication and from the currents of civilization, and the fact that the Turks after the conquest controlled the plains and the lines of inland communication, the social and economic life of the country developed thereafter along very primitive lines. In these areas more than in any other South Slav area, the tribal forces reasserted themselves after the Turkish conquest. The reassertion of the tribal organizations was a result not only of the political conditions, that is, lack of a strong and all-permeating state organism, but also of the geographic factors favoring separation into small territorial units, and of the influence of the earlier mentioned Vlakh *katun* organization. Patriarchalism marked the whole social, economic, and political life of the country. The institutions of the tribe (*pleme*) and the phratry (*bratstvo*)[23] endured as social and economic, if not as political, organizations until the twentieth century.[24] The organization of the nineteenth-century Montenegrin state necessitated the imposition of a governmental framework over these tribal structures, and regular levying of taxes, which proved to be a long and hard task requiring, occasionally, the use of the sword.

The chief source of livelihood in Montenegro was, and still is, animal husbandry, which in most places is based on periodic transhumance.

[22] *Montenegrin Bulletin*, No. 1 (Geneva, December 1917), p. 8.

[23] The literature on Montenegrin tribes is quite voluminous. Among the most detailed are the studies by Jovan Erdeljanović, *Kuči, pleme u Crnoj Gori* and *Stara Crna Gora* (Old Montenegro); in English see M. E. Durham, *Some Tribal Origins, Laws and Customs of the Balkans*, pp. 34–59.

[24] Petar Šobajić, "The Montenegrin Village," in Miloslav Stojadinović (ed.), *Naše selo* (Our Village), pp. 69–73; Nikola Gjonović, *Crna Gora pre i posle ujedinjenja* (Montenegro Before and After the Unification), p. 9.

The bulk of the forests and grazing lands in the mountains was still, during the interwar period, held as the common of the *pleme*, while around the village part of the land was the *bratstvo* common. These lands were freely accessible to the flocks of all members of the respective communities. The tending of the herds while grazing in the mountains was done co-operatively, as in other Balkan lands, by organizing the *bačije* (see p. 191). With the increasing population and the need for more arable land, more and more of the commons were subdivided among individual families and brought under the plow.

According to a rough property census of 1855, when the population of Montenegro was estimated at 80,000, the "wealth" of the country consisted of 68,480 *rali* of arable land; 27,286 *kosa* of meadows (one *ralo* or "plowshare" equals 1,680 and a *kosa* or "scythe" 3,340 square meters); about 315,780 head of sheep and goats; 39,730 head of cattle; 6,000 pigs; 19,300 beehives; 3,200 horses; and about 5,700 hectoliters of wine.[25] Agricultural resources in 1912 were estimated at 160,000 *rali* of arable land; 16,000 *rali* of orchards, vineyards, and gardens; 125,000 *kosa* of meadows; 16,000 horses; 100,000 cattle; 520,000 sheep; 250,000 goats; and 17,000 pigs.[26] The productivity of much of the land and of the livestock was very low. In 1855 there was only roughly one-fourth of one hectare of arable land and meadows per capita in Montenegro, while in 1912 there was a little over one-third of one hectare per capita. The acquisition of more fertile areas in 1878, and again in 1913, did not solve the problem of food for Montenegro.[27]

In pre-1878 Montenegro there were no feudal forms of land tenure. In areas acquired from the Turks in 1878 there existed *čiftlik* estates. According to Article 30 of the Treaty concluded by the Berlin Congress, the Turkish *čiftlik-sahibias* retained their properties, and when expropriated they had to be properly indemnified. The *čifčije* were, however, given a hereditary standing on the *čiftliks* and their relationship with the landlords well defined. Most of the Sultan's property and of the *wakf* lands became Montenegrin state property, for which special payments were made. In areas incorporated in 1913 there existed the same land-tenure conditions as in Macedonia, and the same rules of interwar agrarian reform that applied to Macedonia were applied also to these parts of Montenegro.

[25] Jagoš Jovanović, *op. cit.*, p. 262. This "census" was undertaken prior to the introduction of a system of regular taxes in Montenegro.

[26] *Montenegrin Bulletin*, Nos. 4–5 (Geneva, September 1918), pp. 7–16.

[27] For a detailed discussion of the western parts of Montenegro from the point of view of cultural and economic geography, see Kurt Kayser, *Westmontenegro*.

According to Article 256 of the Montenegrin Code of Civil Procedure of 1905, one *ralo* of land and the house of the peasant, valued up to 200 crowns (at that time about $50) could not be foreclosed for private debts.

Because of the utter poverty, emigration from Montenegro was a continuous process. It was estimated that around 1912 approximately one third or more of all the able-bodied men had permanently or temporarily emigrated. Emigrants' remittances were one of the essential parts of Montenegro's national income in those days. Over two-thirds of the exports before 1914 consisted of livestock on the hoof, hides, wool, and dried meat, while the chief imports were cereals, textiles, coffee, and sugar.

Part of the cereal imports and a grant-in-aid for the payment of a part of government expenditures came in the form of relief from Russia, which Montenegro regarded as its protector. Cash grants-in-aid (reportedly amounting to about 1,000 ducats annually) were initiated in 1715 by Peter the Great and they were granted more or less regularly for 200 years. In return Montenegro served as a pawn of the Russian policy against the Ottoman Empire.

SLOVENIA

In the early Middle Ages the Slovenes had an association of tribes with only rudimentary characteristics of state organization.[28] Unlike other South Slav nations they never had a full-fledged medieval state of their own, and Slovenia is not a historical province. As an idea it is the creation of the Slovene cultural and political renaissance of the eighteenth and nineteenth centuries. As such, it covers the territory inhabited by the Slovenes, namely, all of the territory of the former Austrian crownland of Carniola, a sizable part of Styria, a strip of Carinthia, and parts of Istria and Gorizia and Gradisca. As a political unit Slovenia was created after the collapse of Austria-Hungary, but did not include all the territory claimed as Slovene. The Slovene lands belonged to various Germanic rulers from the eighth century onward. Having been almost half surrounded by the Germans and being located on a strategic spot where the South Slavs meet with the Germans and the Italians and in an area over which the Germans had to pass in their

[28] For the early and rather involved history of the Slovenes and their relations with other Slavic and Germanic groups in the Middle Ages, all of which is still a matter of considerable discussion among Yugoslav historians, see Bogo Grafenauer *et al.* (eds.), *Istorija naroda Jugoslavije* (History of the Peoples of Yugoslavia), I, 131–66, 745–804.

southward drives (from Germany and Austria to Italy and to the Adriatic), the Slovenes were subjugated by the Germans for over a thousand years and exposed to a strong process of Germanization.[29]

One of the advantages that the Slovene lands had through centuries in comparison with other South Slav lands was that they never lived under the Ottoman rule, though they were exposed to periodic Turkish raids for over two centuries. Thus they never experienced the utter devastations and great population shifts of the other South Slav lands.

The cultural renaissance in Slovenia began during the eighteenth century, but the great cultural and political awakening of the Slovenes came in the wake of the French Revolution and following the creation of the Illyrian Provinces by Napoleon, of which the Slovene main city, Ljubljana, was the capital. Real political renaissance came, however, with the revolutionary year 1848. While in the course of the nineteenth century the Slovenes showed little revolutionary zeal, their cultural, political, and economic growth was carried on under more stable conditions and was on more systematic bases than that of their brothers to the southeast. The whole political and economic life of Slovenia until the 1880's was under German control, and the Slovenes had an extremely difficult time to secure some rights in their own land. But this fact also meant that they had in their own midst a population of higher cultural standing and technological skill from which to learn. By 1914 the Slovenes were culturally and economically by far the most advanced South Slav nation. At the turn of the century they obtained a solid political organization along Christian populist lines covering both rural and urban areas. They also had a liberal and a socialist movement, the latter two among the urban population. It should be pointed out that in no other South Slav land did the Church, Roman Catholic or Serbian Orthodox, play such an important role in temporal affairs as did the Catholic Church in Slovenia. This remained true until the end of World War II.

Up to 1848 the land tenure in the Slovene lands was marked by an outright feudal order, as in the remainder of the Dual Monarchy. As the domestic ruling class was eliminated even before the tenth century, feudalism in the Slovene lands had exclusively German forms, includ-

[29] Milko Kos, "History [of Slovenia]," in Anton Melik and Milko Kos (eds.), *Slovenačka* (Slovenia), pp. 33–85; Dragotin Lončar, *The Slovenes: A Social History*, translated from the Slovenian by Anthony J. Klančar, pp. 8–10 and *passim*; Milko Kos, "Colonization and Germanization of the Slovene Land," *Historijski zbornik*, IV, 9–19. See also James W. Thompson, *Feudal Germany*, pp. 580–611.

ing the institution of landless nobility. The main representatives of the feudal order were thus feudal lords of German blood[30] and the Catholic Church.[31]

Together with other lands of Central Europe, Slovene lands went through a series of peasant revolutions between the fifteenth and the seventeenth centuries. The most important was the one led by the Croatian peasant leader Matija Gubec in 1573, in which both Croatian and Slovene peasants took part. One historical force of the same period which affected the Slovene lands profoundly, but had little effect on Croatia and none on the other South Slav lands, was the Reformation. The Counter Reformation carried, however, a complete victory, and Slovenia is now among the purest Catholic lands in Europe.

During the long centuries of German feudal regime in the Slovene lands German principles of peasant property inheritance exercised great influence. This is proved by two facts. On the one hand, the institution of the zadruga, so powerfully developed and generally maintained among the Serbs and Croats until the middle of the nineteenth century, was pushed aside among the Slovenes many centuries ago. On the other hand, most old peasant farms, according to Melik,[32] have been preserved undivided, which indicates a system of inheritance on the principle of primogeniture.

Serfdom in the Slovene lands was abolished by the Austrian laws of 1848 and 1849. It is necessary, however, to point out that in Slovenia the topographic configuration, namely, the largely Alpine character of the land, and the fact that there were no marked shifts in population, periods of depopulation, or large-scale colonization, was not conducive to the formation of latifundia, as was the case in Slavonia and Vojvodina. Most of the feudal estates were actually based on large

[30] In the northeastern parts of the Slovene lands, which have been known since the Middle Ages as wine-producing areas, the relationships between the German landlords and the Slovene viniculturists since the middle of the sixteenth century have been regulated by special rules embodied in a law of 1543, called in German the Bergrechtsbüchel. The administration of these rules was supervised by special courts composed of viniculturists and landlords, which in their decisions relied much on Slovene customary law. Metod Dolenc, "Slovene People's Courts in the Period from the Sixteenth to the Eighteenth Centuries," Yugoslav Academy of Science and Art, *Rad*, CCXXXIX, 1–55.

[31] One of the oldest *urbars* in the Slovene territory was the one of 1377 regulating the conditions of the serfs on the Church properties in the area of Tolmin in the Slovene Littoral, the *Liber censualis ecclesiae Aquilegiensis 1377*. Milko Kos, *Srednjeveški urbarji za Slovenijo*. II: *Urbarji Slovenskega Primorja* (Medieval *Urbars* for Slovenia. II: The *Urbars* of the Slovene Littoral).

[32] Anton Melik, "The Village in Slovenia," in Miloslav Stojadinović (ed.), *op. cit.*, pp. 66–68.

forest holdings, of course with considerable areas of arable and pasture land.

Unlike in other areas of present-day Yugoslavia, with the possible exception of former "civil" Croatia, the village and the peasantry of Slovenia did not go through repeated ordeals of political, social, and economic upheavals. Practically all villages in Slovenia are centuries old, while in most other parts of Yugoslavia old and relatively new villages exist, as well as traces of many destroyed and deserted villages. The Slovene rural population, with the exception of some German enclaves which were formed in the Middle Ages and minor immigrations of other South Slavs from the southeast, is much less mixed than in other parts of the country. Until the middle of the nineteenth century urban population was, however, largely German.

In the Slovene village there are two main types of peasants and farms. First are the old settlers, called the *kmetje* or *gruntari*. They own larger farms on better soil and form the core of the Slovene village, both in terms of the location of their homes and in the economic and social sense. The size of their farms, though varied according to area and topography, enables the peasant families to live without looking for income outside of their farms. Second, there are the newer settlers on much smaller farms, who settled on former common pastures or on forest land, which is poorer soil. They live in much smaller houses or *bajte* on the outskirts of old villages and are known as *bajtari* or *kočari*. Generally these farms were not sufficient to assure a living to their owners, who had to earn additional income by working as farm hands, as workers in forests, industry, mining, and road transport, and as servants in the homes of the *gruntari* and in the towns.[33]

With the rise of industry and mining and the development of railroad transportation, all of which advanced in Slovenia much more rapidly and fully than in other South Slav lands, part of the Slovene peasants, especially those with little land, switched to industrial work. Most of them continued, however, to keep their farms. New employment opportunities did not suffice to absorb the increasing population, and large-scale emigration ensued, especially to the United States. Emigration was at its highest between 1890 and 1910.

Except for some areas which specialize in the production of wine, hops, poultry, or fruits, most of Slovenia follows a mixed type of agriculture with small surpluses for the market. As in other Alpine lands, cattle raising is well developed, and in many peasant households the

[33] Anton Melik, *Slovenija* (Slovenia), Pt. 2, pp. 438–61.

number of cattle can be taken as an expression of their economic strength.[34] One of the basic characteristics of the Slovene peasant economy is that forest exploitation—and the peasants owned during the interwar period about 80 percent of all forests—plays a most important role. Forest farming was put on a rational basis over a century ago, and in several areas of Slovenia sales of timber and/or employment in the timber industry represent the chief source of cash for the peasants.[35]

An organization that played an important role in the economic and political life of Slovenia in the last decades of the Austrian rule, and again in Yugoslavia during the interwar period, was the agricultural co-operative system. It was especially well developed in the field of agricultural credit. Mostly it was controlled by the Slovene People's (Catholic) party. One of the reasons for the greater development and success of co-operatives in Slovenia was the fact that the agricultural property was not so excessively subdivided as in most other South Slav lands. Moreover, the Slovenes, having attained a higher cultural level, were able to appreciate the advantages of modern co-operatives more than the other South Slav nations.

VOJVODINA

Vojvodina—meaning literally a duchy—is located in the northeasternmost part of Yugoslavia. It is not a historically well-defined province as are most of the others, but rather a name used to designate the western part of the Banat of Temesvar, most of Bačka, and a small part of Baranja to the west, in which large Serbian settlements took place between the middle of the fifteenth and the beginning of the nineteenth centuries. Only between 1849 and 1860 was it constituted as a separate province—the Serbian Vojvodina—within the Austrian Empire, but at that time it did not include all of its present territory. Even before the conquest of this area by the Hungarians around A.D. 900, its population consisted partially of South Slavs. But from the time of the Hungarian conquest until 1918, with the exception of the period when most of the Hungarian territory was under Turkish rule (approximately from 1530 to the Peace of Karlovci in 1699 and the Peace of Požarevac

---

[34] *Ibid.*, p. 423.

[35] Ante Ružić, "Small Private Forest Property in Slovenia," in Aleksandar Ugrenović (ed.), *Pola stoljeća šumarstva, 1876–1926* (One-Half Century of Forest Economy, 1876–1926), pp. 279–99. "Small" forest properties are defined variously: 60 hectares in altitudes below 500 meters, 115 hectares in altitudes between 500 and 800 meters, and above 800 meters any forest property which is administered by its owner directly and does not give a larger income than a medium peasant farm.

in 1718), this area was considered an integral part of the Hungarian state territory, though much of it was for a considerable time administered directly from Vienna.

The patterns of land tenure developed in Vojvodina in the same fashion as in the remainder of Hungary and in Slavonia. Before the Turkish invasion the country had a feudal system based on latifundia. The harshness of the system resulted in many peasant revolts, the most important being the one in 1514 which, like the others, was crushed with sword and fire and led to an almost complete elimination of the remaining free peasants. The position of the peasants was so difficult that many were willing, as earlier in Bosnia and other Balkan regions, to serve as a "fifth column" helping the invading Turks, who promised them better treatment. During the Turkish regime in Hungary, the Turks introduced their feudal system characteriezd by the military fiefs: ziamets and timars.

After the Turkish subjugation of the Serbian medieval state, a number of Serbian nobles, who had obtained grants of land from the Hungarian kings, and large numbers of Serbian people emigrated to Hungary, especially its southern parts, and to other territories in the west. Serbian emigration to these parts continued while the Turks were in control, as well as after 1699 and 1718 when these areas were wrested from the Turks. It was a process which lasted several centuries.[36] The Serbs in these areas not only pursued agriculture, but also engaged heavily in handicrafts and in trade and showed considerable cultural achievement. The Serbian cultural renaissance began within, and was largely carried out by, this segment of the Serbian nation.

After the expulsion of the Turks, southern Hungary came under the direct administration of the Austrian Emperor, who considered this land as war booty. The Turks left the land largely depopulated. The remaining population was mostly Serbian and Rumanian. The elaborate policy initiated by the Imperial military administration in this area after its liberation from the Turks had several purposes. The basic task was to colonize the area. Only after colonization was it possible to improve its defensive power against the Turks and to increase the number of subjects devoted to the Emperor in this important outpost of the Empire. Only after colonization was it possible to develop agriculture,

---

[36] For a discussion of the settlement of the Serbs in Vojvodina prior to the seventeenth century and of the conditions in that territory under the Turkish rule, see D. J. Popović, "Vojvodina During the Turkish Rule," in D. J. Popović (ed.), *Vojvodina* (Vojvodina), pp. 145–300. See also Aleksa Ivić, *Istorija Srba u Vojvodini* (History of the Serbs in Vojvodina).

transportation, and agricultural industries and to increase the number of taxpayers. Furthermore, this colonization was intended to further the German element and Roman Catholicism in this part of the Empire. Moreover, by distributing land in this area, the government wanted to reward many devoted servants of the dynasty. Thus, in the course of the eighteenth century a systematic large-scale colonization by Germans, mostly from the Rhineland and from Upper Austria, was carried out in the whole southern Hungarian Plain. This colonization created the basis for the later large and economically powerful German minority in Southeastern Europe, which after World War I was split among Yugoslavia, Rumania, and Hungary.[37] Some Croatian, French, Italian, Slovak, Armenian, Rumanian, and other colonists were also brought in, but the Austrian Imperial government tried to keep the Magyars out until 1867. The Serbs were also colonized throughout the eighteenth century, though in certain areas they were greatly abused and a segment emigrated to Russia. Large numbers of Serbs and a small number of other settlers were established as peasant soldiers in the Banat Military Frontier which was gradually organized in the course of the eighteenth century, and which actually was a continuation of the Croato-Slavonian Military Frontier to the west (see Map 2, p. 75).[38] The Banat Military Frontier was demilitarized in 1871.

In spite of the large-scale colonization of free peasants, large areas of land were left and were distributed as feudal grants to the Roman Catholic and the Eastern Orthodox churches and to various nobles and civilian and military dignitaries of the Habsburg Empire. Some land was sold at low prices to people who had good contacts with the military authorities. Furthermore, many people engaged in ruthless land-enclosure practices, mostly at the expense of the colonists, but also at the expense of the state.[39]

Most colonists were settled as free peasants, who for the first ten years after their settlement were also freed from all taxes. But the latifundia outside of the Military Frontier belonging to the temporal lords and to the churches were settled with serfs, whose obligations in produce

[37] For a detailed discussion of the settlement and development of the German minority in the Danube Basin, see Andreas Dammang, *Die deutsche Landwirtschaft in Banat und in der Batschka*, and articles "Banat" and "Batschka" in *Handwörterbuch des Grenz- und Auslanddeutschtums*, I, 207–86, 291–345.

[38] Rupert von Schumacher, *Des Reiches Hofzaun*, pp. 82–114.

[39] Arpad Lebl, "Land Enclosure in Vojvodina," *Naučni zbornik Matice Srpske*, I, 48–71. As in Slavonia so in southern Hungary only very small amounts of land were returned after liberation from the Turks to the feudal families which owned these lands before the Turkish invasion.

and *corvée* were approximately the same as those of the serfs in Slavonia, and were regulated by the *urbars* of 1767 for Hungary and of
1780 for Banat.[40] The class of peasants with little or no land began
to be formed as a counterpart to the latifundia in the Middle Ages and
grew rapidly after the middle of the eighteenth century.

The struggle between the Austrian and the Hungarian parts of the
Habsburg Empire was almost constant and was carried on also in southern Hungary. The intensification of Hungarian nationalism and Hungarian opposition to the Germanization drives emanating from Vienna
were complicated by the rise of nationalism among nationalities who
themselves were subject peoples in Hungary. Vojvodinan Serbs were
occasionally used by Austria as a tool against the Hungarians. But
after the conclusion of the Austro-Hungarian Compromise of 1867,
which regulated the relations between Austria and Hungary during the
last 50 years of their existence as a federal state, the Serbs of Vojvodina
were left at the mercy of the Hungarians, and their cultural, political,
and economic development, just as that of other nationalities including
the Germans, was systematically hindered by the Magyars. Following
the Compromise the Hungarian government embarked upon a policy
of Magyarization of all those areas in which the Magyar element was
weak. Tools of this policy were political, cultural, and economic discrimination, and planned and subsidized colonization of the Magyars.
This policy continued until World War I. Coming upon earlier colonization drives carried out by the Austrians, this new wave of colonization made Vojvodina and the southeastern parts of pre-1918 Hungary
racially the most mixed area in Europe. The territory of Vojvodina, as
incorporated into Yugoslavia in 1918, showed, according to the Hungarian population census of 1910, that of the total population of 1,347,-
000 there were only 31.93 percent Magyars, as against 28.92 percent
Serbs, 5.26 percent other South Slavs, 4.40 percent Slovaks and other
Slavs, 22.80 percent Germans, 5.74 percent Rumanians, and 0.95
percent people of other nationalities.

As in other parts of Hungary and Austria (with the exception of
Dalmatia) serfdom was abolished in Vojvodina in 1848. Circumstances
which led to this reform were described in Chapter 3. In Hungary the
conditions were greatly complicated by the revolution and the war with
Austria. However, neither in Croatia-Slavonia nor in Hungary did
that reform result in the liquidation of large landed estates or in the
elimination of the political power of the landed aristocracy. In Croatia-

[40] Josip Bösendorfer, *Agrarni odnosi u Slavoniji* (Agrarian Relationships in Slavonia), pp. 89–92.

Slavonia and Vojvodina both ended in 1919 with the Yugoslav agrarian reform, but in Hungary they continued until the end of World War II.

The application of capitalist principles in Hungarian agriculture in the decades following the abolition of serfdom in 1848 favored the continuation of large estates, on the one hand, and the formation of a large number of dwarf farms and the growth of the class of landless agricultural workers, on the other. Both the agricultural workers and the dwarf peasants depended fully or partially for their livelihood on employment on large estates and medium-size and large peasant farms. Under the circumstances existing in Hungarian politics and agriculture, a greater concentration of landed property was inevitable. According to the census of agriculture of 1895 there were in Hungary 3,768 latifundia (each with more than 580 hectares or 1,000 cadastral yokes of land) with a total area of 6,849,000 hectares. In 1913 there were, however, 4,219 such large estates with a total area of 11,242,000 hectares. Only 128 of the largest latifundia, those with more than 20,000 yokes of land, owned more than one-third of this huge area. In 1895 there were, on the other hand, 1,279,718 dwarf farms (53.57 percent of the total number) not exceeding 2.8 hectares (5 cadastral yokes), owning an area of only 1,240,000 hectares (5.85 percent of the total area), that is, on the average, less than one hectare per household.[41] At the same time there were about 2 million agricultural workers, of whom one fifth owned their homes and about one tenth "a little bit of land." Indeed, as the Director of the Hungarian Statistical Office stated in 1908, "exaggerated extremes mark the conditions of land-ownership in the Hungarian Empire."[42] In the three southernmost *comitates* (regions) of pre-1918 Hungary—Torontál, Bács-Bodrog, and Baranya—in 1913 there were 28.9, 25.3, and 37.3 percent of the total area, respectively, or 644,000 hectares of land, in the hands of the large estate owners (each with more than 580 hectares of land).[43]

From the Austro-Hungarian Compromise until World War I Hungarian agriculture made great strides. Construction of railroads and canals made the opening of the rich agricultural resources of the Pannonian Plain possible and enabled Hungarian agriculture to deliver its products to the Central European markets. But in regard to its main product, grains, like the rest of European agriculture, after about 1870

[41] Aladár Edvi Illés and Albert Halász, *Hungary Before and After the War in Economic-Statistical Maps*, p. 55.

[42] Julius von Vargha, *Die wirtschaftlichen und kulturellen Verhältnisse Ungarns*, p. 40.

[43] Aladár Edvi Illés and Albert Halász, *op. cit.*, p. 55.

it was greatly affected by the competition of grain imports from overseas.

Vojvodina was among the leading agricultural areas in the old Austro-Hungarian Monarchy. In the new Yugoslav state it became the breadbasket of the nation. Its high productivity in relation to other areas of the new state had several bases. Its soil was among the most fertile to be found any place in Europe. Large-scale reclamation work undertaken during the second half of the nineteenth century to ensure the land against ravages of the rivers and to transform the marshes into arable land—a task not yet completely mastered—helped to increase the area of fertile land and to preserve its natural fertility. The bulk of the Vojvodina land, which was in the form of large estates and medium-size peasant farms, was in the hands of people of relatively high cultural level, who were capable of applying modern agricultural technology. Vojvodina agriculture produced before 1918 for a large market protected by tariffs. And finally, in the last few decades before 1918, it had rather well-organized and relatively cheap agricultural credit. Moreover, one of its basic assets from the point of view of the individual landowner was the abundant supply of cheap labor.

The mainstay of Vojvodina agriculture, both in the pre-1918 and the post-1918 eras, was the production of wheat and corn. But it also produced on a large scale such crops as potatoes, sugar beets, hemp, oilseeds, vegetables, and wine. It was also a center of livestock production, especially pigs, cattle, and fowl. Many large estates in pre-1918 days were well-integrated units which produced a whole range of agricultural and livestock products and had their own industrial plants—flour mills, hemp mills, industrial alcohol distilleries—to process the raw materials produced on their land. Some of these estates produced improved seed varieties and livestock breeds. Through their advanced agricultural technology and through their industrial activity, some large estates influenced agricultural production in the whole surrounding area.

Vojvodina brought into the agricultural structure of the new Yugoslav state in 1918 three specific factors: relatively high productivity with large food surpluses over the needs of the area itself, large agricultural estates, and several hundred thousand landless peasants.

One of the fringe areas with a majority of Yugoslav population prior to World War I is not included in this survey because it was not a part of Yugoslavia during the interwar period. This is the territory which prior to 1918 was known as the Austrian Littoral. It consisted of three parts: Istria, Gorizia and Gradisca, and Trieste. The first two areas were largely incorporated into Yugoslavia after World War II, while the problem of Trieste has been solved by leaving the city to Italy. According to the Austrian census of 1910, the total population of the Austrian Littoral was 895,000, of which Istria had 404,000, Gorizia and Gradisca 261,000, and Trieste 230,000 people. Of this total number there were 466,400 Croats and Slovenes, 391,600 Italians, 32,200 Germans, and 4,800 other nationalities. Percentagewise that meant 52.1 percent Croats and Slovenes, 43.7 percent Italians, 3.6 percent Germans, and 0.6 percent other nationalities. The relationship between the Yugoslavs and Italians in the three areas was as follows: Istria, 57.8 percent Yugoslavs and 38.2 percent Italians; Gorizia and Gradisca, 61.9 percent Yugoslavs and 36.0 percent Italians; and Trieste, 31.0 percent Yugoslavs and 62.3 percent Italians.[44] As a rule the Italian population was concentrated in cities and towns while the Yugoslavs were in overwhelming majority in rural areas. Under Italian rule during the interwar period the relationship between the Yugoslav and Italian populations in all these areas was shifted by systematic Italian policy to the disadvantage of the Yugoslavs.

The land-tenure system in Istria and in Gorizia and Gradisca, when the owners did not work their land, was characterized prior to 1918 by the colonate system. It is generally conceded that prior to 1918 the Italians owned a relatively large amount of land in spite of the fact that most of them lived in towns. Moreover, they usually owned land of better quality. While the Yugoslav peasants in Istria, Gorizia and Gradisca looked to the land primarily as a source of subsistence, most of the Italian landowners invested in land as a business proposition. Needless to say, the Italians controlled in all these areas most of the trade, a portion of industry (the other portion was controlled by the Austrian government or Austrian interests), and a large portion of the sources of credit.

[44] Robert A. Kann, *The Multinational Empire*, II, 301–2.

CHAPTER 6

CHANGES IN THE POLITICAL FRAMEWORK

AT THE BEGINNING of the nineteenth century all South Slav peoples with the exception of the inhabitants of a portion of tiny Montenegro and the small Republic of Dubrovnik were under foreign rule. Owing to the advancing forces of nationalism and democracy the long process of decay and disintegration of the Ottoman Empire was speeded up. During the nineteenth century the same forces began to undermine the foundations of the Habsburg Empire. Thus, on the ruins and within the wombs of these two supranational empires, all South Slav peoples moved slowly but inexorably toward their national liberation and unification. This process began—in a territorial sense—with the Serbian First Revolt of 1804, took over one hundred years for its completion, and gave the imprint to most political activities and ideological movements during the century preceding 1918. Needless to say, the political conditions prevailing in the South Slav nations that acquired their independence during the nineteenth century differed greatly from those that prevailed in those areas that remained under foreign rule until 1913 or 1918.

As they were a group of small nations locked for centuries within or between the Ottoman and the Habsburg empires, and located at the crossroads of great civilizations, world religions, and the imperialistic drives of the European Great Powers, their political life developed since the beginning of the nineteenth century partly as a result of the general European political trends and partly as a by-product of bargainings among the Great Powers. Owing to all these reasons the South Slav states before 1918, and Yugoslavia since then, were forced to lean always on one Great Power or another. Domestic political and social forces were always at work, however, and at certain crucial points burst upon the European and even upon the world's stage (1876–78, 1908, 1914, 1941, 1948). Because of their exceedingly unfavorable geopolitical position, and the political and economic odds that the South Slav peoples had to contend with since the beginning of the nineteenth century (as in earlier centuries), their political and economic progress was slow and had to be paid for with a high price in blood and treasure. Nevertheless, these peoples have made considerable advances in all aspects of political, economic, and cultural endeavor during the past one hundred and fifty years.

By far the most important and most persistent political force in the South Slav nations during the past century was nationalism. It animated the nations which were under foreign rule, increased their power to resist, and gave them an objective to aim for; it animated the independent South Slav states of the nineteenth century and Yugoslavia since 1918. It was characteristic of the policies of despotic and dictatorial governments and of governments based on genuine popular following, and of the programs of ultraconservative, bourgeois democratic, peasant democratic, Fascist, and Communist political parties. As long as a nation was subjugated, the primary objective of its nationalism as a political movement was national liberation. When states were formally free but in the position of satellites, nationalism was the most important factor leading them to throw off foreign tutelage, or in exchanging one foreign tutelage for a less obvious and dangerous one.

The problem of nationalism in the South Slav lands is an extremely complicated one. Since much has been written about it,[1] we do not intend to pursue this issue here beyond one general statement, which, however, is of great importance. The problem consists of the following: there are two general types of nationalism in the South Slav lands, the nationalism of the individual nations and a common South Slav or Yugoslav nationalism. The special Croatian, Serbian, and Slovene nationalisms have their roots in the early decades of the nineteenth century, while the Macedonian and Montenegrin nationalisms are of more recent origin. The primary objective of the nationalism of the individual South Slav nations is the defense and promotion of their special aims as individual nations without regard to the interests of the other South Slav nations, and often at their expense. But even in regard to this type of nationalism there are great variations: nationalism of the liberal and democratic political forces and groups was usually constructive, reasonable in its approach to various political, economic, and cultural issues, and mindful of the vital interests of other South Slav nations, while nationalism of the ultranationalist and Fascist groups and

---

[1] See, for example, R. W. Seton-Watson, *The Southern Slav Question and the Habsburg Monarchy*, passim; L. v. Südland [Ivo Pilar], *Die südslawische Frage und der Weltkrieg*, passim; Hermann Wendel, *Der Kampf der Südslawen um Freiheit und Einheit*, pp. 113–228, 509–755; Vladimir Ćorović, *Istorija Jugoslavije* (History of Yugoslavia), pp. 506–13; Robert A. Kann, *The Multinational Empire*, I, 233–59, 284–304; Walter Kolarz, *Myths and Realities in Eastern Europe*, pp. 189–212; Viktor Novak, *Antologija jugoslovenske misli i narodnog jedinstva* (Anthology of the Yugoslav Idea and National Unity).

factions was intransigent, virulent, expansionist, and, in the final analysis, destructive of its own professed purposes.

Yugoslav nationalism, on the other hand, professed to be the synthesis of national aspirations of all South Slav nations taken as a unit, fighting for a common Yugoslav state in which the interests of all South Slav peoples would be served better than if they were to go their own separate ways. Yugoslav nationalism has its roots in the Illyrian movement of the 1830's in Croatia, which originally was a literary and cultural movement maintaining that the various South Slav peoples are basically one people with many different names. In turn, this movement was related to certain writings propounded in the South Slav lands during the eighteenth century, to the general cultural renaissance in Europe which influenced the intelligentsia in the South Slav lands in the early decades of the nineteenth century, to the French rule in the South Slav lands between 1809 and 1813, and to the ideas of closer ties among the Slavic peoples in general. The central concept of the Yugoslav idea and thus of Yugoslav nationalism—that is, that all South Slav nations are bound by a specific community of origin, language, and destiny—attracted from the beginning some of the greatest names in the recent history of the South Slav nations and a large portion of the intelligentsia. Prior to 1918 the Yugoslav idea was the strongest in Croatia-Slavonia, which is easily understandable because Croatia-Slavonia was its cradle and because here there was a large Serbian population, so that the collaboration between the Croats and Serbs, which is the chief political problem of the Yugoslav state, was also a matter of practical politics.

The Yugoslav idea and the existence of a free Serbian state were the two basic factors of domestic origin which were leading toward the liberation of the South Slav nations from foreign rule and their unification in a common Yugoslav state in 1918. The Yugoslav idea reached its greatest popularity in the South Slav areas under Austria-Hungary in the decade prior to World War I and immediately after the Balkan Wars, in which Serbia achieved great successes. Thus it was a strong force during World War I, and the establishment of Yugoslavia in 1918 was the realization of the great dream of Yugoslav nationalism. As will be shown in Chapter 13, however, the Yugoslav idea as a principle of practical politics failed completely during the interwar period. Yugoslav nationalism receded before an upsurge of the particular nationalisms of various South Slav nations, which reached their culmination during World War II. But during that war and since then, the Yugoslav idea and Yugoslav nationalism, now a tool in the hands of the Yugoslav Communists, experienced a rebirth also. How successful the Communists are going to be in using this political idea remains to be seen. The nationalisms of the particular nations are undoubtedly still very strong.

THE RISE OF THE BUREAUCRATIC STATE

The nature of the state changed greatly in the course of the nineteenth century in all South Slav lands, whether it was the re-established national state or the state of a foreign master. A bureaucratic and centralized state arose where in the beginning of that century there was only local autonomy under the blanket of Turkish rule and feudal order as in Serbia, or where there was only a loose tribal association as in Montenegro, or where there reigned a kind of feudal anarchy as in the Turkish-held provinces of Bosnia and Herzegovina and in Macedonia, or, finally, where there already existed a strong system of central government but with the feudal class exercising many functions and prerogatives in regional and local government as in the areas under the Habsburgs. While the political power of the former feudatories was eliminated, the power did not accrue in a democratic way to the people as a whole, but rather to the despotic ruler, the army, the bureaucracy, and the small but growing bourgeoisie. And these political forces acted often in unison. After the 1830's, political parties, in the Western European sense, began to be formed, but it was only after the middle of the century, and in some areas toward the end of the century, that they began to play an important political role. Whether formally disfranchised or not, the peasantry exercised in some areas only limited, and in others no, political influence whatsoever.

The expanding functions and apparatus of the state and the increasing costs for military expenditures resulted in a greatly increased burden of taxation and in a rising public debt. In some areas the obligations of the citizenry toward the state in the form of *corvée* for public purposes continued to represent a great and vexatious burden. In addition, general military service was introduced, which represented a new burden. But the institution of the Military Frontier was abolished, reducing drastically the military obligations of the population of this area.

Whether the state power was in the hands of foreigners—the Austrians, the Magyars, or the Turks—or in the hands of the domestic forces, as in Serbia and Montenegro, the state was used as the chief instrument of oppression and as an important instrument of exploitation of the peasantry. State power was the whip and the state treasury was often milked by those who held the power. This use of the state was especially characteristic of those areas which were under the influence of Ottoman rule, such as Serbia, Bosnia and Herzegovina, and Macedonia. The bureaucracy in the Habsburg Empire was quite efficient when compared with the bureaucracy in the areas under the Ottoman Empire, in pre-1912 Serbia, or in Yugoslavia during the interwar period, but it considered itself the elite outside and above the people rather than as a part of the people and their servant.

This character of the state and its bureaucracy and the fact that the state acted primarily or exclusively in the interest of the ruling groups had a profound influence on the attitude of the peasantry toward the state and toward the city from which emanated the power of the state and in which were concentrated the representatives of the new socioeconomic order: the traders, usurers, bankers, and members of professions. Practically the only contact that the peasantry had with the state was while paying taxes and fines, rendering military service, and rendering *corvée* for various public purposes. The state was not an institution that the peasantry, and that is to say the overwhelming portion of the people, considered their own, but it remained to them a foreign, fearful, and often hated organization. The wrath that the peasantry felt through centuries against the feudal class was now transferred to the state bureaucracy and the representatives of the new socioeconomic order from the city. As will become abundantly clear in the course of this study, there was little cause for the peasants to look at the newly emerging state of the nineteenth century either with confidence or benevolence. And yet, owing to his hard and—in the case of a majority of peasant families—economically hopeless situation, the peasant wanted nothing more than, himself, to become a servant of the state and thus a participant in the spoils of power.

FOREIGN RULE AND THE RETARDED ECONOMIC
AND CULTURAL DEVELOPMENT

As long as the feudal system persisted, it was the chief vehicle of oppression and exploitation of the peasantry, because it held in its hands both political and economic power. The fact that feudal lords were mostly foreign, either by religion, "nationality," or culture, influenced considerably the struggle between them and the peasantry. The struggle against feudalism was at the same time a struggle against foreign rule. In areas in which serfdom was abolished in 1848 and the feudal class superseded in its functions by state bureaucracy, semifeudal concepts in the relationship between the bureaucracy and the peasantry continued to operate. In other areas, such as Bosnia and Herzegovina and in Macedonia, feudalism continued in existence until 1918. While Bosnia and Herzegovina were under Austro-Hungarian rule between 1878 and 1918, the Moslem feudal class maintained its landed interests, but the power in the province was exercised by the Austrian military and civilian authorities. In Macedonia and the Sandjak of Novi Pazar, where Turkish rule continued until 1913, the inefficient and corrupt Turkish administration and the prevailing political turmoil and insecurity held up the development of the South Slav population completely. It is very easy to show, by referring to the high degree of illiteracy, the unfavorable land-tenure system, the backwardness of agricultural technology, the lack of railroads and roads, the absence of industrial and mining development, and the general political instability, that the Ottoman rule was detrimental to the South Slav peoples and was impeding their political, economic, and cultural development. That can be seen especially in the conditions in Macedonia and the Sandjak of Novi Pazar when they were liberated in 1913, but to a large extent also in Bosnia and Herzegovina, although there the Ottoman rule ended in 1878.

It is a different question when the effect of the Austro-Hungarian rule is considered in those South Slav areas which continued to be within the Dual Monarchy until 1918. The idea that the Austro-Hungarian Empire in spite of its many political shortcomings was economically satisfactory, or even ideal, for all nations within its borders is a product primarily of Austrian propaganda. However, many of the enthusiasts of the *Grossraumwirtschaft* in Central European and other countries still share this view. The Dual Monarchy, no doubt, served well the interests of the Austrian and somewhat less well the interests of the Magyar ruling groups, their bureaucracy, industry, and banking, though the shortsighted policies of the ruling groups made the position of the Empire less and less tenable in a time of advancing nationalism and democracy. From the point of view of the South Slavs the Habsburg Empire was politically and economically worse than a bad stepmother.[2] The subject nations within the two halves of the Monarchy could not even hope to achieve political and economic equality—without which they could not freely progress—as long as the Empire was

<hr/>

[2] R. W. Seton-Watson, *op. cit.*, pp. 52–117 and *passim*; Hermann Wendel, *op. cit.*, pp. 385–620; Friedrich F. G. Kleinwaechter, *Der Untergang der österreichisch-ungarischen Monarchie*, pp. 148–66. For the Austrian economic policy toward Hungary and Croatia prior to 1860 see Rudolf Bićanić, *Doba manufakture u Hrvatskoj i Slavoniji (1750–1860)* (The Period of Manufacture in Croatia-Slavonia, 1750–1860), pp. 186–205.

ruled in an undemocratic fashion which was inherent in its tradition and the character of its ruling groups.

But all was not well even between the two halves of the Dual Monarchy. In addition to constant political rivalries, disputes, and bickerings,[3] essentially they conducted two distinct and often, to each other, opposed economic policies, e.g., with regard to industrial development, railroad building and railroad rates, agriculture, merchant marine and ports, banking, and the like. Since after 1850 the Empire formed one customs area, the Magyars resorted after 1867 to direct government subsidization of new industries. As time progressed the political and economic separatist tendencies of the Magyars grew more rather than less pronounced. But while Hungary fought stubbornly against the political and economic encroachments of Austria, it pursued a ruthless and intransigent policy in relation to the subject nations within its own half of the Empire.

Of course, once a relatively high degree of industrial development had been reached in the northern and western parts of the Dual Monarchy, namely, in Austria and Bohemia—and the industrial development in these areas had been systematically favored ever since the reign of Maria Theresa (1740–80)—other sections of the Empire could not easily develop their industries even if a policy of economic discrimination had not been practiced against them. In fact, however, Austria continued to pursue a policy of discrimination against the Hungarian half of the Empire whenever it could, while the Magyars followed a policy of economic discrimination against the subject nations within their own half of the Empire.

In no field of economic endeavor was the Magyar policy of discrimination against the Croatian areas so flagrant as in the field of railroad construction and railroad rates. And the railroads were the key to economic development. The Hungarian policy of railroad construction was directed in a manner serving primarily Hungarian interests. It left some rich South Slav areas unopened and prevented the connection of other Croatian areas with the Dalmatian seaports and with the markets in Austria and Italy. The railroad rate policy was so arranged that it systematically stifled industrial development in Croatia-Slavonia.[4]

    [3] F. F. G. Kleinwaechter, *op. cit.*, pp. 75–99; Oscar Jászi, *The Dissolution of the Habsburg Monarchy*, pp. 344–65; Robert A. Kann, *op. cit.*, II, *passim*.

    [4] For a general discussion of the internal working of the economic policies in Austria-Hungary see Oscar Jászi, *op. cit.*, pp. 185–212; and for a short discussion of the discriminatory policy practiced by Hungary against Croatia-Slavonia through railroad building and railroad rates policy, see R. W. Seton-Watson, *op. cit.*, pp. 329–34.

Practically all industrial and mining enterprises, and a portion of railroads which were privately owned, in the South Slav lands within the Dual Monarchy were owned and managed by Austrians and, to a much lesser degree, by the Magyars. The same applies to banks and insurance companies. Austrian and Hungarian investments in the South Slav areas prior to 1918 were only partly financed by Austrian and Hungarian capital, while the other part was financed by Western European capital loaned to Viennese and Budapest industrial concerns and banks. Furthermore, almost the entire wholesale trade was in the hands of Viennese and Budapest firms.

The subsidized colonization practiced by the Magyars in Slavonia after 1868 was also considered detrimental to the established peasantry because the newcomers were favored in many respects. Moreover, this colonization was a tool of a policy of Magyarization and thus was objectionable to the Croats on political grounds.

The economic relationships between the two halves of the Habsburg Empire after 1867, and among various lands within these two halves, and the techniques and consequences of the economic discrimination involved in these relationships represent a long and involved story. It is not our purpose to pursue this issue in any detail. But as an over-all indication of the differences in the economic well-being in the various sections of the Empire on the eve of World War I, we adduce the per capita national income in the two halves of the Empire and in their various parts which were included in the different succession states after the dissolution of the Dual Monarchy in 1918. The disposable average per capita income (population according to the 1910 census) in the Austrian half of the Monarchy during the period 1911–13 was estimated at 531 crowns, but this income averaged as follows:[5]

Territory included in	Crowns per capita
Austria	695
Czechoslovakia	666
Poland	298
Italy	495
Rumania	343
Yugoslavia	350

In the Hungarian half of the Monarchy the average per capita income (population according to the 1910 census) "immediately preceding

[5] Ernst Waizner, "Das Volkseinkommen Alt-Österreichs und seine Verteilung auf die Nachfolgestaaten," *Metron*, VII, No. 4, 97–183, esp. 180–81.

World War I" was estimated at 321 crowns and averaged as follows:[6]

Territory included in	Crowns per capita
Hungary	350
Czechoslovakia	313
Rumania	275
Yugoslavia	320

The figures for the two halves of the Monarchy were not calculated by the same method and should not be taken as strictly comparable. But they serve well to illustrate the differences between the two halves and among various areas within the two halves of the Monarchy. Undoubtedly the differences in the average per capita income in various areas were partly a reflection of the differences in their wealth of natural resources and their development, and in the technological level of their respective peoples. But to a large extent these differences were a consequence of the discriminatory economic policies conducted by the Austrians against the Hungarian half of the Monarchy and by both the Austrians and the Magyars within their respective halves of the Monarchy against their subject nationalities.

The figures of the average per capita income for the areas included in 1918 in Yugoslavia represent averages for the whole territory, obtained from the respective halves of the Empire rather than figures for various Yugoslav provinces. Had we the figures by provinces, there would be considerable differences among them, partly because of the difference in their endowment with natural resources, partly because not all of them were discriminated against or in the same manner. Thus, within the Austrian half of the Empire the Slovene lands were not discriminated against as much as Dalmatia, and Vojvodina was part of Hungary proper and benefited fully from all Hungarian economic policies.

The inclusion of the South Slav lands within the Dual Monarchy did, however, secure a large market for some important branches of agriculture of these lands, such as wheat and wheat flour, cattle, horses, pigs, and fruit. The tenor of the Austrian and Hungarian economic policies was to keep the South Slav lands as sources of agricultural products and raw materials and as markets for their industrial products. Among these industrial products textiles and various metal products played the most important role. The South Slav lands also offered op-

    [6] Friedrich von Fellner, "Die Verteilung des Volksvermögens und Volkseinkommens der Länder der ungarischen heiligen Krone zwischen dem heutigen Ungarn und den Successions-Staaten," *Metron*, III, No. 2, 226–307, esp. 302–3.

portunities for Austrian and Hungarian capital investments, and for the employment of their entrepreneurial talent, traders, skilled workers, and bureaucrats. Thus, generally speaking, Austria and Hungary conducted toward their respective subject nations a policy of political and economic imperialism and treated them essentially as colonies, which did not serve the interests of the latter nations and constituted the basic reasons for the tendency of all these nations to liberate themselves from Austro-Hungarian rule.

Austria and Hungary did not pursue an imperialistic policy solely against those South Slavs who were within their borders. Austro-Hungarian policies toward Serbia and toward Montenegro (the latter was politically and economically insignificant) were of the same cloth. Ever since its liberation, Serbia leaned diplomatically either on Russia or on Austria-Hungary. After the Berlin Congress in 1878, Serbia became an outright Austro-Hungarian satellite. The trade treaties between the two countries, the railroad conventions, the veterinary convention, as well as the state loans that Serbia obtained in Austria-Hungary, reflected the satellite position of Serbia. Between 1881 and 1893 Serbia obtained from Austria-Hungary 60 percent of all its imports and sold to that country 93 percent of its exports. In the period 1894–1905 these shares were 66 and 83.5 percent, respectively. In addition, most of the remaining Serbian foreign trade was carried on over the railroads and river shipping lines of the Dual Monarchy. As long as Serbia had no industry and the livestock and cereal traders exercised the only important influence on the trade policies, this close economic tie-up with Austria-Hungary served well their interests and the interests of the country. When after 1903 Serbia refused to continue to play the role of an Austro-Hungarian satellite, but rather itself began to follow designs involving vital interests of Austria-Hungary (aspirations to some of the Austro-Hungarian territory and to Macedonia and the Sandjak of Novi Pazar, in which the Dual Monarchy was greatly interested), Serbia was subjected to brutal political and economic pressure.[7] The Serbian policy tending toward economic emancipation from Austria-Hungary stemmed partly from the fact that it began to develop its own industries and needed tariff protection. On the other hand, the Austro-Hungarian opposition against livestock imports from Serbia was primarily due to the efforts of the Hungarian latifundia owners to monopo-

---

[7] A close parallel to the political and economic warfare between Austria-Hungary and Serbia from 1906 to 1910, but much more brutally and thoroughly executed, is the policy of the Soviet Union and its satellites inaugurated against Yugoslavia after the break between Yugoslavia and the Communist bloc in June 1948.

lize the Austrian livestock market. The best-known and most important aspect of this economic warfare between Austria-Hungary and Serbia was the tariff war lasting from 1906 to 1910, and often referred to as the "pig war."[8] During this period only 26.6 percent of Serbian exports went to Austria-Hungary and only 32.7 percent of its imports came from that country. Especially hard hit was the Serbian export of pigs and cattle, the chief export products of the country, which during these years sank to little more than one-third of the volume of previous years. Serbia weathered this foreign trade crisis much better than expected, partly by reorienting its foreign trade over Salonika and Braila (on the Danube estuary) and partly by increasing the export of grains and meat products instead of livestock on the hoof. But sacrifices involved in this trade reorientation were great and the chief sufferer was the Serbian peasant.

Austro-Hungarian rule in the South Slav lands was always characterized by discrimination in cultural and educational matters. Thus the Magyars exercised steady pressure on Croatia in order to promote the Magyar language in schools, public administration, and in railroad administration. Censorship of the press and policing of schools was quite regularly applied. That means that progress in the cultural and educational fields was systematically impeded, causing bitter reactions in the body politic and forcing the political parties and the intelligentsia to spend much of their energy on the defense of national heritage and integrity. Similar conditions existed in the Slovene lands under Austria where the German language and schools were pushed at the expense of the Slovene language and Slovene schools, and in Dalmatia where the Austrians used the small Italian minority as a tool in ruling that province. Also in Bosnia and Herzegovina after 1878 Austria-Hungary paid much more attention to the policing function than to the development of education. One of the principal indicators of educational backwardness in the South Slav areas under Austria-Hungary was the high rate of illiteracy which was found at the beginning of the 1920's (see p. 198). Needless to say, this low educational level affected unfavorably both the political and economic development of the South Slav nations within the Austro-Hungarian Monarchy, which was just the objective of the Austrian and Hungarian ruling groups, because subject nations on a lower level of educational and economic development can be more easily controlled and kept in bondage.

[8] Costa Stoyanovitch, *Economic Problems of Serbia*, pp. 40–47; F. F. G. Kleinwaechter, *op. cit.*, pp. 162–63; Wayne S. Vucinich, *Serbia Between East and West*, pp. 165–209.

CHAPTER 7

THE INCREASE IN POPULATION

THERE IS no doubt that one of the most dynamic factors in the economic life of the South Slav lands during the nineteenth century, as well as since the beginning of this century, was the great increase in population. This coincided with the general population trend in the remainder of Europe, and, in fact, in the whole world during the past 150 years. The nineteenth-century population data for most South Slav lands are quite unsatisfactory and, for some of them, nonexistent. The main reasons for this inadequate information were changes in boundaries, poor administration in census and population-estimates work, deliberate manipulation of figures for political reasons, and lack of comprehensive data on migrations. Nevertheless, the available data give the order of magnitude of the population increase, which is all that is needed for present purposes.

INCREASE IN POPULATION PRIOR TO 1914

Table 1 shows the development of population in various South Slav lands from 1840 to 1910 or 1914, respectively. The rise in population during these 70 years was very uneven both in various periods of time and in various areas. The same conclusion, most probably, would apply also to areas for which data are completely lacking or are not readily available. All data indicate, however, that the increase was proceeding at higher rates after 1880 than in earlier periods, though the increase after 1880 was also very uneven. Population developments in various lands, especially in regard to migrations, were greatly influenced by political factors.

In Serbia population increase between 1817 and 1840 occurred to a large extent through immigration, which was systematically favored by Prince Miloš in order to settle the land depopulated under the Ottoman rule, to have more tax heads and consumers of state monopoly products, to further economic activity in the country, and to have a larger number of soldiers for the needs of national defense. By the decision of the Berlin Congress in 1878 Serbia obtained a territory of 10,300 square kilometers with slightly over 300,000 people. Steadily deteriorating political and social conditions in Turkish-held Macedonia

151

TABLE 1.—POPULATION DEVELOPMENT BY PROVINCES, 1840–1914*

(Thousands)

Province	1840	1850	1860	1870	1880	1890	1900	1910	Mid-1914[a]
Serbia[b]	829	927	1,101	1,302	1,700	2,162	2,493	2,912	3,020
Croatia-Slavonia[c]	1,605	1,636	1,629	1,838	1,892	2,186	2,416	2,622	2,700
Bosnia and Herzegovina[d]	930	1,022	1,210	1,042	1,158	1,336	1,568	1,898	1,990
Dalmatia[e]	399	...	416	457	476	527	594	646	665
Slovenia	...[f]	...	...	...	...	...	...	1,181	1,195
Macedonia	...	...	...	...	...	...	...	...	1,665
Montenegro	...	...	...	...	...	...	...	...	238
Vojvodina	...	...	...	...	...	...	...	1,347	1,385

* Sources: A general survey of the demographic developments in the South Slav lands during the nineteenth century is to be found in Fran Vrbanić, "Demographic Conditions of the South Slavs," Yugoslav Academy of Science and Art, *Rad*, CXXIX (Zagreb, 1896), 172–254. Data for years up to 1910 for Serbia from Djurdje Jelenić, *Nova Srbija i Jugoslavija* (New Serbia and Yugoslavia) (Belgrade, 1923), p. 187; for Croatia-Slavonia, data until and including 1890 from Fran Vrbanić, "One Hundred Years of the Development of Population of Croatia-Slavonia," Yugoslav Academy of Science and Art, *Rad*, CXL (Zagreb, 1899), 17–58; for 1900 and 1910 from Josip Lakatoš, *Narodna statistika* (Nationality Statistics) (Zagreb, 1914), p. 3; for Bosnia and Herzegovina from Djordje Pejanović, "Population of Bosnia and Herzegovina for the Past One Hundred Years, 1840–1940," *Pregled* (Sarajevo, March 1948), pp. 186–94; for Dalmatia from Mladen Lorković, *Narod i zemlja Hrvata* (The People and the Land of the Croats) (Zagreb, 1939), p. 142; data for Slovenia and Vojvodina for 1910 and for Macedonia and Montenegro for 1914 from Jože Rus, *Glavni statistički podaci o državi Srba, Hrvata i Slovenaca* (The Main Statistical Data on the State of the Serbs, Croats, and Slovenes) (Ljubljana, 1920), Tables V, VI, VIII, and XI.

ᵃ Population for mid-1914, with the exception of that for Macedonia and Montenegro, estimated by projecting arithmetically the rates of growth between 1900 and 1910 (for Bosnia and Herzegovina from 1895 to 1910). In the case of Serbia the estimate was adjusted by a deduction of 31,000 for the losses suffered during the two Balkan Wars in 1912 and 1913 (cf. Carnegie Endowment for International Peace, *Enquête dans les Balkans* [Paris, 1914], p. 236), and 29,000 as our estimate for the lower number of births and higher civilian mortality during these two wars. Estimate for Slovenia obtained by projecting the increase in the population of Carniola (see p. 154), and for Vojvodina by projecting the increase in the population of Hungary as a whole for the period 1900 to 1910. Thus the following annual percentage increases have been used: Serbia 1.68, Croatia-Slavonia 0.85, Bosnia and Herzegovina 1.40, Dalmatia 0.87, Slovenia 0.35, and Vojvodina 0.85.

ᵇ Data as of 1862 and 1878, rather than 1860 and 1880.

ᶜ Data as of 1857 and 1869, rather than 1860 and 1870.

ᵈ Data as of 1851, 1865, 1871, 1879, 1885, 1895, rather than 1850, 1860, 1870, 1880, 1890, 1900.

ᵉ Data as of 1857 and 1869, rather than 1860 and 1870.

ᶠ Dots indicate that data are not available for any reason, while dashes (see, for example, Table 3, p. 172) indicate that figures are zero, negligible, or not applicable.

after 1870 caused large emigration from that area. Some writers estimated that between 1876 and 1912 more than 400,000 people immigrated into Serbia from the areas to the south and southwest.[1] Demographically the important point in regard to Serbia was, however, that during the three decades before World War I it showed, unlike the other South Slav lands, practically no emigration overseas but, on the contrary, had a large influx of population.[2]

Partial population data for Croatia-Slavonia are available from the 1750's. The first full census took place in 1785 as a part of the drive of Emperor Joseph II of Austria to reorganize the state and tax administration. The increase in population of Croatia-Slavonia from decade to decade was extremely uneven. One of the reasons for such development was cholera epidemics during the 1830's, in 1857, and again between 1872 and 1874.[3] From 1870 to 1880 the death rate, with the exception of three years, was above 40 and, in one year, above 50 per thousand, which, even with the birth rate of above 40 per thousand, gave during the decade of the 1870's only a slight population increase. From 1881 to 1890 the birth rate was every year, except in 1890, above 40 per thousand while the death rate was slightly above 30, so that the population increased during that decade by 15.5 percent, a rate of growth equaled never before or after.[4] Croatian population movement from 1840 to 1914 was profoundly influenced by migrations. On the one hand, there was the immigration of the German and Hungarian element into the land, migrations intended to serve the political purposes of Austria and Hungary. Owing to this immigration the number of Croats and Serbs in the land fell from 98.4 percent of the total population in 1840 to 87.9 percent in 1890 and 87.1 percent in 1910.[5] On

---

[1] Jovan M. Jovanović, *Južna Srbija od kraja XVIII veka do oslobodjenja* (Southern Serbia from the End of the Eighteenth Century to the Liberation), Volume XVI of the collection *Srpski narod u XIX veku* (The Serbian People in the Nineteenth Century), p. 39. In this title "Southern Serbia" means actually Macedonia and other areas acquired by Serbia after the Balkan Wars of 1912–13.

[2] Detailed studies of the origin of families in the main part of pre-1912 Serbia showed that more than 80 percent of the whole population consisted of descendants of immigrants during the eighteenth and nineteenth centuries. Jovan Cvijić, *Balkansko poluostrvo i južnoslovenske zemlje* (The Balkan Peninsula and the South Slav Lands), p. 227.

[3] Fran Vrbanić, "One Hundred Years of the Development of Population of Croatia-Slavonia," Yugoslav Academy of Science and Art, *Rad*, CXL, 46–47.

[4] Milovan Zoričić, "Population of the Kingdoms of Croatia and Slavonia by Profession and Occupation," Yugoslav Academy of Science and Art, *Rad*, CXXV, 79.

[5] The number of Germans in Croatia-Slavonia rose from 13,226 in 1840 to 117,493 in 1890 and to 134,078 in 1910, and the number of Magyars rose from 5,151 in 1840 to 68,794 in 1890 and to 105,948 in 1910. Moreover, other nationalities, that is to say, other immigrants into Croatia-Slavonia, rose from 6,957 in 1840 to 78,404 in 1890. Politically

the other hand, heavy emigration overseas began after 1880 and was greatly intensified after 1900. The number of emigrants from Croatia-Slavonia between 1899 and 1913 has been estimated at 400,000 to 450,000, while the number of returnees during the same period was only 41,760. The bulk of that emigration was directed to the United States of America.[6]

In Bosnia and Herzegovina population increase after 1880 was primarily due to natural growth, although there were practically continuous, though small, immigrations into the provinces after the Austro-Hungarian occupation in 1878. Some emigration both of the Moslems to the Ottoman Empire and of people of all denominations to overseas countries was also taking place. Emigration from Bosnia and Herzegovina between 1895 and 1910 was estimated at only 50,280 people,[7] which was rather insignificant in comparison with the emigration from Croatia-Slavonia, Dalmatia, and Slovenia. A few rather isolated colonies of Germans and Poles were established in Bosnia during the Austro-Hungarian rule, but they were numerically insignificant in comparison with the German and Magyar colonies in Slavonia and especially Vojvodina.

The increase in the population of Dalmatia was also considerable. Large emigration from this land to overseas countries began somewhat earlier than from Croatia-Slavonia and became very intensive after 1890.

Population data for the territory of Slovenia as a whole are not readily available. But data for Carniola, which represented approximately half of the Slovene population, showed that population of that land increased from 466,000 in 1846 to 481,000 in 1880 and to 526,000 in 1910.[8] In comparison with the growth of population in other

most important and by the Croats greatly resented was the systematic settlement of the Magyars, as this was a tool used by the Hungarian government in its policy of Magyarization. Both the Germans and the Magyars settled usually in compact groups as farmers and in towns as professional people, merchants, and artisans; in both cases they brought with them considerable amounts of capital, and the Germans also brought a higher agricultural technology. Data for 1840 and 1890 from Fran Vrbanić, *op. cit.*, p. 55, and for 1910 from Josip Lakatoš, *Narodna statistika* (Nationality Statistics). pp. 12, 27, 40.

[6] *Ibid.*, p. 65. Exact figures on emigration from various South Slav lands before 1914 will never be available. Many emigrants left to evade military service and thus had no passports. It is also impossible to establish the exact number of emigrants to the United States. Data contained in the *Annual Reports of the Commissioner General of Immigration* of the United States, because of the way of classifying immigrants by race, cannot always supply information on their origin by provinces.

[7] Josip Lakatoš, *op. cit.*, p. 66.

[8] Marijan Dobovšek, "The Movement of Population of Carniola . . . ," *Geografski vestnik*, X, 104–16. The number of Slovenes, that is, people whose mother tongue was

South Slav lands, the increase in Carniola between 1846 and 1880 and again between 1880 and 1910 was insignificant. The main reasons for that development were a relatively low rate of natural growth and heavy emigration.

There was probably a considerable increase in the population of Yugoslav Macedonia between 1840 and 1910, but there is less reliable information on the population movement in Macedonia than in any other Yugoslav area. Some Turkish censuses established only the number of Moslems obliged to bear arms and the number of men of other denominations subject to a special military exemption tax. But because of the partial character and the different territory to which these data pertained, they cannot be used. The unofficial population estimates for Macedonia as a whole before 1913, of which there are quite a number,[9] depended on the political view of the author, and, as a rule, are unreliable. Large-scale emigration from Macedonia after 1870 was a very important factor affecting population growth. It is also known that large numbers of people had left Yugoslav Macedonia immediately before and after Serbian entry into the province in 1913. Actually this emigration continued for a few years after World War I. Owing to this, the Bulgarian census of 1934 showed that 47,416 people living in Bulgaria were born in Yugoslavia, and the Turkish census of 1935 showed that 158,145 people living in Turkey in that year were born in Yugoslavia.[10] Undoubtedly a small portion of the latter figure came from Bosnia and Herzegovina. Considering the deaths in the intervening years, the actual number of these emigrants to Bulgaria and Turkey must have been considerably higher. The population figure for Yugoslav Macedonia for 1914, given in Table 1, is an official estimate made by Serbian authorities after they took over the administration of the province in 1913.

Rather primitive population censuses seem to have been undertaken only twice in pre-1914 Montenegro, in 1896 and in 1914. The 1914 figure is given in the table. But there were many official and private population estimates. As a rule, the latter indicated a lower popula-

Slovenian, living in the Austrian half of the Dual Monarchy rose from 1,054,765 in 1846 to 1,140,304 in 1880 and to 1,253,148 in 1910. Thus, from 1846 to 1910 the number of Slovenes increased by 18.8 percent while the total population of the Austrian half of the Habsburg Monarchy rose by 57.5 percent. In addition to low natural increase and heavy emigration, this discrepancy in growth was caused by denationalization of the Slovenes after their urbanization. See Stanoje Stanojević (ed.), *Narodna enciklopedija srpsko-hrvatsko-slovenačka* (National Encyclopedia of the Serbs, Croats, and Slovenes), IV, 247.

[9] Carnegie Endowment for International Peace, *Enquête dans les Balkans*, pp. 9–10.

[10] Dudley Kirk, *Europe's Population in the Interwar Years*, pp. 282–83.

tion for the country, because the actual figures in official estimates were apparently raised by the government by about 30 percent in order to enhance the standing of the country abroad.[11] There is little doubt, however, that during the past century a considerable increase in the population of Montenegro had taken place. Owing to utter poverty in agricultural and other resources of the country, a large portion of its population had to emigrate in search of bread.

Population figures for Vojvodina before 1910 are not readily available since this territory was an integral part of Hungary and population figures would have to be computed by counties, as was the figure for 1910, given in Table 1. As pointed out earlier, Vojvodina, and southern Hungary in general, represented an area with extremely mixed population. And the growth of various nationalities was under the influence of different factors, to a large extent of a political nature. Systematic colonization of the Magyars in these areas after 1867 and the assimilation of other nationalities by them led to an incomparably higher increase in the number of Magyars than of other nationalities. The population of Banat, of which approximately a third was included in Yugoslavia in 1918, rose from 1,082,550 in 1840 to 1,582,133 in 1910, an increase of 46 percent. The population of Bačka, which was almost completely assigned to Yugoslavia, rose in the same period from 459,623 to 812,385, or 77 percent. During these 70 years the numbers of various leading nationalities in Banat rose as follows, in percent: Germans 86, Yugoslavs (Serbs) 43, Magyars 310, and Rumanians 5 percent. In Bačka the Germans increased during the same period by 110 percent, the Yugoslavs (primarily Serbs) by 21, and the Magyars by 110 percent.[12] But while between 1890 and 1910 the number of Germans in these two areas remained almost unchanged and that of the Yugoslavs, Rumanians, and other nationalities showed only a relatively small increase, the number of Magyars increased in those 20 years by 66 percent in Banat and by 23 percent in Bačka. One of the reasons for the stability of the German minority, in addition to heavy

[11] Lazo M. Kostić, "The Population of Montenegro," in Danilo Vulović (ed.), *Cetinje i Crna Gora* (Cetinje and Montenegro), pp. 278–79.

[12] *Handwörterbuch des Grenz- und Auslanddeutschtums*, I, 214, 295. For both areas the 1840 figures are the estimates of Fényes. In order to increase the relative number of "state-building" Magyars in the state, the Hungarian authorities had been known to manipulate the figures of the censuses. The number of Magyars in the Hungarian half of the Dual Monarchy (without Croatia-Slavonia) rose from 44.4 percent in 1869 to 54.5 percent in 1910. While the Magyar population might have had a somewhat higher rate of natural growth, politics undoubtedly played an important role in this growth of the Magyar population, because the Hungarian authorities conducted a systematic policy of Magyarization of other nationalities within the Hungarian borders.

emigration overseas after 1890, was the practice of birth control on a large scale.

To indicate the increase in population in various provinces for which data are available between 1880 and 1910 in a clearer fashion, Table 2 shows the increase in percent by decades as well as the total

TABLE 2.—INCREASE IN POPULATION BY PROVINCES, 1880 TO 1910*
(In percent by decade)

Province	1880–90	1890–1900	1900–1910	1880–1910
Serbia	27.2[a]	15.3	16.8	71.3[b]
Croatia-Slavonia	15.5	10.5	8.5	38.6
Bosnia and Herzegovina	15.4[c]	17.4[d]	21.0[e]	63.9[f]
Dalmatia	10.7	12.7	8.7	35.7
Slovenia[g]	5.6[h]		3.5	9.4
Vojvodina[i]	17.9[j]	7.0	5.9	33.6[k]

* Source: Table 1, p. 152.
[a] 1878–90.   [b] 1878–1910.   [c] 1879–85.   [d] 1885–95.
[e] 1895–1910.   [f] 1879–1910.   [g] Carniola.   [h] 1880–1900.
[i] Bačka or, in fact, *comitate* (region) Bács-Bodrog.
[j] The real increase was smaller because the 1880 base figure did not include infants up to one year of age and foreign citizens.
[k] See preceding note.

increase from 1880 to 1910. According to the growth of population in that period, all provinces can be divided into three groups: Serbia, and Bosnia and Herzegovina with an extremely rapid growth; Croatia-Slavonia, Dalmatia, and Vojvodina with an intermediate rate of growth; and Slovenia with a very low rate of growth. The important point to remember is that during the interwar period these provinces showed similar differences in the growth of their respective populations.

ECONOMIC CONSEQUENCES OF THE GROWTH OF POPULATION

Economic consequences of this great increase in population in the South Slav lands, especially after 1880, were deep and manifold. Owing to the population growth, the predominantly pastoral economy in the areas south of the Sava-Danube line shifted more and more to crop agriculture, concentrating on the production of grains. A great increase in the cultivation of corn and potatoes in practically all areas of present-day Yugoslavia during the nineteenth century was to a large extent caused by this growth of population. As a consequence of the spread

of crop agriculture, the numbers of livestock in relation to both population and to arable land were greatly reduced in most areas.

With the spreading of crop agriculture, the dwindling of free land,
and changed political conditions, large-scale internal migrations characteristic of the earlier times slowed down in some areas and completely
ceased in others toward the end of the century.

By far the most important consequence of this increase in population in many areas was that the population started to push at, and
go over, the limits of the land resources to support it on the basis of
the existing agricultural technology. Even if a very low per capita
area is taken as a basis for calculation, say one hectare (or roughly
2.5 acres) of arable land in grain-producing areas, manifestations of
agricultural overpopulation begin to appear in many areas. The first
worries about agricultural overpopulation in Croatia-Slavonia to be
expressed by economists in print were recorded in 1894,[13] and in Serbia
after the publication of the agricultural census of 1897, which showed
that over 11 percent of all Serbian rural households were landless. Of
course, a long time before the agricultural overpopulation became a
problem for the economists, it existed in almost all mountainous areas
in South Slav lands where the economy was based on an extensive
animal husbandry, and the population was already making the necessary adjustments. Great migrations from the central mountainous area
during the seventeenth, eighteenth, and early nineteenth centuries were
caused largely by overpopulation. While some internal migration from
that area continued also during the last quarter of the nineteenth century, it was greatly reduced. In addition to switching to crop agriculture more and more, the peasants were acquiring new land by clearing
forests, by making former summer shepherds' villages in the mountains
(*katuni, stanovi*) at an elevation of between 3,500 and 5,000 feet into
permanent villages, and by putting a portion of the meadows and pastures under the plow.

After 1880 the emigration overseas became a very important
safety vent for the growing population pressure. Heavy emigration
overseas took place especially from Dalmatia, Croatia-Slavonia, and
Slovenia, but was heavy also from Herzegovina, Montenegro, Macedonia, and Vojvodina. From Vojvodina and Slavonia emigration was
more a result of the presence in these areas of large numbers of landless

[13] Milovan Zoričić, *Statistika ratarske produkcije god.1888–1892 u kraljevinah
Hrvatskoj i Slavoniji* (Statistics of Agricultural Production 1888–1892 in the Kingdoms
of Croatia and Slavonia), p. x; see also the earlier quoted work by the same author,
p. 91.

rural families than because of an unsatisfactory average land-population ratio. From some areas, such as some sections of Macedonia, large-scale seasonal emigration (*pečalba*) of a large portion of all able-bodied men used to take place year in and year out. Seasonal migrations of agricultural workers from northern parts of Croatia and Medjumurje and from Slovenia, and in years immediately preceding World War I also from the eastern counties of Serbia, were also important. And finally, a part of the agricultural population had found employment in industry, mining, forestry, government service, and in other services in urban areas.

Some other developments in the agriculture of the South Slav lands during the decades preceding World War I were fundamentally affected by the large increase in population, such as progressive subdivision of agricultural property, increasing hunger for land on the part of the peasants, and consequently a great rise in prices of agricultural real estate, and impeding of agricultural progress because of the rising number of consumers in agriculture in relation to producers. But these problems will be dealt with later.

CHAPTER 8

CHANGES IN THE ECONOMIC AND
SOCIAL STRUCTURE

ALL South Slav lands underwent, during the nineteenth century, deep changes in their economic and social structure. Bonds of serfdom which had shackled the peasantry for centuries were broken in all lands except in Bosnia and Herzegovina and Macedonia. The peasants became full owners of their land and were granted political freedom. A centuries-old fundamental wish of the peasantry, the acquisition of full owner-ship of the land which they tilled, had been achieved, although it is well known that this fact did not usher the peasants into the millenium of freedom, progress, or plenty. After the traditional enemy of the peasant, the feudal lord, had departed from the political and economic stage, new forces inimical to the peasant's interests took his place: the state bureaucracy, the trader, and the usurer. The state exploited the peasants through the tax system and the *corvée* for public works. Ex-ploitation of the peasants through other classes proceeded, however, through the operation of the market mechanism. Needless to say, the bulk of the state legislation, including the tax system, was enacted pri-marily to serve the interests of the ruling classes. The increase in popu-lation and production for the market led to an increase in the production of crops, primarily grains, and to a reduction in the pastoral economy. The development of communications and the penetration of the money economy in the South Slav lands greatly stimulated the spread of the market economy. The urban sector of the economy grew steadily and so did the internal economic integration and economic contacts with the European and world economy. The traditional peasant way of life was changed in many respects, and economic differentiation in rural areas advanced under the influence of new economic and psychological forces affecting the peasant population.

INCREASE IN CROP PRODUCTION—DECREASE IN PASTORAL ECONOMY

During most of the past century the economic life in the areas south of the Sava-Danube rivers, and to some extent in the lands north of this line, was primarily based on extensive animal husbandry—the raising of cattle, horses, sheep and goats, and pigs. In many areas this animal husbandry was based on seasonal transhumance. This pastoral type of economy was possible because of the sparse population. It was favored also by other factors. Obligations to landlords from animal raising were lower than from field crops. Livestock was easily movable and could be hidden, a factor of great importance in those times of limited personal and property security. Lack of arable land in many areas and relative abundance of pastures in the mountains made animal husbandry the natural economic activity. Finally, this type of economic life was the result of a centuries-old tradition and of a process of adjustment of the peoples of these lands to the insecurities afflicting crop farming in the plains due to wars, Turkish terror, and widespread brigandage.

Large increase in population in practically all South Slav lands, especially after 1880, necessitated an expansion of the area under field crops such as grains, potatoes, legumes, vegetables, as well as under vineyards and orchards. This reduced in all provinces the area kept as permanent meadows and pastures. It also reduced the area under forests, as much of the new land had to be obtained by the clearing of forests.[1] The expansion of the area under field crops, especially under wheat and corn, was not only the consequence of an increase in population, but also an expression of increased production for the market. As in many other areas of the world, grains were and remained the most important product of fully or partially commercialized agriculture. In the present Yugoslav territory, that was especially the case in Vojvodina, Slavonia, and Srijem. Vojvodina was opened and became the leading agricultural area of the Habsburg Monarchy by the building of railroads and canals, which enabled it to put its products on the large markets of the Monarchy in Austria and Bohemia. Large stretches of land were obtained by land reclamation. Animal husbandry in north-

---

[1] The expansion of arable land and the continuation of extensive animal husbandry in areas south of the Sava-Danube rivers, but to a certain extent also in areas north of these rivers, led to widespread abuses of land and forest resources. In many areas this came on top of centuries-old abusive practices in which forests were cut down for construction purposes, to provide raw materials for woodworking handicrafts and charcoal burning and, in areas such as Macedonia, also for security purposes. One of the factors contributing to the abusive use of forests and pastures was that much of the forest and pasture lands was held as a common, and the attitude of the South Slav peasantry toward the common has always been and still probably is that "it belongs to everybody and therefore to nobody." In the common everybody was reaping and nobody sowing. Thus the depletion of forest lands and of common pastures advanced to a dangerous degree. Large-scale industrial exploitation of forests, beginning in the second half of the nineteenth century and carried on almost exclusively by foreign capital with modern technology, was also conducted, to a very large extent, on the principles of "plunder economy."

ern areas, unlike that in areas south of the Sava-Danube rivers, shifted largely to fairly intensive forms. This was brought about by two factors. On the one hand, the enlargement of the crop area and its improvements were possible only with sufficient numbers of draft animals capable of doing efficient work and by an increase in the production of manure. On the other hand, animal husbandry developed into an important cash branch of agricultural production, both on large estates and on smaller farms.

Owing to the growth of population, which required the production of more food per unit of land, and owing to the increase in the production of crops for the market, the number of livestock in relation to population and in most areas also in relation to cultivated land began to fall. The trend of diminishing livestock numbers was one of the outstanding features of the economy of most of the South Slav lands during the past hundred years. The territory of the former Military Frontier in Croatia-Slavonia is the only one in which that process can be followed satisfactorily during the nineteenth century, while for most other areas it can be traced only since about 1880. In the territory of the former Military Frontier the population increased from 1801 to 1890 by 78.25 percent, while the numbers of livestock increased from 1801 to 1895 as follows (in percent): cattle by 64.87; horses by 125.47; sheep by 20.08; and pigs by 20.09. If all livestock is expressed in terms of cattle (one head of cattle equals two-thirds of one horse, ten sheep, ten goats, or four pigs), then the increase in livestock in that period of 95 years amounted to only 58.8 percent. In 1801 there were in the Military Frontier 789 head of cattle (all livestock in terms of cattle) per thousand inhabitants, while in 1895 on the same territory there were only 703 head of cattle per thousand inhabitants. But the number of livestock per unit of cultivated land increased somewhat in that territory during the period under consideration.[2] In this particular area, as elsewhere in areas north of the Sava-Danube rivers, considerable improvement in livestock breeds took place, and animal husbandry became quite intensive. Thus the reduction in numbers, especially of cattle, did not mean a comparable reduction in productivity of livestock.

In areas south of the Sava-Danube rivers animal husbandry remained extensive and there was very little or no change in animal breeds. If the same coefficient for the conversion of various types of

[2] Fran Vrbanić, "Studies in the Economic Development of the Croato-Slavonian Military Frontier During the Nineteenth Century," Yugoslav Academy of Science and Art, *Rad*, CXLIV, 115–21.

livestock to cattle is used for Serbia as was used for the Military Frontier, the number of livestock per thousand inhabitants fell from 1,498 head in 1859 to only 695 in 1895.[3] In Bosnia and Herzegovina the number of livestock in terms of cattle per thousand inhabitants fell from 1,540 in 1895, when the first reliable livestock census was taken, to 1,140 in 1910.[4] The downward trend in livestock numbers both in relation to population and to cultivated land continued until the end of the interwar period and was related to several factors. Therefore, it will be discussed later in more detail.

The increase in hectarage under cultivation during the nineteenth century in the territory of the Military Frontier is indicated by the increase in per capita production of all grains, though a part of that increase has to be ascribed to the increase in yield and the changed composition of grain production. The average per capita production of grains rose from 3.6 hectoliters (one hectoliter of wheat equals roughly 60 kilograms) between 1806 and 1818 to 5.2 hectoliters between 1888 and 1895. However, the composition of grain production changed greatly. Wheat production rose during that period from an average of 0.32 to 0.96 hectoliters per capita; that of corn from 1.06 to 2.09 hectoliters per capita. The average per capita production of barley, spelt, rye, sorghum, and oats either rose little or fell. The production of potatoes rose in the same period from an average of 26 to 121 kilograms per capita.[5] There was also a considerable increase in the production of industrial crops and in the production of feed for livestock. For Serbia, only the more recent data are available. The area under wheat rose from 162,766 hectares in 1889 to 385,584 in 1910 and that under corn from 268,423 hectares in 1889 to 585,226 in 1910.[6]

One of the basic changes in crop production of practically all South Slav lands which took place during the nineteenth century was the spread of the cultivation of corn. This trend was especially strong after the middle of the century. In certain mountainous areas in the central parts of Yugoslavia corn was first introduced as a garden vegetable. Large-scale corn growing in these areas began after 1880, after the

[3] Based on figures in Costa Stoyanovitch, *Economic Problems of Serbia*, p. 48.

[4] Milan Janković and Josip Džuverović, "Animal Husbandry and Livestock Production in Bosnia and Herzegovina," A. Koen *et al.* (eds.), *Bosna i Hercegovina kao privredno područje* (Bosnia and Herzegovina as an Economic Area), p. 53. See also Dragan Ilančić, *Brojčani razvitak stočarstva u hrvatskim zemljama* (The Numerical Development of Livestock Herds in Croatian Lands), pp. 6–38.

[5] Fran Vrbanić, *op. cit.*, p. 98.

[6] Milan J. Komadinić, *Skice i ogledi za jednu istoriju zadrugarstva u Srbiji* (Sketches and Examples for a History of Co-operativism in Serbia), p. 21.

peasants became assured that it could fully ripen in the higher altitudes. It took land from other grains as well as land obtained by new clearance. For several decades now corn has been the most important and the most widespread field crop in the present Yugoslav territory. It is planted in most areas on the best soil, and in the high areas it is occasionally irrigated.[7]

In the field of agriculture much more attention began to be paid to various industrial crops, especially in the Pannonian Plain where, in connection with large estates, agricultural industries were developed. In all areas potatoes also began to be cultivated more, and they served party as a substitute for cereals. But the enlarged area of arable land was used primarily for the growing of grains to provide food for the additional and steadily growing population, in some areas for livestock feed, and finally for the market, including foreign markets.

The changed structure of agricultural production during the nineteenth century resulted, naturally, in great changes in the nutrition patterns of the peasantry. Understandably, statistical data on that change are lacking. But in countries with a predominantly peasant subsistence economy, dietary patterns are simply a reflection of the agricultural production structure. Thus a switch from a predominantly pastoral to a predominantly crop agriculture resulted in a decrease of animal products—meat, milk, cheese, and animal fats—in the regular diet and an increase in the intake of vegetable items, primarily cereals. In fact, under the impact of the increase in population, the relative drop in livestock numbers, and generally low productivity in agriculture, the diet of the peasantry evolved into an almost completely vegetable, cereal diet. A great change also took place in the composition of this vegetable part of the diet. The relative share of such grains as barley, rye, spelt, sorghum, oats, and buckwheat in the total grains production, and thus in their consumption, was greatly reduced. On the other hand, the production and consumption of wheat and corn were greatly increased. Corn in various forms, as bread and cornmeal mush, became in fact a standard component of the peasant diet in most South Slav lands. A large increase in the production of potatoes and legumes took place and these products became important components of the diet. It appears also that the production of leafy vegetables was increased, various types of cabbage taking the most important part. The cultivation of turnips, onions, tomatoes, bell peppers, and various types of pumpkins also spread and greatly increased.

[7] Milisav V. Lutovac, "Geographic Spreading of Corn Cultivation in Yugoslavia," *Glasnik Geografskog društva*, XXII, 59–67, esp. 60–63.

PENETRATION OF MARKET AND MONEY ECONOMY

By far the most important structural change in the economy of the South Slav lands during the nineteenth century was the penetration of money and credit and of capitalist principles into the existing traditional social and economic system. This factor changed the whole institutional framework and the whole psychological basis of the existing system and engendered within the economy of these areas forces that proved extremely dynamic until the end of the interwar period. The penetration of a money and credit economy meant first that all goods and services in the economy obtained a price expressed in money and that, at a price, they began to be bought and sold. In the existing subsistence economy, production was carried on by families for the satisfaction of their immediate needs, for payment of taxes, and rendering of obligations toward the feudal lord. This type of economic organization also used money, as some taxes and some obligations to the feudal lords were paid in money and there also existed a market. But the significance of money and market economy was only of minor importance. Naturally a money and market economy prevailed in cities and towns, but its role in the economic life was at that time much smaller than in later decades. With the development of a market economy, production and other economic activities begin to be undertaken more and more for the market in order to achieve a profit. It should not be forgotten, however, that in peasant economies of a predominantly subsistence character the selling of a part of the peasant's production does not regularly take place to achieve a profit but rather to secure a certain money income in order to be able to meet the family requirements for money, i.e., for the payment of taxes, interest, and debts, and the buying of certain essentials such as salt, some textiles, and the like.

Before the development of a market economy and the penetration of money and credit into the South Slav lands on a large scale, land and livestock were almost the only means of wealth accumulation, and, owing to various factors, they were quite limited. With the appearance of money in everyday life it becomes the general denominator of economic values and thus the general means of wealth accumulation. This was the more so as the development of trade and credit enabled the owner of money to use it in trade, in financing various production branches, and above all for granting of loans at usurious rates of interest. It was only in the last third of the century that investment in industrial activities became more widespread, though the bulk of industrial enterprises was established, financed, and managed by foreigners.

Whether the money was used for granting loans or in trade and industry, it proved to be the most powerful means of further accumulation of wealth. Thereby money helped to stimulate differentiation among economic units both in the villages and in towns, and to increase the antagonism between the village and the city.

The appearance of money in the village as an agent of everyday life had a profound influence on the psychological, economic, and social life of the peasant family and of the village as a whole. Money became the measure of all things economic also for the peasant and a factor which enabled its owner to acquire goods and services as he pleased. There is no doubt that the market economy, made possible by the appearance of money, did have a considerable influence on the structure of agricultural production of the peasant, but this influence was much stronger in areas with better-developed communications and near the markets—as in the Pannonian Plain where a large portion of agriculture became commercialized—than in more isolated areas. Furthermore, it affected the peasants differently, according to the sizes of their farms.

With the appearance of manufactured products in the market place within easy reach of the peasants, particularly of textiles, footwear, jewelry, house utensils, as well as coffee and sugar, and with the development of transportation conveyances facilitating the movement of peasants, the whole structure of the peasants' wants was radically modified. In order to satisfy more of these new wants, the peasant was forced to market a relatively larger portion of his production or to seek additional employment. The increased tax burden acted in a similar fashion. New wants and increased taxes began to compete with old needs for his income. The peasant often lacked proper discrimination in satisfying his wants. Because of low productivity in peasant farming and limited possibilities for earning elsewhere, the wants of the peasant far outstripped his economic ability to satisfy them. He began to borrow. The prevailing usurious interest rates easily led to overindebtedness. Thus, since about the 1830's the problem of overindebtedness in agriculture persisted as one of the basic economic and political problems in Serbia and to a lesser extent in other areas. Changing demand on the market for his products, and thus changing prices, regularly worked against his interests. Thus, both economically and psychologically, he became unhinged from the old economic order, but lacked both means and knowledge to make a success in new conditions. A fact which especially affected the peasant unfavorably was that when selling, buying, and borrowing he was often dealing with one and the same person, the local trader and usurer, who was economically much stronger than the peasant and who used his greater economic, and often political, power to the utmost. Many peasants, especially in Serbia, driven by the desire to earn money, often started to trade and speculate, and in that way many met their economic doom. Because of the growing population, hunger for land became greater from year to year and the price of land rose. To acquire additional land, borrowing was often necessary, and, because this was done at usurious interest rates, newly acquired land often could not be retained. There were many other ways in which money had untoward effects on the peasant, but two features should be specifically mentioned. The spreading of the tavern and the coffeehouse to the village, serving there the function of a social club and political meeting place, kept many a peasant from home and also absorbed an undue share of his income. Second, the innumerable occasions of feasting, which in the subsistence economy were limited by availability of food and drink in the household, became now more elaborate and altogether too expensive. In spite of its irrationality, this type of conspicuous consumption is characteristic even of the poorest peasant in practically all South Slav areas.

THE DEVELOPMENT OF COMMUNICATIONS

The penetration of money and credit and generally of capitalist forces into the economy of the South Slav lands, which began to be especially strong after 1850, was an exceedingly complex and all-pervasive process. It began earliest and was strongest in areas under the Habsburg Monarchy, later and less strong in Serbia, and still later and less pronounced in Bosnia and Herzegovina, Macedonia, and Montenegro. Neither systematic nor comprehensive data for a statistical study of this process are available, but we do have certain indicators which reflect the process. One of the most powerful agents of capitalist development in the South Slav lands was the construction of railroads. The railroad was an essential stimulant of the money economy, first during the construction stage, as it raised the money income of the population through buying of construction materials (other than industrial) and payment or spending of wages.[8] But as a permanent effect it stimulated the selling of products of areas which were thus opened, and made possible the bringing of larger quantities of industrial goods into such areas. Both of these factors had a stimulating effect on the

---

[8] A large portion of labor in railroad building was foreign workers. Thus in Serbia in the 1880's approximately 5,000 Italians were working in railroad construction. Émile de Laveleye, *The Balkan Peninsula*, p. 219.

quantity and variety of production. One of the important consequences
was that the competition of manufactured goods greatly reduced the
relative extent of handicrafts which formerly flourished in these areas,
both on a commercial basis and in many peasant households.

The building of railroads in the present Yugoslav territory progressed in several well-defined periods and advanced from the northwest
and the north toward the south and the southeast. During the first
period, from 1846 to 1868, and the second period, from 1869 to 1878,
the interiors of Austria and Hungary were connected with the Adriatic
ports of Trieste and Rijeka (Fiume). These trunk lines crossed the
territories of Slovenia and Croatia-Slavonia and connected them both
with the two ports and with the central and northern parts of the Dual
Monarchy. The previously great economic role of these cities for the
northwestern and northern South Slav areas was thereby greatly increased, and these cities had a profound effect on the stimulating of
capitalist development in Slovenia, Croatia-Slavonia, and Vojvodina.
The most important period in railroad construction was, however, that
between 1879 and 1891, when the other trunk lines were completed.
These railroads have remained the basis of the railroad network in the
South Slav countries up to the present. In this period were completed
the connections of Western and Central Europe through Serbia with
Istanbul and Salonika. Moreover, the Bosnian line connecting the Sava
River (Brod) with the Adriatic Sea was built in this period. From 1892
to 1914 a considerable number of small and side lines were built. The
basic characteristics of railroad construction on the territory of the
South Slav lands was that, except for the main lines from Belgrade to
Istanbul and Salonika and the Bosnian line, most of the lines were
north of the Sava-Danube rivers.[9] This was largely a result of political
conditions prevailing before 1918. In addition to stimulating commercial traffic in all areas reached by the railroads, their construction was
the prerequisite of an intensified exploitation of natural resources, such
as forests and mineral deposits, and generally of all industrial development.

Another communication factor which greatly stimulated capitalist
forces in industry, trade, and, especially, in agriculture in the Pannonian Plain was the regulation of great rivers (Danube, Tisa, Sava),
the building of canals, and the development of river shipping.

Construction of roads also contributed greatly to the economic
opening of the South Slav lands, to the spreading of the market and

[9] Anton Melik, "The Development of Railroads in the Territory of Yugoslavia,"
Geografski vestnik, XIV, 118–34.

money economy, and to a closer integration of the economy of various regions. Between 1874 and 1882 in Croatia-Slavonia 3,310 kilometers of roads were built and in the following 20 years another 1,400 kilometers. In Serbia intensive road building began in the 1860's. In Bosnia and Herzegovina, only after 1860 did more attention begin to be paid by the Turkish authorities to the construction of roads, but it was after 1878 under the Austro-Hungarian rule that a great road-building program was inaugurated. In 1878 there were only 900 kilometers of roads usable for transportation on wheels. By the end of 1890, 3,570 kilometers of roads were built, much of which was exclusively for military purposes. It is interesting to note, however, that roads were built in Serbia, Bosnia and Herzegovina, Montenegro, and many other areas of the present Yugoslav territory almost exclusively by forced labor (*corvée* for public purposes), for which all citizens were liable and for which the workers had to supply their own draft animals, tools, and even food and feed. Naturally, it was the great mass of the peasantry that suffered most from this vexatious obligation.

Inauguration of regular mail services and building of telegraph and telephone facilities were also a boon to both economic and cultural development.

THE RISE OF GOVERNMENT REVENUE AND EXPENDITURES

A basic indicator of the penetration of money and credit in the economic life of the South Slav lands and of their general political and socioeconomic development was the growth of government revenue and expenditures. In Serbia all taxes paid by the peasants were assessed and payable in money after 1835. In areas under the Habsburg rule such practice was introduced considerably earlier. Moreover, because of the much increased needs of the state to finance the ever-expanding range of public functions and the greatly enlarged military expenditures, the total tax load was greatly increased. In Croatia-Slavonia, Slovenia, and Vojvodina, where serfdom was abolished in 1848, the former serfs were obliged to pay the indemnity for the land which they obtained over a period of 20 years, and these payments had to be met, together with taxes. In order to meet increased tax payments, agricultural producers were forced to raise and sell more of their produce, and that forced them into closer contact with the market.

On the other hand, greater state expenditures increased the amount of money in circulation, especially in the urban sector of the economy. Government expenditures of Serbia rose from 4.9 million groshes in 1834 to 8.5 million in 1840, 19.1 million in 1860, and 28.8 million in 1868, when a currency reform took place and the dinar currency was introduced. From 1869 a great rise in government expenditures both in Serbia and in Croatia-Slavonia was recorded. In the latter, only expenditures for the financing of its autonomous affairs (police, justice, religious affairs, public instruction, and later also economic affairs) are available. The government expenditures rose as follows:[10]

Year	Serbia (*Million dinars*)	Croatia-Slavonia (*Million crowns*)
1869	12.5	4.4
1880	19.3	6.6
1890	46.2	13.0
1900	76.3	18.6
1911	120.1	28.1

Another indication of the penetration of the money and credit economy was the increase in the consolidated government debt. In Serbia it rose from 2.3 million dinars in 1867 to 16.5 million in 1880, 414.0 million in 1895, and 903.8 million in 1914. The rise in public expenditures and, especially, in the public debt in Serbia after 1880 was largely connected with the rise in military expenditures, which proved detrimental to the health of government finances.[11]

The growth in the paid-up share capital of the Serbian banks (except the bank of issue) is also an indication of the advance of capitalism in the Serbian economy. It rose from 3.25 million dinars in 1884, the year when the Serbian bank of issue began to operate, to 7.6 million in 1889, to 15.1 million in 1895, and to 45.2 million dinars in 1911.[12] In South Slav areas under the Habsburg rule most commercial banks were branches of Vienna and Budapest banks, and data on the development of the paid-up share capital would not have the same significance as those for Serbia.

THE GROWTH OF INDUSTRY

The process of industrial growth in the South Slav lands from the beginning or even from the middle of the nineteenth century until

[10] Stanoje Stanojević (ed.), *Narodna enciklopedija srpsko-hrvatsko-slovenačka* (National Encyclopedia of the Serbs, Croats, and Slovenes), I, 302–3.

[11] *Ibid.*, p. 673.

[12] Stanislav Kukla, *Razvitak kreditne organizacije u Srbiji* (The Development of the Credit Organization in Serbia), p. 22. The primitive character of the Serbian monetary and credit organization during much of the nineteenth century can be well seen from the fact that before 1868 only foreign coins circulated in that country. In that year the first Serbian copper coins began to be minted, and in 1873 the first full-bodied silver money was coined. Of course, we speak here of modern Serbia and not of medieval Serbia, whose rulers coined various types of silver coins.

World War I cannot be traced on the basis of statistical data on the number and capacity of industrial enterprises, on the number of workers employed, or on the volume or value of industrial production. Such data are not available.[13] Only a few remarks can therefore be made here and illustrated by certain figures obtained mostly on the basis of backward extrapolation. First, industrial growth started earliest and advanced most in the Slovene lands, followed by Vojvodina, and then Croatia-Slavonia. In areas south of the Sava-Danube rivers it set in later and was much more limited. This statement is supported by two sets of figures. First, in desperation at the inability to trace the industrial development of the South Slav lands because of lack of data, the Yugoslav Ministry of Trade and Industry took existing factories[14] in 1938 and classified them according to the decade of their establishment, thus "reconstructing approximately" the course of industrial development. However crude this procedure was, it shows approximately the timing of industrial growth and the order of magnitude of this growth by areas and by decades, as reflected in the number of factories which were established in the respective decades and which succeeded in surviving until 1938. But how many factories were actually established at various times, what their contribution was to industrial production, and how many did not survive—these statistics do not show. Of 4,257 factories existing in 1938, some 1,831 were established before 1918, and 2,193 were established between 1919 and 1938; the year of establishment could not be ascertained for 233 factories. The 1,831 factories established before 1918, according to the decade of their establishment, were distributed by provinces, as indicated in Table 3.

This table does not include mining enterprises. Mining before 1918 was best developed in Slovenia, but it was considerable also in Serbia, Croatia-Slavonia, Bosnia and Herzegovina, and Dalmatia. In Vojvodina and Montenegro it was nonexistent and in Macedonia it was mostly developed after 1918. Industrial development, as indicated in Table 3, was obviously much greater from the beginning of this century than in the preceding decades. In the case of Bosnia and Herzegovina the effect of Austro-Hungarian occupation in 1878 is clearly visible. The economically depressing effect of Turkish rule is especially visible in Macedonia, as the Turks remained here until 1913.

---

[13] Yugoslavia, Ministry of Trade and Industry, *Statistika industrije Kraljevine Jugoslavije* (Industrial Statistics of the Kingdom of Yugoslavia), p. 8.

[14] The Ministry defined a factory in no fewer than 18 different ways. As a rule, the number of workers employed when at full capacity, mostly 15, and/or horsepower of machines installed, occasionally as low as 5 hp, were used to define a factory. *Ibid.*, p. 25.

TABLE 3.—NUMBER OF FACTORIES ESTABLISHED BY DECADES, 1859–1918,
AND STILL EXISTING IN 1938, BY PROVINCES*

Province	Before 1858	1859 to 1868	1869 to 1878	1879 to 1888	1889 to 1898	1899 to 1908	1909 to 1918	Total
Slovenia	59	20	52	64	48	124	86	453
Croatia-Slavonia	30	18	20	55	58	141	156	478
Vojvodina	22	14	25	51	57	108	129	406
Dalmatia	—	3	5	3	9	29	21	70
Bosnia and Herzegovina	1	—	6	25	51	19	43	145
Serbia	6	5	8	24	37	92	77	249
Macedonia	—	—	—	3	6	8	5	22
Montenegro	—	—	—	—	—	3	5	8
Total	118	60	116	225	266	524	522	1,831

* Source: Yugoslavia, Ministry of Trade and Industry, *Statistika industrije Kraljevine Jugoslavije* (Industrial Statistics of the Kingdom of Yugoslavia) (Belgrade, 1941), p. 73.

The second indicator of the varied industrial development of the lands included in 1918 in the new state of Yugoslavia is supplied by the Yugoslav census of 1931. According to that census (see Table 20, p. 304), of the total population of 13,934,038 at the end of March 1931, only 1,533,052 people made their living from industry, mining, and handicrafts. This figure includes people gainfully employed in those economic activities and persons supported by them. This census was based on the 1929 administrative division of the country into *banovine*, which in some cases allows an approximation to the historical provinces, but in others makes such an attempt useless without a tedious readjustment of the figures by counties (see footnote 7, p. 238).

While from 1919 to 1931 the advance of industry and mining and the development of handicrafts proceeded at various rates in different parts of the country, being relatively the strongest in Macedonia and in Serbia,[15] the occupational structure in 1931, as shown in Table 20, still largely reflected the respective positions reached by 1918 in various provinces.

Three additional points should be made with regard to the pre-1918 development of industry and mining in the South Slav lands. First, the pattern of industrial development reflected the raw materials available and the fact that these lands were discriminated against, owing to their political and/or economic inclusion in the orbit of Austria-Hungary. Of the 1,831 factories included in Table 3, more than one-

[15] *Ibid.*, p. 73.

third were in food and agricultural raw materials processing branches and almost one-sixth in the lumber industry. If power plants in cities and towns were left out of account, these ratios would be even greater. But in such production lines as textiles, leather and shoes, metals, and chemicals, the number of factories was relatively small. Most of the factories, with the exception of some units in the food processing and lumber industries, were small and many of them specialized in products suited to the needs of the home market, which were not readily covered by imports, e.g., rough textiles. The bulk of industrial products was imported from the northwestern portions of the Austro-Hungarian Empire.

Second, industry and mining which developed in the South Slav lands prior to 1914 were mostly established by foreign capital and foreign entrepreneurial talent, namely, capital and industrial managers from Austria and, to a lesser extent, from Hungary. Most of the skilled workers were also foreign. Vienna and Budapest served also as intermediaries for the investment of Western European capital in the South Slav lands. A large portion of the industrial and mining development in Yugoslavia during the interwar period was also financed by foreign capital. The hold of foreign capital on Yugoslav industry, mining, trade, and banking remained exceedingly strong until the end of World War II.[16] The greater portion of domestic capital was used for ventures in trading and in usury, and after 1918 in urban real estate, rather than in industry. Moreover, the bulk of industrial and mining enterprises established by foreign investors, being primarily in the field of extractive industries, produced for export and not for the domestic market. Added to foreign rule, these factors gave the economies of the South Slav lands prior to 1918 a colonial or semicolonial character. This remained so to a great extent also during the interwar period.

Third, industry's share in the national income of Yugoslavia in the early 1920's was still low and testified to the low over-all development of industrial activity. The national income of Yugoslavia during the period 1923–25 was estimated on the average at 69,608 million dinars annually, of which 31,663 million dinars were derived from agriculture, animal husbandry, and fisheries. The value of manufacturing production was estimated at only 5,823 million dinars, to which, however, the value of forestry production of 3,936 million and the value of mining production of 900 million dinars should be added. On the other

[16] On the role of foreign investments in the Yugoslav economy during the interwar period, see Jozo Tomasevich, "Foreign Economic Relations [of Yugoslavia], 1918–1941," in Robert J. Kerner (ed.), *Yugoslavia*, pp. 185–97.

hand, the value of handicraft production was estimated at 7,760 million and that of the cottage industry at 4,837 million dinars.[17] All these figures should, however, be taken only as indications of the order of magnitude of the value of production in these various branches of economic activity. Nevertheless, they show how strong were the handicrafts and the cottage industry, whose products industry was intended largely to replace, and that industrialization was still in the very early stages.

There is another mark characteristic of industry, or, more specifically, of industrial labor power in all South Slav lands. That is the fact that the great portion of industrial labor was and still is half industrial, half agricultural in character. Most of the industrial workers were actually peasant workers. But more is said about this problem later (pp. 406–7, 427–28).

GROWTH OF THE URBAN SECTOR

As a consequence of the growth of transportation, industry and mining, trade, and various services—that is, as a consequence of the growing division of labor in the South Slav lands—and owing to the rise of a state bureaucracy after 1850, an increasing urbanization and growth of population living from nonagricultural pursuits took place.[18] This process has continued ever since. The urbanization in areas which were under the Habsburg Monarchy set in earlier and progressed faster than in other South Slav lands. In Vojvodina, however, a considerable section of the population living in towns (as defined by statistics, in communities with more than 5,000 people), was and still is engaged in agriculture. In other areas a portion of the population in smaller communities was, on the contrary, of a purely urban character.

Looking back at the development of towns in the South Slav lands, one sees clearly that many of them grew out of the ancient and medieval townships and fortresses. Others are of a purely military origin of the last 200 to 300 years. But a large portion of the medieval, and even some of the more recent, towns based on or around fortresses have disappeared. While industry, trade, and railroads have favored the growth of all urban centers, there are few towns in the South Slav lands which are of purely industrial origin, namely, which developed on the

17 V. M. Djuričić et al., *Naša narodna privreda i nacionalni prihod* (Our National Economy and National Income), p. 265.

18 Nikola Vučo, *Privredna istorija naroda FNRJ* (Economic History of the Peoples of the Federal Peoples' Republic of Yugoslavia), pp. 251–53, 323, 342; Zvonimir Dugački and Milan Šenoa, "The Settlements," in Zvonimir Dugački (ed.), *Zemljopis Hrvatske* (Geography of Croatia), Pt. 2, pp. 608–17.

basis of agglomeration of industry, as was the case in Western Europe and particularly in the United States.

As a consequence of the political framework within which the South Slavs lived, the urban population at the beginning of the nineteenth century was almost fully composed of elements foreign by blood and culture. During the nineteenth century towns became largely Slavicized, but most of the economic power positions in the urban centers continued to be held by foreigners. Before 1914 the bulk of industry, trade, and banking, and a large percentage of the liberal professions as well were in the hands of foreigners. While the basic reason for this state of affairs has to be sought in the political situation of these lands, i.e., foreign rule until 1918 in all South Slav lands with the exception of Serbia and Montenegro, at least partly responsible for this situation was the psychological make-up of the South Slavs. During the nineteenth century these peoples brought forth great churchmen, artists, scientists, statesmen, and some great merchants, but no industrial or financial pioneers. These latter functions were performed almost exclusively by foreigners. Naturally, they were favored by foreign regimes —they were an essential part of the foreign rule—and they were able to procure abroad the necessary capital for their industrial, transportation, and financial ventures. But they also showed a typical capitalistic entrepreneurial perseverance and acumen. Industrial and financial ventures of purely domestic capital and talent were always on a much smaller scale and systematically discriminated against in all areas under foreign rule. These ventures showed a greater advance only in the last 20 or 30 years before 1914. Thus, in decades before World War I the primary representatives of capitalist forms of economic activity in all South Slav lands, except in Serbia, were foreign interests. To a lesser extent this was also the case throughout the interwar period.

Because of foreign influence in the South Slav cities, and because this was also considered modern and progressive, the city imitated foreign mores and ways of life and thinking. It ignored the rural population surrounding it in practically all respects except as objects of oppression and exploitation.

The growth of urban centers in the South Slav lands, especially after 1850, greater use of money and credit, increased division of labor and increased production, closer integration of their economies through the development of communications, and the inclusion of the economies of these lands in the nexus of the European and the world economy, stimulated greatly the growth of the domestic market. The chief mark of this process was the great intensification of economic intercourse between the village and the town. As the town was the center of political, commercial, industrial, and financial power, it had all the advantages in its dealings with the village. The natural consequence of this situation was an increasing political and, especially, economic antagonism between the urban and the rural populations. It replaced the centuries-old antagonism between the peasantry and the feudal class. The struggle between the town and the village has remained the chief characteristic of the whole political, social, and economic life in the South Slav lands up to the present day.

INCREASING CONTACTS WITH EUROPEAN AND WORLD ECONOMY

While, after the middle of the nineteenth century, agriculture in the South Slav lands was still struggling to break away from feudal bondage and was in the process of loosening itself from the patterns of the patriarchal system, the development of transportation and international trade brought it into contact with the Central and Western European market and thus, also, into the nexus of world economy. Soon thereafter it experienced for the first time the crushing competitive fight with agricultural products from overseas areas which began to appear on, and soon to flood, the European market. The long depression of the whole of European agriculture from 1873 to the middle of the 1890's affected profoundly the agriculture in all South Slav lands as well.[19]

The transition from subsistence to commercialized or quasi-commercialized agriculture in the South Slav lands was and remained only partial, and the degree of commercialization differed greatly from area to area. But even that part of agriculture which retained a subsistence character, representing the great majority of peasant households, was connected with the market to such an extent as to be affected by economic fluctuations. The export trade in agricultural products and raw materials, whose role began to grow from year to year, and the intensified influx of foreign capital became the two principal avenues of contact between the economies of the South Slav lands and the economy of Europe and the world. Thus, for example, exports from Serbia rose from an annual average of 46.5 million dinars in the period 1889–93 to an annual average of 94.0 million dinars in the period 1908–12. During the same time Serbian imports rose from an average of 38.7 million dinars to an average of 91.0 million dinars.[20] Moreover, the

---

[19] Rudolf Bićanić, "The Agricultural Crisis of 1873 to 1895 and Its Effect on the Economic and Social Structure of Croatia," *Ekonomist*, issues for March, April, and May 1937, pp. 97–108, 151–59, and 199–207, respectively. Nikola Vučo, *op. cit.*, p. 250.

[20] *Ibid.*, p. 255.

commodity composition of both exports and imports became more varied as domestic production and domestic consumption patterns became more diversified. It was through these channels of foreign trade and capital movements that the economic fluctuations in the industrial countries transplanted themselves to the South Slav lands. Large-scale emigration after 1880 also played an important role in this respect, as both the number of emigrants and, especially, their remittances to the folks at home depended greatly on the economic conditions in their new lands.

As the economic fluctuations in industrial countries became more severe and prolonged, so did also the induced fluctuations in the economy of the South Slav lands. Difficulties created by cyclical fluctuations were superimposed in the South Slav lands on an economic situation which became structurally more difficult as time advanced. But this problem will be treated more fully in Chapter 26.

CHAPTER 9

CHANGES IN THE ECONOMIC AND SOCIAL
STRUCTURE (*Continued*)

AMONG changes of basic importance for the peasantry which took place during the nineteenth century in the South Slav lands was the disappearance of the zadruga,[1] or joint family, as the predominant form of rural family and landownership. With the exception of Slovenia and Vojvodina (excluding the Banat Military Frontier) the zadruga was the prevailing type of rural family in all South Slav lands at the beginning of the nineteenth century. It was represented also among the urban Slav population.

ATTRIBUTES OF THE ZADRUGA

The zadruga had existed for centuries, had been subjected to various socioeconomic, political, and legislative influences, had been the organizational form of families pursuing various economic activities, and had existed under various natural (geographic) conditions; so it showed in real life a great number of forms and varieties, in terms of both internal organization and forces of cohesion. While the zadruga in which kindred people were organized predominated, there were also zadrugas whose members were not related by blood at all, in which some of the members were legally, or only factually, adopted into the fold.[2] While zadrugas numbering up to one hundred members existed[3] and attracted the most attention from social scientists, the over-

---

[1] It should be pointed out at the outset that the term zadruga is a literary invention. What the various social sciences refer to as the zadruga, the people in various areas call simply the house or the family (*kuća, hiža, familija*). The same applies to the term *inokoština* for the single family. But the people did and do use in their everyday life the adjective *zadružna*. Its meaning was only that a *zadružna* house or family had sufficient workers without respect to whether it was an extended or a single family. Valtazar Bogišić, *Pravni članci i rasprave* (Legal Articles and Studies), I, 190–94. This collection contains a translation of the famous article by Bogišić, "D'une forme particulière de la famille rurale chez les Serbes et les Croates," first published in Paris in 1884 in *Revue de droit international et de législation comparée*, XVI, 374–409.

[2] Milenko S. Filipović, *Nesrodnička i predvojena zadruga* (The Zadruga of the Nonrelatives and the Split Zadruga), p. 31.

[3] Some of the limited number of large zadrugas still in existence during the interwar period were closely investigated and reported upon. See Philip E. Mosely, "Adaptation for Survival: The Varžić Zadruga," *The Slavonic and East European Review*, XXI,

whelming portion of the zadrugas numbered below ten members.[4] While the cohabitation of all members of a zadruga in one household was the rule, there were zadrugas which were organized on a permanent basis in two households (the split zadruga), often at a great distance, but still owning their property communally and operating under one family head.[5] While generally the zadrugas derived their income from one activity, namely, agricultural pursuits (crop farming and livestock raising), not only zadrugas in towns, but also those in rural areas sometimes derived sizable portions of their income from non-agricultural sources (e.g., wages of their members in seasonal urban employment). While the zadruga owned the bulk of its property communally, both the custom and, later, the written laws allowed various members of the zadruga, and not only the women brought into the zadruga by marriage, to own individually some property, mostly livestock, and also land (*osebunjak, posobac*). Furthermore, according to one of the best Yugoslav experts on the zadruga during the interwar period, the Yugoslav peasants have abandoned in recent decades the idea of maintaining large, multiple-family zadrugas, and as far as the zadrugas continue to exist, e.g., in Croatia-Slavonia, these are overwhelmingly single-family zadrugas. Their basic formal characteristic

---

147–73; Milan Karanović, "Some of the Large Zadrugas in Bosnia and Herzegovina," *Glasnik Zemaljskog muzeja u Bosni i Hercegovini*, XLI, 63–77; *ibid.*, XLII, 133–56; Držislav Švob and Franko Petrić, "Zadruga Domladovac," Yugoslav Academy of Science and Art, *Zbornik za narodni život i običaje Južnih Slavena*, XXVII, Pt. I, 92–110.

See also the works of the most prolific of all modern writers on the zadruga, the French sociologist Emile Sicard: *La Zadruga dans la littérature serbe (1850–1912)*; *La Zadruga Sud-slave dans l'évolution du groupe domestique*; *Problèmes familiaux chez les Slaves du Sud*.

[4] Milovan Zoričić, "Population of the Kingdoms of Croatia and Slavonia by Profession and Occupation," Yugoslav Academy of Science and Art, *Rad*, CXXV, 129–33, shows that most of the zadrugas in Croatia-Slavonia, according to the census of 1890, were actually single families with fewer than ten members. This was the case even more so in 1910; see Dragutin Tončić, *Vrhovne upravne i sudske rješidbe k zakonu od 9.V.1889 o zadrugama i zadružnoj noveli od 30.IV.1902* (Supreme Administrative and Court Decisions Regarding the Law on the Zadrugas of May 9, 1889, and Its Amendments of April 30, 1902), pp. 242, 281. For the distribution of households by size in Serbia, according to the census of 1900, see Milan Marković, *Die serbische Hauskommunion*, pp. 23–24. Large zadrugas were an exception also in medieval Serbia. See Stojan Novaković, *Selo* (The Village), p. 211, and Teodor Taranovsky, *Istorija srpskog prava u Nemanjićkoj državi* (History of Serbian Law in the Nemanid State), III, 53–55. Dinko Tomasic in his *Personality and Culture in Eastern European Politics*, p. 149, says with regard to the number of members in the zadrugas: "The zadruga is economically, as well as emotionally, a self-sustaining community, consisting of a group of families averaging, altogether, from twenty to forty members." This statement completely disregards the statistical evidence. (See also pp. 420–21.)

[5] Milenko S. Filipović, *op. cit., passim.*

becomes then a collective ownership of the farm real estate, with the father of the family unable to dispose freely of any of it.[6]

Because of this, a compact, general definition of the zadruga is all but impossible, though many have been given. In a tentative way, Philip E. Mosely, foremost American authority on the zadruga, defined it as

a household composed of two or more biological or small families closely related by blood or adoption, owning its means of production communally, producing and consuming its means of livelihood jointly, and regulating the control of its property, labor, and livelihood communally.[7]

It is clear from the aforesaid that this definition has to be understood as an approximation and that some elements—e.g., the fact that some zadrugas consist of two rather separate households, that some property is individually owned, and that most zadrugas in recent decades have been single families—are not covered by it.

For some authors the specific ethos ascribed to the zadruga seems to have been of as great importance as its type of landownership and communal work. Thus, in the words of Dragutin Tončić:

The zadruga is an institution of our peasantry, a national product of its spirit, its original creation developed without a foreign model and without the influence of legislation and legal experts. It was created by the legal conscience and by the needs of our peasantry. The peasantry regulated the zadruga by custom as its ownership collective and as a type of its peasant family order with special family law, incorporating in the zadruga not only its property and labor, but also family love and mutual assistance, much earlier than the statutory laws promulgated rules for the regulation of the zadruga.[8]

From the point of view of land tenure the chief mark of the zadruga consisted of the fact that the property was owned collectively by all members of the zadruga. According to customary law of the South Slavs, the head of the peasant family was thus not the owner of the family property in the sense of the Roman law. The property belonged to the family as a collective, and the head of the family, who was the first among equals, was able to dispose of it only with the consent of the majority of the adult zadruga members. It was also impossible for him to bequeath real estate property either during his life or by a will,

---

[6] Dragutin Tončić, *op. cit.*, pp. 246–47.

[7] Philip E. Mosely, "The Peasant Family: the Zadruga, or Communal Joint-Family in the Balkans, and Its Recent Evolution," Caroline F. Ware (ed.), *The Cultural Approach to History*, p. 95.

[8] Quoted from an article by Tončić in Milan Ivšić, *Temelji seljačkoga zakonika* (The Principles of the Peasant Code), p. 18. See also Vinko Krišković, *Hrvatsko pravo kućnih zadruga* (Croatian Zadruga Law), *passim*.

as the real owner of the property was the family collective, which continued to exist. These rules with regard to peasant property applied, moreover, according to customary law, equally to the single peasant family, or *inokoština*, though in it the father had of necessity somewhat greater power than the head of the zadruga. Neither in regard to the disposition of the property nor in other respects were there actually any differences, according to customary law, between the two parallel types of peasant family in the South Slav lands.[9] While customary law did not go so far, Slobodan Jovanović, maintained that

it would have conformed best to the spirit of the zadruga if its members had only the right of usufruct and lacked the right to dispose of the collective property, that is, if they had not been able to dispose of it at all, but had to preserve it intact for their inheritors.[10]

Male members of the zadruga who were of age were able to claim their share of the collective property at any time, but it was up to the majority to decide whether to give them a share of property in kind or an appropriate indemnity. Participants in collective property were only members who lived and worked in the household, and prolonged absence meant loss of property rights (by marriage or transfer into other walks of life). The South Slav peasants expressed this principle with the saying: "Those who work also eat" (*"Ko je pri djelu, taj i pri jelu"*).[11] With the consent of the head of the family—who, in principle, always acted only with the approval of the majority of the adult members of the zadruga—individual members could earn outside of its fold, but if they wanted to preserve their rights in the zadruga they had to give their earnings to the family collective.

The zadruga was directed by a household head (*domaćin, starješina*) either designated by the preceding head or elected by the adult members. As a rule, he was the most intelligent married man in the family, but zadrugas with women as heads were not unknown. The *domaćin* represented the zadruga before the authorities and directed all the work of its members, allocating the work to various members according to their capacities. In this respect the advice of other family members was always sought. The wife of the *domaćin*, or another woman in the family—the *domaćica*—was in charge of the housework and was assisted by other women in the house on the principle of rotation.

[9] Valtazar Bogišić, *op. cit.*, pp. 185–86.
[10] Slobodan Jovanović, *Političke i pravne rasprave* (Political and Legal Studies), Collected Works, III, 97.
[11] Milan Ivšić, *op. cit.*, p. 21.

The zadruga flourished in an economic order in which the market and the use of money were only of incidental importance. It marketed only a small part of its products in order to acquire the necessary money for the payment of some taxes and some obligations toward the feudal lord, and also to buy a few necessities which it was incapable of producing at home, e.g., salt. But essentially the larger zadrugas were economically self-sufficient. One of the great advantages of such zadrugas in relation to the single family was a far-reaching division of labor within the household, which, naturally, increased with the rising number of zadruga members.

In addition to the economic advantage to the zadruga members resulting from the economic co-operation of many family members and from the division of labor within one household, there were other economic reasons for the maintenance of the zadruga. Large families were much better suited to stand the drain on their labor power for *corvée* to the landlord and for public purposes, to stand those taxes which were assessed by households rather than by property or per capita, and in some areas to stand the drain on manpower for military duties. This last factor was of special importance in the Croato-Slavonian and Banat Military Frontiers where the zadruga was the basis of social and economic organization of this militarily organized peasantry and, as such, was codified into law.

Furthermore, the need for greater personal and property security contributed powerfully to the maintenance of the zadruga, primarily in those South Slav areas which were under Ottoman rule. In times when neither personal nor property security was assured by the state, people had to depend on their own resources for protection. And large families were much better able to perform that function than single families, especially in areas of the dispersed village. Need for greater security was apparently the basic reason also for the amalgamation of various smaller tribes (*plemena*) not related by blood into larger ones in some parts of Montenegro.[12] One device which some Albanian families living in zadrugas in the present Yugoslav territory used to increase their security was for the family to have part of its members belong to the Christian and part to the Moslem religion. Under a Moslem regime the family would be headed by the Moslem and under a Christian regime by the Christian branch of the family. Furthermore, the great importance which in most South Slav areas is given to artificial kinship forms, e.g., to the godfather and the best man, can also be related to the need for mutual defense and protection.

[12] Milenko S. Filipović, *op. cit.*, p. 32.

We are primarily concerned with the dissolution of the zadruga during the nineteenth century and its replacement by the single family and individual landownership. It appears helpful, however, to state briefly the various types of theories on the origin and the nature of the zadruga, because disagreements on these points still exist, because various views had different influences on the legislation affecting the zadruga, and because a juxtaposition of these theories is helpful in putting into better perspective the reasons for dissolution of the zadruga. Theories about its origin and nature can be roughly classified into four main groups, each of which has several variations:[13]

1. Theories which, in the zadruga among the South Slavs in the Balkans, see only the continuation of an institution existing among them in their original, trans-Carpathian homeland. To most writers subscribing to this theory, the zadruga is a unique institution resulting from the fundamentally democratic character of the South Slavs (or Slavs in general) and from their urge for communal life and action. The zadruga was considered by many to have been the matrix of their social organization, which in a process of evolution grew into the clans and tribes. In spite of profound political and economic changes undergone by the South Slavs after their settlement in the Balkans, the zadruga, according to these theories, was preserved because it corresponded best to their character and their needs.

2. Theories which maintain that the zadruga is a necessary, and therefore a general transitional, form of landownership and rural settlement between the communal type of landownership and individual private property in land. As such, it was a common occurrence and not a typically South Slav or Slav institution. As the system of private landownership advanced, the zadruga and zadruga-like institutions receded.

3. Theories which maintain that the zadruga in the South Slav lands was simply a consequence of the medieval taxation system, which in its origins goes back to the Byzantine tax by hearths or by chimneys. As the tax unit was a hearth, the combination of several small families into one joint family was a way of lessening the tax burden.

4. Finally, theories which maintain that the zadruga is neither

---

[13] A review of the theories on the origin and nature of the zadruga can be found in an article by Vasilj Popović, "The Zadruga—Theories and Literature," *Glasnik Zemaljskog muzeja u Bosni i Hercegovini*, XXXIII–XXXIV, 73–114; and Zdenko Vinski, *Die südslavische Grossfamilie in ihrer Beziehung zum asiatischen Grossraum*, pp. 43–47. For a recent contribution in this regard from a Marxian point of view, see Oleg Mandić, "The Class Character of the Bourgeois Theories on the Origin of the Zadruga," *Istorisko-pravni zbornik*, Nos. 3–4 (1950), pp. 131–55.

something specifically South Slav or Slav, nor a necessary transitional form in the development of landownership systems, nor a consequence of the medieval taxation system, but rather a general mode of rural settlement and property ownership under primitive economic and social conditions. Zadrugas and zadruga-like institutions, as many authors have pointed out, were widespread among many other peoples and disappeared when the economic and social life evolved to more advanced forms. They were maintained longer among the South Slavs than among other peoples because foreign occupation, feudalism, legislation (e.g., taxation, Military Frontier laws), and the hold of customary law have favored this mode of land tenure and rural settlement. By and large, this writer is inclined to accept this point of view.

FORCES CAUSING DISSOLUTION OF THE ZADRUGA

The reasons for dissolution of the zadruga have been among the most widely treated questions in all discussions of the zadruga. It was to a large extent the tendency of its rapid disintegration, noticed already at the beginning of the nineteenth century and greatly intensified after 1850, which stimulated the discussion of the zadruga as such. The explanations of the dissolution of the zadruga adduced by various writers depended essentially on their views on its origin and nature.

Practically all those authors who thought of the zadruga as a specific South Slav institution originating in their pre-Balkan history, as well as most of those authors who did not bother about the origin of the zadruga but considered it as the expression of the legal ideas and the economic needs of the South Slav peasantry, were of the opinion that the chief reason for the disintegration of the zadruga was to be sought in the introduction of statutory laws based on the principles of unlimited individual property in the sense of Roman law. Obviously, this was a view which put too much stress on legal forms and paid insufficient attention to the economic and social forces behind various social organizational forms and their evolution. Of course, it was rather easy to blame the introduction of statutory laws based on a foreign legal philosophy for the dissolution of the zadruga. This was to a large extent a romanticist and nationalist attitude, which characterized much of the thinking of the social scientists in the South Slav lands (as elsewhere) during the nineteenth century. The importance of this school of thought was primarily in the fact that it fathered the idea that with proper changes in statutory laws directed toward the protection of the zadruga this institution could be saved. Undoubtedly, forces leading to the disintegration of the zadrugas were much more powerful and complicated than the introduction of statutory laws based on an individualistic philosophy. But there can be little doubt that these new statutory laws, by introducing individual ownership and the possibility of individual inheritance, created a completely new situation in the regulation of peasant property and thus became a contributing factor in the process of the zadruga dissolution.

When speaking of property relations and their significance in the dissolution of the zadruga, it is necessary also to point out that the abolition of serfdom in various South Slav lands during the nineteenth century contributed to this dissolution. First, as long as feudalism persisted, division of the zadrugas of the serfs was subject to the approval of the landlord, and as a rule such divisions were not allowed because it was thought that a zadruga with a larger number of working hands was a better source of *corvée* labor. Second, the abolition of serfdom made possible the upsurge of social and economic forces favoring the development of a market and money economy, and, as will be shown later, this development proved to be fatal to the zadruga. Demilitarization of the former Military Frontiers in the 1870's removed the statutory provisions protecting the zadruga and exposed it to social and economic influences working for its dissolution.

The authors who maintained that the taxation by hearths or chimneys which prevailed during the Middle Ages, and in some areas until well into the nineteenth century, was one of the main reasons for the maintenance of the zadruga, are of the opinion that the introduction of taxation by heads and by property was one of the basic reasons for the disappearance of the zadruga. New tax procedures removed the tax-saving incentive connected with living in the fold of the zadruga. While changes in the tax structure did contribute to the dissolution of the zadruga, this view gives to this factor a much greater importance than it deserves.

The dissolution of the zadruga was basically the consequence of changes in the psychology and in the economic and social life of the South Slav peasantry during the nineteenth century. These changes resulted from the penetration of individualistic ideas and from the penetration of a money and market economy into the South Slav lands. Prior to that the family collective as a unit of ownership, production, and consumption was in the foreground, and the individual member was in the background. The definite predominance of the collective aspects of life both in the peasant family and in the village community was a consequence of economic and social conditions and, as such, was taken for granted. There was no other alternative for the individual—the force of conditions kept him in the zadruga fold. The eighteenth and nineteenth centuries brought about the emergence of the individualistic spirit in Western and Central Europe, which, though with a great lag, slowly penetrated into the South Slav peasant community. The old patriarchal system based on subsistence economy, collective spirit, a specific zadruga ethos, and the traditional customs as regulators of relationships between individuals in the peasant family and among families in the village community gradually broke down.

But the chief blow to the zadruga came from the penetration of the money and market economies, those basic vehicles of capitalism, into the former subsistence economic order of the South Slav lands. There were three basic reasons which forced the zadruga to seek a higher money income and thus to become more and more dependent on the market in its function as both producer and consumer. First of all, the new bureaucratic state began to assess and collect all taxes in money and to increase greatly the tax load in order to increase its revenue to finance the growing system of state services and a part of the greatly enlarged military expenditures. The increased tax load in money forced the peasant to take a larger share of his products to the market in order to obtain money for payment of taxes. Second, with the development of communications and the growing sector of the market economy, the peasants began more and more to utilize the products of the handicrafts and especially factory products such as textiles, footwear, jewelry, house utensils, and even cosmetics, and such foods and beverages as sugar and coffee. The factory product caught the imagination of the peasants, especially the young women, and this soon resulted in the enlargement of their traditional consumption patterns. The zadruga could not supply these needs directly, as it was geared to the production of only a few items in addition to food, and these products were often of a very crude nature. The zadruga could satisfy the new consumption needs only by producing more, and especially by selling more, of its agricultural products. It was forced more and more into the market and into the nexus of the money and market economy. Third, if the money income obtained by the zadruga from its sales was insufficient to meet the enlarged money requirements, credit had to be obtained. And credit was obtainable only at usurious interest rates, which easily increased the amount of indebtedness. Payment of interest and repayment of debts meant additional requirements of money and forced the zadruga into closer contact with the market. It had to sell more. Owing to the inability of many peasant households to respond on time to their debt and interest obligations, land began to slip out of the peasants' hands, with all the untoward consequences which this entails for the peasant population.

All these factors put the peasant households under great financial pressure. As a rule, the zadruga was unable to increase its production sufficiently, and to market enough of its produce, to cover increased money requirements. The single peasant family was beset by the same problems, but many members of the zadrugas thought that at least part of their troubles could be solved by division of the zadrugas. The division of the zadrugas served thus also as an outlet for the dissatisfaction of its members under the new economic conditions.

Needless to say, many other factors exerted strong pressure on the zadruga. Among these factors, perhaps the most important was the large increase in rural population. The growth of population was not matched by a corresponding increase in agricultural land; the resources-population ratio worsened and caused an increased hunger for land on the part of the individual peasant households. Insufficiency of land acted as an inducement for individual peasant families, especially those with ample labor resources and displaying greater personal initiative, to try to redress this unfavorable situation by division of the zadrugas. The principle of the zadruga society, "one for all and all for one," gave way to the rule that every single family follow its own interests. This individualistic behavior on the part of many peasants was stimulated by the fact that money had become an agent of everyday life in the peasant community. Now the contribution by, and the "cost" of, every member of the family collective were accountable and if the balance among various biological families of the zadruga was not satisfactory, internal cohesion among these families inevitably suffered. The fact that the process of property and income differentiation and wage labor in the village community became more pronounced as time advanced served as an additional stimulus for individualistic actions.

A consequence of increased single-family selfishness in the zadruga showed itself sometimes in the partial and abusive attitude of the household head, the *domaćin*. He often promoted the interests of the members of his own narrower family at the expense of other members of the zadruga. He was able to do this partly because he held the family purse. On the other hand, as the psychological independence of other members of the zadruga was increasing, the moral and disciplinary hold of the household head over the zadruga members relaxed and cohesion within the zadruga diminished. Young married women, often holding some individual property in the zadruga (*osebunjak*), tended also to become a disruptive factor, first by their unwillingness to submit to the authority of the *domaćin* or *domaćica*, and second by their propensity to consume more of the factory products, especially textiles, footwear, and jewelry. After the division of the zadruga the young matron had to contend only with the authority and resistance of her husband.[14]

The gradual switch from a predominantly pastoral to a predominantly crop type of agriculture in the course of the nineteenth century, as a consequence of growing population, changed considerably the pattern of labor needs of the peasant family in a way not conducive to the maintenance of the zadruga. Another consequence of growing population, the migration of peasant folk from the village either into the urban areas at home or to overseas countries, was also a contributing factor toward the dissolution of the zadruga. In addition, migration from the zadruga fold strengthened individualistic propensities of its members, and also militated against the rule of the zadruga society that only those who work at home have the right to share in the property of the zadruga. Those who emigrated only temporarily and returned home with their savings were often little inclined to share their savings with the zadruga at large, but rather used them to strengthen their individual households after separating from the zadruga.

If one keeps in mind this array of factors which contributed to the dissolution of the zadruga in the South Slav lands during the century preceding World War I, it becomes quite obvious that the taking of any single reason as the cause of that process must necessarily miss the mark. The combination of causes working for the dissolution of the zadruga, and their timing, differed somewhat in various areas. Nevertheless, it must be stressed that it was the penetration of the market and money economy into the South Slav lands, with its psychological and economic consequences, which was the basic reason for the doom of the zadruga. The multiple-family zadruga proved unable to adapt itself to the exigencies of the market and money economy. Its inability to provide a satisfactory economic organization for its member families in the period of nascent capitalism became obvious. Its usefulness came to an end. Changes in the patterns of its production and consumption functions destroyed its economic rationale, and changes in the psychological foundations of the peasant society de-

---

[14] An attempt was made in the late 1930's to interpret the process of zadruga disintegration by the study of the relaxation of authority of the *domaćin* and *domaćica* over younger married people. The fact was stressed that in disputes between the young matron and her mother-in-law, the husband more and more took the side of his wife against his mother. Vera Ehrlich-Stein, "The Southern Slav Patriarchal Family," *The Sociological Review*, XXXII, Nos. 3 and 4, 224–41.

stroyed the zadruga as "a state of mind." Thus, when rapid dissolution of the zadruga began after the middle of the nineteenth century, this process could not be stopped until it had run to its logical end, namely, the transformation of the zadruga society into a society based on individual families and individual property. This process was almost completed when World War I came. A considerable number of zadrugas, some with large memberships, continued to exist, but they obviously were relics of a past age. In the case of single-family zadrugas, the collective ownership of land may, however, under the Yugoslav conditions, be beneficial (see pp. 420–23).

DECAY OF VOLUNTARY FORMS OF COMMUNAL
AGRICULTURAL LABOR

Feudalism, the subsistence economic system with little or no money in circulation, and the settlement of the majority of the peasant population in the zadrugas led in the South Slav lands to special forms of acquisition of labor for public, for communal, and for private needs. Construction and maintenance of fortresses and other military installations, roads, bridges, and public buildings were traditionally accomplished exclusively or predominantly by *corvée* for public purposes. This type of obligation is known in the South Slav lands under the name of *zgon* (herding), *kuluk* (coming from the Turkish word *kul* meaning slave), or *tlaka*.[15] It was used on a large scale in medieval South Slav states, somewhat less by the Turks prior to the nineteenth century, by the French during their short rule in South Slav lands, by the Austrians and the Hungarians, by Serbia and Montenegro prior to 1914, and also by Yugoslavia during the interwar period. The methods of assessment varied, but the extent of the obligation was usually related either to houses, to biological families, to property, to the number of able-bodied males in the family, and on occasions it simply affected all people able to work, without respect to class, age, or sex. In recent times it was possible to redeem this obligation by payment in money. After the middle of the nineteenth century *corvée* obligations were mostly regulated by law, but such laws were never precise, and, what is even more important, they were administered in an abusive way.

Corvée was used not only for proper public purposes, but by many of those in power also for their private needs, such as for agricultural

---

[15] Milan Z. Vlajinac, *Zgon ili kulučenje van mesta stanovanja od srednjega veka do naših dana* (The *Corvée* Outside of the Place of Living from the Middle Ages to the Present). In addition to the above-mentioned public needs, *corvée* was also used for transport services both in peacetime and during the war, for watch duty on the frontiers, for raising of posses, and the like.

work on their estates, building of houses, and transport. Thus, until 1839 *corvée* was rendered on the estates of Prince Miloš in Serbia, as well as on the properties of the local headmen.[16] In Bosnia and Herzegovina Moslem feudal lords depended partly on *corvée* for the working of their *beglik* lands even in the 1850's. The already mentioned dynamic administrator of Herzegovina from 1833 to 1851, Ali Pasha Rizvanbegović, was in ill repute and entered the folk poetry because of his ruthless exactions of labor from his subjects.[17]

From the middle of the nineteenth century *corvée* was used chiefly for building and maintaining roads, public buildings, post offices, schools, and churches. But in Bosnia and Herzegovina it was used also for the laying of telegraph lines. The characteristic of this type of *corvée*, as distinguished from *corvée* of the serfs on the estates of their feudal lords, was that it represented forced draft for work outside of the place of living. Those drafted for work had to bring their own tools and draft animals, and they had to provide food and feed for animals at their own expense. In times of war *corvée* was usually greatly increased. This type of obligation was a mode of taxation in kind and thus constituted a natural concomitant of a type of economy which used little or no money. In later days when the money and credit economy penetrated into the South Slav lands, *corvée* was used instead of paid labor, as government revenues were not sufficient. But *corvée* for public works, like that on feudal estates, was always considered as forced labor and, as such, was deeply resented by the peasantry.

More interesting from the point of view of the economics of labor in agriculture were various forms of voluntary communal or co-operative work widely practiced among the peasantry in all South Slav lands prior to the middle of the nineteenth century, of which the most important were the *moba* (the bee) and the *pozajmica* (labor loan). The *moba* (a corruption of the word *molba*, meaning an appeal or request) was defined as "an assembly of people who get together voluntarily in order to help other people [neighbors] accomplish certain jobs, without pay and without the obligation of a comparable return."[18] According to custom, though, a reciprocal, or nearly reciprocal, counterservice was expected in the case of need. The *pozajmica*, or labor loan, on the other hand, was based on strict reciprocity, namely, loan of labor for a comparable, even if not qualitatively identical, amount of labor at a

---

[16] Milan Z. Vlajinac, *Zgon* . . . , pp. 121–22.

[17] *Ibid.*, pp. 99–103.

[18] Milan Z. Vlajinac, *Moba i pozajmica, narodni običaji udruženoga rada* (The Bee and the Labor Loan—Folk Customs of Communal Labor), p. 21.

later date. There were several types of bee: the regular bee among neighbors in a village; the charity bee, namely, work for a family in exceptional need of neighborly help; the church or other bees for the accomplishment of communally needed work; and, finally, the forced bee for the members of the ruling groups, e.g., for the Turkish land-lords.[19] The last type of labor was, in fact, forced labor, as those who were its beneficiaries had neither moral nor legal right to such services, nor did they ever intend to reciprocate. As a rule, the bee was called to accomplish a pressing job for which even a large rural family did not have enough hands to do. Bee members brought their own tools, but the family for whom the work was done was obliged to feed them, and the fare was usually of a festive character. The entertainment during the work and afterward was provided by the participants them-selves.

In addition to the bee and the labor loan, there existed two other forms of communal co-operative work in common use in the South Slav lands, the *sprega* or co-operative use of draft animals, and the *bačije* or co-operative tending of livestock at the summer pastures.[20] Further-more, some special types of work, such as scouring of wool, wool spin-ning, husking of corn, and pressing of grapes, well suited for evening work, were performed by special bees, called *sijelo* (sitting) or *prelo* (spinning sitting).[21]

The bees and labor loan were widespread in all South Slav lands and were used for grain harvesting, hay cutting and gathering, fruit picking, transport of produce, house building, and the like. Basic features of all bee work were the song and entertainment and compe-tition among individuals and among groups. Song, music, dancing, games, and joking, especially by the younger folks, were an integral part of bees. The evening bees also served as social gatherings during which much of the village gossip was spread and the village youth got together for merriment. This type of work was quite natural for a patriarchal society living largely in the zadruga and using little or no money in its daily life. Many authors considered the *moba* and other types of voluntary communal work simply as implementations of the zadruga constitution of rural life, making the hiring of workers and thus paid labor unnecessary and impossible, and thus an integral part of a patriarchal, subsistence type of economy.

[19] *Ibid.*, pp. 42–80. With regard to the bee, see also Josip Predavec, *Selo i seljaci* (The Village and the Peasants), pp. 249–58.

[20] Milan Z. Vlajinac, *Moba i pozajmica* . . . , p. 15.

[21] For an identical institution, the *sedenka* (sitting) in the Bulgarian village and its social significance, see Irwin T. Sanders, *Balkan Village*, pp. 260–65.

Opinions about the *moba*, and, especially, about the evening bees, both as to their economic advantages and their implications for the moral standards of the village youth, were divided. But the majority of writers, including Vlajinac, considered them as favorable and important features of the peasant society that the South Slav peoples had developed and maintained through centuries. They also had the sanction of public opinion, as the great majority of folk proverbs and folk poems dealing with these institutions spoke approvingly of them.

With other economic and social institutions of the traditional society, the *moba* and other forms of communal co-operative work started to wither away during the second quarter, and, especially, after the middle of the nineteenth century. By the beginning of the twentieth century they were quite rare, though in certain parts of the country they were in use also during the interwar period. The reasons for the disappearance of the *moba* as well as of other types of communal work were akin to those causing the disappearance of the zadruga: penetration of the money economy whereby labor, like all other commodities and services, obtained a price, increased economic differentiation in the village, increase in the number of dwarf and landless peasants needing money wages to make a living, substitution of labor loan for the work bee, improvement in farm implements and draft animals, which increased work performance per man and draft animal, greater selfishness among the peasants, membership in opposing political parties, the unsatisfactory performance of bee work on many occasions, promulgation of laws prohibiting assemblies which the authorities interpreted as including work bees. The over-all reason for the disappearance of the *moba* was simply the penetration of the market and money economy into the South Slav lands, which destroyed most of the social and economic collectivist institutions of the traditional system and replaced them by an individualist system and its institutions. In regard to labor in agriculture that meant introduction of the wage system.

PATTERNS OF PEASANT CULTURE

The peasant societies of these lands have their roots in the tribal formations of the South Slavic peoples who settled in the Balkans in the early Middle Ages. In many areas these formations disintegrated under the impact of the medieval Slavic feudal states, while in the inaccessible mountainous areas remainders of these formations in conjunction with the remainders of the Vlakh elements reasserted themselves during Ottoman rule and lasted until the nineteenth century. These peasant societies lived under various geographic conditions which greatly influenced the nature of their economic activity, favoring in some areas crop raising and in others animal husbandry. These societies lived and developed within different political and socioeconomic frameworks and thus under various internal and external political, social, and cultural influences. In a considerable part of the mountainous region south of the Sava-Danube rivers the Slavic population came into close and long-enduring contact with the strong remainders of the old Balkan population (Vlakhs), both prior to and especially during the period of Turkish rule. This association resulted in an ethnic, institutional, and cultural symbiosis between the Slavic and the Vlakh elements and gradually almost complete assimilation of the latter. In some limited areas of the present Yugoslav territory populations did not shift much, although in most of the territory large and persistent population shifts were taking place during Turkish rule. All this resulted in the development of different ways of life in various areas and different systems of values, and thus in different patterns of peasant culture. Thus far, two main types of this South Slav peasant culture have been discussed in the social sciences: the so-called Dinaric patriarchal culture and lately also the so-called Zadruga culture. These cultures have been differently characterized and interpreted by various authors and these different interpretations have acquired considerable political significance.

In the development and spread of the Dinaric patriarchal culture, Ottoman rule in the Balkans is considered to have been of primary importance. The basic consequence of Ottoman rule in the South Slav lands was the interruption of the trend of social and economic development, which, before Ottoman conquests, had been under the influences of Byzantium and Central and Western Europe and which in the fourteenth and fifteenth centuries was not too far behind the development in Central Europe. Turkish rule led first to economic stagnation in areas conquered by the Turks and later—in conjunction with several other factors—to a general regression in the economic, social, and cultural life. In this process of regression the patriarchal type of culture asserted itself anew. This became possible because of the withdrawal of a part of the population from the plains to the less accessible mountainous areas in order to avoid Turkish pressure, because in the latter areas tribal remainders were still strong and the Turks left the peasant population a large degree of freedom in its local government and religion. Later the population of mountainous areas, owing to increased numbers and other factors, gradually spread its influence over the plains in areas south of the Sava-Danube rivers and spread in large numbers north of these rivers. This pastoral mountaineer element, representing the Dinaric patriarchal culture, became in time the dominant population stratum in much of the areas south of the Sava-Danube rivers and in some areas north of these rivers.

The great Serbian geographer Jovan Cvijić, who initiated large-scale field investigations of the Balkan migrations and shifts in population and cultural zones, formulated the basic characterization and interpretation of the Dinaric patriarchal culture. Cvijić and many of his followers considered the resurgence and spread of the patriarchal culture a process of "ethnic and social rejuvenation" of the peoples of the Dinaric area and the type of culture that thus evolved a type of "perfected and well-developed patriarchal culture."[22] Cvijić maintained that the zadruga had been a basic component of the Dinaric patriarchal culture, especially in the domain of the dispersed village. Within the sphere of this culture the tribe (*pleme*) was primarily a fighting organization, while the zadruga "was always an institution of peace, a family institution, an economic grouping. Under the patriarchal system in which economic life was based on extensive agriculture and extensive animal husbandry, the zadruga seemed to be an economic organization best adapted to the circumstances."[23]

The Dinaric patriarchal culture and the Dinaric man were idealized to a large extent by Cvijić and his followers.[24] To the Dinaric man were ascribed the attributes of a high sense of honor, mutual support for his fellow man, heroism, upholding of tradition, intensive national pride, and constructiveness in a political sense. Undoubtedly, the culture of the Dinaric man evolved through a process of continuous struggle against and adaptation to both hostile political conditions—that is, foreign rule—and scanty natural resources. It, therefore, commanded the admiration of many people. On the basis of such characterization of the Dinaric man—and implicitly or explicitly that meant primarily

[22] Jovan Cvijić, *La Péninsule Balkanique*, pp. 29–30. With regard to the influence of Turkish rule on the social development of the South Slavs, see also Branislav Djurdjev, "The Influence of Turkish Rule on the Development of Our Peoples," *Godišnjak Istoriskog društva Bosne i Hercegovine*, II, 19–82, esp. 41–51.

[23] Jovan Cvijić, *op. cit.*, p. 284.

[24] Among the philosophic interpretations and considerable idealizations of the Dinaric man and culture, following in many respects Cvijić's lead, the most important are the many studies by Gerhard Gesemann, a German scholar of the culture, literature, and national character of the various Yugoslav peoples, and the studies by the Yugoslav philosopher Vladimir Dvorniković. See, for example, Gerhard Gesemann, *Heroische Lebensform—Zur Literatur und Wesenskunde der balkanischen Patriarchalität*; and Vladimir Dvorniković, *Karakterologija Jugoslovena* (The Yugoslav National Character).

the Serbs and the Montenegrins and only parts of other South Slav nations—it was easy to claim for him the leading role in Balkan political life and to idealize his whole history. This theory was developed at the turn of this century at a time of great Serbian nationalist upsurge and expansion. Such thinking was almost tailored for the purposes of Serbian statesmen, educators, soldiers, and administrators. In the Yugoslav state established in 1918 this reasoning was often used to defend and explain the hegemony of the Serbs and the crudely centralistic organization of the new state.

On the other hand Cvijić barely mentioned the Croats of the Croatian Zagorje. Having apparently never studied them, he accepted the view of a little-known Croatian writer and repeated the latter's assertions that they were docile and disciplined, and that because of their past, democratic principles could not take root among them.[25] It appears to us that this political interpretation of Cvijić's theories of the Dinaric man and his culture and of his acceptance of a disparaging, though Croatian, view of the Croats of Zagorje was largely responsible for the emergence of a totally different characterization of the Dinaric culture by Dinko Tomasic, a Croatian sociologist now in this country, and his comparison of the Dinaric culture with the Zadruga culture.[26] In the background of Tomasic's writings is the idealization of the culture of the peasants of the Croatian Zagorje, which he calls the Zadruga culture, and on the other hand a disparaging attitude toward the Dinaric culture. According to Tomasic, the Dinaric patriarchal or tribal culture is the culture of nomadic or seminomadic warlike sheep raisers and robbers in which power-seeking, be it of the father in the family (either zadruga or single family), or the tribal chief, or any individual in a state, is the basic moving force. The basic component of the social organization of the Dinaric culture was also the zadruga, but since it was built on a tribal basis, it was, according to him, essentially an authoritarian institution lacking any democratic spirit. Tomasic fails, in his discussion of the Dinaric zadruga, to elaborate on the collective ownership of land, the division of labor and economic co-operation in the zadruga, and its economic self-sufficiency until the middle of the nineteenth century, although these are the undeniable marks of the Dinaric

[25] Jovan Cvijić, *op. cit.*, p. 517. In this particular passage Cvijić was simply repeating the ideas expressed by a Croatian (Vatroslav Rožić), whose study on the Croatian area of Prigorje was published by the Yugoslav Academy of Science and Art in *Zbornik za narodni život i običaje Južnih Slavena*, XIII (1908), Pt. 1, 111.

[26] Dinko Tomašić, *Društveni razvitak Hrvata* (Social Development of the Croats), pp. 9–83; Dinko Tomasic, *Personality and Culture in Eastern European Politics*, pp. 16–105, 149–205.

zadruga. He concentrates on the problem of "power-seeking" in the Dinaric culture and zadruga, and discusses the mentioned economic characteristics of the zadruga, which were general, only in connection with the zadruga in the area of his Zadruga culture.

The Zadruga culture is the culture of the crop- and cattle-raising peasants of the Croatian Zagorje, a population which in his opinion is averse to migration, imbued with a collectivist-democratic spirit, and, above all, indifferent to power. Unlike the tribal organization which is based on kinship, the social organization in the Zadruga culture is, according to Tomasic, based primarily on the territorial and only secondarily on the kinship principle. The woman has in the latter, unlike the former, equal social standing with the man. Furthermore, according to this theory, it seems that the centralistic and autocratic organization of the state better corresponds to a society with the patriarchal cultural basis, while the Zadruga society avowedly understands the state as a democratic organization for the promotion of collective interest, an organization of social justice.[27] As described by Tomasic, this Zadruga society was an almost idyllic, peaceful, prosperous, and emotionally stable type of society.

It is on the basis of this duality of cultures and cultural background that Tomasic has interpreted the political developments in the South Slav lands up to the present time, and especially the conflict between the Serbs and Croats since the establishment of Yugoslavia in 1918. Since, however, a large part of the Croats have a patriarchal cultural background, he ascribes all political excesses among the Croats, e.g., the bloody Ustaša regime during World War II, to those among them belonging to the Dinaric cultural background.[28]

One cannot suppress the feeling that the theories of both Cvijić and Tomasic represent generalizations and idealizations of the respective types of culture and societies with which they had identified their sympathies. It is therefore essential to remember the political situation in Serbia when Cvijić wrote as well as the political atmosphere in Croatia and Yugoslavia which existed during the 1930's when Tomasic formulated his ideas. There is little doubt, however, that further unbiased study will lead to considerable changes in the characterization and interpretation of these cultures and their significance for the earlier as well as the more recent developments in the history of the Yugoslav nations. In the opinion of this writer, this applies less to Cvijić's work, which is a product of painstaking field studies and great erudition, than

[27] Dinko Tomašić, *Društveni razvitak Hrvata*, p. 45.
[28] Dinko Tomasic, *Personality and Culture in Eastern European Politics*, p. 98.

to Tomasic's writings, behind which there is practically no field study, and which carry all the earmarks of hurry, one-sidedness, and often of political invective.

But even if one assumes that the characterization of the two peasant cultures as given by their respective interpreters would stand, it is necessary to remember that the territory under the sway of the Dinaric culture takes in most of the central portions of Yugoslavia, while the socalled Zadruga culture is limited to a small area in northern Croatia. In other areas of Yugoslavia shifts in population and long-enduring foreign political rule and cultural influences have led to the development of mixed types of rural culture showing a variety of marks. This is especially true of the fringe areas such as Slovenia, Dalmatia, Macedonia, and Vojvodina. In any case, much additional work will be required before a satisfactory "cultural" interpretation of the Yugoslav peasant societies is achieved.

In the discussions of the autochthonous peasant cultures in the South Slav lands, very little attention was given to the problems of adjustment of populations with these cultural backgrounds to the way of life in an industrial society. But the fact that these cultures have been developed exclusively as peasant cultures, and that traditionalism and attachment to land constitute basic components of the personality in such cultures, would suggest that the adaptation of such peasant societies to the mores of an industrial society is not a simple problem. As was already pointed out, the promoters of capitalist forms of economic activity in the South Slav lands prior to 1914 were primarily foreigners. This remained largely so during the interwar period. Needless to say, the increasing need to leave rural areas, owing to the growing overpopulation, forced more and more people to look for a livelihood in nonagricultural pursuits. But most of these people, as will be shown later, still tried to keep one foot in the village and to own a piece of land. Undoubtedly, the transition from agricultural to industrial occupation would have been easier and more readily accepted by the peasants if opportunities for earning in industry or urban economy generally had been more secure and wages more satisfactory. Thus the willingness and capacity of the peasants to accept the way of life of industrial workers depends greatly on the economic and social incentives favoring such transition.

EDUCATIONAL BACKWARDNESS

One of the characteristics of the peasant cultures in the South Slav lands is the great wealth and variety of folklore. This folklore

shows not only the extremely varied and rich spiritual heritage of these
peasant societies, but also it shows better than anything else the specific
ethos of these cultures and their high ethical standards. And yet in
terms of formal educational standards, e.g., the degree of literacy, the
peasant population in all South Slav lands is very much behind the
peasant populations of Central and Western Europe.

While almost the whole area of the present Yugoslav state is marked
by relative educational "backwardness," its degree varies greatly from
area to area. The degree of educational development essentially parallels the level of economic development. Generally, it can be said that
the degree of educational and economic development decreases as one
goes from the northwest and the north toward the southeast and the
south. Education as well as economic life was least advanced in those
areas in which the Ottoman rule persisted until recently. Moreover,
some of the areas which were longest under the Ottoman rule were
quite inaccessible, making their contacts with the outside world and
foreign cultures more difficult.

The spread of education, especially on the elementary level, among
both urban and rural population was considered one of the basic re-
sponsibilities of the state for many decades, but various religious and
humanitarian and political organizations helped also to advance the
cause of education.[29] Actually, the spread of formal education was exceedingly slow. According to the census of 1921, illiteracy in various
provinces of Yugoslavia was as follows:[30]

	Percent of total population above ten years of age
Macedonia	83.8
Bosnia and Herzegovina	80.5
Montenegro	67.0
Serbia	65.4
Dalmatia	49.5
Croatia-Slavonia	32.2
Vojvodina	23.3
Slovenia	8.8
Yugoslavia	51.5

[29] Ruth Trouton, *Peasant Renaissance in Yugoslavia, 1900–1950*. This study covers
the whole range of problems dealing with the Yugoslav peasant society as affected by
education.

[30] V. T. Simić, "Popular Education," *Jubilarni zbornik života i rada Srba, Hrvata
i Slovenaca 1918–1928* (Jubilee Record of Life and Work of the Serbs, Croats, and Slovenes, 1918–1928), I, 410.

The legacy of Turkish rule is best seen in the cases of Macedonia and Bosnia and Herzegovina. Needless to say, the percentage of illiterates in rural areas was much higher than in urban areas. In fact, in some rural areas it was almost 100 percent. Furthermore, the percentage of illiterates was much higher among women than among men. It is also necessary to remember that a large number of people in rural areas who were considered literate were only able to sign their name and were actually only semiliterate.

In modern times illiteracy is by far the greatest stumbling block in cultural development, and it is one of the greatest in economic development. It prevents the people from learning and profiting from the experience of others except where they can perceive directly by hearing or seeing. Illiteracy keeps people tradition-bound and prey to centuries-old superstitions and prejudices and very often makes them helpless victims of abuse and exploitation. Thus prejudice, superstition, fear of the outside, fear of new things and new modes of work and life, and often mental inertia represent the most important components of the spiritual make-up of people lacking education. The spread of education was, therefore, considered one of the basic preconditions of political, cultural, and economic advance.

Foreign rule was undoubtedly one of the basic reasons for the low level of education in most South Slav provinces prior to 1914. In areas under Turkish rule the state paid little attention to the advancement of the ruling population—the Moslems—let alone of the subject nations. In the South Slav areas under Austria-Hungary the spread of education was often considered inimical to the interests of the ruling Germans and Magyars, because in the long run the spread of education among subject nations tended to undermine both their political and their economic interests. Thus, owing to foreign rule, much of the collective energy, and the energy of the leading spirits among the South Slavs since the beginning of the nineteenth century, was spent on the struggle for sheer national survival. Any advance in political, economic, and cultural life took much longer and required much more effort than in the free countries of the West. Besides, most of the advance made was limited to the urban population. Many rural areas saw none of it.

CHANGES IN LAWS PERTAINING TO LANDOWNERSHIP
AND INHERITANCE

Among factors tending to disrupt the traditional social and economic order of the peasantry in the South Slav lands were also the new civil codes introduced in the course of the nineteenth century. Previously, family, social, and economic relationships among the Christian population in rural parts of these lands, so far as they were not regulated by feudal laws and ordinances, were regulated by customary law. This customary law represented a system of traditional legal rules, flowing from the ideas of the common people about justice and order under existing conditions. It differed somewhat from area to area. Being a living doctrine, it was handed down from generation to generation and modified under the influence of changing conditions in order to suit better the changing needs of the people. What is very interesting and indicative of the power of the customary law over the spirit of the peasants is that it continued to exist and operate, in many respects, alongside the statutory laws, although litigations which appeared before the courts had to be settled according to the letter of the statutory law.[31]

Civil law legislation of the Western European type was not introduced at the same time in all areas. Austria promulgated the new civil code in 1811 (based on Code Napoléon), which was introduced in the Slovene lands and in Dalmatia in 1816.[32] In 1853 the Austrian Civil Code was introduced in Croatia-Slavonia. In Serbia Prince Miloš ruled without any written laws from 1817 until 1838. In 1844, five years after his fall, Serbia introduced a civil code which was simply an abridged form of the Austrian code of 1811, though it showed certain changes to suit, purportedly, the Serbian conditions. In Montenegro the Code of Prince Danilo was introduced in 1855 and a General Property Code in 1888. In Bosnia and Herzegovina landownership and land tenure were regulated from the middle of the nineteenth century by the Act of 1858 and the Safer decree of 1859, while matters pertaining to the Moslem family were regulated by *Sheri* law based on the Koran. Some other matters were regulated by Turkish legislation of a civil code nature. After the Austro-Hungarian occupation of Bosnia and Herzegovina in 1878, these Turkish laws were maintained, but many new laws were promulgated, and the Austrian Civil Code was applicable in Bosnia and Herzegovina in a subsidiary fashion (i.e., if other legal regulations did not exist).[33] In Macedonia Turkish legislation applied

---

[31] Mihailo Konstantinović, "The Ideas of Valtazar Bogišić About the Customary and the Statutory Law," *Sociološki pregled*, I, 272–82, esp. 275.

[32] During French rule in the Illyrian Provinces, 1809–13, Code Napoléon was in force in these areas.

[33] For the array of laws in various Yugoslav provinces which were in existence prior to 1914—and most of them continued to be applied also during the interwar period—see the section on "The Courts and the Judiciary," in *Jubilarni zbornik života i rada Srba, Hrvata i Slovenaca, 1918–1928* (Jubilee Record of Life and Work of the Serbs, Croats, and Slovenes, 1918–1928), I, 368–83.

until its liberation in 1913, while Vojvodina was under Hungarian law.

The parts of the new codes affecting the peasantry most profoundly were those relating to the holding, division, and inheritance of farm land. The new civil codes were based on the principles of Roman law, embodying the principles of unlimited individual property and the predominant position of the father in the family and his full liberty to dispose of family property. What was most important was that these laws paid little or no attention to the legal customs, or conceptions, and thus to the needs of the peasant people. Above all, the newly introduced principle of unlimited individual ownership in farm land was directly opposed to the family collectivist principles embedded in customary laws and best exemplified in the institution of the zadruga. Many authors maintained that these individualistic laws were primarily responsible for the many calamities besetting the peasantry under the new conditions, and especially for the disintegration of the zadruga.

The collision between the philosophy of the customary laws and that of the statutory laws as introduced in the various South Slav lands became a famous issue of discussion among legal historians and theoreticians. The most successful collector and interpreter of the South Slav customary law was undoubtedly Valtazar Bogišić, who maintained that statutory laws affecting the peasants should always take into consideration their ideas, convictions, and customs.[34] What Bogišić preached he also practiced in the drafting of the already mentioned Montenegrin General Property Code of 1888. In it he succeeded in capturing the ideas and principles of a portion of the existing Montenegrin customary law and translated them into the statutory law. Another piece of legislation in which a large portion of customary law was translated into statutory law was the Croatian Law of 1889 on the zadrugas, and its amendment of 1902, but this law applied only to those peasant households which were registered as zadrugas in the land property records.

The new legal codes were, however, only one factor which intensified the profound changes in the socioeconomic life of these lands, especially after the middle of the nineteenth century. They were not original causative factors. The new legislation was bound to speed up and to complicate the transition process in which the peasantry was involved. A conscious policy of adaptation of the principles of statutory laws to the existing customary laws, as in the case of Bogišić's law of 1888 for Montenegro, would have perhaps contributed, as far as the

[34] Valtazar Bogišić, *op. cit.*, pp. 1–96.

peasantry was concerned, to a smoother and less painful transition from the old to the new patterns of economic and social life.

It should also be noted that the nascent capitalism in the South Slav lands needed a system of law that would enable free or quasi-free traffic in land and various commodities, and that would guarantee speedy enforcement of contracts. New codes were also essential for the development of various credit instruments. Some interest groups, such as the owners of large estates and the new bourgeoisie class, were also interested in abundant and cheap supply of labor, and new codes were thought of as instruments capable of speeding the transformation of the existing system of peasant property, which would free a considerable segment of the rural population for employment as wage earners. In a word, the introduction of civil law legislation according to the Western and Central European patterns was considered an essential component of social and economic progress. Whether this type of legislation was suitable for the regulation of property and inheritance matters in the rural areas of the South Slav lands and its effect on the economic conditions in these areas remained an issue of debate until the end of the interwar period.

CHAPTER 10

DISTRIBUTION OF FARMS BY SIZE AT THE TURN OF THE TWENTIETH CENTURY

THE abolition of serfdom in most South Slav lands during the nineteenth century, the large increase in population, the changes in legal rules pertaining to division and inheritance of agricultural property, and the economic differentiation in the village as a consequence of the penetration of capitalist forces into the economy of the South Slav lands, were also reflected in the size-structure of farms and in the distribution of agricultural land property. The data given below are the results of the agricultural censuses or special surveys around the turn of the century. Most of these data refer to farm units rather than to units of ownership of agricultural land. But with the exception of Vojvodina (illustrated by data for Hungary as a whole), where tenancy was widespread, and Bosnia and Herzegovina, where until 1918 feudal relationships and a special type of tenancy on *beglik* lands were in existence, the farm size-structure can also be taken as largely representing the distribution of farmland property. Actually, larger ownership units, say above 20 hectares, controlled somewhat more land than indicated by data on the size-structure of farms, because it was primarily the bigger landowners who gave part of their land in tenancy. The following data indicate great differences in the farm size and property structure in agriculture in various provinces and supply another indicator of the variety in the agricultural and social structure of these lands at that time, a variety stemming essentially from the various political and socioeconomic conditions under which these lands developed. These figures are important not only for showing the farm size and property structure around the turn of the century, but also because they represent the only basis for comparison with Yugoslav data on the distribution of farm units by size, obtained through the census of 1931. The latter data showed the farm size and property structure in Yugoslav agriculture after the great undertaking of the post-1918 agrarian reform was almost completed and the population of the whole area had risen since 1900 by approximately 22 percent.

Table 4 gives the distribution of farms by size in Croatia-Slavonia, according to the census of 1895, and shows that the agricultural prop-

TABLE 4.—DISTRIBUTION OF FARMS BY SIZE IN CROATIA-SLAVONIA, 1895*

	Farms		Area	
Size in yokes[a]	Number	Percent of total	Yokes	Percent of total
Below 1	53,886	13.24	24,374	0.52
1–5	126,289	31.00	370,630	7.95
5–10	110,999	27.24	804,805	17.26
10–20	81,657	20.05	1,128,312	24.20
20–50	30,603	7.51	859,288	18.43
50–100	2,830	0.69	184,602	3.96
100–200	550	0.13	73,733	1.58
200–500	263	0.06	84,554	1.81
500–1,000	117	0.03	85,157	1.83
Above 1,000	209	0.05	1,047,540	22.46
Total	407,403	100.00	4,662,995	100.00

* Source: Milan Ivšić, *Les problèmes agraires en Yougoslavie* (Paris, 1926), p. 133.
[a] One yoke equals 0.5755 hectares.

erty structure in Croatia-Slavonia in 1895 was marked by a dichotomy. It remained so until 1919. On the one hand, 44.24 percent of all farms were below 5 yokes and included only 8.47 percent of the land. These were the typical dwarf and small farms (see pp. 393–94). The next two categories, namely, farms from 5 to 10 and from 10 to 20 yokes, represented another 47.29 percent of the total number of farms, holding 41.46 percent of land. Thus 91.53 percent of all farms controlled slightly less than half of all land. On the other hand, 209 latifundia, located almost exclusively in Slavonia and Srijem, or .05 percent of all farm units, held 22.46 percent of all land. In between these two groups there was another 8.42 percent of farms controlling 27.61 percent of all land. The dichotomy applied not only to the size of farms but, to a large extent, also to technology applied in farming and the principles underlying the economic rationale of the small and of the large producers. In the case of dwarf and small farms, agricultural technology was on a much lower level than that on large estates, and the primary purpose of production was the provision of subsistence for the peasant family by direct production on the farm. Large estates and some of the large and medium farms employed advanced agricultural technology and produced exclusively or partly for the market in order to make a profit. Some of the large estates were managed by trained agricultural managers, and all were worked by wage labor.

Somewhat less than one-fifth of all agricultural land, that is, excluding forests, was held in 1895 by other than individual owners. Chief among these were "land associations," cities and communes, the churches, and the state. Smaller owners were the "property communes" in the former Military Frontier, fideicommissa, various foundations, and corporations.[1]

While there are no readily available data on the size-structure of farms or distribution of land property in Vojvodina without reworking the census data by counties, the data for the whole of Hungary (except Croatia-Slavonia) can be taken as indicative of the Vojvodina situation, especially if the remarks made earlier (pp. 137–38) on the situation in the southern parts of old Hungary are taken into consideration. The farm size-structure in the Hungarian agriculture, according to the census of 1895, is shown in Table 5. The dichotomy in the distribution of

TABLE 5.—DISTRIBUTION OF FARMS BY SIZE IN HUNGARY, 1895*

Size in yokes[a]	Farms		Area	
	Number	Percent of total	Hectares	Percent of total
Below 1	562,949	23.57	133,514	0.63
1–5	716,769	30.00	1,106,708	5.22
5–10	458,535	19.20	1,908,860	9.00
10–20	385,381	16.13	3,105,280	14.64
20–50	205,181	8.60	3,459,737	16.31
50–100	36,032	1.51	1,387,822	6.54
100–200	10,275	0.43	807,636	3.81
200–500	6,448	0.27	1,163,262	5.48
500–1,000	3,144	0.13	1,288,410	6.07
Above 1,000	3,768	0.16	6,848,818	32.30
Total	2,388,482	100.00	21,210,047	100.00

* Source: Hungary, *Ungarisches statistisches Jahrbuch*, New Ser., XXIII (Budapest, 1921), 69.
[a] One yoke equals 0.5755 hectares.

agricultural property characteristic of Croatia-Slavonia was even more pronounced in Hungary. On the one hand, 1,279,718 dwarf peasants, or 53.57 percent of the total, held farms up to 5 yokes, including only 5.85 percent of the land. On the other hand, 3,768 owners of latifundia, or 0.16 percent of all agricultural units, owned not less than 32.30 percent of land. Another 9,592 farms of 200 to 1,000 yokes, or 0.40 percent of the total number, owned 11.55 percent of all land. The bulk

[1] Milan Ivšić, *Les problèmes agraires en Yougoslavie*, p. 145.

of other farms was in the category between 5 and 20 yokes, but included only 23.64 percent of the farm area. It is necessary, however, to stress that, unlike Croatia-Slavonia, Hungary had a large landless peasantry, amounting in 1895 to one third of all those gainfully employed in agriculture.[2] Needless to say, all dwarf and a large portion of small peasants had to look for additional income through work for wages. According to M. M. Kosić, in 1910 in Vojvodina 38.3 percent of the total population was in the category of landless peasants.[3]

For Serbia, Dalmatia, and Carniola (Carniolan data are used as an illustration of conditions in the later province of Slovenia) only numbers of farms in the various size categories are available, without indication as to what area of agricultural land they held. While the value of these figures is considerably smaller than in the previous two cases, where the area controlled by the various size categories of farms was given, nevertheless these figures convey an idea of the distribution of agricultural property. Table 6 shows the distribution of farms in

TABLE 6.—DISTRIBUTION OF FARMS BY SIZE IN SERBIA, 1897*

Size in hectares	Number	Percent of total
Rural households without land	34,952	11.34
Up to 1	19,173	6.22
1–2.................................	31,368	10.18
2–5.................................	93,627	30.39
5–20................................	117,939	38.29
20–50	10,277	3.33
50–100	710	0.23
100–200	68	0.02
Above 200	6	0.00
Total	308,120	100.00

* Source: Nikola Konstandinović, *Seljačko gazdinstvo u Jugoslaviji* (Peasant Farming in Yugoslavia) (Belgrade, 1939), pp. 18–19.

Serbia in 1897. In addition to 308,120 rural households, of which 11.3 percent did not possess any land, there were 46,823 households in towns and cities, of which not less than 20,253, or 43 percent, owned farms (not taken into account in this table). While the Serbian agri-

[2] Julius von Vargha, *Die wirtschaftlichen und kulturellen Verhältnisse Ungarns*, p. 40.
[3] Mirko M. Kosić, *Osnovi ekonomne politike* (Principles of Economic Policy), p. 218.

cultural property structure was also loaded with dwarf farms, the category of farms between 5 and 20 hectares, or the medium peasant farms, was still strong, representing 38.29 percent of the total number. In Croatia-Slavonia the roughly comparable categories (10–20 and 20–50 yokes) represented only 27.56 percent of the total number. Moreover, in Serbia there were no latifundia, and thus its agricultural property structure was not characterized by the dichotomy observed in Croatia-Slavonia and especially in Hungary (Vojvodina). The reason for that lay in the nature of the Serbian agrarian reforms of the first half of the nineteenth century and, to some extent, in the protective measures of the state with regard to peasant property. Larger farms depended on hired labor, but there was practically no difference in the agricultural technology employed on the small and on the large farms. The difficult position of the small peasants in Serbia was indicated partly by the fact that 66,756 farms, or 27.6 percent of all peasant households with land, had no draft animals.[4]

The distribution of farms by size in Dalmatia and Carniola, according to the census of 1902, is indicated in Table 7. The 83,455

TABLE 7.—DISTRIBUTION OF FARMS BY SIZE IN DALMATIA AND CARNIOLA, 1902*

Size in hectares	Dalmatia		Carniola	
	Number	Percent of total	Number	Percent of total
Below 0.5	15,553	18.63	9,361	12.40
0.5–1	15,378	18.43	6,307	8.36
1–2	20,411	24.48	8,166	10.82
2–5	21,564	25.86	14,663	19.43
5–10	7,243	8.67	14,921	19.77
10–20	2,243	2.68	14,590	19.33
20–50	762	0.91	6,409	8.49
50–100	147	0.17	728	0.96
Above 100	154	0.17	332	0.44
Total	83,455	100.00	75,477	100.00

* Source: Milan Ivšić, *Les problèmes agraires en Yougoslavie* (Paris, 1926), p. 282.

farms in Dalmatia in 1902 held 1,283,494 hectares of land, of which, however, only 266,437 hectares were arable land, vineyards, meadows, and gardens. The remainder of land was pasture and forest. The farms of over 100 hectares included only 7,543 hectares of agricultural land

[4] Nikola Konstandinović, *Seljačko gazdinstvo u Jugoslaviji* (Peasant Farming in Yugoslavia), p. 19.

proper; 138,000 hectares of their land consisted of pastures and forests.[5] The 75,477 farms in Carniola included 995,521 hectares of land, of which 337,733 hectares were arable land and meadows, the remainder being pastures, forests, and marshes. The 332 large farms of over 100 hectares held only 10,760 hectares of arable land and meadows but over one-fourth of all pastures and almost one-third of all forests.[6]

The data on the number and size of farm units in Bosnia and Herzegovina have been obtained from a special survey of 1906, and they are much less reliable than data for other areas, which were obtained by regular censuses. Furthermore, since in Bosnia and Herzegovina serfdom was still in existence, the survey of 1906, as shown in Table 8,

TABLE 8.—FARMS OF FREE PEASANTS AND OF SERFS IN BOSNIA AND HERZEGOVINA BY SIZE, 1906*

Size in hectares	Farms of free peasants		Farms of serfs	
	Number	Percent of total	Number	Percent of total
Below 2	96,936	51.32	19,281	19.96
2–5	48,138	25.48	27,175	28.13
5–10	26,019	13.78	27,430	28.39
Above 10	17,790	9.42	22,723	23.52
Total	188,883	100.00	96,609	100.00

* Source: Otto von Frangeš, *Die sozialökonomische Struktur der jugoslawischen Landwirtschaft* (Berlin, 1937), p. 149.

separated the farms held by free peasants from those held by serfs. There were, however, some farm units which were held by landlords who had no serfs and some which were held by peasants who were partly free, partly serf. The farms belonging to free peasants and to serfs represented, however, the bulk of all farm units. It is interesting to note that the farms of the serfs were on the average considerably larger than those of the free peasants. But one should not forget that the serfs delivered approximately one-third of their gross production to the landlords.

The census of 1910 in Bosnia and Herzegovina supplies no information on the distribution of farms by size, but it does supply data on the social position of various segments of agricultural population and their religious affiliation. According to that census, in 1910 there were

[5] Milan Ivšić, *op. cit.*, p. 283.
[6] *Ibid.*, p. 163.

10,463 landlords who had serfs or tenants and 4,279 landlords without serfs. Of the former, 91 percent were Moslem agas and begs. There were 136,854 families of free peasants, 79,701 of serfs, and 31,416 part-serf, part-free families, of whom 16,963 held mostly land subject to serf obligations.[7] Of all free peasant families 56.6 percent were Moslems, while roughly three fourths of the serfs and a little over one half of the part-serfs belonged to the Serbian Eastern Orthodox Church. Somewhat more than one fifth of all serfs and about one third of the part-serfs were Roman Catholics, and the remainder were Moslems.

For Macedonia no data on the size-structure of farms or agricultural property are available for the period before 1914. But from our discussion of the land-tenure system in that area, we know that there were a large number of dwarf and small farms, especially in the mountainous areas, and a considerable number of *čiftliks*, located mostly in the plains. In Montenegro *čiftliks* were also present in areas incorporated in 1913. In other areas the dwarf farm was the rule.

The above data indicate clearly that in various South Slav lands great differences in the distribution of farms by size and in the agricultural property structure existed before 1914. Serbia was the only area where there were no large estates and no other survivals of the former feudal order. Data for all areas without exception show, however, that by the turn of the century the excessive subdivision of agricultural property had progressed to a dangerous degree, and that, as a consequence, widespread pauperization and proletarization of the village had taken place. Moreover, there was a strong trend toward further subdivision of agricultural property under the influence of growing population and many other forces. These are important points to remember, because some writers on Yugoslav agriculture in the interwar period uncritically accuse the post-1918 agrarian reform of having been responsible for the predominance of dwarf and small farms in Yugoslav agriculture. In fact, that reform only intensified an already existing and progressing situation. Furthermore, successive divisions of peasant property had already resulted by the turn of the century in far-reaching fragmentation or splitting of individual farms into a great number of parcels, a fact which greatly impeded the rational utilization of the land which a family owned. The trend of further excessive subdivision of agricultural property and of fragmentation of individual farms continued unabated during the interwar period.

[7] Karl Grünberg, *Die Agrarverfassung und das Grundentlastungsproblem in Bosnien und der Herzegowina*, pp. 117–19.

CHAPTER 11

CONCLUDING REMARKS ON THE
DEVELOPMENTS DURING THE CENTURY PRECEDING
WORLD WAR I

THE preceding five chapters have depicted in a brief manner the transformations in the political, social, and economic life which took place in the South Slav lands during the century preceding World War I. These transformations, and the forces responsible for them, can be summarized as follows:

During that century the political framework within which the South Slav nations developed changed completely under the influence of the forces of nationalism and other political trends in Europe and the world. Throughout that period there developed a growing conflict between the forces of rising South Slav nationalism, which demanded national liberation and later also unification of all South Slavs, and the Ottoman and Habsburg empires, culminating in the disintegration of both empires and establishment of a whole series of states, including Yugoslavia, on their ruins. The rise of nationalism was associated with the ideas of political democracy and socioeconomic reform, primarily the liquidation of feudal and quasi-feudal forms, of which the two multinational empires were strong citadels until their very end. The struggle of the South Slavs during the nineteenth century was thus stimulated by both political and socioeconomic forces which—as the history of the last two centuries shows—have proved irresistible in their advance. The formation of the new Yugoslav state in 1918, which represented the final consummation of the Yugoslav nationalist drive, was thus accomplished on the ruins of the two multinational empires which for centuries controlled Southeastern Europe and oppressed politically, socially, and economically all South Slav nations.

The liquidation of the feudal order in a formal sense took place in most South Slav areas in the 1830's and in 1848. In the South Slav areas within the Habsburg Empire, where feudalism was formally abolished in 1848, certain quasi-feudal forms remained extant until 1918. In Bosnia and Herzegovina and in Macedonia, the latter under the Ottoman Empire until 1913, feudal forms were in force until 1918.

210

Thus the removal of feudal and quasi-feudal forms took almost a whole century. Meanwhile the nature of the state in all South Slav areas changed radically. Either by replacing feudal forms, or on the basis of tribal formations, as in Montenegro, there developed a centrally organized, bureaucratically administered state. The main representative of the new state power, the bureaucracy, took, from the point of view of the peasants, the place that formerly was held by the feudal lords. Except for insuring peace and order, and providing for some education and communications, the new state did very little for the peasant, while in terms of his obligation in taxes, in military service, and to a certain extent in forced labor, it represented a heavy burden.

The economic life in these areas changed gradually from a subsistence type of economy, based on the division of labor either within the rural family or within the large feudal estate and producing relatively little for the market, to a system producing wholly or partially for the market. While still remaining essentially the producer for the direct satisfaction of the needs within the household, the peasant family became attached to the growing market economy and thus subject to its all-pervading dynamics. As far as large agricultural enterprises continued to exist, many of them became capitalist enterprises, following in their production patterns the requirements of the market. This shift from the subsistence to the more market-orientated economy was by far the most important structural change which took place in the economy of these lands during the century preceding World War I. A large proportion of the peasants continued to produce with the methods of the Middle Ages, and the yield in agriculture remained low. The increase in rural population worsened the land-population ratio to a point creating a strong hunger for land and agricultural overpopulation in many areas. The declining amount of arable land, both actual and potential, per peasant household, together with primitive techniques of production, proved insufficient to assure the peasants a decent plane of living. In spite of the fact that after the liquidation of serfdom the peasant obtained his land in full ownership, he remained poor, ignorant, and dissatisfied. Moreover, there was a tendency for the land to slip out of his hands.

The penetration of capitalist economic forms into the South Slav lands, marked by the use of money and credit as agents of everyday life, an increased production for the market, and the profit motive, led to the breakdown of both the feudal system and the closed village economy based on the division of labor within the peasant family, primarily the joint family or zadruga. Already in the eighteenth century, under the blanket of the decaying feudal order, a new process of differentiation with regard to wealth and income in agriculture was beginning to take shape as a result of the somewhat larger development of a money and market economy. After the liquidation of serfdom in most Yugoslav lands during the second quarter of the past century, this process of class and property differentiation—a process closely associated with the development of capitalism—continued, but with greater force. It was reinforced by many other factors, such as the development of communications, introduction of modern technology by some agricultural producers, and inclusion of the South Slav lands in the nexus of world economy. In areas where feudalism, albeit modified, continued to exist until 1918, as in Bosnia and Herzegovina and in Macedonia, capitalist economic forms grew alongside the feudal forms and gave a new imprint to the economic, social, and political patterns of these areas. This process of economic differentiation and, in consequence, the shifting of power relationships have continued up to the present time and have colored all social developments in the South Slav lands during the past 150 years.

As an exceedingly dynamic and revolutionary economic system, capitalism conquered and transformed the traditional economic order, and in turn greatly enlarged the urban sector of the economy in the South Slav lands. Still, one should remember that the advance of capitalism in these lands, especially in areas south of the Sava-Danube rivers, was rather slow and that all these areas have remained up to the present essentially areas of peasant subsistence agriculture. But capitalism did actually penetrate into the old patriarchal economic and social system and dissolved its psychological, social, and economic fabric. Capitalism subjected the entire economy to its exploitative sway but failed to create sufficient employment opportunities outside of agriculture to absorb the increased labor power in the economy, especially in agriculture. The great shortcoming of capitalist development in the South Slav lands, as in many other underdeveloped areas, was in the fact that it was not strong and varied enough to provide employment for the increasing population and that the bulk of population which became redundant in agriculture was forced to remain on the land, thus worsening the land-population ratio. Thus, the great mass of population of the rural areas derived little benefit from the development of the new economic system. This is, of course, not to say that capitalism was not an advance over the old feudal and zadruga systems, which had outlived their usefulness. Capitalism in the South Slav lands never attained complete fruition. It was not an economic system which grew out of the internal sources of the economy, but rather, it was the appendage of Central and Western European capitalism and it was introduced into the South Slav lands primarily by foreigners. Whether its representatives were foreigners or nationals, capitalism in the South Slav areas remained essentially rapacious and exploitative rather than creative, a corrupting crust rather than a well-developed economic system. And while it exploited the peasant masses and the nascent labor class through the market and credit mechanisms, its typical forms of enterprises in production and service industries remained so limited that only small numbers of peasants could switch either into the class of the bourgeoisie or that of the industrial workers. Capitalism destroyed the social and economic system that the peasantry had developed through a centuries-old process of adaptation, without replacing it with another which would have enabled the peasantry to improve its economic lot. The great mass of the peasant population in these lands remained hanging between the old system, which was destroyed or made impotent, and the new system, which was unable to meet its needs, especially in furnishing it with adequate employment opportunities. Various measures intended to protect the peasants from the untoward influences of the market and money economy proved of no avail as the advance of the new economic and social forces had the nature of an inevitable necessity once the economies of the South Slav lands were included in the framework of European capitalism.

The development of a market economy, the inroads of money and credit, and the replacement of former customary law with regard to collective family ownership and inheritance of peasant property by statutory laws conceived in the spirit of individual, unlimited private property concepts of Roman law had also profound influences on the ownership relations of land. The above factors led to the individualization of the peasant mind, to the disappearance of the zadruga, to assessment of all values in money, to a tendency to capital accumulation in the form of money. The fast-growing agricultural overpopulation induced large migration overseas as long as the outlets for large-scale emigration were open, namely, until World War I. Following all this development on the land was a growing differentiation in peasant property whereby more and more peasants were pushed into the category of dwarf peasants or became altogether landless. Thus pauperization and proletarization of the village—a great issue in the heated debates on the zadruga during the second half of the nineteenth century—materialized and continued unabated until the end of World War II, when the Yugoslav agriculture and peasantry entered a new phase.

The development of transportation, especially of railroads, roads, and shipping, brought about not only greater internal economic integration, but also enabled agriculture and the raw materials-producing industries of these lands to export a larger quantity and a greater variety of their products to European markets, thus enmeshing the economy of these lands in the nexus of world economy. Especially important was the fact that agriculture in the South Slav lands came into direct competition on European markets with the more cheaply produced commodities of extra-European areas. This uneven competitive struggle which began in the 1870's continued until World War I and throughout the entire interwar period.

As in most other countries, a general urge for "progress" in the cultural, political, and economic fields was at work in the South Slav lands. The underlying philosophy of this urge for progress was in the uplifting of these nations from the social and economic conditions of the Middle Ages into modern times. But the difference to be made up was tremendous, and since the industrial countries kept advancing, and at a faster rate, the difference became greater as time went on. All work toward progress had to contend with strong traditions, utter poverty, great ignorance, and, above all, with foreign and, to a lesser extent, domestic political and economic vested interests. Moreover, many measures undertaken with good intentions were poorly prepared, were often ill-fitted to actual conditions, and resulted in shaking the will of the peasants to partake of progress as brought to them by the state or the city. The fact was that under the conditions in which the peasantry lived it could not afford any risky experiments. Failure meant starvation. Much of this so-called progress, actually most of it, was buried in various laws, regulations, plans, and good wishes rather than translated into practical reality. No doubt largely responsible for this failure was the nature of the political framework under which most of the South Slav nations lived, i.e., foreign rule.

The history of the South Slavs since the beginning of the nineteenth century was thus marked by profound convulsions in their political, social, and economic life. At the beginning of the nineteenth century these nations entered upon an age of revolution, breaking down gradually the old regime in all its aspects. In fact, this age of revolution is still continuing, recently at a much increased rate. The process as a whole was marked by a relentless drive for national liberation and, later, national unification, for the introduction of democratic principles and practices in government, for the limitation of the power of bureaucracy, and for the solution of the agrarian question as the foremost social and economic problem of the overwhelming portion of the people. As time advanced, some problems were solved, but new ones arose or the old ones reappeared, and, in general, the solution of the political and especially the socioeconomic issues became more and more complicated.

On the eve of World War I a considerable portion of the intelligentsia in the South Slav nations was in a revolutionary frame of mind. In some areas, e.g., in Bosnia and Herzegovina where serfdom was still in existence, a large portion of the peasantry was also ripe for revolution. Generally speaking, however, it was World War I which woke the great mass of peasantry in all areas of Austria-Hungary and in other parts of Eastern and Southeastern Europe. Two factors characterized the situation in years immediately preceding World War I: the national issue—that of national liberation and unification of all South Slav peoples into one state—and the issue of agrarian reform in those areas in which feudal and quasi-feudal forms still persisted. At the bottom of peasant dissatisfaction in all South Slav areas was the worsening land-population ratio and thus the growing agricultural overpopulation and the need of the peasantry to seek employment outside of agriculture, partly at home, partly abroad. World War I contributed mightily to the speeding up of the revolutionary process, pushing both the political and the socioeconomic issues to a climax and, at least, to a partial solution. Of course, the formation of the new state of Yugoslavia in 1918 did not bring about a complete solution of the national problem, it did not mean the establishment and maintenance of a democratic form of government, it did not mean a reduction but rather an increase in the power of bureaucracy; and while serfdom and serfdom-like institutions were eliminated in all areas of the country, this did not mean the achievement of a satisfactory plane of living for the great mass of people. And, what was worse, prospects for an improvement in the general conditions of the peasantry continued to be dim. Thus, revolutionary ferment in the body politic persisted. In this respect, conditions in Yugoslavia were akin to conditions in the great majority of other countries of predominantly peasant subsistence farming.

Finally, it should be pointed out that certain trends which characterized the conditions of Yugoslav agriculture and peasantry during the interwar period were already quite definite and pronounced in the years before World War I. Among them were the trend of a rapidly rising population, the trend toward enlargement of the sector of the market and money economy, together with increased need of the village economy for credit, the trend toward further subdivision of peasant property, and, finally, the closely related trend toward increased pauperization and proletarization of the peasantry. In fact, all these trends became stronger during the interwar period. Another trend which prevailed during the 30 years prior to World War I, the growing emigration overseas, came to an end in 1914.

This long review of the historical background of the various South Slav provinces and of the general trends of their political and socio-economic development since the beginning of the nineteenth century was necessary to set the stage for the detailed treatment of the course of events during World War I and especially during the interwar period in Yugoslavia. Without this background the developments between 1914 and 1941 could not be viewed in proper perspective.

CHAPTER 12

WORLD WAR I AND ITS EFFECTS ON THE PEASANTRY AND AGRICULTURE OF THE SOUTH SLAV LANDS

BESIDES the factors reaching far into the past, such as varied political developments, cultural differentiation and varied levels of cultural advance, uneven economic development, varied property relationships, and differences in agricultural technology, the peasantry and agriculture of Yugoslavia during the interwar period were also greatly affected by World War I and its consequences. The basic fact, of course, was that the new Yugoslav state was the product of that war and that after 1918 the peoples of the South Slav lands lived within a totally changed political and economic framework. From 1918 on agriculture and peasantry of Yugoslavia developed, in principle, under one system of political and legal institutions, under one system of economic policy, and, in comparison with pre-1918 days, with greatly changed conditions in regard to the internal market, foreign markets, taxation, credit institutions, and emigration. In this chapter, however, we are interested only in briefly describing the course of that war and its effects on the population, agriculture, and economy of the various South Slav lands which in 1918 were consolidated into the new state of Yugoslavia.[1]

[1] This particular period in the history of the South Slav peoples is not satisfactorily covered either in the Yugoslav or in the non-Yugoslav literature. This is especially true in regard to the social and economic developments. The study by Dragolioub Yovanovitch, *Les effets économiques et sociaux de la guerre en Serbie*, in the Carnegie Endowment for International Peace series, Economic and Social History of World War, refers exclusively to Serbia and leaves much to be desired. The Austro-Hugarian military administration of Serbia and Montenegro during World War I after their occupation is described in considerable detail in the same series by General Hugo Kerchnawe *et al.*, *Die Militärverwaltung in den von den österreichisch-ungarischen Truppen besetzten Gebieten*, pp. 53–282. General Kerchnawe pictures the record of the Austro-Hungarian military government in Serbia and Montenegro in a very favorable light, but it should not be forgotten that he was a leading member of that administration. Various other studies in the same series, such as Alexander Popovics, *Das Geldwesen im Kriege*, and Gustav Gratz and Richard Schüller, *Der wirtschaftliche Zusammenbruch Österreich-Ungarns*,

DEVELOPMENTS LEADING TO THE BIRTH OF YUGOSLAVIA

But first a brief synopsis of political and military developments during World War I in so far as they pertain directly to the South Slav lands. As is very well known, the spark which ignited World War I was the assassination of the Archduke Francis Ferdinand, the heir to the Habsburg throne, in Sarajevo on June 28, 1914, by Bosnian revolutionary youths. As the Austro-Hungarian government took the position that the assassination was planned in Serbia under the eyes of the Serbian government, it made that government morally responsible for the act and presented it with an ultimatum containing conditions which the Serbian government considered to be infringements of its national sovereignty. Since Serbia refused to accept all the conditions of the ultimatum, an Austro-Hungarian declaration of war against Serbia followed immediately. Within four weeks this act led to a general European and later to a world-wide military conflagration.

It is generally agreed that the basic cause for the outbreak of World War I was not the assassination at Sarajevo but rather the European system of conflicting alliance blocs which automatically transformed every diplomatic dispute into a major crisis. Various areas and factors had created disputes and crises during these years, including the Alsace-Lorraine question, the disposition of Morocco, the Anglo-German naval rivalry, and the general imperialist rivalry throughout the colonial world. To this list should be added the collision between Habsburg imperial interests and South Slavic national aspirations.[2]

By 1914 a large portion of the intelligentsia in all South Slav nations was in a strong nationalistic revolutionary mood. In areas in which serfdom still persisted, as in Bosnia and Herzegovina, this nationalistic revolutionary trend was closely interwoven with social revolutionary trends, and here it had a much broader basis. The idea of liberation and unification of all South Slavs received a strong push after the Balkan Wars of 1912 and 1913, in which the Balkan nations proved victorious and liberated Macedonia and the Sandjak of Novi Pazar after more than 500 years of Ottoman rule. The successes of Serbia and

---

supply a great deal of information pertaining to the Dual Monarchy as a whole. But specific information relating to the South Slav lands of the Monarchy is hard to cull from these sources.

  [2] For the discussion of the causes of World War I dealing specifically with the South Slav contribution, see Bernadotte E. Schmitt, "Serbia, Yugoslavia, and the Habsburg Empire," in Robert J. Kerner (ed.), *Yugoslavia*, pp. 41–65; Bernadotte E. Schmitt, *The Coming of the War 1914*; R. W. Seton-Watson, *Sarajevo—A Study in the Origins of the Great War*; Hermann Wendel, *Der Kampf der Südslawen um Freiheit und Einheit*; Leo Pfeffer, *Istraga u sarajevskom atentatu* (The Investigation of the Sarajevo Assassination).

Montenegro in these wars, and the essentially democratic regime which existed in Serbia after 1903, made a unification with Serbia more attractive to the South Slavs of the Dual Monarchy. This, of course, collided directly with the imperial interests and, in fact, endangered the very survival of Austria-Hungary. Hence the severity of the Austro-Hungarian ultimatum after the assassination in Sarajevo, and also the immediate declaration of war against Serbia when the ultimatum was not accepted unconditionally.

The first proclamation of the Serbian commander in chief, Regent Alexander, and the Serbian government to the people after the declaration of war by Austria-Hungary ended with the impassioned call: "Serbs, defend with all your might your homes and the Serbian people."[3] However, soon thereafter, on December 7, 1914, the Serbian government in an official declaration stated the following as the Serbian objective of war:

Convinced of the determination of the whole Serbian people to persevere in the holy struggle for the defense of their sacred homes and their liberty, the government of the Kingdom considers as its foremost and, in these fateful moments, its only task to see through to the successful conclusion this great struggle, which from the moment it started became at the same time the struggle for the liberation and unification of all our subjugated brothers, Serbs, Croats, and Slovenes.[4]

This statement was soon followed by declarations of the newly organized Yugoslav political exiles from Austria-Hungary residing in Allied countries, which proclaimed the destruction of Austria-Hungary and the creation of a unified Yugoslav state as the objective of the war. This common aim of the Serbian government and the Yugoslav political exiles became formalized in the so-called Corfu Declaration of July 20, 1917, signed by the representatives of the Serbian government and of the Yugoslav Committee of London, which represented the Yugoslav political exiles from Austria-Hungary.[5] The representatives of other subjugated nationalities of Austria-Hungary, especially the Czechs and the Slovaks, also organized in Allied countries with the aim of helping the war effort of the Allies and attaining full liberation of their nations after the war. Thus, from the beginning of the war not only the victory over, but the total destruction of, the Habsburg Empire was made an

---

[3] Ferdo Šišić, *Dokumenti o postanku Kraljevine Srba, Hrvata i Slovenaca, 1914–1919* (Documents on the Establishment of the Kingdom of the Serbs, Croats, and Slovenes, 1914–1919), p. 3; quoted hereafter as Šišić, *Dokumenti.*

[4] *Ibid.,* p. 10.

[5] *Ibid.,* pp. 96–99. For the activity of the Yugoslav Committee see Milada Paulová, *Jugoslavenski Odbor* (The Yugoslav Committee) ; P. D. Ostović, *The Truth About Yugoslavia,* pp. 54–62.

objective of war not only of Serbia and Montenegro but of a well-organized and ably led group of political exiles from Austria-Hungary. These organized political exiles, especially the Czechoslovaks, though meeting with great obstacles in the beginning, contributed materially in persuading the Allies and the United States that the dissolution of the Habsburg Empire and the self-determination of its nationalities were necessary. In the closing stages of World War I these objectives became declared war aims of the Allied and associated powers.[6]

On the other hand, internal conditions within Austria-Hungary were developing from bad to worse under the stress of war. The co-operation between the two halves of the Empire, Austria and Hungary, was deteriorating, though in war it was more necessary than ever,[7] the morale of the troops was poor, and large-scale desertions of the soldiers of Slavic nationalities in the Austro-Hungarian army on the Russian front continued until the end of hostilities on that front. The internal political fabric of the Empire was in a state of disintegration. And economic and financial exhaustion caused by the war helped to push the state closer and closer to disaster. Military reverses, domestic political disintegration and dissatisfaction, and economic exhaustion induced Emperor Charles early in 1918 to offer far-reaching political concessions to various nationalities and to sue for a separate peace. But it was much too late. There was nothing more to keep the Habsburg Empire together and the old "prison of nations" simply crumbled to pieces in the closing weeks of World War I.

THE TOLL IN BLOOD

But this ignominious end was preceded by more than four years of struggle during which the Habsburg Empire and its allies, Germany and Bulgaria, were for almost three years in full control as occupying powers of the whole Serbian and Montenegrin territory. World War I cost Serbia in blood, suffering, and wealth relatively more than any other country participating in that first world-wide industrialized slaughter.

In the second decade of this century Serbia actually fought three different wars. Serbia and its allies—Montenegro, Greece, and Bul-

---

[6] Malbone W. Graham, Jr., *New Governments of Central Europe*, pp. 273–76, 339–45.

[7] For the political relationships between Austria and Hungary in these days see Friedrich F. G. Kleinwaechter, *Der Untergang der österreichisch-ungarischen Monarchie*, pp. 65–99, 218–84, and for the economic developments see Gustav Gratz and Richard Schüller, *op. cit., passim.* For the lack of co-operation between Austria and Hungary during World War I in regard to the vital issue of food supply, see *ibid.*, pp. 225–307.

garia—fought first in the First Balkan War against the Ottoman Empire, which ended the Turkish rule in the Balkans except for a small but politically and strategically important area of the Straits. With this the centuries-old dream of all Christian peoples of the Balkans was fulfilled. Immediately upon the conclusion of this war, the so-called Second Balkan War broke out between Bulgaria, on the one hand, and Serbia and Greece, on the other, over the division of spoils in Macedonia. The Serbian and Greek armies were victorious. These two wars brought Serbia great gains in territory and population. Serbia's territory was enlarged by about 39,500 square kilometers, or 79 percent. Its population was increased by about 1,660,000, or 55 percent. During the Balkan Wars Serbia mobilized 402,000 men out of an estimated population, at the end of 1912, of approximately 3 million.[8] Its casualties in these two wars were estimated at 12,000 to 13,000 killed, approximately 18,000 dead of wounds and disease, and about 48,000 wounded.[9] In addition to these losses in manpower, the two Balkan wars cost Serbia the bulk of its military supplies (this was badly felt during World War I). Agricultural production of the country suffered substantially because of the draft of manpower and of livestock (Serbia's artillery and supply columns were almost exclusively oxen-drawn). Exports were reduced, taxes were increased, and, finally, the war resulted in the increase of the foreign public debt by about 40 percent.

The losses in life and wealth suffered by Serbia during the Balkan Wars were, however, almost insignificant in comparison with its losses during World War I. From the Serbian point of view World War I could be divided into five periods: (1) from July 1914 until December 1914, a period of Austrian invasion and successful Serbian counteroffensives which cleared the Serbian territory of the invading troops; (2) from December 1914 until October 1915, a period of lull in military operations but in which the Serbian army and people were exposed to an even worse enemy, the great typhus epidemic; (3) the period of the combined Austro-German-Bulgarian offensive in October and November 1915 which overran the whole of the Serbian territory; (4) the withdrawal of the remnants (about 20 percent of the total) of the Serbian forces through Albania and Montenegro to the Adriatic seacoast and their evacuation to Corfu and other Greek islands and later transfer to the Salonika front;[10] and (5) the final phase including

---

[8] Djurdje Jelenić, *Nova Srbija i Jugoslavija* (New Serbia and Yugoslavia), p. 290.

[9] Carnegie Endowment for International Peace, *Enquête dans les Balkans*, pp. 236, 246.

[10] The story of the first four phases, but especially of the dreadful Serbian retreat

the break-through of the Serbian[11] and Allied armies on the Salonika
front and the liberation of Serbia and Montenegro, and the taking over
of the South Slav areas of Austria-Hungary, where the Austro-Hungarian
rule was already broken and a new state, the State of the Slovenes,
Croats, and Serbs (that is, South Slavs who were living within the Habsburg Empire), was already proclaimed.

Serbia entered World War I with an estimated population of 3,020,-
000 in the pre-1912 area and a population of about 1,660,000 in the
areas acquired in 1913 in Macedonia and the Sandjak of Novi Pazar.
On the whole, mobilization was much more complete in the old than in
the newly acquired areas and affected practically all men capable of
carrying a gun. Before the retreat through Albania at the end of 1915,
Serbia mobilized an estimated 707,000 men. According to one of the
best comparative studies on the direct and indirect losses of life
during World War I, Serbia's and Montenegro's[12] losses in armed forces
were estimated at 300,000. Of these, Serbian losses were 275,000
or close to 40 percent of all mobilized men, and Montenegrin losses
approximately 25,000.[13] Thus, Serbian losses in armed forces were
relatively two and a half times as high as those of France, three times
as high as those of Great Britain and Italy, and four times as high as
those of Belgium.[14] All Serbian official and private estimates are considerably higher than those of Hersch.[15]

This loss of life among Serbian armed forces during World War I
was, however, only one part of the frightful loss of life suffered by the
population as a whole. Practically throughout the whole war Serbia
was ravaged by epidemics of typhus, typhoid fever, relapsing fever,
and other contagious diseases. But the typhus epidemic of 1915 was

through Albania to the sea is told in John C. Adams, *Flight in Winter*. See also Dragolioub Yovanovitch, *op. cit.*, pp. 27–56.

[11] The Serbian troops on the Salonika front were joined by approximately 25,000
volunteers recruited partly from the former Austro-Hungarian soldiers (South Slavs)
taken prisoner by Russia and partly from South Slav emigrants to the United States and
other countries. All these volunteers were promised free land after the liberation of the
homeland and the creation of the new state of Yugoslavia. Stanoje Stanojević (ed.),
Narodna enciklopedija srpsko-hrvatsko-slovenačka (National Encyclopedia of the Serbs,
Croats, and Slovenes), I, 610–11; P. D. Ostović, *op. cit.*, pp. 62–68.

[12] Montenegro was fully subdued and occupied by the Austro-Hungarian troops in
March 1916.

[13] L. Hersch, "La mortalité causée par la guerre mondiale," Part I, *Metron*, V, No. 1,
89–133; Part II, *Metron*, VII, No. 1, 3–82. In Part I, p. 106, Hersch estimated the losses
of Serbia and Montenegro at 325,000, but in Part II, p. 76, he reduced his estimate for
the two countries to 300,000.

[14] *Ibid.*, V, No.1, 106–7.

[15] Dragolioub Yovanovitch, *op. cit.*, pp. 302–6.

the great killer, and during the six months before it was checked, more than 150,000 deaths were registered.[16] Owing to the ravages of disease, as well as to other causes connected with the war and occupation, an even greater number of deaths occurred among the civilian population than was estimated for the armed forces. Summing up his findings with regard to the indirect losses of life in Serbia and Montenegro during World War I, L. Hersch said: "The number of deaths caused indirectly by World War I in the two Balkan kingdoms was thus in round numbers 450,000, of which 195,000 were males and 255,000 females."[17] Thus, according to this neutral source, the loss of life caused directly and indirectly by World War I in Serbia and Montenegro was between 750,000 and 800,000.

The loss of life during World War I in those South Slav areas which until 1918 formed a part of the Habsburg Empire was relatively much smaller than that of Serbia, but still very heavy. The Dual Monarchy entered World War I with a population of about 53 million and those South Slav areas which in 1918 were included in the new state of Yugoslavia with a population of slightly over 8 million, or about 15.4 percent of the total. The total number of mobilized manpower of the Dual Monarchy was estimated at about 8 million men and its total losses 1,100,000 to 1,200,000 men, of whom about 60 percent were killed and 40 percent died of wounds and disease.[18] If it is assumed that both the draft and the losses of the South Slav areas were proportionate to their population, their contribution to the total mobilized manpower of the Dual Monarchy was about 1,230,000 men and the number of lost men in the neighborhood of 150,000.

While epidemics raged also among the civilian population in various areas of the Habsburg Monarchy and the general death rate had

---

[16] According to an eyewitness, "The epidemic of typhus which occurred in Serbia in 1915 was one of the most severe which the world has known in modern times. It was particularly characterized not only by its magnitude, but by its high virulence and high mortality. During the height of the epidemic the number of new fever cases entering the military hospitals alone reached as high as 2,500 per day, and the number of reported cases among the civilian population was approximately three times this number. How many more unreported cases actually occurred, one will never know. The mortality during the epidemic varied at different periods in different localities between 30 and 60 per cent, and in complicated cases sometimes reached 70 per cent. Over 150,000 deaths occurred within six months before the epidemic could be suppressed. Coincident with the epidemic of typhus there occurred an epidemic of relapsing fever, and there was present much typhoid fever." Dr. Richard P. Strong, "The Anti-Typhus Campaign in 1915 in Serbia Considered in Connexion with the Present Typhus Epidemic in Poland," *International Journal of Public Health*, I, No. 1, 7.

[17] L. Hersch, *op. cit.*, VII, No. 1, 76.

[18] Gustav Gratz and Richard Schüller, *op. cit.*, pp. 149–64.

increased during the war, we have no data on the number of deaths caused indirectly by World War I either for the Monarchy as a whole or for the South Slav areas which until 1918 formed parts of it (see, however, footnote *d*, Table 9).

But in addition to the killed and missing in World War I and the deaths caused indirectly by that war, there was another great loss in population which has to be taken into account, namely, the loss of potential births which were prevented because of the separation of sexes and the much reduced rate of marriage during the war years. There is, of course, a great economic difference between the actual loss in population due to death from whatever causes originating in war and the loss of potential births as a result of war, though they affect the size of the population at the end of the period under consideration in the same fashion. In the first case, the greatest number of deaths occurs among men in the best productive age, though increased death rate among the civilians due to war affects primarily the children and the old. These losses represent actual or potential labor power on which the community has already expended resources. In the loss of potential births no such cost is involved.

Assuming that the rates of population growth would have been the same during the second as they had been during the first decade of this century, the total loss in population of the South Slav lands as a consequence of World War I, including the loss of potential births, can be obtained by comparing the potential population which would have been reached in 1920 with the actual population found in various provinces by the census of population of January 31, 1921. It should not be forgotten, however, that this census took place more than two years after the end of World War I and that, in addition to a heavy birth rate in 1919 and especially in 1920, it also showed effects of sizable migrations both internally and across national frontiers. Table 9 shows the population in various South Slav provinces in 1910 (or 1914), the theoretical population for 1920, the actual population as found by the census of January 31, 1921, and the difference (rounded) between the two latter series, representing the total loss in population which can be ascribed in Serbia to the effects of the First and Second Balkan Wars and World War I and in other provinces to the effects of World War I.

The combined loss of population, as a result of the wars between 1912 and 1918, suffered by all South Slav provinces which since 1918 form the state of Yugoslavia, amounted to the staggering figure of about 1.9 million. Of this number Serbia alone lost about 43 percent

TABLE 9.—COMBINED LOSS OF POPULATION DUE TO WORLD WAR I, BY PROVINCES

Province[a]	Population in 1910[b]	Annual rate of growth 1900–1910[c]	Theoretical population in 1920	Population according to the census of 1921[b]	Combined loss in population[d] (rounded)
Pre-1912 Serbia ...	2,911,701	1.7	3,406,690	2,595,430	811,300
Macedonia	1,664,807	0.9	1,754,705	1,442,208	312,500
Montenegro	238,423	0.9	251,298	199,857	51,400
Bosnia and Herzegovina	1,931,802	1.4	2,202,254	1,889,929	312,300
Dalmatia	333,112	0.9	363,092	329,070	34,000
Croatia-Slavonia...	2,731,738	0.9	2,977,594	2,726,379	251,200
Slovenia	1,063,767	0.4	1,106,317	1,056,464	49,900
Vojvodina	1,352,844	0.8	1,461,071	1,380,413	80,700
Total	12,228,194		13,523,021	11,619,750	1,903,300

[a] While after 1918 considerable changes in the territory of various provinces have taken place, the areas as used in this table are identical in 1910 and 1921 when the census was taken. Dalmatia's figure pertains only to the area covered by the census of 1921. The then Italian-occupied part of Dalmatia had in 1910 a population of 292,359. Croatia-Slavonia includes Medjumurje, the island of Krk, and the city of Kastav, but excludes the city of Sušak. Slovenia includes Prekomurje.
[b] Figures from Kingdom of the Serbs, Croats, and Slovenes, *Résultats préliminaires du recensement de la population dans le Royaume des Serbes, Croates et Slovènes* (Sarajevo, 1924), p. xiv.
[c] Rates of population growth based on Table 1, p. 152. For Macedonia and Montenegro, where no population figures were available for periods before 1914, it was assumed that the rate of growth was identical with that for Dalmatia, namely, 0.9 percent.
[d] If the loss in population in that part of Dalmatia which was not covered by the census of 1921 is taken as 30,000, then the total loss in areas, which until 1918 formed part of the Habsburg Monarchy, amounted to 757,000 persons. An almost identical figure is obtained if one takes the proportionate share for the South Slav areas, namely, 15.4 percent of the combined loss of population of the Habsburg Empire during World War I of 4,920,000 as estimated by the Austrian general, Hugo Kerchnawe. Kerchnawe's estimate quoted by Gustav Gratz and Richard Schüller, *Der wirtschaftliche Zusammenbruch Österreich-Ungarns* (Vienna and New Haven, 1930), p. 162.

which, both in absolute and in relative numbers, represented a much larger toll than that suffered by other provinces. The loss of population as a result of World War I in the South Slav areas, as elsewhere, was and is still being felt. The great loss of young males during the war years, which is the common result in all warring nations and which was fully revealed by the Yugoslav census of 1921, represented a permanent loss of potential parents, as lack of marriageable men had forced a portion of females of corresponding ages to remain single and/or childless. Furthermore, the loss of births in war years represented also a loss of potential parents at a later stage.[19]

[19] For the influence of World War I and World War II on the age structure of the Yugoslav population see Ivo Lah, "L'Âge moyen et la vie moyenne de la population en R.P.F. de Yougoslavie," *Statistička revija*, I, No. 1, 86–112, esp. p. 100.

Two additional factors have to be mentioned with regard to the influence of World War I on the population of the South Slav lands: (1) wartime privations and sufferings no doubt had an unfavorable effect on the health conditions of the population in postwar years, raising the morbidity rates and reducing the working capacity of many people. In this category one should count also the scores of thousands of those fully or partially incapacitated in the war.[20] (2) The war has caused an unduly high loss of trained people (intelligentsia), such as teachers and physicians, and arrested completely further schooling. This was especially true in Serbia. Economically and culturally under-developed areas can ill afford the loss of trained people. In fact, many shortcomings in Yugoslav life during the interwar period in the fields of politics, public administration, education, and so forth, have been ascribed to loss of the flower of the intelligentsia, especially in Serbia, during the period 1912 to 1918.

AND THE TOLL IN TREASURE

In addition to this staggering loss in population and labor power, World War I caused grave destruction in the productive power of all South Slav lands and great dislocations in their economic activity. Needless to say, areas which often experienced actual combat and enemy occupation, such as Serbia and Montenegro, suffered much more damage than the South Slav areas of the Habsburg Monarchy. Except for military operations of very short duration in eastern Bosnia and Srijem, the latter areas were not a scene of military operations and remained free of wanton destruction characteristic of Serbia. One of the foremost Yugoslav economists of the interwar period, Professor Velimir Bajkić, wrote thus about the effect of the war upon Serbia: "World War I brought about a great evenness in the distribution of wealth in Serbia. Everybody became more or less a beggar."[21]

It is not our purpose to review the destruction and losses in various branches of the economy in the South Slav lands during World War I. Agriculture, as well as other sectors of the economy, was put into the service of winning the war. In areas occupied by the enemy, the objective was to secure as large a contribution in goods and services to the enemy war machine as possible. Since the bulk of agricultural labor was drafted for military service, it was necessary not only to

[20] Milutin Mrvaljević, "The Question of War Invalids," *Jubilarni zbornik života i rada Srba, Hrvata i Slovenaca, 1918–1928* (Jubilee Record of Life and Work of the Serbs, Croats, and Slovenes, 1918–1928), II, 672–81.

[21] Velimir Bajkić, *Seljački kredit* (Peasant Credit), p. 76.

utilize the remaining labor in agriculture most fully, but also to husband systematically the reduced supplies of agricultural products. To
compensate for the lack of manpower and animal draft power in agriculture, mechanization in agriculture made considerable strides where
it was feasible, as in the Pannonian Plain. It would have surely progressed even further had it not been for shortages of steel and other
supplies limiting the production of agricultural machinery. In addition
to the lack of manpower and animal draft power, agriculture was
plagued also by reduced supplies of manure, farm implements, commercial fertilizers, insecticides, and pesticides. The supply of these
products became shorter as the war advanced, and yields were reduced
in all branches of agriculture. Reduced supplies of feed grains and
especially the use of corn (maize) for human consumption in larger
amounts greatly lowered the numbers of pigs and thus the supply of
fats.

A system of obligatory delivery of food production was introduced,
not only in the occupied areas but also in all areas of the Dual Monarchy. Naturally, the armed forces had the first claim on food supplies.
The producers of food in the territory of the Dual Monarchy were
assured of a more liberal supply which they were able to retain for food
and seed, as well as for feed for livestock. In urban areas a system of
food rationing was introduced and the rural food-deficit areas obtained supplementary supplies. One of the great difficulties with regard
to the food economy in the Habsburg Monarchy during World War I
was the fact that an almost completely separate food policy was conducted for each of the two halves of the Empire, resulting in great
inequalities of supply to the population at large. Moreover, Croatia-
Slavonia had a separate food policy and Bosnia and Herzegovina were
treated in a special way.

Austria-Hungary imported certain amounts of various foodstuffs,
primarily grains and meat, from various occupied areas such as Galicia,
Rumania, and Serbia. These supplies were also distributed among the
armed forces and to the two halves of the Empire according to a special
formula.

Agricultural production in Serbia suffered greatly during 1914 and
1915 because its richest agricultural regions were transformed into
battlefields and the lack of manpower and draft power in agriculture
was much more severe in Serbia than in Austria-Hungary. Partly responsible for the lack of manpower was the great typhus epidemic of
1915. According to the account of General Kerchnawe, the Austro-
Hungarian military government in Serbia (autumn 1915 to autumn

1918) was more than eager to re-establish agricultural and livestock production in Serbia in order to provide supplies not only for the army of occupation and the minimum for the civilian population, but especially for export to Austria-Hungary. To assure the cultivation of lands temporarily deserted—and a considerable portion of arable land was in this category—the military government resurrected and applied certain old Serbian laws on forced labor.[22] Agricultural production was apparently already restored in 1917 almost to the prewar level. More important from the Austro-Hungarian point of view was the fact that Serbia delivered more in agricultural products and animal foodstuffs to the occupation forces than any other occupied area and more than its assigned quota and thus, from the standpoint of the occupying powers, proved decidedly a great economic asset.[23] Naturally the securing of these supplies from the Serbian peasantry did not go without pressure, and as the war advanced and the food conditions in Austria-Hungary worsened, the pressure was increased and larger amounts of food and livestock were taken. As in most other areas, the city population in Serbia fared much worse than the rural population with regard to food. The rations were small and not regularly available and in time were reduced. In addition, prices were several times as high as before the war. Among all South Slav areas Montenegro fared, perhaps, the worst in regard to food supplies during World War I and experienced periods of outright starvation.

One of the indicators of the deterioration in the food supply in the Dual Monarchy during World War I was the great rise in the cost of living. Obviously, this rise partly reflected the great increase in the amount of money in circulation but also was caused by the decreased supplies of food and other items whose prices make up the cost of living.[24]

Toward the end of the war, in 1918, difficulties in providing the necessary food supplies for the military forces and for the urban population increased greatly as the peasants refused to live up fully to their obligations to deliver their quotas of crops. In some areas, such as Croatia-Slavonia, local authorities seem to have knowingly tolerated such behavior on the part of the peasants.[25]

The primary effect of World War I on the agriculture of the South

22 Hugo Kerchnawe *et al.*, *op. cit.*, pp. 100–107, 121–36.
23 *Ibid.*, pp. 136–77.
24 Gustav Gratz and Richard Schüller, *op. cit.*, pp. 178–85.
25 *Ibid.*, pp. 84–87.

Slav lands was the diminishing of its productive capacity. This was caused by the worsened cultivation of the soil, owing to the shortage of manpower and draft power, the lack of manure and commercial fertilizers, and lack of pesticides; by the destruction or wearing out of farm implements, the destruction of housing facilities of the peasants in such areas as Serbia, the loss of personal belongings, and the loss of savings due to inflation. But one of the most serious losses suffered by agriculture was that of a large portion of livestock. The estimated loss of the principal types of livestock for all South Slav areas, due to World War I, was as follows:[26]

Type of livestock	Heads in 1914	Heads in 1919	Loss in percent
Horses	1,555,776	1,008,980	35.1
Cattle	6,276,855	4,555,220	27.4
Pigs	5,233,950	2,792,503	46.6
Sheep	11,570,260	5,249,667	54.6
Goats	2,445,370	1,200,296	50.9

As will be shown later, these areas never succeeded during the interwar period in making good the losses of their livestock during World War I, although in that period many other factors were responsible for the stagnation or even reduction of livestock numbers, but especially of cattle and pigs. The loss of livestock during World War I differed from type to type as well as from area to area. The large reduction in the number of pigs is easily explainable as a result of the lack of feed. Area-wise, Dalmatia, Slovenia, and Bosnia and Herzegovina suffered the greatest losses. In spite of occupation, Serbia apparently did not suffer a much larger loss in livestock than other areas. Moreover, its loss in cattle was made good within two years after the end of the war by natural growth, by imports from other areas of Yugoslavia, and partly by receipts from reparations.

The destruction of production facilities in the agriculture of the South Slav lands during World War I, as well as other material losses suffered by the peasantry, made it necessary to spend much energy and resources during the first postwar years in order to rehabilitate the agriculture and village life in general. Much of this reconstruction work had to be financed by credit, and it is in this period that a large portion of the peasant indebtedness originated, which later in the period of low agricultural prices proved to be such a vexing problem.

[26] V. M. Djuričić *et al.*, *Naša narodna privreda i nacionalni prihod* (Our National Economy and National Income), p. 63.

WORLD WAR I AS A SCHOOL
FOR THE SOUTHEASTERN EUROPEAN PEASANTRY

Practically all Yugoslav writers who dealt with the peasant problem during the interwar period agreed that World War I had some important and favorable political and socioeconomic effects on the broad peasant masses not only in Yugoslavia but in all countries of Southeastern and Eastern Europe.[27] Generally speaking, in addition to bringing about a great political and social revolution, World War I was also a great and hard school for the peasantry of those lands, and the peasant of the interwar period was much changed in relation to what he was before 1914. First, the peasants had plenty of opportunity to observe that, in times of war, food which they were producing was a key factor for both the military and the civilian economy. This realization of being the key factor in the national economy as producers of food and many raw materials is generally taken as one of the basic factors which raised the political and social self-confidence of the peasants during and after World War I. This situation was revealed also in the fact that the terms of exchange between agricultural and industrial products moved to the favor of the peasants.

Second, as a fighting soldier or as a prisoner of war, the peasant from all South Slav provinces became during World War I a great "traveler." He was able to observe not only the difference between the life in his village and in the cities, but also the difference between the ways of working and living of the peasants in countries and areas on a much higher level of cultural and economic development than the way of life to which he and his neighbors were accustomed. He saw that peasants who were able to acquire a basic education and use advanced methods of farming were able to attain a decent level of living, while he was accustomed in most cases to an existence not much different from that of cattle. No doubt these experiences during the war served as an impetus in the attempts of many peasants during the interwar period to improve their economic lot and the conditions of life in the village generally. As a rule, however, too small farm holdings, lack of capital and knowledge, limited incentives, and complete absence of any systematic help from the government were responsible for the fact that this striving for progress became stifled. The great mass of peasants was forced to continue on the traditional paths of working and living.

Third, the peasant had grown politically during the war. Many

[27] See, for example, Dragoljub Jovanović, *Agrarna politika* (Agrarian Policy), pp. 21–23; Josip Predavec, *Selo i seljaci* (The Village and the Peasants), pp. 223–24; Adam Pribićević, *Seljak* (The Peasant), pp. 111–12.

Yugoslav peasants in the Austro-Hungarian army responded very soon to the nationalist propaganda and they surrendered in droves, especially on the Russian front. As the war advanced and the expectation of victory of the Central Powers vanished, both the Austro-Hungarian military and civil administrations began to lose their grip on the army and civilian population. This resulted, on the one hand, in mass desertion from the armed forces and, on the other, in the already mentioned refusal of the peasants to obey the rules with regard to obligatory delivery of their produce to the authorities. As far as deserters were concerned,

The number of deserters enrolled in "green companies" [bands of men living in forests to avoid detection and capture] at the end of the war was from 40,000 to 50,000; and the military tribunal at Zagreb had to deal in the area of Croatia-Slavonia with over 100,000 cases of desertion.[28]

What was involved in both military and civilian disobedience was the realization that the old political and social order was not worth fighting and suffering for, and that the old regime could not any longer enforce its will. The reverberations of the Russian Revolution of 1917 were felt also among the peasantry and peasant soldiers of the South Slav nationalities within the Dual Monarchy. Thus, toward the end of the war and in the first postwar years the peasantry of Yugoslavia, as well as of other peasant countries of Southeastern and Eastern Europe, was in a political and social revolutionary ferment. In the socioeconomic direction the liquidation of all serfdom and serfdom-like institutions, with the full ownership of land by those who till it, was the main objective of this revolutionary trend. In the political domain the dissolution of the Dual Monarchy, peace, self-determination of various nationalities, and complete political equality among all citizens were the objectives. In fact, the revolutionary ferment in Yugoslavia, as in some other Southeastern and Eastern European countries, was channeled by the undertaking of a radical agrarian reform and the granting to the peasants of complete franchise. Thus World War I brought the fulfillment of centuries-old dreams to the peasants in all those areas of Yugoslavia where serfdom and serfdom-like institutions existed up to 1918.

Fourth, immediately after World War I the peasantry became one of the most important factors in the political life of all peasant countries of Southeastern and Eastern Europe. Peasant parties, which before 1914 were just beginning to take root among the peasant masses and were trying to awaken them politically, became powerful political

[28] Otto von Frangeš, "The Agrarian Reform in Yugoslavia," in International Institute of Agriculture, *Bulletin of Agricultural Economics and Sociology* (1934), p. E 90.

organizations. In some countries, like Bulgaria and Rumania, the peasant parties controlled the government temporarily, while in Poland and Czechoslovakia peasant parties formed important components of coalition governments. In Yugoslavia the Croatian Peasant party became practically the only political force of consequence in Croatia, but peasant parties in other parts of the country showed only very limited strength. But while the peasant parties continued to claim and actually hold the allegiance of the broad peasant masses in all these countries, political forces controlled by the respective dynasties, the armed forces, and small city cliques removed completely the representatives of the peasant parties from the affairs of government in all peasant countries with the exception of Czechoslovakia. While the peasant parties in the interwar period had little success in acquiring and keeping political power, nevertheless their political significance was immeasurably greater than in pre-1914 days.

Finally, the great loss of actual and potential rural population during World War I had somewhat improved the unfavorable land-population ratio. In other words, agricultural overpopulation, which in some South Slav areas was quite pronounced before 1914, was somewhat relieved. This relief, however, was only very temporary in character.

After World War I the peasantry of the South Slav lands entered a new period of its political, social, and economic development. By one of those odd turns in history the two multinational empires—the Ottoman Empire and the Habsburg Empire—which had fully controlled and greatly affected the destinies of the South Slav nations for centuries, met their doom within a period of six years. This fact changed completely the political face of the whole area of Central and Southeastern Europe. Swept away with the two empires were social and political institutions which, like the crumbled empires, had long since outlived their usefulness. Liberation and unification of the South Slavs into one state meant the victory of the nationalist idea over the ideas of the multinational empire. But the national issue reappeared in a new form. The realization of political democracy, which was one of the main objectives of World War I, remained only a dream. And the achievement of a satisfactory economic and social order which, with the final abolition of feudal and quasi-feudal forms, appeared to many peasants to be at hand, proved even less possible than the achievement of political democracy. And so, throughout the interwar period, the peasantry of Yugoslavia continued in search of a more just and more satisfactory political and economic system. But in vain.

CHAPTER 13

POLITICAL ORGANIZATION AND DEVELOPMENT, 1918–41

YUGOSLAVIA of the interwar period was a state made possible by the outcome of World War I and the peace treaties following it. With its 11.9 million inhabitants, according to the census of January 1921, and a territory of 247,542 square kilometers (95,558 square miles), the new state was a conglomeration of five closely related but different nations, which up to that time were never under one state roof. These nations were the Serbs, the Croats, the Slovenes, the Montenegrins, and the Macedonians. The latter two nations were not officially recognized as such during the interwar period. Both officially and by many members of these nations they were considered Serbs. In addition, the state had four large minority groups with a total population of about 1.5 million, consisting of Germans, Hungarians, Albanians, and Turks of Macedonia. Other minorities were of small significance.

CONSTITUTIONAL DEVELOPMENTS

From a constitutional and administrative point of view, the new state was created by consolidation of the former independent kingdoms of Serbia and Montenegro; Croatia-Slavonia, which was a quasi-autonomous province of the Hungarian half of the Habsburg Monarchy; Vojvodina, which formed an integral portion of Hungary; Slovenia (combining Carniola and small portions of Styria and Carinthia) and Dalmatia, territories which were parts of the Austrian half of the Habsburg Monarchy; and, finally, the province of Bosnia and Herzegovina, which was an Austro-Hungarian condominium administered by their joint Ministry of Finance.[1] Serbia in 1918 included the Yugoslav part of Macedonia and a part of the Sandjak of Novi Pazar, acquired after the Balkan Wars of 1912 and 1913. The Serbian gov-

---

[1] Istria with approximately half a million people, the cities of Rijeka (Fiume) and Zadar (Zara) on the east Adriatic coast, and some Adriatic islands came in 1918 (Rijeka in 1922) under Italy and remained officially so until 1945.

ernment considered these territories nationally and politically as integral parts of Serbia, Macedonia being officially called Southern Serbia. Montenegro was also greatly enlarged after the Balkan Wars by the acquisition of a part of the Sandjak of Novi Pazar and some territory near Lake Scutari. All these areas are shown in Map 1.

After its establishment Yugoslavia became a cog in the French system of post-1918 diplomacy, dedicated to the preservation of the status of Europe as created by the peace treaties concluding World War I. This continued to be so until about 1934 when the French influence in general, and in Southeastern and Eastern Europe in particular, was removed by the rising might of Nazi Germany and, to a much lesser degree, of Fascist Italy. Yugoslavia tried for a short while to ride the fence between the Axis and the Western democracies. But the increasing German hold on the Yugoslav economy, Germany's bloodless territorial expansion which brought it to the borders of Yugoslavia, the weak support from the Western powers, and the profascist propensities of some Yugoslav political leaders soon forced the country to take the pro-Axis course. This course continued until a few days before the Axis invasion of Yugoslavia in April 1941, when this unpopular affiliation was broken. The basic point with regard to the Yugoslav foreign policy during the interwar period was that, like Serbia and Montenegro in previous decades, it also, as a small power, had to lean on a powerful friend abroad. One interesting point from the realm of foreign policy during the interwar period was that Yugoslavia refused to establish diplomatic and economic relations with the Soviet Union until late in 1939, although traditionally Russia was the main "protector" of both Serbia and Montenegro. But in spite of this constant policy of leaning on a powerful friend abroad, there runs like a red line through the policy of the South Slav states in the pre-1918 period—and of Yugoslavia since then—the readiness to shake off this foreign protection the moment it becomes incompatible with what is considered an acceptable degree of foreign interference. This has often happened through revolutionary changes in the domestic regime, and also in exchanging a more dangerous foreign "protector" for what was considered a less dangerous one. The developments since the end of World War II are a perfect illustration of this traditional policy.

But while Yugoslavia was politically orientated toward Western democracies for most of the interwar period, its most important markets and sources of supplies abroad were in Germany, Italy, and Austria. This dichotomy in its foreign orientation was a vexing problem, as foreign trade was affected by political issues, and the export of agricultural surpluses played a key role in the situation of Yugoslav agriculture throughout the interwar period.[2]

The liberation and unification of various South Slav nations into one state in 1918 was the consummation of plans and tendencies of long standing. Once achieved, the new unity needed constant and intelligent nursing, which, unfortunately, was lacking. The varied historical background and the mixture of nations make Yugoslavia a country of profound contrasts. Yugoslavia is the area where the West has been colliding with the East for centuries in religious, cultural, and social respects, as well as in political ideas, institutions, and practices. The population belongs to three main religions. According to the 1931 census it was 48.7 percent Serbian Eastern Orthodox (Serbs, Montenegrins, and Macedonians), 37.5 percent Roman Catholic (Croats and Slovenes and part of the Hungarian and German minorities), and 11.2 percent Mohammedan (in Bosnia and Herzegovina, Macedonia, and Montenegro). The remaining 2.6 percent belonged to other denominations. The Serbs, Croats, and Montenegrins speak the same language, the Serbo-Croatian, while the Slovenes speak a closely related but different tongue, the Slovenian. The separate Macedonian language, standing somewhere between the Serbo-Croatian and the Bulgarian, was not recognized officially during the interwar period, and no literature to speak of existed in Macedonian. The grammar of this language has been developing since 1945 and literature published in Macedonian is rapidly growing. The Yugoslavs use both the Latin and the Cyrillic scripts. The levels of cultural and economic development and of general and political education, the relation of the citizen to the state, and the hold of tradition on the mind and mores of the people differed greatly from area to area. But in a period when states tend to be identical in territory with nations or groups of closely related nations with similar interests, Yugoslavia is a logical and necessary political structure. Its history during the past 15 years confirms this assertion. In all aspects of political, economic, and social life, diversity and contrasts, rather than uniformity and unity, were the rule. One of the consequences of this varied historical background was that the new state contained seven different legal and administrative systems. Many of the differences in regard to legal and administrative matters persisted up to the beginning of World War II. The nature of this

[2] Other close Yugoslav regional diplomatic ties, e.g., within the Little Entente (Yugoslavia, Czechoslovakia, and Rumania) and within the Balkan Pact (Yugoslavia, Greece, Rumania, and Turkey), also lacked strong economic foundations (except with Czechoslovakia), as the economies of these nations were competitive rather than complementary.

background of the new state would have made the task of the rulers during the interwar period extremely exacting even if they had been philosophers and saints rather than politicians.

This varied political and cultural background, the varied level of economic development, the strong nationalist feelings of various nations, and the religious prejudices made a federal organization of the new state the only logical solution. Historical individuality and territorial lines of the various provinces were well defined and, as such, each commanded a special allegiance from a great majority of its population. Each had an operating legal and administrative apparatus. But the Serbian political parties, helped by some groups from other areas, were intent on monopolizing the power in the new state and on gathering the spoils of victory, so they imposed upon the country a crude centralism through the adoption of the Constitution of June 28, 1921, and made of the new state what, in essence, was an enlarged Serbia.[3] Not only the Serbian political parties,[4] but also the two other

[3] The Constitution was adopted by 223 out of 419 votes in the parliament (Skupština), 35 votes were cast against it, and 161 members of the parliament abstained. Of the yes votes, 183, almost evenly split, belonged to the People's Radical party and the Democratic party, both almost exclusively Serbian, but especially the former. Twenty-four Bosnian Moslem votes were secured by the government parties by liberal promises with regard to indemnities for property which was affected by the agrarian reform, as this party represented the interests of the landlords. Eight Turkish minority votes from Macedonia were also secured by promises of better treatment of lands affected by the agrarian reform in Macedonia, as this party represented primarily the interests of the landlords. Eight votes of a small peasant party from Slovenia were apparently secured with other concessions. Against the Constitution were the Croatian Peasant party, which at that time abstained from the work in the parliament, the Serbian peasant party "Union of Peasants," the Slovenian People's (Catholic) party, the Social Democratic party, the Communist party, and various other minor parties. In fact, the parties which voted for the Constitution represented less than half of the popular vote cast for the representatives of the Constitutional Assembly. Čedomil Mitrinović and Miloš Brašić, *Les Skoupchtinas et les Diètes Yougoslaves*, pp. 353 ff.; Josip Horvat, *Politička povijest Hrvatske, 1918–1929* (Political History of Croatia, 1918–1929), pp. 254–55; Malbone W. Graham, Jr., *New Governments in Central Europe*, pp. 356–60.

[4] A synopsis of the Yugoslav political parties during the interwar period seems to be in place here as an aid to better understanding of the following discussion, although more will be said later about some of these parties. Political party life in interwar Yugoslavia can be divided into three periods: from 1918 to the royal coup d'état in January 1929; from January 1929 until September 1931, when the king granted a Constitution to the people, a period during which no political parties were allowed to function; and from September 1931 until 1941, when only parties fulfilling certain conditions were able to exist officially. In fact, these were only government-sponsored parties, which disintegrated as various prime ministers were changed, to be again organized. Most of the pre-1929 parties continued to exist, however, and some even increased in importance, though they were illegal. Before 1929 the following political parties existed: The People's Radical party, a party of long tradition and considerable achievement in Serbian history, was almost exclusively a Serbian party. The Democratic party was organized after 1918 out of several pre-1914 Serbian parties and out of those

Serbian-controlled political factors, the Crown and the Military, tended toward the establishment and perpetuation of Serbian hegemony in the new state. This was the basic reason for the emergence of various unsolved national questions in the new state of Yugoslavia. The central issue was the "Croatian Question," as the Croats never unreservedly recognized the constitutional or political form which robbed them of their autonomy.[5] The Croatian Question, as the expression of the struggle between the forces of centralism and the forces of federalism, became the principal internal political question immediately upon the creation of the new state and remained so until the downfall of the interwar Yugoslavia in April 1941. Of the same character, but of lesser importance, were the Macedonian and the Montenegrin national questions, as these provinces also did not wholeheartedly accept the centralistic form of government and the complete Serbian control of their

---

political forces from other Yugoslav areas which, prior to 1914, co-operated in the so-called Croato-Serbian Coalition, organized in Croatia-Slavonia and Dalmatia in 1905. The Radical and Democratic parties included both the bourgeois and peasant elements. The Independent Democratic party split off from the Democratic party in 1923; it included the elements from the former Croato-Serbian Coalition, and allied itself in 1926 with the Croatian Peasant party into what became known as the Peasant Democratic Coalition. The Yugoslav Moslem Organization was the party of Moslems from Bosnia and Herzegovina. It primarily represented the interests of the former Moslem landlords. The Slovenian People's party was purely Slovenian in membership and was the only Yugoslav political party under the control of the Catholic Church. The Croatian Peasant party was purely Croat in membership, at first without any bourgeois elements, but after the small Croatian bourgeois parties disintegrated during the early 1920's, it included Croats from all walks of life, commanding the allegiance of perhaps more than 90 percent of all Croats. Among the major parties, although with greatly fluctuating membership, was the peasant party "Union of Peasants," with membership among peasants in Serbia and Bosnia. During the 1920's there was a plethora of small political parties, all of which disintegrated. One of these was the Social Democratic party. Finally, there was the Yugoslav Communist party, which was outlawed in 1921. It continued to operate underground, however, and after undergoing many internal crises emerged after the collapse of Yugoslavia in April 1941 as an exceedingly well-organized and ably led political force which during and after World War II captured undisputed control of the country. Between 1931 and 1941 there were a number of government-sponsored parties, which in some instances were created *ad hoc*, and in others were composed of the old political parties.

As is usual, all political parties had high-sounding programs. With the exception of the Communist party, all these programs propounded principles of democratic government and civil liberties, while those of the Communist party and, to a lesser extent, of the Croatian Peasant party, the Slovenian People's party, and the "Union of Peasants" propounded far-reaching social and economic reforms. Again as usual, the behavior of the political parties in opposition was totally different from when they were in power, as in the latter case power rather than principles was the issue.

[5] The answer of the main Croatian party, the Croatian Peasant party, to the centrally organized new state and the Serbian hegomony which it made possible was the abstention from the parliament. In this policy it endured from 1919 to 1924 and again from June 1928 to August 1939.

affairs. It is now beyond any doubt that the unsolved national questions were the chief political problem of Yugoslavia in the interwar period and the basic cause of its political instability.

The Constitution of 1921 obliterated the historical provinces as political or administrative units. It foresaw the establishment of regional governmental bodies at an intermediary level between the central government and the counties (the latter were divided into communes), the so-called *oblasti*. Territorially the *oblasti* were supposed, according to the Constitution, to be based on "natural, social, and economic conditions" and were not to have more than 800,000 people. As it was impossible to reach an agreement among the political parties on the size and the capitals of the *oblasti*, the government divided the country by a special Decree of April 1922 into 33 *oblasti* varying in population between 109,000 and 808,000, and special laws implemented the provisions of the Constitution on the organization and functions of all types of local government. In fact, these rules, especially those relating to the legislative functions of local government, remained almost a dead letter. Various types of local government operated essentially, and in some cases exclusively, as the agents of the Ministry of the Interior.[6]

After the royal coup d'état in January 1929 the internal administration of the country was reorganized. Historical provinces were disregarded as before. Instead of 33 *oblasti* the country was now divided into nine *banovine*,[7] or regions, as indicated in Map 3. The central rule was strengthened still further. By means of gerrymandering, six out of nine *banovine* showed a Serbian majority. Counties, as before, continued to be important administrative organs of the state. This condition of affairs remained unchanged until August 1939, when a partial

---

[6] Stevan Sagadin, "Our Local Governments," *Jubilarni zbornik života i rada Srba, Hrvata i Slovenaca, 1918–1928* (Jubilee Record of Life and Work of the Serbs, Croats, and Slovenes, 1918–1928), II, 612–21.

[7] The names of the *banovine* are derived from the various rivers of Yugoslavia and the Adriatic maritime area. For the convenience of the reader, instead of using the adjective form of, say, "dravska" *banovina*, which is the only proper form in the Serbo-Croatian language, we use throughout this study the noun form, *banovina* "Drava."

The territorial relationship of the nine *banovine* to the historical provinces was approximately as follows: *banovina* Drava was identical with Slovenia; Sava related to Croatia-Slavonia without its eastern zone; Dunav included all of Vojvodina, the north central portion of Serbia except Belgrade, and the eastern zone of Croatia-Slavonia or Srijem; Morava included the eastern and central portion of Serbia; Drina and Vrbas the bulk of Bosnia, but Drina also parts of Serbia and Slavonia; Primorje covered the bulk of Dalmatia with parts of Bosnia and Herzegovina; Zeta covered all of Montenegro with southern Dalmatia, parts of Herzegovina, and most of the Sandjak of Novi Pazar; Vardar included Macedonia. The Prefecture of Belgrade included the cities of Belgrade, Zemun, and Pančevo.

Map 3

solution of the Croatian Question was achieved by the Agreement (Sporazum) between the Croatian Peasant party and the Belgrade government. This Agreement resulted in the consolidation of two *banovine* with an overwhelming Croatian majority, Sava and Primorje, and a few counties from several neighboring *banovine* into the *Banovina* Croatia with a certain degree of autonomy. This political Agreement changed little, if at all, either the nature of the Yugoslav government as a whole or the administration of the *banovine* except in *Banovina* Croatia. It is safe to assume, however, that not even this limited reform would have taken place had it not been for the critical political situation in Europe. The objective of the Agreement was to strengthen the internal cohesion of the country.

This review of the changes in the administrative organization of the country during the interwar period is of interest for two reasons. First, it shows one facet of the political framework under which the peasantry of Yugoslavia lived during that period. Second, these changes make it very hard to utilize agricultural and other statistical data for interregional comparisons over the whole period. Reduction of the 33 regions in existence from 1922 to 1929 to the eight historical provinces is not difficult, as it requires only minor adjustments. But the comparison of data for the nine *banovine* in existence from 1929 to 1939 (or eight from August 1939 to April 1941) with either the previous 33 *oblasti* or the still earlier eight historical provinces is impossible. Thus, most of our interregional comparisons which span the whole interwar period or which compare data of the interwar period with those of the pre-1918 years have of necessity to be only approximations.

THE CONTROLLING POLITICAL FORCES

Politically, the whole interwar period of Yugoslav life was marked by the hegemony of the Serbs from pre-1912 Serbia. Actually, if not formally, the citizens from all other areas of the country were considered as second-class citizens. The Serbs held almost all key power positions in the state, with the dynasty at the helm and as a shield. All opposition to unsatisfactory constitutional and political conditions, to abuse of power and maladministration and large-scale corruption, however well founded and reasonable, was branded as antistate activity. Until 1929 freedom of speech, assembly, press, and political organization existed, except for the Communist party and temporarily for the Croatian Peasant party, but was of no avail. With the royal coup d'état of January 1929,[8] all political parties were officially prohibited and such political laws promulgated that made normal political activity impossible. It remained so even after King Alexander granted a new Constitution to the country in September 1931. This Constitution established a sham parliament and allowed the creation of political parties, but under such conditions that no traditional party was able to attain official recognition. Thus, only government-created parties were in a position to operate.[9] The new Constitution simply sanctioned the personal rule of the king. Royal dictatorship, in somewhat milder form after the assassination of King Alexander in October 1934, re-

[8] The parliamentary era ended actually, if not formally, with the assassination in the Belgrade parliament of three members of the Croatian Peasant party, including its leader, Stjepan Radić, in June 1928. Thereupon the Peasant Democratic Coalition withdrew from the parliament. Radić actually was wounded on that occasion and died on August 8, 1928.

[9] Political parties could not be formed on nationality or confessional lines. To participate in national "elections" they had to present lists with a minimum of 60 signatures in more than half of all counties spread over two-thirds of the *banovine* and had to fulfill many other impeding requirements. Moreover, each candidate had to pledge

mained in force until the collapse of Yugoslavia in 1941 and, formally, until 1945.

There were always some Croats, Slovenes, or Bosnian Moslems who participated in the Yugoslav cabinets of the interwar period. But even when they held important portfolios they were powerless, if not outright tools of the Serbian ruling groups. Even during the parliamentary period before January 1929, these men, while occasionally representing powerful political parties, in the words of Stjepan Radić—who himself participated in two cabinets in 1925 and 1926—were "not in the government but attached to the government" (*Mi nismo u vladi nego pri vladi*). The basic purpose for having the non-Serbs in the various cabinets was essentially "decorative": the government leaders could point to these men and state that Croats, Slovenes, and the others were represented in the government.

Throughout the interwar period the basic political forces in the state—the dynasty, the army which supported and was under the control of the dynasty, and a core of the Serbian political and economic forces and high government officials usually referred to as the Belgrade clique (*čaršija*)—controlled fully the political destinies of the state. In spite of this, that period was marked by a great instability of cabinets. Reportedly, none of them was overthrown by a true vote in the parliament, but rather by the maneuvers of the Crown. Nothing better than the membership of these cabinets could indicate the degree of Serbian hegemony in the new state during the interwar period. During the so-called parliamentary period, from December 1918 to January 1929, lasting 121 months, there were 24 different cabinets, headed by seven various prime ministers. There were 127 various ministers in these cabinets (and a considerable number of undersecretaries), of whom 55 belonged to the People's Radical party, 16 to the Democratic party, seven to the Independent Democratic party, eight to the Yugoslav Moslem Organization, seven to the Slovenian People's party, and seven to the Croatian Peasant party.[10] The remaining ministers belonged to other political groups which were or soon became without significance. The Ministry of the Army and Navy was always in charge of a general on the active list. During that period of 121 months the Serbs held the office of Prime Minister for 117 months, Ministry of the

---

his allegiance to the existing political order in the state. In the 1931 elections only the government party list was presented, but in the elections of 1935 and 1938 the opposition parties, existing informally, succeeded in presenting a united list.

[10] Based on Stevan Sagadin, "State Government," *Jubilarni zbornik života i rada Srba, Hrvata i Slovenaca, 1918–1928* (Jubilee Record of Life and Work of the Serbs, Croats, and Slovenes, 1918–1928), I, 99–102.

Army and Navy for 121 months, Ministry of the Interior (controlling the police) for 111 months, Ministry of Foreign Affairs for 100 months, Ministry of Finance for 118 months, Ministry of Education for 110 months, and the Ministry of Justice for 105 months.

In the period of royal dictatorship, from January 1929 to March 1941, lasting 147 months (without counting the last cabinet, formed after March 27, 1941, which was in office only two weeks before it went into exile), Yugoslavia had seven various prime ministers and 15 cabinets in which 121 ministers served, 34 of them having served as ministers before 1929. Of these 121 ministers 73 were Serbs, 33 Croats, ten Slovenes, and five Bosnian Moslems. Of these Serbs 36 were formerly prominent in the Radical party and five in the Democratic party. Twenty-four Serbs and 24 Croats were considered either as experts, belonged to minor political groups, or were simply willing individuals. Five Croats belonged to the Croatian Peasant party when it took part in the government between August 1939 and March 1941, while four of its pre-1929 members took part in various cabinets between 1929 and 1936 as renegades. During this second period the Serbs held the premiership, the Ministry of the Army and Navy, and the Ministry of Foreign Affairs for 147 months, the Ministry of the Interior for 129 months, the Ministry of Finance for 98 months, the Ministry of Education for 126 months, and the Ministry of Justice for 132 months.[11]

In addition to the control of all main ministries, the Serbs were also in absolute control of the armed forces. Of the 165 generals in active service in 1938, 161 were Serbs, two were Croats, and two were Slovenes.[12] All important diplomatic posts, such as the legations in Paris, Rome, London, and Berlin, were always in charge of Serb diplomats. Furthermore, the four tremendously important state financial institutions—the National Bank (the central bank), the State Mortgage Bank, the Postal Savings System, and the Chartered Agricultural Bank—were always headed by Serbs (the Postal Savings System was headed by a Croat from September 1939 to April 1941). Being in control of all focal points of power and thus of employment opportunities in government service, the Serbs took full advantage of patronage as a political weapon, a fact that was bitterly opposed by the other nationalities.[13]

[11] All data for the period 1929 to 1941 computed from *Službene novine*, the official organ of the Yugoslav government, issued in Belgrade, 1929 to 1941.

[12] Rudolf Bićanić, *Ekonomska podloga hrvatskog pitanja* (The Economic Basis of the Croatian Question), p. 120.

[13] *Ibid.*, pp. 70–77.

One of the basic calamities of Yugoslav political life from 1918 to 1934 was the dictatorial proclivity of King Alexander. The same, though to a somewhat lesser extent, was true also of his cousin, Prince Paul, who as the first regent (of three), from October 1934 to March 1941, had all the power centered in his hands. It is true that Alexander enjoyed a great personal prestige, which went back to his successful leadership as commander in chief during the wars between 1912 and 1918. But the real reason for his power lay in the fact that after the Salonika trial of 1917 the army had been effectively under his control, strengthening tremendously his position vis-à-vis the political parties, especially the People's Radical party.

There is as yet no dependable study of the political history of Yugoslavia during the interwar period. It is generally agreed, however, that King Alexander, even in the days of the parliamentary period, did not scrupulously play the role of a constitutional monarch. Naturally, from January 1929 until his assassination in October 1934, plotted by Croatian extremists in exile but executed by a Macedonian, he was also formally an autocrat. It is evident that without the "softening" of the political parties of great standing and powerful hold over the people, he could not have abolished the Constitution and introduced his personal rule simply by a stroke of his pen. King Alexander considered strong political parties and strong political leaders the chief obstacles to his complete personal rule. Being in an extremely strong position, and with the army under his control, he easily and frequently evaded parliamentary rules and played one political party against the other, one faction of a political party against the other, one political leader against the other. "The confidence of the Crown" was the most important asset needed for a politician to prosper in the Alexandrine period. The democratic and parliamentary system had no chance under Alexander. Of course, there were many other ills afflicting Yugoslavia at that time, primarily the dissatisfaction of all nations except the Serbs with the Constitution of 1921, the large number of political parties, and the ruthless scramble for power and for the spoils of power without respect to any moral principles.

The fact that political parties could not operate freely after 1929 and that the royal dictatorship, in a period of spreading dictatorships, seemed there to stay, led to a far-reaching attrition of party political life and widespread defection of party politicians from their parties. In the cabinets of King Alexander after 1929, and of Prince Paul from 1934 to 1941, practically all of the important posts were in the hands of various members of the former political parties, especially the Radical party and the Democratic party. When the organization of political parties was permitted in September 1931, it was only the party sponsored by the government which could be organized. In addition to the renegades from the old political parties, the government party became the refuge of political opportunists of all shades and of such people who could be herded into these parties, e.g., government employees. There is no doubt that the period of royal dictatorship was a period of moral trial for everybody in Yugoslavia, and especially for professional politicians. A large number of politicians accepted and collaborated actively with the dictatorial regime, a portion tried to sleep through these years, biding their time,[14] while a third group openly opposed the dictatorship throughout the 1930's, or for most of that period. While they were incapable of breaking the royal dictatorship, their resistance prevented its developing into an outright fascist one with complete totalitarian paraphernalia, because they continued to hold the support and allegiance of large masses of their following—which, in fact, increased as time went on. The Yugoslav regime during the 1930's was therefore much more akin to the old forms of government based on military and police forces than to the totalitarian regimes of either fascist or communist type.

By far the strongest opposition party was the Croatian Peasant party, since 1928 under the leadership of Vladimir Maček. While in the "elections" of 1931 the opposition did not take part, in those of 1935 and 1938 Maček headed the election list of the combined opposition. The Croatian Peasant party also suffered considerable defections. This party gained in membership during the period of royal

[14] One of the important reasons for the lack of opposition on the part of most former ministers against the dictatorial regime was purely pecuniary. Former ministers enjoyed government pensions. According to law a minister acquired a lifelong personal pension after having served as minister or undersecretary for two years and a family pension after having served for three years. But the practice was to count all the time spent in "official retirement" (*ministar na raspoloženju*) for the pension right, and since, again according to usage, all retiring ministers were put in "official retirement," it was sufficient to spend only one year as an active minister to obtain a pension. This pension amounted to 5 percent of the salary for every six months (including the official retirement) in service. See Stevan Sagadin, "State Government," *op. cit.*, p. 98. No essential change in this respect took place after the introduction of royal dictatorship in 1929. There is no doubt that this system of ministerial pensions, the opportunity for graft while in office, and the social prestige which went with the ministerial office and was materially helpful after leaving it, have been important factors contributing to the political corruption of many Yugoslav politicians during the interwar period.

It is only fair to mention that King Alexander had an annual salary of 24 million dinars (approximately $500,000), which under the Yugoslav conditions was inexcusable. He was also known to be an astute financier with considerable financial interests at home and abroad.

dictatorship and was considered a model by many Serbs and Slovenes who felt that the peasants of these nations had to follow their Croatian brothers in organizing or strengthening their own peasant parties. In spite of extremely rigorous laws pertaining to political assemblies and the press, in spite of the great police terror and the open ballot, the united opposition gained in the 1935 elections 37 percent, and in those of 1938, 45 percent of the total vote cast. In both cases Prince Paul, the first regent, considered that the government party had lost the elections, but the only change which he undertook was to replace the respective prime ministers (Jevtić in 1935 and Stojadinović in 1938). The nature of the electoral law of 1931, which was extremely complicated, is best shown by the way in which the election results were reflected in the parliament. In 1935 the government party obtained 1,746,982 votes and 303 seats in the lower house of the parliament. The opposition gained 1,076,345 votes and only 67 seats. In 1938 elections the government party obtained 1,643,783 votes and 306 seats in the lower house while the opposition gained 1,364,524 votes and only 67 seats.[15] The election procedure for the senate was even less favorable for the opposition, as many of the senators were named directly by the Crown.

It has been necessary to stress these political developments in the country because in the attrition of many political parties which prevented the normal growth and rejuvenation of political leadership lay one of the basic weaknesses of the state. All parties became bound in their past, blind to general national issues, and bent on protection of their particular national or group interests. Had political freedom existed, the political and economic difficulties of the country, and especially the dismal position of the peasantry, would have occupied the center of political attention and perhaps some worth-while measures would have been taken to alleviate these difficulties. Those in power used all possible means to stay in power and to prevent any change in the political conditions of the country. Improvements in economic and social conditions were for them of little importance. Preventing or at least delaying changes in the body politic became the leading principle of their policy. This was quite understandable from their point of view, as any basic change would have meant either drastic curtailment or complete exclusion from power of those who now had everything. From the point of view of the general national interest it was a disastrous policy to follow.

[15] Data on the elections of 1935 from *Službene novine* (Belgrade), May 30, 1935, and for the elections of 1938 from Yugoslavia, *Annuaire statistique 1938–1939*, pp. 478–79.

The opposition parties commanded the support of the large masses of population, but they neither held together[16] nor were capable of developing a constructive political and economic program for the country as a whole. In fact, the opposition asserted itself as a united force only during the elections, which was simply a demonstration of protest against the existing regime. Their's was a unity against a political situation rather than for a definite and generally acceptable program of political and economic action.

Thus the country drifted along from year to year without a single party or group of parties being able to offer a program of political and economic reconstruction acceptable to all nations and to the overwhelming majority of the population, the peasantry. In fact, constitutional (national) and other primarily political issues used up so much energy and created so much ill feeling in the country that little time and energy remained for proper consideration or solution of the pressing economic and social issues.

In a political and social sense the interwar period in Yugoslavia was characterized by the rule of a very small minority, the Balkan version of the bourgeoisie. This minority consisted basically of higher government bureaucracy, including the military, the well-to-do urban people composed of the *rentiers* and business and professional people, and a thin layer of others living in rural areas, composed again of government bureaucrats, merchants, loan sharks, and of some wealthier peasants. The dynasty might be said to have served as the top and shield of this group. The churches, especially the higher clergy, were largely allied with these groups. This minority, which certainly did not amount to more than 5 or 10 percent of the total population, not only controlled the political power but also kept in its hands the overwhelming bulk of the economic power of the land. The essence of this type of rule in general, and in the Balkans in particular, is that the ruling group serves only its own interests, and in the promotion and defense of its interests it uses the power of the state in an extremely brazen and ruthless fashion. As the productive forces of the country were insufficiently developed, the state was not only the chief employer of all salaried people, but also the most important and the quickest source of enrichment. Thus, the conquest and retention of state power

[16] Thus, various supposedly opposition groups of the Radical party, the Slovenian People's party, and the Yugoslav Moslem Organization shifted into and out of the dictatorial governments on several occasions. The Croatian Peasant party, the staunchest opponent of the dictatorship, entered the government in August 1939 after obtaining a limited degree of autonomy for Croatia, letting down much of the opposition with which it went into the elections in 1935 and 1938.

become the supreme objective of such a group for economic purposes as well as political. Large-scale corruption was considered a natural concomitant of power. The service for the state, business with the state, and abuse of state power were the primary sources of wealth. In addition to outright corruption and graft, the ruling groups advanced their interests in many other ways. The system of direct taxes favored the rich, especially those possessing urban real estate and government bonds, the tariff protection was established for many industries which had no real basis for success, the cheap credit of the government credit institutions was largely distributed on the basis of political favor or good connections, and cartels were permitted to operate freely. Thus the state of Yugoslavia during the interwar period could be regarded as a domain of the few for the few. Needless to say, the Serbian control of almost all political and most economic key power positions in the country enabled the Serbian bourgeoisie, and especially its center, the Belgrade clique, to be the principal beneficiary of this regime.

PEASANTRY AS AN OBJECT IN POLITICS

Those who suffered most from this state of political and economic affairs were the great mass of the peasantry, the small working class, still half-peasant, and other low-income groups. The peasantry, forming three-fourths of the total population, was actually, if not formally, disfranchised. Its influence on government policies, in spite of the fact that the peasant vote was numerically the largest, was virtually nonexistent.

The primary means of keeping the peasantry under control were the use of the police force and economic power, especially in the form of credit. It did not matter that this apparatus of government force was composed of people who only recently had left the village themselves. In fact, that was an advantage from the point of view of the ruling groups. The life in the village was so hard and for many so hopeless that, to get away and stay away from it, these erstwhile peasants were willing and ruthless tools of oppression of their own brothers. The great Serbian social scientist Slobodan Jovanović, speaking of the conditions in Serbia around the middle of the nineteenth century, aptly said,

Nobody was so well fitted to beat up and keep down the peasant in the moccasin as another peasant who has put on the city coat. And nobody could teach and direct the peasant less than this peasant in the city coat.[17]

[17] Slobodan Jovanović, *Ustavobranitelji i njihova vlada* (The Defenders of the Constitution and Their Rule), Collected Works, V, 71. For the meaning of the terms "moccasin" and "city coat," see p. 250.

As time passed and conditions in the village worsened, this became even more true than it had been previously. It is generally agreed that most of those peasants' sons who succeeded in leaving the village and in establishing themselves either in government service or in business and professions were far worse in their relations with the peasantry than the people with a longer bourgeois tradition. This, however, seems to be a general, rather than a specifically Yugoslav, pattern of behavior of upstarts. What an uneducated or half-educated peasant in government service lacked in education and professional training, he more than compensated for by ruthlessness and callousness. In a somewhat poetic but extremely forceful fashion, this type of people was described in an article dealing with the problems of the village in Herzegovina during the 1930's as follows:

Even in wealthier families people will tighten their belts during the winter months and empty stomachs will growl. And we will continue to sing about the "violent type" and about the "manliness and heroism" of our people because we have been taught so by our folk poetry. Meanwhile the "violent type," who until yesterday was a shepherd, who in moccasins jumped from rock to rock, carved beautiful pictures on the distaff for his girl, and who with a bird's eye looked down from his mountains into the misty plain, will tomorrow, after having gone through a few grades of high school and acquired some position, be prepared to skin his brother, who is still in moccasins and with whom until yesterday he has eaten corn-meal mush from the same wooden bowl and with the same spoon. As forester, county chief, or a member of the parliament, as a simple clerk or as a sergeant in the *gendarmerie*, he will understand nothing and will not want to understand anything of the dismal conditions of his native community. On the contrary, in the unbridled way of a barbarian and a *nouveau riche*, he will jump on the back of his hungry people and soil even the bloody spot which he hit with his forehead when his mother gave him birth in a field furrow.[18]

This portrait of the Herzegovinian upstart is essentially valid for his brothers from other parts of Yugoslavia.

One of the chief economic tools with which the ruling groups in Yugoslavia controlled the peasantry was credit. For many reasons, which will be explained in Chapter 27, the peasant was dependent on credit almost year in, year out. And creditors' pressure can be easily used for political purposes. In no other area of Yugoslavia was peasant credit used so much for political purposes as in Serbia. "Any Serbian

---

[18] Dr. Branimir Gušić, "Today's Herzegovina," *Nova Evropa*, Nos. 7–8 (July–August, 1936), p. 207. The "violent type" referred to here is the product of the so-called patriarchal, hero-worshiping Dinaric culture. The close connection between hero-worshiping and the willingness to submit to those in power is a special characteristic of the political practice in the South Slav countries, with its attendant danger to democratic institutions. This was especially pointed out by Adam Pribičević, *Seljak* (The Peasant), pp. 180–87.

politician worthy of his salt," said Professor Bajkić, "must have his bank."[19] Somewhat earlier in the same study he said that loans of the provincial banks "were mostly given to peasants in small villages in the province, because the peasant in debt is the safest voter."[20]

But the ruling groups used regularly two other devices in their policy toward the peasantry. First, they appealed to various prejudices of the masses, for which Yugoslavia, as a multinational and multireligious country with varied historical background and a low level of economic and cultural development, offered sufficient opportunity. By incensing the peasants with prejudice against members of other nations, religions, or political views, they were able to draw their attention from basic issues of social and economic significance and present themselves as the protectors of their political and other interests. In no other area were the ruling groups as successful in this respect during the interwar period as in Serbia. But that cost the Serbian peasant his political liberty. Second, the ruling groups used the method of delaying the pressing issues of both political and economic nature, making in the meantime as much political capital out of them as possible. Some concessions were even made, as in the case of peasant debts. All this in order to gain time and in the hope that with the passage of time some way out would be found which did not jeopardize their political or economic interests.

PEASANTRY AS A SUBJECT IN POLITICS

Political oppression, social abuse, and economic exploitation, to which the Yugoslav peasantry was subjected during the interwar period, was nothing new. This had been the fate of peasants through centuries in the South Slav and most other lands, although changes had taken place in the ruling classes and in the methods of suppression and exploitation of the peasantry. Nevertheless, the peasants in the South Slav lands made some advances, and the nature of their struggle against this oppression and exploitation had changed. It changed from the sporadic armed rebellions of the serfs against individual feudal lords or groups of feudal lords, or against the heavy hand of bureaucracy, to the struggle through political organizations in the form of political parties and economic organizations, such as co-operatives. It changed from short, impulsive, bloody outbursts to long, more or less well-organized, and disciplined methods of modern party political warfare.

The struggle of the peasants for their rights and for a better life in

[19] Velimir Bajkić, *Seljački kredit* (Peasant Credit), p. 76.
[20] *Ibid.*, p. 17.

political, social, cultural, and economic respects had, in recent decades, one basic mark in all South Slav lands: it was a struggle against the city and all that the city represented. The city represented government bureaucracy, which in the eyes of the peasants had essentially replaced the former feudal class because it collected the taxes, it drafted the people for military service and forced labor, and it had all the power in its hands. The city represented the market where the peasant (most of the time) sold his products cheaply and bought dearly what he had to buy. It represented the chief source of credit on which the peasant depended and could get only at usurious rates of interest. Finally, it represented different social and cultural mores, a different system of life values. Its people had a different clothing, and altogether a different way of thinking and living. Figuratively speaking, the struggle between the village and the city has been epitomized both in literature and in political oratory as the struggle between the peasant moccasin (*opanak*) and the city coat (*kaput*). It has been the chief theme of politics in the South Slav lands for many decades. But although the grievances of the village against the town grew more numerous and better founded as time advanced and the political and economic hold of the town over the village increased, the peasantry alone was unable to formulate and still less to translate its political and economic yearnings into action. Political action has become a complicated business. It needed an ally from the town, and that ally was the small part of the intelligentsia which sided with the village and identified its interests with those of the village. In fact, it was this portion of the intelligentsia, later in the jargon of peasant politics known under the name of "honest people's intelligentsia," which initiated the process of modern political mobilization of the village. While that portion of the intelligentsia which associated itself with the ruling groups and gained a vested interest in the political and economic status quo was one of the peasantry's worst enemies, the "honest intelligentsia" was not only its indispensable ally but actually its leader. How well the peasants organized, what course of action they took in the political, cultural, and economic fields, and what they achieved depended essentially on how this "honest intelligentsia" kept faith with the needs and interests of the peasants and the programs which they formulated but which the peasants accepted as their own.

In terms of ideas the political mobilization of peasantry in the South Slav lands represented essentially the application of the ideas of the French Revolution and other political and social revolutionary movements of Western Europe on the peasant masses. This application took place with a time lag, often of over a century. In many cases these ideas began to be propagated in the South Slav lands after having passed through the Russian sieve and taken on some of the specifically Russian or Slavic features. The nature and record of organized political activity of the peasants in the South Slav lands before 1941 varies greatly from area to area.[21] If this record in any area is measured by the standard of attaining and holding power, by organizing the state and conducting the state policies in the interests of the peasants, or if the achievements are compared with the programs, this record was one of failure. But in a larger sense, it is quite impressive. Through the peasant movements the broad peasant masses, before this almost completely inactive politically, entered actively into the political arena. They have since been politically educated to a considerable degree, and they have come to appreciate the meaning of political organization and discipline. Any regime in Yugoslavia, as in other countries of Southeastern and Eastern Europe, has to consider the peasantry as one of the basic political forces in the country. Prior to the advent of the peasant movements, the peasants, from a political point of view, could be considered as just so many cattle.

In Serbia the loosely organized Liberal party was the first to try in the 1860's to fight the entrenched bureaucracy by leaning somewhat on the political support of the peasantry. But the first real political movement in Serbia giving expression to the political and economic aspirations of the peasantry came at the beginning of the 1870's. The originator of this movement was Svetozar Marković (1846–75), a socialist, who, while studying in Switzerland and later Russia, became a disciple of the Russian socialist, N. S. Chernyshevsky, and who tried to apply socialist ideas to the conditions of a peasant country—Serbia. Like some of the Russian reformers he thought that Serbian peasantry, by building up on the house collective, or zadruga, could slide into a socialist economy with modern technology without going through the "purgatory of capitalism." But more important, Svetozar Marković was the spiritual father of the People's Radical party, established in 1881 by Nikola Pašić, himself originally a disciple of Bakunin, and others (Pera Todorović, Adam Bogosavljević), and based on peasant masses. Soon after its establishment the Radical party became the chief popular political force in Serbia and controlled Serbian political life from 1903 to 1918 and the Yugoslav party political life from 1918 to 1929. It

---

[21] A good review of the nature, record, and achievements of the peasant movements in various South Slav nations up to the late 1930's is to be found in a special issue of the Sarajevo journal of opinion, *Pregled*, for July–August, 1937, dedicated to the theme, "The Village and the Peasantry."

originally became great because of its opposition to state bureaucracy, and by its struggle for political liberties, the rights of the parliament as against the Crown and bureaucracy, local self-government, and improved agricultural credit. This party acquired its great prestige partly also because of its nationalist program and its opposition to the pro-Austrian foreign policy of the Obrenović dynasty. But as soon as the Radical party went into power, as soon as it became a government party, it forgot its propeasant program. In fact, it soon became the main party of the nascent Serbian bourgeoisie, and, what is even more significant, it became the most corrupt party in all Serbian history. Nevertheless, the Radical party commanded the support of most of the Serbian peasants, at least until the end of the 1920's. This support was maintained by the tight hold of the Radical party machine over the peasants, by the great prestige of its leader Pašić (who died in 1926) and his hold over the popular mind, distribution of patronage, and by the use of credit to peasants as a tool of political control. Of course, after 1918 they used, perhaps more than any other party, the fanning of prejudice of the Serbian peasants against other nations, especially against the Croats and their leaders.

The other leading Serbian party of the interwar period, the Democratic party, also commanded considerable support among the Serbian peasantry and was somewhat less corrupt than the Radical party, though in essence it was also a party which only paid lip service to the interests of the peasants.

According to its program and according to the actions of a part of it leaders, the only purely peasant party during the interwar period in Serbia was the Union of Peasants (Savez zemljoradnika). It approached the peasant issue as a class issue, and in its socioeconomic program, which included many features of agrarian socialism, it was quite radical. The Union of Peasants was organized in 1919 as a peasant party embracing all areas of Yugoslavia, and in the beginning it had adherents in most of them. Soon thereafter it remained of importance only in Serbia and the northwestern parts of Bosnia, where its roots went back to the peasant movement of the first two decades of this century when it was led by Petar Kočić. In Serbia itself the leadership of the party became split between the "liberals" and the "reactionaries" and because of it largely lost any value it may have had as a vehicle for the political expression of Serbian peasantry. Various attempts at the rejuvenation of leadership of the Union of Peasants, and the activity of some political mavericks to salvage and rebuild the peasant movement in Serbia during the 1930's, remained without any appreciable result.[22] Because of the small political significance of the Union of Peasants in Serbian politics during the interwar period and the outspoken bourgeois character of the two other Serbian political parties, one can say with justification that during that period the Serbs had no peasant party of great strength. While the absence of feudal forms in Serbia since 1830, the absence of large estates, and the considerable engagement of the Serbian peasant in politics induced many people to talk of Serbia, especially between 1903 and 1914, as a true peasant democracy, most of it was without foundation. In this regard, one of the Serbian scholars said in 1920, "The peasant as a person was less esteemed than the worst city dweller and his shortcomings were healed more by police methods than by schools and education."[23] And Professor Velimir Bajkić refers to the Serbian peasant of pre-1914 days as "a martyr," and simply says, "The peasant lives like a dog."[24]

In Slovenia, the Slovenian People's (Catholic) party also had its chief support in the village. Its leadership was challenged, but not with much success, by both the liberals and a small peasant party. More perhaps than any political party in the history of the South Slavs, the Slovenian People's party paid constant attention to the economic and cultural improvement of its membership. In this it reaped impressive results. Through systematic efforts and persistence it developed an extremely well-organized and efficient co-operative system and a well-managed and huge program of popular education. Thanks to the efforts of its co-operative arm, it solved with considerable success the problem of cheap and ample agricultural credit, a problem which proved insolvable in all other South Slav areas. True to its origins and its Catholic political philosophy, this party had a paternalistic attitude toward peasantry and its following from other classes of the population. Considering the successses of this party in regard to the solution of some of the basic problems of the peasantry, one should not forget that it dealt with a population on a relatively high cultural level, emotionally very stable, thrifty, and diligent, and above all willing to work for fruits which take time to ripen. The chief consideration of this political party during the interwar period was to maintain its hold on the Slovenian masses, in which it fully succeeded, and to secure for Slovenia a virtual,

[22] For good statements on the Serbian peasant movement during the interwar period see Miloš S. Moskovljević, "The Peasant Movement Among the Serbs," *Pregled*, July–August, 1937, pp. 418–27, and Dragoljub Jovanović, "The Unity of the Peasant Movement," *ibid.*, pp. 440–48.

[23] Tihomir Ostojić, "Peasant Democracy," *Nova Evropa*, I, No. 1 (September 1920), 19.

[24] Velimir Bajkić, *op. cit.*, p. 80.

if not formal, autonomy. In the latter aim it also succeeded by following a shrewd and opportunistic political line. But in Slovenia, just as in Serbia, during the interwar period there was no typical peasant party with a large following.

THE CROATIAN PEASANT PARTY

The most interesting, and by far the strongest, peasant party in Yugoslavia during the interwar period was the Croatian Peasant party. Its membership was almost 100 percent Croatian. This party was originally established in 1905 but came into prominence only after World War I. It was the creation of two intellectuals of peasant stock, the Radić brothers: Antun, the creator of its principles and ideology, and Stjepan, its political organizer and moving power. Peasant parties of a general populist character rose in almost all peasant countries of Eastern and Southeastern Europe toward the end of the nineteenth and at the beginning of the twentieth century under the influence, on the one hand, of the democratic ideas of the French Revolution, and, on the other, of the ideas of the Russian Populists (Narodniki), romanticizing the common peasant. But perhaps in no other country did the peasant ideology aspire to wider horizons than in Croatia, even though it contained a large amount of confusion and contradiction and a liberal dose of utopia.

The fundamental idea of the Croatian Peasant party is that the state and political life should be based on the principles of social justice. This was not the case either in Croatia, where the peasants numbered about 80 percent of the total population, or in other peasant countries at that time. The power was in the hands of a small minority, the remainders of the feudal class, the Church, and the small bourgeois class. These forces used the state power to further their own interests. The aim of the Peasant party was, therefore, to take the power from the hands of this minority and to put it into the hands of the vast majority, the peasantry. In peasant countries the peasantry, or the "fifth estate," has the natural right—that is, the right of the majority—to rule, but this rule has to be a rule of justice for all.[25] The basic political tenet was that in peasant countries the will and the needs of the peasants have to take precedence over the will and the needs of other classes; that is, the interest of the peasants is the general, the national, interest. The

---

[25] It maintained that the rule of the "third estate," or the bourgeoisie, in peasant countries was detrimental to the peasantry because the ruling class used the peasantry as an object of exploitation, keeping it in a state of poverty, ignorance, and political and economic bondage. It also maintained that the rule of the "fourth estate," or the working class, was inacceptable because the workers also formed a small minority.

Radić brothers proceeded to educate and organize politically the peasant masses of Croatia with that aim in mind.[26] It was generally considered prior to World War I that this objective could not be reached, and the brilliant but demagogic Stjepan Radić was laughed at by the Croatian bourgeoisie for many years. The Croatian peasant masses were in the beginning also quite unresponsive, and the Radić brothers likened the peasantry to a "blind giant" lacking belief in his own strength. The philosophy of the Peasant party maintained that the Croatian peasantry alone forms the Croatian nation and that it alone is the creator and repository, on a collective basis, of a genuine, autochthonous, national, peasant culture. Because of this original culture and a particular peasant honesty, the peasantry in its politics is liberty- and justice-loving, village-collective-minded rather than individualistic, social (humanitarian), and pacifist. Its aim was to establish a peasant state based on the above political and social tenets.

Two marks were characteristic of the political program of the Croatian Peasant party from the beginning: it was strongly nationalistic, of a Pan-Slav orientation, and it was strongly anticlerical. What especially attracted the Radić brothers, in their Pan-Slav or pro-Russian orientation, was the body of values attached to the heart and soul of the peasantry, as shown in much of the Russian literature, and the teachings of the Russian Populists. Their anticlericalism was pure and simple opposition to the antinational and reactionary political and social role played by the political forces which were controlled by the Catholic Church in Croatia, and not the expression of an antireligious feeling. The Radić brothers could not hope to penetrate the village politically without breaking the hold of the rural clergy over the minds of the peasants. On the other hand, they knew that the peasant was greatly attached to religion. Hence it was necessary to combine reverence for religion and anticlericalism in one package.[27] Before 1914 the party

[26] The activity of the two brothers in educating the peasant masses began in 1900 with the publishing of a weekly newspaper called *Dom* (The Home), and continued at an increasing rate in the following years. The study of the village of Croatia was begun in a systematic fashion by Antun Radić in the mid-1890's, and much of his work was published by the Yugoslav Academy of Science and Art in Zagreb in a special series on the life and customs of the Croatian peasantry, a series that is still appearing—*Zbornik za narodni život i običaje Južnih Slavena.*

[27] Stjepan Radić used sometimes to open his political meetings with the greeting, "Praise be to Jesus, down with the clergy!" (*Hvaljen Isus, dolje s popovima!*). Talking about the roles of religion and the churches among the Slavic nations, Stjepan Radić said, "Thus it is clear that the antagonism between nationality and religion and the antagonism between Church and State, in which both clericalism and anticlericalism are rooted, are foreign to the Slavic spirit. To this spirit nothing is as wicked as touch-

showed an extremely slow, though steady progress. It should also be pointed out that the activity of the party at that time was concentrated in northern and central Croatia. To appreciate the magnitude of the task undertaken by the two brothers, it should be repeated that in 1905, when the party was organized, perhaps not even 1 percent of the Croatian peasants had the franchise, and that a large part of the Croatian bourgeoisie was denationalized and willingly doing the bidding of the ruling groups of Hungary and Austria.

As in other areas of Southeastern and Eastern Europe, World War I led to an upsurge of the political activity of the Croatian peasantry. Building upon the more than two decades of educational and organizational political work of the two Radić brothers, there ensued after 1918 a general political mobilization of the peasant masses in Croatia. As the general franchise was introduced, the "politization" of the peasantry became visible in election results. The reaction of the peasants to the war and the establishment of the new state of Yugoslavia forced Stjepan Radić to adjust his political program to the new situation. He did this by stressing and elaborating the pacifist plank of his program and accepting republicanism and the principle of national self-determination as other leading planks. The principle of national self-determination, as announced by President Wilson in his Fourteen Points, was accepted as an important idea of practical politics under the new conditions in Yugoslavia. Radić's wrath was as much directed against the Serbian ruling groups, which controlled the new state, as against the Croatian bourgeois parties (especially the successors of the pre-1914 Croato-Serbian Coalition), which accepted a centrally organized Yugoslav state without securing proper rights for the Croatian nation, that is, without insisting on a federal organization of Yugoslavia. His great skill as a leader of an underprivileged class—which for the first time in history thought of itself as a subject, a deciding factor in politics—his ardent nationalism, republicanism, and pacifism attracted to the Croatian Peasant party practically the whole peasantry and, soon thereafter, also the bulk of the Croatian intelligentsia and bourgeoisie. After the elections of March 1923 the Croatian Peasant party became the only important political force among the Croats, a true representative of the nation. The outlawing of the party, incarceration of its leadership early in 1925, and assassination of Radić and several other leaders in June 1928 in the Belgrade parliament made the party

---

ing into the religious teachings and nothing so godless and hateful as amassing of wealth and the struggle for power in the name of religion." *Savremena Evropa* (Contemporary Europe), p. 212.

stronger rather than weaker. It remained so until the end of the inter-war period. As such, it became the envy of most other political parties in Yugoslavia. Almost throughout the interwar period, except for a short interval in 1925 and 1926 and again from August 1939 onward, the Croatian Peasant party conducted a constant struggle against the existing political organization of Yugoslavia. Actually its energy spent itself almost completely in the field of purely political struggle for the national rights of Croatia. But as long as the national question is not solved, this is the usual function of any political party aspiring to or actually holding national leadership.

As far as the ideology of the party is concerned, no new additions were made after the death of Antun Radić in 1919.[28] Both Stjepan Radić and his successor Vladimir Maček were primarily political prac-titioners, rather than creators of political ideologies or programs. One of the chief interpreters of the ideology of the party during the interwar period was Rudolf Herceg, the chief of its cultural arm—the Seljačka Sloga. In a speech in May 1940 over Radio Zagreb, Herceg referred to his organization as the "ideological purifier of the Croatian, and the nursery of the world's peasant movement." It cannot be said that his interpretations were penetrating, that they clarified much of what was nebulous in the teachings of the Radić brothers, or that they helped to make the party's ideology forward- instead of largely backward-looking.

On the other hand, there was a group of younger economists and sociologists who tried to apply some of the principles of the Croatian Peasant party to practical economic and social issues. This undertak-ing was greatly stimulated by the ravages of the Great Depression among the peasants of Croatia. Since the government was undertaking no measures to alleviate the economic distress in the village, the Peas-ant party, having full sway among the Croatian peasantry, had to take some steps or else lose at least part of its great prestige and following. Thus, this group organized the co-operative arm of the Peasant party— the Gospodarska Sloga—and undertook through it to improve the eco-nomic lot of the peasants (see pp. 616–18). In general, it preached and helped to organize, and partially also to finance, self-help among the peasants. Furthermore, this group engaged in a systematic study of the economic structure and the economic needs and problems of the

---

[28] The core of the ideology of the Croatian Peasant party can be found in the *Temeljni nauk ili program hrvatske republikanske seljačke stranke* (Basic Principles or the Program of the Croatian Republican Peasant Party), adopted and proclaimed in 1921. The fact that the two Radić brothers have written a tremendous amount of ma-terial, much of it relating to the program of the party, made different interpretations possible.

Croatian peasantry, an essential task to which the originators of the party, and practically all of its later leaders, paid little or no attention. The moving spirit of this group, as far as organization and management of economic measures were concerned, was Dragutin Toth, who apparently was greatly liked and enjoyed the full confidence of the peasants. The best-known spokesman of the group and the organizer of its research activities was Rudolf Bićanić.

Proclaiming itself the general national movement and branding all Croats outside of its ranks as traitors, the party opened its doors to all social classes (which was in agreement with its teaching) and all political groups (which was not), and thus in its ranks showed the whole spectrum of political colors, with the exception of the extreme left. During the 1930's it was infiltrated by Croatian fascist elements and a wing of the Peasant party came under the influence of the Croatian ultranationalists. Meanwhile it dropped most of its original anticlericalism, and post-1918 conditions led to the abandonment of its Pan-Slavic orientation.

Had the Peasant party ever had an opportunity to hold or effectively participate in power for a longer period of time, there is no doubt that contradictions of interests of the various groups and social classes united in it would have led to differences and probably to splits into factions. Thus, for example, one of its basic misconceptions of great political, economic, and social import was the view that the village as a social unit, and the peasantry as a whole, are economically and socially homogeneous. It was manifest, however, that economic and social differentiation in the village and among the peasants was pronounced and that this differentiation was becoming greater from year to year. Furthermore, while committed to the proposition of raising the plane of living of the peasant masses, it considered mass industrialization as an untoward development. Industrialization and the transformation of peasants into industrial workers en masse were bound to destroy the peasant cultural heritage and ethos, the greatest asset of the Croatian peasantry (people), according to the ideology of the party. The increasing agricultural overpopulation would, no doubt, have forced in time a revision of these views.

The ideology of the party was opposed to the philosophy and practices of capitalism, socialism, and communism. It was groping after the solution of the political, economic, and social problems of the peasant countries in a specific, peasant fashion. The economic and social program of the movement included, however, very radical reforms, though of a conditional nature. The party was against all those institutions and policies which it considered as sources of privileges for the urban population or special interest groups, and for a system of political and economic policies that would serve the peasants.[29] Nobody can say how the Croatian Peasant party would have performed had it ever achieved a fully autonomous Croatia in normal political conditions and kept power for a long time. The experience in other peasant countries of Europe during the interwar period shows that with the exception of Czechoslovakia, where the Peasant party participated steadily in coalition governments, the peasant parties were a great force in opposition, but as political vehicles for capturing, and especially for holding, power they proved a failure. After a few years in power, these parties were either broken up, thrown out of office, or made impotent by small but strong traditional power groups in these countries: the dynasties, military cliques, the upper strata of the city bourgeoisie, and high bureaucracy.[30] Relying on the operation of democratic principles and abhorring violence, peasant parties proved absolutely incapable of holding power in these countries against the above groups, which never shrank from using brute force to seize and maintain themselves in power. Thus, while the leaders and programs of the peasant parties attracted practically the whole peasantry in their respective countries during the interwar period, the establishment of a peasant democracy and of peasant states remained only a distant dream. But, unfortunately, one must largely agree with the following diagnosis by Professor Mijo Mirković of the relationship between the peasant parties and the peasantry:

Peasant ideologies and peasant movements in countries of peasant farming show very little knowledge indeed of the real conditions of peasant property and of the peasants. These ideologies and movements are based on irrational elements—the past, religion, and nationality—and take little into account the economic facts of life.[31]

The peasantry is praised, the value of peasant property is praised, peasant ideologies are created, but at the same time there is complete absence of any positive program favoring the peasants. This situation is typical of all countries

[29] The best source of information on the economic philosophy of the Croatian Peasant party is the pamphlets and numerous articles by Rudolf Bićanić written during the second half of the 1930's. But in spite of his close association with the leader of the party, Vladimir Maček, and the important position he held in the Gospodarska Sloga, many people in the party, especially those in its center and the right wing, maintained that Bićanić was not a true spokesman for the party either in economic or other matters.

[30] Hugh Seton-Watson, *Eastern Europe Between the Wars 1918–1941*. A good review of the political developments in Yugoslavia between the two world wars is found on pp. 216–41.

[31] Mijo Mirković, *Održanje seljačkog posjeda* (The Preservation of Peasant Property), p. 106.

in which the peasants form an overwhelming majority. Ideologists, political parties, and governments fight for the support of the peasants but do not know how to improve the economic conditions of the peasantry. In a word, the more the peasants are praised the worse becomes their position.[32]

As will be shown later (Chapter 17), it was becoming more and more obvious during the 1930's that the solution of the problem of agriculture and peasantry could not be found within agriculture itself but rather in a policy directed toward rapid development of industry and modernization of agriculture. A reorientation in this direction would have required a revision in the ideology and programs of most peasant parties of Southeastern and Eastern Europe.

CONCLUDING OBSERVATIONS

While the establishment of Yugoslavia in 1918 was a product of historical necessity and was greeted favorably by a large majority of the population in all South Slav nations, it cannot be said that it was a success during the interwar period. Yugoslavia as constituted and governed during that period showed little political, ideological, and social cohesion, and little concern for the general welfare. The legacy of the past proved too difficult to erase. The difficulties of adjustment of the new state internally as well as within the new Balkan, Danubian, and European political and economic frameworks proved such that the Yugoslav state of the interwar period was really never consolidated. It was kept together by force alone. The Yugoslav national idea, which had been accepted before 1914 by a segment of the population especially among the intelligentsia in all South Slav nations and which apparently triumphed in 1918, was abused by the successive regimes of Belgrade and made into a servant of Serbian hegemony. Thus the political idea, which should have served as the pivot around which all South Slav nations could gather, became completely discredited. As time advanced, conditions became worse. For political, social, and economic reasons—unsolved national questions, the precarious international situation, the worsening position and dissatisfaction of the broad peasant masses, the dissatisfaction of a large portion of the intelligentsia, inability or unwillingness of the ruling groups to tackle the burning political and economic issues in the country, and finally the absence of hope for a better tomorrow—the existing order was in the process of disintegration and the state more and more ready for revolution. It would be wrong, however, to put the whole blame for this de-

---

[32] Mijo Mirković, *Održanje selačkog posjeda*, p. 19.

velopment on the ruling groups in Yugoslavia, or primarily on their controlling, Serbian faction, though the latter's share of blame was overwhelming. Part of the blame has to be carried by all the citizens of Yugoslavia and by the political forces which spent practically the whole of the interwar period in opposition. Part of the blame has also to be assigned to the general European political situation, which did not favor democratic forces, especially in the small countries which were appendages of one or another of the European Great Powers or power blocs.

When the test came—the invasion in April 1941—the whole fabric of the state simply disintegrated. Whole nations and the great bulk of population, especially the peasantry, apparently felt that the state in the form in which it existed was nothing that belonged to them and thus was not worth fighting for. The speed and the manner in which Yugoslavia collapsed, the nature and extent of the fifth-column activity, the formation of quisling states, and the following fratricidal warfare gave the impression that Yugoslavia would never fight its way back into any kind of unity. With the total collapse of the old regime, with the discrediting of the dynasty, the army, and almost all former political parties and their leaders, Yugoslavia was a wreck wallowing in the turbulent seas of Europe at war, seething with internal revolutionary and counterrevolutionary fires. But that also meant that a new political force would attract some support from all South Slav nations, if it were capable of organizing effective resistance against the enemy and the domestic quislings and of presenting a new political program on which, from the very beginning, a portion of all Yugoslav nations could agree. As the experiences during World War II and the years following its termination show, the role of the re-creator of the Yugoslav state, based on a new Yugoslav synthesis, was played, ironically enough, by the Yugoslav Communist party, the party which was outlawed as early as 1921 and which throughout the interwar period was the target of all regimes. Yugoslavia has been reconstituted along federal lines, granting autonomy to national units which largely coincide with historical provinces. The basic political problem of the interwar Yugoslavia—the national question—has been solved as well as is possible under the tangled national conditions in Yugoslavia.

Nevertheless, Yugoslavia of the interwar period was a great improvement over the political conditions under which the South Slav nations lived until 1918.

CHAPTER 14

THE NATURAL RESOURCES BASE OF
YUGOSLAV AGRICULTURE

AFTER having placed the Yugoslav agriculture both in its historical perspective and within the political framework of the interwar period, a third step must be made before entering upon a more detailed analysis of its development during the 1918–40 period, that is, placing the agriculture of Yugoslavia in its physical setting. This involves a brief description of the physical configuration of the country, its climate, soils, and other factors which form the natural basis and the natural limits within which the agriculture of the country developed. Finally, a brief outline of the various agricultural regions of Yugoslavia will be given. Even a brief description of the physical characteristics of the country will show that—as in political, social, and economic matters— differences and contrasts, rather than uniformity, are characteristic of the natural resources base of the Yugoslav agriculture in various areas.

LOCATION AND TOPOGRAPHY

Yugoslavia of the interwar period had a territory of 247,542 square kilometers (95,558 square miles).[1] It is located between 40° 51′ and 46° 53′ north latitude and between 13° 43′ and 23° 02′ east longitude. It is therefore approximately in the middle latitudes of the Northern Hemisphere.

One of the most interesting geographic characteristics of Yugoslavia is its varied relief (Map 4), which influences profoundly its climate and soil and thereby is of primary importance for the whole agricultural and livestock production. Within its territory there are six separate and well-defined mountain systems. In the northwestern corner of the country, or Slovenia, are the eastern ranges of the Alps. In the Yugoslav territory the Alps split in several distinct ranges of mountains, the Karawanken Alps and the Kamniški Alps extending in an easterly direction, and the Julian Alps to the southeast.

Southwest of Ljubljana the Julian Alps pass into the Dinaric System,

[1] The area of Yugoslavia during the interwar period was slightly larger than that of the United Kingdom (94,279 square miles) and slightly smaller than that of the state of Oregon (96,981 square miles).

262

MAP 4

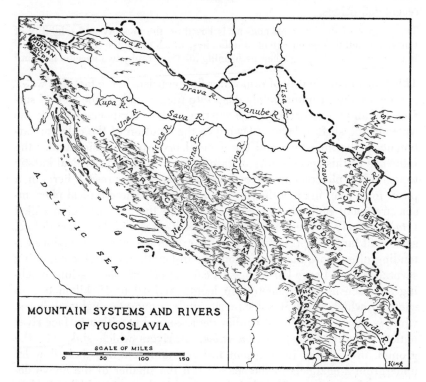

MOUNTAIN SYSTEMS AND RIVERS
OF YUGOSLAVIA

•

SCALE OF MILES

0   50   100   150

the largest and most characteristic mountain range of Yugoslavia. It
follows the eastern coast of the Adriatic Sea and becomes wider as it
extends toward the southeast and covers practically the whole central
area of the country (about 40 percent of the total territory). It occupies a considerable portion of Slovenia, all of southwestern Croatia,
the whole of Dalmatia, Herzegovina, and Montenegro, almost all of
Bosnia, and the western and southwestern portions of Serbia. The Serbian geographer, the late Jovan Cvijić, the greatest authority on the
Dinaric System, divided it into three distinct parts according to their
topographic characteristics: the coastal, relatively low area, or *primorje*; the area of the high mountains, or Dinaric Alps, or *planine*;
and the transitional zone between the two, or *zagora*.[2] Most of the
Dinaric area is characterized by the karstic phenomena, namely, specific morphological formations giving to this area distinct geographical

[2] Jovan Cvijić, *La Péninsule Balkanique*, p. 73.

features and the specific name of karst. According to one of the most recent definitions,

The essence of the karst phenomena is based on the porosity and solubility of limestone, and to a lesser extent of dolomites, which cause the rain water to flow in a typical (karstic) way, thereby forming the topography in a specific fashion.[3]

This typical karstic way of rain-water flow consists in the fact that water percolates almost immediately deep into the ground, as the lack of surface soil and the structure of the existing surface strata cannot keep the water in the surface layers. Owing to the solution of the calcium carbonate in the limestone and the general process of erosion under the influence of this specific way of rain-water flow, certain typical karstic topographic phenomena have developed and are present here in a purer form than in any other part of the world. These typical phenomena are small hollows or *škrape*; gullies in the *zagora* region called *vrtače*, namely, depressions of a few tens of meters in diameter; *doline*, somewhat larger depressions than *vrtače*; and *uvale*, or depressions extending often more than one kilometer in length and often comprising several *doline*. Large karstic basins called *polja* are depressions reaching as much as 60 kilometers in length and 10 to 15 kilometers in width, in which rain water disappears underground through sink holes, while *kotline* are somewhat similar depressions but with a surface river outlet. Finally, there are *ponornice*, or rivers which sink into the ground, often in an intermittent fashion, and continue their flow by underground channels to the sea.[4] Even the smaller of the above depressions have some soil on their bottoms, but the *polja*, which are often inundated for much of the year because the great mass of water cannot flow fast enough through the sink holes, and the *kotline* are the only important areas in the karst region suitable for agriculture. However, along the coast and on the northeastern slopes of the Dinaric System there are some river valleys and other areas suitable for raising crops. Owing to the specific type of rock formation and water flow in the karst, sources of fresh water are rare.

The karst area includes, roughly, the territory between the Adriatic coast and the line which runs approximately from the Gulf of Trieste northeastward to Ljubljana in Slovenia, then southeastward to the town of Kolašin in Montenegro, and thence down the Morača and Bojana

[3] Alfred Šerko, "The Karst Phenomena in Yugoslavia," *Geografski vestnik*, XIX, 43.
[4] Cvijić, *op. cit.*, pp. 72–73; Alfred Šerko, *op. cit.*, p. 45. For the genesis of karstification see Anton Melik, *Jugoslavija—Zemljopisni pregled* (Yugoslavia—A Geographic Survey), pp. 40–46, hereafter quoted as Melik, *Jugoslavija*. A pictorial illustration of some of these phenomena can be seen in Raymond E. Crist, "The Peasant Problem in Yugoslavia," *The Scientific Monthly*, May 1940, pp. 385–402.

rivers back to the Adriatic coast.[5] The whole karst area with regard to
the vegetation cover can be roughly divided into four zones: the ever-
green, the montane, the subalpine, and the alpine zones; but more
precisely the area is divided in that regard into seven different zones.
These zones and their vegetation cover depend primarily on the altitude, but modified by specific local factors.[6] One of the specific marks
of the karst area, especially near the Adriatic coast, is the so-called bare
karst, which, in fact, is nothing but a mountainous and hilly stone
desert. Much of the whole karst area is referred to in Yugoslavia as the
"passive regions," that is, areas greatly deficient in food production as
well as in other earning opportunities and therefore depending for
livelihood, to a large extent, on outside earnings. The need for reforestation is one of the basic economic problems of these regions. But
a portion of the karst area, especially in the interior, is covered by
deciduous and coniferous forests representing the most important timber resources in Yugoslavia.

Toward the north (Bosnia) and toward the northeast (all of western Serbia) the Dinaric System slopes gradually, though less so toward
the southwestern portions of Serbia where it forms a plateau. The
slopes toward the north and northeast and the plains along the rivers
which flow from the Dinaric System toward the Sava River form the
southern limit of the great Pannonian Plain.

The third system of mountains continuing on the southern ranges
of the Dinaric System is the Pindus–Šar Mountain (or the Greco-Al-
banian) range, occupying in Yugoslavia the southwestern portion of
Macedonia. Like the Alps and the Dinaric System the Pindus–Šar
Mountain range is a relatively young system of mountains and of rugged
landscape, but in its morphology it differs considerably from the Dinaric System. Limestone formations play an insignificant role here.

The fourth system of mountains in Yugoslavia is the Rhodope
Massif, which occupies the remainder of Macedonia and all of central
Serbia, reaching to the outskirts of Belgrade. The Rhodope Massif is
the only range of relict mountains in Yugoslavia, and as such it has
rounded mountaintops with mild slopes. Because of climatic and soil
conditions and because its original forest cover had been destroyed,
a large portion of the Rhodope Massif area, so far as not cultivated,
is covered with grass. This is especially true in Macedonia where in
summer these mountain grasslands turn dry and form what is locally
called *suvati*. The Rhodope Massif range is richer in minerals than

---

[5] Alfred Šerko, *op. cit.*, p. 50; Josip Balen, *Naš goli krš* (Our Bare Karst), p. 5.
[6] For a detailed discussion of this problem, see L. Adamović, *Die Pflanzenwelt der
Adrialänder*, pp. 153–62; see also Josip Balen, *op. cit.*, pp. 37–51.

any other mountain system in Yugoslavia, particularly in nonferrous metals.

The fifth system is the Balkan range entering Yugoslavia from the east (Bulgaria) and occupying a relatively small part of territory in the east of Serbia. Finally there is the Carpathian mountain range which protrudes from Rumania across the Danube River into the north-easternmost corner of Serbia. This range is marked by a considerable area of volcanic rock formations and, as such, is rich in minerals. Both of these ranges are also exceedingly rugged, largely deforested, and to a certain extent marked by karstic phenomena.

The northern and northeastern areas of Yugoslavia are occupied by the southern part of the great Pannonian Plain, consisting of the valleys of the Danube, Tisa (Tisza, Theiss), Sava, and Drava rivers and the whole or portion of the valleys of their tributaries. This essentially flat area, reaching in the south to the slopes of the Dinaric System, in the southeast including flat parts of Serbia along the Sava, Danube, and the lower reaches of the Morava rivers, and in the west reaching into the northeastern section of Slovenia, is agriculturally by far the most important area—in fact, the granary of Yugoslavia. The core of this area is, however, Vojvodina, Srijem, and parts of Slavonia.[7]

Thus, geographically, Yugoslavia can be roughly divided into three great regions: (1) the Pannonian Plain, just identified, (2) the central, mountainous area occupying most of the country's territory and characterized by either high mountain ranges or lower mountains and hilly regions, and (3) the coastal area along the eastern shore of the Adriatic Sea. Needless to say, each one of these three areas, and especially the central region, can be divided, and usually is divided for the purpose of closer study, into a great number of smaller areas and regions, forming specific geographic units.

According to Melik, the total Yugoslav territory, which within its 1945 frontiers amounted to 256,850 square kilometers, was distributed as follows with respect to elevation above the sea level:[8]

Elevation in meters	Percent of total territory
Up to 200	29.4
200 to 500	25.4
500 to 1,000	27.4
1,000 to 1,500	14.0
1,500 to 2,000	3.3
Above 2,000	0.5

[7] For a detailed geographer's description of the main river valleys of Yugoslavia, see Borivoje Ž. Milojević, *Glavne doline u Jugoslaviji* (The Main River Valleys in Yugoslavia), pp. 227–440.   [8] Melik, *Jugoslavija*, pp. 12–14.

Of the 29.4 percent of total land below 200 meters in altitude, 25 percent is located in the Pannonian Plain, as defined above, 3.2 percent in the coastal region along the Adriatic, and the remainder in Macedonia and along the Timok River in northeastern Serbia. There is no doubt that this relatively high altitude of most of Yugoslavia represents one of the natural limits for the availability of good agricultural land. Owing to the mountainous character of the country, much land is too steeply inclined and thus unsuitable for cultivation.

CLIMATE

The climate of Yugoslavia is influenced by two basic factors: the geographic location of the country and its topographic configuration. Yugoslavia's location in Southeastern Europe places it in an area in which three different climatic zones meet: the zone of the Mediterranean climate, the zone of the modified Atlantic or Central European climate, and the zone of Continental or Eastern European climate. Its topographic configuration, on the other hand, is responsible for the fact that the various zonal climates are greatly modified by the terrain. The Dinaric Range represents an effective barrier against any considerable penetration of the mild influences of the Mediterranean climate into the interior of the central and northwestern parts of the country, while the Pindus–Šar Mountain and the Rhodope Massif ranges prevent the penetration, on a large scale, of the Mediterranean climate from the Aegean Sea into Macedonia. But while these three mountain ranges limit the influences of the Mediterranean climate to the fringe areas of the country in the south and southwest, the openness of the country toward the north and northeast allows unobstructed penetration of the Central European and Eastern European climates from the north and the northeast. Differences in altitude, openness to, or isolation of various areas from the influences of the principal zonal climates, variations in the surface and vegetative cover, and regional winds make for great variations in prevailing temperatures and in total precipitation as well as in their distribution by months and by seasons. It is often stated that few countries of the same size have as many climatic variations as does Yugoslavia.[9]

Yugoslav authors usually divide the country in a number of principal and transitional zones. The best-known Yugoslav climatologist, Pavle Vujević, divides Yugoslavia into three main zones: the Mediter-

[9] M. Y. Nuttonson, *Agricultural Climatology of Yugoslavia and Its Agro-Climatic Analogues in North America*, International Agro-Climatological Series, No. 4 (Washington, D.C., 1947), p. 9.

ranean, the Central European, and the Continental zones, and the local zone of mountain climate with various other transitional areas.[10] Aleksandar Stebut's climatic division of Yugoslavia, which is essentially based on the Vujević classification, distinguishes four main zonal and three transitional types of climate.[11] Of the four basic zones three are, so to speak, extensions of the surrounding climatic zones, namely, of the Mediterranean, the Central European, and the Continental or Eastern European climates, while the fourth basic zone, the zone of mountain climate, is of local character and a result of high altitudes prevailing in the center of the country. The Mediterranean climate in its modified form prevails along the Adriatic coast and is characterized by mild winters and hot summers. The range between the January and the July average temperatures is lower than in any other area of Yugoslavia. This climatic zone is marked by a relatively heavy rainfall (e.g., Dubrovnik 1,500 mm.), and its rainfall is more unevenly distributed than in any other area, heavy rainfall being characteristic of autumn and winter months while summers are relatively very dry. The Central European climate characteristic of all Slovenia and the southwestern parts of Croatia is among the coldest in the country, with an annual average of about nine degrees centigrade and a range between January and July average temperatures of about 22 degrees. This area has heavy precipitation (e.g., Ljubljana 1,546 mm.), which is lower in winter than in other seasons when the precipitation is relatively evenly distributed. Continental or Eastern European climate is most characteristic of Vojvodina. Here also winters are very cold, but summers are quite hot, giving thus a January-July temperature range of between 23 and 24 degrees centigrade. Precipitation in this area is among the lowest in the country (e.g., Vršac 682 mm.), but, as characteristic of the Continental climate, it is heaviest in the latter part of spring and in early summer, which makes it possible for the plants to utilize more of the available precipitation in the period of most intensive growth. The zone of mountain climate, taking essentially the center of the Dinaric System, shows lowest average annual temperatures with low winter and low summer average temperatures, and very heavy precipitation (e.g., Kolašin 2,670 mm.), concentrated in the autumn and winter months. The mixed Central European–Continental climatic zone takes most of Croatia-Slavonia and northern Bosnia, while the mixed Continental-

10 Pavle Vujević, "The Climate of the Kingdom of the Serbs, Croats, and Slovenes," in Pavle Vujević (ed.), *Recueil des travaux offert à M. Jovan Cvijić*, pp. 625–46.

11 Aleksandar Stebut, *Naši glavni poljoprivredni reoni* (Our Main Agricultural Regions), pp. 9–23 and Map No. 1.

mountain climate is characteristic of most of central and eastern Serbia. The third transitional climatic zone is that in which the Continental climate is basic and Mediterranean climatic influences are secondary. This area includes most of Macedonia. In some parts of Macedonia, as in the lower (Yugoslav) reaches of the Vardar River and in the valley of the Strumica River, the influences of the Mediterranean climate are very pronounced because these areas are relatively open to the influences of the Aegean Sea. However, the area around Skoplje is quite Continental.

The effect and sufficiency of precipitation are not judged solely by its total amount. Even greater in importance may be its seasonal distribution, the force and form in which it falls, and the nature of the terrain on which it falls. Thus, while the areas of the Mediterranean and of the mountain climate are the "wettest" areas of Yugoslavia, the bulk of precipitation is concentrated in the autumn and winter, regularly resulting in the inundation of the only fertile areas in these regions—the *polja*, while in spring and summer several months may pass without a drop of rain. Moreover, much of the rain comes in downpours, forming torrential creeks (*bujice*) of short duration, which wash the slopes to the bare rock, accumulate gravel and rock in cultivated patches, and, in general, contribute much to soil erosion. Furthermore, owing to the nature of the terrain (limestone) the rain water rapidly sinks underground. Thus, in these areas, there is a constant struggle between man, who wants to conserve and control water, and the insatiable ground. One might say that here the rainfall comes at the wrong time, in the wrong way, on the wrong surface, and thus cannot fail but be dissipated in the wrong way.

In the Pannonian Plain, characterized by the Continental climate or climatic varieties under its influence, two problems arise. First, a large portion of the late spring and summer precipitation is in the form of sudden downpours preceded and followed by heat spells which lead to excessive evaporation, so that only a part of the rainfall is effectively utilized by the crops. Second, heavy spring precipitation leads often to large-scale flooding of the Danube, Tisa, Sava, and Drava rivers and their tributaries. The basic reason for this condition is the mild gradient of all these rivers in the Pannonian Plain so that heavy rains often cause more damage than good to agriculture.

Winds, in addition to temperature and precipitation, are important factors in the nature of these climates. Strong winds in Yugoslavia are characteristic only of southwestern Croatia, Dalmatia, and the areas of Bosnia and Herzegovina nearer the coast, as well as in the areas of northeastern Serbia and southeastern Vojvodina. In the former areas a southeasterly, warm, and moist wind, the sirocco, prevails in the rainy season, while in the dry spells of the rainy season a northeasterly wind coming from the interior, the bora, is most common and characteristic of this area. Being often of high intensity and very erratic, the bora dries and carries away the soil and is one of the basic contributing factors to the soil erosion and bareness of the karst. In Vojvodina and Serbia the strongest wind is a rather cold southeasterly wind called the košava, prevailing during most of the autumn and winter.

The long growing season makes it possible for Yugoslavia to raise a great variety of crops, ranging from subtropical fruits such as citrus, figs, and olives to rye, among the cereals. What is most important from an economic point of view, however, is the fact that summer temperatures in the Pannonian Plain and most of the other territory range between about 22 and 24 degrees centigrade and are combined with sufficient summer rainfall, allowing a very successful culture of corn, the most important single crop in Yugoslavia. The almost perennial droughts in the area of the bare karst, while a vexing problem from the local point of view, influence very little the over-all agricultural production of the country. Occasional droughts in the Pannonian Plain, on the contrary, are great calamities for the whole economy of the country, as they endanger not only the food supplies for the country, but also important items in the export trade, primarily wheat, corn, and livestock products.

There is very little irrigated farming in Yugoslavia. It is estimated that shortly before World War II there were only between 30,000 and 40,000 hectares of land that were irrigated, which, when related to the total cultivated area of 8,219,000 hectares in 1938, is of small significance. There is no irrigation in Vojvodina, the most important agricultural region of the country, but a considerable portion of this region could be economically irrigated. Practically all irrigated land in Macedonia and southern Herzegovina relies to a large extent on installations and methods many centuries old. In mountainous areas south of the Sava-Danube rivers a small portion of fields under corn are irrigated by using water from small mountain creeks, which is stored in and conducted by exceedingly primitive contrivances.

But while irrigation plays only an insignificant role in Yugoslav agriculture, dams, dikes, canals, and pumping installations protecting agricultural land and providing for drainage are of fundamental importance for agriculture of much of the Pannonian Plain because practically all Yugoslav rivers in this area spill over their banks occasionally and inundate or threaten with inundation large areas of farm land. As will be shown later, considerable progress was achieved during the interwar period in regard to the protection of agricultural land against the ravages of the rivers.

Owing to the configuration of terrain and the type of soil in many areas of Yugoslavia, especially in the karstic areas where it would be most needed, irrigation is technically a very difficult proposition and therefore too costly. One factor which would open new vistas in respect to irrigation would be the construction of hydroelectric power plants and large artificial lakes, because this would help regulate the flow of water in rivers and would provide cheap power to run the pumps and other irrigation installations.

SOILS

Soil investigations in Yugoslavia have not progressed to the point where satisfactory soil maps are available, although several soil maps of the country have been published.[12] Professor Stebut, a Russian soil scientist who has been working in Yugoslavia for over 30 years, and the man responsible for most of the existing soil maps published during the interwar period, had this to say in 1947:

In Yugoslavia there exists a whole series of soil types whose pedological—that is to say, pedogenetic, dynamic, and morphological—qualities as well as their chief virtues and defects have already been established. The existence of these soil types in our country is known, but their distribution is barely intimated, so that neither the limits of their spread nor their area is known.[13]

Regional investigations of soils in Yugoslavia have shown that in regard to soils, just as in regard to other natural phenomena, Yugoslavia presents a mosaic-like picture.[14] This reflects the variety of

[12] *Ibid.*, pp. 37–54 and Map No. 5; Paul Krische, *Bodenkarten und andere karto-graphische Darstellungen der Faktoren der landwirtschaftlichen Produktion verschie-dener Länder*, pp. 54–57, contains Stebut's map (footnote 11) as well as a soil map of Yugoslavia by Professor Ferdo Koch, a geologist.

[13] "Report of the Federal Conference on Agricultural Research," Yugoslavia, Min-istry of Agriculture and Forestry, *Arhiv za poljoprivredne nauke i tehniku*, II, No. 2, Supplement, p. 64.

[14] From a considerable number of these regional and local soil investigations a few may be mentioned: Aleksandar Stebut, *Zemljišta Drino-Savo-Moravske oblasti* (The Soils of the Drina-Sava-Morava Region); Mihovil Gračanin, *Pedološka istraživanja vriština Ličkog polja* (Pedological Investigations of the Lika polje); Mihovil Gračanin, "A Contribution to the Geography of Podzol Soils in Croatia," *Hrvatski geografski glasnik*, Nos. 8–9–10, pp. 59–61; Dobroslav B. Todorović, "The Mechanical Analysis of the Principal Soil Types of Serbia," University of Belgrade, *Yearbook of the Faculty of Agriculture and Forestry*, II, 7–30; Dobroslav B. Todorović, "The Principal Agricultural Characteristics of the Skoplje *kotlina*," *ibid.*, I, 5–29; Djordje Zloković, *Prilog pozna-*

geological substrata on which various soils were formed, the result of the lake disappearance and river flows, and, above all, the soil-forming influences of various climates. To a lesser extent man has influenced the development of soils through deforestation, land reclamation, and various agricultural techniques. These regional soil investigations have thus shown that in Vojvodina the following types of soil are represented: chernozem, but with a humus content of only 3 to 5 percent (much less than the typical Russian chernozems), degraded chernozem, alluvial soils, marsh and meadow black soils, quicksands, and various types of saline soils. Chernozem and degraded chernozem are the most important categories. In Serbia three main types of soil prevail: the *smonica*, a black soil of postlake marsh origin, chestnut soils, and podzol soils. The latter are the most widespread. Because of the existing climatic conditions podzolization is continuously affecting all these three types of soil. Naturally, alluvial soils in some areas, and skeletal soils in southwestern Serbia where the climate is under the influence of higher altitudes, and some high-altitude black soil are present. In Macedonia, which has a mixed Continental and Mediterranean climate, a great variety of soils is found, the main types being the *smonica*, chestnut soil, podzol, alluvial soil, skeletal soil, terra rossa, and the saline soils. In the zone of the mountain climate, podzols, skeletal soil, rendzina, and terra rossa prevail. The latter is regularly of low fertility in its natural form as it often lacks various plant nutrients. In the area of the Mediterranean climate skeletal soils and terra rossa are the basic types. In most of Croatia-Slavonia and northern Bosnia, podzol soils in various stages of podzolization, depending on the degree of humidity and prevailing temperatures, are the climatic zonal soil types. But the greatest area in this climatic zone is taken by such intrazonal soil types as skeletal soils, alluvial soils, rendzina, etc. In the area of pure Central European climate, namely, in Slovenia, podzols, skeletal soils, and in the high altitudes the alpine black soil are the main soil types.

This review shows clearly how varied the soils of Yugoslavia are. Chernozem, degraded chernozem, and the alluvial soils, all of them typical of and most widespread in the Pannonian Plain, are the most fertile. But *smonica* and some of the chestnut soils, if they are not in an advanced stage of podzolization, are counted also as quite fertile soils. A considerable portion of podzol soils in which the leaching

---

vanju zemljišta Metohije (A Contribution to the Study of Soil of Metohija); Viktor Neugebauer, *Vojvodjanski černozem, njegova veza sa černozemom istočne i jugoistočne Evrope i pravac njegove degradacije* (Vojvodina's Chernozem, Its Relation to the Chernozem of Eastern and Southeastern Europe and the Direction of Its Degradation).

process has greatly advanced (the gray soils), saline soils of all types, skeletal soils, and terra rossa are, however, soils of poor natural fertility. And in most areas south of the Sava-Danube rivers these are the basic soil types. With regard to soil fertility, it should be stressed that soils in almost all areas except in the Pannonian Plain are mined or starved out to a great extent, owing to crop rotations which exhaust the soil, the application of only small amounts of stable manure, and the almost complete absence of application of green manure and commercial fertilizer. Thus, low natural fertility of most soils in areas outside of the Pannonian Plain has been further decreased by the action of man.

AGRICULTURAL LAND RESOURCES

The topographic character of Yugoslavia, namely, its predominantly mountainous nature, determines the amount of land available for agricultural purposes and affects basically its over-all utilization. Of the total territory of 24,754 thousand hectares, 14,438 thousand hectares are recorded in 1938 as agriculturally productive land (not counting 121 thousand hectares of marshes) and about 7,300 thousand hectares as land under forests. The remaining territory is taken by lakes, rivers, inhabited places, communications, etc.

The relationship of the agriculturally productive land to total territory and the over-all nature of its utilization are indicated in Table 10. This table also contains data for a selected group of other European countries for purposes of comparison.[15] The 1938 figure of 14,438 thousand hectares of agriculturally productive land, or 58.3 percent of the total territory, gives Yugoslavia a relatively less favorable position than that of any other country included in the table. This relationship, as indicated by official Yugoslav statistics, is, however, considerably better than the actual situation. According to this table Yugoslavia records 43 percent of its agriculturally productive land as land under permanent meadows and pastures, which is a much larger proportion than in any other of the included countries. This item, amounting to 6,219 thousand hectares, is divided into two categories: the permanent meadows taking 1,841 thousand hectares and the pastures taking 4,378 thousand hectares. But the latter include not only pasture lands which

---

[15] These countries, which are going to be used also for other comparisons such as density of agricultural population, have been so selected that they contain typical industrial countries like Germany, balanced industrial-agricultural countries like France, Italy, and Czechoslovakia, balanced industrial-agricultural countries with thoroughly specialized agriculture like Denmark, and a group of countries whose agriculture shows many similarities with the agriculture of Yugoslavia: Bulgaria, Hungary, Poland, and Rumania.

TABLE 10.—AGRICULTURAL LAND AND ITS UTILIZATION IN YUGOSLAVIA AND SELECTED EUROPEAN COUNTRIES IN 1938*

(*Thousand hectares and percent*)

Country	Total area	Agricultural land		Cultivated land					Permanent meadows and pastures	
		Area	Percent of total	Arable	Tree and bush crops	Total			Area	Percent of agricultural land
						Area	Percent of total territory	Percent of agricultural land		
Yugoslavia	24,754	14,438	58.3	7,552	667	8,219	33.2	56.9	6,219	43.1
Bulgaria[a]	10,315	—	—	4,082	170	4,252	41.2	—	—	—
Czechoslovakia	14,051	8,358	59.5	5,857	175	6,032	42.9	72.2	2,326	27.8
Denmark[b]	4,293	3,099	72.2	2,674	—	2,674	62.3	86.3	425	13.7
France[c]	55,099	34,534	62.7	20,731	2,112	22,843	41.5	66.1	11,691	33.9
Germany	47,071	28,537	60.6	19,166	858	20,024	42.5	70.2	8,513	29.8
Hungary	9,309	7,560	81.2	5,611	339	5,950	63.9	78.7	1,610	21.3
Italy[c]	31,008	21,118	68.1	13,003	2,298	15,301	49.3	72.5	5,817	27.5
Poland	38,863	25,588	65.8	18,557	552	19,109	49.2	74.7	6,479	25.3
Rumania	29,505	18,451	62.5	13,445	633	14,078	47.7	76.3	4,373	23.7

* Source: International Institute of Agriculture, *International Yearbook of Agricultural Statistics* (Rome), for 1938–39 and 1939–40.
[a] In the case of Bulgaria, areas under permanent meadows and pastures are combined with those under forests.
[b] Rural communes.
[c] For 1937.

are actually productive and supply grazing lands for livestock but also a large area of bare karst whose value as grazing land is either nil or almost nil. How large the area of bare karst is—and thus the area of these unproductive pastures recorded as productive in the official figure of 4,378 thousand hectares—is not known. It is probable, however, that in the figure officially recorded as "pastures" about one million hectares are either absolutely unproductive or show only a minimal productivity which hardly entitles them to be called "pastures."

A much better indication of the availability of land resources in Yugoslavia is obtained by using the area of cultivated land, namely arable land and land under tree and bush crops, for various comparisons. This comparison for Yugoslavia and nine other European countries is also supplied in the preceding table and shows that cultivated land in Yugoslavia amounts to only 33.2 percent of the total territory and to only 56.9 percent of the agriculturally productive land, as officially defined. These ratios are lower in Yugoslavia by as much as 8 to 30 percent than in the other European countries, indicated in the above table. As almost all land that can be put under the plow or hoe is actually cultivated under Yugoslav conditions of relative agricultural overpopulation, the low percentage of cultivated land is the expression of its natural scarcity rather than of any socioeconomic factors, e.g., an unfavorable land tenure system, which would tend to keep the potentially arable land out of cultivation. It is beyond any doubt that the shortage of actual and potential cultivable land is the basic, natural, limiting factor for the expansion of the Yugoslav agricultural production. If one disregards a limited amount of potential arable land which can be obtained by land reclamation (see Chapter 17) and some transfers from the category of the permanent meadows and timberland into cultivated land, Yugoslavia cannot expect any considerable increase in its agricultural production from an increase in cultivated land. For this increase in production it will have to rely primarily on the increase in the productivity of the presently cultivated land.

The availability of agricultural land resources, combined, of course, with both their natural productivity and the agricultural technology prevailing in the country, determines largely the way in which the land is utilized. Needless to say, the availability of other production resources, both natural and man-made, and their comparative productivity are of basic importance in the determination of the over-all use of national economic resources. As far as Yugoslavia is concerned, the relatively low development of nonagricultural production resources forces the population of Yugoslavia to concentrate on agricultural production; and, since the ratio between the land resources and the population that these resources have to support is unfavorable, the agricultural production concentrates on the output of foods, primarily cereals, and among the cereals on the production of corn, which gives the largest yield in terms of calories per unit of land.

UTILIZATION OF ARABLE LAND IN 1938

Table 11 shows the utilization of arable land in 1938 in Yugoslavia and nine other European countries. After Rumania, Yugoslavia had the largest proportion of its arable land, 81.9 percent, under cereals. In the industrial and quasi-industrial countries, as well as in Denmark, this percentage was much lower. The Yugoslav area under vegetables and potatoes, amounting to 5.7 percent of the arable land, is rather low when compared with the area under these crops in Poland, Germany, Czechoslovakia, and France. But potatoes in these countries serve as an important substitute for cereals. The area under industrial crops is low, but this is common in practically all European countries. Area lying fallow, amounting to 5.3 percent of the arable land in Yugoslavia, represents approximately the average for the European countries included in the above table.

One of the most revealing characteristics of the pattern of the over-all utilization of land resources in Yugoslavia, next to the high proportion of land devoted to cereals, is the low share of arable land (4.7 percent of the total) under rotation meadows and feed crops. This fact is characteristic also of other typical peasant countries like Bulgaria and Rumania, and to a lesser extent Poland and Hungary, and is a consequence of the relative agricultural overpopulation prevailing in these countries. There is, however, one factor which has to be taken into account in the case of Yugoslavia in regard to feedstuffs. A considerable portion of the corn and barley produced and practically all of the oats are used for animal feeding. If this factor were taken into account, the ratios of areas under cereals and under feed crops to total arable land would be considerably changed.

UNEVEN DISTRIBUTION OF LAND RESOURCES BY BANOVINE

Our discussion of the topographic configuration and of the climatic zones of Yugoslavia indicated a very uneven distribution of agricultural land within the country. This extremely uneven distribution of land resources, with regard to both amount and quality in various regions, is one of the most important characteristics of the natural re-

TABLE 11.—UTILIZATION OF ARABLE LAND IN YUGOSLAVIA AND SELECTED EUROPEAN COUNTRIES IN 1938*

(Thousand hectares and percent)

Country	Arable land Area	Cereals Area	Cereals Percent	Rotation meadows and feed crops Area	Rotation meadows and feed crops Percent	Vegetables and potatoes Area	Vegetables and potatoes Percent	Industrial crops Area	Industrial crops Percent	Crops for seed Area	Crops for seed Percent	Other use Area	Other use Percent	Fallow Area	Fallow Percent
Yugoslavia[a]	7,552	6,185	81.9	356	4.7	428	5.7	184	2.4	—	—	—	—	399	5.3
Bulgaria	4,082	2,777	68.0	271	6.6	204	5.0	350	8.6	—	—	—	—	480	11.8
Czechoslovakia	5,857	3,534	60.3	1,180	20.1	821	14.0	238	4.1	4	0.1	9	0.2	71	1.2
Denmark	2,674	1,350	50.5	1,127	42.1	90	3.4	40	1.5	34	1.3	—	—	33	1.2
France[b]	20,731	10,467	50.5	5,946	28.7	2,212	10.7	387	1.8	—	—	—	—	1,719	8.3
Germany	19,166	11,402	59.5	3,609	18.8	3,057	15.9	664	3.5	66	0.4	11	—	357	1.9
Hungary	5,611	4,119	73.4	848	15.1	393	7.0	117	2.1	—	—	30	0.5	104	1.9
Italy[c]	13,003	6,901	53.1	2,500	19.2	1,374	10.6	308	2.4	3	—	922	7.1	995	7.6
Poland	18,557	11,693	63.0	1,877	10.1	3,204	17.3	409	2.2	127	0.7	76	0.4	1,171	6.3
Rumania	13,445	11,272	83.9	731	5.4	482	3.6	486	3.6	—	—	—	—	474	3.5

* Source: International Institute of Agriculture, *International Yearbook of Agricultural Statistics* (Rome), for 1938–39 and 1939–40.
[a] Area sown.
[b] For 1937.
[c] For 1937. Areas bearing two crops counted only once.

source base of Yugoslav agriculture. Regional differences in the supply of agricultural land would be even more pronounced if they were considered by historical provinces. As we have to consider them by *banovine*, since statistics are available during the 1930's only on this basis, these differences are somewhat blurred because of the political gerrymandering which was involved in the drawing of the banovinal boundaries.

Table 12, in addition to giving the total area of each *banovina*, shows the area of agriculturally productive land, as defined by the Yugoslav official statistics, the cultivated area subdivided into arable land and land under tree and bush crops (including gardens), the area of permanent meadows and pastures, and, finally, the number of livestock in terms of cattle. The fact that pastures include a great deal of absolutely unproductive bare karst in some *banovine*, especially Primorje and Zeta, makes it necessary to state land resources of each *banovina*, both in cultivated land and in the numbers of livestock as an expression of the feed-producing capacity of the land under meadows and pastures. While the production of feed crops, and thus stable feeding, plays a considerable role in the livestock economy of Dunav, Drava, and Sava, in most other *banovine* livestock is almost exclusively dependent on the permanent meadows and pastures for feed. Thus the numbers of livestock reflect the value of these lands as feed producers.

A clearer view of the differences in the abundance of land and livestock in various areas is presented in Table 13. This table shows the relative numbers pertaining to the share of each *banovina* in the total territory of the country, the cultivated area, permanent meadows and pastures, and livestock in terms of cattle units. Best supplied with land is, of course, Dunav, lying almost completely in the Pannonian Plain. With 12.6 percent of total territory and 5.9 percent of all permanent meadows and pastures, it has not less than 28.2 percent of all cultivated land and 16.9 percent of all livestock in the country. On the other extreme are Primorje and Zeta with 7.9 and 12.5 percent of all territory and 14.1 and 17.8 percent of all meadows and pastures, but with only 3.9 and 4.3 percent of all cultivated land and 6.1 and 9.6 percent of all livestock, respectively. Other *banovine* range between the two extremes, showing a more or less even, relative distribution of their cultivated land and livestock in relation to the total area and meadows and pastures, respectively.

Some *banovine* have a larger proportion than others of their land under gardens, vineyards, and orchards, which are, as a rule, more productive than the plowed land and, for purposes of comparison

TABLE 12.—TOTAL AREA, LAND IN VARIOUS USES, AND LIVESTOCK BY BANOVINE IN 1938*

(Thousand hectares; livestock in thousands)

Banovina	Total area	Productive area[a]	Cultivated area				Permanent meadows and pastures			
			Arable	Tree and bush crops	Total area	Percent of total area	Meadows	Pastures	Percent of total area	Livestock[b]
Drava	1,585	819	315	60	375	23.6	248	195	27.9	544
Drina	2,784	1,445	782	116	898	32.3	242	305	19.6	946
Dunav	3,123	2,681	2,179	138	2,317	74.2	133	232	11.7	1,409
Morava	2,547	1,417	755	89	844	33.1	171	402	22.5	718
Primorje	1,965	1,201	247	77	324	16.5	111	766	44.6	508
Sava	4,053	2,355	1,295	97	1,392	34.3	431	532	23.7	1,532
Vardar	3,667	1,970	907	28	935	25.5	105	930	28.2	1,106
Vrbas	1,892	1,074	733	32	765	40.4	167	142	16.3	765
Zeta	3,100	1,463	328	29	357	11.5	233	873	35.7	802
Prefecture of Belgrade	38	13	11	1	12	31.6	—	1	2.6	10
Total	24,754	14,438	7,552	667	8,219	33.2	1,841	4,378	25.1	8,340

* Source: Yugoslavia, Annuaire statistique 1938–1939 (Belgrade, 1939), pp. 164–65, 180–81.

[a] Excluding marshes.

[b] All livestock in terms of cattle. In converting all types of livestock to cattle, the following conversion coefficients were used: one head of cattle equals two-thirds of one horse (one horse equals one mule or three asses), one water buffalo, four pigs, ten sheep, and ten goats. Needless to say, the productivity per head of various types of livestock and therefore also of these composite units varies greatly from area to area.

TABLE 13.—PERCENTAGE DISTRIBUTION OF LAND RESOURCES AND LIVESTOCK
BY BANOVINE IN 1938*

Banovina	Total area of the country	Cultivated area	Meadows and pastures	Livestock
Drava	6.4	4.6	7.1	6.5
Drina	11.2	10.9	8.8	11.3
Dunav	12.6	28.2	5.9	16.9
Morava	10.3	10.3	9.2	8.6
Primorje	7.9	3.9	14.1	6.1
Sava	16.4	17.0	15.5	18.4
Vardar	14.8	11.4	16.6	13.3
Vrbas	7.7	9.3	5.0	9.2
Zeta	12.5	4.3	17.8	9.6
Prefecture of Belgrade......	0.2	0.1	0.0	0.1
Total	100.0	100.0	100.0	100.0

* Source: Based on Table 12.

among regions, could be reduced to a common denominator.[16] But in view of the relatively small hectarage of these forms of land utilization and their very uneven and often low productivity (see Table 15), we count land under tree and bush crops and gardens hectare for hectare with the plowed land and exclude permanent meadows and pastures from direct comparison.

UNEVEN QUALITY OF LAND RESOURCES REVEALED BY YIELDS AND CADASTRAL NET INCOME

In addition to this extremely uneven distribution of land resources among the various regions, it is necessary to stress the differences in the productive capacity or yields per unit of land in various regions. Since an overwhelming percentage of all arable land is under cereals, the yield of the principal cereals per unit of land reflects quite well the differences in the quality of land in various areas. To illustrate these differences in yields, Table 14 gives first the average percentage of arable land devoted to cereals between 1934 and 1938, as well as areas

[16] Wilbert E. Moore, *Economic Demography of Eastern and Southern Europe*, p. 196, "following the method suggested" by the Polish writer J. Poniatowski, reduces all types of land utilization to the common denominator of "arable equivalents," by giving to the land under gardens and orchards (presumably also vineyards) a coefficient of 3, meadows a coefficient of 0.4, and pastures a coefficient of around 0.2 in relation to plowed land. We will have more to say about Moore's calculations with regard to Yugoslavia on a later occasion.

TABLE 14.—AVERAGE PERCENTAGES OF ARABLE LAND UNDER CEREALS, POTATOES, AND FALLOW, AND AVERAGE YIELDS OF CEREALS, POTATOES, AND HAY BY BANOVINE, 1934–38*

(Percent, quintals per hectare)

Banovina	Percent of arable land				Yields					
	Cereals	Potatoes	Fallow	Total	Wheat	Barley	Rye	Corn	Potatoes	Hay
Drava	61.7	18.1	0.7	80.5	9.7	9.6	8.4	14.1	59.7	23.7
Drina	88.5	2.5	3.8	94.8	9.5	9.7	8.6	15.2	51.4	14.4
Dunav	89.2	1.3	0.3	90.8	13.7	15.8	13.4	23.5	81.4	19.0
Morava	92.3	1.0	1.8	95.1	10.8	9.9	8.5	12.3	31.2	11.6
Primorje	76.3	6.3	7.2	89.8	10.2	9.0	9.7	14.3	60.0	12.8
Sava	75.7	7.4	2.4	85.5	11.1	10.2	9.1	18.6	68.4	22.2
Vardar	77.8	1.1	14.4	93.3	8.4	8.3	7.3	10.5	39.1	13.7
Vrbas	68.5	2.7	23.6	94.8	8.9	8.5	8.6	12.6	63.5	13.6
Zeta	84.2	4.0	7.8	96.0	8.7	7.9	7.7	11.6	30.9	13.5
Prefecture of Belgrade	—	—	—	—	—	—	—	—	—	—
Yugoslavia	81.9	3.5	5.7	91.1	11.4	9.6	8.2	17.6	62.0	17.3

* Source: Yugoslavia, Ministry of Agriculture, *Statistique agricole annuelle 1937* (Belgrade, 1938), pp. 2–81, and Yugoslavia, *Annuaire statistique 1938–1939* (Belgrade, 1939), pp. 164–76.

devoted to the production of potatoes and left fallow, and then average 1934–38 yields for the principal cereals, potatoes, and hay. While average yields for cereals and potatoes illustrate the differences in the productivity of arable land, hay yields illustrate the quality of soil under permanent meadows. The area devoted to cereals varies between 61.7 percent in *banovina* Drava and 92.3 percent in Morava and gives a national average of 81.9 percent. The area under potatoes is highest in Drava, 18.1 percent—where the area under cereals is the lowest— and is lowest, 1 percent, in Morava—where the area under cereals happens to be the highest. In other *banovine*, area under potatoes ranges from 1.1 to 7.4 percent. Finally, the table shows the area left fallow in each *banovina*. The purpose of including fallow land was simply to prove better the statement that cereals, especially if potatoes are added in certain *banovine*, and their yields represent the utilization and quality of the overwhelming bulk of arable land.

The regional differences in yields, especially of the basic crops— wheat, corn, and potatoes (this latter only in Drava and Sava)—show that there are, roughly speaking, three general areas with regard to soil quality in Yugoslavia: (1) the high-yield area—*banovina* Dunav; (2) the areas in which the yields are much below the national average—Primorje, Zeta, Vardar, and Vrbas; and (3) the remaining *banovine* in which yields vary between these extremes and approach, more or less, the national averages. In the case of hay, Drava has the best yields, followed by Sava and Dunav. With the exception of Morava, which had the lowest yields in hay, it is again the *banovine* Primorje, Zeta, Vrbas, and Vardar which are much below the national average. The greatest differences exist in the yield of corn, which is the chief cereal crop in Yugoslavia both for food and feed. In the period 1934–38 the yield of corn in Dunav averaged 124 percent higher than in Vardar, 100 percent higher than in Zeta, 86 percent higher than in Vrbas, and 26 percent higher than in Sava, the area with the next best yield of corn. The yield of wheat was higher in Dunav than in Vardar, Zeta, and Vrbas by 60 to 63 percent. In the case of barley and rye the difference in yield between Dunav, on the one hand, and Zeta, Vardar, and Vrbas, on the other, ranges between 75 and 100 percent. The potato yield in Zeta and Morava was a little more than one-third of that in Dunav. However, the yield of potatoes in Sava, which grows almost half of the total Yugoslav potato crop, was only 16 percent lower than in Dunav. The yield of hay in Drava and Sava was roughly twice that of Morava and approximately 75 percent higher than the yield in Primorje, Vardar, Vrbas, and Zeta.

As will be shown later, productivity of livestock, especially of cattle, which is the most important type of livestock in all regions of Yugoslavia, also varies greatly from area to area (see Chapter 23). Again, in Dunav, Drava, and Sava productivity is much higher than in the *banovine* south of the Sava-Danube line.

It would be a mistake, however, to ascribe the differences in land productivity, as shown in the preceding table, exclusively to the differences in soil and climatic conditions. Though they are the basic factors, methods of land working—e.g., better rotation of crops, better plowing, better seed selection and preparation, use of more fertilizers and pesticides—exert a profound influence on yields. Owing to a number of cultural and socioeconomic factors, working methods in the agriculture of *banovina* Dunav, as well as in Drava and most of Sava, were on a much more advanced level than in the *banovine* south of the Sava-Danube rivers. The working methods thus account for a part of the differences in yields between the various *banovine*. One of the basic reasons for the low yields in the latter group of *banovine*, however, is to be found in the agricultural overpopulation of these areas. Owing to the insufficiency of other means of making a living and to the high relative density of population, the peasants are forced to plant cereals on land which under the existing soil and climatic conditions is wholly unsuitable for these crops. The use of unsuitable land for cereals, which is a consequence of socioeconomic factors (overpopulation), is thus one of the basic reasons for average low yields in these areas.

Perhaps the best indicator of differences in the quality of soil and productivity of agriculturally used land in various *banovine* is the cadastral net income per hectare of land in various forms of utilization, which served as the basis for the assessment of the land tax. Cadastral net income per hectare of land was the difference between gross income and the regular cost of production involved in the utilization of that land. Table 15 shows the cadastral net income calculated on the basis of conditions existing in 1938 and according to regulations based on the Law on Direct Taxes of February 8, 1928. The differences in the cadastral net income reflect actually not only differences in the quality of soil and other natural conditions, but also differences in the type of land utilization and the levels of agricultural technology.

However complex the causes of these differences in yields are, they must be kept in mind in considering the natural resources base of agriculture in different parts of Yugoslavia. Only then is one able to appreciate fully the impact of the tremendous regional unevenness in

TABLE 15.—CADASTRAL NET INCOME PER HECTARE OF LAND UNDER VARIOUS
FORMS OF UTILIZATION, BY BANOVINE IN 1938*

(*Dinars*)

Banovina	Arable land	Gardens and orchards	Vineyards	Meadows	Pastures	Average
Drava	354	558	506	295	62	163
Drina	237	780	853	180	41	156
Dunav	978	1,095	1,475	480	262	760
Morava	268	522	938	233	67	145
Primorje	153	213	263	156	11	54
Sava	383	875	874	406	57	223
Vardar	246	802	730	310	40	101
Vrbas	203	683	410	159	26	113
Zeta	133	341	298	178	17	43

* Data received by correspondence from the Yugoslav Federal Geodetic Administration in
Belgrade. Data on the cadastral net income were not officially published during the interwar
period. A similar table with cadastral net income for 1929 was, however, published in 1938 by
Djordo Krstić, "Agrarian Policy in Bosnia and Herzegovina," in A. Koen *et al.* (eds.), *Bosna i
Hercegovina kao privredno područje* (Bosnia and Herzegovina as an Economic Area) (Sarajevo,
1938), p. 136. Krstić apparently obtained his data through his personal contacts in the Ministry
of Finance.

the distribution of these resources. The basic economic meaning of
these regional differences in land productivity consists in the fact that
a certain area of arable land, permanent meadows, or vineyards in
practically all areas south of the Sava-Danube line is capable of supporting a much smaller number of people than in Vojvodina and a few
fringe areas in the Pannonian Plain. The situation is aggravated by
the fact that areas which have low yields are at the same time areas
with a relatively much lower proportion of arable land and good
meadows in their territory. It will also be seen that the areas with a
small percentage of arable land and with low yields often have a much
higher rate of population growth than areas with a high proportion of
arable land and high yields. Furthermore, these areas have much less
opportunity to market their products and have much greater technical
difficulties and higher cost to reach the market.

THE CHIEF AGRICULTURAL REGIONS

The structure of agricultural production in various parts of Yugoslavia is not a product of conscious agricultural policy, but rather a
result of many natural and socioeconomic factors: soil and climate,
tradition, domestic and export market conditions; and, above all, it is
a consequence of the subsistence character of the overwhelming portion

of Yugoslav agriculture. There was much discussion about scientific zoning of agricultural production in Yugoslavia during the interwar period. All plans remained, however, in the talking stage. Zoning of agricultural production according to scientific criteria would first have required a great deal of scientific investigation to determine the zones for various crops and various types of livestock, which would have taken many years. Second, such zoning of agricultural production would have involved great changes in the structure of agricultural production in many areas, and these changes could not be undertaken while the population pressure in practically all parts of the country made it imperative that the peasant households strive to produce a sufficient amount of food, primarily cereals, on their own land.

The division of Yugoslavia into various agricultural areas can be undertaken along several lines—some more, others less, clearcut. As far as topographic, soil, and climatic conditions—and thus over-all agricultural production—are concerned, the country can be divided, as is done by most geographers, into three basic areas: (1) the Pannonian Plain in the north and northeast, showing a rather prosperous and relatively well-developed system of agriculture and an often intensive animal husbandry; (2) the mountainous area, including the bulk of the country in the center, extending from its borders in the northwest (Slovenia) to the southeast (Macedonia), with much less developed agricultural production and with extensive animal husbandry; (3) the rather narrow strip of land along the Adriatic coast and the Adriatic islands, depending greatly on specialty crops such as grapevines, olives, and in some parts tobacco. According to the degree of marketability of agricultural products, the country could be divided into two main areas: (1) the area north of the Sava-Danube line, in which agriculture is more market-orientated and sells a considerably larger proportion than other areas, and (2) areas south of these rivers, in which agriculture is much more of a subsistence character. In the latter area there are, however, specific sections which devote a considerable area to cash crops: Dalmatia to wine and olive oil production, Herzegovina and Macedonia to tobacco, northeastern Bosnia and northwestern Serbia to prunes.

As a mixed cereals production and a mixed animal husbandry are the basic lines of production in all parts of Yugoslavia, it is impossible to have a clear-cut division of the country along single production lines. However, if specialty crops or special branches of animal husbandry are superimposed on this general production basis, agriculture in various parts of the country can be more or less clearly characterized. Thus, taking into account the cereals and livestock production and special production branches in various areas, the U.S. Department of Agriculture prepared in 1943 a rather complex map on zoning of agricultural production in Yugoslavia. In addition, this map showed the areas with a surplus of cereals and areas with a deficit in cereals as well as areas which supplied the surpluses for export of various agricultural and livestock products (corn, wheat, fruits, pigs, cattle, poultry).[17]

Regarding the division of the country from the point of view of the adequacy of cereal production for the needs of various areas, more will be said in Chapter 24.

In spite of the great unevenness in the distribution of agricultural land resources in Yugoslavia and the fact that agricultural and livestock economy are often carried on in a primitive fashion and show exceedingly low productivity, Yugoslavia as a whole was, during the interwar period, on an export basis for a large number of agricultural and livestock products. It exported wheat and corn; industrial crops such as hemp, tobacco, hops, opium, medicinal herbs; and fresh and dried prunes. It exported relatively large numbers of live cattle, horses, fat pigs, sheep, and poultry, and such livestock products as meat, lard, light hides, cheese, sausage casings, and, especially, eggs. The extent of these exports and their foreign markets will be discussed at a later stage. Except in the case of tobacco, prunes, opium, hops, sheep, cattle, eggs, and poultry, the bulk of agricultural exports came from *banovina* Dunav and eastern sections of *banovina* Sava. These areas not only accounted for the bulk of shipments to the domestic food-deficit areas, but also supplied most of all Yugoslav agricultural exports. These areas rightly deserve the name of the Yugoslav food basket, and their agricultural and general economic importance is far out of proportion to either their size or population. Without them, Yugoslavia would indeed be a much poorer country.

---

[17] U.S. Department of Agriculture, Neg. 134, Office of Foreign Agricultural Relations.

CHAPTER 15

THE DEVELOPMENT OF POPULATION BETWEEN
THE TWO WORLD WARS

In Chapter 7 we followed the development of population in various South Slav areas from approximately 1840 to 1914. There it was shown that population in all South Slav lands was rapidly increasing, especially after 1880, but that the increase in population differed greatly from area to area. Areas which were on a higher level of cultural and economic development, such as Slovenia, Vojvodina, Croatia-Slavonia, and Dalmatia, long before 1914 showed a much lower rate of population growth than Serbia and Bosnia and Herzegovina. This difference was due to lower birth rates and to heavy emigration from the former provinces. While there are no data on the growth of population in Montenegro before 1914, it apparently did not exceed that of Dalmatia, and that possibly was the case in Macedonia, for which data are also lacking. Another pronounced characteristic of the population movement in most South Slav lands between 1880 and 1914 was heavy emigration, especially from Dalmatia, Slovenia, Croatia-Slavonia, Montenegro, and Vojvodina. The same seems to have been true of Macedonia. Bosnia and Herzegovina showed a relatively much smaller emigration, while Serbia appears to have had a considerable net immigration balance. For political reasons there was much immigration, especially of the Magyar element, into Vojvodina and Croatia-Slavonia.

World War I, as explained in Chapter 12, resulted in large losses of population in all South Slav lands, but especially in Serbia and Montenegro. It also affected greatly the sex and age composition of population in all areas. A considerably higher ratio of females to males in all provinces was shown in the census of 1921 than in the censuses before 1914, because the war losses were heaviest among the men of fighting age. The age structure of population also appeared "older" than before 1914 because births were greatly reduced during the years of war, owing to the separation of sexes, loss of males, and the low marriage rate.

The development of the population of Yugoslavia during the interwar period must be considered with these previous trends and developments in mind. It cannot, however, be studied with the same degree of

287

certainty for the whole period between the two world wars. There were only two censuses, in January 1921 and in March 1931. For the period after 1931, in addition to the official estimates of total population for the country as a whole and for the nine *banovine*, birth and death rates are also available, and thus the rates of natural growth and data on migrations across the frontiers. But nothing is available on internal migrations or on changes in the age, sex, and occupational structure of population. Furthermore, because of the administrative changes in the country, which obliterated historical provinces, population developments cannot be followed by provinces. This precludes a continuation of data supplied for the pre-1914 years in Tables 1 and 2 (pp. 152, 157) to include the interwar period. Especially confusing in this respect was the drawing of banovinal frontiers in 1929, which often combined areas with populations displaying totally different trends of growth.

The purpose of this chapter is to show the general development of the population of Yugoslavia during the interwar period, with pertinent comparisons to the developments in some other European countries, differences in the development of various areas within Yugoslavia, changes in the occupational structure of population, important changes in the sex and age composition, and migrations across the frontiers.

THE GROWTH OF POPULATION, 1921–39

In our discussions of the Yugoslav population growth during the interwar period it is best to disregard the first two years after World War I. Data for these years are extremely scanty, and this period was marked by considerable shifts in population for political reasons, resulting from changes in international frontiers after that war.[1]

We therefore start with the census of January 1921. From 11,984,-911 at the end of January 1921 the population of Yugoslavia rose to 13,934,038 at the end of March 1931. Calculated by geometric progression, rectified by changing trends of population movement, especially the falling trend in the rates of growth during the 1930's, the population of Yugoslavia increased, according to official estimates, to 15,703,000 at the end of 1939. Total increase in population during these 19 years amounted thus to 3,718,000, or 31 percent. If one disregards Albania, which, because of its small population (slightly over

[1] The order of magnitude of these shifts can be gauged from data on the place of birth in Yugoslavia of people living in Bulgaria, Austria, Hungary, and Turkey, and on the country of birth of population present in Yugoslavia around 1930, though by that time the number of original transferees had been considerably thinned by death. Dudley Kirk, *Europe's Population in the Interwar Years*, pp. 282–83.

one million, about which very little demographic information is available), is insignificant in the European population picture, and Greece, whose population was swelled during the 1920's by approximately 500,000 as a net balance resulting from the mass population exchange with Turkey, Yugoslavia's population growth during these 19 years was the highest in Europe. It was closely followed by that of Bulgaria (30.0), Poland (29.9), the Netherlands (28.7), Rumania (28.2), and Portugal (27.0), but was very much higher than the population growth in the industrial countries of Western, Northern, and Central Europe.[2] If rates of growth used officially for 1938 are projected by geometric progression until the end of March 1941—a point of time just one week before the invasion of the country by the Axis powers— the population of the country rose to 15,973,000. Thus the estimated gain in population of Yugoslavia between January 1921 and March of 1941 amounted to 3,988,000, or 33.3 percent.

This large increase in population was due to a high birth rate which, in spite of a high death rate, resulted in a high rate of natural population growth. Table 16, in addition to the estimated total population for the country, shows the number of births and deaths and the surplus of births over deaths by year from 1921 to 1939, as well as birth and death rates and the rate of natural growth per thousand. The latter series show conclusively a falling trend in all rates. While there is a certain degree of irregularity in the behavior of all these rates from year to year, the five-year averages (four-year average for 1936–39) show clearly the falling trend in all of them. Between the five-year average for 1921–25 and the four-year average for 1936–39 the birth rate fell from 35.0 to 27.4 per thousand, or 21.7 percent. The death rate fell from 20.2 to 15.7 per thousand, or 22.3 percent, and the rate of natural growth fell from 14.8 to 11.7 per thousand, or 20.9 percent. The fall in the death rate was pronounced during the whole decade of the 1930's, while the fall in the birth rate and in the rate of natural growth was especially strong in the second half of that decade. The downward trend in the vital rates was characteristic, however, of practically all European countries during the 1930's, but was especially strong in areas of highest fertility in Eastern and Southern Europe.[3] The falling rates of births and natural growth in Yugoslavia during the second half of the 1930's were somewhat related to the fall in the birth rates during World War I. Young people who would have been the most productive parents during the 1930's were less

2 *Ibid.*, p. 24.
3 *Ibid.*, pp. 59–60.

TABLE 16.—ESTIMATED TOTAL POPULATION; THE NUMBER OF BIRTHS, DEATHS,
AND SURPLUS OF BIRTHS; BIRTH, DEATH, AND NATURAL
GROWTH RATES, 1921–39*

Year	Total population	Births	Deaths	Surplus of births	Births	Deaths	Natural growth
		(*In thousands*)			(*Rate per thousand*)		
1921	12,149	442.5	252.1	190.4	36.7	20.9	15.8
1922	12,330	420.9	254.5	166.4	34.4	20.8	13.6
1923	12,514	432.8	252.5	180.3	34.8	20.3	14.5
1924	12,701	442.8	254.5	188.3	35.1	20.2	14.9
1925	12,891	437.1	239.4	197.7	34.2	18.7	15.5
Average 1921–25					35.0	20.2	14.8
1926	13,083	459.0	244.8	214.2	35.3	18.8	16.5
1927	13,279	451.6	276.3	175.3	34.3	21.0	13.3
1928	13,477	437.5	272.6	164.9	32.7	20.4	12.3
1929	13,678	452.5	286.2	166.3	33.3	21.1	12.2
1930	13,883	489.3	261.5	227.8	35.5	19.0	16.5
Average 1926–30					34.2	20.0	14.2
Fall from 1921–25 to 1926–30 average in percent					2.3	1.0	4.7
1931	14,077	470.3	276.8	193.5	33.6	19.8	13.8
1932	14,271	465.9	272.2	193.7	32.9	19.2	13.7
1933	14,468	452.2	243.7	208.5	31.5	17.0	14.5
1934	14,666	460.9	248.9	212.0	31.6	17.1	14.5
1935	14,868	441.7	249.0	192.7	29.9	16.9	13.0
Average 1931–35					31.9	18.0	13.9
Fall from 1926–30 to 1931–35 average in percent					6.7	10.4	2.1
1936	15,073	435.9	240.9	195.0	29.1	16.1	13.0
1937	15,280	424.4	242.3	182.1	28.0	16.0	12.0
1938	15,490	411.4	240.3	171.1	26.7	15.6	11.1
1939	15,703	403.9	233.2	170.7	25.9	15.0	10.9
Average 1936–39					27.4	15.7	11.7
Fall from 1931–35 to 1936–39 average in percent					14.1	12.8	15.8
Fall from 1921–25 to 1936–39 average in percent					21.7	22.3	20.9

* Source: Based on Yugoslavia, *Annuaire statistique 1940* (Belgrade, 1941), pp. 84, 103.

represented, owing to that war. This can be observed also in the number of marriages. The number of marriages fell from an average of
127,589 during the five-year period 1927–31 to an average of 108,385
during the period 1932–36. Of course, partially responsible for this

great fall in marriages was the Great Depression. In the period 1937–39 the number of marriages rose again to an average of 121,046.[4] This higher number of marriages, however, had no visible influence on the birth rate, except perhaps that without that increase in marriages it would have been somewhat lower during these years. The whole development thus appears to indicate a definite fall in fertility, as practically all observers of the European population movements during the 1930's maintained.

MOVEMENT OF VITAL RATES IN YUGOSLAVIA AND SOME SIMILAR COUNTRIES

It is interesting to compare the movement of the Yugoslav vital rates during the interwar period with those of some other European countries. The movement of vital rates in Western, Northern, and Central European industrial countries is, however, so basically different from those in the countries of Eastern and Southeastern Europe that we compare the Yugoslav rates only with those of countries with a similar population development. Table 17 shows the development of these rates in five-year averages (four-year averages in the last period) during the interwar period. This comparison shows that, throughout the interwar period, Rumania had a higher birth and a higher death rate than Yugoslavia, but that, with the exception of the 1921–25 period, its rate of natural growth was lower than that of Yugoslavia. During the two earlier periods, 1921–25 and 1926–30, both Bulgaria and Poland had a higher rate of natural growth than Yugoslavia, but their birth and death rates were lower than those in Yugoslavia during the 1930's, resulting in a lower rate of natural growth than that prevailing in Yugoslavia. The most important conclusion, on the basis of these comparisons and the comparisons with the rates of natural growth in other European countries, is that during the 1930's the Yugoslav population showed a trend of faster, though declining, rate of growth than any other European country with the exception of the Soviet Union. The net reproduction rate was 1.72 for the Soviet Union (1926–27), 1.45 for Yugoslavia (1930–32), 1.40 for Rumania (1930–31), 1.25 for Poland (1931–32), and 1.20 for Bulgaria (1934–35).[5]

This high fertility was also responsible for the fact that the age structure of the Yugoslav population was very "young." According to the census of 1931, 34.6 percent of its total population was in ages

---

[4] Yugoslavia, *Annuaire statistique 1936*, p. 71, and *Annuaire statistique 1940*, p. 102.
[5] Dudley Kirk, *op. cit.*, p. 56.

TABLE 17.—VITAL RATES IN YUGOSLAVIA AND SOME SIMILAR COUNTRIES,
AVERAGES 1921–25 TO 1936–39*

(Per thousand of population)

Period	Rates	Yugoslavia	Bulgaria	Poland	Rumania
1921–25	Births	35.0	39.0	34.7	37.9
	Deaths	20.2	20.8	18.5	23.0
	Natural growth	14.8	18.2	16.2	14.9
1926–30	Births	34.2	33.1	32.2	35.2
	Deaths	20.0	17.9	16.8	21.2
	Natural growth	14.2	15.2	15.4	14.0
1931–35	Births	31.8	29.3	27.6	32.9
	Deaths	17.9	15.5	14.6	20.6
	Natural growth	13.9	13.8	13.0	12.3
1936–39	Births	27.3	23.6	25.2[a]	30.0
	Deaths	15.6	13.7	14.0	19.2
	Natural growth	11.7	9.9	11.2	10.8

* Source: League of Nations, *Statistical Year Book of the League of Nations 1940/41* (Geneva, 1941), pp. 36–39.
[a] 1936–38 average.

0–14 and only 15.4 percent was in ages of 50 and above. The age structure according to the census of 1931 showed a somewhat "younger" population than the census of 1921. Another change noticeable between the two Yugoslav population censuses was the fact that the ratio of women to men fell from 51 to 49 in 1921 to 50.5 to 49.5 in 1931. Both of these developments were a consequence of the fact that the 1931 census was more removed from World War I, which affected greatly both the age and the sex structure of the Yugoslav population.

FALLING INFANT MORTALITY RATES

One of the encouraging developments in the Yugoslav as well as the general European population picture during the interwar period was a certain fall in infant mortality. Its fall in Yugoslavia and other countries in Eastern and Southeastern Europe was neither regular nor uninterrupted. Data on infant mortality in Yugoslavia prior to 1924 are lacking, and those for later years are considered not completely reliable. The average infant mortality in five-year averages between 1926 and 1935 and the annual rates between 1936 and 1938 were as follows:

	Per thousand infants
1926–30 average	151
1931–35 average	153
1936	137
1937	141
1938	144

Infant mortality in Rumania was considerably higher than that in Yugoslavia throughout the interwar period, and in Hungary and Bulgaria it was higher than in Yugoslavia in many years. In Poland, however, it was somewhat lower. Generally speaking, infant mortality in agricultural countries of Eastern and Southeastern Europe is approximately twice as high as in the industrial countries of Western, Northern, and Central Europe.[6]

Needless to say, infant mortality varied greatly from area to area in Yugoslavia, but one of the most interesting facts in this respect is that infant mortality is the highest in the agriculturally and economically most prosperous areas of the country, namely, in Vojvodina, Srijem, and Slavonia. In 1938–39 infant mortality in 12 of the 33 counties of *banovina* Dunav north of the Sava-Danube line (Srijem and Vojvodina) averaged over 200, reaching 242 in the county of Kovačica. In *banovina* Sava, infant mortality in the same years averaged over 200 in ten counties—that is, practically all Slavonian counties—with the highest, 234, being in the county (not city) of Osijek. Insanitary living conditions, lack of care in infant nutrition, and polluted water have been occasionally given as basic reasons for high infant mortality in these areas. It should be noted, however, that in these areas repeated abortions (popularly known as the "white plague") were practiced as a means of birth control and that many families strove to have no more than one or two children. It is possible that a certain connection existed between these practices and the high infant mortality. In the remaining 300-odd counties of the country outside these areas of uncommonly high infant mortality, in 1938–39 this rate exceeded 200 in only six counties in Macedonia, two counties in Bosnia, one county in Montenegro, and one county in Dalmatia.[7]

[6] League of Nations, *Statistical Year Book of the League of Nations 1940/41*, pp. 39–40.

[7] Yugoslavia, *Annuaire statistique 1940*, pp. 129–36.

It is conceivable, however, that the differences in infant mortality rates among various areas might be accounted for in part by varying degrees of underreporting of infant deaths.

INTERNATIONAL MIGRATIONS

The movement of population in Yugoslavia during the interwar period was little influenced by migrations across the frontiers (apart from the shifts in population for political reasons immediately following the conclusion of World War I, of which we have already spoken). Legislation of the early 1920's limiting immigration in those countries to which the South Slavs mainly emigrated (especially the United States and the British Dominions), and later the economic depression which discouraged emigration to the Latin-American countries, broke the trend of heavy transoceanic emigration so pronounced before 1914 in most South Slav lands. This represented a basic change in the development of the Yugoslav population movement when compared with the pre-1914 years. But while the transoceanic emigration was reduced, especially after 1930, to insignificant proportions, emigration to the European industrial countries, France, Belgium, and Germany, increased greatly after 1927 and reached its top level in 1930.

The picture of the Yugoslav interwar migrations across the frontiers is supplied in Table 18. The Great Depression affected profoundly not only the transoceanic emigration, but also that to the European countries, although the latter recovered somewhat in the second part of the 1930's. While data are lacking to draw a complete balance sheet of the Yugoslav migrations during the interwar period, data for 1930 and later years are complete and are included in this table. One of the most interesting problems is, of course, the development of emigration to and the number of returnees from the United States. According to United States official sources, between July 1, 1919, and June 30, 1927, the United States admitted a total of 47,488 people from Yugoslavia (in the last year of free immigration, between July 1, 1920, and June 30, 1921, a total of 23,666), while during the same period a total of 64,527 people returned from the United States to Yugoslavia, giving a balance of 17,039 to the returnees.[8] In the period 1930 to 1938 total emigration, both transoceanic and Continental, amounted to 152,750, while the number of returnees was 95,513, the surplus of emigrants

[8] U.S. Department of Labor, *Annual Report of the Commissioner General of Immigration* (annually for the fiscal years 1919 to 1927). For a general review of the problem of Yugoslav emigration, including various laws and regulations pertaining to emigration up to 1928, see Christa Stamenkovitch, *L'émigration yougoslave* (Paris, 1929).

TABLE 18.—EMIGRANTS AND RETURNEES, 1919–38*

Year	Emigrants			Returnees		
	Transoceanic	Continental[a]	Total	Transoceanic	Continental[b]	Total
1919 1920	6,279			41,167		
1921	12,965					
1922	6,086					
1923	11,473			1,981		
1924	19,575			5,244		
1925	17,643			5,691		
1926	18,230			5,554		
1927	21,976	6,560	28,536	5,753		
1928	21,789	12,538	34,327	5,827		
1929	18,189	19,425	37,614	5,992		
1930	13,560	25,409	38,969	7,607	7,395	15,002
1931	4,808	10,560	15,368	8,089	10,046	18,135
1932	2,454	6,642	9,096	6,031	8,209	14,240
1933	2,221	7,508	9,729	3,385	3,895	7,280
1934	2,907	11,004	13,911	2,309	4,421	6,730
1935	3,345	10,120	13,465	1,887	3,969	5,856
1936	3,860	8,625	12,485	1,861	3,345	5,206
1937	5,378	14,287	19,665	2,462	4,303	6,765
1938	5,686	14,376	20,062	2,070	14,229	16,299

* Source: Yugoslavia, *Annuaire statistique 1929* (Belgrade, 1932), p. 122; *Annuaire statistique 1936* (Belgrade, 1937), pp. 78–82; and *Annuaire statistique 1940* (Belgrade, 1941), pp. 137–51.
[a] No official data available for years before 1927. ·
[b] No official data available for years before 1930.

being 57,237. The excess of emigrants over returnees during the interwar period was not large, definitely not comparable with the excess prevailing during the two decades prior to World War I, but the economic character of these two groups was quite different and economically important. The emigrants were recruited from among the young people, mostly male peasants, going abroad in search of work. The returnees, on the contrary, were mostly older people, who, as a rule, used to bring back considerable savings and considerable skills or business experience. There is, however, no doubt that the virtual cessation of large emigration characteristic of the pre-1914 years had dire consequences, because emigration was previously one of the chief safety vents for the mounting population pressure in rural areas. It had also dire consequences for the country's balance of payments and the income of population in areas which had depended heavily on emigrants' remittances.

ESTIMATED AVERAGE LIFE EXPECTANCY

There are two other general issues with regard to the Yugoslav population movement during the interwar period: the average life expectancy and the trend of the future population growth. The average life expectancy can be taken as the over-all indicator of economic and social conditions under which a population lives. It is therefore much higher in countries on a high level of economic and cultural development than in the underdeveloped countries, including Yugoslavia. Exact data on average life expectancy during the interwar period are not available for Yugoslavia as a whole. They exist only for Slovenia (*banovina* Drava) and are based on the mortality tables for the three-year period 1931–33. Average life expectancy in Slovenia for children born in those years was 50.08 years for males and 54.15 years for females.[9] But Slovenia was not then and is not now typical of Yugoslavia as a whole. Rather, it was the most advanced area of the country. However, an approximate calculation (margin of error one to three years) of the average life expectancy of people in Yugoslavia is obtained by multiplying the average age of population of the country with the coefficients obtained by dividing the average life expectancy of males and females in Slovenia by their average age (1.77 and 1.81). If this formula is applied, then the average life expectancy in Yugoslavia in 1931 was 46.51 for males and 49.57 years for females.[10] Keeping in mind the margin of error, this seems to be a reasonable estimate, since the average life expectancy in Bulgaria was 45.92 for males and 46.64 for females (1925–28), in Poland 48.20 for males and 51.40 for females (1931–32), and in Hungary 48.27 for males and 51.34 for females (1930–31).[11] According to the average age of population in Yugoslavia, shown by the census of March 15, 1948, the average life expectancy in the country, calculated by the same method as above, was 48.60 for males and 53.01 for females, an improvement over a period of 17 years, which seems reasonable.[12]

[9] Ivo Lah, "L'Âge moyen et la vie moyenne de la population en R.P.F. de Yougoslavie," *Statistička revija*, I, No. 1, 98.

[10] *Ibid.*, p. 96.

[11] League of Nations, *Statistical Year Book of the League of Nations 1942/44* pp. 82–85.

[12] Ivo Lah, *op. cit.*, p. 98.

TRENDS OF FUTURE POPULATION GROWTH

The final general problem to be discussed is the trend of population growth as revealed by the Yugoslav vital rates prevailing during the 1930's. The only existing population forecast for Yugoslavia going to 1970, as far as this writer is aware, is the one developed by the Office of Population Research of Princeton University, undertaken for the League of Nations.[13] Before calculating the future growth, Professor Notestein and his associates introduced certain corrections in the Yugoslav pre-1940 official population estimates to account for the under-registration of births and deaths. The order of magnitude of this correction is indicated by the fact that their estimate of Yugoslav population at the beginning of 1940 was 15,200,000 as against the official estimate for the end of 1939 of 15,703,000. Using the census figures of 1931 and the vital rates of 1936–38 as the "base fertility schedule" and taking into account their rectification, they estimated the Yugoslav population in 1970 at 18,500,000.[14]

Estimates of future population on the basis of the trend in the vital rates of the 1930's proved to be only of academic interest for many countries. This seems to be notably true also of the forecasts for Yugoslavia, though the Princeton Group itself stated:

In general, the results for the whole of Eastern Europe must be taken as more reliable than those for any of the constituent countries, and the results for Rumania and Yugoslavia are particularly open to question.[15]

The above estimate did not explicitly take into account the population losses of World War II. In Yugoslavia these losses were staggering and resulted from direct military losses, excess civilian mortality, reduced births during the war years, politically induced mass exterminations of population, and, finally, from the politically conditioned mass migrations. In the latter category the most important item was the exodus of the German minority from Yugoslavia, which in 1939 numbered about 450,000 and was reduced in March 1948 to a bare 55,328.[16] In the closing stages of World War II certain pro-Axis Croatian and Serbian military formations fled the country, and their number, including the civilians who left with them, was estimated by Yugoslav authorities at between 50,000 and 60,000. On the other hand, after

[13] Frank W. Notestein *et al.*, *The Future Population of Europe and the Soviet Union—Population Projections 1940–1970.*

[14] *Ibid.*, pp. 310–11.

[15] *Ibid.*, p. 196.

[16] Yugoslavia, Federal Bureau of Statistics, *Bulletin statistique*, No. 1, July 1950, p. 16.

World War II Yugoslavia obtained the bulk of Istria, the cities of Rijeka (Fiume) and Zadar (Zara), and several Adriatic islands, which during the interwar period were under Italy, with a population of approximately 500,000.[17] In spite of this and two and a half years of peacetime population recovery, the population of Yugoslavia, according to the census of March 15, 1948, was only 15,751,935.[18] If one subtracts from this figure the 500,000 of population in the newly acquired territory, 266,744 people as the surplus of births over deaths from January 1947 to March 15, 1948[19] (the date of the census), and 200,000 which we assume as the surplus of births over deaths in 1946, the population of Yugoslavia in the pre-1941 territory at the end of 1945 was 14,785,000. As the estimated population of Yugoslavia (geometric progression using the coefficient of growth of 1938) at the end of 1945 would have been 17,144,000, the total direct and indirect losses of population, including the reduction in births and mass emigrations, in Yugoslavia due to World War II amounted to about 2,360,000.

Another basic factor in considering the Princeton Group estimate of Yugoslav population is that its forecast was based on vital rates as they prevailed during the period 1936–38. This was a period characterized by relatively low and declining birth rates and declining rates of natural growth. But after World War II Yugoslavia experienced, with several other European countries, a pronounced increase in birth rates and a drop in death rates, thus achieving a higher rate of natural growth. Compared with average vital rates for 1936–38, the post-World War II vital rates moved in Yugoslavia as follows:[20]

	Births	Deaths	Natural growth
	(Per thousand of population)		
1936–38 average	27.9	15.9	12.0
1947	26.3	12.6	13.7
1948	28.2	13.5	14.7
1949	30.0	13.5	16.5

Thus both components of population in 1970, the one born before 1940 which was greatly reduced during World War II, and the one which

[17] Anton Melik, *Jugoslavija—Zemljopisni pregled* (Yugoslavia—A Geographic Survey), pp. 365–69.

[18] Yugoslavia, Federal Bureau of Statistics, *Preliminary Results of the Population Census of March 15, 1948*, p. 13.

[19] Yugoslavia, Federal Bureau of Statistics, *Bulletin statistique*, No. 5, June 1951, p. 36.

[20] *Ibid.*, p. 39.

already was or will be born between 1940 and 1970, will probably differ greatly from estimates calculated by the Princeton Group. Wartime losses will, obviously, tend to reduce, and the post-1947 changed vital rates to increase the actual population in the foreseeable future. There are many other factors which will exert an important, but definitely not predictable influence on the future development of Yugoslav population. It is impossible, for example, to gauge how the industrialization drive pursued at present and the resulting greater urbanization are going to influence vital rates. What will be the influence of the continuing low plane of living, which is, for the time being, a result not only of low productivity of the country's economy but also of the great investment activity and of large defense expenditures? What will be the results of the extended educational services and of the apparently extended and improved health and care services for infants and children in general? It is interesting to note that infant mortality as officially reported for 1949 has already been markedly reduced, namely to 102.38.[21] Thus far Yugoslavia has not announced any policy favoring a higher birth rate, but its whole economic and cultural policy is orientated in a direction which in the future may result in considerably reduced death rates, so that even a lowered birth rate would result in a high rate of natural growth. The basic fact which has to be remembered is that Yugoslavia is now undergoing a political, socioeconomic, and cultural revolution and that this revolution is going to affect profoundly, but hardly in a predictable fashion, both the quantitative and qualitative aspects of the Yugoslav population.

But if it is assumed that the rate of population growth (about 230,-000 annually) which prevailed between the censuses of March 15, 1948, and March 31, 1953,[22] is going to continue, Yugoslavia's population will reach the 18.5 million mark by 1960, in spite of the great losses during World War II (but counting the population from the enlarged territory). If approximately the same rate of growth is assumed for another ten years, the population of Yugoslavia in 1970 will exceed 21 million.

INTERREGIONAL DIFFERENCES IN POPULATION GROWTH

Great differences in population trends in various South Slav lands, which were pronounced before 1914, continued to prevail during the interwar period. This is best illustrated by Table 19, which shows population by *banovine* according to the censuses of 1921 and 1931

[21] *Ibid.*, p. 38.
[22] *Borba*, May 1, 2, and 3, 1953.

TABLE 19.—POPULATION BY BANOVINE ACCORDING TO THE CENSUSES OF 1921
AND 1931; ESTIMATED POPULATION FOR MARCH 31, 1941, AND THE RESPECTIVE
PERCENTAGE GROWTH BETWEEN THESE PERIODS*

(In thousands; in percent)

Banovina	Census 1/31/21	Census 3/31/31	Increase 1921–31 (Percent)	Estimate 3/31/41[a]	Increase 1931–41 (Percent)	Increase 1921–41 (Percent)
Drava	1,060.3	1,144.3	7.9	1,214.0	6.1	14.5
Drina	1,205.5	1,534.7	27.3	1,914.0	24.7	58.8
Dunav	2,179.3	2,387.3	9.5	2,575.0	7.9	18.2
Morava	1,200.3	1,435.6	19.6	1,690.0	17.7	40.8
Primorje	804.2	901.7	12.1	994.0	10.2	23.6
Sava	2,424.4	2,704.4	11.5	2,975.0	10.0	22.7
Vardar	1,323.5	1,574.2	18.9	1,845.0	17.2	39.4
Vrbas	850.0	1,037.4	22.0	1,243.0	19.8	46.2
Zeta	784.7	925.5	17.9	1,076.0	16.3	37.1
Prefecture of Belgrade	152.7	288.9	89.2	447.0	54.7	192.7
Yugoslavia	11,984.9	13,934.0	16.3	15,973.0	14.6	33.3

* Source: Census figures from Yugoslavia, *Annuaire statistique 1931* (Belgrade, 1934), pp. 50–51.

[a] The estimate for March 31, 1941, obtained by geometric progression, using official growth coefficients as applied in the Yugoslav official estimates for banovinal population in 1938. Yugoslavia, *Annuaire statistique 1938–1939* (Belgrade, 1939), p. 111.

and the estimated population for March 31, 1941, as well as the percentage increases between these various periods. Two *banovine* with an outstanding population growth were Drina and Vrbas, where the increase in population between 1921 and 1941 amounted to 58.8 and 46.2 percent, respectively. In the second group are the *banovine* Morava with an increase of 40.8 percent, Vardar with 39.4 percent, and Zeta with a population increase of 37.1 percent between 1921 and 1941. All these *banovine* were south of the Sava-Danube rivers and economically and culturally on a considerably lower level of development than the areas north of these rivers. This is only an additional illustration of the almost general rule that higher economic and cultural development usually results in a lowered birth rate and a generally lower rate of natural population growth. A third group was formed by the *banovine* Primorje with an increase in population between 1921 and 1941 of 23.6 percent, and Sava with an increase of 22.7 percent. In the fourth group were the *banovine* Dunav with an increase of 18.2, and Drava with an increase of 14.5 percent. The population of the

Prefecture of Belgrade, including the city of Belgrade proper and certain communities which actually were its suburbs, rose between 1921 and 1941 by 192.7 percent. But the case of Belgrade cannot be taken as representative of the growth of the urban population of Yugoslavia.

THE GROWTH OF URBAN POPULATION

The growth rate of urban population undoubtedly has greatly increased during the interwar period. But the criteria of defining urban population are not simple. Generally speaking, in Yugoslavia all communities with 5,000 and more inhabitants are officially considered as urban. According to the census of 1931 a total of 2,607,072 people, or 18.7 percent of the total population of the country, lived in such communities. It was estimated that at the end of March 1941 about 3,640,-000 people, or 22.8 percent of the total population, lived in communities of 5,000 and more people. This meant a rise of more than one million during a period of ten years. A considerably smaller percentage of the total population lived in cities of 20,000 and more inhabitants. The percentage of total population living in such communities rose from 7.8 percent of the total in 1921 to 9.3 percent in 1931, and to an estimated 10.6 percent in March 1941. But living in communities of 5,000, or even in those of 20,000 and more people, does not mean that all their inhabitants have typical urban occupations, namely, that they are not engaged in agriculture. In fact, many communities with fewer than 3,000 inhabitants along the Adriatic coast and in Macedonia are purely urban, while in Vojvodina some communities with 10,000 to 15,000 people are purely agricultural. Generally speaking, a considerable proportion of the "urban" population in the Pannonian Plain was engaged in agriculture. Thus, for example, 52 percent of the total population of the largest city in Vojvodina, Subotica, which in 1931 had a population of 100,058, derived a livelihood from agriculture.

DIFFERENCES IN POPULATION GROWTH WITHIN REGIONS

It would be wrong to think that population growth either before 1914 or during the interwar period was similar in all parts of various *banovine*, even when the *banovine* included historically and economically quite homogeneous areas. Studies of population growth by counties have shown that from 1880 to 1931 population had increased in 14 counties of northern Bosnia and five counties in Serbia by well over 100 percent.[23] There were only three such counties in Croatia-Slavonia

[23] Svetozar Ilešič, "The Increase in Population in the Territory of Yugoslavia, 1880–1931," *Geografski vestnik*, XVI, 3–25.

and one in Herzegovina. On the other hand, there were a few counties in Slovenia, southwestern Croatia, and Dalmatia in which population had decreased between 1880 and 1931. In a series of counties in these areas and a few isolated counties in other areas population increased by less than 10 percent during those 50 years. In most counties in Bosnia and Herzegovina, Serbia, Dalmatia, and Croatia-Slavonia population increased during that period by 50 to 100 percent. In practically all Bosnian and Serbian counties in which population grew between 1880 and 1931 by more than 100 percent, this growth had to be ascribed to a surplus of births over deaths rather than to immigration, as these counties are not characterized as industrial or mining areas. While counties known for rapid population growth have shown the same tendency also during the whole interwar period, data are available only for the decade of the 1920's.

DIFFERENCES IN THE GROWTH OF POPULATION
AMONG NATIONALITIES

It is noteworthy that, as a rule, areas populated by Croats and Slovenes, who are Roman Catholics, and by the German and Magyar minorities, who are either Roman Catholic or Protestant, showed a much lower rate of population growth than areas populated by Serbs, Macedonians, and Montenegrins, all of whom are Eastern Orthodox. Moslems of Bosnia and Herzegovina, who are racially South Slavs, also showed a considerably lower growth than the Serb population. The same seems to be true of the Moslems of Macedonia, who are racially Turkish, but not of Moslems of the present Kosovo-Metohija autonomous area and western Macedonia, who are Albanians and who showed rapid growth. In most areas of mixed population the Eastern Orthodox element is growing faster than other denominations.

This discrepancy in the rate of growth between the Serbian and especially the Croatian portion of the Yugoslav population also had political implications, as it tended to tip the numerical relationship between these two main and competing nations of Yugoslavia even more to the advantage of the Serbs. Faster growth of the Serbs sustained an old tendency of the Serbian element to expand into areas north of the Sava-Danube rivers and, during the interwar period, also into Macedonia. This first tendency created a considerable amount of political and economic apprehension among the Croats. At least one of the Croatian organizations, the co-operative society Zemlja (The Land) which became connected with the Gospodarska Sloga of the Croatian Peasant party, had as its economic aim to facilitate colonization of peasants from Croatian Zagorje (the area north of the Croatian capital of Zagreb), the most overpopulated Croatian region, into Slavonia and Srijem; and it had as its political aim the counteracting of Serbian colonization in these "threatened areas." There is no doubt that the higher rate of natural growth of the Serbs than of the other Yugoslav nations—assuming that this situation would continue to prevail in the future—will produce in the long run specific problems of demographic adjustment of considerable economic and political significance. It will require from the future political leaders in Yugoslavia a great deal of political wisdom to deal equitably and intelligently with this problem, even if in the meanwhile the poisonous fangs of the Serbian and Croatian chauvinisms have been extirpated.

POPULATION DEPENDENT ON AGRICULTURE

Both of the interwar censuses have shown that the bulk of the Yugoslav population depends for its livelihood on agriculture. According to the census of 1921 not less than 78.9 percent, and according to the census of 1931, 76.5 percent, of the total population depended on agriculture. The population depending on industry, handicrafts, and mining for a livelihood rose from 9.9 percent in 1921 to 11.0 percent in 1931. Trade, transportation, and banking supported 4.3 percent in 1921 and 4.9 percent in 1931; public service, professions, and armed forces served as a source of livelihood for 3.8 percent of the total population in 1921 and 4.1 percent in 1931. Finally, there was 3.1 percent of the population in 1921 who lived by other occupations, were without occupation, or did not indicate their occupation. Their number increased by 1931 to 3.5 percent. Thus, during the 1920's there was a definite trend resulting in the reduction of the relative importance of agriculture as a source of livelihood of the population of Yugoslavia and in an increase of the importance of industry, trade, transportation, professions, and public service. This, however, was a trend which had been operating ever since the beginning of the nineteenth century.

It is safe to assume that this trend continued also during the 1930's and that by 1941 a somewhat smaller proportion of the Yugoslav population depended on agriculture and a greater proportion on other occupations, especially industry, than in 1931 (see Table 22, p. 317). But conclusive data in this respect are not available. An indicator of such a development was a relatively large increase in the average number of workers and employees insured with the Central Office of Workers Insurance, with private employees' insurance societies, and with the brotherhoods of miners, which rose from 654,246 in 1931 to 794,523 in 1939.[24]

Agriculture is of varying importance as a source of livelihood in various areas of Yugoslavia. There are no statistical data which would show us this relationship at the beginning and at the end of the inter-war period. But data for 1931, supplied in Table 20, are indicative

TABLE 20.—POPULATION ENGAGED IN AGRICULTURE AND IN INDUSTRY, HANDICRAFTS, AND MINING, BY BANOVINE IN 1931*

(In thousands; in percent)

Banovina	Total population	Engaged in agriculture		Engaged in industry, handicrafts, and mining	
		Number	Percent of total	Number	Percent of total
Drava	1,144.3	689.8	60.3	253.4	22.1
Drina	1,534.7	1,263.2	82.3	119.4	7.8
Dunav	2,387.3	1,783.6	74.7	321.7	13.5
Morava	1,435.6	1,232.0	85.8	103.6	7.2
Primorje	901.7	753.2	83.5	57.6	6.4
Sava	2,704.4	2,037.2	75.3	326.8	12.1
Vardar	1,574.2	1,228.3	78.0	148.2	9.4
Vrbas	1,037.4	914.6	88.2	53.8	5.2
Zeta	925.5	758.5	82.0	52.1	5.6
Prefecture of Belgrade..	288.9	10.2	3.5	96.4	33.3
Yugoslavia	13,934.0	10,670.6	76.5	1,533.0	11.0

* Source: Yugoslavia, *Annuaire statistique 1936* (Belgrade, 1937), pp. 38–43.

of the whole period. This table shows the total and the percentage of population in various *banovine* which had as the principal source of livelihood (*a*) agriculture and (*b*) industry, handicrafts, and mining. Here again a division of the country into two basic regions is indicated, i.e., the region south of the Sava-Danube line and the region north of this line. The first depends relatively much more on agriculture and

[24] Yugoslavia, *Annuaire statistique 1936*, pp. 456–60, and *Annuaire statistique 1940*, pp. 409–11. It would be wrong to think, however, that all these people were industrial workers. These figures include, in addition, domestic servants, employees of health institutions, theaters, restaurants and coffee houses, trade, credit and insurance institutions, employees of municipal enterprises, and those of privately owned transportation facilities. But they exclude the employees of the government-owned transportation facilities, primarily the railroads, which had a special insurance scheme. Their number in 1931 was about 70,000 and rose in 1939 to 84,554. Agricultural wage workers are also excluded.

animal husbandry than the latter. Least "agricultural" was *banovina*
Drava where only 60.3 percent of the total population was engaged in
agriculture while 22.1 percent was in industry, handicrafts, and mining. On the other extreme was *banovina* Vrbas in which 88.2 percent
of the total population was engaged in agriculture and only 5.2 percent
in industry, handicrafts, and mining. The remaining *banovine* ranged
between these two extremes. In *banovina* Dunav 74.7 percent, and in
Sava 75.3 percent of the total population were engaged in agriculture.
In this respect these two regions were also below the national average.
In all other *banovine*, with the exception of Vardar, more than 82 percent of the total population depended on agriculture. If one remembers
that the growth of population is greatest in areas in which the relatively
largest proportion of people depend on agriculture, the relationship
between rural population and agricultural resources, and the potential
growth of both, acquires an even greater meaning.

THE EMPLOYED AND THE SUPPORTED POPULATION

A basic issue in regard to population is not only the source of its
livelihood but also the relationship between the employed and the supported population in various branches of economic activity. In agricultural countries like Yugoslavia this relationship is of special importance. Another problem closely related to this issue is the way in which
the new labor force resulting from population growth has been able to
find employment. In both respects important changes took place in
Yugoslavia between 1921 and 1931 and most probably continued to
take place during the 1930's, but conclusive statistical information for
the latter period is lacking. Of the total population of 11,684,767
covered by the census of 1921 (about 300,000 were not covered), only
6,033,111, or 51.6 percent, were gainfully employed. In 1931, of the
total population of 13,934,038 only 6,682,615, or 48.0 percent, were
employed. Thus, in the whole economy a shift occurred which bur-
dened those who were gainfully employed with a larger number of
those who were supported. Two factors were responsible for this: the
relatively younger population, namely, a relatively larger proportion of
children in the population of 1931, and, to a much lesser extent, the
economic depression. While the total increase in population between
1921 (area covered by the census) and 1931 amounted to 2,249,271,
the number of gainfully employed people was only 649,504 larger in
1931 than in 1921, and the number of supported people was larger in
the latter year by 1,599,767. The number of employed in agriculture
rose between 1921 and 1931 by 250,450, or only 5.2 percent, while

the number of supported people in agriculture rose by 1,204,601, or 27.6 percent. In industry, handicrafts, and mining the number of employed rose between the two censuses by 37.3 percent and the number of supported people by 28.4 percent. Coefficients of increase similar to those in industry were recorded in trade, credit, transportation, public service, professions, and armed forces. Indeed, agriculture provided the greatest number of new jobs during the 1920's, but industry, handicrafts, and mining provided not less than 194,911 new jobs, which shows the great importance of industry as an outlet for the increasing labor force. All other occupations provided another 204,143 new jobs.[25] But while the distribution of new jobs between agriculture and all other occupations was on a basis of 38.6 to 61.4 percent, the distribution of the load of caring for those people who were not gainfully employed was 75.3 to 24.7 percent between agriculture and other occupations, respectively.

The increase in the number of people dependent on agriculture for their livelihood between 1921 and 1931 was accompanied by two developments. On the one hand, the amount of cultivated land increased between 1922 and 1931 from 6,955,526 to 7,635,023 hectares, or by 679,497 hectares (9.8 percent). On the other hand, the number of households making a living in agriculture increased between the two censuses from 1,741,092 (area covered by the census of 1921) to 1,963,403, or by 222,311 (12.8 percent). Perhaps 40,000 to 50,000 new households were created during the 1920's by the division of large estates and internal colonization in the course of the agrarian reform. A few thousand peasant households were created by using land obtained by clearance of forest land. The remainder of approximately 170,000 new peasant households were created by the subdivision of the existing farms. Thus, the chief outlet for new jobs which were found in agriculture between the censuses of 1921 and 1931 was the creation of new farms by the subdivision of existing ones.

It is not known how large was the population dependent on agriculture at the end of 1938 or at the end of March 1941, how great was the number of households depending on agriculture, or how great was the number of employed people and the number of supported people in agriculture at those two points of time. But if we assume that the trend of the 1920's continued during the 1930's this percentage in 1938 was 74.8 and the estimated population depending on agriculture was 11,586,000 at the end of 1938 (see Table 22, p. 317). It is not known

25 Figures for 1921 from Yugoslavia, *Annuaire statistique 1929*, pp. 90–91, and for 1931 from Yugoslavia, *Annuaire statistique 1936*, pp. 32–43.

what percentage of the increase in population during the 1930's became employed and what percentage swelled the ranks of supported
people, or how the increase in employed and in supported people was
distributed between agriculture and other occupations. Most probably
the trend prevailing during the 1920's was continued whereby agriculture provided the largest proportion of new jobs and was saddled
with a relatively much larger share of the supported people than other
occupations. Undoubtedly industry continued to be the second most
important outlet for the growing labor force.

It is also most probable that the greatest proportion of new jobs
in agriculture was created not by the increase in the cultivated area,
though it rose from 7,635,023 hectares in 1931 to 8,218,505 hectares
in 1938, or by 7.6 percent, but by further subdivision of the existing
farms, as was the case during the 1920's. The tendency of further subdivision of the existing farms was perhaps somewhat weaker during the
1930's than during the 1920's for several reasons: the increase in
total and in rural population was smaller than during the 1920's, the
number of marriages between 1921 and 1930 averaged 129,265 and
between 1931 and 1938 only 113,415 for the country as a whole. And
new marriages are perhaps the most important single cause of division
of peasant households. Finally, the division of peasant households involved, as a rule, considerable expenditures in cash, which often had
to be obtained by going into debt, and during the 1930's, because of the
legislation with regard to the existing peasant debts, the peasants were
almost totally excluded from obtaining credit. On the other hand, one
could argue that the depression of the 1930's, which in Yugoslavia
lasted until 1935 in a severe form, put additional psychological and
financial strains on the peasant family, thus contributing to the division
of peasant households. Be that as it may, owing to the lack of census
data around 1940, the developments in the Yugoslav agriculture and
in the agriculture of many other European countries during the 1930's
will remain a matter of estimates and conjectures.

CHAPTER 16

AGRICULTURAL OVERPOPULATION

WE HAVE now arrived at the point of considering the basic problem of the Yugoslav agriculture and rural population during the interwar period—the development in the relationship between land resources and livestock numbers, on the one hand, and the population dependent on agriculture for its livelihood, on the other. Livestock numbers are, however, in themselves variables depending essentially on the relationship between the two other factors. It seems best to show first the relative conditions of Yugoslavia in this respect as compared with those existing in a series of other European countries and then proceed with the discussion of these relationships among various regions of Yugoslavia itself.

DENSITY OF AGRICULTURAL POPULATION IN YUGOSLAVIA AND SELECTED EUROPEAN COUNTRIES

Table 21 presents the census results for the years around 1930 for Yugoslavia and nine other European countries, showing the percentage of total population dependent on agriculture for its livelihood and the relative density of this population in relation both to cultivated land and to livestock numbers expressed in terms of cattle. To indicate the differences in the quality of land among the various countries, the 1930–34 average yields for wheat and potatoes, as crops widely grown in all of these countries, are given. Differences in yields of livestock, though they were as much or even more pronounced than the differences in the crop yields, are left out of account because we deal in composite animal units, and the computation of yields would involve insurmountable statistical difficulties. But this factor has to be kept in mind. This table shows that in Yugoslavia and other countries of Southeastern and Eastern Europe a much larger percentage of the total population is dependent on agriculture and that the relative density of agricultural population to each hundred hectares of cultivated land is much higher than in the industrial or quasi-industrial countries of Western and Central Europe. As pronounced or even more so were the differences among these countries in regard to the relationship between agricultural population and livestock numbers. And finally, there are great differ-

TABLE 21.—PROPORTION OF TOTAL POPULATION DEPENDENT ON AGRICULTURE AROUND 1930, AGRICULTURAL POPULATION AT THE END OF 1931, RELATIVE DENSITIES OF AGRICULTURAL POPULATION PER 100 HECTARES OF CULTIVATED LAND AND 100 ANIMAL UNITS IN 1931, AND 1930–34 AVERAGE YIELDS OF WHEAT AND POTATOES, IN YUGOSLAVIA AND SELECTED EUROPEAN COUNTRIES

Country	Percent of total population dependent on agriculture[a]		Estimated agricultural population at the end of 1931[b] (Thousands)	Agricultural people		Average 1930–34 yields (Quintals per hectare)[e]	
	Census year	Percent		Per 100 hectares cultivated land[c]	Per 100 animal units[d]	Wheat	Potatoes
Yugoslavia	1931	76.5	10,771	140	141	10.5	58.8
Bulgaria	1934	73.2	4,441	116	102	11.5	53.0
Czechoslovakia .	1930	34.5	5,114	85	79	17.0	127.2
Denmark	1930	31.2	1,116	42	21	28.9	165.5
France	1931	28.0	11,746	48	51	15.5	110.5
Germany	1933	20.8	13,473	63	44	21.5	160.0
Hungary	1930	51.8	4,529	76	115	13.1	61.3
Italy	1936	43.2	17,918	111	153	14.0	60.0
Poland	1931	62.8	20,207	106	112	11.7	112.9
Rumania	1930	72.4	13,249	94	142	9.0	87.8

[a] Data for all countries except Yugoslavia, Bulgaria, and France from C. J. Robertson, "Population and Agriculture, with Special Reference to Agricultural Overpopulation," in International Institute of Agriculture, *Documentation for the European Conference on Rural Life 1939* (Rome, 1939), p. 13. For Yugoslavia the census of 1931 percentage of 76.5 instead of 76.6; for Bulgaria the percentage as found in the census of 1934 instead of 1926; for France, the estimate from Dudley Kirk, *Europe's Population in the Interwar Years* (League of Nations, 1946), p. 200.

[b] League of Nations, *Statistical Year Book of the League of Nations 1932/33* (Geneva, 1933), pp. 22–23.

[c] Calculated on the basis of data on cultivated land in International Institute of Agriculture, *International Yearbook of Agricultural Statistics 1931–32* (Rome, 1932), *passim*, and *International Yearbook of Agricultural Statistics 1932–33* (Rome, 1933), *passim*, by relating cultivated land to estimated agricultural population (col. 3). Cultivated land includes arable land and land under tree and bush crops.

[d] Livestock calculated into animal units on the basis of the formula given in Table 12 (footnote *b*), p. 279, from figures on livestock in International Institute of Agriculture, *International Yearbook of Agricultural Statistics 1931–32* (Rome, 1932), *passim*, and *International Yearbook of Agricultural Statistics 1932–33* (Rome, 1933), *passim*, and relating the number of animal units to estimated agricultural population (col. 3).

[e] International Institute of Agriculture, *International Yearbook of Agricultural Statistics 1940–41* (Rome, 1941), pp. 10–11, 36–37.

ences in average crop and livestock yields, a fact which simply means that, assuming the same standards of comparison for all countries, the same amount of land or the same number of livestock can support a different number of people.

The second and most important conclusion to be obtained from this table is that Yugoslavia showed a far greater relative density of agricultural population per 100 hectares of cultivated land than any other country included in the table, either in Western and Central or in Southeastern and Eastern Europe. As far as the relationship between agricultural population and livestock numbers is concerned, Yugoslavia had a worse relationship than any other country in the table except Italy. Rumania was, in this respect, on a par with Yugoslavia. But if the more favorable relationship between cultivated land and the agricultural population in Italy and Rumania is taken into account, the over-all relationship between the agricultural population and agricultural resources was worse in Yugoslavia than in any other country included in the table. If the differences in the quality of land and agricultural technology, as expressed in the differences in yields, were taken into account, then the position of Yugoslavia would further deteriorate in relation to the other countries.

INDICATORS OF AGRICULTURAL OVERPOPULATION

There is obviously a certain relationship between agricultural population, on the one hand, and the agricultural land resources, on the other, which enables the agricultural population of a given country or area to have a satisfactory level of living. Of course, it must be remembered that the differences in the quality of land resources and the prevailing agricultural technology modify substantially these numerical relationships because they affect the yields and quality of products and thus the capacity of agricultural land to support a certain number of people. Furthermore, it is necessary to stress that the differences in the planes and standards of living among the agricultural populations of various countries are often great and that they are mostly related to cultural and socioeconomic factors. Owing to these differences a considerably lower income may be as acceptable in terms of economic welfare in a country with a low plane of living as a much higher income in a country with a high plane of living. This problem cannot be solved statistically. But we must be aware of it when establishing the standard relationship between agricultural population and agricultural resources for various countries.

The choice of a standard relationship between the agricultural population and agricultural land resources is admittedly a difficult and always arbitrary one. The problem is made difficult because of the differences in the structure of agricultural production, differences in the productivity of land and livestock due either to natural or to socioeconomic causes, differences between prices of products the farmers sell and those they buy, differences in the tax burden carried by agriculture, differences in the availability of agricultural credit and the rates of interest which the farmers have normally to pay, and, finally, because of the differences in the planes and standards of living. The difficulties arise not only when international comparisons are made, but also, to a lesser degree, in interregional comparisons in the same country. It is obvious that all these factors cannot be statistically taken into account on the basis of the existing data.

The simplest procedure in order to arrive at an indicator of over-population is to take a certain number of agricultural population per unit of agricultural land as the norm and to consider all excess population as "surplus" and a country or area in which the agricultural population has surpassed the norm as characterized by a state of over-population. While this is admittedly a mechanistic approach, if the norm is established with regard to the over-all structure of agricultural production, and if due regard is taken of the productivity in agriculture and the prevailing ideas about an appropriate amount of land to assure fairly full employment and a satisfactory plane of living, this method is quite acceptable. It is essential, however, to compare only countries with similar structures of agriculture, similar agricultural techniques, and similar planes of living.

Most of the Yugoslav economists used this method during the interwar period to gauge the degree of agricultural overpopulation. They related the agricultural population to agriculturally productive land as defined by the official statistics—that is, including the permanent meadows and pastures—and to arable land, thus obtaining a double index of the relative density of agricultural population.[1] Others used only arable or only cultivated land as the basis for their calculations of population density in agriculture.[2] Differences in the quality of soil and in the level of agricultural technology, as expressed in varied levels of yields and differences in cropping patterns as well as differences in the number of livestock per given area of cultivated land, were pointed out by almost all authors as factors influencing the significance of ratios between agricultural population and land resources in various areas. None of them had, however, attempted to assign specific co-

[1] Otto von Frangeš, "The Problem of Relative Overpopulation in Yugoslavia," Yugoslavia, Ministry of Agriculture, *Arhiv*, V (reprint), 7; Nicholas Mirkowich, "Die Bevölkerungsentwicklung Jugoslawiens und das Problem der agrarischen Übervölkerung," *Weltwirtschaftliches Archiv*, L, No. 1, 115–20.

[2] Rudolf Bićanić, *Agrarna prenapučenost* (Agricultural Overpopulation), p. 7; Anton Melik, "The Density of Population in Yugoslavia," *Geografski vestnik*, XVI, 88–104.

efficients of importance to these factors. Generally, agricultural population—land resources ratios were related to the average crop structure in Yugoslavia, in which cereals play the determining role, and to the rather low average yields. It was pointed out by most of these writers, however, that, owing to the different productivity of various crops per unit of land, areas with more intensive cropping patterns (e.g., vineyards, orchards) can support a larger number of people per unit of land than the areas concentrating on the production of cereals. Explicitly or by implication an area of one to one and a half hectares of agricultural land per person in agriculture was taken as a satisfactory relationship between agricultural population and agricultural land.

Another way of arriving at an indicator of the degree of agricultural overpopulation is to establish the labor requirements of the existing system of agriculture, thus taking into account both the structure of agricultural production and the prevailing agricultural technology, and add the dependent population. Population above this level is then considered as "surplus." This method had been widely used by the pre-1914 Russian agricultural economists and by various economists in Eastern and Southeastern Europe during the interwar period. Considering the extensive patterns of agricultural economy in Eastern and Southeastern Europe, any population in agriculture of these states which exceeds about 30 working people, or a total of 60 to 70 working and dependent people per 100 hectares of agricultural land (exclusive of pastures like those in the Balkans), was considered as surplus population.[3] Some Yugoslav writers used this method in the late 1930's (see pp. 450–57). Since the removal of the surplus population from the land may not reduce production at all, the marginal productivity of labor in much of agriculture is zero. One might say that it is actually negative, because the removal of much of the surplus population from the land is one of the preconditions of any marked rise in agricultural output.

An extremely complicated undertaking, to show the relative agricultural overpopulation of Eastern and Southern European countries in comparison with the average European conditions during the first half of the 1930's, was made by Wilbert E. Moore of the Office of Population Research, Princeton University. Professor Moore has calculated the value of the total agricultural production (crops and livestock) expressed in crop units (CU) in all European countries, and

[3] Doreen Warriner, *Economics of Peasant Farming*, pp. 61–78; P. Lamartine Yates and Doreen Warriner, *Food and Farming in Post-War Europe*, pp. 47–57; The Royal Institute of International Affairs, *Agrarian Problems from the Baltic to the Aegean*, pp. 51–53.

compared the resulting per capita levels (relating both to males employed in agriculture and to total population dependent on agriculture) with the value of the average European production. The average European level of production is taken as standard (100), and the production value in various countries is expressed in the form of an index related to the European standard as base. This enabled him to calculate for each country the "standard" population—the population which under the existing production can meet the average European standard—and the "surplus" population, or the percentage of overpopulation, in each country. In fact, he has calculated these indexes of standard and surplus (or shortage) population not only for various countries as units, but also for each of their provinces. In the case of Yugoslavia, Moore arrives at a degree of overpopulation amounting to 61.5 percent (53.0 percent for Bulgaria, 22.4 percent for Hungary, 51.3 percent for Poland, and 51.4 percent for Rumania).[4]

If one had complete data on crop and livestock production, utilization of this output, differences in qualities of products, and satisfactory information on the percentage of the production marketed and on prices received by the farmers for each commodity in each country, if satisfactory information existed on prices paid by farmers for products they buy and on the tax load imposed on agricultural income, and if interest payments of agriculture were known, this method would, no doubt, furnish a much better picture than other methods of the relationship between agricultural population, on the one hand, and agricultural resources and their income-producing capacity, on the other hand, related to any particular level of production or plane of living as standard of comparison. But in the case of many countries of Eastern and Southeastern Europe such data, with the exception of those on crop production, are scanty, often quite unreliable, and in many cases outright nonexistent. Yugoslavia of the interwar period was notorious for lack of systematic statistical information with regard to the structure and dynamics of its agriculture, as we have had the opportunity of mentioning repeatedly in the course of this study and as Moore himself mentions. In such a case an elaborate statistical procedure, like the one followed by Moore, seems to us to involve so many sources of error and to require so many qualifications that its value is greatly reduced. Moore himself says: "The index [of production] here presented has serious shortcomings, but if interpreted cautiously seems to reveal regional differences in the effectiveness of European agricul-

[4] Wilbert E. Moore, *Economic Demography of Eastern and Southern Europe*, pp. 63–64.

tural production."[5] Thus, when it comes to his calculations for Yugoslavia we have many differences with him.[6]

Because of the paucity of statistical information, we are forced to use the simple procedure of relating agricultural population to land resources in order to obtain an indicator about the degree of agricultural overpopulation in Yugoslavia. We stress that in this way we are obtaining only an indicator and not an adequate "measure" of the degree of overpopulation. But, in fact, we are primarily interested in

[5] *Ibid.*, p. 180.

[6] The following are some of his unacceptable calculations for Yugoslavia: (1) He estimates the "net" production in the Yugoslav agriculture at 90 percent. In Moore's opinion, in the calculation of "net" production in agriculture "reliance must be placed on the relatively small samples available in farm accountancy statistics" (*ibid.*, p. 49), published annually by the International Institute of Agriculture in *Farm Accountancy*. But there are no such "data" for Yugoslavia. There is no doubt that the percentage of "net" production in agriculture as defined by Moore is considerably less than 90 percent in Yugoslavia. For example, in his calculation of the "net" production of basic cereals and potatoes (*ibid.*, p. 151), the net being arrived at after subtracting the shrinkage, wastage, seed requirements, and the portion of the crop used for feed, he estimates that in Yugoslavia 92 percent of the corn crop is "net." He obviously takes into account only shrinkage, wastage, and the seed requirements. The fact is, however, that approximately 25 to 35 percent of the total corn crop, which averaged 4.7 million metric tons in the period 1934–38, was used for feed. (2) Another source of error seems to be involved in Moore's estimate of the output of livestock products in Yugoslavia. As no official or private estimates of this production existed for Yugoslavia before World War II, he must have estimated this production "by analogy," that is, on the basis of the output of livestock products in some neighboring country or countries. But he does not give any information in this respect. The following figures suggest, however, that the results are quite questionable. In his table on page 181 (*ibid.*) Moore estimates the average 1931–35 output of livestock products in Hungary at 87.9 million crop units, in Rumania at 114.3 million crop units, and in Yugoslavia at 62.0 million crop units. However, a check of their livestock numbers for 1934, as published by the International Institute of Agriculture, shows that Yugoslavia had more than twice as much cattle, about 10 percent more pigs, and ten times more sheep and goats than Hungary and that it had only about 7 percent less cattle and pigs and 16 percent less sheep and goats than Rumania. As differences in the productivity of livestock, especially between Yugoslavia and Rumania, could not have been appreciable, if there were any, either the output of livestock products had been estimated on totally different bases or prices which Moore applied to obtain his crop units differed extremely much among the three countries. Furthermore, the production of meat from poultry is of such importance in Yugoslavia, both as a cash product of the peasant population and as an export article (see pp. 533–34), that it should not be left out of account as Moore did. (3) Moore's procedure in calculating the "arable land equivalents" is inapplicable to Yugoslavia in view of the information presented in our Table 15, showing the cadastral net income per hectare of land under various types of utilization in various *banovine*. This source of error becomes very important when he calculates the density of agricultural population in relation to "arable-equivalent agricultural land" on a banovinal basis (see his Table 1, Appendix II, pp. 197–204), because *banovine* where overpopulation is most acute (Primorje and Zeta) have an unduly high ratio of low-value pastures, and the high coefficient he uses for pastures puts them in a better light than corresponds to facts.

seeing the trend in the relationships between agricultural population and land resources during the interwar period in Yugoslavia and not in obtaining an accurate picture of the degree of overpopulation at one point of time, even if this were possible. By using a simple ratio we were enabled to calculate the relationship between the Yugoslav agricultural population and its land resources throughout the interwar period and to see whether the position of the peasantry was improving or deteriorating. As there was little change in the structure of the Yugoslav agricultural production and in the level of agricultural technology during the interwar period, the changes in the ratios of the agricultural population to land resources acquire an even greater meaning.

Taking into account the over-all structure of agricultural production in Yugoslavia and the average yields, we could take about one and a quarter hectares of cultivated land per person, or about 80 persons dependent on agriculture per 100 hectares of cultivated land, as the norm which would assure the peasant population a decent plane of living under Yugoslav conditions. All agricultural population above this standard can be taken as surplus population, and all areas showing this or a less favorable relationship between agricultural population and cultivated land resources can be taken as overpopulated. This norm is much less arbitrary than it appears at first glance. First, peasant families try to adjust their farm size in a way which would enable them to provide reasonably full employment for their family labor and, if one remembers the level of agricultural technology in Yugoslavia, a farm of six to seven hectares of cultivated land would provide the necessary work for a family of five. Second, farms providing between one and one and a half hectares per person in the peasant family have been a basic political and economic aim of the peasantry in the South Slav lands, because the peasants consider that such a farm can assure for them a decent level of living. Third, the agrarian reform during the interwar period used as standard a five-hectare farm, and the norm here accepted is only a little more liberal than the norm used by the agararian reform. Thus we cannot be accused of using a very liberal norm which would result in increasing the portion of "surplus" population in rural areas. The chief objection to our procedure is perhaps to be found in our using the same norm for the whole country, although considerable differences exist among various areas in regard to cropping patterns, levels of technology, yields of land and livestock, and in the levels of real income considered as satisfactory by the rural population. But here, too, paucity of statistical information was mainly responsible for our procedure.

AGRICULTURAL OVERPOPULATION IN YUGOSLAVIA,
BULGARIA, AND RUMANIA, 1921–38

Before seeing what portion of agricultural population in Yugoslavia and in Bulgaria and Rumania—the two neighboring countries whose agricultural structure and agricultural technology are very similar to that of Yugoslavia—has to be considered as surplus population on the basis of this norm, it is interesting to see the respective development in the ratios between agricultural population, on the one hand, and cultivated land and livestock, on the other, in these three countries. This information is supplied in Table 22 for the years 1921, 1931, and 1938. This table shows several interesting things. First, relatively more people were dependent on agriculture for their livelihood in Yugoslavia during the interwar period than either in Bulgaria or Rumania, though the difference was rather small. The rate at which the part of population dependent on agriculture was decreasing was very similar in all three countries. Second, Yugoslavia had a relatively much greater number of people per 100 hectares of cultivated land than either Bulgaria or Rumania. Third, a small improvement in the population–cultivated land ratio took place between 1921 and 1938 in both Bulgaria and Rumania, but in the case of Yugoslavia a slight worsening occurred. The development between 1921 and 1931 and 1938 differed considerably in the three countries. Fourth, in all three countries the number of agricultural population per 100 animal units was markedly increased between 1921 and 1938.

If the above norm of one and a quarter hectares of cultivated land per person, or 80 persons dependent on agriculture per 100 hectares of cultivated land, is taken as the basis of calculation, the "surplus" agricultural population in Yugoslavia, Bulgaria, and Rumania during the interwar period was as follows:[7]

Country	"Surplus" population (*Thousands*)			Percent of agricultural population		
	1921	1931	1938	1921	1931	1938
Yugoslavia	3,892	4,663	5,011	41	43	43
Bulgaria	970	1,388	1,158	27	31	25
Rumania	2,912	1,969	2,952	25	15	21

This comparison confirms the earlier statement that the degree of agricultural overpopulation was much higher in Yugoslavia than either in Bulgaria or Rumania. What is more significant is the fact that both in Bulgaria and Rumania the degree of overpopulation as here measured

---

[7] Based on Table 22.

TABLE 22.—AGRICULTURAL POPULATION AND RELATIVE DENSITIES OF AGRICULTURAL POPULATION PER 100 HECTARES OF CULTIVATED LAND AND 100 ANIMAL UNITS IN 1921, 1931, AND 1938 IN YUGOSLAVIA, BULGARIA, AND RUMANIA

Country	Percent of total population dependent on agriculture[a]			Population dependent on agriculture[b] (Thousands)			Number of agricultural people per 100 hectares of cultivated land			Number of agricultural people per 100 animal units[c]		
	1921	1931	1938	1921	1931	1938	1921[d]	1931	1938	1921	1931	1938
Yugoslavia ...	78.9	76.5	74.8	9,456	10,771	11,586	136	141	141	113	142	139
Bulgaria	75.0	73.2	72.7	3,635	4,441	4,560	109	116	107	84	102	114
Rumania	74.0	72.4	71.6	11,570	13,249	14,214	107	94	101	113	142	147

[a] The percentages for 1921 are those of the Yugoslav census of January 1921, the Bulgarian census of December 1920, and are estimated for Rumania. For 1931 the percentages are those of the Yugoslav census of March 1931, the Bulgarian census of 1934, and the Rumanian census of 1930. For 1938 the percentage for Yugoslavia is estimated by projecting the development between 1921 and 1931; for Bulgaria by projecting the development between the censuses of 1926 and 1934; for Rumania the percentage is obtained from the census of agriculture of 1941, cf. Roman Cresin, *Recensământul agricol al României din 1941* (Agricultural Census in Rumania in 1941) (Bucharest, 1945), p. 73.

[b] Agricultural population in 1921: for Yugoslavia as obtained by the census of January 1921; for Bulgaria as obtained by the census of December 1920; for Rumania as officially estimated for the end of 1920. Agricultural population in 1931 and 1938 represents figures for the end of the year.

[c] Animal units calculated on the basis of coefficients given in Table 12, p. 279, footnote b.

[d] Basis: cultivated land in Bulgaria for 1921; in Yugoslavia and Rumania for 1922.

was somewhat reduced between 1921 and 1938, though the development was mixed in the two countries. In Yugoslavia it increased from 41 percent of the agricultural population in 1921 to 43 percent in 1931 and remained on the same level in 1938.

These figures have to be qualified in one important respect. It is well known that in Yugoslavia a portion of landless, dwarf, and small peasants derived a part of their income from activities outside of agriculture, that is, by working in lumber and textile industries, mining, urban construction industry, and the like. It is not known what percentage of their income was so derived. Obviously, some of the peasants in Bulgaria and Rumania were similarly employed. Considering the fact that the lumber industry and mining seem to have been relatively more important sources of employment in Yugoslavia than in Bulgaria and Rumania, the higher degree of agricultural overpopulation should be somewhat reduced to be more comparable with that of the two neighboring countries. How large this adjustment should be is impossible to say.

There is no doubt that in Yugoslavia and its neighboring countries as well as in other countries of "peasant" Europe we have an area of severe agricultural overpopulation. Its degree depends, naturally, on the ratio between land resources and agricultural population, which is taken as the basis of comparison. The norm applied by us is quite low, but, in our opinion, that makes it more realistic. The state of overpopulation in Yugoslavia and other countries of Eastern and Southeastern Europe can be seen not only from the relationship between the agricultural population and land resources, but also from other characteristics prevailing in overpopulated areas. H. J. Seraphim, who wrote extensively on the problems of agriculture in Eastern and Southeastern Europe, stated the following as the symptoms of agricultural overpopulation:

. . . small size of farms, strongly rising prices and rentals of land, exodus from the land, expansion of secondary sources of income of the agricultural population, falling wages, falling farm income and pauperization, reduction in the area of pastures, meadows, and under fallow, reduction in the number of livestock on farms, and reduction in the gross product of agriculture.[8]

And C. J. Robertson of the International Institute of Agriculture indicated the following facts as being among the principal symptoms of agricultural overpopulation: the small size of agricultural holdings,

---

[8] H. J. Seraphim, "Die statistische Erfassung der landwirtschaftlichen Übervölkerung und Untervölkerung," Germany, Ministry for Food and Agriculture, *Berichte über Landwirtschaft*, XIII, 203.

the high proportion of cereals or other food crops with respect to arable area, the low unit yields, the low density of livestock, undernutrition, and cultural stagnation.[9] If added to the underutilization of labor, these are all of the important indicators of agricultural overpopulation. Almost every one of these symptoms was noticeable in the agriculture of the South Slav lands since the turn of this century and became more pronounced as time advanced.

Two additional factors should be specially pointed out. First, the increased number of people on the land meant relatively fewer producers and more consumers per unit of land. The inescapable consequence of this development was that the portion of current income for consumption had to be increased, while the portion that could be saved and invested in the improvement of the techniques of production had to be reduced. And since increased investment is the basic precondition of economic progress, one could say that the most important and most disastrous economic consequence of agricultural overpopulation is the lessening of the ability to save and invest in order to increase production in the future. Increasing population and decreasing ability to invest, and thus to increase production, form a vicious circle which is characteristic of all areas suffering from agricultural overpopulation. If the low current income (production) is incapable of satisfying the minimum needs of the peasants, the consumption of the capital substance of the rural family begins by depletion of livestock, soil, farm implements, household utensils, and, above all, by depletion of human capital in the form of reduced health and working capacity. The unavoidable result of agricultural overpopulation is thus a lowering of the peasants' plane of living. And since the standard of living—expressed either as a certain schedule of consumption wants or more often as a certain area of cultivated land per person which could ensure a certain income—does not fall at all, or at least does not fall at the same rate as the plane of living, this thinning of the economic basis of life of the peasantry has far-reaching social and political consequences.

Second, politically and socially, agricultural overpopulation is usually a reason for dissatisfaction and unrest among the peasant masses. The fact that the peasantry saw its economic and social position becoming worse and worse, with little prospect for betterment, gave rise to two lines of development: (a) on the one hand, the peasantry became more and more characterized by mental inertia and an air of

[9] C. J. Robertson, "Population and Agriculture, with Special Reference to Agricultural Overpopulation," International Institute of Agriculture, *Documentation for the European Conference on Rural Life 1939*, pp. 32, 52–61.

gloom about the future. Obviously, people who feel that they cannot expect a better future and who are thus robbed of all hope lose an essential attribute of full life. Under the circumstances of acute agricultural overpopulation, few indeed are the opportunities for the "pursuit of happiness" in life. Instead, life becomes a struggle—almost a torture—from the cradle to the grave. (*b*) On the other hand, the peasantry became more and more inclined as a dissatisfied mass to follow revolutionary political and social creeds. Partly responsible for the latter development was the fact that in the typical peasant countries of Eastern and Southeastern Europe, including Yugoslavia, the peasants had little or no influence on the political life and state policies either in pre-1914 days or during the interwar period. On the contrary, the peasantry was the chief object of both political oppression and economic exploitation by the groups in power. But the time of peasant uprisings, as they often occurred in the Balkans during the nineteenth century, was definitely past. Owing to modern military technology, small armed forces (police, army) at the disposal of the state can easily keep at bay large numbers of peasants to whom access to arms under normal conditions is impossible. In the twentieth century, revolutions in peasant countries have become preconditioned on wars, or, rather, on lost wars. Lost wars result in the disintegration of the political and administrative organization, or power fabric, of the state. During a war large numbers of peasants get into possession of modern arms and form large, more or less disciplined bodies of men. Here again, however, the peasants did not act independently. The history of World War I and its aftermath in Southeastern and Eastern Europe outside of Russia has shown that in its revolutionary moves at that time the peasantry was led by bourgeoisie. The history and the aftermath of World War I in Russia and the history of World War II in Southeastern and Eastern Europe, in China, and in various parts of Southeast Asia showed that the peasantry, or the part of it that was willing to follow revolutionary movements, had been led by the Communist professional revolutionaries who avowedly are the representatives of another social class, the labor class. However, the fighting manpower in all these revolutions in predominantly agricultural countries consisted primarily of the peasants. It is beyond any doubt that large bodies of peasants would not have followed the new revolutionary leaders if they had been satisfied with the old social and economic regime, or if they did not think that the revolution would be a change for the better. Although the honeymoon between the Communists and the peasants is of short duration and the overwhelming majority of the peasants resists collectivization of agriculture and the unfavorable taxation and price policies pursued by the Communist regimes with regard to the peasantry, the fact is that in most underdeveloped areas in which the Communists have acquired power or are fighting for power the bulk of their fighting contingents were recruited from among the peasants.

REGIONAL DIFFERENCES IN THE DEGREE OF AGRICULTURAL OVERPOPULATION

There existed great differences in the degree of agricultural over-population in various areas of Yugoslavia. Table 23 shows the agricultural population, cultivated land, livestock numbers in terms of cattle, and the ratios of agricultural population to cultivated land and to livestock by *banovine* for the years 1921, 1931, and 1938. Owing to variations in the structure of agricultural production and in the yields per unit of land, as a consequence of differences in the quality of soil and in the level of agricultural technology, considerable adjustments would be necessary to make the factor "cultivated land" strictly comparable for various *banovine*. On the basis of the available data, however, we were unable to undertake this adjustment. But these differences have to be kept in mind. Thus the norm of 80 people per 100 hectares of cultivated land is taken as the basis of comparison for the relative density of agricultural population in various areas. All population over 80 per 100 hectares of cultivated land has therefore to be considered as "surplus" population.

This table shows, first of all, that differences in the population–cultivated land ratio among various regions of Yugoslavia were as much pronounced as the differences between Yugoslavia as a whole and the various European countries (see Table 21, p. 309). The most satisfactory agricultural population—cultivated land ratio was in *banovina* Dunav, where the norm of 80 people per 100 hectares of cultivated land was passed only slightly. Furthermore, in this *banovina* the increase in cultivated land was capable, at least up to 1938, of keeping pace with the increase in population dependent on agriculture, as there was no increase in the number of people per unit of cultivated land between 1921 and 1938. Also the agricultural population–livestock ratio in this *banovina* was somewhat better than the national average. On the other extreme were the *banovine* Primorje and Zeta in which about two-thirds of the total agricultural population was surplus population on the basis of the norm here accepted. These were by far the most overpopulated areas in Yugoslavia, which during the interwar period were referred to as the "passive regions," that is, regions

TABLE 23.—AGRICULTURAL POPULATION, CULTIVATED LAND, LIVESTOCK, AND THE RATIOS OF AGRICULTURAL POPULATION TO CULTIVATED LAND AND TO LIVESTOCK IN 1921, 1931, AND 1938, BY BANOVINE

Banovina	Agricultural population[a] (Thousands)			Cultivated land[b] (Thousand hectares)			Livestock in animal units[c] (Thousands)			Agricultural people per 100 hectares cultivated land			Agricultural people per 100 animal units		
	1921	1931	1938	1921	1931	1938	1921	1931	1938	1921	1931	1938	1921	1931	1938
Drava	639	690	722	324	362	375	639	558	544	197	191	193	100	124	133
Drina	993	1,263	1,499	732	819	898	1,098	840	946	136	154	167	90	150	158
Dunav	1,628	1,784	1,891	1,979	2,213	2,317	1,630	1,227	1,409	82	81	82	100	145	134
Morava	1,030	1,232	1,398	705	788	844	759	610	718	146	156	166	136	202	195
Primorje	672	753	813	286	320	324	339	460	516	235	235	251	198	164	158
Sava	1,825	2,037	2,192	1,207	1,349	1,392	1,580	1,472	1,532	151	151	157	116	138	143
Vardar	1,033	1,228	1,388	763	853	935	893	1,021	1,111	135	144	148	116	120	125
Vrbas	750	915	1,054	544	608	765	834	669	765	138	150	138	90	137	138
Zeta	644	759	853	279	312	357	568	699	806	231	243	239	113	108	106
Prefecture of Belgrade	5	10	14	9	11	12	18	10	10	55	93	117	28	102	140
Yugoslavia[d]	9,219	10,671	11,824	6,828	7,635	8,219	8,358	7,566	8,357	135	140	144	110	141	141

[a] Agricultural population for 1931 by *banovine*, according to the 1931 census. As no data are available on agricultural population for 1921, we have taken the percentage of agricultural population for various *banovine*, as shown in the 1931 census, to apply also to 1921. The figure of 9,219,000 gives for 1921 an agricultural population of 76.9 percent of the total population while, in fact, it was higher—namely, 9,456,000, or 78.9 percent of the total. But this difference is insignificant. For total population by *banovine* for 1921 see Yugoslavia, *Annuaire statistique 1931* (Belgrade, 1934), pp. 50–51. To calculate the agricultural population by *banovine* for 1938 we have taken the official estimates of total population by *banovine* for 1938, *Annuaire statistique 1938–1939* (Belgrade, 1939), p. 111, and assumed that the same percentage of the total population was engaged in agriculture in various *banovine* as in 1931. This procedure gave us a slightly larger agricultural population than the one estimated for the country as a whole for 1938 and given in Table 22, p. 317.

[b] Cultivated land (arable land, gardens, orchards, and vineyards) for 1931 and 1938 according to official data in Yugoslavia, *Annuaire statistique 1931*, pp. 82–83, and in Yugoslavia, *Annuaire statistique 1938–1939*, pp. 164–65, respectively. For 1921 the total of 6,828,000 hectares of cultivated land is the official figure (Yugoslavia, *Annuaire statistique 1931*, pp. 82–83), but lacking data for *banovine*, the total was divided among the various *banovine* according to the ratios of 1931.

[c] Livestock numbers in terms of cattle obtained by using the conversion coefficients supplied in Table 12, p. 279, footnote *b*. For 1931 and 1938 livestock figures from *Annuaire statistique 1931*, p. 98, and *Annuaire statistique 1938–1939*, pp. 180–81, respectively. These figures actually represent official estimates for the end of the year. Livestock figures for 1921 are those obtained by the census of 1921; see Yugoslavia, *Annuaire statistique 1929* (Belgrade, 1932), p. 153. These figures refer to slightly different areas of most *banovine*. *Ibid.*, p. 136, and *Annuaire statistique 1931*, p. 82.

[d] Differences in final figures, especially the ratios, from figures in Table 22, are the result of differences in basic figures or dates to which they refer, and, as such, are explained in various tables. But these differences are small.

which were unable to feed their population owing to the paucity of their land and capital resources. The unsatisfactory agricultural population—cultivated land ratio in these areas is accentuated by the fact that here the yields of both land and livestock are much lower than in the country as a whole. Especially striking was the difference between *banovina* Dunav and these "passive regions." There is no doubt that in Yugoslavia areas which are least economically developed and poorest in land resources are at the same time the relatively most overpopulated areas. It is true that livestock economy played a greater role in these areas than in the country as a whole, but while *banovina* Zeta had a quite satisfactory population–livestock ratio, that for *banovina* Primorje was considerably worse than the national average ratio. Thus, while practically all areas of Yugoslavia suffer from agricultural overpopulation, it is in these two *banovine* and in some surrounding areas, covering the historical provinces of Montenegro, Herzegovina, Dalmatia, and southwestern Croatia, that the issue of agricultural overpopulation is overshadowing all other economic issues.

Next to the *banovine* Primorje and Zeta the least satisfactory population–cultivated land ratio was in *banovina* Drava, followed (in 1938) by *banovine* Drina, Morava, Sava, Vardar, and Vrbas. It was, however, only in Vrbas in addition to Dunav in 1938 that this ratio was more satisfactory than the national average ratio. As far as agricultural population–livestock ratio was concerned, least satisfactory was the position of *banovina* Morava. Only in the *banovine* Zeta, Vardar, Drava, and Vrbas was the population–livestock ratio better than the national average.

Table 24 indicates the percentage of "surplus" agricultural population in various *banovine* in 1938 (percentage of agricultural population over the norm of 80 per 100 hectares of cultivated land), the increase in total population between 1921 and 1941 in percent, and the percentage changes in the number of people per 100 hectares of cultivated land and per 100 animal units between 1921 and 1938 by *banovine*. The differing degree of agricultural overpopulation, as indicated in column one, has already been discussed. Data in column two are taken from Table 19, page 300, and are supplied here in order to show the growth of total population during the interwar period in various *banovine*, as this had an important influence on the degree of agricultural overpopulation in various areas. The two remaining series in this table are highly interesting. The percentage changes in the ratio of population to cultivated land and in the ratio of population to livestock between 1921 and 1938 varied greatly among various areas.

TABLE 24.—"SURPLUS" POPULATION IN AGRICULTURE IN 1938, INCREASE IN TOTAL POPULATION 1921 TO 1941, AND PERCENTAGE CHANGES IN THE NUMBER OF PEOPLE PER 100 HECTARES OF CULTIVATED LAND AND PER 100 ANIMAL UNITS FROM 1921 TO 1938, BY BANOVINE

Banovina	"Surplus" population as percentage of existing agricultural population in 1938[a]	Increase in total population 1921–41 in percent[b]	Increase (decrease) in the ratio of agricultural population in percent 1921–38 in relation to [a]	
			Cultivated land	Livestock
Drava	58.5	14.5	—2.0	33.0
Drina	52.1	58.8	22.8	75.5
Dunav	2.4	18.2	0.0	34.0
Morava	51.8	40.8	13.7	43.4
Primorje	68.1	23.6	6.8	—20.2
Sava	49.0	22.7	4.0	23.3
Vardar	45.9	39.4	9.6	7.8
Vrbas	42.0	46.2	0.0	53.3
Zeta	66.5	37.1	3.5	—6.2
Yugoslavia	44.4[c]	33.3	6.7	28.2

[a] Based on Table 23, p. 322.
[b] Based on Table 19, p. 300.
[c] This percentage is slightly higher than the 43 percent indicated in the tabulation on p. 316. The estimated population figures on the basis of which the percentages in this table are calculated were made on the assumption that the relative number of people engaged in agriculture was the same in 1938 as in 1931. The percentage of 43 on p. 316, on the other hand, was calculated on the basis of the estimated population which was obtained by projecting to 1938 the rate of reduction in agricultural population which was observed between 1921 and 1931.

The population–livestock ratio deteriorated much more than the population–cultivated land ratio. Under the prevailing circumstances this was to be expected. But looking at these changes from the point of view of various regions, some striking differences in the development are easily observed, which simply show the variety of factors at work in various areas with regard to the relationship between population and the means of subsistence.

The greatest deterioration in the ratio of agricultural population to cultivated land between 1921 and 1938 was in *banovina* Drina, which also showed the greatest deterioration in the ratio of population to livestock. This *banovina*, however, had the highest estimated increase in population between 1921 and 1941. But this parallelism between the growth of total population and the deterioration of the population–cultivated land ratio does not hold in all cases. Despite the second largest increase in population between 1921 and 1941, *banovina* Vrbas

showed no increase in the number of people per 100 hectares of cultivated land in 1938 as against 1921, though this ratio deteriorated considerably between 1921 and 1931. In only one other *banovina*, Dunav,
did the population–cultivated land ratio remain the same during the
interwar period. And only in *banovina* Drava did this ratio improve
slightly (2 percent). But in these two areas the growth of total population between 1921 and 1941 was relatively much smaller than in the
country as a whole or any other area of the country.

In *banovine* Zeta and Primorje, the two areas in which the degree
of agricultural overpopulation is far above the national average and
which represent the most difficult problem in this regard in Yugoslavia, the population–cultivated land ratio deteriorated relatively little
during the interwar period, namely by 6.8 and 3.5 percent. There was
no parallelism between the growth of the total population and the
deterioration of the population–cultivated land ratio in these areas.
But what is very interesting is the fact that in both of these areas, and
in them alone, the ratio between population and livestock improved
between 1921 and 1938. That can be at least partly ascribed to very
low livestock numbers in 1921 in these areas as a consequence of
World War I. A more important reason for this development is perhaps to be found in the nature of livestock economy in these areas.
Livestock competes here very little with population for arable land.
It is essentially supported by meadows and pastures. Similar factors
were most probably operative in *banovina* Vardar, in which the deterioration of the population–livestock ratio was rather small (7.8
percent). In all other areas including *banovine* Drava, Dunav, and
Vrbas in which there was no deterioration in the population–cultivated
land ratio, the ratio of population to livestock became much less satisfactory in 1938 than it was in 1921. The deterioration of the population–livestock ratio in the *banovine* Drina, Morava, and Vrbas between
1921 and 1938 may, however, be somewhat less than indicated by the
above figures. It seems that a certain improvement in the breed composition of cattle in these areas had taken place during the interwar
period, so that the same number of cattle may represent a larger total
value.

Data on these banovinal averages with regard to the relationship of
agricultural population to the land and livestock resources often cover
conditions of great divergence. The relationship between agricultural
population and cultivated land in Yugoslavia in 1931 by counties was
worked out by the Slovenian geographer Anton Melik. He showed, for
example, that in the Montenegrin county of Kolašin (*banovina* Zeta)

there were 994 agricultural people per 100 hectares of cultivated land
and in the county of Senj in the Croatian coastland (*banovina* Sava)
there were 940 people per 100 hectares of cultivated land.[10] Obviously,
in such cases as well as in other areas of acute agricultural overpopulation, the rural population was deriving a large part of its livelihood
from livestock, work in the lumber industry, and the like. Several
studies dealt with regional problems of agricultural overpopulation in
Yugoslavia.[11] Space limitations make it impossible, however, for us
to go into further details here.

[10] Anton Melik, *op. cit.*, especially map, p. 95; Slava Lipoglavšek, "Cultivated Land
in Yugoslavia," *ibid.*, pp. 76–88, especially map, p. 79.

[11] Zvonimir Dugački, "The Settlements and the Density of Population in the Croatian
Zagorje," *ibid.*, pp. 41–67. The Croatian Zagorje, the area north and northeast of the
Croatian capital of Zagreb, is one of the most densely populated areas of Yugoslavia,
which suffered from overpopulation for decades, and still does. Svetozar Ilešič, "The
Agrarian Overpopulation in Slovenia," *Tehnika in gospodarstvo*, VI, 60–70.

CHAPTER 17

ADJUSTMENTS TO AND REMEDIES FOR
AGRICULTURAL OVERPOPULATION

THE USUAL procedure, after showing the degree of agricultural over-population in a country or in its various areas, is to discuss the different ways out of this economically and socially unenviable position. Usually the following possibilities are reviewed: emigration abroad, internal colonization, migration from rural areas into urban areas, birth control, increasing the amount of cultivated land, increasing the productivity of land by modernization of agricultural technology, reform in land tenure if the existing system is impeding an increase in productivity, better-ment in the quality and in the marketing of agricultural products, and, finally, industrialization. It seems to us more fruitful to proceed in a slightly different way, namely, to review what the Yugoslav agricul-tural population actually did during the interwar period in order to better its relationship to resources, or to limit the unfavorable effects of the growing agricultural overpopulation. This approach will also reveal which of these ways of mitigating agricultural overpopulation have proved most and which least effective during the interwar period and which of them would seem to be most promising for the future. With the exception of internal colonization, we are not going to com-ment upon policy developments in this regard since 1945.

Table 23 (p. 322) shows that the agricultural population of Yugo-slavia did not improve its relationship to cultivated land and livestock during the interwar period. Agricultural population grew faster than either cultivated land or livestock. The worsening in the ratio of popu-lation to both cultivated land and to livestock took place especially during the 1920's, which were generally regarded as a period of rela-tive prosperity in the Yugoslav economy. During the 1930's, mostly characterized by severe depression, the ratio of agricultural population to cultivated land remained unchanged, and the ratio of population to livestock improved slightly. But under the blanket of these over-all developments in the ratios of agricultural population to cultivated land and to livestock, a great number of adjustment processes were at work, and they are going to be briefly reviewed here.

EMIGRATION

One of the avenues of adjustment of the agricultural population to increasing numbers was emigration abroad. In the three decades before World War I this was considered the primary cure in the South Slav and many other lands, and the same ideas persisted after 1918 among the peasants in many areas. But as we have seen from Table 18 (p. 295), emigration was of considerable extent only until 1930. During the early 1930's it was greatly reduced because of the world-wide economic depression. Toward the end of that decade it recovered somewhat. The reason for the fall in emigration during the interwar period was not lessened population pressure in the Yugoslav village or the lessened willingness of the Yugoslav peasants to emigrate, but rather the restrictive legislation with regard to immigration in various overseas countries, especially the United States. After the virtual cessation of emigration to the United States in 1922, the chief overseas areas for Yugoslav emigration were Brazil, Canada, and Argentina. But the Great Depression reduced the incentives to emigrate as employment opportunities abroad were reduced. Furthermore, it became almost impossible to obtain loans for the payment of passage expenses. Thus, overseas emigration fell during the 1930's to insignificant numbers. The relatively larger emigration to European countries during the interwar period could not compensate for the fall in emigration overseas. Besides, most of the emigration overseas was actually of a permanent character, while this was not the case with emigration to the European countries. What is of fundamental significance is that, after World War I, emigration ceased to be an important factor in alleviating agricultural overpopulation. There is no doubt that the legislation restricting immigration in the United States was one of the important factors contributing to the increasing overpopulation in Yugoslavia as well as in many other countries. Moreover, had the emigration continued at the pre-1914 rate, emigrants' remittances would have been larger than they were and thus of greater importance both to the Yugoslav balance of payments and to the income of the regions in which the emigrants originated. Nevertheless, emigrants' remittances were an important credit item in the balance of payments of Yugoslavia, especially during the 1920's, and represented an important source of income for the population of "passive regions."[1] While emigration

---

[1] According to the estimates of Arthur Benko Grado, a leading expert on problems of emigration in interwar Yugoslavia, emigrants' remittances between 1919 and 1938 amounted to $244.0 million. The maximum of $20.0 million was reached in 1924 and the minimum of only $2.0 million in 1935. Quoted in J. N. Dunda, "The Role of Emi-

played only a very limited role during the interwar period as a means of relieving population pressure, it is perhaps safe to say that hereafter emigration will play an even lesser role in that respect.

But World War II led to voluntary withdrawal or to the expulsion of the bulk of the German minority from Yugoslavia, numbering approximately 400,000 people. As has been pointed out above, this minority had inhabited Vojvodina, Slavonia, and Srijem and had been the most advanced segment of the Yugoslav agricultural population before 1941. A large portion of the other political emigration resulting from World War II was most probably recruited from urban elements.

INTERNAL COLONIZATION

Internal colonization as a means of relieving agricultural overpopulation in certain areas of Yugoslavia was only of minor importance during the interwar period. It was a concomitant of the post-1918 agrarian reform and was practiced primarily in Vojvodina, Macedonia, and the Kosovo-Metohija region. In all these areas it had also a political objective, namely, the strengthening of the Yugoslav element in areas in which national minorities were strong (Germans and Magyars in Vojvodina, Albanians and Turks in Macedonia, and Albanians in the Kosovo-Metohija region). Colonists were recruited not only from among the people in specially overcrowded areas, but also from among the transferees from Hungary and Italy after World War I. Moreover, many colonists acquired the land because they could qualify as volunteers during World War I. The bulk of colonists did, however, originate from the overcrowded karst regions (for more details on the numbers involved in internal colonization during the interwar period, see pp. 361 and 367).

Generally speaking, internal colonization seems not to have appealed too much to the people in the overcrowded areas. Considering the ease with which the people from these areas used to emigrate abroad, this sounds surprising. Of course, in internal colonization whole families had to move while normally only individual family members emigrated abroad. Another reason for this lay in the fact that the colonizing was not well organized and supported by the government. The colonists obtained from the government the land and, in some areas, also houses, but little financial help, tools, or proper advice. Some areas in which colonization was carried out suffered from lack

grants' Remittances in the Yugoslav Balance of Payments," *Ekonomist*, April–May, 1940, p. 143.

of security, both personal and property, e.g., parts of Macedonia. Some of the areas earmarked for colonization were actually not fit for settlement without previous large investments (for the drainage of marshes, supply of potable water, etc.). As things stood in 1939, internal colonization seems to have contributed all that could be expected from it toward the alleviation of population pressure in overcrowded areas. In fact, little more land was then available for such programs. It was only because of the departure of the German minority that internal colonization acquired considerable importance immediately after World War II, when approximately 60,000 families, mostly from the various karst areas, were settled on the vacated farms.[2] But this was only a temporary and rather limited relief. This colonization after World War II had two specific political objectives: distribution of land to colonists had the nature of a veteran's bonus for the members of the National Liberation Army of World War II, and colonization was to serve as a spearhead of collectivization of agriculture. The immediate effect of this elimination of the German minority from Yugoslav agriculture and replacement by the mountaineers from areas south of the Sava-Danube line was reduced agricultural production and worsening of the quality of products. This result was quite natural, considering the disparity in the cultural level of the two populations, the low level of agricultural technology among the mountaineers, and the difficulties involved in shifting from a predominantly pastoral to a primarily crop type of agriculture. But the transfer of the German minority at the time when it took place, whether it was voluntary or forced, was politically unavoidable.

EMPLOYMENT OUTSIDE OF AGRICULTURE

Since neither emigration abroad nor internal colonization resulted in relieving markedly the pressure of population in rural areas, the need to find employment in the country but outside of agriculture, either on a permanent or on a temporary basis, grew stronger and stronger. It is impossible for us to go into detail with regard to the growth and nature of employment opportunities that the peasant population was able to secure in the urban economy in the course of the interwar period. Some over-all figures will have to suffice. Between 1921 (area covered by the census) and 1931 there was an increase of 1,455,051 in the population which was living from agriculture, for-

---

[2] *Zakon o agrarnoj reformi i kolonizaciji* (The Law on the Agrarian Reform and Internal Colonization), p. xii.

estry, and fisheries. The population which lived from typical urban pursuits, such as industry, handicrafts, trade, transportation, and professions, increased during the same time by 794,220. Less than half of this number, 375,294, was the increase in population which lived from industry and handicrafts. Naturally, a large proportion of the increase in urban population and in population employed in urban economy came from the villages.

The increase in total population between 1931 and 1941 was estimated at 2,039,000. As no basic structural changes took place in the Yugoslav economy during the 1930's, although the economy was affected by a severe depression, it might be assumed that the increased population during the 1930's found sources of livelihood similar to those found by the increased population during the 1920's. There can be no doubt that the growth of the urban economy provided a very basic outlet for the growing rural population during the interwar period. The ability of the urban economy to provide these new employment opportunities depended, naturally, on the development of the general economic conditions in the country. The exceedingly low wage level which prevailed in Yugoslavia during the interwar period was directly related to the chronic oversupply of labor due to agricultural overpopulation and formed a specific stimulus to the urban economy to employ more labor.[3] A considerable portion of the work in the industrial economy in which peasants engaged was of a seasonal character. This was especially true of the urban construction industry and of lumbering. An important field of work for the surplus labor in rural areas was road transport with horses and carts in lumbering, mining, construction work, and hauling of commercial cargo. The motor truck, however, was becoming a menacing competitor.

While urban economy was a powerful factor in the employment of part of the surplus labor from rural areas, it was not able to siphon off all the surplus rural population during the interwar period. The agricultural population grew much faster than the absorptive power of the urban economy. Moreover, a large portion of employment opportunities in the urban economy was in the field of services, whose contribution to the increase in the production of goods was limited, but whose influence on the distribution of national income was profound and to a considerable extent at the expense of the rural population.

[3] Bogdan Krekić, *Radnička nadnica kao privredni, socijalni i kulturni faktor* (The Worker's Wage as an Economic, Social, and Cultural Factor), pp. 7–30; Mijo Mirković, *Ekonomska struktura Jugoslavije, 1918–1941* (Economic Structure of Yugoslavia, 1918–1941), pp. 43–48.

REDUCTION OF THE BIRTH RATE

The Yugoslav peasantry was also partly adjusting itself—though as a rule unconsciously—to the relatively decreasing means of subsistence by the reduction of the birth rate. As shown in Tables 16 and 19 (pp. 290, 300), the birth rate and the natural growth rate were falling during the interwar period, and especially during the 1930's, in all areas of Yugoslavia. But as noted earlier, birth control in rural areas was widespread only in Vojvodina, Srijem, and Slavonia. These areas also showed the highest rate of infant mortality during the interwar period. As widespread birth control had been practiced in these areas for several generations, it had greatly slowed the growth of population. Hence, the more satisfactory population–cultivated land ratio in these areas was at least partly caused by birth control. Actually in such areas as Vojvodina and Slovenia (*banovine* Dunav and Drava) the birth rate was already very low during the interwar period. This was true also of certain portions of Croatia-Slavonia and Dalmatia.

Birth control should obviously be regarded as one of the means of combating population pressure. But its proper practice presupposes a much higher level of education than is found among the great majority of the Yugoslav peasants. Abominable housing conditions and the mores of peasants in many areas of Yugoslavia, especially in areas south of the Sava-Danube rivers, also militate against proper practice of birth control. Furthermore, any educational drives and propaganda in support of birth control would have to show the peasants in areas in which it is not practiced that having fewer children would be economically advantageous to the parents. This would not be too difficult to show to a peasant with a large or even a medium-size farm. But in the case of peasants with dwarf and small farms, especially when there is a chance for some earnings outside of the home farm, that might be altogether impossible. In a village the child, if he survives, becomes a producer at a very tender age. Thus, children are considered the poor peasants' only hope and insurance against old age. In such families it is hard to find an economic incentive to practice birth control. Birth control propaganda would therefore have to overcome great obstacles of a cultural, psychological, and economic nature in many overcrowded areas. Nevertheless, birth control should be systematically propagated in practically all overpopulated areas, because it would be advantageous for those areas taken as a whole. Whether any results of such propaganda could be expected in Yugoslav rural areas of high fertility within a decade or two, it is impossible to predict.

INCREASE IN CULTIVATED LAND

The people who could not emigrate abroad or find work outside of agriculture within the country itself remained in agriculture and in time built new households. As stated earlier, the bulk of the increase in population during the 1920's and 1930's was forced to remain in agriculture. The number of households whose heads derived their livelihood primarily from agriculture rose from 1,741,092 in 1921 to 1,963,403 in 1931, or 12.8 percent. The number of households in all other occupations rose during the same period by 194,143, or 35 percent. During the 1930's a similar increase took place in both fields. Thus, between 400,000 and 450,000 new households have been created during the interwar period in Yugoslav agriculture. This was one of the basic effects of the rise in agricultural population. While part of the land needed for the livelihood of these families came from the increase in the area of cultivated land between 1921 and 1938, as will be shown presently, several other adjustments were also necessary. It can be said with assurance that the great majority of these new rural households did not arise on the basis of land newly taken into cultivation, but rather on the basis of division of the existing farm households. Dwarf and small farms, which were characteristic of the Yugoslav agriculture at the beginning of the interwar period, became even smaller as a result of this process (see Chapter 19).

The area of cultivated land rose from 6,828,000 hectares in 1921 to 7,635,000 in 1931, and to 8,219,000 in 1938, or by 20.5 percent over a period of 18 years. This increase in cultivated land has come from several sources, but the available statistical information makes it impossible to obtain a clear picture in this respect. Part of the new land, no doubt, came from the clearance of forests and some came from the reclamation of marshes, as, according to official statistics, both of these categories of land were reduced. It is interesting to note that land reclamation which was undertaken in Yugoslavia during that period was concentrated in the Pannonian Plain, namely, in *banovina* Dunav and the eastern portions of *banovina* Sava. It consisted of erecting dikes against inundations, building of canals, and installation of pumping stations. Through land reclamation work between 1918 and 1938 a total of 1,284,218 hectares of land was improved, of which only about 50,000 hectares was outside of *banovine* Dunav and Sava. The bulk of the work was financed by the so-called water co-operatives. On the basis of the existing legislation, the joining of water co-operatives was compulsory as soon as a majority of landowners in a certain area decided that they wanted such installations built. Charges for their services were paid in the same manner as the land tax. The land reclamation projects in the karst regions remained on paper during the interwar period, although their execution might have greatly reduced the cereal deficiency in these areas.[4] In addition to the protection of land against inundations (almost all rivers in Yugoslavia spilled over their banks periodically) and the drainage of marshy lands, another basic problem of land reclamation in Yugoslavia was present in the karst regions, the need for reforestation. In fact, reforestation held the key to the improvement in the over-all productivity of much of these regions. The total area reforested during the interwar period amounted to only 47,000 hectares, and of this a large portion was outside of the karst region.[5] Thus, it can be safely said that during the interwar period little attention was paid to acquiring the potential cultivable land through systematic land reclamation.

The area of arable land increased between 1921 and 1938 by 20.5 percent. The most interesting and most easily understandable development with regard to the arable land was that the area under cereals was greatly increased. It rose from 4,625,000 hectares, or 73.8 percent, of arable land in 1921 to 6,183,000 hectares, or 81.9 percent, of the total in 1938. Actually, the greatest relative increase in the area under cereals occurred in 1924. The increase between 1921 and 1938 was 1,558,000 hectares, or 33.6 percent. The rate of this increase exceeded slightly the rate of increase in total population of the country. An important change in the utilization of arable land was a reduction in the fallow by almost half a million hectares between 1921 and 1938.

Although the growth in cultivated land during the interwar period did not keep pace with the increase in population, it was still very impressive. The trouble was, however, that while agriculture population had the tendency of continued growth at a high rate, the increase in cultivated land was nearing its natural limits. There is no doubt that a certain increase in the cultivable land was still possible at the end of the interwar period through the reclamation of permanent and periodic marshes and karstic *polja*, clearance of forests, and plowing up of permanent meadows. But this reclamation was possible only at the cost of heavy capital investment; forest clearance, from now on, would bring in, as a rule, only land of inferior quality for agricultural purposes; and plowing up of meadows would tend to reduce livestock

[4] Yugoslavia, *Annuaire statistique 1940*, pp. 174–75; *Annuaire statistique 1938–1939*, pp. 182–85.

[5] Yugoslavia, *Annuaire statistique 1929*, p. 162; *Annuaire statistique 1940*, p. 176.

numbers and would have unfavorable consequences for the quality of land cultivation. Finally, a reduction in the area under fallow would increase the area under crops, but in many areas that presupposes considerable changes in agricultural technology. The increase in cultivated land as an avenue for counteracting agricultural overpopulation is still open in Yugoslavia in a very limited way, but it will soon completely disappear.

INTENSIFICATION OF AGRICULTURAL PRODUCTION

From statistical data on agricultural production in Yugoslavia during the interwar period there is not much indication that under the stress of agricultural overpopulation there was any considerable shift from extensive to more labor-intensive crops or to a systematic effort to increase yields, except that the relative importance of corn in total agricultural production rose considerably. Industrial crops, which took 1.42 percent of the arable land in 1921, took only 1.96 percent in 1931, and 2.47 percent in 1938. The increase in the area under feed crops rose from 4.16 percent of the arable land in 1927 (strictly comparable data for earlier years are not available) to 4.71 percent in 1938. The area under vegetables and potatoes fell from 5.74 percent of the arable area in 1927 to 5.67 percent in 1938. Moreover, the increase in area under industrial and feed crops was relatively much larger in the areas north of the Sava-Danube rivers, especially in Vojvodina, than in areas south of these rivers, and the latter areas are much more overpopulated. One basic indication of more intensive farming was that the area left as fallow was greatly reduced. It fell from 889,161 hectares in 1921 to 328,237 hectares in 1931, but it rose again to 397,877 hectares in 1938. The reduction in fallow occurred, however, largely in areas south of the Sava-Danube rivers. The increase in relative figures between 1921 and 1938 pertaining to industrial crops and even feed crops looks quite impressive, but in absolute terms the increase in land under these crops (see Table 31, p. 474) is very limited indeed.

From information on the use of farm implements and commercial fertilizer (see pp. 440–50) one has to conclude that there was little if any improvement in the general land cultivation techniques in order to derive from the same land area an increased amount of agricultural products. The fact that Yugoslav peasants continued to till their soil during the interwar period as they did during the preceding decades and that lower-quality soils were put to crops would suggest that a lowering of yields was inevitable. This conclusion, however, is unwarranted for the 20-year period here under consideration. The three-year moving-average yields of potatoes and sugar beets show considerable improvement in the late 1930's as against the yields during the 1920's. There was even a tendency, though a very weak one, toward improvement in the yields of wheat and corn during the late 1930's as against earlier years. Among the major crops, only hay showed a definite tendency toward lower yield during the interwar period, which would indicate that better meadows were put under the plow. As most of the increase in yield was during the late 1930's, it is most probable, however, that favorable weather conditions played an important role. In the long run a maintenance in yields, let alone an improvement, could not be achieved, except by improved agricultural technology.

In spite of the fact that the cultivated area increased by 20 percent between 1921 and 1938, the possibility of further increase in arable land is quite limited. Thus the increase in agricultural production from the existing cultivated land area is actually the foremost avenue of increasing agricultural production, and thus the primary means of fighting against agricultural overpopulation from within agriculture itself. It is beyond any doubt that the intensification of agricultural production and industrialization are the only two promising ways of combating agricultural overpopulation. Both of these closely interdependent approaches to the problem of agricultural overpopulation are long-run propositions and ones beset with great economic, psychological, and political difficulties.

REDUCTION OF LIVESTOCK HERDS

An important way of adjustment to the relatively reduced land resources in comparison with rural population followed by the Yugoslav peasantry was to reduce the number of livestock. As we have seen earlier, the number of livestock in terms of cattle decreased from 8,458,000 units in 1921 to 7,566,000 units in 1931, and rose again to 8.340,000 units in 1938. That means that while agricultural population rose between 1921 and 1938 by 22.5 percent and the amount of cultivated land by 20.5 percent, livestock numbers first fell from the 1921 stand and then recuperated slowly, but in 1938 they were still below the 1921 level. If the 1938 livestock figures were compared with the pre-1914 data, the comparison would be even more disastrous. The falling trend of livestock numbers in comparison with cultivated land and agricultural population started during the nineteenth century and continued also during the interwar period. But in addition to the fact that livestock figures were reduced, there was also a worsening in the composition of livestock. Thus cattle, which in 1921 formed 59.9 percent of all livestock units in terms of cattle, fell to 51.7 percent of the total in 1931 and to 51.5 percent of the total in 1938. The relative percentages of horses rose somewhat. Those of pigs remained the same. But the numbers of sheep and goats, which did not compete with people for arable or potentially arable land, rose from 10.2 percent of all animal units in terms of cattle in 1921 to 13.7 percent in 1931, and to 14.4 percent of the total in 1938. By keeping down the number of livestock the peasant population simply made more room for the production of food for the people. A certain compensation for smaller numbers of livestock was perhaps to be found in improved breeds and increased average weight of animals, especially of cattle, but this compensation factor was not too important during the interwar period. Reduction of livestock is one way of adjustment of the agricultural population to increased population pressure, but definitely not a recommended way of combating agricultural overpopulation, because it has the tendency to affect unfavorably agricultural production, cash income, and nutrition of agricultural population. It should be mentioned, however, that two other factors partly contributed to the decline of livestock in Yugoslavia during the interwar period: relatively low prices of livestock and livestock products in comparison with the cost of feed and the reduced demand for exports.

DEVELOPMENT OF COTTAGE INDUSTRIES

Another of the typical adjustment processes to increasing population pressure, which was urged in order to increase the labor opportunities for the peasants, was an increase in cottage industries. Not long ago the Yugoslav village was largely self-sufficient economically; hence, many cottage industries were still widespread during the interwar period. Among the most important were the processing of the domestic wool clip and domestically produced vegetable fibers into clothing, the making of footwear, carpets, blankets, embroidery, cordage, furniture, sieves, brooms, baskets, clay pots, carts; the making of household utensils out of wood, and the burning of lime and charcoal. A group of Yugoslav economists in 1927 had estimated for the years 1923 to 1925 the value of the cottage industry's production for sale at 1,073 million dinars per annum, and production for domestic use at 3,764 million dinars, or a total annual average of 4,837 million dinars. This compared with an estimated total production value of the handicrafts of 7,760 million dinars and that of the factory production of 5,823 million dinars.[6] While all these estimates are rather crude, we supply them only to indicate the order of magnitude of the cottage industry. But as factory production grew, the position of the cottage industry became more and more difficult. This was especially true of the textile and footwear production. It is also true, however, that during the Great Depression of the 1930's the Yugoslav village had a tendency to withdraw more and more from the market because of the great fall in prices of agricultural products and the impossibility of obtaining any credit, and this probably increased somewhat the relative value of the cottage industry's production during the early 1930's.

A greater development of cottage industries, especially of textiles, was advocated by the Croatian Peasant party during the 1930's as a means of furthering the economic autarky of the village in order to make the village more resistant to the influences of the depression. The effect of this endeavor is not known. The important point to remember is that the cottage industry, which was engaged for decades in a losing battle with factory production, was unable to contribute substantially to the reduction of population pressure. On the contrary, the destruction or reduction of the size of most cottage industries tended to increase the pressure of population in the village. While some types of cottage industries will no doubt continue to exist, it is safe to say that most of them have no future and that they should not be counted upon as an important means of combating agricultural overpopulation. Only in some limited areas where some quasi-artistic cottage industries working exclusively for the market are practiced could one expect, with proper promotion, consolidation and further development of these sources of earning. Furthermore, the maintenance of the general type of cottage industries indicated above would tend to reduce the demand for factory products in the village, limiting still further the narrow domestic market for industrial products, thus impeding some branches of industry.

INDUSTRIALIZATION AS A CURE FOR AGRICULTURAL OVERPOPULATION

A realization of basic significance, which became clear during the 1930's to most Yugoslav economists and to some politicians and administrators, was that the problem of agricultural overpopulation was the central economic issue of the country and that it had far-reaching political and social significance and ramifications. This meant that in the long run the solution or marked amelioration of agricultural

---

[6] V. M. Djuričić *et al.*, *Naša narodna privreda i nacionalni prihod* (Our National Economy and National Income), pp. 161–79, 265.

overpopulation was to be the chief task of the Yugoslav governments, and their achievements in this direction the basic yardstick for judging their activities and successes. It also became abundantly clear to practically all those who investigated the problem of the relationship between the agricultural population and the agricultural resources and their respective trends of development that the solution of the problem of agricultural overpopulation could not be found within agriculture itself. Since mass emigration was impossible, the only avenue of approach to a permanent solution of the problem of agricultural overpopulation outside of agriculture was through industrialization. This is how the problem was put by a series of Yugoslav economists:

> The scarcity of land, that is, a great number of agricultural people on limited land, leads us to the conclusion that in our country the solution of the agrarian issues cannot be found in agriculture alone . . . Expressed more clearly, the preconditions for the improvements in peasant farming are first of all: (1) orderly employment of the surplus of labor in the village by intensifying agricultural production and by creating employment opportunities in industry, public works, forestry, etc.; (2) favorable exchange of commodities the peasants sell and those they buy (removal of price scissors, customs duties, indirect taxes, etc.); (3) direction of capital into the village economy in order to intensify agricultural production and for the creation of employment opportunities.[7]
>
> A permanent solution of our peasant question is to be sought outside of agriculture.[8]
>
> Industrialization is the indispensible precondition for a betterment of conditions in agriculture. . . . Only industrialization on a large scale and over a long period of time can create a larger and better domestic market . . . , only industrialization can free agriculture from its surplus population and create conditions for the formation of larger and more satisfactory farms.[9]
>
> The most effective way of counteracting the unfavorable consequences of relative overpopulation is industrialization, that is, a change from the status of a purely agricultural to the status of an agricultural-industrial country.[10]

It should be stressed that these authors represented the whole spectrum of political opinion in Yugoslavia during the 1930's, from the ultra-conservative Otto von Frangeš to the chief economic expert of the Croatian Peasant party, Rudolf Bićanić, an independent like Mijo Mirković, and the Communist Maksim Goranović.

[7] Rudolf Bićanić, *Pogled iz svjetske perspektive i naša ekonomska orientacija* (Our Economic Orientation in International Perspective), pp. 54, 58–59.

[8] Maksim Goranović, *Naš seoski posed i tehnika* (Our Peasant Property and Technology), p. 13.

[9] Mijo Mirković, *Agrarna politika* (Agrarian Policy), pp. 300–301.

[10] Otto von Frangeš, "The Problem of Relative Overpopulation in Yugoslavia," Yugoslavia Ministry of Agriculture, *Arhiv* V (reprint), 40.

Thus, the cry of the decade became the cry for industrialization. Furthermore, there was an almost unanimous opinion in support of planned industrialization and, generally, for a planned economy in which the leading criteria would be the needs and the interests of the large mass of the peasant population. Of course, this did not mean that the need for improvements in agricultural technology were forgotten. But as long as agriculture remained overburdened with surplus population, no chances of marked improvement existed within agriculture.

As we have seen earlier, some industrialization took place in most South Slav provinces before 1914. Industrial development obtained fresh impetus in the new state after 1918. It was aided by the protective tariff, especially after 1925, by exchange controls, by far-reaching concessions to foreign capitalists willing to invest in Yugoslavia, by direct investment on the part of the state in transportation and heavy industry. The industrial development of the interwar period in Yugoslavia, while of considerable proportions, was incapable of absorbing the bulk of the increasing labor force in the country.

In principle, industrialization is an acknowledged remedy for agricultural overpopulation. But to be successful in this respect, industrialization, first of all, has to proceed on a large scale and be sustained over several generations. Otherwise, its growth would not provide a sufficient outlet for the growing labor force. Second, industrialization is not supposed only to siphon off the surplus labor from the village, but also to increase the productivity of labor both in the urban and in the agricultural economy and thus provide for a rising plane of living for the population as a whole. As soon as the aim of industrialization is understood in this way, the rate of growth of industry or its speed becomes a basic issue. If industrialization is to provide employment opportunities for the incoming new labor in the urban and rural areas that cannot be employed elsewhere, and also to provide for an increase in the plane of living, the rate of the industry's growth has to outweigh the rate of population growth by a certain margin commensurate with the desired rise in the plane of living. A rise in the productivity due to industrialization, to technological improvements in agriculture, and to the increase in cultivated land, comparable only to the growth of population, would simply enable the population to prevent its present plane of living from falling.

It is not our intention to discuss various problems which arise as soon as a policy of forced industrialization is inaugurated, either generally or under the Yugoslav conditions. Only a few questions are indicated which arise and have to be answered in one way or another. First of all, it should be stated that a policy of industrialization is not followed only to relieve the pressure of population, but to achieve a series of various aims: to increase productivity in industry and agriculture and to raise the level of living, to diversify the economy of a country and to increase its stability, to increase the defensive or aggressive potential of the country, and the like. Among the questions raised in connection with a policy of industrialization would be the following: whether to concentrate first on developing light industries or industries of capital goods; whether to fit completely the industrial development to the raw material supplies available at home; what should be the role of private enterprise and what the role of the government in industrialization; how much economic planning should there be; should economic development be financed exclusively out of domestic capital formation or should foreign capital be attracted; where should new industries be located; what and how much to export in order to pay for needed imports of machinery and industrial appliances (disregarding foreign loans and/or aid); how to develop a skilled labor force and managerial staffs; how to provide for the necessary domestic capital formation and how to distribute the financial burdens, on the one hand, and the benefits of industrialization, on the other; what would be the best domestic and what the best international political framework for the prosecution of an industrialization program; what would be the effect of large national defense expenditures on industrialization. In spite of all difficulties and the limited results of industrial development both during the interwar period and since 1945, industrialization remains the most important means of relieving the agricultural overpopulation in Yugoslavia and of raising, in time, the level of living of the whole population.

WARS AS A MEANS OF CURING OR ALLEVIATING AGRICULTURAL OVERPOPULATION

Finally, one might ask if war could be considered a means of curing or reducing agricultural overpopulation. Two possibilities are to be distinguished here: the enlargement of the territory and the reduction of population in the same territory. Use of force for territorial expansion, together with conquest of additional resources for the growing population of one group at the expense of others, is as old a method of dealing with population pressure as recorded human history. In recent times some of the Great Powers, notably Germany, Japan, and Italy, used, among other measures, wars of conquest for relieving their population pressure. At least temporarily, Japan had some success in this regard but, in the end, the attempted conquests of all these three powers failed. Small powers, which, depending on their geographic location and possession of strategic raw materials, are more or less pawns in the hands of the Great Powers, cannot even attempt to engage in wars of conquest at the present time. On the contrary, they are most often objects of conquest. But if they cannot engage in wars of conquest, small nations cannot regularly keep out of modern wars. This is so partly because they are pawns of the Great Powers; partly because they are objects of oppression or conquest and have to defend themselves; partly because in their territories the competing imperialistic drives of the Great Powers collide; partly because their territories often serve as the token money, so to speak, in diplomatic bargains among the Great Powers. The Balkans have long been famous for serving in these capacities. The sacrifices in blood and treasure of the small powers due to war are often relatively much greater than those of the Great Powers. The Yugoslav nations have had the unenviable distinction of being objects of conquest, and of suffering a formidable toll in blood and wealth, during both World War I and World War II. The struggles that the Teutons, hungering for an enlarged *Lebensraum,* have imposed upon the Slavic nations during the two world wars were only phases in a centuries-long struggle between Slavs and Teutons. Moreover, other nations such as the Magyars and Italians have also claimed Yugoslav land. Wars to defend the land they already hold or to liberate themselves, rather than wars to conquer new land, have been the lot of the South Slavs for centuries.

It is important to note, however, that as a consequence of World War I further immigration of the German and of the Magyar elements in that part of the Pannonian Plain that was incorporated into Yugoslavia in 1918 had ceased. On the contrary, a few thousand families from the areas south of the Sava-Danube rivers were settled in Vojvodina, Srijem, and Slavonia, continuing, so to speak, the long trend of migration from the mountainous parts of the Balkans into the Danubian Plain. The same sealing of the frontiers happened in 1918 to the south, as it stopped the persistent infiltration of Yugoslav Macedonia and much of the area of the former Sandjak of Novi Pazar by the Albanians. Here also some colonization from other parts of Yugoslavia took place. Thus the political changes brought about by World War I stopped immigration into the territory of the new state. World War II was also very important in this respect, as it resulted in virtual elimination, either by withdrawal or by expulsion, of the German minority of over 400,000 people from Yugoslavia. In their place several scores of thousands of families from the overcrowded mountainous areas were settled. The two world wars, which were supposed to obliterate the statehood of the South Slavs, to reduce them to servility, and to reduce their numbers, helped, in fact, to create and then to regenerate the common Yugoslav state, to insulate its territory against further immigration from the neighboring areas, and even to clear its territory of the minority belonging to the most dangerous of the would-be conquerors.

But the two world wars, in which the Yugoslav nations were involved, caused a formidable loss of population. This, naturally, reduced the number of people in relation to land resources. But these wars also reduced the area of cultivated land, despoiled orchards and vineyards, agricultural buildings and implements, and cut down the number of livestock. The improvement in the population–cultivated land ratio was far overweighed by the loss of other resources in agriculture. Besides, this type of betterment in the population–land ratio usually lasts only a short time, as experience shows that after wars the birth rate of the peasant population increases and thus creates a tendency for a faster growth of peasant population. Above all, however, the price paid for this temporary betterment in the population–cultivated land ratio is so frightfully high that wars as a means of relieving the population pressure have to be discarded from consideration.

CHAPTER 18

THE POST–1918 AGRARIAN REFORM

In Chapter 10 we reviewed briefly the size-structure of farms and the land tenure as it existed in various South Slav lands at the turn of this century. In Chapter 12 we showed the influences of World War I on the political and economic developments in Central and Southeastern Europe and the emergence of a revolutionary spirit within Austria-Hungary both among the soldiery and among the civilian population. The political objective of these revolutionary forces was the breaking up of the multinational and quasi-feudal Austro-Hungarian Empire and the creation of a series of national states with a democratic form of government. The socioeconomic aim of this revolutionary ferment, as far as peasantry was concerned, was a radical agrarian reform which would abolish all vestiges of the feudal order and still the land hunger of the peasant masses by realizing the principle that "land belongs to those who till it."

The first logical step in the study of the land-tenure system in Yugoslavia during the interwar period is therefore a review of the nature and the effects of the post-1918 agrarian reform. Changes in the land tenure were also produced by other forces such as the increasing agricultural overpopulation, continuing penetration of capitalist forces into the peasant economy, and specific pieces of legislation. The post-1918 agrarian reform in Yugoslavia can be understood only as a phase, albeit a very important and almost final phase, in the realization of the idea that the land belongs to those who till it—an idea which served as the prime mover of the peasantry of various South Slav lands throughout the feudal period, and in particular since the beginning of the nineteenth century when the democratic and liberal ideas of Western Europe started to penetrate to the Balkan peasantry. This idea was realized in Serbia after its liberation from the Turkish yoke early in the nineteenth century. And after 1918 it was considered as the socioeconomic concomitant of the national liberation in all those areas in which feudal forms or strong vestiges of feudalism still existed. The idea that the land belongs to those who till it was formalized by a decree of February 25, 1919, and by the Constitution of 1921, but it was necessary to deal with the reform in various provinces by specific legislation.

Needless to say, the agrarian reform became from its inception in the new Yugoslav state a plaything of party politics. Owing primarily to this fact, though other influences were also at work, it took over 14 years to pass the laws settling finally the problem of agrarian reform in all provinces. But even at the end of the interwar period some administrative work connected with the reform, including the indemnification of some of the former landowners, was not completed, except in Bosnia and Herzegovina. The long provisorium between 1918, when the peasantry who worked land belonging to various types of landowners took possession of that land, and the time when their right to ownership was fully ensured by acquisition of a formal legal title, affected very unfavorably both the holders of land who were not sure of their ownership and the old owners who tried to regain their rights. It also gave much opportunity for graft and administrative bungling. All of this greatly reduced the effect of the reform from an economic point of view.

THE CORNERSTONE OF THE REFORM: THE INTERIM DECREE OF FEBRUARY 25, 1919

The cornerstone of the Yugoslav post-1918 agrarian reform was the Interim Decree on the Preparation of the Agrarian Reform of February 25, 1919. It provided the ideological framework of the whole reform. The philosophy of this decree—the idea that the land belongs to those who till it—corresponded to the centuries-old ideals of the peasantry of the South Slav lands. The decree was preceded by a series of official statements conceived in the same spirit, which had a direct bearing on the formulation of various stipulations in this decree. As we have shown in Chapter 12, the revolutionary ferment in Austria-Hungary toward the close of World War I affected large numbers of men in the military services as well as large segments of the peasantry. As the power of the Dual Monarchy began rapidly to disintegrate during the summer and early fall of 1918, the peasantry began to refuse the payment of rents and started to occupy lands belonging to large estates. The latter process was intensified after the collapse of the Dual Monarchy and the proclamation of the State of the Slovenes, Croats, and Serbs on October 28, 1918. The National Council (Narodno Vijeće) in Zagreb proclaimed itself both as the legislative and the executive organ of this new state. Its first act which dealt with the land problem was the Message to the Peasants of November 14, 1918, in which it was stated that in the new state every family would be able to obtain enough land without doing force, injustice, or damage to anybody. The Council promised to settle the land issue by law and called upon the peasants, who now had obtained full franchise, to co-operate with the state authorities.[1] The next step of the National Council was the Decision of November 26, 1918, in which the Council stated that the basic principles of its policy with regard to the agrarian reform were the "abolition of all feudal relationships which still existed in the provinces of the State of the Slovenes, Croats, and Serbs with a just indemnity and the abolition of all those privileges which resulted from the feudal relationship." Furthermore, it promised to expropriate, again with an appropriate indemnity, and to distribute among the needy peasants all the estates which, according to the conditions prevailing in various areas, could be considered as large estates and all landed properties acquired during the war with war profits.[2] There is no doubt but that these proclamations were an expression of the determination of the liberal political forces in the new state to abolish all the vestiges of feudalism and break any remaining vestiges of the political power of former feudal lords. They were intended to appease the peasantry, which was in a revolutionary state of mind and bent on satisfying as much as possible its perennial hunger for land either peacefully or by force.

Even if pre-1912 Serbia was not directly interested in agrarian reform within its own territory, some pronouncements of its government prior to 1918 had a direct bearing on that reform in some other areas. First, in the Royal Proclamation of October 5, 1912, which was made concurrently with the declaration of war (First Balkan War) on the Ottoman Empire, it was promised that the peasantry of Macedonia (Southern Serbia) was to obtain economic and social freedom in addition to national liberation and full equality with the Serbs.[3] This meant an abolition of serfdom. Second, in a special decision of February 20, 1917, of the Serbian government in exile, a promise was made to all volunteers, coming essentially from the territories of the Austro-Hungarian Monarchy, that they would obtain five hectares (three hectares for noncombatants) of land after liberation.[4]

---

[1] Ferdo Šišić, *Dokumenti o postanku Kraljevine Srba, Hrvata i Slovenaca, 1914–1919* (Documents on the Establishment of the Kingdom of the Serbs, Croats, and Slovenes, 1914–1919), pp. 246–48; quoted hereafter as Šišić, *Dokumenti.*

[2] *Ibid.,* pp. 256–57.

[3] Stanoje Stanojević, *Srpsko-turski rat 1912 godine* (The Serbo-Turkish War of 1912), pp. 82–84.

[4] Kingdom of the Serbs, Croats, and Slovenes, Ministry of Agrarian Reform, *Agrarna reforma—uredbe, naredbe i raspisi* (Agrarian Reform—Decrees, Orders, and Circulars), I, 271; hereafter quoted as *Agrarna reforma.* With Volume II, published in 1925, this publication represents the best collection of official documents pertaining to the agrarian reform until 1925.

On December 1, 1918, the unification of the State of the Slovenes, Croats, and Serbs (former Yugoslav areas of Austria-Hungary) with the former Kingdom of Serbia and the Kingdom of Montenegro into one common state, the Kingdom of the Serbs, Croats, and Slovenes (between 1929 and 1945 officially Kingdom of Yugoslavia) was consummated. The agrarian issue was one of the most urgent questions in the new state. The first pronouncement of the government of the new state was made by the Regent Alexander in his Manifesto to the People of January 6, 1919, in which, among other things, he said:

I wish that we immediately begin with a just solution of the agrarian question, and that serfdom and large land estates be abolished. In both cases the land will be distributed among the poor peasants, and the former owners will be justly indemnified. Every Serb, Croat, and Slovene should be full owner of his land. In our free state there can and will be only free landowners. I have asked my government to form immediately a commission which will undertake all the necessary preparations for the solution of the agrarian question. I call upon the peasant-serfs to have full confidence in my royal word and to wait peacefully for the government to hand over to them the land in a lawful manner, the land which in the future will be only God's and theirs as it has been for long in Serbia.[5]

These were the various official pronouncements that preceded the promulgation of the "Interim Decree" of February 25, 1919. Because of the fundamental importance of this decree we give in the following its main provisions, either in quotation or in summary:

Art. 1. "The institution of serfdom is Bosnia and Herzegovina and in the new areas of Serbia and Montenegro is abolished and the re-establishment of this institution is prohibited."

Art. 2. "Former serfs are hereby proclaimed to be free owners of the land they till."

Art. 3. "Former owners will be indemnified for the land taken from them and this indemnity is guaranteed by the state. The extent of the indemnity and the way in which it will be paid will be regulated by a special law."

Art. 5. "Until the issue of indemnity had been settled, former owners, if they should desire so, will be entitled to an interim rent which will be pro-rated according to their previous income from these lands . . ."

Art. 6. This article arrests all legal actions resulting from the serfdom relationship such as suits, executions, etc., pending at that time until new legal rules have been promulgated.

Art. 7. "The colonate and other serfdom-like institutions in Istria, Gorizia, Dalmatia, and other areas of the Kingdom of the Serbs, Croats, and Slovenes are abolished in the sense of the preceding articles (1–6)."

Art. 9. "All large landed estates within the territory of the Kingdom of the Serbs, Croats, and Slovenes are hereby expropriated. Land thus ob-

[5] Šišić, *Dokumenti*, p. 299.

tained will be distributed to those citizens who till the land, but who do not own any land or do not own enough land, and they will obtain only so much land as they can work with their own family. War invalids, widows and orphans of soldiers killed in action, and former soldiers and volunteers who have fought for the liberation and unification of the Serbs, Croats, and Slovenes have first call on such land. The disposition of the remainder of the expropriated land and the definition of large estates in various areas will be regulated by special law." (What is meant here is that land belonging to large estates above a certain minimum is expropriated.)

Art. 10.   This article defines, provisionally and quite vaguely, what the large estates are. They include all fideicommissa and properties in excess of a minimum size beginning in some areas with 100 cadastral yokes, but in some areas not before they reached 500 cadastral yokes. Estates which were leased or not under cultivation were declared large estates even if they were smaller than the respective minimum in their particular area. All these lands were subject to immediate interim subdivision (see Art. 14).

Art. 11.   "Indemnity to large estate owners for the expropriated land in regard to its amount and the manner of its payment will be regulated later by law; temporarily the provisions of Art. 5 will apply."

Art. 12.   "The following estates are expropriated without indemnity: (*a*) those belonging to the Habsburg dynasty and its members; (*b*) those estates belonging to dynasties of other enemy powers; (*c*) those estates which were granted to foreigners for services to the Habsburgs and which did not yet pass into third hands."

Art. 13.   This article states that indemnity for estates which were presumably bought with war profits will not be paid before the issue of war profits is settled by law.

Art. 14.   "Until the final division of large estates in the sense of Art. 9, the state will lease the estates mentioned in Art. 10 to persons mentioned in Art. 9 in smaller or larger lots. The rent to be paid will be established later according to local conditions."

Arts. 15 and 16.   These articles regulate the issue of land leases, abolishing certain of their forms. Subleasing of land is prohibited.

Art. 17.   "All larger forest properties are declared state property. The peasants have the right to use these forests for grazing and for cutting of wood for household and construction needs." Indemnity for these lands and the regulation of peasants' rights will be regulated by law.

Art. 19.   This article allows the revision of certain earlier settlements between landlords and serfs (segregations) if the interests of the serfs were impaired.

Art. 21.   "The provisions of this decree do not affect the territory of pre-1912 Serbia."

Art. 22.   "Land received under the provisions of this Decree cannot be sold, mortgaged, or transferred to third persons into possession, until this is allowed by further legislation."

Art. 23.   "Those persons who after the proclamation of this Decree should engage in seizing, dividing, or plundering of landed estates belonging to other persons and are convicted of such action, forfeit all rights to profit from the provisions of this Decree."[6]

The ideological basis of the interwar agrarian reform in Yugoslavia contained in this decree is marked by three main features: abolition of all feudal and quasi-feudal institutions, expropriation of a portion of land from large estates above a certain minimum in order to satisfy the need for land of at least a part of landless, dwarf, and small peasants; and recognition of the principle that former landowners have to receive an indemnity for their land. Politically, the reform liberated the serfs, and, together with later provisions about the general and equal franchise (except for women), it destroyed all vestiges of political strength of the feudal class or of its remainders. Socially and economically, the reform made the peasants who were serfs or in a serflike position into freeholders of their farms. In some cases and to a certain level this was done without any obligation on the part of the beneficiaries to pay for the land, which now became their property; in other cases they were supposed to pay a part or the whole indemnity for the acquired land. Nationally, the reform was important because it broke the political and economic power of large estate owners, most of whom were foreign, either by birth, political affiliation, religion, or political attitude. The agrarian reform was an important step in strengthening of the South Slav element in Vojvodina and Macedonia and in the political strengthening of the Christian sector of population in Bosnia and Herzegovina and Macedonia. In Vojvodina and Macedonia, which had and continued to have strong and compact minorities, this strengthening of the Yugoslav element was also furthered by internal colonization, which, in those areas, was a part of the agrarian reform. Finally, agrarian reform served also as a means of rewarding those who had fought during World War I as volunteers for Yugoslav national liberation and unification, and thus it had, in a specific way and for a limited number of fighters, the character of a veteran's bonus.

If the peasantry of Southeastern Europe in general, and of such areas as Bosnia and Herzegovina and Macedonia in particular, had any desires for economic and social changes to be brought about by World War I, it was the desire for agrarian reform. That was a social, economic, and political necessity long overdue. In fact, the reform was largely carried out by the peasants themselves by refusing to render tithes or pay rents on land they worked already, or by occupying some new land. No government in Yugoslavia after 1918 could have upheld the serfdom and serfdom-like institutions.

[6] *Agrarna reforma*, I, 12–17.

In addition to including the basic principles of the agrarian reform, the Interim Decree also contained the seeds of most of the shortcomings of that reform. The obvious shortcomings of the decree were the following: (1) It was provisional. The complete execution of the reform was left to later regulation by special legislation for each province, thus giving time to groups which would be unfavorably affected by the reform to marshal their political and propaganda forces against it. (2) The formal transfer of full ownership of the land to the former serfs and other beneficiaries of the reform was delayed, in some areas for more than 15 years, thus creating a sense of insecurity on the part of the beneficiaries of the reform and a faint hope in the hearts of the former owners that some land affected by the reform might be saved. (3) The decree left open the definition of large estates, part of whose land was to be expropriated, which gave rise to complications in the following years. (4) The fixing of interim rents was left open for the leased land from the large estates which were to be expropriated, pending their distribution, as well as for land which was immediately distributed but where the indemnity was not yet fixed. (5) The decree granted a priority treatment to volunteers of World War I and thus opened the way for considerable abuse with regard to their definition and identification. (6) It prohibited alienation of land obtained by the agrarian reform until the final legal settlements, a fact which has been appraised both favorably and unfavorably.

It was with these numerous handicaps and against considerable political and propaganda pressures from organized landlords, some of whom were abroad and, as citizens of other countries, exercised pressure through diplomatic channels, that the Yugoslav agrarian reform began after World War I and made its arduous way to legal conclusion in 1933; but administratively and financially it was not completed in some areas even by 1940. Any appraisal of the reform, however, has to distinguish between the basic principles of the reform, which under the existing conditions in Yugoslavia in 1918 were good, and the way in which the reform was actually executed, which deserves considerable criticism.

From the start the agrarian reform was an important political issue and thus a matter of horse trading among political parties. The most interesting instance in this regard was the passage of the Constitution of 1921 (see pp. 236–38). The government parties (essentially Serbian), which lacked the necessary majority to pass the Constitution in the Constituent Assembly, managed to secure 32 votes from the former Moslem landlords in Bosnia and Herzegovina and Macedonia by promising concessions in regard to the agrarian reform in these provinces. And a group of 8 Slovene votes was secured by other concessions.[7]

THE REFORM AFFECTS TWO DIFFERENT PATTERNS
OF AGRICULTURAL ECONOMY

Economically speaking, one could distinguish two basically different situations in regard to the agrarian reform in Yugoslavia after World War I, which were bound to affect the agricultural production of the country differently, and they must be appraised differently. In Bosnia and Herzegovina and Macedonia the reform consisted of breaking up an outlived feudal and semifeudal order. While in these provinces large ownership units of a special type existed in the form of *agalik, beglik*, and *čiftlik* lands they were not operated as farming units, except very rarely in the latter two cases. Rather, they consisted of a multitude of small farms held by the serfs and tenants, who were obliged to pay tithes or rents in kind or in money to the landlord. Here large ownership units did not mean large farm units and advanced technology, but rather small units, and, because of feudal or quasi-feudal relationship, primitive techniques and the absence of any incentive on the part of the tillers of the land to improve its productivity. The basic problems of the reform were to declare what land was affected by the reform, to transfer formally the ownership of this land from the former landlords to the new owners, and to indemnify the former landlords. The breaking up of the feudal order in these provinces was a political and legal, not an economic, process. Economically the reform resulted in increased efficiency because it created incentives for the new owners to work the land better, as the increment in production was solely to their advantage.

The problem in Vojvodina, Croatia-Slavonia, and Slovenia was totally different, because here there were large ownership units, though as a rule of feudal origin, which were operated as large farming units with part of the land being affected by the agrarian reform. Here the agrarian reform consisted of determination of what portion of the large estates was to be expropriated, distribution of the expropriated land to various types of claimants, and indemnification of the former owners. This was a much more complicated problem. It had important

---

[7] The agreement between the government parties and the Moslem (Turkish minority) representatives from Macedonia was in written form, while the agreements with the representatives of Moslems from Bosnia and Herzegovina and with the Slovenian group were oral but promptly and fully carried out. Josip Horvat, *Politička povijest Hrvatske, 1918–1929* (Political History of Croatia, 1918–1929), pp. 254–55.

consequences for both the large estates affected by the reform and for the agricultural production of these areas as a whole.

It is not necessary to go into details of the procedures followed by the reform in various provinces. That has been done many times before and there is a large body of literature on the subject, both in Serbo-Croatian and in various other languages, though a considerable portion of this literature is biased in one way or another.[8] This is quite natural because in these discussions emotions and material interests are often involved. What seems to this writer to be most important here is to sketch the reform as undertaken in various provinces, to present statistical information on the amount of land affected in various areas and on the number of peasant households which benefited from the reform, to indicate changes which it brought about in the structure of agricultural property in the country, and to appraise economic and social consequences which it produced for the Yugoslav agriculture.

REFORM IN BOSNIA AND HERZEGOVINA

The Interim Decree of February 25, 1919, provided in Articles 1 to 6 that the serfdom (*kmetstvo*) in Bosnia and Herzegovina be abolished and its re-establishment in the future prohibited. The *agalik* lands were affected by this decision. The relationship between the

[8] Ivan Z. Galić, *Problem agrarne politike u Hrvatskoj i Slavoniji* (The Problem of Agrarian Policy in Croatia-Slavonia) ; Dragan Turk, *Osnovi naše agrarne politike* (Principles of Our Agrarian Policy) ; *Agrarna reforma u Hrvatskoj, Sloveniji i Vojvodini* (Agrarian Reform in Croatia, Slovenia, and Vojvodina), opinion of the professors of the Department of Agriculture and Forestry of the University of Zagreb; Čedomir Marjanović, *Agrarni udar i zadužbinska, crkvena i manastirska imanja* (The Agrarian Reform and the Endowment, Church, and Monastic Properties) ; Dragoljub Jovanović, *Agrarna politika* (Agrarian Policy), pp. 277–89; Slavko Šećerov, *Iz naše agrarne politike, 1919–1929* (On Agricultural Policy, 1919–1929) ; Teofan Ristić, *Borba za zemlju i naša agrarna reforma* (The Struggle for Land and Our Agrarian Reform) ; Mijo Mirković, *Agrarna politika* (Agrarian Policy), pp. 105–25; Milan Ivšić, *Les problèmes agraires en Yougoslavie*, pp. 97–371; A. H. Hollmann, *Agrarverfassung und Landwirtschaft Jugoslawiens* (Germany, Ministry for Food and Agriculture, *Berichte über Landwirtschaft*, N.F., Sonderheft No. 30), pp. 28–66; Blagoje Nikosavić, *Die Agrarverfassung und der landwirtschaftliche Kredit Jugoslawiens* (Germany, Ministry for Food and Agriculture, *Berichte über Landwirtschaft*, N.F., Sonderheft No. 112), pp. 18–37; Otto von Frangeš, *Die sozialökonomische Struktur der jugoslawischen Landwirtschaft*, pp. 159–231. Among articles the following three are the most important: Djoko Bogojević, "The Agrarian Reform," *Jubilarni zbornik života i rada Srba, Hrvata i Slovenaca, 1918–1928* (Jubilee Record of Life and Work of the Serbs, Croats, and Slovenes, 1918–1928), I, 299–316; Mijo Mirković, "On the Twentieth Anniversary of Our Agrarian Reform," Yugoslavia, Ministry of Social Welfare, *Socijalni Arhiv*, March–April, 1939, pp. 65–72; Otto von Frangeš, "The Agrarian Reform in Yugoslavia," International Institute of Agriculture, *Bulletin of Agricultural Economics and Sociology* (1934), pp. E 89–100, 125–36, 174–98, 209–30, 269–87, 311–27.

landlords and serfs or kmetovi was of a purely feudal character, though the harshness of this relationship was somewhat softened by the Turkish legislation of the 1850's and later by Austro-Hungarian administrative decisions. In addition to the *agalik* lands, the reform also affected the *beglik* lands, when it was considered that the tenancy relationship between the landlord and people who tilled the soil had similarities with serfdom. In practice that meant that practically all *beglik* lands were also affected by the reform.

A number of laws, decrees, decisions, and regulations, issued over a period of more than 15 years, were necessary to carry out the agrarian reform in Bosnia and Herzegovina. Owing to a number of factors, however, the basic issues of the reform in these provinces—such as decisions as to what lands were to be affected by the reform and the transfer of property rights from the landlords to the new owners—were solved between 1919 and 1921. First of all, land property records were in fairly good order and made the legal and purely technical part of the reform much easier than in some other provinces, e.g., in Macedonia. Second, the former serfs and tenants were mostly Serbs, and Serbian representatives from Bosnia carried considerable political weight in Belgrade and could effectively defend their interests and press for speedy definite decisions. Third, owing to the already mentioned political arrangements between the Serbian political parties and the political party of the former Bosnian Moslem landlords, the issue of indemnities, at least for the former *agalik* lands, was speedily solved.

The first decree pertaining specifically to the Bosnian agrarian reform was issued on July 21, 1919. It ordered the authorities to transfer ownership and legal title from the landlords to the serf families. The former serf families were recorded as collective owners of their farms in the sense of the customary zadruga law. This decree provided also that land thus obtained could not be sold, foreclosed, divided, or encumbered for any other purpose but for the payment of taxes. By a special law of May 17, 1928, this family collective property was transformed into individual property and the institution of a protected minimum homestead was introduced into Bosnia and Herzegovina (p. 417). Former serfs obtained the land that they worked free of any charge. In accordance with the principles embodied in the Interim Decree and an agreement with the Serbian political parties, the former owners of the *agalik* lands obtained from the state an indemnity of 255 million dinars for all their rights. This indemnity was paid on the basis of the Decree on the Financial Settlement of Agrarian Reform in Bosnia and Herzegovina of May 12, 1921. Of the total amount, 125 million dinars was paid in cash and 130 million dinars in 4 percent, 50-year, government bonds. Smaller landlords obtained a relatively higher indemnity, and a larger portion of their indemnity was paid in cash. Generally, the indemnity for land was below its market value. Furthermore, from late 1923, when these bonds began to be traded on the Yugoslav stock exchanges, until June 1925 their price was below 30 percent of par, and since, during that time, most of the original recipients were forced to sell them because they had little or no other source of income, they actually received much less for their land than would appear on the surface.

Considerably more involved was the issue of the *beglik* lands. The claims of the prospective beneficiaries of the reform program for these lands constantly grew and found their expression in political pressures. On the other hand, the affected landlords sought to safeguard their interests through the political maneuvering which has already been mentioned. During 1919 only certain decisions with regard to the current crops and rents for *beglik* lands were made. A decree of basic importance for these lands was promulgated on February 14, 1920, but it was very unfavorable for the landlords. The tenants were also dissatisfied because the decree stipulated payment for the land by the prospective beneficiaries in some cases. Soon new regulations followed, of which the most important was the Decree on the Agrarian Reform on *Beglik* Lands of May 12, 1921 (the same day as the decree on financial settlements regarding the *agalik* lands). The final effect of these decrees was that those *beglik* lands which were worked in tenancy forms similar to serfdom (the relationships of *pridržnik, priorac, prisjevnik,* and *četvrtar*) were to be treated like *agalik* lands, provided they had been worked by the tenant uninterruptedly for ten years prior to February 25, 1919, that the duration of the tenancy contract was not limited, and that the livelihood of the tenant's family depended on keeping such land (which was true in most cases). Further legislation in regard to *beglik* lands was promulgated by the Law of December 3, 1928, the Law of September 14, 1929, and the Law of November 24, 1930. These laws made more potential beneficiaries of *beglik* lands eligible and, most important, specified that the state alone would pay all the indemnities to the landlords. In order to indemnify the former owners of the *beglik* lands, the government issued 500 million dinars worth of 6 percent government bonds, to be amortized in 43 years. When these bonds began to be traded on the Yugoslav stock exchanges in July 1930, their price was around 76 percent of par. But most of these bonds were also soon sold to speculators and various types of creditors. According to a special law, another 50 million dinars was paid to the former landlords for certain forest lands, but again in the form of 6 percent government bonds.

Approximately 4,000 families of former *agas* and *begs* were affected by the agrarian reform in Bosnia and Herzegovina. Many of them were actually reduced to poverty because they had lost their rents and tithes and the indemnity was insufficient to assure them a new start. The beneficiaries of the reform were, first of all, 113,103 families of former serfs (kmetovi), who obtained a total of 775,233 hectares of land (of this 566,076 hectares were cultivated land, 161,978 hectares forest land, and 47,179 hectares pastures).[9] Second, 54,728 families of various types of tenants on *beglik* lands (*beglučari*) obtained a total amount of 400,072 hectares of cultivated land. Undoubtedly, a considerable number of families in the above two groups were counted twice.

Two additional measures relating to the agrarian reform in Bosnia and Herzegovina were undertaken. First, the government undertook a limited program of internal colonization by distributing, between 1918 and the end of 1928, a total of 34,364 hectares of land, almost exclusively forest land from government property, to 13,806 families, mostly volunteers of World War I.[10] Second, because of steady encroachments of the peasants upon government-owned forest and pasture lands and their transformation into cultivated land, the government was forced to settle this issue. By the Decree of June 12, 1936, the government legalized all usurpations of state land by the peasants and stipulated the procedures about future granting of government land to peasants who needed it. In 1938 it was estimated that the number of peasants who had already usurped some state land and others who were waiting for the government to grant them some land was not less than 100,000, and that the land involved was approximately 600,000 hectares, most of which was already under cultivation.[11]

Because of the nature of the pre-1918 land-tenure system in Bosnia and Herzegovina, the agrarian reform had little effect on the number and size of the farm operating units. However, in other respects the reform brought about important changes. After the insecurities about the outcome of the reform had passed, the area of land under fallow was reduced, the planting of forage crops and industrial crops was increased, and, generally, the efficiency of agricultural work seems to

[9] Djoko Bogojević, *op. cit.*, p. 315.

[10] Yugoslavia, *Annuaire statistique 1929*, pp. 452–53.

[11] Djordjo Krstić, "Agrarian Policy in Bosnia and Herzegovina," A. Koen *et al.* (eds.), *Bosna i Hercegovina kao privredno područje* (Bosnia and Herzegovina as an Economic Area), p. 76.

have been improved. This was quite natural, as the increment in production did not need to be shared with the landlord. Needless to say, all these advances were rather slow in coming and were limited in extent, because the government was giving little assistance to the peasants, price developments and the tax load were unfavorable for the peasants, and the proverbial traditionalism and backwardness of the Bosnian peasants could not be overcome without much greater effort and perseverance.

REFORM IN DALMATIA

Article 7 of the Interim Decree of February 25, 1919, abolished the colonate system as well as all the vestiges of the feudal land-tenure institutions in Dalmatia. The former *coloni* and other long-term tenants in Dalmatia refused thereafter to pay tithes and rents to the landlords, whether these were defined in money or as a part of the crop. Owing to the great complexity in the land tenure in Dalmatia before 1918, and the political ramifications of the land reform issue, the definite solution of the problem in that province was delayed until 1930. The details of the reform were formulated in the Law of October 19, 1930 (effective November 5, 1930), and somewhat amended by the Law of March 6, 1931, but the actual processing of claims for land affected by the reform did not begin until 1933.

According to these laws, and in agreement with the principles embodied in the Interim Decree, the former *coloni* and various other types of tenants, including the so-called perpetual hereditary tenants and subtenants, became owners of the land they tilled, provided they or their ancestors had held that land for at least 30 years prior to November 5, 1930, and only up to ten hectares per family of six members (one-half hectare for each additional family member). To prove their right to various pieces of land they worked, the beneficiaries had to submit the necessary proof to county courts, which were handling the legal side of the reform. Only after the clearing of their right to the land were they recorded as full owners in the land property records. A survey of 1925 showed that in Dalmatia there were 96,953 families working about 53,000 hectares of land belonging to other people, but by May 1938 a total of about 102,000 petitions were submitted to the courts by the various types of claimants of land under the laws on agrarian reform in Dalmatia.

The indemnity for the land taken from the landlords was estimated by local mixed-claims commissions composed of one representative of the landlords, one representative of the beneficiaries, and the county agricultural agent as chairman. Land was classified into four different categories, depending on its quality, and the indemnity was assessed according to the following rules: (1) for all former feudal and other land which was held by former serfs, *coloni*, and different types of tenants and subtenants from before the beginning of 1878, the former owners were to receive a maximum indemnity of 10,000 dinars per hectare; (2) for land that had been leased after 1878 but had been held for at least 30 years prior to November 1930, a maximum of 20,000 dinars per hectare was to be paid. If the amount of land belonging to one landlord was less than five hectares, he himself was considered in a needy position and the indemnity for such land was set at a maximum of 30,000 dinars per hectare. The indemnity for land in the first category was to be fully paid by the state without any charge to the tiller of that land. In the second category the payment of the indemnity was to be equally shared between the beneficiary and the state. The same principle obtained for the payment of the arrears in rents. The beneficiaries alone paid the indemnity for the buildings and the state shouldered alone the court and administrative costs connected with the execution of the reform. The beneficiaries paid their charges to the state, together with regular land taxes, and their properties were mortgaged by the state for the respective amount. In the case of land that was subleased by the original tenant, it was given to the subtenant currently working on the land, while the original landlord got one portion of the indemnity and the original tenant the other portion for any improvements that he might have made on the land (planting of fruit or olive trees, vineyards, etc.).

All payments by the state were to be made in 6 percent, 30-year, government bonds. The government apparently contemplated the issuance of 400 million dinars of such bonds, which, on the average, would have been approximately 8,000 dinars per hectare for the 53,000 hectares of land estimated to be involved in the reform. This indemnity was considered very low. The legal and administrative procedures connected with the reform were, however, exceedingly slow and it appears that a considerable portion of claims for land under the above laws remained unprocessed when World War II broke out.

Regardless of the great delay in the processing of individual claims for land and the formal assumption of ownership, the Interim Decree of 1919 actually severed the semifeudal relationships between the former landlords and the peasants who worked their land, and led to the cessation of payment of rents and other obligations that attached to the land affected by the agrarian reform. How much the peasants paid on account of indemnity and arrears of rents between 1933 and 1940 is not known, but it could not have been much.

REFORM IN MACEDONIA AND IN THE SANDJAK OF NOVI PAZAR

In these areas the issue of the agrarian reform after 1918 was complicated by political, legal, and administrative factors. Until the liberation of these areas from the Ottoman Empire in 1913 there existed a degenerated system of feudal land tenure, its most important feature being the *čifči* tenure on large ownership units called *čiftliks*, though there were several other forms of relationships between the landlord and the people who worked the land.

Soon after the incorporation of these areas into Serbia and Montenegro, respectively, World War I broke out and there was no time either to execute the agrarian reform or to do much of anything else in or for these provinces. The consequences of the Balkan Wars and of World War I greatly complicated the issues involved in the reform. First of all, a great number of Turkish landlords left the area for Turkey either in 1912–14 or after 1918, and their lands were seized either by the *čifčije*, other tenants, or other independent landowners. Some simply remained unoccupied. The occupation of these areas during World War I by Bulgaria, Austria-Hungary, and Germany led, on the one hand, to additional expulsions and, on the other, to intrusions of new peasant population, complicating further the actual occupancy and ownership of land. Moreover, in these areas there were no land tax assessment roles (cadaster) or satisfactory land property records. The right to land use was attested by the *tapu*, but a great number of these documents proved on close inspection to be forgeries.

The Interim Decree of February 25, 1919, provided for the abolition of the *čifči* and similar land-tenure relationships. And as in other parts of the country, the peasants refused thereafter to pay the rents. In considering the agrarian reform in Macedonia and the Sandjak of Novi Pazar, referred to officially as the "reform in southern areas," two distinct issues have to be kept apart: the agrarian reform proper—that is, the abolition of *čifči* and like relationships—and the internal colonization. Both of these steps were important not only from a socioeconomic but also from a political point of view. They were ways of strengthening the Serbian or the pro-Serbian Macedonian element in areas which had large Albanian and Turkish minorities and a large pro-Bulgarian Macedonian segment. As explained earlier, the Macedonian nation was not recognized by official Yugoslavia during the interwar period, and the Serbs and pro-Serbian Macedonians were the element which was considered by the government to be in need of reinforcement. A certain proportion of *čifčije* were Moslem (Turkish or Albanian), and it appears that, by and large, they were treated in the same way as the Christian *čifčije*. In certain cases the Moslem and Christian landlords and Moslem and Christian *čifčije* were deprived of their lands in order to make room for colonists or for land grants to former members of the border police for their services to the government.

In spite of the fact that Macedonian Moslem landlords participated in the political horse trading involved in the adoption of the 1921 Constitution for concessions in regard to the agrarian reform, the solution of this problem in Macedonia was delayed until 1931 or 1933. The Law of December 5, 1931, on the agrarian reform "in the southern areas" distinguished between the former *čifčije*—that is, those people who worked the land of the landlords in a long-term relationship without a time limit uninterruptedly for at least ten years, beginning with October 1, 1912 (roughly the beginning of the First Balkan War)— and various other types of tenants, mostly with a time limit to their contracts (sharecroppers, tenants on private land, tenants on monastic land, farm hands), who were occupying particular plots of land on the day of the promulgation of the Interim Decree of February 25, 1919, without respect to how long that relationship had lasted. The *čifčije* were to obtain land up to five hectares free of any charge. If a *čifčija* had a large family or his farm was situated on poor soil, he could retain another ten hectares, but was supposed to pay as much to the state for that land as the state paid to the landlords. Unlike the *čifčije*, the other types of tenants had to pay for all of the land they obtained over a period of 30 years with 5 percent interest, but again only as much as the state paid to the landlords. As long as these people were indebted to the state, their farms were to remain mortgaged for the account of the state.

In 1931 it was contemplated that the indemnity for the land and the arrears in rents would be paid to the landlords in 5 percent, 30-year, government bonds, of which 300 million dinars were to be issued. But this was not the end of the story. On June 24, 1933, a new law was passed which changed considerably the provisions of the previous law. According to this law the state took over the obligation to pay the complete indemnity for all land the *čifčije* received, but all other claimants had to pay for the land they received. The old landlords were to be permitted to retain a relatively small amount of land if they needed it to make a living. Furthermore, the law provided that all indemnity for land would be paid in cash, for which a special fund of 100 million dinars was established with the State Mortgage Bank and also that the arrears of rents (the state had been paying these rents more or less regularly) would be paid in cash. It is generally agreed that the Macedonian landlords, by being able to obtain payment of the indemnity for the land and of rents in cash, fared much better than the landlords in any other area of Yugoslavia. This feat of the Macedonian Moslem landlords can be explained only by the fact that the dictatorial regime needed their support and this was one way of securing it.

The execution of the reform was handled by special county courts established for that purpose. Until the end of 1936 these courts received 38,592 claims for land. Claims of 20,457 *čifčije* and other claimants were processed and these families were proclaimed full owners of 125,550 hectares of land, or, on the average of 6.2 hectares per family. Another 154,264 hectares of land had been surveyed and partly processed. Until the end of 1936 a total of 40.7 million dinars had been paid to 4,687 former landlords as indemnity for their land. Thus, only about 40 percent of the anticipated indemnity had been disbursed by that date. More interesting is the fact that from 1919 until the end of 1936 the Macedonian landlords received 140.6 million dinars from the state as rent for the lands taken over by the *čifčije* and other claimants.[12] The processing of claims for land continued between 1937 and 1940, but the whole job was still unfinished when World War II broke out.

The colonization of peasants from other areas of Yugoslavia into Macedonia began almost immediately after World War I. To a certain extent it was only the putting into effect of a plan which was propounded by the Serbian government after the liberation of these areas in 1913. The legal framework which represented the basis of the colonization work in the beginning was the Decree of September 24, 1920, which was replaced by the Law of May 20, 1922. But for years this program remained poorly organized and even less satisfactorily financed and supervised. The basic rules of the colonization were as follows: The land for colonization was obtained from that owned by the state or local governments, unoccupied land, and from the landlords' surplus after the claims of their respective tenants had been satisfied. The standard farm for a colonist family was five hectares, but

---

[12] A. Urošević, "The Agrarian Reform and Colonization," Aleksa Jovanović (ed.), *Spomenica dvadesetpetogodišnjice oslobodjenja Južne Srbije, 1912–1937* (Jubilee Record of the Liberation of Southern Serbia, 1912–1937), pp. 827–28.

large families or families who brought along draft animals and farm implements could get additional land. The colonists were freed from all state and local taxes for a period of three years. The grant of land could not be leased. The full ownership of such land was obtained only after ten years of continuous living upon and working the grant. The state gave indirect help to the colonists by some land-reclamation work, by helping to build the facilities to supply potable water, etc. Some houses were built by the state for the colonists and it also helped with credit for building houses, buying animals and farm implements. This financial help, which was very limited in extent, was granted through special co-operatives established for the colonists, the so-called agrarian associations (*agrarne zajednice*).[13] In addition to colonists from outside the province, local landless and small peasants could also take advantage of the colonization scheme. One of the few limitations attached to these land grants, both before and after they had become the absolute property of the colonists, was the prohibition of utilizing credit from private sources without permission from government authorities. Their sole sources of credit were intended to be government organizations for agricultural credit.

In June 1931 a new law pertaining to colonization was passed, which, coupled with the laws on the agrarian reform in these areas, served thereafter as the legal basis for the colonization. By the end of 1936 the government had already earmarked about 350,000 hectares of cultivable land for colonization. Of this amount 161,637 hectares were already divided among 30,566 families. Of these, 14,972 families were natives who obtained 40,391 hectares of land, an average of 2.7 hectares per family. In most cases, native families obtained a supplementary grant to their already existing farm land, which they had as independent peasants or had obtained through the agrarian reform as former *čifčije* or tenants; while 15,594 families from other parts of Yugoslavia (about half of them from Montenegro) obtained 121,246 hectares of land, an average of 7.8 hectares per family.[14]

In spite of the meager economic and financial aid on the part of the government and the fact that, at least in the early stages, it operated in a haphazard way, the colonization in Macedonia during the interwar period was considered a successful experiment.

[13] Slavko Šećerov, *op. cit.*, pp. 143–50; A. H. Hollmann, "Kolonisation und Entwicklung der Landwirtschaft in Südserbien (Makedonien)," Germany, Ministry for Food and Agriculture, *Berichte über Landwirtschaft*, VIII, 269–94.

[14] A. Urošević, *op. cit.*, pp. 823–33.

REFORM IN VOJVODINA, CROATIA-SLAVONIA, AND SLOVENIA

As explained earlier, the land-tenure system in these areas in 1918 was very different from those in other areas of the newly created Yugoslav state. Here the problem of the agrarian reform was to separate a portion of land from the large estates and to divide it among the various types of claimants envisaged in the Interim Decree. These claimants were partly local landless, dwarf, and small peasants, partly colonists from other areas, partly volunteers, and partly refugees from the neighboring states, primarily Hungary. The first step was to define the size of the large estates. This was accomplished in an interim fashion by the Decree of July 21, 1919. Since the expropriation was not definite, the distribution of land to the claimants could not be definite, and the government resorted to temporary leasing of the land tentatively scheduled for expropriation. The Decree of April 10, 1919, provided that the expropriated lands could be leased for one year only, but the Decree of September 3, 1920, made four-year leases possible and provided that they could be extended until the final settlement of the reform and the transfer of ownership to the claimants. The land could be leased only to potential claimants under the agrarian reform legislation. A special Decree of February 11, 1920, put all large estates under the supervision of the state and many of them were temporarily sequestrated. Thus, the state had to see to it that they were worked and that the interests of the potential land claimants and, to a certain extent, those of the landlords were not prejudiced.

A Law of May 20, 1922, added some new categories of potential land claimants, e.g., poor local handicraftsmen. While other decrees provided that the volunteers were to obtain five hectares of land, this law of 1922 provided that local claimants obtaining supplementary land were to be limited to a maximum of ten cadastral yokes, including the land they previously held. The same limit applied to colonists and refugees. Exceptionally large families were able to obtain additional land. Since the distribution of land to the claimants was provisional in the form of leases, it was also necessary to establish and provide for payment of interim rents. The Decree of September 3, 1920, set the rents at eight times the pre-1914 cadastral net income, but in some cases the rents could be increased. However, the landlords had to turn over one-fourth of the amount received as rent to a special colonization fund established by the government.

A special provision was made in 1925, allowing the claimants entitled to obtain land from large estates to make individual arrangements with the landlords for the purchase of the land on relatively satisfactory terms. The conditions of these "elective purchases" were left to the parties concerned, but the government reserved the right to supervise the terms and even to forbid these arrangements if they were judged detrimental to the purchasers.

The issue of the agrarian reform in Vojvodina, Croatia-Slavonia, and Slovenia—or, as it was officially referred to, "reform in the northern areas"—was further complicated by the fact that some large estate owners were foreign citizens. The Hungarian nationals among them carried their grievance against the Yugoslav state's expropriation of their properties to the Permanent Court of International Justice in The Hague. The claims of these landlords (including similar claims in Rumania and Czechoslovakia) were finally combined with the issue of the so-called Eastern Reparations and settled by a treaty concluded in Paris, April 28, 1930. According to this treaty, a special fund, Fund "A," was established within the Bank for International Settlements in Basel, Switzerland, and this fund assumed the responsibility of paying the indemnity for the expropriated land belonging to the Hungarian landlords. This fund was to be financed partly by the Hungarian payments of reparations to various of its former enemies, and partly by the contributions of countries which expropriated the landed estates of Hungarian citizens in the course of their respective agrarian reforms.[15] This scheme collapsed, however, even before it was put into operation, together with the whole edifice of the German and Eastern Reparations. But, had there been no Treaty of Paris of April 1930 nor any so-called Protocol of The Hague of January 1930, which obliged Yugoslavia to settle definitely the agrarian reform in northern areas before July 20, 1931, this problem might have been delayed for a few more years. With the exception of those landlords of Hungarian and other foreign nationality, part of whose land was bought and paid for under the provisions of elective-purchase provisions established in 1925, it seems that foreign owners of large estates had not obtained any indemnity for the land expropriated from them.[16]

The agrarian reform in northern areas was essentially carried out

[15] Jozo Tomašević, *Die Staatsschulden Jugoslaviens*, pp. 65–66.

[16] The claims of former Turkish landlords who emigrated from Macedonia after the Balkan Wars or after World War I for the land affected by the agrarian reform have apparently been settled and paid for by a special agreement of 1935. The former landlords in Dalmatia who elected to move to Italy after World War I had a choice of accepting the same indemnity for their land that was given to Yugoslav citizens or of awaiting a special arrangement between Yugoslavia and Italy. It appears that such an agreement between the two countries was concluded in 1939. It is not known, however, whether any monies have been paid by Yugoslavia for these claims.

by the Law on Agrarian Reform on Large Estates of June 19, 1931.[17] Within less than six months an amendment to this law was enacted, granting certain additional concessions to the large estate owners (Law of December 5, 1931). By another Law of June 24, 1933, these concessions of December 1931 to the landlords were practically eliminated and certain other provisions were made which brought some additional land under the agrarian reform (additional forest land, land near the cities, additional land from monasteries and churches, and elimination of some types of land which formerly could be retained by the large landowners).

According to the Law of June 19, 1931, large estates were finally defined. Their size depended greatly on the quality of soil, the prevailing utilization of land, and the relationship between agricultural population and cultivated land in various areas. In the most overpopulated areas, such as Herzegovina and Dalmatia, large estates were defined as those having 87 cadastral yokes of cultivated land or 174 yokes of land in general. The size of large estates was gradually increased as the quality of land improved and as the relationship between agricultural population and cultivated land became more favorable, and in some areas, such as Vojvodina, Srijem, and some counties in other parts of the country, large estates were defined as those which had 521 cadastral yokes of cultivated land or 869 yokes of land in general. However, in all areas holdings of 100 or more yokes of cultivated land were considered large estates and thus were subject to the reform legislation if they were worked by tenants and not under the direct management of the owner. It must be stressed that the post-1918 agrarian reform in Yugoslavia affected large estates not only when they were owned by individuals (nationals or foreigners), but also when they were owned by churches, monasteries, municipalities, land associations and property communes in Croatia-Slavonia, and private corporations. In fact, landholdings of local governments which were leased to tenants were expropriated without respect to size. State properties which were managed by government employees, or government properties which served as experimental stations or in similar capacities, were not affected.

The Law of June 19, 1931, provided for expropriation of land from all large estates, with the following provisos: (1) The owners were left the so-called lower maximum of land, namely, an amount of cultivated

---

[17] This law applied primarily to the provinces of Vojvodina, Croatia-Slavonia, and Slovenia where the great majority of the large estates were located. But a few large estates were located in other areas of the new state outside of pre-1912 Serbia and Montenegro and the provisions of this law also covered these estates.

land identical with the limit of large estates in various areas, the lower
maximum varying thus between 87 and 521 yokes of cultivated land.
The landlord was at liberty to choose one-half of this lower maximum
from the whole estate, with the exception of land already distributed
to entitled claimants. For the second half of the lower maximum the
landlords were primarily entitled to vineyards, orchards, and land with
such improvements as drainage and flood control. (2) The landlord
was left a so-called upper maximum, which included the land with his
housing facilities, parks, uncultivated land surrounding land included
in the lower maximum, and additional pasture and forest land, but all
of this was actually included within the lower maximum of land for
that particular area as defined by the law. (3) Some large estate owners
were left a so-called supermaximum, consisting of lands and facilities
which served a public purpose, such as land producing quality seed,
orchard and grapevine nurseries, land producing rice, animal-breeding
stations, fish farms, etc. The supermaximum was granted only on the
basis of special investigations, and their special activities had to be
continued for at least 15 years. The state, furthermore, reserved the
right to buy a part of their production. Vineyards and parts of cultivated land which were given to employees of the large estates as part
of their remuneration, if such arrangements existed in March 1919,
were also included within the supermaximum. Churches, monasteries,
and local governments could apply for a supermaximum if it was needed
to carry out any of their special religious and cultural activities. The
Law of June 24, 1933, revised considerably the rules with regard to the
supermaximum. Thereafter, this special concession could not be
granted for grapevine and orchard nurseries, fish farms, or rice-growing.

The indemnity for land finally expropriated under this legislation
was set at the amount of the pre-1914 cadastral net income (crowns
taken as dinars) for second-class land multiplied by 160. This was the
indemnity per cadastral yoke for the first-class land, while for the three
lower-quality types of land it was reduced by 20, 20, and 50 percent,
respectively, below the preceding class. In overpopulated counties the
multiplier could be raised from 160 to 200 (this provision was removed
in 1933, leaving a general multiplier of 160). The indemnity was to
be paid, at the choice of the landlord, either in 4 percent bonds issued
by the Chartered Agricultural Bank (carrying government guaranty),
which had to be amortized in 20 years, or in annual cash payments with
5 percent interest paid by the beneficiary directly over a period of 20
years. When the landlord chose to take the payment in bonds, the
beneficiary who obtained the land paid his annual installments to the

Chartered Agricultural Bank. In both cases the land of the beneficiary was mortgaged for the amount of the indemnity outstanding. But the landlord had to pay the state, for administrative expenses and the colonization fund, between 10 and 20 percent of his receipts, depending on the extent of cultivated land in his original estate. It is not known what amount of 4 percent bonds was issued before 1940 for the payment of the expropriated large estates, or what amounts were paid by the beneficiaries of the reform directly to the landlords. But it is known that the agrarian reform in the northern areas was not fully completed when World War II began.

The number of large estates affected by the agrarian reform in the northern areas amounted to 720 at the end of 1935. Of these, 369 estates were owned by private persons, 50 by private corporations, 77 by churches and monasteries, 171 by municipalities and other communes, 44 by the central government, and nine by others. The total area of the estates at the end of 1935 was 2,219,149 cadastral yokes or 1,277,045 hectares. Of this area only 33.3 percent was expropriated by the end of 1935, 10.1 percent was bought from the large estate owners through the system of elective purchases, and 56.6 percent of the whole area was left to the landlords. Of course, the percentage of expropriated land varied considerably in the case of various groups, and, in addition, the expropriated portion of the large estates consisted predominantly of cultivated land while the area which was left to them was primarily forest land and pastures, although a sizable area of cultivated land was also left. From the area of 1,030,391 yokes of land owned by 369 individual persons, 429,911 were expropriated by the end of 1935 and 104,509 were bought from them, or altogether 534,420 yokes, while 495,971 yokes of land were left to them. A certain additional amount of land was expropriated from the large estates during the second half of the 1930's, but not so much as to change the picture markedly from what it was at the end of 1935. The most important point revealed by these figures is that the large estates were not fully but only partially expropriated. To most of them was left an area of land which permitted continued application of modern farm technology and continuation of any special farming functions which these large estates might have had before 1918.

It is interesting to note that among the 369 private persons who were owners of large landed estates affected by the agrarian reform 310 were foreign nationals. Of these, 142 were Austrians, 126 Hungarians, 10 Italians, 8 Czechoslovaks, 4 Rumanians, 3 Germans, and 17 others.

By the end of 1934 a total of 172,975 families benefited by obtaining land expropriated from the large estates. Another 54,874 families obtained land from these estates by elective purchases provided for by the legislation of 1925. Between 1935 and 1940 an additional number of families benefited from the reform, but this number could not have been high. Among the 172,975 families first mentioned there were, first of all, 143,891 local families who obtained, on the average, somewhat less than two yokes of land. But only a part of these families were formerly landless. The others obtained land to supplement their farms, and the limit of these farms was, as a rule, set at ten yokes. Second, there were 20,348 volunteers of World War I who obtained land through the reform. On the average they received 7.8 yokes per family. As in Macedonia, so in northern areas internal colonization was closely connected with the agrarian reform. In fact, 64 percent of all volunteers who obtained land in these areas came from other parts of the country as colonists. In addition, 4,271 other colonist families were brought in from other areas, and approximately 2,700 refugee families from the neighboring countries were colonized on the land obtained from the large estates.[18]

While the colonists in the northern areas, primarily in Vojvodina, Srijem, and Slavonia, had somewhat lesser difficulties to contend with than those in Macedonia, the state also gave these colonists only small assistance in addition to providing them with land. As in Macedonia, the assistance, especially in the form of credit, was administered through the agrarian associations. One difficulty which arose with the colonization in the northern areas was that these flat and sometimes marshy areas were colonized mostly by people from the karst region, who could not easily accustom themselves either to the climate or to the topographic situation in their new home, which also required a different type of farm work (primarily agricultural instead of largely pastoral). But as in Macedonia, the great bulk of the colonists in the northern areas overcame the difficulties and the colonization was generally considered a successful undertaking.

THE BALANCE SHEET OF THE REFORM

Though statistical data on the agrarian reform carried out in Yugoslavia during the interwar period are neither complete nor available for the late 1930's and while, in fact, that reform was not fully completed at the time World War II began, the available data make it possible to estimate approximately the number of landlords who were affected

[18] Otto von Frangeš, *Die sozialökonomische Struktur der jugoslawischen Landwirtschaft,* pp. 186–88.

by the reform, the number of people who benefited from the reform, and the approximate total area of land involved. In Bosnia and Herzegovina approximately 113,000 serf families and another 55,000 families of various tenants (some of these families counted twice) obtained approximately 970,000 hectares of cultivated land from approximately 4,000 landlords. Another 14,000 families in Bosnia and Herzegovina obtained about 34,000 hectares of state-owned forest land until the end of 1928 (other families obtained land from the state by usurpation). In Dalmatia perhaps several scores of thousands of families benefited from the reform by obtaining reportedly somewhat more than 53,000 hectares of land. The number of landlords in Dalmatia who were affected, many of them with very small properties, is not known. In Macedonia upward of 50,000 local families and colonists benefited from the reform, acquiring approximately 290,000 hectares of land from about 4,700 landlords and the state. The area of land earmarked for both agrarian reform and colonization in Macedonia during the interwar period was considerably greater and was estimated at approximately 600,000 hectares. In Vojvodina, Croatia-Slavonia, and Slovenia 250,000 families, mostly local but with some colonists from other parts of the country, obtained, roughly, 500,000 hectares of land until the end of 1935 at the expense of some 700 large estate owners, of whom only 400 or so were private persons and corporations while the others were local governments, churches, the central government, and other institutional holders.

Thus, a total of perhaps 500,000 peasant families (until about 1935), or more than one out of every four peasant families, benefited from the agrarian reform at the expense of about 10,000 to 12,000 landlords and various institutional landowners. The amount of land involved in the reform, including the land which was earmarked for that purpose by the mid-1930's, was well over two million hectares, not counting forest land.* This approximated one-fourth of all cultivated

---

* When this study was already in galley proofs we obtained a copy of a small statistical compendium—*La Yougoslavie par les chiffres*—published in Belgrade in 1937 by the Central Press Bureau (the information and propaganda office attached to the office of the Prime Minister), which gives (pp. 42–44) a balance sheet of the agrarian reform between 1919 and 1937. According to this source 637,328 households (242,259 in northern areas, 249,580 in Bosnia and Herzegovina, 48,536 in southern areas, and 96,953 households in Dalmatia) obtained a total of 2,484,481 hectares of land (555,137 in northern areas, 1,286,227 in Bosnia and Herzegovina, 593,117 in southern areas, and some 50,000 hectares in Dalmatia). The greatest difference between our figures and the figures supplied in this source refers to Bosnia and Herzegovina. As for the number of beneficiaries, there is no doubt that a certain number of households benefited both from the distribution of the *agalik* lands on which they were formerly serfs (kmetovi)

land in 1938. Needless to say, peasants did not benefit from the agrarian reform to the same degree in all provinces. In fact, in pre-1912 Serbia and Montenegro there was no reform whatsoever because here it was thought to be unnecessary when the reform program was initiated in 1918.

AN APPRAISAL OF THE POST-1918 AGRARIAN REFORM

The appraisals of the Yugoslav agrarian reform of the interwar period differed greatly among both domestic and foreign writers. A brief review of these differences of opinion seems to be in order here. It will also serve as a way of presenting our own ideas in regard to these points of difference.

It is necessary to distinguish between the appraisals of the reform in Bosnia and in Macedonia from those on the large estates in Vojvodina, Croatia-Slavonia, and Slovenia. The appraisals of the reform in Dalmatia, of which little was known, did not differ much. It was generally conceded that the reforms in Bosnia and Herzegovina and Macedonia were necessary for both political and socioeconomic reasons and that, owing to the very unsatisfactory land-tenure systems that previously existed, the productivity of land was increased after the reform, though not immediately. The liberated serf and the long-term tenant, who no longer needed to divide the product of their labor with a landlord, found it profitable to intensify their productive efforts, as the increment in production was solely to their own benefit. One of the important consequences of the reform in these areas was the reduction of area of land kept as fallow.

The differences of opinion regarding the reform in the northern

---

and from the distribution of the *beglik* lands which they held as tenants (*beglučari*). The actual number of households which benefited from the reform was thus smaller than here indicated because of double counting. The difference in the area of land distributed in Bosnia and Herzegovina between the two sets of figures is not too great if the forest and pasture lands are included. Moreover, our figures refer to an earlier date. As for the southern areas, it is quite certain that the area of land indicated in the compendium as already distributed to various beneficiaries includes not only the area actually distributed by 1937, but also the area earmarked for distribution, but not yet distributed. Figures for the end of 1936 given by us have been collected by a responsible author from the authorities on the spot, namely in Skoplje. The incongruity of figures relating to southern areas is indicated by another factor. According to this publication the average amount of land received by the local beneficiaries amounted to about 13 hectares, while the generally favored group of colonists received on the average only 10 hectares per family.

The same publication indicates that a large number of landlords of foreign citizenship (primarily Hungarians and Austrians) who were affected by the agrarian reform in northern areas became Yugoslav citizens by 1937. Undoubtedly, they did this in order better to protect their interests.

areas are many, and, occasionally, they are of a fundamental nature. However, it should not be forgotten that discussions of the effects of the agrarian reform in these areas were often greatly biased. These differences can be classified in the following order:

1. Some authors, especially von Frangeš, maintained that the Yugoslav agrarian reform after 1918 was a matter of charity. According to this view, the state distributed land which was affected by the agrarian reform in the northern areas in a manner which did not give to the overwhelming portion of the beneficiaries enough land to make them prosperous, medium-size peasants. In the opinion of this group, the medium-size peasants were not only able to be efficient agricultural producers, but could also (together with big peasants) serve as the conservative political and social backbone of the state. This latter fact was of basic significance in Yugoslavia and other nations of Southeastern and Eastern Europe which were exposed at that time to strong revolutionary ferment and communist influences. The small amount of land distributed to the bulk of the beneficiaries thus made the reform a matter of charity rather than a systematic policy operation aimed at maintaining or increasing production and achieving a greater social and political stability.

No author in Yugoslavia tried to deny that the agrarian reform had among other aims the objective of promoting social welfare. But some of the most important writers on the subject, such as Mijo Mirković, Dragoljub Jovanović, Dragan Turk, Blagoje Nikosavić, deny explicitly or by implication that charity was involved. Professor Mirković says that nobody gave any land or charity to the peasants, but rather that the peasants took the land as they always did when they saw that the old regime had broken down and that they could not be forced to old obligations or to renunciation of the acquired land. The new state was thus faced with a revolutionary *fait accompli* and matched this situation with a revolutionary act of its own by abolishing serfdom and serfdom-like institutions and expropriating a portion of land from the large estates in order that the peasants who had already taken the land could keep it. Actually the first stage of the agrarian change in post-1918 Yugoslavia was a truly revolutionary undertaking by the peasants themselves, and the whole legislation of the following 15 years was in essence only the legalization of the situation created in that early period.

Even if the government wanted to, which it did not, it could not have restored to the landlords their former rights. The times were revolutionary both in a national and a social sense. It should not be forgotten that in the northern areas five out of every six private, large-estate owners were foreigners, primarily of Austrian and Hungarian nationality, and thus the representatives of a foreign rule which had finally ended in 1918. On the other hand, there was the communist danger. In addition, the new state was exhausted by war, politically unsettled, and insecure in its international situation. Not even its frontiers were settled. It was, therefore, imperative to have as many peasants as possible behind the new state and there was no way of marshaling the peasant support other than by radical agrarian reform. The agrarian reform was thus an act of political, social, and economic necessity, and not an act of charity.

The need for the promotion of medium-size farms was a favorite theme of almost all Yugoslav agricultural economists during the inter-war period, because it was felt that the dwarf and small farms were incapable of utilizing most of the modern advances in agricultural technology and must, by definition, be considered inefficient. If the reform had attempted to assure a medium-size farm for its beneficiaries in the northern areas—that is, farms of about 7 to 15 hectares of cultivated land according to area (depending on the quality of soil, crops raised, density of population, etc.)—a much smaller number of families could have benefited from the reform. The additional number of families which actually did benefit from the reform would have remained either landless or with farms which were much less than five hectares. There are, however, several points which have to be considered in this connection. To acquire the land for distribution in these larger lots it would have been necessary for the government, first of all, to dispossess a great number of people who had already taken the land in the closing stages and immediately after World War I. Second, if the government had tried to allocate so much land to the beneficiaries of the reform, it would have created a small favored group of peasants, since more than 70 percent of the peasant families had farms of less than five hectares or were landless. For both of these reasons a policy of creating these larger farms by the reform would have been opposed by the over-whelming portion of the peasants. Moreover, the farm of about five hectares, which generally was taken as the standard for an average family benefiting from the agrarian reform, was popularly considered as sufficient to assure the customary plane of living in the Yugoslav village. A policy of creating a much smaller number, but potentially more efficient farms, was thus not feasible politically. Even if that had been possible, the few tens of thousands of medium-size farms would have been a drop in the sea of dwarf and small peasant farms and landless agricultural households already in existence in the northern areas. Moreover, without special precautions with regard to subsequent division of these farms, without ample provision of cheap credit, and without a satisfactory over-all situation in agriculture (especially regarding the terms of exchange between agriculture and industry)—none of which existed—most of these farms would have been reduced within one or two generations to the status of small or dwarf farms. Such a reform would have increased the cleavage between the landless, dwarf, and small peasants, on the one hand, and the medium-size and big peasants, on the other, and would have made the situation in the village politically and socially more rather than less explosive. Furthermore, the problem of criteria for selection of the few among the mass of landless and dwarf peasants who were to obtain the land from the large estates would have presented great difficulties. A mere listing of the possibilities—need for land, nationality, political pull, volunteering during World War I, good training as a farmer, physical presence—indicates the potential explosiveness of such a course of action.

Nobody would have been more satisfied than the Yugoslav peasants with an agricultural policy which would have made it possible for every peasant family to own a medium-size farm. However, such a solution of the land problem was and remained an impossibility for a very simple reason: there were too many people in relation to the available and potentially available agricultural land. Those who advocated medium-size farms of about 7 to 15 hectares in Yugoslavia of the interwar period could have secured them only by excluding approximately half of all peasant families from landownership. No one would have dared to even dream of such a course of action. In the dilemma between partially satisfying a large number of peasant households and completely satisfying only a fraction of them, the government chose the first, and only, possible avenue. Propaganda for the creation of these medium-size farms of 7 to 15 hectares through the post-1918 agrarian reform was thus quite naïve under the circumstances existing in Yugoslavia at that time.

2. It has often been claimed that the post-1918 agrarian reform was an important cause of the excessive subdivision of agricultural property in Yugoslavia. Undoubtedly, by taking a five-hectare farm as standard for an average family of volunteers, settlers, and landless local peasants, and by granting to other local claimants only enough land to raise their farms to that norm, the agrarian reform resulted in an increase of the relative proportion of small and dwarf farms in Yugoslavia. Moreover, many beneficiaries, even if they did not have land

of their own prior to the reform, did not obtain the theoretical standard allocation, but much less. The data supplied in Chapter 10 shows clearly, however, that already before the end of the nineteenth century the dwarf and small farms predominated in all Yugoslav provinces. In fact, the number of dwarf and small farms and of landless peasantry had been steadily increasing since the middle of the nineteenth century, owing to the growing rural population, the gradual disintegration of the zadruga, and the continuing penetration of capitalism into agriculture, which engendered a process of economic differentiation in the village. The larger percentage of small and dwarf farms in 1931, compared with the pre-1914 censuses (Table 27, p. 389), was a consequence of a complex long-term trend which was only strengthened by the agrarian reform.

3. It was claimed by some writers that by increasing the number of dwarf and small farms and by reducing large estates through expropriating a part of their land, the reform in the northern areas reduced efficiency in agriculture and thereby increased unit costs and in turn weakened the capacity of Yugoslav agriculture to compete successfully on foreign markets. In principle, production costs on dwarf and small farms, which cannot use advanced technology and cannot fully utilize their family labor, would tend to be higher than those on large farms, which can take advantage of modern technology and can achieve a better combination of their production factors. However, the fact that farms are large does not in itself mean that they are more efficient than the smaller ones, and the fact that the farms are small does not necessarily mean that they have to be inefficient. Efficiency depends on the nature of the product and the method of production on various sizes of farms, as well as on their location in relation to the market. It does not depend solely on size as such. Moreover, efficiency in farming in a region or a country should not be considered only with regard to one category of farms, but rather by relating the total population in agriculture to total agricultural production. With or without the reform, assuming that other factors had remained the same, the ratio of agricultural population to cultivated land would have been the same, and thereby the relationship between agricultural population and agricultural production also nearly the same. While in all of Yugoslavia the most important cause of low agricultural efficiency is the unfavorable ratio of agricultural population to agricultural land, there were many other reasons. Agrarian reform played only a minor role in this regard, and that only in northern areas.

As far as large estates were concerned, it is essential to remember that approximately 40 percent of these were owned not by individuals or private corporations, but rather by institutions like churches, monasteries, land associations, and by the local governments. In all these cases of institutional ownership the tendency was most probably toward low efficiency. Of the large estates owned by private persons, most of which were of feudal origin, there is little doubt that many of them did not switch to capitalist techniques of farm management, although they might have used some modern implements. The estates being to a great extent properties of absentee gentry, a large portion of them were exploited by their managers according to the principles of pillage economy. Many such estates, especially in Croatia-Slavonia, became overindebted, owing to the fact that they were mismanaged or that they had some other shortcoming, e.g., location on poor soil. As a result, they began to be subdivided and sold in small lots to the surrounding peasants or colonists even before the turn of this century.

Some of the large estates of feudal origin and others which arose as large capitalist enterprises in agriculture were administered by trained managers with an idea of realizing a profit on a sustained basis. Such estates used modern production methods, were usually well diversified in their production, and were efficient producers. However, it would be misleading to generalize on the conditions on such estates and to claim explicitly or by implication that these conditions existed on all large estates. Thus, while expropriation of land in excess of the legally allowed maxima might have and most probably did unfavorably affect productivity on the new farms, in comparison with the efficiently managed large estates, it is very doubtful whether it did so in comparison with the productivity on estates owned by institutions, local government bodies, the central government, or private persons who were poor managers.

It is generally recognized, however, that during the 1920's the productivity of agriculture in northern areas, as elsewhere in the country, was unfavorably affected and that the agrarian reform, as yet incompleted, was partially responsible. The peasant who benefited from the reform, having not yet obtained the title to the land—and that was the thing he believed in—continued to produce as before, lacking a genuine incentive to improve his production. The owners of large estates, not knowing exactly how much of their land would finally be expropriated nor how much they would receive in indemnity, were also reluctant to improve their production.

The fall in productivity of Yugoslav agriculture during the 1920's, reflected in the lowered yields and possibly in some lowering of quality,

was caused by many other very tangible factors in addition to the
agrarian reform. The following come readily to mind: disorganization
and exhaustion of agriculture during World War I, destruction and
deterioration of farm machinery and implements, reduction in the number of livestock and thus in the availability of draft power and stable
manure, the more urgent necessity for farmers to concentrate on putting
land under crops rather than on the increasing of unit yields. The tax
load of agriculture was greatly increased, and agricultural credit became harder to obtain and much more expensive. After about 1927
the foreign market for the products of Yugoslav agriculture gradually
shrank, and somewhat later a growing disparity developed between the
prices of agricultural and industrial products. All these factors tended
to push the yields down or to prevent them from rising.

A German agricultural economist, A. H. Hollmann, has pronounced
perhaps the most devastating judgment on the supposed consequences
of the agrarian reform in regard to productivity in Yugoslav agriculture:

If various branches of the [Yugoslav] national economy, and especially agriculture, are now behind what they were before World War I, this is for quite
some time not any more a consequence of that war, as many think, but a consequence of the planless breaking up of large estates by the agrarian reform. Ten
years of experiments in agricultural policy and the mistakes of the often changing parliamentary governments cost Yugoslavia a great deal more than all the
wars since 1912.[19]

Hollmann spoke with great confidence, though his conclusions seem to
have been based primarily on a series of estimates by Otto von Frangeš
(who in 1930, when Hollmann wrote, was Yugoslav Minister of Agriculture) regarding the drop in the yields of wheat, corn, and oats, and
on figures showing the reduction in the value of exports of horses and
cattle.[20] Later on, Frangeš used Hollmann as an additional authority
for his continuing criticism of the Yugoslav agrarian reform, but could
not fully accept the harshness of Hollmann's conclusions.[21]

Whatever was said during the 1920's and 1930's in Yugoslavia and
abroad about the reduced productivity in agriculture of the northern
areas as a consequence of the agrarian reform, it was entirely in the
nature of conjecture and not based on statistical evidence. It is obvious
in the light of the factors mentioned earlier that the unfavorable influ-

---

[19] A. H. Hollmann, *Agrarverfassung und Landwirtschaft Jugoslawiens*, p. 14.
[20] *Ibid.*, pp. 37–42.
[21] Otto von Frangeš, "The Agrarian Reform in the Northern Areas of Yugoslavia,"
Ekonomist, November 1935, pp. 343–53.

ence of the agrarian reform on productivity—and there is no doubt that there was some during the 1920's—is impossible to isolate from other causes. But if statistical proof is necessary that the agrarian reform alone could not be made responsible for reduced yields in agriculture, it is furnished by neighboring Hungary. In Hungary there was no agrarian reform during the interwar period worthy of the name.[22] The latifundia system remained intact throughout the interwar period (the short-lived Communist regime of Bela Kun from March to August 1919 meant no change), and still a decline in yields of wheat, rye, barley, oats, corn, potatoes, and sugar beets took place as against the pre-1914 years. Even the average yields of these crops in the period 1930–34 were still lower than those for 1911–15. These yields, in quintals per hectare, developed as follows:

Average	Wheat	Rye	Barley	Oats	Corn	Potatoes	Sugar beets
1911–15	13.0	11.6	13.4	...	17.2	78.9	250.1
1920–24	11.1	9.8	10.0	9.8	14.7[a]	58.2	174.6[a]
1925–29	14.0	11.4	11.4	13.4	16.7	74.5	220.8
1930–34	13.0	11.2	11.2	11.8	16.5	61.4	199.9

[a] Averages for 1922–24.

Source: Karl Geller, *Die Strukturänderung der ungarischen Volkswirtschaft nach dem Kriege und die Stellung Ungarns im mitteleuropäischen Wirtschaftsraum* (Münster in Westfalen, 1938), p. 32.

However, writers like Frangeš and Hollmann never mention the trend in Hungarian yields. It would have deprived them of their favorite criticism of the Yugoslav agrarian reform in the northern areas.

Even if a certain fall in yields had taken place in the northern areas of Yugoslavia and was an unavoidable price of the agrarian reform, it would be inadmissible, under the conditions prevailing in that country, or for that matter in any country of peasant farming, to take the yields or the efficiency of agricultural production as the sole criterion for judging agrarian reforms. This is an attitude that is always taken by

---

[22] The Hungarian government, controlled throughout the interwar period by the latifundia owners, also went through the motions of carrying out an agrarian reform. Between June 1921 and the end of 1928 the government acquired 539,727 hectares of land for subdivision. Of this, 33,545 hectares were granted to 258,378 families, or, on the average, 1,300 square meters as lots for houses, and 398,252 hectares were distributed to 403,980 families. Karl Geller, *Die Strukturänderung der ungarischen Volkswirtschaft nach dem Kriege und die Stellung Ungarns im mitteleuropäischen Wirtschaftsraum*, p. 68. The average amount of land thus distributed exceeded slightly one hectare per family. While the "hunger for land" of the Hungarian landless agricultural workers was probably slightly stilled, the obvious objective of this "agrarian reform" was to tie still closer to the land the landless agricultural workers and keep the agricultural labor cheap for the latifundia owners. This is a classic example of an "agrarian reform" on terms and for the pleasure of the latifundia owners.

the landlords and those who defend their interests. It is also often taken by those who for other reasons oppose these reforms; for example, out of fear that agrarian reforms may endanger the institution of private property or that they might lead to important political changes. Since, in Yugoslavia, only the agrarian reform in the northern areas was criticized on the basis of its alleged unfavorable influence on productivity, and since it is impossible to accept this criticism for most of the large estates, only productivity on land formerly belonging to a relatively limited number of efficiently managed, large estates could have been reduced permanently to any appreciable extent.

Finally, it can be asked, what advantage would the Yugoslav national economy and, above all, the Yugoslav peasantry have had from the preservation of the efficient, large estates owned by absentee, foreign landlords who siphoned off all profits abroad? It should not be forgotten that Yugoslavia was suffering from an acute case of agricultural overpopulation and that relieving of the population pressure was one of the foremost economic and social problems of the interwar period. To give only one example: The estate of 32,084 yokes of Count Czekonics in Banat was before 1918 a well-managed estate, producing grains, sugar beets, hemp, flax, tobacco, and high-quality livestock (it kept about 2,600 head of good cattle and 600 horses). The state expropriated from this estate 30,763 yokes of land and distributed it among about 4,000 families, partly colonists and former war volunteers, and partly local people. While it is not known how much the productivity on this land was reduced nor how much poorer the quality of the livestock became, the most important effect from the point of view of an overpopulated country was that an additional 4,000 families or thereabouts owned their own land. In addition, there were political advantages. Count Czekonics was a Hungarian and minorities were strong in Banat. The agrarian reform strengthened the Yugoslav element in that particular province.[23]

In the opinion of this writer—and in this regard he is in agreement with the overwhelming majority of Yugoslav economists as well as with the traditional view of the Yugoslav peasantry with regard to the ownership of land—a more just distribution of land and thus of income in agriculture is economically and socially more important than a small decline in productivity. Moreover, socially and politically the advantages of a just agrarian reform are immeasurable. Peasants in all lands yearn to own the land they till. Since democratic political and social ideas have penetrated into the huts of the peasants and they have

[23] Slavko Šećerov, *op. cit.*, pp. 103–5.

learned the advantages of political organization, the peasants have been on the move, and this movement will hardly come to an end until they obtain a system of land tenure that, by and large, they consider just. It is immaterial that agrarian reforms, especially in overpopulated, underdeveloped countries, do not solve completely either the economic or the political problems faced by the peasantry. The important point is that in all countries in which great differences in the distribution of land exist and in which no other opportunities are open to the peasants to make a living, the peasants think that an agrarian reform will improve their position, if not permanently at least temporarily. Besides, a just agrarian reform satisfies in many lands a fundamental need of the peasants as human beings because it frees them from one or the other kind of social bondage.

4. Some writers have maintained that one of the consequences of the agrarian reform was also a reduced export of cereals from the South Slav lands in comparison with the pre-1914 years. It appears to be true that exports of cereals, especially of wheat and flour, from the territory that since 1918 has formed the Yugoslav state were reduced in comparison with the exports prior to 1914, but because of the changes in boundaries it is impossible to illustrate this with exact statistics. There are several other reasons, however, which contributed to this development aside from the reduction in yields. The foremost change in this respect was the fact that prior to World War I the bulk of agricultural surpluses from the territory that in 1918 was incorporated into Yugoslavia was shipped into the domestic market, namely, the deficit areas of the Austro-Hungarian Monarchy. After 1918 most of these areas became foreign territory, and as foreign markets they became subject to customs duties, exchange controls, and other forms of protectionism. Second, the increase in population and increased urbanization of the country raised domestic requirements for grains, leaving relatively less for export. This factor became ever more important throughout the interwar period as the population kept growing. Third, all European industrial countries to which grains from the Danube Basin were sold inaugurated during the 1920's and strengthened during the 1930's policies of reagrarization behind tariff walls, quantity import controls, exchange controls, and administrative protectionist measures. Special efforts were made to increase their production of wheat. Fourth, owing to the mechanization of agriculture, the costs of production in extra-European cereals-exporting areas were greatly reduced and the countries of the Danube Basin, where agricultural technology did not advance in that period and where the

prices of land had a strong tendency to rise, found themselves at a great competitive disadvantage. Thus, again, it is impossible to isolate the influence of the agrarian reform on the export of cereals from Yugoslavia during the interwar period.[24]

There are a number of other criticisms of the post-1918 agrarian reform on which most of the writers agree, whatever might have been their differences in regard to the issues discussed above:

1. Most of the early reform measures, beginning with the Interim Decree, were promulgated without sufficient preparatory work. Shortcomings in this regard, as well as political pressures used by various interest groups, resulted in an avalanche of laws, decrees, orders, regulations, and clarifications. The effect was a constant change in procedures relating to the reform, which in turn resulted in administrative frustration, a sense of insecurity and frustration on the part of various land recipients, and encouragement of those whose lands were being taken away to push for concessions.

2. There was from the beginning too much politics in the agrarian reform, and this continued to be so until its legal completion in 1931. There was no government and no political party which in these years was not bent on making political capital out of the agrarian reform. If one keeps in mind the fact that the ministers in charge of the agrarian reform ranged from socialists in early 1919 to ultraconservatives between 1929 and 1931, it is easy to understand that the reform could not have followed either the same political line or the same economic line. Actually, as time advanced and the country moved from a parliamentarian state to a royal military dictatorship, the reform became less and less radical.

3. The long provisorium with regard to the reform in the northern areas, which lasted until 1931, necessitated not only temporary leasing of land taken away from the large estates and fixing of interim rents, but also the temporary management by government officials of the large estates sequestrated by the government. This last activity especially gave sufficient opportunity for graft. But it could not be expected that the administration of the agrarian reform program would be free from corruption when the whole government administration was graftridden.

---

[24] For a detailed analysis of similar effects of the post-1918 agrarian reform on agricultural production and livestock economy in neighboring Rumania, see David Mitrany, *The Land & the Peasant in Rumania*, pp. 284–365. See also his *Marx Against the Peasant*, pp. 99–117.

4. It was also generally agreed that tying of the issue of a bonus in land for the volunteers of World War I with the agrarian reform and colonization brought in a political factor which was bound to complicate matters. Here also there was considerable graft. The number of people who were able to secure documents testifying that they were volunteers and enabling them to benefit from the agrarian reform apparently exceeded by a large percent the number of bona fide volunteers. Moreover, many of the volunteers never even tried to farm the land which they were allotted but used it for leasing.

5. A further criticism referring to the treatment of various types of settlers was that the government provided these people only with land (in some cases it also built homes for them), while it failed to supply them with the necessary tools, draft power, sufficient and cheap credit, and expert advice in order to enable them to become prosperous farmers. Since the government paid practically no attention in this respect to other peasants, it is hard to imagine how it could have done all these things for those who obtained the land through the agrarian reform. The government left the whole peasantry to shift for itself. Moreover, it was generally thought that the acquisition of land was the chief problem. The volunteers and other colonists did actually obtain some help, but this help was very limited.

6. Finally, various writers have pointed out that the indemnification of former landlords was much below the market value of the land which was taken away from them. That was true also of the interim rents which were paid to them, though not regularly and not in all areas, during the provisorium. Besides, the overwhelming portion of the indemnities was paid in government bonds, which were selling at a high discount. This criticism, too, was in place, but under the Yugoslav conditions during the interwar period such an indemnity policy toward the former landlords was quite unavoidable. The landlords who were affected were not from the territory of pre-1912 Serbia, but rather from other areas which during the interwar period played a subordinate role in politics. The landlord class in general, and especially landlords of other nationalities or of the Moslem religion, had little power in Yugoslavia at that time, although on some occasions (e.g., the adoption of the Constitution of 1921) the latter managed to exercise a certain influence which secured for them special concessions. Moreover, there were many other examples of government policy which affected unfavorably the property rights of citizens. Those citizens who obtained from the government the indemnity for losses during World War I were paid in 2½ percent government bonds; former owners of Austro-

Hungarian crowns were unfavorably affected when that currency was changed into dinars through an exchange rate below the market value; the holders of Austro-Hungarian war bonds in the Yugoslav provinces got nothing; foreign and domestic owners of pre-1914 bonds of various Yugoslav provinces got only a percentage of the value of their holdings, or in most cases nothing; and, finally, some of the bonds issued in payment for wheat during the "wheat regime" of the early 1930's depreciated immediately after the issue. Moreover, through the legislation on peasant debts of the 1930's, the property rights of most classes of creditors of agriculture were unfavorably affected. Thus, it appears fair to say that the landlords did not fare worse than many other groups of people whose property rights were affected by the state directly or indirectly.

In conclusion this can be said: Agrarian reform in Yugoslavia after World War I was unavoidable. Both politically and economically it was unimaginable to maintain any vestiges of the feudal or semifeudal system under the conditions existing in the country at the close of World War I. The most important political consequence of the reform was the removal from the agenda of an issue that for almost a century was the focus of political discussion and activity. With the reform the peasantry in areas outside of pre-1912 Serbia and Montenegro achieved the same status as the peasantry of Serbia. From the Yugoslav point of view World War I had two objectives: national liberation and unification and the introduction of a democratic form of government. And while an appropriate agrarian reform may not result in the introduction and maintenance of democratic government, the persistence of a feudal or semifeudal landlordism in a country in which the overwhelming majority of the population lives from agriculture excludes a democratic form of government by definition, because it implies the existence of two types of citizens: a small favored minority, and a great majority with few or no rights but dependent for its livelihood on the first group. The agrarian reform after 1918 was also intended to stem the revolutionary ferment among the peasantry and to make the peasants willing to support the newly established order. The fear of more radical developments also explains the fact that the reform was accepted by the landlords in the beginning practically without opposition.

Socially and economically the reform freed the serfs and various types of serflike tenants from obligations toward their former landlords and declared them to be full owners of the land they tilled. In areas where large estates were the only vestiges of feudalism, these estates were reduced in size and the expropriated land divided among the needy peasants. In both cases a spreading of landownership ensued and thereby a more even distribution of income from agriculture.

While the revolutionary ferment among the peasants was temporarily stemmed and while the reform was a great political achievement and a decided socioeconomic advance, it neither solved the problem of the peasant's yearning for political democracy nor answered his quest for a basic improvement in his plane of living and economic security. The growing agricultural overpopulation during the interwar period, the unsatisfactory relationship between prices of products the peasant sold and those that he bought, the increasing need for credit, and the growing tax load caused an increasing number of peasants to look outside of agriculture for a part of their income. Still, the peasant remained tied to his land psychologically and economically—as he always has been—and he continues to consider his farm, however small and primitive, as his and his family's "place in the sun"; and the agrarian reform helped him to acquire that land.

CHAPTER 19

SIZE-STRUCTURE OF FARMS

FOR LACK of statistical data it is impossible to follow accurately the interwar development of the Yugoslav agriculture in terms of the number of farming units, property units,[1] or changes in the size-structure of farms. Only data on the number and size of farms and the area of land included in various size categories in 1931 are available. As we shall see presently, these data are unacceptable with regard to the land area. They can serve only as information with regard to the number of farms and as indicators of the order of magnitude of the amount of land agriculturally exploited by various size categories of farms.

FARMS BY SIZE IN 1931

Table 25 shows the distribution of farms by size, according to the census of 1931, and the area included in each category, both in absolute numbers and as a percentage of the total. According to that census there were 1,985,725 farms in Yugoslavia at the end of March 1931, which covered an area of 10,645,980 hectares. The area of land productively used, as given in the census, understated considerably the actual amount of land being utilized. This was so partly because the census covered only land owned by individuals and left out of consideration land owned by legal entities, such as churches, religious and other endowments, land associations, property communes, and governmental bodies, and partly because the peasants feared that a truthful declaration of their property might lead to higher taxation and therefore they had the tendency to understate the size of their farms. In areas where the cadaster and the land property records were in good order and the statements of the peasants could be checked, and in areas where institutional ownership of land was small, the differences between the census figures and the figures of the Ministry of Agriculture, which were based on all land recorded in the cadaster or otherwise estimated, were small. In other areas where cadaster and land property records were lacking or were poorly kept, and where institutional landownership was considerable, these differences occasionally exceeded one-

[1] As was pointed out earlier (p. 203), farm units in all South Slav lands, both before 1914 and during the interwar period, can be taken for all practical purposes as synonymous with units of ownership.

TABLE 25.—DISTRIBUTION OF FARMS BY SIZE ACCORDING
TO THE CENSUS OF MARCH 31, 1931*

(Number; area)

Size of farm in hectares	Farms		Area of land	
	Number	Percent of total	¹Hectares	Percent of total
Up to 0.5....	158,904	8.0	43,410	0.4
0.5 to 1......	175,532	8.8	135,760	1.3
1 to 2......	337,429	17.0	514,372	4.8
2 to 5......	676,284	34.0	2,287,570	21.5
5 to 10......	407,237	20.5	2,873,155	27.0
10 to 20......	174,068	8.8	2,380,826	22.3
20 to 50......	49,314	2.5	1,388,570	13.0
50 to 100......	5,156	0.3	338,076	3.2
100 to 200......	1,099	0.1	147,868	1.4
200 to 500......	494	0.0	146,549	1.4
Over 500.........	208	0.0	389,824	3.7
Total	1,985,725	100.0	10,645,980	100.0

* Source: Yugoslavia, *Annuaire statistique 1936* (Belgrade, 1937), pp. 88–89.

third and sometimes approximated one-half of the total agriculturally used area. The difference was especially important in arable land where the statistics of the Ministry of Agriculture for 1931 showed for the country as a whole an area 23.5 percent larger than the census. Except in this connection with agricultural units, the data on agricultural area as shown by the census of 1931 are never used in this study because they are obviously an understatement. We use data as published by the Ministry of Agriculture.[2]

[2] The census data and the data published by the Ministry of Agriculture for the same year, and by the same categories of land utilization, were as follows:

Type of land utilization	Census of 1931	Ministry of Agriculture statistics for 1931
	(In thousand hectares)	
Arable land	5,701.8	7,042.3
Gardens	143.0	150.7
Vineyards	179.8	199.1
Orchards	174.1	243.0
Meadows	1,473.2	1,818.9
Pastures	952.7	4,183.1
Forests	1,581.0	not given
Fish farms, marshes, etc.	167.3	155.9
Unproductive land	273.1	not given
Total	10,646.0	13,793.0

Census data from Yugoslavia, *Annuaire statistique 1936* (Belgrade, 1937), pp. 88–89; Ministry of Agriculture statistics from Yugoslavia, *Annuaire statistique 1931* (Belgrade, 1934), pp. 82–83.

Of the 1,985,725 farms, shown in Table 25, 16.8 percent were one hectare or less, 17.0 percent were between one and two hectares, and 34.0 percent were between two and five hectares. Thus, 67.8 percent of all farms in Yugoslavia in 1931 were five hectares or less in extent. Only 29.3 percent of all farms were more than five but less than 20 hectares, 2.8 percent of all farms were between 20 and 100 hectares, and only 0.1 percent, or 1,801 farms, exceeded 100 hectares in size.

According to the census of 1931, in 85,475 (26 percent) of 334,436 farms of one hectare or less, agriculture was a secondary occupation of the head of the household. This was also true in 10 percent of the farms between one and two hectares, as well as in 5 percent of farms between two and five hectares. While formally that may be true, there is no doubt that the bulk of farms of less than two hectares could not support a peasant family, even though the plane of living was exceedingly low, with the exception of labor and capital intensive farming such as wine production. These households, as well as a considerably larger proportion than 5 percent of those households with farms between two and five hectares, had to derive a portion of their income from other sources. Primarily it came from wage work in agriculture, from nonagricultural pursuits (lumbering, mining, industrial work, cottage industries), and from relatives abroad.

The average farm in Yugoslavia, according to the census of 1931, was only 5.36 hectares of land, most of it productive, but some of it of low productivity, such as pastures, and a small part of it completely unproductive. Considering the farm size-structure in 1931, Yugoslavia had to be characterized as a country of predominantly dwarf and small farms. This is a factor of basic significance because it influences all aspects of agricultural exploitation in the country. It influences the decisions on what to produce, the technology applied in agriculture and, thus, the productivity of agriculture, the level of employment that peasant families have assured on their own farms, the quantity and quality of agricultural production, the portion of production that is marketed, and the ability of agriculture as a whole to provide the people depending on it with a livelihood.

SIZE-STRUCTURE OF FARMS BY BANOVINE IN 1931

The 1931 data on the number and size of farms and the area of land they included were collected and published on the basis of nine *banovine*. As a rule, banovinal boundaries cut across the boundaries of the historical provinces. Because of this, the differences in sizes of farms among *banovine* were less pronounced than they would have been if these data had referred to historical provinces.

Table 26 shows the percentage distribution of various sizes of farms and the area of land they included in 1931 by *banovine*. These data indicate, as did the data obtained around the turn of the century, considerable differences in the size-structure of farms in various areas. The over-all indicator of the differences in the size-structure of farms is to be found in their average size in various *banovine*, which was as follows (in hectares): Drava 8.27, Drina 5.73, Dunav 6.37, Morava 5.22, Primorje 3.35, Sava 4.17, Vardar 4.63, Vrbas 5.57, and Zeta 5.74.[3] These figures show that the size of the average farm was largest in the *banovine* Drava and Dunav, while it was smallest in *banovina* Primorje. This situation in Drava and Dunav was at least partly caused by the fact that in some of their sections or among some of their people (e.g., the German minority in *banovina* Dunav), the principle of primogeniture governed the inheritance of agricultural property. In addition, in *banovina* Drava a considerable portion of forest land was included as agricultural land, population growth in this area had been smaller than in any other South Slav area since the middle of the nineteenth century, and the census coverage of agricultural land in 1931 was here relatively more complete than elsewhere because of the good cadaster. If only cultivated land had been taken into account, *banovina* Dunav would show by far the largest average farm unit. It may be mentioned here, though it will be discussed in more detail later, that *banovine* Dunav and Drava had a relatively much higher percentage of landless agricultural population than any other area in the country. This factor was also partly responsible for the larger average size of farms in these two areas.

FARM SIZE-STRUCTURE IN 1931 AND PRE-1914 YEARS
COMPARED BY HISTORICAL PROVINCES

In this chapter, as elsewhere, it has been necessary to use census and other statistical data on the basis of *banovine* as regional units because all statistics during the 1930's were collected on this basis. Unfortunately, these data on the size-structure of farms and the area of land included in each size group by *banovine* for 1931 cannot be compared without adjustment with similar data for various provinces obtained by the censuses around the turn of the century and presented in Chapter 10.

Since it is important, however, to show as closely as the available data permit the changes which took place in the size-structure of farms in the South Slav lands between the turn of the century and the census

[3] Yugoslavia, *Annuaire statistique 1936*, pp. 86–87.

TABLE 26.—PERCENTAGE DISTRIBUTION OF FARMS BY SIZE AND BY LAND AREA INCLUDED IN EACH SIZE GROUP, BY BANOVINE, IN 1931*

Size of farm in hectares	Yugoslavia	Drava	Drina	Dunav	Morava	Primorje	Sava	Vardar	Vrbas	Zeta
				NUMBER						
Up to 0.5	8.0	11.8	6.7	7.7	3.9	15.0	8.1	8.7	4.8	8.6
0.5 to 1	8.8	8.5	7.9	8.2	5.8	18.4	9.3	8.9	6.6	9.4
1 to 2	17.0	12.7	15.6	15.9	14.9	25.4	19.9	17.2	14.4	16.1
2 to 5	34.0	24.4	33.7	30.9	39.8	27.7	38.7	36.0	35.9	30.7
5 to 10	20.5	18.7	22.2	21.3	25.2	9.3	18.4	20.8	26.1	20.9
10 to 20	8.8	15.8	10.6	11.3	8.8	3.0	4.8	7.0	10.1	10.4
20 to 50	2.5	7.0	3.1	4.1	1.5	1.0	0.7	1.3	2.0	3.4
50 to 100	0.3	0.8	0.2	0.5	0.1	0.2	0.1	0.1	0.1	0.4
100 to 200	0.1	0.2	0.0	0.1	0.0	0.0	0.0	0.0	0.0	0.1
200 to 500	0.0	0.1	0.0	0.0	0.0	0.0	0.0	0.0	0.0	0.0
Over 500	0.0	0.0	0.0	0.0	0.0	0.0	0.0	0.0	0.0	0.0
Total	100.0	100.0	100.0	100.0	100.0	100.0	100.0	100.0	100.0	100.0
				LAND AREA						
Up to 0.5	0.4	0.4	0.3	0.3	0.2	1.4	0.5	0.6	0.3	0.4
0.5 to 1	1.3	0.8	1.1	0.9	0.9	4.3	1.6	1.5	1.0	1.3
1 to 2	4.8	2.3	4.4	3.7	4.6	11.5	7.0	5.7	4.1	4.3
2 to 5	21.5	9.8	20.4	16.4	26.4	26.6	30.2	26.5	22.9	18.4
5 to 10	27.0	16.2	27.9	23.5	34.2	19.3	30.0	31.5	33.8	25.9
10 to 20	22.3	26.9	25.9	24.4	22.8	12.2	14.9	20.5	25.2	24.9
20 to 50	13.0	24.0	15.4	18.3	7.7	8.3	4.6	7.9	9.8	17.0
50 to 100	3.2	6.5	2.7	5.0	1.2	3.2	1.2	1.4	1.5	5.1
100 to 200	1.4	3.1	0.9	2.0	0.3	2.3	1.0	1.0	0.6	1.3
200 to 500	1.4	3.0	0.6	2.1	0.2	1.1	1.7	1.0	0.5	0.5
Over 500	3.7	7.0	0.4	3.4	1.5	9.8	7.3	2.4	0.3	0.9
Total	100.0	100.0	100.0	100.0	100.0	100.0	100.0	100.0	100.0	100.0

* Source: Yugoslavia, *Annuaire statistique 1936* (Belgrade, 1937), pp. 86–87. Data for the Prefecture of Belgrade, which was almost completely urban, are not included.

of 1931, Table 27 was prepared. It was arrived at partly on the basis of an official recalculation (referred to in the table) of the 1931 census data to fit the territories of the peoples' republics as they exist since 1945, and partly by readjusting county data presented in that official recalculation to fit the old historical provinces. Table 27 shows the percentage distribution of the number of farms in various size categories both according to the pre-1914 censuses for the various historical provinces (not available for all of them) and according to the 1931 census for Yugoslavia as a whole and for the corresponding territories of all historical provinces.

Except for Croatia-Slavonia, data are not available for any other historical province on both the number of farms according to size and the land included in the various size groups in the pre-1914 years. Thus, we have to rely for our analysis on the relative numbers of farms in various size groups. Needless to say, it would be much more satisfactory if, in addition to relative numbers of farms, we had also the relative amounts of land included in the various size categories of farms in the respective periods.

The average farms in territories which corresponded to the historical provinces were in 1931 as follows (in hectares): pre-1912 Serbia 5.60, Croatia-Slavonia 4.39, Bosnia and Herzegovina 5.03, Dalmatia 2.98, Montenegro 4.85, Macedonia 4.49, Slovenia 8.27, and Vojvodina 7.15.[4]

THE TREND TOWARD EXCESSIVE SUBDIVISION
OF FARM LAND PROPERTY

A general conclusion, reached on the basis of the absolute numbers of farms in various areas, is that the growth in the number of farms was very great. By far the largest increase took place in Serbia, where the number of farms between 1897 and 1931 increased by roughly 74

---

[4] The historical provinces as presented here include all but about 25 of the 350-odd counties which existed in Yugoslavia in 1931. The excluded counties were, until 1913, parts of the Sandjak of Novi Pazar belonging to the Ottoman Empire. After the Balkan Wars they were divided between the kingdoms of Serbia and Montenegro. Since 1945 some of these counties have been directly incorporated into the People's Republic of Serbia, others into the People's Republic of Montenegro. But a majority of these counties now form the autonomous region of Kosovo-Metohija within the People's Republic of Serbia. This special status was given to this region because its population is mostly Albanian. The counties of Bosiljgrad and Caribrod, which until 1918 belonged to Bulgaria and were added to Yugoslavia after World War I, were also left out of consideration. All this was done in order to arrive at the pre-1912 territories of Serbia and Montenegro. Some very minor changes in the territories of Croatia-Slavonia and Dalmatia between pre-1914 years and 1931 were disregarded.

TABLE 27.—PERCENTAGE COMPARISON OF THE SIZE-STRUCTURE OF FARMS ACCORDING TO PRE-1914 CENSUSES AND THE CENSUS OF 1931, BY HISTORICAL PROVINCES*

Size in hectares	Yugoslavia	Serbia[a] 1897	Croatia-Slavonia[b] 1895	Bosnia and Herzegovina 1906	Dalmatia[c] 1902	Slovenia[d] 1902	Macedonia[e]	Montenegro[a]	Vojvodina[f]
PRE-1914 CENSUSES									
Up to 2		18.5	44.3	40.7	61.5	31.6			
2 to 5		34.3	27.2	26.4	25.8	19.4			
5 to 20		43.1	27.6	} 32.9	11.4	39.1			
20 to 50		3.8	0.7		0.9	8.5			
50 to 100		0.3	0.1		0.2	1.0			
Above 100		0.0	0.1		0.2	0.4			
Total		100.0	100.0	100.0	100.0	100.0			
1931 CENSUS									
Up to 2	33.8	24.4	36.5	34.0	64.2	33.1	40.7	48.2	33.8
2 to 5	34.1	37.7	37.9	34.6	25.4	24.4	33.6	27.7	27.2
5 to 20	29.2	35.6	24.4	29.2	9.6	34.4	24.0	19.9	32.4
20 to 50	2.5	2.2	1.0	2.0	0.7	7.0	1.5	3.4	5.6
50 to 100	0.3	0.1	0.1	0.2	0.1	0.8	0.1	0.7	0.8
Above 100	0.1	0.0	0.1	0.0	0.0	0.3	0.1	0.1	0.2
Total	100.0	100.0	100.0	100.0	100.0	100.0	100.0	100.0	100.0

* Source: The upper part of the table is based on Tables 4, 6, 7, and 8, pp. 204–8; the lower part is recalculated on the basis of data presented in Yugoslavia, Federal Bureau of Statistics, "Poljoprivredna gazdinstva predratne Jugoslavije prema popisu od 1931 g." (Farms in Prewar Yugoslavia on the Basis of the 1931 Census) (Belgrade, 1945), mimeographed.
[a] Territory prior to the annexation of areas acquired during the Balkan Wars.
[b] In 1895 Croatia-Slavonia used cadastral yokes (1 c.y. = 0.5755 hectares) instead of hectares. Thus the first category, 0 to 2 hectares, actually represents farms from 0 to 2.88 hectares, followed by categories 2.88 to 5.76, 5.76 to 28.77, 28.77 to 57.55, 57.55 to 115.1, and, finally, above 115.1 hectares. This has to be kept in mind when comparing relative figures for 1895 and 1931. Let the same relative figures for properties of 50 to 100 hectares and above 100 hectares, in both cases 0.1 percent for 1895 and 1931, give a false impression, it should be stated that this resulted from the need of rounding these figures to one decimal. The respective figures in 1895 were 0.135 and 0.144 percent, and 0.105 and 0.076 percent in 1931.
[c] In 1931 Dalmatia was without the small area annexed by Italy.
[d] In 1902 Carniola was taken as representative of the territory of post-1918 Slovenia.
[e] Territory of the People's Republic of Macedonia.
[f] Without Srijem.

percent. This increase was caused by the natural growth of population, by the disintegration of the zadruga, by the economic differentiation in the village, and immigration into Serbia from areas to its south and southwest, which was apparently very large prior to 1913 (see p. 153). Post-1918 agrarian reform had nothing to do with the increase in the number of farms in Serbia, as it did not affect this province. The next largest growth in the number of farms was probably in Bosnia and Herzegovina, followed by Dalmatia, and finally Croatia-Slavonia. For other areas such information cannot be supplied.

Table 27 enables us to see the trend of development of the size-structure of farms for a number of historical provinces over a period of more than three decades and for others for a shorter period of time. For some other provinces, such as Macedonia and Montenegro, data simply do not exist for the years before 1931, and the data for Vojvodina for the pre-1914 period could be obtained only by painstaking recalculations county by county on the basis of Hungarian statistics. The forces which influenced the development of the size-structure of farms in these years were many, but the most important among them were the following: the increase in agricultural population, the further disintegration of the zadruga and the general process of individualization of farm property, continuing economic differentiation in the village as a consequence of further penetration of capitalism into the economy of the South Slav lands, and finally (in areas outside of the pre-1912 Serbia and Montenegro), the post-1918 agrarian reform. Despite their many shortcomings, the figures in Table 27 show a strong tendency toward the growth of dwarf and small farm units, that is, units below five hectares, and a relative decline in all units of a larger size. To show this point, and to direct attention to it, was the chief objective in working out this table. This progressing excessive subdivision was the most outstanding development in the size-structure of farms in the South Slav lands during the past several decades. It not only reflected changes in the property structure of farm land, such as those that followed the agrarian reform of the 1920's, and the final stages in the process of zadruga disintegration, but most of all it reflected a growing discrepancy between the number of agricultural households, on the one hand, and the available agricultural land, on the other. Basically it meant that a process of pauperization was advancing in the village. Furthermore, under the conditions prevailing in Yugoslavia, it also indicated, in a large number of farms, a tendency toward lower productivity or at least an inability to advance technologically.

The growth of the dwarf and small farms has been going on at the expense of the medium and large peasant farms and also at the expense of the large estates (beyond and above the effect of the agrarian reform in this regard). In all provinces for which data for pre-1914 years are available, the percentage of medium and large peasant farms (those between 5 and 50 hectares) as well as of the large estates was reduced. In addition, there can be no doubt that the number of landless rural households which depended on agricultural and other wage workers was growing, though at varying rates in different parts of the country. While the process of pauperization in the village is obvious from the growth of the dwarf and small farms and from the increase in landless peasantry, the process of concentration of agricultural land in fewer hands, which is commonly accepted as the other side of the advance of the economic differentiation in the village, is not statistically provable in the Yugoslav case (see pp. 403–6).

A most interesting piece of statistical information bearing upon the problem of excessive subdivision of peasant property in the long run is the following series comparing the size-structure of farms in two groups of villages in Croatia-Slavonia in the late 1850's and again in 1924. According to these statistics, the number of farms by size groups was as follows:[5]

	Farms in late 1850's		Farms in 1924	
	Number	Percent	Number	Percent
WELL-TO-DO VILLAGES				
Total number of farms....	332	100.0	780	100.0
Up to 5 cadastral yokes...	77	23.2	545	70.0
5 to 15 cadastral yokes....	199	59.9	219	28.1
15 to 40 cadastral yokes...	48	14.5	15	1.8
Over 40 cadastral yokes...	8	2.4	1	0.1
POOR VILLAGES				
Total number of farms....	171	100.0	309	100.0
Up to 5 cadastral yokes...	104	60.8	209	67.6
5 to 15 cadastral yokes....	37	21.6	89	28.8
15 to 40 cadastral yokes...	20	11.7	9	2.9
Over 40 cadastral yokes...	10	5.9	2	0.7

The interesting disclosure contained in these figures is that in the wealthier villages there was a tremendous increase in dwarf farms up

[5] Both sets of figures as quoted in Mijo Mirković, *Održanje seljačkog posjeda* (The Preservation of Peasant Property), pp. 55–57. The figures for the late 1850's were published in 1859 by Og. M. Utiešenović, *Die Hauskommunionen der Südslaven*, p. 121; the figures for 1924 are those obtained by a survey of the same villages by Professor Stjepan Jurić of the University of Zagreb. Professor Jurić apparently failed to survey five of the original 14 villages, of which two were originally in the group of well-to-do and three in the group of poor villages.

to five yokes (about two and a half hectares), while the relative numbers of all categories of farms above that size were severely reduced. In the poorer villages there was a considerable increase in the relative numbers not only of dwarf farms up to five cadastral yokes, but also of small farms of five to 15 yokes. But again the relative proportion of farms above 15 yokes was greatly reduced. Here too it is impossible to see the process of concentration of land property in fewer hands. Professor Jurić, who surveyed these villages in 1924, gave the disintegration of the zadruga and the successive divisions of farm households as the principal reasons for the excessive subdivision of peasant property in these villages.

No figures are available that would show the development in regard to the number of farms and their sizes between the census of 1931 and the time Yugoslavia was invaded ten years later. It is probably safe to assume, however, that the old and persisting trend of further subdivision of agricultural property continued during the 1930's, and that in 1941 there was a relatively larger proportion of dwarf and small farms than in 1931. Furthermore, it is safe to assume that the bulk of farms which were formed during the 1930's did not arise by taking additional land under cultivation, but rather by subdividing the already existing farms.

THE PREVAILING CLASSIFICATION OF FARM UNITS

Because tenancy played a small role in Yugoslav agriculture and few people operated more than one farm, the number and type of farms reflected at the same time the property structure in Yugoslav agriculture. Judging by the land property scale—but always remembering that quality of soil, type of land utilization, agricultural technology in use, and nearness to the market greatly affect the economic position of individual agricultural households and of whole areas—the agricultural households in Yugoslavia of the interwar period could be divided into several categories. Going from the bottom to the top of the scale, the following six categories of farms can be distinguished:

1. There are the landless peasants, who are essentially agricultural wage-workers but who also work in rural and urban construction activity, in various industries, road transport, lumbering, and mining. The ways in which landless peasants make their living differ considerably in various parts of the country. In some areas, e.g., in Vojvodina and most of Slovenia, their income is earned while living at home or moving within a small area. In practically all other areas there is a periodic migration. Needless to say, the dwarf and many small peas-

ants follow the same pattern in order to earn needed additional income. According to the census of 1931 there were 1,963,403 households in Yugoslavia in which the head of the family derived the main income from agriculture while the number of independent agricultural owners and tenants was 1,769,948. The difference of 193,455 is a rough estimation of the number of landless agricultural households. The number of landless families was actually higher, since most of the tenants had no land of their own. The total number of people employed in agriculture in 1931 was 5,098,888, of which the bulk was self-employed because only 489,018, or 9.6 percent, were working for wages; 199,-432, or more than 40 percent, of the latter number were in *banovina* Dunav. The percentage of those employed in agriculture as wage workers was the highest in *banovine* Drava and Dunav, where it amounted to 22.7 and 22.5 percent, respectively. In other *banovine* it was much lower (in percent): Sava 9.5, Vardar 5.3, Primorje 4.6, Zeta 3.9, Vrbas 3.8, Drina 3.3, and Morava 2.0 percent. The people who worked for wages in agriculture supported 373,638 persons in 1931, so that the total number of persons living from agriculture and having no land amounted to 862,656, excepting tenants and their families who had no land of their own. Thus, whether one takes the households or the people employed in agriculture who did not own land, the result is roughly the same: approximately 10 percent of all the people living from agriculture were landless.[6]

2. The dwarf peasants with farms of up to two hectares of land accounted for 33.8 percent of all agricultural units with land in 1931, but the area which they controlled amounted to only 6.5 percent of agricultural land as shown by the census. These farms were quite evenly distributed over the entire country. While in a large portion of these households income from agriculture was of subsidiary significance and livelihood had to be largely based on income earned outside the home or even outside of agriculture, in the majority of these households, the farm, though small, was a primary means of livelihood. The economic position of the dwarf peasants was well characterized by Maksim Goranović when he said,

These farms cannot, even in years of bumper crops, produce enough grains and other essential foodstuffs to feed their families. For these peasants and their families these dwarfish farms are only a refuge giving them a roof over their heads and only a part of their annual food requirements. The share of these farms in the total agricultural production is negligible. In fact these are predominantly consumer and not [agricultural] producer households, which have to buy bread

6 Yugoslavia, *Annuaire statistique 1936*, pp. 36 53.

and other foodstuffs. To be in a position to buy these necessities, these peasants are forced to look for work outside of their farms, either as workers in agriculture, or as workers in industry, etc. Their interest is best served if prices of grains and of other agricultural products are low. All those factors which are favorable for the big and medium-size peasants, such as cheap agricultural machines, cheap agricultural credit, high prices of agricultural products, are of little significance for this category of peasants. They are much more vitally interested in the conditions of the labor market in industry, construction, etc. This is the core of peasant paupers.[7]

Together with the landless peasants, the owners of these farms of less than two hectares made up 42 to 44 percent of all rural households in 1931. They were undoubtedly the most difficult problem in the Yugoslav agriculture from the political, economic, and social point of view.

3. There are the small peasants with farms of two to five hectares. In 1931 they accounted for 34.0 percent of all farm units with land, but owned only 21.5 percent of agricultural land. This class of peasants is also quite evenly distributed over the entire country. Many of them, especially in areas of poor soil, primitive agricultural technology, and extensive cereal farming, are, in their economic position and psychological make-up, very close to or identical with the dwarf peasants. However, the larger among them who operate under more favorable conditions are very like the lower strata of the medium peasants.

Together with the group of dwarf peasants this category in 1931 represented 67.8 percent of all farm units with land, but held only 28.0 percent of agricultural land. Thus, more than two thirds of all peasants (except about 10 percent landless households in agriculture) owned just a little over one-fourth of all agricultural land.

4. There are the medium peasants with farms of between 5 and 20 hectares. They had 29.3 percent of all farms and controlled 49.3 percent of agricultural land in 1931. This category was the economic backbone of the Yugoslav agriculture, and the one that most Yugoslav agricultural economists and politicians of the interwar period wanted to expand. It is useful, however, to distinguish two subgroups here: farms with 5 to 10 hectares and farms with 10 to 20 hectares. The former represented 20.5 percent of the total number of farms and owned 27.0 percent of agricultural land, and the latter amounted to 8.8 percent of the number of farms and owned 22.3 percent of land. As far as economic and social standing was concerned, peasants with 5 to 10 hectares, depending on the region, were usually the lower strata of the

    [7] Maksim Goranović, "Our Peasant Property and Technology," Reprint No. 3, p. 4, in his collection of reprints: *Položaj seljaka u Jugoslaviji* (The Situation of the Peasants in Yugoslavia).

gazde (well-to-do peasants, *kulaks*). Only those peasants with 10 to 20 hectares, again with variations according to area, were considered as *gazde*. According to Yugoslav standards of the interwar period, the latter category was definitely considered as one of wealthy peasants.

5. The big peasants or *veliki gazde* with farms of 20 to 50 hectares accounted for only 2.5 percent of all farms, while they owned 13.0 percent of all agricultural land.

6. Finally, there are the farms and estates of more than 50 hectares. Farms in this category were only 0.4 percent of the total number, but held 9.7 percent of all land in 1931. Of these, 1,801 farms, or only 0.1 percent of all farms, had more than 100 hectares, and held not less than 6.5 percent of all land. It must be remembered, however, that the latter category of farm units accounted for only 2.8 percent of cultivated land. About two-thirds of their land consisted of forests and pastures. If this qualification is not made—and often it is not made on purpose— these 1,801 farms contained the same amount of land as 671,865 households with farms of less than two hectares.

Even if one takes into account all the qualifications with regard to the various types of utilization of land, the fact is that the few owners with farms of more than 50 hectares controlled a relatively large proportion of agricultural land in Yugoslavia while there was a great number of landless and dwarf peasants. Thus, in spite of a rather radical agrarian reform after World War I, the dichotomy in the agricultural property structure was not removed although the size-structure of farms became more uniform in all provinces than it was before 1914. Because of this continuing dichotomy in landownership and the growing pressure of population, there were many people who were arguing that the work of the post-1918 agrarian reform was not finished. They thought that among various measures which could help provide land for the growing number of peasant households there was a more equitable division of land, a new agrarian reform.

There were writers who, because of their special political or socio-economic proclivities, drew somewhat different lines of demarcation between various categories of farms. These differences were, however, not too pronounced, and the above classification approximates the opinion of an overwhelming majority of Yugoslav writers.[8] Since 1945

[8] *Ibid.*, pp. 3–4; Otto von Frangeš, *Die sozialökonomische Struktur der jugoslawischen Landwirtschaft*, p. 194; Nikola Konstandinović, *Seljačko gazdinstvo u Jugoslaviji* (Peasant Farming in Yugoslavia), pp. 12–16; Mijo Mirković, "Contemporary Problems of Yugoslav Agriculture," *Spomenica I Kongresa ekonomista Kraljevine Jugoslavije* (Proceedings of the First Convention of Economists of the Kingdom of Yugoslavia), pp. 132–35.

the Yugoslav writers have followed a somewhat different classification of farms, which, in fact, reflects the official viewpoint of the new Communist regime. According to this classification there is again the group of landless peasants, then the group of peasants with farms of up to two hectares who are referred to as "poor peasants with little land," the peasants with farms of two to five hectares who are called "medium-size peasants," the peasants with farms of 5 to 10 hectares or "the well-to-do peasants," and peasants with farms of over ten hectares who are classified as the "big peasants or village *gazde.*" Of course, this classification has now a more profound political and socioeconomic meaning than any classification in the interwar period could ever have had, because it now serves as a guiding line for the varied approaches of the government to the peasants.

The classification of farms in terms of area of land is an essential one. The size of individual farms exercises a profound influence on all aspects of the economic existence and behavior of their owners. Generally speaking, all peasants with farms of five hectares or more were able to produce all the necessary food for their families, while practically none with less than two hectares and only a portion of those with two to five hectares could do so. In a country with agriculture of an essentially subsistence character this is of fundamental importance. Although some peasants with farms of less than five hectares had the necessary draft power, it was, as a rule, only peasants with farms of more than five hectares who had sufficient draft power.[9] Needless to say, only peasants with farms of about ten hectares and above were able to take advantage of modern agricultural technology (and they did not always take that advantage). They could make the necessary capital outlay and take the risk of investment and innovation. As stated earlier, the landless peasantry and the great bulk of dwarf and small peasants had to look for work outside of their farms in order to live. A survey made in Croatia-Slavonia indicated that peasants with farms of five hectares of cultivated land and above did not look for work outside their farms, while peasants with farms of 15 hectares and above employed wage labor throughout the year. Of course, the type of crops raised was of basic importance in this regard. On the whole, the peasant family strove to do two things: first, to own enough land in order to employ its whole family labor force, that is, to have about two hectares of agriculturally used land per man labor unit, and second, to supply its food and other needs by its own production. That required about 1.5 hec-

9 Milan J. Komadinić, *Problem seljačkih dugova* (The Problem of Peasant Debts), p. 57.

tares of agriculturally used land per consuming unit.[10] The rate of marketability of production and the nature of the products marketed, as between crop and livestock products, differed with the size of the farm. As a rule, in areas in which specialty crops were not raised, only larger medium farms had genuine surpluses for the market, though small and even dwarf farms had to sell some of their production if they did not secure the needed minimum cash income in some other fashion. The need for and the use of credit also differed with the different categories of farms.

BASIC ECONOMIC SIGNIFICANCE OF MEDIUM AND BIG PEASANTS

The numerical strength of landless, dwarf, and small peasants and their economic and social problems are dealt with in detail in this study for two reasons. First, because these farm households form the overwhelming majority in the country as a whole and in each of its provinces and, second, because these households, which grew at an annual rate of 15,000 to 20,000 during the interwar period, represented the most outstanding difficulty in the Yugoslav village from a political, social, and economic point of view. But from the point of view of agricultural and livestock production, these farms, in spite of their great numbers, are much less significant, except in the case of some types of specialized farming, such as the production of wine, fruits, and some industrial crops (tobacco).

From the production point of view the core of Yugoslav agriculture is represented by the medium and large peasants with farms of 5 to 50 hectares. According to the 1931 census 31.8 percent of all farms were in this broad category and they included 62.3 percent of all agricultural land. The number of farms with more than 50 hectares and the land controlled by these farms were relatively so small that their contribution to total agricultural production and total marketed surpluses was not large. It is therefore the group of medium and big peasants, the strata of *gazde*, owning slightly less than one-third of all farms but including close to two-thirds of all land, which was the most important sector of Yugoslav agriculture from the point of view of production and surpluses for the market.

As explained earlier, the psychology of the lower strata of medium peasants is often very much akin to that of small peasants, though this depended on the area and the pattern of cropping. The psychological make-up of the medium and big *gazde* and their social position in all

---

[10] Slavoljub Dubić, *Prilog istraživanju seljačkoga gospodarstva* (A Contribution to the Study of Peasant Farming), pp. 57–60.

parts of Yugoslavia were those of an upper social group, one of prestige and leadership in the village affairs. Partly this goes back to the traditional leadership function of this stratum of village population; partly it was a result of the fact that they were economically much stronger than the other peasants, that they were always employing hired labor, and that they were often able to play the role of creditors in the village. Needless to say, their social position and greater economic strength are reflected in their whole level of living, which is shown in better houses, better nutrition, better clothing, and greater conspicuous consumption.

As far as the management of farming was concerned, medium and big *gazde* were the only ones who were able to produce sizable surpluses of farm and livestock products for the market and thus they were more influenced by the market situation than the other peasants. Many of them were also able to make capital investments in farm implements or better types of livestock and thus improve their production. But there were areas, as, for example, those south of the Sava-Danube rivers, where the management and technology on large farms differed very little from those on the small ones.

In most areas the big peasants were consciously trying to preserve the size of their farms, but the growth of population and the formation of new agricultural households by subdivision were responsible for the reduction in the relative number of these farm units.

It has already been shown, and it will become still clearer from further discussion, how different the problems of dwarf and small peasants were from those of the medium and big peasants in all aspects of agricultural economy. But it is necessary to stress at this point the key significance of the medium and large farms from the point of view of agricultural production. It should also be stressed that it was only this group of peasants which was capable of markedly improving agricultural technology and thereby increasing the total agricultural production and marketable surpluses. Of course, that was predicated on the creation and maintenance of incentives for increased production and marketing.

We have called naïve the propaganda for the establishment of medium peasant farms through agrarian reform and as a way of solving the problem of agriculture in Yugoslavia during the interwar period. This was done not because this type of farm was not desirable, but because a policy in that direction was impossible under the conditions which existed in Yugoslavia, since no other source of livelihood could be found for peasants who would have been displaced by this policy. Such policy could succeed only if the bulk of the surplus population present in agriculture could be assured of livelihood outside of agriculture.

A considerable number of farms between 5 and 50 hectares and a large percentage of those over 50 hectares were not owned by peasants, but rather by people who came into possession of land either through foreclosure of peasant land for debts or by buying of land for investment and speculative purposes, and who did not make their living by working the land. No information in this respect is available, although such information would be very valuable for better understanding of this sector of agriculture, and especially for seeing what portion of agricultural land was owned by nonpeasants, because limitation of that ownership had been discussed during the 1930's (see p. 423) as a means of making more land available for the peasants.

FRAGMENTATION OF INDIVIDUAL FARMS, AND THE PROBLEM OF LAND CONSOLIDATION

In addition to the fact that the bulk of agricultural units was in the category of dwarf and small farms, most dwarf, small, and medium farms as well as some larger ones were split into a myriad of separate parcels, lots, or scraps of land. This condition arose from the repeated division of farms as a consequence of population growth, disintegration of the zadruga, and the general process of economic differentiation in the village. To some extent this situation was connected also with the great variety in the topographic conditions, great differences in soil within small areas, and lack of land reclamation and improvement works. A diffused possession of parcels, often miles away from the family's homesite, served as a kind of primitive partial insurance against drought, floods, and hail.

The difficulties connected with and waste resulting from excessive fragmentation of individual farms were observed decades ago in most European countries, including both halves of the Habsburg Monarchy. The cure for it was thought to lie in the consolidation of farm property. Consolidation consists of putting together all land property of a village and the subsequent subdivision of the whole mass among the participating proprietors according to their individual contributions, whereby their consolidated property was reduced to only one or a few individual parcels. In both halves of the Habsburg Monarchy various laws intended to facilitate land consolidation were promulgated during the nineteenth century. In Croatia-Slavonia a special law for the same purpose was passed in 1902. Apparently in no other South Slav area belonging to the Habsburg Monarchy, with the exception of Croatia-Sla-

vonia, was any use made of the legislation on farm consolidation prior
to 1918. In Croatia-Slavonia consolidations began after 1902 and proceeded until the end of the interwar period. Consolidation was often a
precondition of land-reclamation work and was undertaken in many
cases together with such work. Some people thought that land consolidation and land improvements connected with it could have increased agricultural production in half of the villages of Croatia-Slavonia by 30 and even 50 percent.[11] This was undoubtedly too optimis-
tic a view. The consolidation work was progressing very slowly (it was
thought in the late 1930's that 25 additional years would be needed to
complete the task in Croatia-Slavonia), and because of its high cost it
was not too popular among the peasants.

The absurd degree to which fragmentation of farms had advanced
and the salutary effect of consolidations can best be seen by a few examples. In the tax commune of Brod on the Kupa River (all these
localities are in Croatia) there were, in 1939, approximately 400 families which owned 1,565 cadastral yokes of cultivated land, which in
turn were distributed in about 12,000 individual parcels. In the tax
commune of Krapina there were 1,032 families owning 3,980 cadastral
yokes of cultivated land, divided into 14,693 parcels. On the other
hand, in the tax commune of St. Helena, county of Križevci, one family
owned 13 cadastral yokes of cultivated land, which before the consolidation was split into 173 individual parcels. After the consolidation its property consisted of 12 parcels.[12] According to information
quoted by Otto von Frangeš, consolidation was carried out until the
end of 1935 in 201 tax communes in Croatia-Slavonia and covered
507,173 cadastral yokes of land. On the average, the number of parcels
was reduced through consolidation in the proportion of 5 or 6 to 1.
Moreover, this consolidation work resulted in building of a considerable
network of drainage and flood prevention dikes which otherwise could
not have been built.[13]

Fragmentation of farms is especially great in the karst region where
land is extremely scarce and every patch of it is worked, and where in
some areas, e.g., the Dalmatian islands, terrace agriculture is practiced.
To give one example: The farm on which this writer was born on the
Peninsula of Pelješac in Dalmatia was never and could not be exactly

[11] Viktor Setinski, "The Meaning and Importance of Land Improvements," *Gospodarska Sloga*, November 15, 1939, p. 4.

[12] Jure Petričević, "The Importance of Consolidation," *Gospodarska Sloga*, December 24, 1939, p. 5.

[13] Otto von Frangeš, *Die sozialökonomische Struktur der jugoslawischen Landwirtschaft*, p. 242.

measured. Its size in 1936 was carefully estimated at 2.85 hectares of cultivated land (since then divided into two parts, one family obtaining five-eighths, the other three-eighths). In comparison with other farms in the same commune, it was in 1936 probably among the top 20 percent of all farms. It was quite a specialized farm. The only cash crop was wine production, which was the basis of livelihood, though the farm also produced a considerable portion of the family's food requirements (some grains, olive oil, meat, and lard, and all potatoes, vegetables, fruits, and eggs). In 1936 this farm (actually consisting of two sections, one near the seacoast and the other on a plateau at an altitude of about 900 feet about three miles away) had 153 parcels, of which about 120 parcels were intensively cultivated. However, that particular area was characterized by very individualistic peasants, by capital and labor intensive agriculture, and by great differences in the quality of soil within small areas, and the peasants did not even think of the possibility of consolidation. On rare occasions individual parcels of land were exchanged if that served well the interests of all concerned.

This senseless fragmentation of individual farms into a myriad of parcels was, no doubt, a great barrier to technical improvements in agriculture and thus an important contributing factor to low yields. It is an extremely wasteful nuisance, causing not only great loss of time in going to and from different parcels, or groups of parcels, but presenting definite impediments in regard to the use of agricultural machinery, types of crops, and protection against floods. Requiring, as it does, innumerable trails in order to reach each parcel and a larger number of lines of property demarcation, it also is wasteful of precious land.[14]

LIMITED SIGNIFICANCE OF FARM TENANCY

In spite of the considerable dichotomy in the property structure in the agriculture of Yugoslavia during the interwar period and the large number of landless and dwarf peasants, only a relatively small amount of land was worked in tenancy. According to the census of 1931, only 439,490 out of 10,645,980 hectares of agricultural land were held in tenancy proper (the ratio of land held in tenancy to cultivated land was higher). Of this amount 222,899 hectares were leased with the rent

[14] For the influence of property fragmentation and long distance of individual parcels from the farmyard on crop rotation and on the profitability of farming see Stjepan Poštić, "The Influence of the Distance of Parcels on the Profitability of Individual Crops and Crop Rotations on Peasant Farms in the Neighborhood of Osijek [Slavonia]," University of Zagreb, *Godišnjak Sveučilišta Kraljevine Jugoslavije u Zagrebu za školske godine 1924/25–1928/29* (Yearbook of the University of Zagreb for the Academic Years 1924/25–1928/29), pp. 577–97.

defined in money, and 216,591 hectares were leased with the rent being a share of the crop. Furthermore, 182,628 hectares were held in usufruct and another 176,839 hectares were held by other arrangements. Unfortunately, there are no data on the number of farming units held or partly held in tenancy. The bulk of the area held in tenancy was, however, in the categories of farms of between 5 and 20 hectares, and that means that the number of units was not very high.

It is an interesting fact that in these four types of land tenancy *banovina* Dunav (actually Vojvodina) represented by far the largest area. Of the total the following amounts were located in *banovina* Dunav: of land where rent was paid in money 41.7 percent, of land where rent was a share of the crop 46.2 percent, of land kept in usufruct 25.1 percent, and of land held by other arrangement, probably including arrangements where the rent was given in the form of labor or management, 50.0 percent. Considerable amounts of land were also held in tenancy in *banovine* Sava and Drava, while in the six *banovine* south of the Sava-Danube line the area held in tenancy was very limited.[15] The prominence of *banovina* Dunav in regard to the spread of tenancy is easily understood. In Vojvodina agriculture was most specialized and commercialized, and there was a relatively greater number of large and medium farms as well as a large landless rural population. All these factors contributed to the spread of tenancy.

The smallness of the area held in tenancy may, perhaps, be partly understood as an outgrowth of the powerful urge of the Yugoslav peasantry to own the land they tilled and against tilling somebody else's land. The radical character of the agrarian reform in Yugoslavia after 1918 and the fact that it also affected certain relationships which were generally considered as matters of private contracts (*beglik* lands in Bosnia and Herzegovina and colonate in Dalmatia) made the owners of land probably less inclined to lease land for fear that after some time it might be affected by a new agrarian reform. However, it had been maintained, in connection with the idea of the progressing economic differentiation in the Yugoslav agriculture, that tenancy was on the rise. This was said to be true not only for Vojvodina where tenancy had a long tradition, but also for Bosnia, and for other areas. As far as sharecropping was the form of tenancy, it seems that a fifty-fifty arrangement prevailed. A special factor which furthered a rise in tenancy in Vojvodina and other northern areas during the 1920's was the agrarian reform whereby a considerable number of people who were not farmers obtained land (volunteers), and since some of them did

15 Yugoslavia, *Annuaire statistique 1936*, pp. 88–109.

not want to work it and could not sell it as long as the provisorium in regard to the reform persisted, they gave such land into tenancy.

The lack of more systematic data on tenancy during the interwar period, and especially the absence of this problem from the perennial discussions of agricultural problems during that period in Yugoslavia, tend to show that this issue was not considered a pressing and important one.

THE PROCESS OF ECONOMIC DIFFERENTIATION IN THE VILLAGE

It was generally accepted among Yugoslav scholars and administrators that the penetration of capitalism, in its psychological, economic, and institutional aspects, into the areas of patriarchal subsistence farming led inevitably to an economic (property) and social differentiation in the village. This process was supposedly marked by a growth in the number of landless, dwarf, and small peasants, on the one hand, and the strengthening of the larger farms, on the other. The basic idea underlying this view was that, when exposed to the influence of the market economy and competition, the family farm units are not capable of making a successful adjustment to new conditions or of withstanding the competition of the larger ones which could take advantage of modern technology and thus would be more efficient producers. The reasoning was similar to that of the relationship between handicrafts and industry.

Generally speaking, this theory is plausible. But to trace its working in this simple and elegant form in the South Slav lands and to prove it statistically is another matter. There is no doubt, however, that the basic idea behind the introduction of the protected minimum homestead in Serbia in 1836 and behind the discussions since 1850 in support of the zadruga in practically all South Slav provinces where it existed was to prevent the pauperization and proletarization of the village, on the one hand, and to prevent the concentration of land in few hands, on the other.

Actually, the beginning stages of the economic and social differentiation in the South Slav village did not take place as a consequence of better farming technology employed by the larger landowners. Originally the differentiation was the result of feudal and quasi-feudal factors, of the more ruthless land enclosure practices of those who already had more than the average amount of land or who had political power in their hands, of the fact that many wealthy peasants began to engage in trade and invest part of their trade profits in land, etc. As in most other respects with regard to economic development in the South Slav provinces, so in regard to the process of economic differentiation in the village, the situation differed from area to area. This especially applies to the differences in the effect of the technology and management on the differentiation process in agriculture. Generally speaking, in areas north of the Sava-Danube line, and especially in Vojvodina, Slavonia, and Srijem, a great majority of the larger farming units were using modern technology, and many of them were managed as business enterprises, so that their competitive advantage over the smaller units was an important factor reinforcing the differentiation process. But in some areas north of these rivers, e.g., in the extremely overpopulated Croatian Zagorje, dwarf and small peasant farms grew partly at the expense of large estates. Here, as once was observed, "the dwarf and small peasants ate up the large estates like rats." In areas south of the Sava-Danube line larger units seldom used a more advanced agricultural technology than the smaller units. Here production efficiency was not much higher on larger farms and could not have much affected the differentiation process in the village.

It was definitely not only the agricultural technology, and the resulting difference in the efficiency of production on larger and smaller farms, that contributed to the differentiation of agricultural property, nor was the degree of economic differentiation in the village mirrored solely or primarily in the difference in land property. On the whole, it is very easy to show statistically the growth in the number of dwarf and small farms (it is not easy to show the growth of landless peasantry) and the reduction in the number of the medium-size and large peasant farms. Thus, it is easy to see the process of pauperization and proletarization in the village, because the farm size reflected the whole property of small and dwarf peasant families. It is an altogether different and really unsolvable task to try to prove the process of concentration of land in fewer hands, because such concentration apparently did not take place in the South Slav provinces in recent decades.

It would be folly to think, however, that the absence of concentration of land in fewer hands as time passed meant at the same time that the process of economic differentiation did not operate in the South Slav village. The fact is that in the case of the wealthy peasants, rural usurers, merchants, and tavern keepers, and especially of nonrural absentee landowners, the ownership of land did not fully reflect their economic position and power. A part of the wealth acquired by these people in dealing with the village and exploiting it was kept in money form as usury capital or as trading capital in rural areas, was used for financing the education of the children of these families as the first step in their transplantation into the urban areas, or was completely pulled out of the rural areas and invested in those branches of the economy in which profits were higher or more secure, such as urban real estate, industry, or banking. Had these people not considered this diversification of investment advantageous, or had the land been the only means of wealth accumulation, a much larger proportion of agricultural land would have had to be concentrated in fewer hands in the form of larger farms. But the need for the diversification of investment and the pronounced propensity of the wealthier people in the rural areas of Yugoslavia to transfer part of their families to the towns[16] help to explain that, while the economic differentiation process was constantly at work in the village and the great mass of the peasantry became more and more pauperized and proletarized, the concentration of land in fewer hands did not need to take place. Thus, whatever the extent of dichotomy in the size-structure of farms in Yugoslav agriculture during the interwar period, it did not reflect the measure of economic differentiation between various groups of population in the village. It was only one of its components.

There have been authors who tried to prove the theory of the progressing land concentration in various Yugoslav provinces, though the usual procedure was to accept it without trying to prove it. Nikola Konstandinović, for example, based his proof on the fact that the number of farms with 100 or more hectares rose in Serbia from 74 units in 1897 to 136 units in 1931, a rise of 84 percent.[17] But the fact is that the relative share of farms of between 20 and 50 hectares fell in Serbia during that period from 3.8 to 2.2 percent of the total, or in absolute numbers it rose only from 10,277 units in 1897 to 10,458 units in 1931, and the relative number of farms from 50 to 100 hectares fell from 0.3 percent in 1897 to 0.1 percent of the total in 1931, or in absolute numbers it fell from 710 units in 1897 to 665 units in 1931 (see Table 27, p. 389). Finally, in 1931 all farms of 50 hectares and more in Serbia controlled only 87,530 hectares of land out of the total recorded amount of land of 2,667,273 hectares. That is 3.3 percent of the total and is hardly an argument with which to prove the theory of land concentration.

---

[16] The rural areas in Yugoslavia supplied the cities with two different groups of people: (*a*) landless and poor peasants who were looking for work in industry, transportation, police, and as domestics, and (*b*) children of wealthier peasants who could finance their schooling and prepare them for government service, professions, and white-collar jobs.

[17] Nikola Konstandinović, *Agrarna politika* (Agrarian Policy), Part I, pp. 105–7. He has slightly different figures, that is, a rise from 83 in 1897 to 143 in 1931. This is related to the differences in the adjustment of territory for pre-1912 Serbia.

Of course it should not be forgotten that even if a peasant formally owns his land, both his land and his labor may actually be pledged to his creditors, who in the form of usurious interest rates may be reaping practically all surplus above a sustenance barely sufficient to maintain life. In that case the fact that the peasant holds the land makes little difference from an economic point of view, as its fruits are impounded by creditors. There is no doubt that this condition was widespread in Yugoslavia in the interwar period (see Chapter 27).

The growth of dwarf and small farms was furthered by a great variety of factors. In one way or another most of these factors were related to the penetration of capitalism into the rural areas. Perhaps the most important single factor was the growth of rural population and the impossibility of increasing the amount of cultivated land in the same proportion. This worsened the rural population–cultivated land ratio and directly and indirectly helped the growth of small and dwarf farms because it stimulated repeated divisions of the existing farms. Second, the disintegration of the zadruga under the pressure of growing population and changes in the psychological and economic bases of life in the village also resulted in repeated splitting of peasant farms and the reduction in their size. Third, during the 1920's in all areas of Yugoslavia, with the exception of pre-1912 Serbia and Montenegro, the number of dwarf and small farms was increased as a consequence of the agrarian reform.

One of the important reasons for the numerical growth of dwarf and small farms and their persistence in the South Slav lands was also the psychology of the Yugoslav peasants. Even if they worked full time in mining or industry, or most of the year in some other occupation of the urban economy, and derived most of their income from that occupation, they wanted to keep or acquire a small farm. As explained above, dwarf and small farms, in spite of the fact that they were not able to secure a livelihood for the peasant family, were considered an indispensable part of that livelihood as a refuge in the case of need, as an insurance, or as a "place in the sun." Such farming was not considered a business proposition and it was not in competition with specialized and commercialized farming, except for land. The peasant did not want to sell his farm, however small it had become through repeated divisions or through other causes that reduced the amount of land in the hands of the individual families (sale, foreclosure, dowry, etc.). Thus an overwhelming number of these dwarf and small farming units were maintained, many of which would have been given up in other countries as hopeless propositions. This great propensity of the Yugoslav peasants to hold onto their land did not detract much from the tendency toward economic differentiation in the village. On the contrary, it probably contributed to the exploitation of the peasants, as they were willing to pay high prices for the land and exorbitant interest rates for the credit that helped them to maintain life on the land, and they were willing to accept extremely low wages in agriculture and industry to complement their meager income from the land.

SOME FACTORS CONTRIBUTING TO THE MAINTENANCE
OF LARGER FARMS

Some specific factors were contributing to the formation and maintenance of larger farms. First, some wealthier people besides the wealthier peasants, such as industrialists, merchants, lawyers, physicians, government officials, and artisans, invested a part of their investable funds in agricultural land and worked it either by hired hands or by leasing it. In this propensity of nonpeasants to own agricultural land one could detect several motives. As most of these people were recent descendants of the peasants, they probably felt a strong emotional attachment to the land. Many of them must have also felt that under the conditions existing in Yugoslavia during the interwar period land was one of the safest investments. And, finally, low wages in rural areas and the high rents for leased land made the investment profitable.

Second, a special factor which tended to keep larger peasant farms intact was the expanding custom of asking a dowry in land. This custom, which appeared since the disintegration of the zadruga, has undergone a great change in the past 60 years. Originally the dowry was given in the form of gold coins, commonly referred to as "ducats." But in more recent times land has become the chief consideration in the dowry, though the ducats, a good cow, and the regular bridal outfit of clothing were also important components. Because of this custom wealthier peasants allowed their sons to marry only girls who were able to bring some land into the family. And the parents of the girl, especially her mother, wanted their daughters to marry only into families which already had comparable property. The dowry was kept as a special property of the young matron, thus increasing her personal independence in the husband's family. This dowry was inheritable through the female line in most areas. Thus an appropriate matching of land became more important than proper matching of the newlyweds. This custom was especially widespread in Croatia-Slavonia and Vojvodina and became almost a curse in the village.[18] There is little doubt that this expanding custom of the dowry in land was only another expression of the general problem of hunger for land and of the fear of wealthier peasants that their farms might be reduced in size. The dowry in land and its inheritance through the female line became problems of such importance that in all interwar discussions on the reform of landownership and inheritance the idea was propounded that girls when they marry could not take any land from their father's family, but should become full-fledged participants in the ownership of land in their husband's family.

Third, a special group of people, numerically small but represented in all parts of the country and easily identifiable, who often owned larger farms were the returnees from overseas emigration, known under the common name of "Amerikanci," though they might have spent their years abroad in Australia, New Zealand, South Africa, or a dozen countries other than the United States. But most of them were, actually, returnees from emigration in the United States. After their return home these people generally used a part of their savings to build or repair their houses and to enlarge their farm, and quite a number among them used a part of their savings in business ventures, including usury in the villages.

A specific factor contributing to the economic differentiation in the village, which operated during the whole interwar period, was the usurpation of state forest and pasture land and its transformation into privately held cultivated land. According to Judge Djordjo Krstić, a leading expert on problems of agricultural policy during the interwar period, official surveys of these usurpations in Bosnia showed that it was the wealthier peasants who took the largest share of these lands, knowing well that as pillars of the existing political regime they would be able to get away with it.[19]

Finally, among the members of the German minority in Vojvodina,

[18] Nada Sremec, "The Dowry in Land," Rudolf Bićanić and Željko Macan (eds.), *Kako živi narod* (How the People Live), II, 173–81. The issue has been masterfully discussed by Slavko Kolar in his stories dealing with peasant life in the Croatian Zagorje. See, for example, "His Body's Master" and "The Marriage of Imbro Futač." For Serbia, Jelenko Petrović, *Okućje ili zaštita zemljoradničkog minimuma* (The Protected Minimum Homestead), p. 155, reported that where before 1914 there was the custom to give a sum of money as "price" for the bride, giving of a dowry in land became the rule after World War I. This development in Serbia was, however, partly related to the scarcity of marriageable men due to great losses in the war, so that the dowry in land made the bride more attractive to the bridegroom.

[19] Djordjo Krstić, "Agrarian Policy in Bosnia and Herzegovina," A. Koen *et al.* (eds.), *Bosna i Hercegovina kao privredno područje* (Bosnia and Herzegovina as an Economic Area), pp. 76–78.

Slavonia, and Srijem, the maintenance of larger farms was a conscious policy of all farmers. To that effect they practiced land inheritance according to the principles of primogeniture, used early marriage and dowry as deliberate tools of maintaining or increasing the size of farm units, and practiced a very strict system of birth control (the rule was to have one or two children). Birth control and dowry as means of maintaining the size of farm units were used by all national groups and religious dominations in these areas, although not to the same extent.

USURY AS A FACTOR CONTRIBUTING TO ECONOMIC DIFFERENTIATION IN THE VILLAGE

The factor which contributed greatly to the economic differentiation in the village was the spread of the use of credit by the peasant population, and this was a direct result of the penetration of a money and market economy in the South Slav village. The need for credit was related, to a large extent, to the fact that the wants of the peasant population under the influence of the spreading market economy rose faster and continued to rise faster than the income of the population. Use of credit was also related to the wish of many peasants to own more land, to unfavorable terms of trade for the peasantry, and to the mounting tax load imposed upon the peasant population.

Because of the onerous interest rates, sometimes because of outright fraudulent actions on the part of creditors, and because of the unfavorable terms of trade between agriculture and industry, debts easily grew into overindebtedness, and foreclosures for nonpayment of debts followed. Foreclosures were a way in which a certain amount of land was steadily slipping out of the hands of the medium and small peasants into the hands of wealthier peasants and those nonpeasants who dealt closely with the village as country storekeepers, tavern keepers, lawyers, and professional usurers. Often these people did not keep the land thus acquired, since it was usually possible to profit more by selling it and using the proceeds again in usury and/or in trade. We know from earlier discussion—and this issue will be raised again—that in order to prevent mass transfer of agricultural land from the hands of the indebted peasants into the hands of their creditors, government intervention was invoked in some areas by the institution of a compulsory protected minimum homestead, and the peasants were urged not to use credit. When a large transfer of agricultural land into the hands of the creditor group threatened during the Great Depression, a moratorium for peasant debts was proclaimed (see Chapter 27).

The large indebtedness of agriculture in 1932 serves as partial evidence that there was a strong process of economic differentiation at work in the Yugoslav village during the interwar period. Even if approximately 90 percent of all peasant households owned some land, a large portion of them did not derive sufficient income from that land to live upon it. Furthermore, a third of all peasant households were indebted, and most of them were paying a tribute in the form of extremely high interest rates to the creditors. The expansion of the compulsory, protected, minimum homestead legislation, discussed in the following chapter, showed that further separation of the peasants from the ownership of land was considered a persistent threat, and for political and socioeconomic reasons the government was called upon to forestall this development.

CHAPTER 20

STATE MEASURES TO SAFEGUARD THE LAND
IN THE HANDS OF THE PEASANTS

THE GREAT line of development from the beginning of the nineteenth century to World War II in the South Slav lands was toward the breaking down of all feudal and quasi-feudal land-tenure relationships and the establishment of peasant freeholds. But it was soon found that the achievement of freehold alone does not solve the problem of the peasant's quest for land. There was a tendency for the land to slip out of the peasants' hands. It was also found that to secure the land for the peasants was hardly less difficult or less important than the conquest of the freehold. This task became harder as time advanced and brought about a worsening of the population–cultivated land ratio, greater dependence of agriculture on the market and credit, greater pressure upon agriculture because of recurring business fluctuations, and finally it became harder as the tax load of agriculture grew. The classic reaction of a large portion of peasantry in Western Europe to this general process was the mass exodus from the land into the domestic urban economy, which grew rapidly under the impact of industrialization, or into overseas emigration. Both of these currents also developed in the South Slav lands. However, because of its relatively limited development the domestic urban economy could not absorb a large percentage of the rural population, and the overseas emigration got under way rather late and then was made impossible by prohibitive immigration legislation in the countries to which South Slav emigration was primarily directed. Thus the bulk of the increase in population remained on the land. This made the general economic position of agriculture more precarious, and the ability of a large portion of the peasants to own land, and especially to keep enough of it in their hands, became more difficult.

From our discussion of pre-1914 conditions in Serbia and Croatia-Slavonia we saw that various measures to secure the land in the hands of the peasants were undertaken with the avowed objective of forestalling the pauperization and proletarization of the village. Although these measures were purely defensive and hardly capable of achieving their basic aim, the maintenance of a minimum amount of land in the hands

411

of the peasants and the prevention of an increase in the numbers of rural landless proletariat were considered by most people to be a rule of economic and social policy as well as a rule of political wisdom. It is, therefore, not surprising that during the interwar period, and especially during the 1930's, when the position of the peasantry worsened rather than improved, considerable attention was directed to various reform and protective measures which were supposed to have some salutary effect on the condition of the peasantry. There were three different courses of action for securing the land in the hands of the peasants: (1) prohibition against the disposition or encumbrance of land obtained by the agrarian reform until specifically allowed by law; (2) moratorium for peasant debts incurred before April 19, 1932, and their later reduction and consolidation; (3) establishment of a minimum homestead protected against foreclosure for debts to private persons and for taxes owed to the government. Furthermore, a need for reform of landownership and inheritance principles for the peasants was widely discussed.

LIMITED FREEDOM IN DISPOSING OF LAND OBTAINED BY AGRARIAN REFORM AND COLONIZATION

As shown earlier, Article 22 of the Interim Decree on the Preparation of the Agrarian Reform prohibited those who received land under that decree from selling, mortgaging, or transferring it until this had been permitted by special legislation. Furthermore, a special Decree of July 21, 1920, prohibited the owners of large estates which were affected by the agrarian reform from selling or encumbering any part of their property. In both cases the idea of the legislator was to allow no action that might prove prejudicial to the intents and purposes of the agrarian reform as formulated in the Interim Decree. Special legislation which regulated the disposal of land obtained by the agrarian reform in Bosnia and Herzegovina was passed in 1928. The limitations that were placed upon the disposal of that land will be shown presently. In Dalmatia, Macedonia, Vojvodina, Croatia-Slavonia, and Slovenia the power of free disposal of land obtained by the agrarian reform was acquired a certain number of years after all formalities connected with the execution of the agrarian reform legislation were completed. As stated earlier, in areas where a considerable number of volunteers of World War I obtained land, the limitation on free disposal, pending the completion of the agrarian reform, favored its leasing into tenancy. But after the volunteers had acquired full ownership of this land, many of them, especially those who were not peasants of plow and hoe or who had acquired easier ways of making a living, sold their grants. The wealthier peasants were apparently the chief buyers of such land. As far as the people who benefited from the agrarian reform and who remained bona fide peasants were concerned, these limitations on the free disposition of land helped them to hold onto their land or to hold it for a longer period of time. These rules, as long as they remained in operation, prevented the peasants who obtained land through the agrarian reform from using it as collateral for credit that, some people argued, might have been applied to improve the production. But these were all small farms, and encumbering of the land would have been done, as a rule, for consumption credit, so that agricultural production was probably little affected by these limitations.

MORATORIUM FOR PEASANT DEBTS OF 1932

The moratorium for peasant debts became effective as of April 19, 1932. The same legislation provided for an elective moratorium for all commercial and savings banks in the country. In the process of settlement of the peasant debts, which was mapped out in subsequent years and culminated in the Decree of September 25, 1936, a large portion was canceled outright, and the remainder was consolidated and payable, beginning in 1936, at a reduced rate of interest, over a period of 12 years. Already in 1939 it had become obvious that a revision of this supposedly "final" 1936 scheme of settlement was necessary, but the outbreak of the war prevented it. (For a detailed discussion of agricultural credit and the settlement of peasant debts see Chapter 27.) The important point to stress here is that through the intervention of the state the chief mechanism by which land was slipping out of the hands of the small and medium peasants into the hands of wealthier peasants and nonpeasant creditors of agriculture was temporarily arrested in its operation at a time when it otherwise would have been most potent. The moratorium for peasant debts made the peasants unable to obtain credit as before and forced a part of the peasants to operate on a practically moneyless and creditless basis. But had the mass foreclosures been allowed, assuming that the peasants would have remained inactive, which is hardly probable, a large percentage of the peasants would have remained landless, or with only a protected minimum homestead, and thus unable to obtain credit through regular channels. On the other hand, the wealthier peasants and the nonpeasant creditors of agriculture would have taken over considerable amounts of additional land. This, naturally, would have greatly increased the economic differentiation in agriculture. Mass foreclosures, as in many other countries, could not be allowed during the Great Depression for both socioeconomic and political reasons, so that the forces working for increased economic differentiation in agriculture through the mechanism of credit were temporarily prevented from exercising their full effectiveness.

It is interesting to note that during the 1930's the state itself formally allowed a longer time for the payment of tax arrears, including the overdue land taxes of the peasants. Payment of the bulk of these tax arrears was, however, unenforceable, and toward the end of the 1930's some tax debts of the peasants were written off. On the whole, the relief in direct taxes granted to the peasants during the 1930's under the stress of the depression was slight. This was the more so as the tax collectors were instructed by the Ministry of Finance not to observe the letter of the various laws with regard to the easing of the payment of tax arrears. As in earlier times in Serbia, so also during the interwar period in Yugoslavia the government was willing to protect the peasant against the private creditor and even against himself, but showed only limited willingness to protect him against itself as tax authority.

LEGISLATION ON THE PROTECTED MINIMUM HOMESTEAD

A very interesting set of measures designed to secure the land in the hands of the peasants refers to legislation regarding the protected minimum homestead. In our earlier discussion we saw that such an institution had existed in the Croato-Slavonian Military Frontier from 1807 until its demilitarization in the 1870's and in Serbia (with an interruption) since 1836. In Montenegro also there was, after 1905, a protected minimum homestead measure against foreclosure for debts.

In order to present the development better, it is advisable to distinguish between the legislation against foreclosure for taxes on the smaller protected minimum homestead and that against foreclosure for private debts on the larger protected minimum homestead. In both cases, in addition to the protected minimum homestead, there was also a protected minimum of movable accessories.

The protected minimum homestead measure against foreclosure for tax debts continued in Serbia after 1918 in its formulation of 1907. Protected against foreclosure were the house of the peasant, the lot around the house up to 2,000 square meters, one pair of draft animals (oxen, cows, horses), one cart, and one plow. Such protection did not exist in areas outside of Serbia between 1918 and 1929. An almost identical provision was incorporated in Article 151 of the Law on Direct Taxes of January 8, 1928. This law unified the direct tax legislation for the whole country and became effective on January 1, 1929. It appears, however, that in this law the protection of the minimum of movable property was made conditional; that is, it was protected against foreclosure as long as the peasant had other movable or immovable property from which the payment of the tax could be enforced. Furthermore, Article 34 of the Decree of November 19, 1928, which regulated the procedure for enforcement of tax payments, protected against foreclosure the necessary clothing, food, and fuel needed by the tax debtor and his family for 14 days, one cow (or two goats or three sheep) with the necessary feed for one month, monies obtained by the tax debtor from public funds as assistance in the case of natural disasters, and monies obtained as insurance against natural disasters. These provisions remained in force until the end of the interwar period. It was well known, however, that the tax collectors often disregarded the letter of the law in this respect and attached supposedly protected property, especially livestock, as means of exerting pressure upon the peasants to pay their taxes.

The development of the protected minimum homestead legislation against foreclosure for private debts had after 1918 an interesting and somewhat involved history. The best way to follow it seems to be by provinces. In the Interim Fiscal Act for the period July–September, 1923, the government obtained, at the proposal of a Serbian deputy, the power to extend the Serbian protected minimum homestead legislation in full or in part over the whole of the remaining territory of the new state. This enabling legislation was opposed in practically all areas outside of Serbia by many individuals (agronomists, agricultural economists, politicians) as well as by federations of credit co-operatives. They based their opposition on the grounds that this legislation would reduce the capacity of the peasants to use credit and therefore that it would hinder the modernization of agriculture, that the institution was not applicable to more advanced economies, and finally that the institution of the protected minimum homestead was claimed to be unsuccessful in Serbia itself. Faced with such opposition and lacking any support from the peasantry in areas outside of Serbia, the government failed to use its powers.[1] The chief reason that this proposed legislation failed to evoke any interest among the peasantry outside of Serbia can most probably be found in the fact that at that time Yugoslav agriculture still enjoyed the prosperity which followed World War I.

In Serbia the first change came about with the passing of the new, unified Bill of Exchange Act of October 17, 1928, which became effec-

---

[1] Jelenko Petrović, *Okućje ili zaštita zemljoradničkog minimuma* (The Protected Minimum Homestead), pp. 138–42; quoted hereafter as Petrović, *Okućje*.

tive in 1929. This law granted the Serbian peasant the right (denied to him by Article 77 of the Serbian Commercial Act of 1860) to borrow money on the basis of bills of exchange, but if enforcement of the bills of exchange became necessary, it was impossible to invoke the protection under the minimum homestead legislation. More important for the development of the institution in Serbia was the passage of the Law on the Chartered Agricultural Bank, April 16, 1929. An Act of February 25, 1930, amending the Law on the Chartered Agricultural Bank, provided in its Article 55 that peasants in Serbia, as well as in other areas in which the institution of the protected minimum homestead existed, who obtained loans from the bank lost protection in regard to the minimum homestead in case foreclosure became necessary. Thus the old argument that the institution of the protected minimum homestead was preventing a modern and rational organization of agricultural credit won out. While opening a possibility for cheaper agricultural credit to the Serbian peasant, the establishment of the Agricultural Bank, so far as he used it, robbed him of the traditional protection. In 1936 the Agricultural Bank took over peasant debts to commercial and savings banks and credit co-operatives which existed as of April 19, 1932 (see Chapter 27), and the peasants had to repay them to that bank, thus losing the traditional protection in regard to these debts. The Law on Execution and Safeguarding of Judgments (roughly corresponding to sections dealing with execution, attachment, and garnishment of the California Code of Civil Procedure) of July 9, 1930, valid for the whole country, failed to include provisions similar to those for the Serbian protected minimum homestead. The effective date of this law was postponed, however, and when it became effective by a special Decree of June 4, 1937, it was expressly provided that both the Serbian and the Montenegrin legislation on the protected minimum homestead should continue to be valid.[2] Thus, with the exception of the indebtedness toward the Agricultural Bank and the indebtedness on the basis of the bills of exchange, the famous Serbian institution continued in operation until World War II. There is no doubt in the mind of this writer, however, that had the Agricultural Bank ever attempted to enforce the payment of its loans, including claims resulting from the consolidation of peasant debts of 1936, by large-scale foreclosures, its privileged position would have been eliminated. Such is the inescapable conclusion from the history of the institution of the protected minimum homestead in Serbia.

[2] Živojin M. Perić, "The Institution of the Protected Minimum Homestead in the Serbian Agrarian Law," *Ekonomist*, July–August, 1939, p. 311.

According to the legislation of 1919, the former serf and tenant families who benefited from the agrarian reform in Bosnia and Herzegovina were declared to be collective owners of the land so obtained in terms of the customary zadruga law and, as such, recorded in the land property records. This, admittedly, was a temporary arrangement. By a special Law of May 17, 1928, passed unanimously by the parliament, this collective type of landownership was replaced by individual ownership. But in order to forestall excessive splitting of these farms, certain provisions with regard to their division, to the rights of women in the family's land property, and to inheritance and priority in buying of land from relatives who might be selling it were incorporated into this law. In addition, this law established the institution of the protected minimum homestead (*najmanja površina*) for Bosnia and Herzegovina. This protection gave mandatory coverage only to land obtained by the agrarian reform, but was elective to other peasants in Bosnia and Herzegovina if they wanted it and made the necessary public declarations. The protected minimum homestead could be neither encumbered nor foreclosed nor freely disposed of except after securing a corresponding amount of land in another locality. These actions were allowed only in specified cases and required previous permission from government authorities. The protected minimum homestead (Article 28) included the house of the peasant, a lot around the house, other buildings necessary for the orderly conduct of the peasant's farm, and one hectare of land for each member of the family, of which at least six-tenths must be cultivated land.[3] The minimum homestead could be encumbered as security for loans, but only for loans from government credit organizations, for productive (not consumption) credits, and with government permission. This minimum was not protected against foreclosure for taxes, or for debts incurred with government permission from specified credit organizations, or for debts toward the former members of the household for land or alimony, or for damages caused by criminal acts.[4] This protection was not valid for debts to the Agricultural Bank or debts on the basis of bills of exchange.

With the exception of the moratorium legislation on peasant debts in 1932 and its amendments in the following years, the passing of the Law on the Chartered Agricultural Bank and its later amendments, and the passing of the Law on Execution and Safeguarding of Judgments (Zakon o izvršenju i obezbjedjenju) of July 9, 1930, there was no new

---

[3] For certain counties in Herzegovina, where land is scarcer than in Bosnia and cultivation more intensive, the protected minimum is smaller.

[4] Petrović, *Okućje*, pp. 143–49.

legislation aiming at or affecting the existing protection of a minimum peasant homestead against foreclosure for private debts until October 1939. On October 17, 1939, less than two months after the conclusion of the Agreement (Sporazum) whereby the Croatian Peasant party entered the Belgrade government and obtained a limited degree of autonomy for Croatia (p. 239), the government in Belgrade passed a decree establishing a protected minimum homestead in the territory of *Banovina* Croatia. It covered existing as well as future debts. By this decree the minimum of immovable property protected against fore-closure for private debts comprised the house, the yard and lot around the house up to 2,000 square meters, a minimum of one-half hectare of cultivated land per person in the family or a minimum of three hectares of cultivated land per family, and buildings necessary to conduct suc-cessfully the operations on the protected minimum homestead (Articles 1 to 3 of the decree). The protection did not extend to foreclosures for damages caused by criminal acts.[5] As in other parts of the country, there was no protection against foresclosure for debts to the Agricul-tural Bank and debts evidenced by bills of exchange.

The important difference between the provisions of this decree and the provisions of the laws pertaining to the protected minimum home-stead in Serbia and Bosnia and Herzegovina was that the decree for Croatia did not prohibit or limit the sale of land by the peasant himself. The institution itself was intended, of course, to deter him from encum-bering the minimum property by precluding foreclosure (except as shown above). The zadruga households in Croatia-Slavonia, as we saw earlier, were prevented by the Law of 1889 (Article 12) from encum-bering the so-called minimum area or homestead (*najmanja izmjera*) except in specified cases. It was also provided that zadruga households could not be divided if the resulting households would be smaller than the minimum area foreseen by the law (three to eight cadastral yokes, depending on area).[6] The Decree of 1939 did limit the capacity of the peasant to use credit, as did similar laws in other provinces. As could be expected, this became the chief point of criticism of the De-cree of October 17, 1939. It was answered by the laconic explanation that the peasant needs first the roof over his head and then credit. With

---

[5] *Gospodarska Sloga*, November 6, 1939, p. 1.

[6] As we have mentioned earlier (p. 88) this provision of the laws of 1889 and 1902 was evaded by a mass recourse to "secret divisions" which were real and complete, except that they could not stand up in the courts. But periodically the government would sanction by special legislation the existing secret divisions and thus make them legal. Such a legalization of secret divisions of the zadrugas in Croatia-Slavonia as of March 30, 1939, occurred also through Art. 125, sect. 8, of the Fiscal Act for 1939/40.

the introduction of the protected minimum homestead, the Croatian Peasant party fulfilled one of the planks of its program of 1921.[7] This decree was the only important agraro-political measure of the Croatian Peasant party in its second participation in government during the interwar period.

The decree on the protected minimum homestead for *Banovina* Croatia did not mention the protection of a minimum of movable accessories for the peasant household. This was unnecessary since such protection had already been provided in the Law on Execution and Safeguarding of Judgments of 1930, which became effective in 1938. This law applied to all citizens, but parts of it were of special importance for the peasantry. Article 209 provided for protection against seizure and execution on the clothing and furniture necessary for the life of the debtor and his family, food and fuel necessary for four weeks, and several other items of lesser importance. In addition, the following movable items, of special interest for the peasants, were also included: one plow, rake, cart, hoe, pick, ax, and scythe; two oxen, or two buffaloes, or two horses, or two asses; one cow or buffalo cow with calf up to one year; ten sheep, or five pigs, or five goats; as much food (or the produce used to buy food) as necessary for the peasant and his family until the new harvest; feed for the protected livestock until the new harvest; and sufficient seed to cover the needs of the peasant. This enumeration of the protected minimum of movable goods included in the law of 1930 was almost an exact copy of the provisions contained in Article 471, Section 4a, of the Serbian Code of Civil Procedure enacted in 1873 (p. 44).

Thus, at the end of the interwar period, for the protection of a minimum amount of peasant property against foreclosure for debts, provision was made on the statute books of Yugoslavia for (1) a smaller minimum homestead, with certain movable accessories, protected against foreclosure for taxes and applicable to the whole country; (2) a minimum of movable accessories protected against foreclosure for private debts by the Law on Execution and Safeguarding of Judgments of 1930, applicable to the whole country, and (3) a larger minimum home-

[7] The Program of the Croatian Peasant party as formulated in 1921 stated in its Article 5, entitled "The Free Peasant Household," as follows: "The peasant state is a regulated community of free and orderly households. For the purpose of the general advancement of the peasant household [or home], a special law will be passed about the inheritance of peasant land and economic freedom in the spirit of the old customary zadruga law, but in accordance with the contemporary ideas and needs of the peasant people; furthermore a special law will be passed whereby the peasant home will be protected against foreclosure, as well as a special law about the peasant home order and obedience, which will regulate also the free establishment of new zadrugas."

stead, established by separate legislation of various dates, for Serbia, for Montenegro, for those peasant households which obtained land through the agrarian reform in Bosnia and Herzegovina, and for the territory of *Banovina* Croatia. However, this minimum homestead was not immune from foreclosure for debts owed to the Chartered Agricultural Bank or for debts evidenced by bills of exchange. In spite of the fact that the institution of the protected minimum homestead continued in force in Serbia and Montenegro and was introduced in Bosnia and Herzegovina and *Banovina* Croatia, it remained a controversial issue until the end of the interwar period.

PROPOSALS FOR REFORM OF LANDOWNERSHIP AND LAND INHERITANCE LAWS

Some administrators and social scientists were of the opinion during the interwar years that a reform of ownership and inheritance laws with regard to peasant property in agreement with the old zadruga philosophy was one of the basic points for any policy directed toward the improvement in the economic and social position of the Yugoslav village. The most sensible and realistic suggestions in this regard came from people who administered the zadruga laws of 1889 and 1902 in Croatia-Slavonia. They observed the functioning and shortcomings of these laws and peasant reaction to them. They had at their disposal statistics on the number of zadrugas, their divisions, and the number of members. They surveyed in 1911 and 1912 the opinion of the peasants in all parts of the province to ascertain their ideas and wishes with regard to the handling of peasant property and its inheritance. One of the principal authorities on the zadruga in Yugoslavia during the interwar period, Dragutin Tončić,[8] belonged to this group. He had an abiding faith in the zadruga and thought that it was the most convenient and most satisfactory way of property and economic organization of the

[8] Dragutin Tončić, *Zakon od 9.svibnja 1899. o zadrugama i Zakon od 30. travnja 1902 o promjeni odnosno nadopunjenju nekih ustanova zak.od 9.svibnja 1889. o zadrugama* (The Law on the Zadrugas of May 9, 1889, and the Law of April 30, 1902, on the Amendments to the Law of May 9, 1889); Dragutin Tončić, *Vrhovne upravne i sudske rješidbe k zakonu od 9.V.1889 o zadrugama i zadružnoj noveli od 30.IV.1902* (Supreme Administrative and Court Decisions Regarding the Law on the Zadrugas of May 9, 1889, and Its Amendments of April 30, 1902). The latter publication contains, in addition to a large number of administrative and court decisions and regulations regarding the zadrugas in Croatia-Slavonia, the most complete statistical data on the zadrugas in that province as of 1910. Tončić was of the opinion that these statistical data applied largely also in the early 1920's. This publication contains also (pp. 235–69) the results of the surveys conducted in 1911 and 1912 by the provincial government on the zadruga laws, their application, and the views and wishes of the peasant population regarding the regulation of peasant property and inheritance.

peasant family in the South Slav lands. Considering the fact that 77,234 zadrugas from the 112,065 recorded in land property books in Croatia-Slavonia in 1910 consisted of one biological family, Tončić concluded that the peasants themselves had abandoned the institution of the zadruga as an agglomeration of several families. The new phase in the development of the zadruga was marked by the constitution of the "closest family members" as zadrugas and not by large zadrugas consisting of several biological families. The latter were exceptions. His principal proposals were, first, a revision of the laws of 1889 and 1902 to eliminate their obvious shortcomings and inequities pertaining to the existing zadrugas, and second, the passing of a general zadruga code for the whole country, incorporating the basic idea that "peasant property belongs to the family and that the head of the family is limited in disposing of that property."[9]

Another devoted supporter of the same ideas among the Croats was Professor Milan Ivšić who proposed the codification of the zadruga principles in a separate Peasant Code. He thought that by the enactment of this code the peasantry of Croatia (and generally the peasantry of Yugoslavia) would obtain an appropriate legal basis for the reconstruction of its whole economic and social life, which (1) would be in the image of the legal and social ideals that permeated the life of the Croatian and South Slav peasantry for centuries, (2) would serve its real economic needs, and (3) would be absolutely modern, because it would be based on the principles of collectivism, albeit zadruga or family collectivism. By resurrecting the zadruga type of collectivism, he wanted to remove the application to the peasantry of the rules of civil law based on the principles of unlimited individual property, and to prevent further division of peasant property and further proletarization and pauperization of the village with all their unfavorable political and economic consequences.[10]

It is here necessary to repeat also that the Croation Peasant party (p. 419, footnote 7) was committed to a revision of the land property and inheritance laws in the spirit of the zadruga philosophy. While this general principle was supported throughout the interwar period, no further elaboration in that regard came from the party or its leaders.

There were also numerous supporters of the idea of the resurrection of the zadruga philosophy and institutions among the Serbs and Montenegrins. The most important among them was Professor Živojin M.

[9] Dragutin Tončić, *Vrhovne upravne i sudske rješidbe* . . . , p. 268.
[10] Milan Ivšić, *Temelji seljačkoga zakonika* (The Principles of the Peasant Code), pp. 25–31.

Perić of the University of Belgrade,[11] and toward the end of the inter-war period his pupil, Ananije V. Ilić.[12] Legally the conditions under which the zadruga existed in Serbia and Montenegro were different from those which existed in Croatia-Slavonia. In Serbia the zadruga was regulated by the civil code, and its legal nature was one of co-ownership rather than collective ownership, while in Montenegro only a small portion of rules regarding the zadruga were written law and most of them were still unwritten customary law. Both of these authors supported the idea of full codification of zadruga principles as the basis for the regulation of landownership and inheritance for the peasants.

The revival of the interest in the zadruga during the 1930's, when the Yugoslav village experienced one of its deepest crises, was to a large extent a criticism of the existing order and the expression of a groping for a new solution. But that did not make the zadruga more capable of rejuvenation or more fit to cope with the problems of the Yugoslav village and peasantry during the 1930's.[13] A resurrection of the zadruga legal and social philosophy and of the corresponding economic and social forms of organization, even if it had been possible or desired by a majority of the peasant population, could have done little to ameliorate—to say nothing of solving—the distress of the Yugoslav village in the 1930's. The Yugoslav village and agriculture suffered from ills that were intractable by a reform of laws pertaining to owner-ship and inheritance of land. Above all, the resurrection of the zadruga could have done nothing about the unfavorable rural population–culti-

---

[11] Živojin M. Perić, *Porodično zadružno pravo u Crnoj Gori* (Zadruga Law in Montenegro); Živojin M. Perić, "Obituary for Dragutin Tončić," *Arhiv za pravne i društvene nauke*, February 1937, pp. 198–205.

[12] Ananije V. Ilić, *Sistem prava o kućnoj zajednici u Crnoj Gori* (The System of Law on the Zadruga in Montenegro). Although this study concentrates on the discussion of the zadruga law in Montenegro, it is to a large extent a study in comparative law, because it repeatedly draws comparisons of the Montenegrin with the Serbian and the Croatian legislation on the zadruga as well as with the customary zadruga law.

[13] One of the indications that the great majority of Yugoslav lawyers, politicians, and high government officials were skeptical toward the idea of a concerted effort to preserve, let alone resurrect, the zadruga on a large scale was the following: There was after 1922 a plan under way to codify the written and customary law pertaining to the zadruga in the form of a general Yugoslav Zadruga Code. The already quoted Croatian laws of 1889 and 1902 were to serve as the basis of the new code, with the inclusion, whenever necessary and advisable, of material referring to the zadruga from the Serbian and the Montenegrin legislation, as well as from zadruga customary law never before codified. In fact, a draft of such a code was prepared in 1931. While awaiting the passage of this general zadruga code for the whole country, a draft of the amendments to the Croatian zadruga laws was made in 1933. But neither of the two drafts was ever put on the statute books.

vated land ratio, which was the chief difficulty facing the Yugoslav agriculture and peasantry. Nevertheless, it is probable that such a reform would have acted beneficially in the case of many peasant households and that it would have helped in reducing somewhat further excessive subdivision of peasant property.

There was hardly anybody in interwar Yugoslavia who would advo-cate the system of primogeniture in regard to the inheritance of peasant property according to the German model. This system of inheritance of peasant property would be at least as far from the traditional con-cepts of the Yugoslav peasants as is the inheritance according to the principles of unlimited individual property in the sense of Roman law. Inheritance of peasant property according to primogeniture had been the customary law in some parts of Slovenia for centuries and also among the German minority in Vojvodina, and continued to be so dur-ing the interwar period.

It should be mentioned that some representatives of the peasant parties in Yugoslavia during the interwar period, mindful of the state of overcrowding in the village, proposed, though quite vaguely, that ownership of agricultural land by nonpeasants be narrowly limited. Thus, for example, Mihailo Avramović of the Serbian "Union of Peas-ants," said as early as 1921: "The land should be owned by those who till it and to the extent that they till it."[14] In 1940 Rudolf Bićanić of the Croatian Peasant party proposed for consideration the idea that in the future those people who live from pursuits other than agriculture be allowed to own only a very limited amount of agricultural land. He supported his proposal by stressing the shortage of land and by saying that such a measure would be nothing new in Croatia, since prior to the demilitarization of the Croato-Slavonian Military Frontier in the 1870's such limitations were observed in that area.[15]

The institution of such measures would have actually meant another radical agrarian reform. But it was generally understood that the effect of such a reform in providing additional land for the peasants who needed it would be very limited. There were too many peasant house-holds who needed additional land, even if only a farm of five hectares were taken as standard, and too few larger farms from which some land could have been taken.

---

[14] Mihailo Avramović, "The Agrarian Reform and the Peasant Movement," *Nova Evropa*, II, No. 7, 245.

[15] Rudolf Bićanić, "The Land to the Peasant," *Gospodarska Sloga*, No. 4, Feb-ruary 15, 1940, pp. 1–2; this idea was also supported by another leader of the Croatian Peasant party, Ljudevit Tomašić, *Gospodarska Sloga*, Nos. 1–2, January 15, 1941, p. 5.

Another item should be mentioned in regard to the problem of landownership during the interwar period. Large stretches of pasture and forest land were owned as village common and commune common (the commune being the lowest administrative unit in the country) in practically all areas of Yugoslavia, and large areas were owned by the state. In Croatia-Slavonia these commons were known as "land associations" and "property communes," and their ownership, administration, and utilization were regulated by special laws. Elsewhere in the country the ownership and utilization rights of the common were generally arranged by local custom. Since most of the people thought that "when the pasture and forest is everybody's, it is nobody's" the exploitation of the common was marked by abuse and lack of any care and much of the pasture and forest stands was destroyed. Furthermore— and this is the problem which interests us at this particular point—a process of transformation of the valuable land from the common into privately owned land has been under way for decades. This happened primarily by usurpation, but to a certain extent also by division. The process of transformation of the common into private land became more intensified as the pressure of population in rural areas increased.[16] As far as the worthless areas in the karst region which were held as common were concerned, almost all experts and administrators who were interested in the systematic and sustained rehabilitation of these wastelands through reforestation and similar measures thought that this rehabilitation was predicated on the distribution of this land into private ownership.[17]

KEEPING THE LAND IN PEASANT HANDS
BY STATE INTERVENTION

The changed attitude outside of Serbia toward the protected minimum homestead after 1923 can be explained by several factors. Among them the most important were perhaps the following: the general influence of the agricultural depression, the overindebtedness of the village, the growing agricultural overpopulation, and the unsatisfactory relationship between the prices of agricultural and the prices of industrial

[16] Sreten V. Vukosavljević, "About the Land Property in the Village," *Istorisko-pravni zbornik*, I, No. 1, 37–77. His book *Istorija seljačkog društva*, Vol. I, *Organizovanje seljačke zemljišne svojine* (History of the Peasant Society, Vol. I, Organization of the Peasant Land Property), which elaborates more fully some of the ideas presented in the above article, arrived too late to be consulted while writing this chapter.

[17] Josip Balen, *Naš goli krš* (Our Bare Karst), pp. 272–85, quoting two resolutions of experts, dealing with the problem of reforestation and general reclamation of the karst area.

products. All these factors made the economic position of the village more difficult and increased the danger of the peasants' losing their land. The need to protect a minimum of land in peasant hands became more imperative. While it was generally agreed that the institution of the protected minimum homestead had reduced the capacity of the peasant to obtain credit from legitimate sources, it was also true that as a protected "minimum of existence" it had increased his sense of security.

In a larger sense, however, the legislation on the protected minimum homestead was part and parcel of a defensive approach to the economic problems of agriculture and peasantry in the South Slav lands. This approach attempted largely to isolate the peasant household from, and to protect it against, the forces of economic differentiation in the village, and to safeguard a minimum of land in the hands of the largest possible number of peasants. The legislation tried to counteract the tendency for many peasants to lose their land either because they were inefficient as producers or because their income was so low in relation to their needs that they were forced to eat into the chief component of their capital, their land. If the peasants were unable to keep the land in their hands as its most efficient users, state intervention was used to help them keep it. This legislation is more understandable if two factors are kept in mind: The political and social aim of the legislation was to prevent the pauperization and/or proletarization of the village which the existing regimes considered undesirable; and, further, the peasantry of the South Slav lands would not have accepted without opposition the concentration of a large amount of agricultural land in the hands of a few.

With the growing overpopulation, the increasing proportion of dwarf and small farms, the growing pressure on the peasant agriculture of Yugoslavia resulting from its weakened competitive position in foreign markets, and the growing needs of the peasant household, it became progressively more difficult to keep the land in the hands of the peasants in small units where both the land and the labor available to the peasant family were inefficiently utilized. While agrarian reform, the moratorium for peasant debts, and the legislation on the protected minimum homestead were socially and economically necessary, they have to be understood to a large extent also as measures of political appeasement for the broad masses of peasantry. The very limited success of these measures and of the whole defensive approach to the problem of agriculture and peasantry in Yugoslavia showed ever more as time advanced that the solution of the basic problems of agriculture in Yugoslavia—the problems of overpopulation and pauperization of the village—could not be found within agriculture itself.

We have delved in detail into the issues bearing upon the problem of landownership and the securing of land in the hands of the peasants. A deep interest in the problems of landownership was quite understandable in a country where until 1918 there existed feudal and quasi-feudal relationships—a country which was marked by growing agricultural overpopulation and a process of economic differentiation in the village, both leading to the pauperization and proletarization of the peasantry. The agrarian policy of the Yugoslav government during the whole interwar period consisted essentially of measures which had as their object the ownership of agricultrual land. However, these measures were not facing the two basic problems of agriculture in Yugoslavia during this period: the growing agricultural overpopulation and the advancing pauperization of the village. From a long-run economic point of view, the absolute necessity for the agricultural policy in Yugoslavia during the interwar period was to increase the amount of cultivable land through land reclamation, to increase the productivity of agriculture in general by creating incentives for higher productivity and by spreading knowledge about better farming, and, above all, to undertake systematic measures to reduce the number of people depending on agriculture for their livelihood by making it possible for them to transfer to other walks of life. The last point was essential, for as long as so many people remained in agriculture their situation could not be markedly improved. Only by reducing the nuber of people that agriculture had to support would it have been possible to increase the savings and investments and thus modernize and increase production and create a basis for the raising of the level of living of the peasantry. That would have been a positive, an aggressive, approach to the problems of Yugoslav agriculture.

Generally speaking, an agricultural policy corresponding to the needs of the country was not developed. Considering the property structure in Yugoslavia during the interwar period, which was marked by a large number of dwarf and small farms and a relatively small number of medium and larger farms, it would have been necessary to develop agricultural and economic policies in order to serve the needs both of the dwarf and small peasants and of peasants who produced largely or wholly for the market. Actually, the government did follow a type of policy which was characteristic of Yugoslavia of the interwar period, namely, that of letting things drift and thereby delaying as long as possible the day on which the vital issues must be faced. In regard to agriculture this had, however, the unfortunate consequence of making the problems more difficult, their treatment more painful, and their solution require both a longer time and greater sacrifices. It is a sad commentary on the ability and social consciousness of the regimes of the interwar period that in their policies the peasantry served primarily as an object of oppression and exploitation while its welfare should have been their prime interest and preoccupation.

THE HUNGER FOR LAND IN THE YUGOSLAV VILLAGE

It is in relation to the general background of the worsening quantitative relationship between the agricultural population and cultivated land, the tendency toward growing pauperization in the village, and the foster-motherly attitude of the state toward the peasants, that we must consider the final question in his chapter—the question of the proverbially strong attachment of the Yugoslav peasants to their land and the issue of the so-called "hunger for land." It should be immediately stated that the strong attachment of peasants to their land is characteristic not only of Yugoslav peasants, but also of practically all peasants in countries of peasant farming, especially when these countries suffer from agricultural overpopulation. The psychological relationship to the land is the most fundamental trait in the whole conscious and subconscious behavior of the Yugoslav peasant. It controls practically all his actions. In most Yugoslav areas the peasants consider their land as a sacred thing. The peasant and his family have been traditionally bound to a farm; it was his father's, it is his, and it will be his son's "place in the sun." It is the staff of life that was bequeathed to him by his forefathers and that he is supposed to leave undiminished to his sons. In a country where opportunities for earnings outside of agriculture were not only very limited but also insecure, and in which the growing population made the land relatively more scarce and wages for work relatively lower, possession of land gave the peasant the only security and safety that he knew. In a society in which the peasant was at the bottom of the social structure, downtrodden and exploited by everyone, only the possession of sufficient land gave him freedom and the personal satisfaction of having full power over something, namely, his land. There lies the source of the saying so dear to the heart of the peasant in all parts of Yugoslavia, that the land is only "God's and his." The possession of sufficient land meant freedom, work for the family, security, and life itself. Thus, the characteristic urge of the Yugoslav peasants to own sufficient land is not an unfounded urge, but rather an urge born of centuries of experience, which taught him that possession of land was security-giving and life-maintaining. The hunger for land is therefore a very natural feeling, considering the conditions under which the Yugoslav peasants lived and still live. From this same source also stems his readiness to defend every inch of his land with his life against any stranger, neighbor, or brother.[18]

While discussing the property structure in the Yugoslav agriculture, we showed the large proportion of dwarf and small farms and mentioned the determination of the peasants to keep these farms. According to the social standards of the village and thus of the overwhelming majority of the peasants taken individually, a peasant without land would have been considered a nobody, an uprooted tramp much like a "naked gypsy." Thus, while the actual economic difference between a landless peasant and a dwarf peasant was often not very great, there was a considerable difference between them in a social sense. In fact, in the case of most dwarf and small peasants there was nothing for them to do but to stick to their farms, however small and low in productivity they had become. For the great mass of the peasantry there was no alternative either at home or abroad. Only a large and continuous growth of the urban economy, which would have guaranteed to the peasant not only an attractive wage but also a reasonable security of employment, would have successfully counteracted the urge to own some land as a safeguard for the livelihood of his family. Even then, the process of weaning the Yugoslav peasant from a psychological dependence on the land might take a long time. Thus far, however, the urban economy in the South Slav lands has not been able to give the peasants such a guaranty. It is, therefore, quite understandable why many peasants in Yugoslavia today look with suspicion on employment in industry as an exclusive source of livelihood for the surplus peasantry and continue to keep one foot in agriculture. This attitude of the Yugoslav peasants is derisively marked by many representatives of the Communist regime as a lower-middle-class attachment to property. In fact, this attachment is a much older and stronger bond than an attachment to property. It is the attachment to the land as the most dependable source of livelihood under the Yugoslav conditions, an attachment that has long become a basic component of the Yugoslav peasant culture.

[18] Peasant land in Yugoslavia was not only soaked with the sweat of the peasant's brow, but also often sprinkled with blood spilled in its defense. It is probable that a large majority of the thousand-odd killings that occurred annually in the Yugoslav villages during the 1930's, and the infliction of grave bodily wounds in another 3,000 cases, occurred in disputes over the possession of land. This is, however, a personal opinion of this writer. The official source of these figures, Yugoslavia, *Annuaire statistique 1938–1939*, pp. 438–39, gives no indication of the reasons behind these crimes.

It would be wrong, however, to think that only landless, dwarf, and small peasants were showing an intense hunger for land. This was also characteristic of other strata of peasants during the interwar period as well as of a part of the nonpeasant population. This is best shown by the fact that a large portion of the debts of the medium and large peasants, as reported in April 1932, were contracted in order to buy land (Table 45, p. 655). The only difference between the hunger for land of the big peasants and wealthier nonpeasants and that of the landless, dwarf, and small peasants was that the former group was able to gratify its hunger for land, though it was not a matter of survival, while the latter group could never do so except partially, and then primarily with the help of the government, such as in the agrarian reform, internal colonization, or distribution or usurpation of government-owned land.

Next to the passion to own the land he tilled, the Yugoslav peasant had the passion to own more and better land. Practically all peasants apparently wanted a farm large enough to employ the whole family and to produce enough food for the family, feed for the livestock, and a surplus for sale to buy the other necessities for the household. In addition, peasants wished to have more and better land, because land was considered an important factor of wealth accumulation and gave its owner more economic and political power and more social prestige. In many cases, to own a piece of good and well-located land is considered a matter of pride just as the possession of a beautiful house or of a rare and costly object of art would be in the case of a wealthy urban family.

There is no doubt that the worsening of the quantitative relationship between rural population and cultivated land, or the growing hunger for land, has left a deep imprint on the physical and spiritual constitution of the peasant population in many areas of Yugoslavia. There are authors—as, for example, Otto von Frangeš[19] and A. H. Hollmann[20]—who were of the opinion that the hunger for land in Yugoslavia has destroyed much of that specific "peasant ethos" which they considered of special value in a peasant population and that it had led to a physical and spiritual degeneration of much of the peasantry. While there is some truth in these assertions, one should be cautious in drawing any

[19] Otto von Frangeš, *Die sozialökonomische Struktur der jugoslawischen Landwirtschaft*, p. 109. Speaking about the landless and dwarf peasants, Frangeš had this to say: "This is the peasant proletariat in the worst meaning of the word. These are social elements whose constant hunger for land, coupled very often with physical hunger, controls all their ideas and actions, and who hardly could be helped."

[20] A. H. Hollmann, *Agrarverfassung und Landwirtschaft Jugoslawiens* (Germany, Ministry for Food and Agriculture, *Berichte über Landwirtschaft*), N.F., Sonderheft 30, p. 68.

general conclusions with regard to the effect of the worsening population-land ratio on both the body and the psyche of the Yugoslav peasants. It is interesting, for example, that the infant mortality is highest in Vojvodina and Slavonia, which otherwise are the most advanced and agriculturally best-situated areas of the country. It is also generally accepted that the most outstanding physical specimens of the Yugoslav peasants are to be found in areas where the ratio of population to cultivated land is the most disadvantageous, that is, in the karst area. To arrive at acceptable conclusions in this regard, it would be necessary to investigate various areas of Yugoslavia separately rather than try to find a general formula for the country as a whole. Such a formula would omit more than it would include.

In spite of the fact that about 90 percent of all Yugoslav peasants owned the land they worked during the interwar period, the ownership of a farm, in the case of a majority of the peasant households, proved incapable of solving the peasant's quest for a decent living or for economic security. The basic reason for this lay in the small size of the majority of farms, which was basically a consequence of the unfavorable relationship between the cultivated land and the number of people these farms were supposed to support. The peasants continued to hold on tightly to their land, as they knew well that it was better to own and hold some land than none. But it is always necessary to remember the truth that the lot of the peasants in countries of peasant farming cannot be improved as long as there are so many of them.

It is interesting to note that during the interwar period there was practically no talk in Yugoslavia of co-operative working of land or of co-operative owning of agricultural machinery (although there were some co-operatives established for the latter purpose) as ways of overcoming the excessive subdivision of land property and assuring a better utilization of farm machinery and implements. Certain remainders of the old forms of communal work such as the bee, the labor loan, co-operative use of draft animals, co-operative tending of herds in summer pastures, etc., continued to be used in various areas, but on a small and decreasing scale. In regard to both landownership and agricultural labor the development continued during the interwar period, as in the several preceding decades, along the paths of greater individualization.

CHAPTER 21

LAND, LABOR, CAPITAL,
AND TECHNOLOGY IN AGRICULTURE

IN REGARD to the general stage of development, one finds in Yugoslavia, within a few hours' walking distance, agricultural systems which are centuries apart from a socioeconomic point of view. This fact is perhaps best illustrated by the differences in the spirit of the peasants and in the agricultural techniques that are used in various parts of the country, and also in various sections in the same areas.

Here again one of our standard reminders bears repeating. In most of the northern areas and northeastern plains agriculture was considerably specialized and commercialized or quasi-commercialized, and agricultural techniques were on a much more advanced level than in areas south of the Sava-Danube rivers. This was so not only because of the differences in topography and soil, although in the northern areas and especially in the Pannonian Plain these were very conducive to the application of modern agricultural technology, but for a number of other reasons. In the northern areas the cultural level of the peasant population was considerably higher; there was a higher proportion of larger farms which could provide and apply more advanced agricultural implements and a larger supply of draft power; here a large and better-organized market for agricultural and livestock products was near; and there was a more favorable ratio between rural population and cultivated land.

THE PREDOMINANCE OF PEASANT SUBSISTENCE FARMING

The basic motivation in the economic activity of the overwhelming portion of Yugoslav farm households was to provide food and other necessities for the family, including feed for livestock, by direct production of goods and services on the family's farm by members of the family, rather than the maximization of total money revenue from farming for the market. The overwhelming majority of Yugoslav farm households were thus primarily subsistence units and not agricultural business enterprises. Only a small part of farm units were commercialized or quasi-commercialized, producing for the market in order to maximize total money revenue.

Yet practically every farm household had to sell a part of its production or earn some money income by selling labor services of its members. The need for all farm units to acquire some money revenue was due to the fact that they could not produce all their necessities at home and had to buy them and that some of their fixed charges, such as direct taxes, debt repayment, and interest, had to be paid in money. That is the reason that many economists in Yugoslavia during the interwar period characterized its agriculture as "mixed" agriculture, in which farm households were working both for subsistence and for the market.

The portion of production sold differed greatly from farm to farm, depending on the size of the farm, the size of the peasant family, the type of cropping and livestock economy carried on by the household, special circumstances (sickness, need for dowry, amount of indebtedness, tax load, buying of implements, building or repairing of housing) in the peasant family, the nearness of the market, and the relationship between prices of agricultural and other products (see Chapter 26). As has already been pointed out, 67.8 percent of all farms were dwarf and small peasant farms, which, as a rule, had negligible surpluses for the market. But there were many dwarf and small specialized farms in some areas, such as those producing wine, fruits, and tobacco, which, in spite of the fact that they sold the bulk of their production, were in their character subsistence farms. They were specialized because that was the best way of assuring indirectly the subsistence of the family. Peasants produced these crops year in, year out, with little or no regard for price movements, considering them on the basis of long experience more satisfactory than other production alternatives.

Another factor which shows the subsistence character of the overwhelming portion of Yugoslav agriculture was the almost complete absence of even the simplest accounting records.[1] What shifts in farm production took place in areas which marketed a large portion of their production, e.g., in Vojvodina, Srijem, and Slavonia, were primarily the result of the obvious fact that certain products were easier to sell and that their prices were better than those of other products. With

---

[1] The examples of peasant farm accounting records collected and published by Slavoljub Dubić and Josip Predavec are so few and unreliable that it does not pay to discuss them here. Slavoljub Dubić, *Prilog istraživanju seljačkoga gospodarstva* (A Contribution to the Study of Peasant Farming in Yugoslavia), pp. 45–56. Dubić published accounting records for only four farms. He especially stressed (p. 5) the tendency of the peasants to understate their receipts in money and to overstate their expenditures. Josip Predavec, *Selo i seljaci* (The Village and the Peasants), pp. 290–97, and Appendix tables. Predavec supplied accounting data for only six peasant farms.

rare exceptions, these changes were made not on the basis of estimates of recorded costs, but by relating the approximate cost of input of factors with the expected value of output, or by the rule of the thumb (*od oka*). Without cost accounting as a means of adjusting the combination of production agents in a satisfactory manner and of appraising their relative contribution to the value of total output, it is hard to talk about "commercialization" of a farm unit, or of its being a "firm."

Since the great majority of farm units in interwar Yugoslavia did not produce primarily for sale but for their own use, they were not compelled to compete with other producers, either by trying to reduce costs or by improving their products. Thus, competition, the great stimulus of economic development tending to improve the methods of production and to shift production to suit better the market situation, was of little significance for subsistence or predominantly subsistence farming. The production technology of the peasants and their outlook were tradition-bound. This did not mean, of course, that the subsistence peasants did not try to improve their methods of production and to increase their output and revenue. No society and no state of societal arts is stationary. But in societies marked by peasant subsistence farming, especially when they exist within a political and economic framework which discourages incentive, as did those in the South Slav lands, the advance in societal arts is often barely noticeable.

In more recent decades the situation of subsistence farming in Yugoslavia was becoming worse owing to the appearance of acute agricultural overpopulation. One of the consequences of growing overpopulation was the growth of farm units during the interwar period at an annual rate of 15,000 to 20,000, almost exclusively of dwarf and small size. Agricultural overpopulation and decreasing size of farms reduced still further the ability of peasant farmers to save and to invest and to take risks of technological innovations. The main problem for an overwhelming and steadily growing number of farm households in Yugoslavia during the interwar period was to keep their people alive rather than to grow and progress. Needless to say, the decline of agricultural prices and reduced possibilities of selling agricultural products during the Great Depression, increased greatly the difficulties in Yugoslav agriculture during the 1930's.

But while the general conditions prevailing in the subsistence sector of Yugoslav agriculture precluded a marked increase in the per capita production and led, in fact, in many households to a reduction of per capita production due to growing agricultural overpopulation, the variety and the extent of wants of the peasant population greatly increased and kept increasing. The resulting inability of the peasant population to satisfy their increased wants from current income forced them to rely more on credit, to eat into their land, and to look more intensively for jobs outside of their households. These jobs, however, were created at a much smaller rate than the increase in population in rural areas. This whole development increased the peasant's economic insecurity and robbed him of a hope in the future. Frustration, discontent, and tension kept mounting in rural areas, and the solution of the basic problems of the Yugoslav village — the agricultural overpopulation and pauperization — became daily more difficult.

Since it was impossible to shift the surplus labor power in agriculture to the urban economy within the country itself, or into emigration, as there was no demand for it in the first case and no opportunities for emigration on a large scale, it remained as an economic burden in the village. As was mentioned on an earlier occasion, agriculture was overburdened with "eaters" in comparison to people that could be employed (both self-employed and hired). Small farms, primitive technology, and the impossibility of fully utilizing either the available labor or draft power, and in many cases also farm equipment, kept the productivity in agriculture low. Low productivity kept the total production low. Low production, in turn, kept the consumption of the agricultural population low and narrowly limited the possibilities of capital formation in agriculture. Limited land resources and dearth of capital, in turn, prevented agriculture from growing and assuring a rising plane of living in agriculture. Since in many countries of peasant subsistence farming, including Yugoslavia, agricultural population grew faster than agricultural resources, there resulted a tendency toward a falling rather than a rising plane of living. Moreover, low consumption power of the agricultural population limited their demand for industrial products and this acted as an impediment to industrial development.

CAPITAL ASSETS IN PEASANT AGRICULTURE

With the exception of a study by Slavoljub Dubić regarding the organization and management of a sample of 116 peasant farms in Croatia-Slavonia, published in 1933, there has been no systematic study of the pattern of organization of production factors in Yugoslav farming published during the interwar period. The main shortcoming of Dubić's survey is that the land factor was not represented in money terms in various size categories of farms, so that the money value of other assets cannot be compared properly with the value of land. Moreover, the whole sample was taken from a relatively narrow area

of Croatia-Slavonia, which reduced its representative value. During
World War II, however, a similar study by Jure Petričević pertaining
to conditions existing in 1940 was published. This survey was based
on a sample of only 60 peasant farms, which in regard to size were
distributed as follows:[2]

Area in hectares	Number of farms	Average farm in hectares, including forest land
0 to 3	18	1.62
3 to 5	12	3.52
5 to 10	16	7.14
10 to 15	7	10.66
15 and above	7	19.48
Total sample	60	6.39

This study is much more detailed than the one by Dubić and furnishes
considerable insight into the organization and relationships among
various assets in peasant farms of different sizes. These farms are well
selected in regard to the nature of their production and are taken from
a wide area, namely, from Croatia-Slavonia, Bosnia and Herzegovina,
and Dalmatia (15 from Slavonia, 6 from central and northern Croatia,
11 from southwestern Croatia, 6 from central and southern Bosnia, 10
from northern Bosnia, and 12 from Herzegovina and Dalmatia). But
the average area per farm of 6.39 hectares and the average number
of members per family of 7.2 and of man-labor units of 3.75 are too
high to be representative, thus reducing somewhat the value of the
sample.

The core of data collected in this study relating to the combination
of capital assets of the surveyed farms is presented in Table 28. The
valuation of assets followed, by and large, these rules: land was valued
according to the purchase price or the average market value; buildings,
improvements in land, and trees and crops in fields were valued according to their production costs; livestock, equipment, and circulating
capital were appraised according to purchase price, costs of production,
or average market value. In all cases where necessary, depreciation
was taken into account. The same table shows also the average money
value of all capital assets for the average farm unit covered by the survey
in order to convey an idea of how low these assets were. It should be
remembered, however, that during the 1930's the relative purchasing
power of the dinar in Yugoslavia in terms of various domestically

---

[2] Jure Petričević, *Untersuchungen über die Betriebsformen der Bauernbetriebe
Kroatiens*, p. 8.

TABLE 28.—CAPITAL ASSETS OF 60 SURVEYED FARMS BY SIZE GROUPS IN 1940*

(Percent; dinars)

Type of capital asset	Size in hectares					Average farm	
	0–3	3–5	5–10	10–15	Above 15	Dinars[a]	Percent
Land	33.37	39.75	38.94	43.25	47.02	77,039	40.97
Improvements ..	0.66	0.13	0.13	0.01	0.03	305	0.16
Buildings	42.89	31.98	32.70	27.65	25.28	58,968	31.40
Trees and crops in fields	8.99	11.28	7.10	6.01	4.85	13,908	7.40
Livestock	3.99	4.76	6.60	6.80	8.24	11,898	6.33
Equipment	3.50	2.68	4.00	4.54	3.56	6,886	3.66
Circulating capital	6.60	9.42	10.53	11.74	11.02	18,943	10.08
Total	100.00	100.00	100.00	100.00	100.00	187,947	100.00

* Source: Jure Petričević, *Untersuchungen über die Betriebsformen der Bauernbetriebe Kroatiens* (Aarau, Switzerland, 1942), pp. 16–17.

[a] In the original the monetary unit is *kuna*, the monetary unit of the Independent State of Croatia, but at the time of the survey in 1940 the dinar currency was in circulation.

produced goods and services was perhaps two times as high as its equivalent of two cents in the United States. But in regard to agricultural land that was surely not the case. Petričević discovered, for example, that in extremely overpopulated areas the price paid for agricultural land was occasionally as high as 50,000 dinars per hectare (Croatian Zagorje) and even 100,000 dinars per hectare (Dalmatia), that is, approximately $1,000 and $2,000, respectively.[3] This survey does not make it clear whether these prices included fruit trees or grapevines on the land, but this was most probably the case.

While the sample in the Petričević study conveys well an idea of the composition of capital assets in peasant farming in most of Yugoslavia, it would be folly to consider it as anything more than an illustration of the order of magnitudes involved. There is thus no need to go into any detailed analysis of data supplied in Table 28. Only a few remarks suffice. One of the interesting facts shown in this table is the low amount of land and high relative value of buildings in the dwarf farms. This relative overburdening of dwarf farms with buildings, and therefore costs to erect and maintain buildings, was stressed in Yugoslav literature as a powerful drain on the savings of peasant households. This relationship improves as farms grow in size, but remains large in farms of all size categories. This survey shows that there are almost no

[3] *Ibid.*, p. 19.

land improvements in peasant farms, a fact which is primarily connected with the absence of irrigated agriculture in the country and
with the virtual absence of flood protection installations in those parts
of Yugoslavia in which the surveyed farms are located. The value of
trees and crops in the fields is highest among dwarf and small farms because a considerable portion of these farms which were surveyed were
engaged in wine and fruit production. As far as equipment is concerned, 25 percent of the amount shown was transport equipment and
another 23 percent equipment for processing grapes and cooperage,
while agricultural machines, implements, and tools for field work
amounted to only 15.8 percent of the total. The value of land per
hectare is almost twice as high in the dwarf and small farms as in the
three remaining classes. This resulted from the fact that the valuation
of land was often made on the basis of purchase price, and the peasants
with dwarf and small farms, in order to acquire a certain minimum of
land, were willing to pay prices for land out of all proportion to its yield
capacity.

The average amount of debt for the 60 surveyed farms was 6,149
dinars, but these were only debts made for production purposes. Debts
for financing of consumption of the peasant households, which in many
of the surveyed farms were large, were not taken into account.[4] Thus,
the difference between the average capital assets of these farms, as given
in Table 28, and the above average amount of debt per farm does not
give the average net worth of these farms. Their net worth is lower.

This survey has confirmed some generally held ideas about the
characteristics of Yugoslav agriculture, of which more will be said in
the following pages. But the confirmation of two basic propositions
was most important. First, the lack of balance between the available
land resources and the available labor force in agriculture has been
confirmed. While it is usually assumed that peasant families endeavor
to have about two hectares of agriculturally used land per man-labor
unit, this survey showed that only 1.22 hectares of agricultural land
per man-labor unit was available in these farms, resulting in an underutilization of their labor resources. Second, it was generally known—
and this survey confirmed—that the relationship between land and
other assets at the disposal of dwarf and small farms is unfavorable,
that they often had too much invested not only in buildings but also
in farm equipment and in livestock. In other cases they had too little
of both. These disproportions worsened still further the economically
precarious position of dwarf and small farm units.

[4] *Ibid.*, p. 29.

UNSATISFACTORY CROP ROTATION

One of the most general features of the agricultural technology in Yugoslavia, which contributed markedly to the low yields in agriculture, was that the overwhelming portion of peasants did not follow a satisfactory crop rotation. There were many reasons for that, but among the most important were the following: the unfavorable relationship between agricultural population and cultivated land, the preponderance of dwarf and small farms, the tendency of most Yugoslav peasants to produce on their own farms all the basic foods which they needed for their families, lack of knowledge about the importance of good crop rotation, and the relatively weak market for livestock and livestock products, which reduced the incentive to produce forage crops.

No official or other satisfactory information exists on crop rotation practices in Yugoslavia during the interwar period. However, agricultural statistics, which furnish information on the uses of agricultural land, state that in the period 1934–38 not less than 81.9 percent of all arable land was under cereals. This 81.9 percent was composed of 29.2 percent under wheat, 36.9 percent under corn, 14.2 percent under secondary grains (barley, oats, and rye), and 1.6 percent under minor grains (meslin, millet, spelt, buckwheat, and rice). Thus a continuous rotation of wheat with corn, or what was popularly known as the two-field system, was the necessary rule for the great majority of farms. The remaining 18.1 percent of arable land was utilized, in the period 1934–38, as follows: industrial crops 2.1 percent, vegetables and potatoes 5.7 percent, feed crops 4.6 percent, and fallow 5.7 percent, but only a part of this area was entering into rotation with grains. However, even if this whole area had been regularly rotated with grains, it was still too limited to provide a balanced rotation.

It is important to stress, however, that one of the grains was corn and that it played a very favorable role in the predominant pattern of crop rotation. First, because it required intensive cultivation it contributed to the control of weeds; second, because it was common practice to interplant corn and string beans and the latter helped somewhat to maintain the plant nutrients in the soil; and third, because it was common practice to apply manure when corn was planted. Had small grains been sown year in, year out, on the same land, most probably a much larger portion of the arable land would have been kept as fallow. There were two main difficulties resulting from the wheat-corn rotation. First, there was not sufficient time after the corn harvest to properly prepare the land for the winter wheat, and any delay in the sowing of winter wheat usually has unfavorable consequences. Second, under such a crop rotation the work load on the farm was very unevenly distributed, with high peaks in June–July and September–October when even families with small farms needed additional labor if they wanted to accomplish the work on time, while the family's labor supply was badly underutilized during much of the remaining months of the year.

The Dubić study, which investigated farm practices on 116 farms in Croatia-Slavonia in 1931, covered also the problem of crop rotation. In terms of size these 116 farms were distributed as follows: 17 included less than 2 hectares of agriculturally used land, 45 had 2 to 5 hectares, 40 had 5 to 10 hectares, 9 had 10 to 15 hectares, and 5 had 15 or more hectares of agriculturally utilized land. This investigation showed that on the largest number of farms the common rotation was corn–winter wheat. When the food requirements, mainly cereal, for the family were assured—and that was the case on somewhat larger farms—and the families lacked sufficient meadows and permanent pastures to maintain their livestock, the rotation followed was: winter wheat–lucerne (or clover)–corn. On about the same number of farms as those with the preceding crop rotation, but farms of the smallest size and especially those located on mountain slopes, there was really no crop rotation whatsoever, but corn was planted on the same parcels of land year in, year out. The basic objective was to assure the largest possible production in terms of calories for direct human use. Finally, on a very small number of farms, primarily those of 10 hectares and more, which usually kept a considerable number of livestock for the market in that particular area, the following rotation was practiced: corn–winter wheat–lucerne–lucerne. There were some deviations from these cropping patterns on some of the investigated farms, but the above four patterns were the basic ones to which practically all others could be reduced.[5]

The results of the Dubić survey, which was made in one of the relatively more advanced agricultural areas of Croatia-Slavonia, could not be projected for the whole of Yugoslavia, but they are quite indicative of the conditions in areas north of the Sava-Danube rivers where livestock raising was on a relatively advanced basis. In some other areas, e.g., on good alluvial soils in the river valleys of Serbia and Bosnia, occasionally wheat and especially corn were grown year after year on the same plots of land.[6]

[5] Slavoljub Dubić, *op. cit.*, pp. 29–30; Jure Petričević, *op. cit., passim*; Božo Turina, *Poljodjelstvo u Nezavisnoj Državi Hrvatskoj* (Agriculture in the Independent State of Croatia), pp. 56–65 and *passim*.

[6] Otto von Frangeš, *Die sozialökonomische Struktur der jugoslawischen Landwirtschaft*, pp. 97 106; Jovo Popović, "Agricultural Production," A. Koen *et al.* (eds.),

In northwestern areas of Bosnia and in Macedonia there was a considerable area of arable land left as fallow. Prior to 1918 that was partly a consequence of the feudal order existing in these areas. While the area under fallow was greatly reduced during the interwar period, it was still very large in these two regions. For Macedonia this large area under fallow has been connected partly with the absence of proper crop rotation, lack of draft power, and lack of manure, and partly ascribed to the generally primitive state of agricultural technology.[7] In those parts of Macedonia which have low precipitation black fallow may be required for the accumulation of moisture.

The problem of appropriate crop rotations, primarily for the chief grain-producing areas of Yugoslavia in the northeast and north has often been discussed during the past few years. Most of the Yugoslav agricultural experts now propose a multiple field-rotation system in which all grains would take approximately 60 percent of arable land, while the remainder would be devoted to forage and industrial crops. This crop rotation, which would make it possible to keep a much larger number of livestock, resulting in larger production of manure, they think would allow the grain production to be maintained and would put the livestock economy on a much broader and stronger feed basis.[8]

EQUIPMENT IN AGRICULTURE

The only official data on the farm equipment used in Yugoslav agriculture during the interwar period were those collected in the special census of 1925. According to this census there were in Yugoslavia 783,762 steel plows, 326,879 wooden plows, 647,371 harrows, 63,395 rollers, 78,775 grain drills, and 219,892 dusters and cultivators. Of harvesting machinery, there were 9,813 harvesters, 6,244 mowers, 7,967 motor threshers, and 25,882 other threshers. Furthermore, there were 117,438 winnows, 18,334 seed cleaners, 58,130 corn shellers, and 90,748 straw, ensilage, and beet cutters.[9]

Statistics for 1925 ought, however, to present a fairly accurate picture for the second half of the 1930's as well, because it can be as-

Bosna i Hercegovina kao privredno područje (Bosnia and Herzegovina as an Economic Area), pp. 22–23.

[7] Relja Dimitrijević, "Problems of Crop Production in Macedonia," University of Belgrade, *Godišnjak Poljoprivrednog fakulteta* (Yearbook of the Faculty of Agriculture), II, 293.

[8] Compare, for example, Lazar Stojković, "Crop Rotation in the Grain-Producing Areas," *Socijalistička poljoprivreda*, April 1951, pp. 12–30, and Artur Starc, "Some Problems of Land Fertility and Land Utilization," *ibid.*, July–August, 1951, pp. 1–21.

[9] Novak Popović and Dušan Mišić, *Naša domaća privreda* (Our National Economy), p. 143.

sumed that whatever increases in agricultural machinery and implements were made in years of relatively favorable economic conditions
in agriculture—that is, until and including 1930—were more than off-
set by wear and tear and lack of replacements in the period 1930 to
1940. Since most of the agricultural equipment, with the exception
of plows and farm tools like hoes, picks, sickles, and scythes, were imported, the imports of these items give a general picture of the new
additions which were made for replacement purposes as well as for
increasing the number of agricultural implements. The volume and
value of imports of agricultural machinery, implements, and tools from
1928 to 1937, and the volume and value of imports of all types of
threshers, plows, and plow parts from 1921 to 1937 are given in
Table 29. It is impossible to give data for the total volume and value
of these imports prior to 1928 because some changes were made in the
customs classification of various items. Furthermore, up to and in-

TABLE 29.—TOTAL IMPORTS OF AGRICULTURAL MACHINERY, IMPLEMENTS, AND
TOOLS, 1928–37, AND OF THRESHERS, PLOWS, AND PLOW PARTS, 1921–37*

(Metric tons; million dinars)

Year	Total imports[a]		Threshers		Plows and plow parts	
	Metric tons	Million dinars	Metric tons	Million dinars	Metric tons	Million dinars
1921....	...	...	1,659.7	8.95	4,390.5	15.27
1922....	...	...	2,458.8	18.72	4,614.3	24.57
1923....	...	...	973.9	10.94	1,515.8	11.10
1924....	...	...	627.4	6.88	1,068.7	9.27
1925....	...	...	1,290.8	17.71	1,531.3	12.02
1926....	...	...	1,042.8	19.20	1,576.1	11.98
1927....	...	...	1,019.0	15.66	2,442.8	15.76
1928....	10,266.8	137.79	2,311.2	37.40	3,562.7	26.55
1929....	12,358.5	182.94	3,700.3	57.89	2,832.3	21.23
1930....	7,898.2	106.39	1,579.8	24.28	1,755.8	13.40
1931....	3,547.7	41.23	248.3	2.96	1,325.4	9.80
1932....	727.4	9.20	63.5	0.70	205.1	1.43
1933....	421.6	4.39	31.5	0.41	150.7	1.04
1934....	576.0	7.69	25.3	0.26	198.1	1.30
1935....	796.0	9.93	31.5	0.35	393.6	2.35
1936....	1,593.9	14.97	139.9	1.61	668.8	3.70
1937....	3,857.0	33.80	361.7	4.12	1,680.9	9.08

* Source: Data for 1921 to 1927 from Kingdom of the Serbs, Croats, and Slovenes, Ministry of
Finance, *Statistique du commerce extérieur* (annually); for 1928–37 from Yugoslavia, Ministry
of Agriculture, *Statistique agricole annuelle 1933* (Belgrade, 1934), and *Statistique agricole
annuelle 1937* (Belgrade, 1938).

[a] Comparable data for the years 1921 to 1927 are not available.

cluding 1927, tractors, locomobiles, and some of the machinery for
road construction were recorded together in the import statistics. Import data for threshers, plows, and plow parts for the period 1921 to
1927 are, however, as revealing of the general situation in Yugoslav
agriculture as data for the imports of all agricultural machinery, implements, and tools. Heavy imports of threshers, plows, and plow parts
in 1921 and 1922 were obviously connected with the endeavor of the
Yugoslav peasants to replace the losses suffered during World War I
through wear and tear and lack of replacements, and also to take advantage of the satisfactory conditions in the market for agricultural
products. The slump in imports during 1923 and 1924 was related to
the downward readjustment in the Yugoslav economy following upon the
postwar inflation, caused, among other factors, by a certain degree of
deflation and marked by a great drop in agricultural prices. The increase in these imports in 1925, and especially in 1928 and 1929, was
related to the relative prosperity in Yugoslav agriculture in these years.

The total imports of agricultural equipment between 1928 and 1937
indicate to a large extent the general conditions in Yugoslav agriculture during those ten years. Data presented in Table 29 are not only
proof of the low rate of maintenance and almost complete absence of
replacements during the long years of the Great Depression, but, above
all, they provide a telling example of the crippling influence of that
depression on Yugoslav agriculture. The volume of imported agricultural machinery, implements, and tools reached its peak in 1929,
when it amounted to 12,358.5 metric tons valued at 182.94 million
dinars. In 1933, when the imports of these items reached their lowest
point, the volume was only 421.6 metric tons, valued at 4.39 million
dinars. The importation of threshers, which in 1929 was valued at
57.89 million dinars, slumped in 1933 to 410,000 dinars. Imports of
plows and plow parts, which reached a maximum of 26.55 million
dinars in 1928, fell to 1 million dinars in 1933. Imports of agricultural
machinery, implements, and tools began to rise slowly after 1933, but
in 1937 they were still little more than one-third in volume and a little
less than one-sixth in value of the level reached in 1929. This increase
in imports after 1935 was related to a considerable revival in the
country's economy, and undoubtedly also to the lack of imports in the
preceding years.

To some extent the replacement of simple implements and tools was
carried out by the domestic production, but this could not have been
done on a large or satisfactory scale. Further, it should not be forgotten
that the rate of wear on agricultural equipment in Yugoslavia is high

because of difficult soil conditions in many parts of the country, and because equipment is often not properly maintained, repaired, and stored when not in use.

A good indicator of primitive agricultural technology in Yugoslavia as a whole is the large percentage of wooden plows in use. The quantitative relationship between the wooden plow (there are two main varieties) and the part-steel and steel plow (and there are innumerable varieties of these) gives a general picture of the state of agricultural technology in various areas. The widespread use of the wooden plow indicates to some extent the degree of cultural and socioeconomic backwardness in various areas. According to the agricultural implements census of 1925, wooden plows made up an insignificant portion of all plows in Slovenia, Croatia-Slavonia, and Vojvodina, as well as in northern Serbia. But in the remainder of the country they were much in use. In Montenegro there were roughly ten wooden plows for each steel plow; in Macedonia two wooden plows for each steel plow; in Dalmatia two wooden plows for every three steel plows; in Bosnia and Herzegovina one wooden plow for one steel plow; in pre-1912 Serbia approximately one wooden plow for every three steel plows.[10] There were counties in some of these provinces in which a steel plow was a rarity.

While there was a tendency during the interwar period for the relative number of wooden plows to decrease, the conditions were such during the 1930's that many peasants could not afford to buy steel plows and thus the wooden ones persisted. The census of March 15, 1948, found that the Yugoslav agriculture (the territory of the country now slightly enlarged because of the incorporation of Istria) had 1,078,114 steel and part-steel plows and 307,772 wooden plows. In Slovenia there was one wooden plow for about every ten steel plows, in Croatia (including Dalmatia) one wooden plow for every seven steel plows, in Vojvodina one wooden plow for every 23 steel plows. But in most areas south of the Sava-Danube rivers they were still, as before 1940, very much in use. In Serbia proper there was one wooden plow for every 3.5 steel plows; in Bosnia and Herzegovina one wooden plow for every three steel plows; in Macedonia one wooden plow for one steel plow; and in Montenegro four wooden plows for one steel plow.[11]

[10] Ljudevit Prohaska, "Agriculture and Its Advancement," *Jubilarni zbornik života i rada Srba, Hrvata i Slovenaca, 1918–1928* (Jubilee Record of Life and Work of the Serbs, Croats, and Slovenes, 1918–1928), I, 321.

[11] Yugoslavia, Federal Bureau of Statistics, *Bulletin statistique*, No. 6, August 1951, pp. 50–52.

The harrow, often homemade, was in general use during the inter-war period, but rollers, grain drills, dusters, harvesters, threshers, and other more complicated and more expensive farm machines and imple-ments were used primarily in the Pannonian Plain, and especially on the larger farms. The use of tools in agriculture, such as hoes, spades, spade forks, picks, rakes, sickles, and scythes, was very great, because a large portion of farm work, especially in cultivation and harvesting, was and still is done manually. In some areas and for some crops, as for example in grapevine cultivation in Dalmatia, agriculture was capital- and labor-intensive, but still was based on the hoe. The num-ber of implements for cultivation, cleaning of seed, shelling of corn, straw and other cutters, hay presses, dusters, and sprayers, all of which had to be imported, was very limited, and again concentrated mostly in areas of advanced agricultural technology north of the Sava-Danube rivers.

One of the most unfortunate and at the same time expensive features in regard to farm equipment in Yugoslavia was and is the great variety of types and models. This meant that adequate supply of spare parts and proper servicing were impossible. As a result, the purchase and use of farm equipment were much more expensive and risky. The basic reason for this situation was the fact that imports of machinery and implements came, in varying quantities, from practically all European countries which produced them in large quantities, as well as from the United States and Canada. There are no data on the variety of models of farm machinery and implements during the interwar period, but data collected by a survey made in 1950 would have also applied, by and large, for the interwar period. This survey has shown that there were in use in Yugoslavia 300 different types of hoes, 88 various models of tractors from 46 different manufacturers (at the end of 1951 there were in Yugoslavia approximately 7,300 tractors), 79 different models of tractor plows, 30 different types of grain and other drills, 64 dif-ferent models of grass mowers, 74 different types of mechanical har-vesters, 143 different models of threshers, over 100 different models of industrially manufactured plows, and an uncounted number of plows of pre-1940 domestic origin "when practically every local blacksmith had his own plow model."[12]

Needless to say, the quality of work performed in agriculture, which

[12] A. V. P., "Our Agricultural Machinery and the Problem of Its Standardization," *Socijalistička poljoprivreda*, February 1951, pp. 47–51. A survey of the supply of Yugo-slav agriculture with farm equipment, according to data collected by the census of March 15, 1948, is to be found in Borislav Kostić, "Equipment of the Serbian Agriculture with Machinery, Implements, and Tools," *ibid.*, April 1951, pp. 31–53.

had an important bearing on the yields, greatly depended on the type of draft power and the quality and type of farm implements used. Since larger farms were capable of keeping and utilizing better draft power and better machines and implements than the small and dwarf farms, their productivity was presumably higher. But this was definitely not a fixed rule, especially in areas south of the Sava-Danube rivers where technology on small and large farms was practically identical. The explanation for this can probably be found in the lower cultural level of the peasants in these areas, their great conservatism and, thus, their aversion to innovations, and also in the low wage level because of the pressure of population in rural areas, which made manual work and use of primitive agricultural methods economically more advantageous. Generally speaking, under the conditions existing in Yugoslavia during the interwar period, it was much more important that implements and machinery were yield-raising than labor-saving.

LIMITED SUPPLY OF MANURE, ARTIFICIAL FERTILIZERS,
AND PESTICIDES

Because of the absence of satisfactory crop rotations, the Yugoslav peasants would have needed an even greater than normal supply of manure and/or artificial fertilizers to keep the fertility of their land intact. But actually their supply of manure was much below their needs, and, as will be shown presently, their use of artificial fertilizers was negligible. The low production of manure was due to the fact that most of the time the livestock grazed in the open, and that, while in the stables, the animals did not have enough feed, nor was enough straw used for stable bedding.

No estimates exist on the production of stable manure in Yugoslavia as a whole during the interwar period.[13] The differences in methods of raising livestock, in the size of livestock, in the availability of straw for bedding, and in the feeding methods of livestock made such an estimate very difficult. In addition, the manure requirements differed from area to area because of differences in soil quality and in cropping. It is perhaps safe to assume that during the interwar period Yugoslavia did not produce more than about one-third of its minimum needs of stable manure. Although the discrepancy between the needs for and the supply of stable manure was so extreme, a large portion of stable manure was lost. Thus, for example, satisfactory traps for the catching

---

[13] Božo Turina, *op. cit.*, pp. 66–68 and *passim*, supplies detailed estimates of the stable manure production in Croatia-Slavonia, Bosnia and Herzegovina, and Dalmatia in 1940.

of liquid manure were built only in parts of Slovenia and in some sections of Croatia-Slavonia. Generally speaking, manure pits were either
lacking or were primitive in construction. This was due, in part, to
the high price of cement, but more fundamentally it resulted from a
lack of knowledge about, and appreciation of the role manure played
in advanced agriculture. In some areas where wood for burning was
scarce, e.g., in some sections of Macedonia, manure was used instead
of firewood. In some parts of Yugoslavia, however, the peasants are
very much aware of the value and the need for manure, and try not
to waste it.

One type of manuring, green manuring, was little known and seldom
practiced in Yugoslavia before World War II. It was occasionally used
by big and more advanced peasants. Furthermore, the stubble of small
grains left after harvest was not, as a rule, plowed under and used as
fertilizer, but rather livestock was let into the fields to feed upon it,
thus serving a more immediate need. This practice did, of course, result in returning the plant nutrients to the soil, but the physical improvement of the soil which results from the introduction of vegetable
matter through plowing in the fall was absent. In some areas south
of the Sava-Danube rivers, notably in Bosnia, livestock was corralled
by movable fences for purposes of direct manuring, for a day or two.
These fences, and livestock with them, would be moved until the whole
field was thus manured.

Because of the shortage of stable manure, no regular manuring of
fields could be achieved. Thus only the crops with the highest priority
in the production plan of the peasant family, such as corn, potatoes,
vineyards, industrial crops, and vegetables, were manured. Naturally,
these practices varied greatly from area to area and from farm to farm.
They depended, of course, on the type and number of animals and the
manner in which they were kept by various families, and this, in turn,
depended to a great extent on the size of the individual farms. Manure
was seldom bought or sold.

In spite of the great shortage of stable manure, Yugoslavia was
one of the relatively lowest users of artificial fertilizers in Europe. During the 16-year period 1924–39 it used, on the average, only 34,400
metric tons of artificial fertilizers, varying between the maximum of
77,685 metric tons in 1929 and the minimum of 13,533 metric tons
in 1933. The consumption of artificial fertilizers for the period
1924–39 is given in Table 30, showing the total amount as well as
various types of artificial fertilizers consumed. The bulk of the consumed fertilizers was superphosphate. During the period 1924–39 it

TABLE 30.—CONSUMPTION OF ARTIFICIAL FERTILIZERS, 1924–39*

(Thousand metric tons)

Year	Total	Super-phosphate[a]	Other phosphate[b]	Nitrogen fertilizers[c]	Potash	Other fertilizers[d]
1924.....	26.0	22.0	1.5	0.8	1.7	—
1925.....	30.6	26.0	1.6	1.4	1.6	—
1926.....	39.1	35.0	1.7	1.0	1.4	—
1927.....	57.1	51.0	1.3	3.0	1.8	—
1928.....	65.5	58.0	1.4	4.0	2.1	—
1929.....	77.7	61.0	2.7	3.9	10.1	—
1930.....	43.2	35.0	1.9	2.0	2.1	2.2
1931.....	34.0	28.1	1.1	1.3	1.5	2.0
1932.....	16.4	13.3	0.6	0.9	0.8	0.8
1933.....	13.5	10.3	0.6	1.0	0.9	0.7
1934.....	14.1	10.3	0.4	1.2	1.1	1.1
1935.....	15.6	11.7	0.6	1.1	0.8	1.4
1936.....	25.3	17.5	1.3	1.4	1.1	4.0
1937.....	27.2	17.6	1.9	2.4	1.6	3.7
1938.....	31.9	21.3	2.0	1.9	1.4	5.3
1939.....	33.2	19.9	2.3	1.5	2.4	7.1

* Source: Yugoslavia, Ministry of Agriculture, *Glasnik*, Belgrade, July 1937, XV, 338, for the years 1924–36; for 1937 *ibid.*, October 1938, XVI, 565; for 1938 *ibid.*, July 1939, XVII, 494; and for 1939 *ibid.*, March 1940, XVIII, 83.

If the quantities of artificial fertilizers given in this table were converted to plant nutrients they, especially N, would differ considerably from data supplied in K. G. Clark and Mildred S. Sherman, *Prewar World Production and Consumption of Plant Foods in Fertilizers*, U.S. Department of Agriculture, Misc. Publ. No. 593 (Washington, D.C., April 1946), p. 40, for the years 1937–39. The totals involved are so small that it really does not matter. But for the record it should be stated that Clark and Sherman have made some mistakes in their calculations regarding Yugoslavia. Thus, for example, they assume that the import of ammonium nitrate, which in the period 1937–39 averaged about 2,500 metric tons per year, supplied 61 percent of all nitrogen used as fertilizer (p. 20). It was, in fact, used almost exclusively for the production of explosives. The imports of sodium nitrate and ammonium sulfate cannot be taken as identical with their use for fertilizer either. A large portion of the former and practically all of the latter were used for industrial purposes.

[a] The average P_2O_5 content of the superphosphate was about 16 percent. It was produced domestically from imported phosphate rock.

[b] This figure contains basic slag, most of which was imported, rock phosphate produced after 1934 from domestic raw material, and small amounts of superphosphate of bones.

[c] The bulk of it came from domestically produced calcium cyanamide, with an N content of about 20 percent, imported sodium nitrate, and bonemeal.

[d] This is a domestically produced mixed fertilizer. There is no indication in the official statistics of its chemical composition.

was consumed, on an average, at the rate of 27,400 metric tons per year. This table shows how insignificantly small was Yugoslavia's consumption of artificial fertilizers during the interwar period. It is also apparent that its consumption of artificial fertilizers, like the purchase of agricultural machinery and implements, was profoundly affected by the respective phases of prosperity and depression in Yugoslav agriculture. The consumption of plant food in the form of artificial fertilizers per hectare of arable land in Yugoslavia during the period 1935–37 was estimated on the average to be 0.1 kilogram of N, 0.4 kilogram of P_2O_5, and 0.1 kilogram of K_2O.

Before 1940 artificial fertilizers were used in Yugoslavia almost exclusively in the commercialized and quasi-commercialized agriculture of the Pannonian Plain and Slovenia. They were primarily used in growing export crops such as hemp and hops and crops which, by one method or another, had prices assured in advance, such as sugar beets and oil seeds. Some superphosphate fertilizer was used also for lucerne. In areas south of the Sava-Danube rivers they were little known and even less utilized.

It is interesting to note that practically no research was undertaken by either the government or private agricultural organizations (e.g., federations of agricultural co-operatives) or producers of artificial fertilizers during the interwar period to determine the effects of the application of various fertilizers on the yield of different crops in various areas of Yugoslavia. Thus, the application of the artificial fertilizers that were used was always done on a trial-and-error basis in which the farmer assumed not only all the cost but also all the risk of innovation. The absence of irrigated farming added to the risk of application of artificial fertilizers.

There were two basic reasons for the low consumption of artificial fertilizers by Yugoslav agriculture during the interwar period. First, there was a lack of knowledge about advanced agricultural technology and about the function of artificial fertilizers in it. Second—and this was of fundamental importance—there was an unfavorable relationship between the prices of fertilizers and the prices of agricultural products, so that the producers lacked any incentive to apply artificial fertilizers. It did not pay. According to the calculations of Karlo Šoštarić-Pisačić, the Yugoslav peasant had to pay, on the average, 149 percent more in terms of agricultural products than the farmers in Germany, France, and Italy for superphosphates in 1938; for potash fertilizers, 219 percent more than the farmers in these three countries; and for calcium cyanamide, 104 percent more.[14]

While Yugoslavia had to import the phosphate rock for the pro-

---

[14] Karlo Šoštarić-Pisačić, "Consumption of Artificial Fertilizers in Yugoslavia and Abroad," *Ekonomist*, January 1940, pp. 1–11, and February-March, 1940, pp. 100–110. This is one of the best discussions of the problem of consumption of artificial fertilizers in Yugoslavia during the 1930's.

duction of superphosphate, as well as the small quantities of sodium nitrate (Chilean nitrate), potash, basic slag, and ammonium sulfate that it consumed, the country used to be an exporter of other artificial fertilizers. It exported primarily calcium cyanamide, and small quantities of bonemeal, mixed fertilizer, and, until 1931, it was also a net exporter of superphosphate. The most interesting was the case of calcium cyanamide, the exports of which averaged 28,707 metric tons yearly between 1924 and 1937, while total domestic consumption in that period averaged only 799 metric tons annually, or 2.8 percent of the exported quantity. Needless to say, the artificial fertilizer industry enjoyed a high tariff protection. Furthermore, all artificial fertilizers were subject to a small testing fee and to the payment of a general sales tax, which, according to product, varied between 2.5 and 5 percent.

The consumption of pesticides, insecticides, and fungicides for the control of plant diseases and pests was negligible, the basic reason being that these means of control were not known to the overwhelming portion of the Yugoslav peasants. But even if they had been known, their prices would probably have been such as to make their use, like the use of artificial fertilizers, a rare exception rather than a rule. The only important exception was products for the control of grapevine diseases, namely, copper sulfate and sulfur, both of which were successfully and generally applied in all parts of the country in which grapevines were raised. Without them, there often would have been no grape harvest. Their application was thus a matter of economic survival for the peasants depending for their livelihood on the production of wine.

The part of Yugoslav agriculture in which diseases make the greatest ravages and where the application of means of control would pay the highest dividends is, perhaps, fruit growing. That, of course, does not mean that various diseases are not important in other crops. Actually, small grains, corn, potatoes, sugar beets, etc., are subject to many diseases that cause the loss of a considerable portion of the crop. In some years and in some areas such common pests as field mice also take an undue share of the crop, especially of grains. But to return to fruit crops, as we shall see later, fruit growing is an important branch of agriculture in many parts of Yugoslavia. The most important type of fruit is the prune. The ravages of diseases in this particular case can best be judged from the drop in the number of bearing trees. The number of prune trees of fruit-bearing age fell from the interwar maximum of 60.9 million in 1922 to 49.4 million in 1924. After a respite, and slight increase in the number of trees, it fell from 50.4 million trees in 1929 to 44.7 million in 1930, 39.3 million in 1931, and 38.5 million in 1932. In 1938 there were 42.7 million prune trees. The most destructive disease was undoubtedly the San Jose scale, although half a dozen or more other diseases were also affecting them. Furthermore, the San Jose scale proved to be particularly destructive of the most valuable variety, the Požegača prune, which is used for the production of dried fruit, while its effects on the varieties used for the production of marmalade and prune brandy were much less severe. This made the problem of prune diseases even more costly, because dried prunes were an important export article. While the loss of trees is, of course, the greatest loss in fruit growing, there has been a considerable loss in the quality of fruit almost every year. If there had been any standard controls for marketed fruit in Yugoslavia, except some control regarding fruit destined for export, a large portion of fruit that used to appear on urban markets would never have reached the market.

In regard to fruit growing, there was another unfavorable factor which sounds almost unbelievable. Many orchards in areas south of the Sava-Danube rivers were practically never pruned—or at least not scientifically—although pruning is essential in fruit growing. Furthermore, in many areas orchards and olive groves had little cultivation, to say nothing of irrigation or application of either manure or artificial fertilizers. A large portion of Yugoslav peasants would merely plant a young tree and wait for it to start bearing. Their general attitude with regard to fruit growing was, "If the Lord grants, there will be a good crop." In regard to tree crops, it can be said that a large portion of Yugoslav peasants had not, during the interwar period, come to the full realization that for a good tree crop the Good Lord requires a great deal of help from mortals. But in some areas the techniques of fruit growing were fairly advanced.

UNDEREMPLOYMENT OF THE LABOR FORCE AVAILABLE
IN AGRICULTURE

Factors responsible for the underutilization of a large portion of the available labor power in Yugoslav agriculture during the interwar period were small farms, large families in rural areas, concentration on the production of cereals, and acute agricultural overpopulation. Since only a very small number of Yugoslav peasants could conduct a labor-intensive type of cropping, there being no possibility of selling more than a limited amount of special crop products, the consequence was that Yugoslavia had a labor-extensive type of agriculture in spite of an oversupply of labor.

During the interwar period many Yugoslav writers maintained that a medium-size farm, owned and operated by the peasant family, of 5 to 15 hectares of cultivated land—depending on the area and the pattern of cropping—following a moderate degree of production specialization and capable of fully utilizing the family's labor force, would be the most desirable type of farm for Yugoslav conditions. In this they followed a great number of pre-1914 Russian and many Central European agricultural economists who were the proponents of a system of peasant family farming that would be economically quite stable and technically fairly efficient. Considering the psychological make-up of the Yugoslav peasants, there could hardly be any dispute over the desirability of such farms. In fact, the 29.3 percent of all farms with 5 to 20 hectares of land, which accounted for 49.3 percent of all land according to the census of 1931, were the backbone of Yugoslav agriculture from a production point of view during the interwar period. But while the securing of family farms of satisfactory size would have been the most desirable situation from the point of view of the overwhelming portion of the Yugoslav peasantry, as well as from that of many economists including this writer, it is abundantly clear that such a solution could not be achieved in Yugoslavia for the simple reason that there were too many peasants in relation to the available cultivated land or land that potentially could be brought under cultivation.

Since the overwhelming portion of the farms in Yugoslavia during the interwar period suffered from a discrepancy in the proportions of land, capital, and labor at their disposal, there was a tendency among the Yugoslav peasant households to increase their farms by buying land, or by dowry, or occasionally even by renting it in order to have about two hectares of land per man-labor unit in areas of cereals growing, and thus to assure the employment of the available family labor and the subsistence of the family on the farm. This tendency was especially strong in families with a large number of young men, and growing boys and girls, and parents still in good health and capable of work. But when the peasant family farm reached a size that was capable of providing full employment for the family's labor and thus food for the family, feed for the livestock, and other necessities for the family, that is, a real income and security commensurate with the ideas of peasant well-being in that particular area, the urgency to grow in size was very much reduced. On the contrary, as soon as the sons in the family got married the farm was usually divided. Of course, only a portion of the families with abundant labor could gratify their need for more land, because there was no room for a great number of farm units to grow and to round themselves out into farms sufficiently large to employ the whole family labor.

Owing to the predominantly subsistence character of Yugoslav agriculture and the fact that about 90 percent of all peasant households owned at least some land, the overwhelming portion of all work in agriculture was done by members of the peasant families who owned the land. There were areas such as Vojvodina, Srijem, parts of Slavonia, and Slovenia where a considerable amount of farm work was done by hired labor. In other parts of the country this was much less the case, although practically all medium-size and big farmers throughout the country used some hired help. The use of hired labor depended on the degree of agricultural overpopulation, the size-structure of farms, the amount of labor-saving machinery and implements at the disposal of various farms, the type of cropping, and the relative number of landless households and dwarf farms in various areas. A small amount of farm work was occasionally done by neighborly help without pay, which was a remainder of the earlier widespread custom of voluntary communal labor without pay (pp. 190–92). According to Dubić 50 percent of the surveyed households with less than 2 hectares of land, 40 percent of households with farms from 2 to 5 hectares, and only 10 percent of households with farms from 5 to 10 hectares earned some income outside of their farms. Thus, he was of the opinion that peasants with farms of 5 hectares and more under the conditions existing in Croatia-Slavonia around 1930 did not look for and did not need work outside of their farms. On the other hand, most of the households with farms from 10 to 15 hectares of land and all those with farms above 15 hectares of land employed hired labor throughout the year.[15] Similar conclusions were reached for Slovenia in 1938 when it was said that members of households with farms up to 5 hectares of land looked for outside employment, while households with 10 and more hectares regularly employed hired labor.[16]

The oversupply of labor was an important contributing factor to the very limited use of labor-saving machinery and implements. On farms where work was done exclusively by family labor, the buying of such machinery and implements, even if it had been possible, would have displaced labor power for which there was no other opportunity for employment and would have decreased the degree of its utilization.

---

[15] Slavoljub Dubić, *op. cit.*, pp. 16–19.

[16] Filip Uratnik, "Agricultural Workers in Slovenia," Hrvoj Maister and Filip Uratnik, *Socialni problemi slovenske vasi* (Social Problems of the Slovene Village), II, 10.

Further, the low wage level for hired labor in agriculture reduced the incentive for those who had to hire labor to buy and use labor-saving machinery and implements. In both cases it was more economical to use more manual labor because a scarce production factor (capital) would have been used to replace the more plentiful and cheaper one (labor).

Unfortunately no systematic investigations were made for Yugoslavia as a whole during the interwar period to determine the rate of utilization of labor power available in agriculture. The available information refers to particular regions of the country; different methods of calculation were used for the estimates, and they referred to various periods of time. These estimates can, therefore, at best serve only as indications of the rate of utilization of available labor in agriculture and as nothing more.

The first study which investigated, among other problems of peasant economy, the utilization of the labor power available in agriculture was made in Serbia in the period 1910–12 by Mihailo Avramović, but its results were published only in 1928. Because of the great loss of population in Serbia during World War I, and because of the fact that no marked changes took place either in the social structure of Serbian agriculture or in agricultural technology and rural customs after World War I, the results of the Avramović survey were probably as valid in 1928 as they were at the time it was made. This survey covered 835 peasant farms of various sizes and types in 324 villages, "different in regard to production and the distance from the town markets," in 12 of the 18 administrative districts of the country. According to this survey, the average utilization of the available labor power in these households was as follows (in percent):

	Men	Women
In field work	45	51
Away from home	5	—
In the home	9	38
Sick	7	3
Unutilized	34	8

One of the contributing factors to this underutilization of labor was the number of holidays, which totaled as many as 120 days a year including Sundays. In spite of this great number of holidays, the basic reasons for the underutilization of labor in agriculture were insufficiency of land, draft animals, and farm implements.[17]

[17] Mihailo Avramović, *Naše seljačko gazdinstvo* (Our Peasant Farming), pp. 27–32.

Two other studies, pertaining to the problem of utilization of labor available in Yugoslav agriculture, were made in the late 1930's at a time when the problem of agricultural overpopulation was uppermost in the minds of many Yugoslav economists. One of these studies referred to Slovenia (*banovina* Drava). Its calculations were based on the census of 1931. Counting the growth of population in the intervening years, it was estimated that in 1938 there were in Slovenia about 424,000 persons capable of agricultural work. All persons between 15 and 64 years of age were considered as labor units without distinction between various ages or between men and women. After assuming that 68,000 persons were employed in housekeeping and 58,000 persons in the raising of livestock throughout the year, the remaining labor force of 298,000 persons, using an average of 280 working days per year, had at their disposal a total of 83.44 million working days. Of these they utilized only 63.31 million working days. A two-week vacation for everybody was taken into account in this calculation. Thus, disregarding people employed in housekeeping and livestock raising, but taking into account employment in cottage industry, road transport, lumbering, and the like, the remaining labor force, according to this calculation, was utilized only at the rate of 76 percent. Naturally, its utilization was much higher in the period March–October than in the period November–February.[18]

The second study of this kind, by Božo Turina, covered the territories that in 1941 were included in the quisling Independent State of Croatia, that is Croatia-Slavonia, Bosnia and Herzegovina, and Dalmatia. It was based on the estimates, but only for Croatia-Slavonia, by county agricultural agents of labor requirements in man-labor and woman-labor days for various crops and all other activities in agriculture and rural households (for other areas the same labor requirements for various activities as in Croatia-Slavonia were assumed). These surveys established that labor requirements differed from area to area and that the available labor power was utilized at different rates, depending on the pattern of agricultural production and the prevailing intensity and quality of agricultural work. On the average, however, men worked between 200 and 245 days, housewives 346 days, young girls below the age of 20 between 100 and 150 days, and farm hands 315 days per year. Children below the age of 14 and old people above the age of 64 were excluded from consideration. From this total amount of workdays 2–3 percent was deducted for sickness, and for men another 2 percent

[18] Hrvoj Maister, "The Employment of Peasant Population," Hrvoj Maister and Filip Uratnik, *op. cit.*, pp. 91–116.

for the average absence in military service in peacetime. On the basis of these assumptions, Turina estimated that the total available amount of labor power in the Independent State of Croatia in 1941 was 358,-127,680 man-labor days and 542,078,156 woman-labor days. Labor requirements, on the other hand, were 252,536,386 man-labor days and 483,278,246 woman-labor days. This meant that roughly 70 percent of man-labor days and 90 percent of woman-labor days were utilized.[19] Two things have to be remembered, however, in considering Turina's data. First, Turina himself was of the opinion that the rate of labor utilization was lower than indicated in the above figures, especially in Bosnia and Herzegovina and southwestern Croatia, where the intensity and quality of agricultural work was lower than in other areas covered by his survey. Second, his study indicates a work load of 200 to 245 days per year for men and 100 to 150 days per year for young girls, which could hardly be considered as full employment. Thus, his figures overestimate considerably the rate of labor utilization in rural areas of the provinces covered by this survey.

Neither on the basis of the above studies nor on the basis of scattered references to the underutilization of labor available in Yugoslav agriculture, found in the writings of such Yugoslav authors of the interwar period as Otto von Frangeš, Mijo Mirković, Maksim Goranović, Slavoljub Dubić, and Rudolf Bićanić, is it possible to arrive at an over-all percentage of labor that remained unutilized in Yugoslav agriculture, say in the second half of the 1930's. A well-organized and conscientious survey carried out in the mid-1930's in neighboring Bulgaria, where the general agricultural conditions were quite similar to those prevailing in much of Yugoslavia, but where agricultural overpopulation was not as severe as in Yugoslavia (see tabulation, p. 316), showed that only roughly 63 percent of the available labor power in agriculture in terms of man-labor units was utilized.[20] Because of this and because of the fact that Yugoslav agriculture showed a considerably higher degree of overpopulation, it appears probable that the rate of underutilization of labor available in agriculture in Yugoslavia was higher than in Bulgaria, and that for the country as a whole, assuming a 280-day annual work load as standard, it amounted in the second half of the 1930's to approximately 40–45 percent. Needless to say, conditions differed greatly from area to area, depending on the relationship

[19] Božo Turina, *op. cit.*, pp. 141–44 and *passim*.
[20] Pawel P. Egoroff, "Die Arbeit in der Landwirtschaft," Janaki St. Molloff (ed.), *Die sozialökonomische Struktur der bulgarischen Landwirtschaft*, pp. 131–59, esp. 152–53.

of agricultural population to cultivated land and livestock, on the types of crops raised, and on the labor and capital intensity of agriculture and animal husbandry.

The extensive type of cropping and the extensive type of animal husbandry in most of Yugoslavia contributed to the underutilization of labor in agriculture. Landless peasantry, and a great portion of dwarf and small peasants, had to look for work outside of their farms or outside of agriculture in order to live. Thus many able-bodied peasants in parts of Macedonia, Montenegro, Herzegovina, Dalmatia, southwestern Croatia, the Croatian Zagorje, Medjumurje, and northeastern Slovenia (Prekomurje) had to migrate periodically in search of work and bread. The bulk of this migration was seasonal and was related to increased seasonal demand for labor in industry (construction, lumbering) or in agriculture. The main areas of immigration of seasonal agricultural workers were Vojvodina, Srijem, and Slavonia, and most of the migrants' earnings were paid in the form of grains (as most of their work dealt with grains). On the other hand, in Vojvodina and Slovenia a considerable portion of rural population, which was landless (p. 393) and dependent for its income on wage work, was of necessity underemployed because of the seasonal character of agricultural work. Moreover, because of the oversupply of agricultural labor from local resources in Vojvodina and the competition of labor which immigrated for seasonal work, the wages of agricultural workers were exceedingly low. According to information published by Professor Mijo Mirković, the agricultural workers in Vojvodina who were not steadily employed as servants or as farm hands with fixed annual incomes in kind and/or in money, worked in agriculture only about 90 days a year, and all of them could not get employment for that long.[21]

It is extremely interesting to see from the Avramović survey that the labor power of women in Serbian agriculture was much more fully utilized than that of men. This was the usual situation in all parts of Yugoslavia, though more so in some areas than in others. In fact, it is a part of the cultural pattern of this peasant society in which the women are in an underprivileged position. But in Montenegro, parts of Macedonia, Dalmatia, and Herzegovina, women had to do most of the field work in agriculture because a large portion of able-bodied men were working away from home either overseas, in other areas in Europe, or in other areas within the country itself. This relatively better utilization of woman labor power in Yugoslav agriculture has been corrobo-

[21] Mijo Mirković, "The Agricultural Proletariat in Vojvodina," *Ekonomist*, March 1937, pp. 114–17.

rated by systematic surveys in Croatia carried out by Božo Turina shortly before World War II, which showed that in areas in which the main cropping pattern consisted of a rotation of small grains and corn, women's labor power in field work was utilized 42 percent more fully than that of men.[22]

Some specific factors contributed to the underutilization of labor power available in agriculture, such as the already mentioned great number of holidays, while others were responsible for its unrational utilization. Thus, in many areas it was necessary to spend a great deal of time in going from one parcel of the farm to another (p. 401), in water hauling, and in the collecting and hauling of firewood. The peasant often traveled many miles to the neighboring town in order to sell a small load of firewood, a few eggs, a chicken, a few liters of fresh milk, or a few kilograms of vegetables or fruits, and to buy a few necessities. The government authorities (tax collector, police, courts) are always located in townships, and any need to visit them took a great deal of time traveling and waiting. The same applied when medical help, veterinary help, or the need for credit was involved. Finally, there was, in many areas of the country, the village tavern or coffee house which took further time. But all these factors should not deter us from the idea that the basic cause of underutilization of labor power in Yugoslav agriculture during the interwar period was the lack of land in comparison with the existing agricultural population.

MALDISTRIBUTION AND UNDEREMPLOYMENT OF DRAFT POWER IN AGRICULTURE

One characteristic of the agricultural technology in Yugoslavia during the interwar period was that almost the only source of draft power was horses and cattle. Only in the Pannonian Plain were there some tractors in use on large farms.

There are no data or acceptable estimates on the distribution of draft teams in various areas of the country, or among various sizes of farms, or on the rate of utilization of the available draft power in agriculture. Thus only a few general remarks based on statistical data regarding livestock herds and some generally accepted notions based on repeated observation of the existing conditions can be stated.

It is generally known that cattle, both oxen and cows, and horses were and are used for draft in agriculture throughout the country. Our rather rough estimates suggest that for approximately every two to

[22] Božo Turina, *op. cit.*, pp. 69–70; Slavoljub Dubić, *Sociologija sela* (Rural Sociology), pp. 163–67.

three oxen (and cow) teams there was only one horse team. Furthermore, the geographic distribution of these teams was very uneven over
the country. Oxen and cows were the primary source of draft power
in all areas of Yugoslavia except in Vojvodina and the eastern parts
of Croatia-Slavonia (Slavonia and Srijem). But in these latter areas
small and dwarf farms also used cattle (especially cows) for draft if
they had any. The predominance of oxen and cows as draft beasts in
areas south of the Sava-Danube rivers and in northwestern Croatia and
Slovenia is easily seen from the relationship between the numbers of
horses and cattle. One of the basic reasons for such practice in the
areas south of the Sava-Danube rivers lies in the fact that the domestic
cattle of these areas are relatively more powerful than the small Bosnian
domestic horses which largely predominate in those parts. And while
these horses are also used for draft, a large percentage of them are used
exclusively as pack animals. The importance of oxen as draft animals
in these parts of the country is also shown by their relative numbers
in the total cattle stock. While in *banovine* Dunav and Sava in the
period 1934–38 oxen represented on the average only one-ninth, and
in Drava only one-seventh of the total cattle stock, in *banovina* Vardar
they represented two-fifths, in Morava one-third, in Vrbas, Zeta, and
Primorje one-fourth, and in Drina one-fifth of the total cattle stock.
The relatively small number of horses in *banovina* Drava and in northwestern Croatia, plus the relatively small number of oxen in the total
cattle stock, shows clearly that a large portion of draft power was supplied by cows. Cows were used as draft animals especially on small and
dwarf farms which could not afford, and did not need to keep, either
horses or oxen. On large farms in the Pannonian Plain there were
some of the long-horned, domestic, Podolian cattle which are extremely
satisfactory as work cattle because of their build and great power.

In Vojvodina, Slavonia, and Srijem most of the draft power in
agriculture was provided by horses belonging to two long-established
and, for these areas, very satisfactory breeds of horses, Nonius for
Vojvodina and Lipica for Slavonia, and crosses of various other breeds
of horses. In the period 1934–38 *banovina* Dunav had 29 percent of
all horses in the country and with the adjoining *banovina* Sava more
than 50 percent. Horses in these areas are strong because the above
breeds are large and people can provide proper feed and care for them.

It was generally thought that farms of five hectares and more had
at least one pair of horses or oxen (and cows) for use as draft animals.
Larger farms which needed more draft power could and did have more
draft teams. But if it is understood that, under Yugoslav conditions,

a team of horses or cattle could work eight to fifteen hectares of arable land, it becomes quite obvious that a large portion of farms with five and more hectares which possessed draft teams could effectively use only a part of the available draft power. Farms with less than five hectares which happened to have draft teams could utilize only a small part of the draft power at their disposal. On the other hand, a large majority of farms below five hectares did not have draft teams to work their land. They had to either hire draft teams at exorbitant wages, combine their one animal with that of a neighbor, or work their land by hoe.

As a general conclusion it can be said that the total available draft power in agriculture was more than ample, but that most farms with teams could not fully utilize their available draft power, especially horses, and the smaller farms often lacked sufficient draft power. In the first case, this situation increased the total costs of production. In the latter, lack of draft power often caused delays and lower quality of farm work, especially of plowing. It can also be said that as a result of weak draft animals and often primitive wooden and part-steel plows, the working of land in practically all areas south of the Sava-Danube rivers was generally poor. Very often plowing looked more like scratching of the land surface than real plowing. Deep fall plowing was seldom practiced. However, in some areas, such as in arid sections of Macedonia, this type of poor plowing proved more advantageous in terms of yields than deep plowing, which some of the interwar colonists began to use and had soon to abandon. The advantage of shallow over deep plowing in arid regions seems to be recognized also by some modern soil scientists, but the issue is still controversial.

Only a small portion of the draft power used by Yugoslav agriculture during the interwar period was supplied by tractors. In 1938 their number was estimated at 2,400. On the other hand, there were probably between 1 and 1.2 million draft teams of horses and oxen (cows) in that year. Tractors were used almost exclusively on large farms in Vojvodina, Slavonia, and Srijem. The survey of *banovina* Drina in 1938 showed that there were in the whole *banovina* only 22 tractors as compared with 219,279 farms.[23] In all areas south of the Sava-Danube rivers there were, in 1938, probably less than 100 tractors.

But there were many impediments in the way of greater use of

[23] Milan M. Obradović, *Selo Drinske banovine u brojevima* (The Village of *Banovina* Drina in Figures), p. 25. This is a report containing data collected in a survey conducted by the Chamber of Agriculture of *banovina* Drina. On page 24 Obradović says that 43 percent of all rural households in that *banovina* had no draft teams, that is, two horses, two oxen, or two cows.

motorized equipment in Yugoslav agriculture in addition to small farms and the conservatism of the overwhelming majority of the peasants. Among these factors were the disparity between the prices of agricultural products and prices of agricultural machinery. High prices of fuel and the high tax on fuel made the use of tractors extremely expensive. Low wages of farm labor and low price of feed enabled the larger farms to raise, keep, and use draft animals at a relatively much lower cost than the cost of using motorized equipment. Lack of proper servicing and repair facilities and provision of spare parts added to the cost of motorized equipment and to the risk of using it. Inability of the peasants to obtain cheap credit before 1932, and any credit at all after April of that year, made the purchase of expensive farm equipment more difficult or completely impossible.

The utilization of draft power and farm equipment was increased somewhat, but not to any appreciable extent, by hiring draft animals and implements for wages. Communal utilization of draft power used to be more widespread in earlier times, but this practice largely disappeared or was supplemented by the just-mentioned hiring for wages. Only a systematic development of co-operative use of both draft power and of the major farm implements and machines could have guaranteed their fuller and therefore more economical utilization.

AGRICULTURAL EDUCATION

In our previous discussions of various policies pertaining to agriculture, both in pre-1918 South Slav states or provinces and in Yugoslavia during the interwar period, it was shown that the government intervened very actively in property relationships in agriculture; and that in some parts of the present Yugoslav state, e.g., in Serbia, the government tried to protect the village population from the effects of the penetration of money and credit economy in the rural areas. In Chapter 27 we will discuss the activities of the government in providing or in regulating credit to agriculture.

There are, however, a whole series of other governmental activities pertaining to agriculture which have been carried on in all civilized countries and so, to a certain extent, also in the South Slav lands. These activities relate to agricultural education; to research regarding various crops and animal husbandry, farm management, marketing, and soils; to services to agriculture in terms of advice, help, and protection; to regulations of various activities of interest to agriculture; to price supports and other types of subsidization of agricultural production; to foreign trade policies which affect agriculture; and to taxation of the agricultural population. The three latter problems will be dealt with later. In this section we will briefly consider only the problems of education, research, services, and certain government regulations pertaining to agriculture.

In some of these matters, a number of the South Slav lands have a rather long record. Thus, since about 1840, there has been considerable discussion and legislation on the advancement of agriculture and animal husbandry in Croatia-Slavonia, in provinces which now make Slovenia, in Serbia, and in Bosnia and Herzegovina after the occupation of 1878. The actual achievements were, however, modest. But it must be remembered that all these efforts were hindered by the unfavorable political framework under which the South Slav nations lived, the low cultural level and strong traditionalism of the peasantry, the difficulties originating in the subsistence farming which gave little room and opportunity for advancement, isolation from the markets, the growing number of dwarf and small farms, and by growing agricultural overpopulation. In some areas outright feudal or semifeudal land-tenure relationships, e.g., in Bosnia and Herzegovina and in Macedonia, which lasted until 1918, were an unsurmountable barrier to technical advance in agriculture. In other areas, e.g., in Vojvodina, the remainders of the feudal order in the form of large estates, some of which shifted to capitalist farm management methods, were, on the contrary, a boon to agricultural advance. There were, finally, changes in the market for agricultural products which influenced the advance in agriculture. The long agricultural depressions of the last quarter of the nineteenth century, and later of the 1930's, were not conducive to the technical improvement of agriculture in the Balkan countries.

One of the first special agricultural schools, in the present Yugoslav territory, was established in Topčider near Belgrade in 1853. In this age when the problem of technical assistance to economically underdeveloped areas commands considerable interest in the United States and abroad, the curious genesis of this school is worth relating. It was an outgrowth of the efforts of Atanasije Nikolić who, as a Serbian from the culturally and economically advanced Austria-Hungary, was employed with scores of other experts by the small, nascent, and backward state of Serbia in order to help it develop its administration, laws, schools, and economy. He was active in agricultural administration and thought that, to improve Serbian agriculture, it was necessary to teach Serbian peasants advanced methods of agricultural work. His first venture was to publish a weekly paper for the peasants (1847), which soon ceased to appear because of the lack of subscriptions. The second decision of the government on his advice (1848) was to teach the inmates of the country's main prison in Topčider the advanced methods of agricultural work in the hope that after their return to the villages the former prisoners would translate their newly acquired agricultural knowledge into practical use and serve as trail blazers of progress in Serbian agriculture. With the help of these prisoners a model farm was developed by 1851, next to which a regular, two-year agricultural school was established in 1853. Every county, depending on its size, sent one or two youngsters to this school at government expense. In 1852 a stud farm in Ćuprija, another Serbian town, was established at Nikolić's suggestion. It was generally agreed, however, that neither this school, which had to be closed in 1858, nor the stud farm made a notable contribution to the advancement of agricultural technology in Serbia. One of the basic reasons will be related presently. It is important, however, to stress that there existed a basic difference in the philosophy of Atanasije Nikolić and of the politicians and leading officials of Serbia with regard to the appropriate methods for advancing agricultural techniques in Serbian agriculture. While he thought that training and good example were the ways of progress, the latter thought that the Serbian peasant really knew how to distinguish good from bad work in agriculture and that only force was necessary to persuade him to do good work.[24] The later, well-known, agricultural high school in Križevci, Croatia, was established in 1860. And in the following decades more agricultural schools, model farms, stud farms, and nurseries were developed.

There was no agricultural school of college standing in the present Yugoslav territory before 1918. Soon after the establishment of the new state, however, colleges of agriculture and forestry were established at the universities in Zagreb and Belgrade, and so were colleges of veterinary medicine. In the academic year 1937/38 Yugoslavia had 2 colleges of agriculture and forestry, 2 colleges of veterinary medicine, 3 agricultural high schools, 46 junior high and special agricultural schools, and 114 permanent and mobile schools of housekeeping for the training of peasant girls.[25] Furthermore, some students went to foreign universities for training in agricultural sciences. And, at least on one occasion, in 1930, in-service training on Swiss farms for a group of 86 young men from Yugoslavia was organized.

One of the basic difficulties in translating scientific progress in agri-

---

[24] Slobodan Jovanović, *Ustavobranitelji i njihova vlada* (The Defenders of the Constitution and Their Rule), Collected Works, V, 134–36.

[25] Yugoslavia, *Annuaire statistique 1938–1939*, pp. 354–73.

cultural sciences into real use in the South Slav lands was the lack of incentive and, therefore, the unwillingness on the part of trained agriculturists, especially those with high-school and college training, to return to agriculture. This seems to be the case in all countries of peasant farming. There were many reasons for that in Yugoslavia, but the principal one consisted in the fact that even in years of best crops and satisfactory prices it was extremely difficult to make a decent living in agriculture, except on large farms. And the basic reason for that was the unfavorable relationship between agricultural population and cultivated land and the predominance of subsistence farming. The intention of the overwhelming number of students from rural areas enrolling in agricultural high schools and colleges was actually to get out of agriculture, to cease to be a "peasant" and to become a *gospodin* or "gentleman," which almost always meant a government employee, and to make a living as a pencil-pusher, law-enforcement officer, or the like. Thus almost all graduates of agricultural high schools and colleges, both before 1918 and during the interwar period, sought employment in government service and to a lesser degree in private service in urban economy. The conditions in this regard during the 1930's were well illustrated in the annual report for 1938/39 to the Budget Committee of the parliament, by the Minister of Agriculture when he said

Although we have only three agricultural high schools, the graduates of these schools find little employment. The government and banovinal authorities employ mostly graduates of agricultural colleges at the universities, but not even all of these can be employed. Both groups seek only [central] government and banovinal employment. Very few find employment in agriculture itself. Government and banovinal services are getting more and more saturated and the number of unemployed agronomists grows.[26]

It was stated in 1935 that only about 10 percent of the graduates of the Agricultural High School at Križevci, the best school of its kind in the country, went back to agriculture.[27]

It should also be pointed out that in the opinion of many experts the curriculum of agricultural junior high and high schools was not well adjusted to the actual needs of agriculture and that the working on the school farms took altogether too much time of both teachers and students, which could have been much better utilized in the training

[26] Yugoslavia, Ministry of Agriculture, *Glasnik*, XVI (March 1938), 69.
[27] Quoted by Mijo Mirković in his *Agrarna politika* (Agrarian Policy), p. 205, from an article by Slavoljub Dubić, "Instruction in Agricultural High Schools," published in *Agronomski glasnik* in 1935.

of the youngsters. Thus, also, those few graduates of the agricultural schools who returned to agriculture could not contribute a full measure toward improvement in agricultural technology and management.

AGRICULTURAL RESEARCH

Research activities relating to agriculture and animal husbandry were carried on in the South Slav lands on a small scale for several decades prior to World War I. Some of these activities were connected with the agricultural schools, others were pursued by special organizations established in order to improve certain specific agricultural branches. Before 1918 there were, however, several large agricultural estates in Vojvodina which engaged in systematic improvement and development of crop varieties and of livestock breeds, which greatly helped their own production as well as that of the surrounding peasants. Only in some cases and on a reduced scale were such activities continued after 1918, because the political changes of 1918 and the agrarian reform disrupted the management of these estates and reduced the incentives to continue with such selection and improvement work.

Agricultural research activities during the interwar period were not of particular consequence. They were carried on almost exclusively by various government organizations either connected with the institutions of agricultural learning or existing as special agencies. There is no point in going into their activities beyond mentioning the leading organizations and their chief fields of interest. The most important agrcultural experiment and control stations were the following: in Topčider for wheat and barley, in Ljubljana for wheat and barley, in Zagreb for corn and forage crops, in Skoplje for poppies, rice, and hard wheat, and in Goražda (Bosnia) for fruit. There was an institute for the examination of farm machinery and implements at Belgrade which had to test and pass upon every type of farm equipment entering trade in Yugoslavia. An institute for wool research in Belgrade was working on the improvement of wool from domestic sheep. There were also several cattle, horse, and sheep selection stations in various sections of the country, three veterinary and bacteriological institutes (Belgrade, Ljubljana, and Križevci) and a veterinary experimental institute in Zagreb. The institutes at Zagreb and Belgrade also produced various drugs for the control of animal diseases and sold them to the peasants at cost. To direct, supervise, and co-ordinate agricultural research there was established in the Ministry of Agriculture in December 1938 a Central Advisory Board on Agricultural Research and Experiment Stations. Research activities of all these agencies were, however, impeded and in some cases kept at a minimum by two factors. On the one hand, most of these organizations were charged with a great number of purely administrative and control functions which hindered their research work; and, on the other, lack of funds and of trained personnel, as well as lack of real understanding and appreciation for the need of research work, kept their research activity at a minimum. Thus scientific information did not exist in Yugoslavia during the interwar period even on such essential problems as classification of soils (except in very limited areas), the effect of artificial fertilizers on the yield of various crops, the farm machinery and farm implements best suited to various soils, the strains of plants and breeds of animals best suited to various areas, the possibilities of and problems connected with the shifting of crops and their zoning in order to correspond better with the climate and soil conditions in different parts of the country, and the incidence and possible means of control of pests, insects, and diseases of plants and animals. There was practically no information on the productivity of livestock, the dynamics of livestock herds, and the production of animal food products. There was especially no systematic information on the changes in the supply of and the demand for agricultural and livestock products and their influence on the prices of these products and on the welfare of the agricultural population. There was no information on, or facilities for proper storage of agricultural products, their preparation for the market, and packaging. And there was no systematic information on the consumption of agricultural and livestock products in Yugoslavia and, thus, on the nutrition of the people.

But while research activities in agrotechnical and zotechnical fields had a long tradition, if not many or important achievements to their credit, these government agencies engaged only occasionally and superficially in the study of economic and social problems of agriculture and the peasantry. The first governmental agency which was supposed to concentrate its attention on these issues was the Administration for the Study of Agriculture and Nutrition, which was established in September 1939. Its research activities did not even get under way before the invasion of the country in April 1941. But, like practically all other agricultural and livestock research agencies, this administration was charged with work in the field of agricultural and food administration, for which it was primarily established. It was also charged with the stockpiling of food reserves for the periods of national emergency—i.e., in time of war. One of the basic difficulties in regard to research on the economic and social problems of Yugoslav agriculture was the unreliability of the existing statistical information, and complete lack of any statistical information on some basic issues pertaining to the structure and dynamics of Yugoslav agriculture. In this regard Yugoslavia was perhaps in a worse position than any other country in Europe with the exception of Albania, though the need for reliable information on the structure and dynamics of agriculture was an essential precondition for charting appropriate agricultural policies, and especially for the development and undertaking of a systematic program of agricultural development.

A group of organizations which did considerable research on the problems of disease, nutrition, housing, and related matters in rural areas of Yugoslavia during the interwar period were the Central Institute of Hygiene in Belgrade, the School of Public Health in Zagreb, and the Federation of Health Co-operatives. Furthermore, all of them engaged in spreading health and sanitary education in the village (see Chapter 25).

The absence of governmental organizations and efforts for the study of socioeconomic problems of agriculture resulted, understandably, in the attempt of private organizations and individuals to at least partially fill the gap. Thus, the founder of a very progressive school of thought in the field of public health in Serbia, the late Dr. Milan Jovanović-Batut of the University of Belgrade, investigated population movements, nutrition, working and living habits, and many other problems facing the Serbian peasantry after the 1880's. The agricultural co-operative movement in Serbia and its leader, Mihailo Avramović, did a creditable job in surveying the economic problems of Serbian agriculture in the decade before World War I. In the second half of the 1930's, when the issues of the agrarian reform and peasant debts ceased to command the primary attention of agricultural and other economists in Yugoslavia, and the problems of the structure and dynamics of agriculture and the issue of agricultural overpopulation became recognized as the central economic issues of the country, several private organizations were formed for or became interested in the study of these problems. The most interesting, perhaps, was the Research Institute on Peasant and National Economy within the Gospodarska Sloga, the co-operative economic arm of the Croatian Peasant party. The Socioeconomic Institute in Ljubljana and the Sociological Society in Belgrade also paid considerable attention to the socioeconomic issues of agriculture and peasantry. But counting both governmental and private efforts, it must be concluded that, before World War II, only beginnings were made in the study of the socioeconomic structure and dynamics of Yugoslav agriculture.

It is interesting to note that, on the other hand, the Yugoslav village had been for over a century an object of research on a large scale. This research was, however, directed primarily in three directions: linguistic, ethnographic, and with regard to customary law. This is to be understood partly as an outgrowth of the political bondage in which the Yugoslav nations lived, because the results of this kind of research could be effectively used as means of national reawakening and national cultural and political resistance. They were the emanations of cultural and political nationalism and were used for the strengthening of both. The two academies of long standing in Yugoslavia, the Yugoslav Academy of Science and Art in Zagreb and the Serbian Academy of Sciences in Belgrade, concentrated most of their energy, money, and publications on these aspects of the life of the Yugoslav village. The perusal of their many tomes yields little systematic information on the economic and social problems of the peasantry or the economic and social history of the South Slavs. It was thus unavoidable that a distorted, romantic picture of the life in the Yugoslav village emerged and persisted for a long time. The peculiar attitudes of the peasant parties in this respect helped to maintain this falsehood. A great deal of information and often penetrating qualitative analysis about the conditions in the village of the South Slav lands since about 1880 is to be found in novels, short stories, and plays of the realistic group of fiction writing.

The bulk of government funds "for the advancement of agriculture," and thus also for agricultural research, came from a share in the profits of the state lottery. Research and control work in special fields, such as sugar beets, cotton, oil seeds, and silkworm cultivation, was mostly financed by a special tax imposed on the producers of these crops. A large portion of work on the improvement of animal husbandry was shifted, after 1930, to the co-operatives for the improvement of various types of livestock which were subsidized by the government to a certain extent. Some funds for the "advancement of agriculture" came from special appropriations of the central bank and other government financial institutions, and some came from a number of private endowments. But the total was a mere pittance in comparison with the need.

In one very important respect very little if any advance was made during the interwar period, namely, in the improvement of the quality of agricultural and animal food products, their preparation for the market, and in marketing techniques themselves. It is perhaps safe to say that the quality of more agricultural and animal food products deteriorated rather than improved during that period of time.

It is well to remember, however, that natural, cultural, and socio-economic conditions put rather narrow limits on the improvements in Yugoslav agriculture within a short period of time. There were people who, especially during the 1920's, talked a great deal about the so-called "danization" of Yugoslav agriculture, i.e., its development, intensification, and specialization along the lines of Danish agriculture. But all those who looked closer into the problem soon saw that this talk represented wishful thinking. "Danization" of agriculture in Yugoslavia and other areas of Southeastern and Eastern Europe is an absolute impossibility for a long time to come, perhaps for ever.

But in spite of the rather narrow limits that are put on the improvement of agricultural production by the natural and socioeconomic conditions in Yugoslavia, it is nevertheless essential to stress that the increase in yields per unit of land and head of livestock rather than an expansion of the area of agricultural land is the principal frontier of advancement of agriculture in Yugoslavia and similar countries. It is because of this that agricultural education, agricultural research, reforms in land-tenure patterns, and creating of proper incentives for greater exertion on the part of agricultural producers—that is, all those measures which tend to increase agricultural productivity—acquire basic significance for Yugoslav agriculture.

SUNDRY ACTIVITIES OF THE GOVERNMENT AND OF PRIVATE ORGANIZATIONS ON BEHALF OF AGRICULTURE

There existed in Yugoslavia, during the interwar period, a system of agricultural and veterinary service with one field representative of each branch in almost every county of the country. Prior to 1929 these were organized on the basis of various laws which were supplanted by the Law on the Advancement of Agriculture of 1929 and the Law on the Advancement of Animal Husbandry of 1930. These services were, to a certain extent, comparable to the Extension Service in the United States, and the functions of the field representatives somewhat resembled those of the county agricultural agents in the United States. In regard to these laws and the services based upon them, it is imperative to distinguish between language and stated aims of the statutes, and their practical execution. The laws were conceived in and marked by a great deal of wishful thinking, but the appropriations for their execution were meager, and they were administered by people whose hearts were not always in what they were doing. As a result they accomplished little. Both the agricultural and the veterinary field services were primarily administrative and control organizations for enforce-

ment of laws and regulations affecting agriculture and animal husbandry. Their functions also included the making, in co-operation with
special communal committees, of annual statistical estimates on the
area under various crops, their yields, and the number and types of
livestock. Essentially it was a bureaucratic apparatus and was considered by the peasants not as something that was there to serve them
and to help them, but as just another branch of government administration. The Ministry of Agriculture and its various organizations spent
very little time, money, or energy on the extension work proper, namely,
searching for scientific methods of farming and animal raising and
making them available and understandable to the peasants, and actually
applicable on the farms under the prevailing conditions. Thus there
was little for the field agricultural and veterinary agents to "extend" to
the peasants of Yugoslavia. Many of these agents had, furthermore,
only limited notions of the conditions that existed in the areas under
their supervision, the real needs of the peasants, and the ways in which
these needs could be filled.

Nevertheless, there were a number of services that the central government or local government bodies rendered to the peasantry, but
their extent was limited by the small financial means earmarked for
such purposes. Thus, for example, the government had, for decades,
been importing good breeds of livestock from abroad or buying domestically produced breeding material for distribution among the peasantry
in order to replace and improve the existing livestock breeds. This
was especially true of cattle and, to a lesser extent, of horses, pigs, goats,
sheep, and poultry. This government program was definitely an important contribution to the improvement of livestock. During the
1930's the government bought considerable quantities of the Bankut
variety of wheat and distributed it among the peasants for seed in
areas where wheat was grown for the market, especially the export
market. In areas where the wheat yield, and not its quality, was the
basic consideration, the government was distributing the so-called
Prolifik wheat variety, which is rust- and drought-resistant and yields
approximately one-fourth more than other wheat varieties. The government maintained nurseries for grapevines and for various types of
trees, and thus helped the peasants to acquire better varieties. Two government veterinary laboratories were producing various drugs for the
control of livestock diseases, e.g., hog cholera, and sold them at cost. The
government passed special laws for the insurance of crops against
damage by hail, but these laws were never satisfactorily implemented.
The insurance of some types of livestock was carried on in some

areas by the co-operatives for the advancement of animal husbandry. The government also tested, in its laboratories, agricultural machinery and implements, artificial fertilizers, and drugs, thus providing a certain degree of protection for the peasants who were able to buy and use them. During livestock epidemics the government imposed various controls on transportation and sale of livestock.

The most telling proof of the very limited activity in agricultural research, field services, and assistance to agriculture on the part of the central government is the small share that the Ministry of Agriculture had in the purely administrative (personnel and matériel) expenditures of the government, but this issue will be discussed in Chapter 28.

Some service in the form of information and advice was given to the peasantry also by a great number of more or less well-conceived and variously effective private organizations. The oldest among them were the societies for the advancement of agriculture, of which the three best known were the Croato-Slavonian Agricultural Association in Zagreb and Osijek, which was established in 1840; the Serbian Agricultural Association in Belgrade, established in 1869; and the Slovenian Agricultural Association in Ljubljana, with its beginnings in 1767 and reorganization in 1870. All of them had hundreds of branches with many thousands of members, and each of them published special periodicals for the peasantry. The activity of these associations led, however, to their engaging in trading operations, which were not always successful. There were also professional organizations of college-trained agronomists and veterinarians from private and government services who, in their meetings, discussed not only their purely professional problems as lobbying groups, but also issues of importance to agricultural sciences and issues affecting agriculture and animal husbandry, and legislation pertaining to them. They also published their own periodicals. Further, there were the co-operative organizations, which, through their studies of the economic and management problems in agriculture, close contact with the peasantry, and the confidence that some of the agricultural co-operative organizations enjoyed among the peasantry, were able to exercise considerable influence upon and give help and advice to the peasants. The producers of such crops as sugar beets, hops, and a few others were organized in their special associations which were rendering information and assistance to their members. In addition, various political parties often had a special "extension-like organization" of their own which was usually organized in the form of a co-operative.

A special semipublic type of organization relating to agriculture was the chambers of agriculture, which were formed on the basis of a special decree of 1937. It was planned to have one of these chambers in each *banovina* and a co-ordinating federation in Belgrade. The chambers were supposed to develop both into organizations for the systematic study of the conditions and needs of agriculture in the various *banovine* and into lobbying organizations for the protection of the specific interests of agriculture in legislation and in various government policies and actions. By the beginning of World War II an agricultural chamber had been established in each *banovina*, except *Banovina* Croatia where its establishment was opposed by the Croatian Peasant party, which considered that the Peasant party itself and its organizations fully safeguarded the interests of the peasantry.

It must be understood, however, that there existed great psychological difficulties and formidable economic barriers in the way of any attempt to induce the peasants in most Yugoslav areas to change their old-established ways of thinking and doing things. The thinking of most peasants was tradition-bound, backward-looking. The peasantry in most Yugoslav areas had only limited contacts with the outside world, and little or no knowledge had penetrated into these areas about modern advances in agricultural technology. The impact of the penetration of money and market economy, while of profound consequence, still left the peasants largely in a situation in which, as before, the subsistence of their families on the basis of their own production, rather than production for the market, was the chief consideration. Thus, the importance of reducing costs of production by applying more modern methods of work in order to increase their competitive power was not a compelling issue as it was for the commercial farmers. Innovations in agriculture were looked upon by many peasants with suspicion, or else were considered to be beyond their ability to translate into practical use. Thus the peasants stuck to the old ways of production.

In fact, innovations were beyond the ability of many peasants for economic reasons. Among the economic barriers working against the introduction of more modern methods of agricultural technology, the most important were as follows: (1) The small size of farms was responsible for low production per household and for the small or nonexistent capacity to save and thus to finance the innovations or to incur the risks connected with them. Moreover, small farms would not have allowed full utilization of various implements or draft power, and their underutilization would have greatly increased their costs. (2) The price relationships between products that the peasants sold and those that they bought, including the products needed in the modernization of agricultural technology, were unfavorable to the peasants most of the time. (3) If credit was necessary to finance the innovations in farming, the exorbitant interest rates greatly increased their cost. Thus, some of these factors prevented any innovation in agricultural technology and others drastically reduced the economic incentives to introduce the innovations. In a great number of farms, technical advance was not noticeable and almost medieval methods of production were still used. In others the pace of advance was a mere crawl.

Of course, in areas in which a considerable portion of farm units was commercialized or quasi-commercialized, namely, in areas north of the Sava-Danube rivers, a considerable portion of the peasants showed a favorable attitude toward the application of more advanced methods of farming. They possessed not only the psychological willingness but also the economic possibilities to do so. Many of them possessed larger farms, had better conditions for marketing their products, could obtain credit at satisfactory terms, and could see the results of modern agricultural technology on neighboring large estates which were conducted as capitalist farm enterprises, and, as a rule, the natural fertility of the land they worked was much higher than in areas of predominantly subsistence farming. They were quite aware of the fact that through the application of better methods of production their costs would be lowered, their competitive power improved, and their revenue increased.

Had the research activity in agriculture been organized on a large scale, had it been properly adjusted to the needs of the peasant agriculture in Yugoslavia, and had appropriate ways been devised for communicating the results of agricultural education and research to the peasants, a greater advance in agriculture would have undoubtedly been made. The basic need was to bring the technical know-how to the individual farmer in ways understandable to him and applicable advantageously under the conditions in which he worked. The peasants could not be expected to seek knowledge in experiment stations or in books. Besides, many Yugoslav peasants were illiterate, and others lacked appropriate books. Peasants the world over learn best by seeing and doing things, because for them, more than for any other group of people, seeing means believing. Naturally, the spreading of agricultural know-how in this fashion is an expensive, arduous, long-term task requiring from those who undertake it not only knowledge but also patience and dedication.

CHAPTER 22

PRODUCTION OF CROPS

AN OVER-ALL discussion of the availability of land resources and their utilization in Yugoslavia during the interwar period was furnished in Chapter 14. The intention in this chapter is to discuss more fully the structure of crop production, the main characteristics of the more important crops, and the forces behind the changes in the amount of land devoted to various crops. The prevalence of dwarf and of small farms made it impossible for the great majority of the peasants to specialize in the production of crops for the market, but forced them generally to concentrate on the crops which, year in, year out, assured them of the highest possible return in terms of calories; that is, it forced them to concentrate on the production of cereals. But even when Yugoslav peasants produced for the market, a large proportion of their production was in grains, although a part of it was ultimately marketed in the form of livestock and livestock products. As we shall see in the course of this chapter, Yugoslavia raised a great variety of crops, but their importance was of a subsidiary nature in comparison with the importance of cereals.

THE GENERAL PATTERN OF THE UTILIZATION OF ARABLE LAND

Table 31 shows the utilization of arable land in selected years between 1921 and 1938. If we disregard, in the figures for 1921, the relatively low percentage of land under cereals and the relatively high percentage of the area held as fallow, both of which can be ascribed to the effects and aftereffects of World War I, there was very little change in the over-all pattern of utilization of arable land during the interwar period or in the relative hectarage of arable land devoted to various crop groups. The ratios of the arable land devoted to various groups of crops and to fallow remained relatively unchanged between 1925 and 1938. Meanwhile, however, the total area of arable land rose by exactly 25 percent. Of course, the areas under individual crops in various crop groups varied considerably during that time. That was especially true in the case of cereals, forage crops, and industrial crops.

The most important characteristic of the utilization pattern of arable land in interwar Yugoslavia was the overwhelming proportion of the total area taken by cereals. From 1924 until the end of the inter-

TABLE 31.—UTILIZATION OF ARABLE LAND IN SELECTED YEARS, 1921–38*

(Thousand hectares; planted area)

Year	Arable land	Grains	Potatoes	Vegetables and legumes	Industrial crops	Forage crops	Fallow
1921......	6,265	4,625	214	169	89	279	889
1925......	6,017	4,953	234	144	118	270	298
1930......	7,076	5,877	245	145	159	275	375
1935......	7,485	6,118	265	167	140	336	459
1938......	7,552	6,183	270	158	187	356	398
			IN PERCENT				
1921......	100	73.8	3.4	2.7	1.4	4.5	14.2
1925......	100	82.3	3.9	2.4	1.9	4.5	5.0
1930......	100	83.1	3.4	2.1	2.2	3.9	5.3
1935......	100	81.7	3.6	2.2	1.9	4.5	6.1
1938......	100	81.9	3.5	2.1	2.5	4.7	5.3

* Sources: For the years 1921 and 1925 from Yugoslavia, *Annuaire statistique 1931* (Belgrade, 1934), pp. 82–89; for 1930, 1935, and 1938 from *Annuaire statistique 1938–1939* (Belgrade, 1939), pp. 164–71. Classifications of vegetables, legumes, and forage crops for 1921 and 1925 have been adjusted to the pattern used in later years.

war period approximately 82 percent of all arable land was devoted to cereals. As already pointed out, and as will be shown even more conclusively in the following section, this was a concomitant of the predominantly subsistence character of the Yugoslav agriculture, and also of the fact that in areas of quasi-commercialized or commercialized agriculture cereals were the most important crops grown for the market. The area under potatoes averaged, throughout the interwar period, about 3.6 percent of the arable land area, that under vegetables and legumes about 2.3 percent, that under industrial crops about 2 percent, and that under forage crops about 4.5 percent. Between 1924 and 1938 the area held as fallow averaged between 5 and 6 percent of the total arable land, and, as we mentioned earlier, it was relatively much larger in *banovine* Vardar and Vrbas than in other *banovine*. The area of land devoted to crops other than grains showed the subsidiary position of these crops, though, as we shall see later, some of these crops had a considerably greater importance for agriculture and the national economy than would be indicated by the proportion of arable land devoted to their cultivation.

It is necessary to point out that areas devoted to various groups of crops, as indicated in Table 31, are in need of qualification. Thus, for example, a part of the cereals production was used for animal feed, and the overwhelming portion of straw and stover production in Yugoslavia was and is used for feed. A small portion of the potato production was also used for feed and some was used for industrial purposes. A small amount of corn production was also used for industrial purposes. The areas under forage crops and under industrial crops were thus somewhat larger than indicated in the table. The area under vegetables and legumes, as indicated in the same table, represents only the area on which vegetables and legumes were the sole or chief crop. In fact, both vegetables and legumes, and such forage crops as pumpkins, were interplanted with other crops, especially corn, on a large scale. But all these facts will be dealt with as we move along.

GRAIN HECTARAGE AND GRAIN PRODUCTION

As just pointed out, the production of grains formed the basis of Yugoslav crop production during the interwar period. Table 32 indicates the development of the area under all grains;[1] the areas under the two primary grains—wheat and corn; the area under the group of secondary grains—barley, rye, and oats; and the area under the group of minor grains—meslin, spelt, buckwheat, millet, and rice; and their respective production during the period 1921–38. The total area under all grains rose constantly, with slight interruptions only in 1923 and 1932; and between 1921 and 1938 the area increased by 33.6 percent. The development of the area under various grains differed, however, considerably. Until 1929 the wheat area grew at a somewhat higher rate than the area under corn. But while the area under wheat remained almost stationary between 1929 and 1938, the area under corn grew each year.[2] We shall see later that there were many reasons for the relatively faster growth of the area under corn than under wheat in Yugoslavia during the 1930's. On the other hand, the area under secondary grains showed rather small changes. It was only slightly over 5 percent larger in 1938 than it was in 1921, and throughout the period 1921–38 it fluctuated between the minimum of 918,000 hectares in 1925 and the maximum of 1,131,000 hectares in 1930. What is even more interesting, there were no basic shifts among the three secondary grains in regard to area. The area under minor grains was actually smaller in 1938 than it was in 1921 and 1922. But in this group of grains there

[1] The area devoted to grains, given in Table 32 and elsewhere, was the sown area. The harvested area was somewhat smaller. Thus, for example, during the period 1934–38 the harvested area under wheat was, on the average, 2.5 percent smaller than the area sown, and that under corn, 3.6 percent smaller than the area sown. Similar differences existed in regard to other grains. Only in years of droughts and big floods was that difference greater.

[2] It is interesting to note that in 1939 this trend was sharply reversed. The area under wheat rose from 2,156,000 hectares in 1938 to 2,260,000 hectares in 1939, while at the same time the area under corn fell from 2,842,000 to 2,661,000 hectares.

TABLE 32.—GRAIN HECTARAGE AND PRODUCTION, 1921–38*

(Thousand hectares; thousand metric tons)

Year	Total grain		Primary grains				Secondary grains[a]		Minor grains[b]	
	Area	Production	Wheat		Corn		Area	Production	Area	Production
			Area	Production	Area	Production				
1921	4,626	4,067	1,544	1,410	1,954	1,874	992	714	136	69
1922	4,711	4,185	1,531	1,210	2,045	2,281	993	621	142	73
1923	4,632	4,666	1,624	1,662	1,943	2,154	955	768	110	82
1924	4,844	6,183	1,789	1,572	2,003	3,795	944	736	108	80
1925	4,954	6,963	1,785	2,140	2,146	3,791	918	940	105	92
1926	5,032	6,369	1,798	1,944	2,174	3,410	950	923	110	92
1927	5,264	4,532	1,874	1,595	2,276	2,109	1,004	757	110	71
1928	5,307	5,656	1,921	2,811	2,304	1,819	979	952	103	74
1929	5,728	7,806	2,149	2,585	2,381	4,148	1,090	973	108	100
1930	5,877	6,628	2,171	2,186	2,467	3,465	1,131	888	108	89
1931	5,886	6,817	2,183	2,689	2,496	3,203	1,099	850	108	75
1932	5,873	7,215	2,125	1,455	2,625	4,793	1,014	872	109	95
1933	5,949	7,380	2,127	2,629	2,638	3,578	1,074	1,079	110	94
1934	5,989	8,051	2,102	1,860	2,700	5,154	1,072	939	115	98
1935	6,118	5,954	2,210	1,990	2,712	3,028	1,075	850	121	86
1936	6,179	9,164	2,247	2,924	2,738	5,180	1,070	959	124	101
1937	6,162	8,677	2,195	2,347	2,786	5,336	1,053	888	129	106
1938	6,183	8,873	2,156	3,030	2,842	4,756	1,055	975	130	112

* Sources: For the period 1921–23 Yugoslavia, *Annuaire statistique 1929* (Belgrade, 1932), pp. 138–39; for 1924–27 Yugoslavia, Ministry of Agriculture, *Statistique agricole annuelle 1933* (Belgrade, 1934), pp. 14–17; for 1928–37 Yugoslavia, Ministry of Agriculture, *Statistique agricole annuelle 1937* (Belgrade, 1938), pp. xviii–xxi; for 1938 Yugoslavia, *Annuaire statistique 1938–1939* (Belgrade, 1939), pp. 166–69.

[a] Includes barley, rye, and oats. In the period 1934–38 the respective average hectarage (thousand hectares) and production figures (thousand metric tons) were as follows: barley 432 and 403; rye 260 and 206; and oats 373 and 313.

[b] Includes meslin, spelt, buckwheat, millet, and rice. In the period 1934–38 the respective average hectarage (thousand hectares) and production figures (thousand metric tons) were as follows: meslin 66 and 56; spelt 17 and 12; buckwheat 5 and 3; millet 33 and 26; and rice 3 and 4.

were some basic changes in the area sown. The area under buckwheat in 1938 was only a fraction of what it was in the early 1920's, while the area under meslin rose by about 75 percent in the same period of time.

Since corn and wheat were by far the most important of the grains, a few remarks will suffice to deal with both secondary and minor grains. All three secondary grains are grown in all parts of the country where climatic and soil conditions made their production more advantageous than that of other grains or other crops. *Banovina* Vardar had, however, a relatively much larger area under rye (in the period 1934–38, 45 percent of the country's hectarage) and barley (in the period 1934–38, 25 percent of the country's hectarage) than any other part of the country. Here these two grains, to a large extent, took the place of corn, because corn growing in that area, though extensive, was impeded by unsuitable climatic conditions. Two other regions of relatively large barley production, *banovine* Primorje and Zeta, have climatic conditions somewhat similar to those of *banovina* Vardar. All three areas lacked the necessary humidity for successful corn growing, and on their poor soils barley did better than other grains. In these areas barley was grown where corn could not be, and was used instead of corn. But peasants of these areas often sold barley, rye, wheat, and oats in order to buy corn, which "went further." Thus, there were different ways in which the production of calories per unit of land could be maximized. In addition to *banovina* Vardar, rye growing was of importance only in *banovine* Drava, Sava, and Morava. The production of oats was more evenly distributed over the country than the production of either barley or rye. It was relatively most important in *banovina* Vrbas, followed by Drina and Vardar. In some localities in Serbia and Bosnia oats were used for making bread. Interestingly enough, the growing of secondary grains was of very little significance in the most important grain-growing area of the country, the Pannonian Plain. Here conditions were best suited for wheat and corn.

Most of the minor grains, with the exception of rice, were also grown throughout most of the country, although no spelt and buckwheat at all were grown in *banovina* Dunav. The growing of millet was concentrated primarily in *banovine* Sava and Zeta, which together had about five-sevenths of the total area. The largest area under buckwheat was in *banovina* Zeta, followed by Drava. Spelt was mostly grown in *banovine* Zeta, Sava, and Primorje, and meslin in *banovine* Morava, Primorje, and Sava. Rice was grown exclusively in *banovina* Vardar during the interwar period. Its area more than doubled between 1931 and 1938. But actually the area taken by the minor grains and their production, while of some importance in certain limited regions, was of no real consequence from a national point of view.

Before going into a more detailed discussion of wheat and corn, a few general remarks about the Yugoslav grain economy of the interwar period should be made. The climatic and soil conditions prevailing in Yugoslavia make it suitable for the production of wheat, almost exclusively winter wheat, and corn. The growing of these crops is also a matter of tradition, though, as was mentioned earlier, the tradition of corn growing is of relatively recent origin in some parts of the country. Had the Yugoslav agriculture been economically in a position to specialize its production for the market in all areas, it is almost certain that the growing of both wheat and corn would have been limited to the areas in the Pannonian Plain and in more suitable flat areas in the remainder of the country. The subsistence character of the Yugoslav agriculture resulted, however, in the growing of these crops in areas which were absolutely unsuitable, from the point of view of soil and climate, for the production of grains. This was, and still is, simply a consequence of the fact that peasant families tried, and try, to meet the basic food requirements of the household by their own production. Thus, even in such areas as *banovine* Primorje and Zeta, which were indeed poorly suited for the production of cereals, 75.7 and 81.7 percent, respectively, of all their arable land area in 1938 was under cereals. The low level of cereal yields in these areas as well as in most other Yugoslav areas is shown clearly in Table 14, page 281. However, it should not be forgotten that, under the conditions which existed in Yugoslavia, no better alternative use for that land was then available.

In the period 1934–38 the Yugoslav area under wheat amounted to 1.3 percent of the world's wheat area (including the U.S.S.R. and China), with an average production amounting to 1.5 percent of the world's total wheat crop. In the same years its area under corn represented, on the average, 3.1 percent of the world's corn area (including the U.S.S.R. and China) and its corn production 4.1 percent of the average production of corn in the world. In this period Yugoslavia was thus the fourteenth largest producer of wheat and the sixth largest producer of corn in the world.[3] The area which was consolidated into Yugoslavia in 1918 was, in the period 1909–13, a relatively larger wheat producer and perhaps a more important supplier of wheat and wheat flour to the European market than in the period 1934–38. But

[3] Food and Agriculture Organization of the United Nations and International Institute of Agriculture, *Les grands produits agricoles—Compendium international de statistique 1924–1938*, pp. 28, 90.

Yugoslav participation in the world corn area and corn production was greater in 1934–38 than before World War I. Throughout the interwar period Yugoslavia was a net exporter of both wheat and corn (and pigs).

There was no clear-cut distinction in Yugoslavia between grains grown for direct human consumption and grains grown for livestock feed. With the exception of oats and millet—the overwhelming portion of which was used for feed and only a small portion for breadmaking— and, to a lesser extent, corn and barley—which in many countries are grown primarily for feed or industrial purposes—most of the grains production was used for direct human consumption in Yugoslavia. This is of special importance in the case of corn, since corn used as grain provided a larger amount of the total caloric supply of cereals for human consumption than wheat in Yugoslavia during the interwar period (Table 40, p. 548). As feed for pigs, corn was also the chief raw material for the production of animal fats in the country.

From the point of view of Yugoslav agriculture as a whole, the production of wheat and corn, their marketing and utilization, was the central problem of the whole agriculture. The importance of these crops was increased by the fact that they were important export products (corn partly in the form of pigs and pig products) and the fluctuations in their exports, whatever the causes, were of fundamental significance for the Yugoslav balance of payments during the interwar period. Wheat was also the crop in which the government tried to follow a policy of price support, but more will be said about that in Chapter 26.

The most important area for wheat production lies in the northeastern plain, or in the territory which, between 1929 and 1941, was included in *banovina* Dunav. The wheat area in *banovina* Dunav in the period 1934–38 represented, on the average, 40.3 percent of the total area under wheat in the country, but it produced 48.5 percent of the total wheat crop. As pointed out on several occasions, this can be explained by the fact that the soil, climatic, and agrotechnical conditions in this area were much better for wheat growing than in any other part of the country.

Yugoslavia grows almost exclusively winter wheat. The production of spring wheat in the period 1934–38 averaged only about 30,000 metric tons annually and showed a falling trend. According to some estimates, there were during the interwar period as many as 200 different varieties of wheat grown in Yugoslavia, though differences among varieties were often very small and depended on special soil and cli-

matic conditions in various areas.[4] In reference to wheat which entered the channels of trade, there was ample room for confusion. Thus,
for example, the general public called all wheat grown in Vojvodina
"Banat" wheat. In trade, however, Banat wheat was only wheat which
was loaded into barges or railroad cars in Banat proper. "Tisa" was
a trade name for wheat loaded into barges on the river Tisa or on railroad cars within 30 kilometers of that river, whether it came from Banat
or from Bačka. As a rule it commanded a somewhat better price than
the Banat wheat, especially Banat wheat loaded on the Danube, because
the trade considered it somewhat better in quality. To capitalize on this
general attitude of the market, some Banat-grown wheat was marketed
as "Tisa-Banat." "Serbian" wheat was wheat loaded into railroad cars
along the main Serbian railroad line in the Morava Valley.[5]

During the 1930's the state favored the growing of a variety called
"Bankut" wheat, which was developed by commercial selection in
neighboring Hungary. While it degenerated under the Yugoslav conditions after two or three years and was susceptible to rust, it was still
considered somewhat better than some domestic wheats raised in Vojvodina, especially because of the somewhat higher weight and the
higher protein content. It was generally considered that the export
possibilities for that wheat were somewhat better than for other wheats.
The state favored its growing by distributing seed among the growers.
Agricultural co-operatives were also helpful in this regard. From 1930
to about 1936 the state also furthered the growing of a rust- and
drought-resistant wheat variety known under the commercial name of
"Prolifik." It usually yielded about 20 to 30 percent more than other
wheats, but its protein content and baking qualities were poor and its
growing was favored only in areas in which wheat did not enter the
channels of trade. Its growing in the Danubian area was discouraged
after 1936 because the mills and the government corporation handling
the export of wheat instituted certain penalties for accepting it. It was
obvious, however, that Yugoslav agriculture and the grain trade needed
an improvement and standardization of wheat varieties. The extent of
selection work which was under way in Yugoslavia during the interwar

[4] For a discussion of the qualities of wheat varieties grown in Yugoslavia in the late
1920's see Karlo Šoštarić-Pisačić, "The Qualities of Our Wheats," University of Zagreb,
*Godišnjak Sveučilišta Kraljevine Jugoslavije u Zagrebu za školske godine 1924/25–
1928/29* (Yearbook of the University of Zagreb for the Academic Years 1924/25–
1928/29), pp. 513–31.

[5] Information received in 1945 by correspondence from Leo Gotlib, who in the late
1930's was Director General of the Chartered Corporation for the Export of Agricultural
Products (PRIZAD), which handled the government monopoly of wheat exports (see
pp. 629–35).

period was limited, and it produced no marked results for the improvement of wheat varieties.

While wheat from the northeastern plains in Yugoslavia which entered domestic trade and export channels (Banat, Tisa, and later Bankut) had a high protein content (over 15 percent), one of the basic deficiencies of these wheats from the point of view of international trade was their high content of impurities.[6] The standard price quoted on the commodity exchanges in Novi Sad and Belgrade during the interwar period was based on the weight of 78 kilograms per hectoliter, with 2 percent impurities, f.o.b. barge Bačka. Regularly, the percentage of impurities was higher. In areas south of the Sava-Danube rivers the rate of impurities in wheat rose as one went farther south and, in Macedonia, reached astounding percentages. But very little of the wheat and other grains grown in these regions entered any but the local markets. Disregarding the question of admixtures and impurities, the quality (e.g., the gluten content and baking qualities) of wheat in these areas is much poorer than those grown in Vojvodina.

Corn growing in Yugoslavia, as stated earlier, took the largest area and was, during the interwar period, by far the largest and the most important single crop of the country. Like wheat, corn is also grown throughout the country, but former *banovina* Dunav produced the largest share of the total crop. In the period 1934–38 this *banovina* had 34.9 percent of the total area under corn and produced 47.1 percent of the country's corn crop. Because of this, *banovina* Dunav (especially Vojvodina) was a heavy exporter of corn in the form of grain and animal products. In Vojvodina, Slavonia, and Srijem, corn was little used as a bread grain. But in practically all other areas of the country the corn produced was used almost exclusively for direct human consumption.

Compared with wheat and other small grains, corn growing in the present Yugoslav territory is of relatively recent date. As was stated earlier, the spread of corn cultivation was one of the basic changes in the structure of crop production in the South Slav areas during the nineteenth century. Corn entered agricultural production in the present Yugoslav territory from the north, where it was introduced by the Austrians, and from the southeast, where it was brought in by the Turks.[7]

[6] For the characteristics and qualities of the Danubian wheats, see also Vladimir P. Timoshenko, "The Danubian Basin as a Producer and Exporter of Wheat," *Wheat Studies*, VI, No. 5 (March 1930), 232–37.

[7] Because of this, corn is known in various Yugoslav areas under different names, often quite colorful. The official name is *kukuruz*, but in some places it is called *framentun*, *carevica* (Tsar's grain), *kolomboć* (Columbus grain), and *turčica* (Turkish grain).

After having spread from both directions into the plains and river valleys, corn began to spread into higher altitudes. In some areas of the central mountain region of present Yugoslavia, corn was grown as a garden crop as recently as 70 years ago. After the peasants established that corn could fully ripen under the climatic conditions prevailing in these areas, it soon became the leading crop there. Today corn is grown at altitudes of up to 1,200 meters in places where the land is exposed to sun. Owing to the climatic conditions in these altitudes, only fast-ripening varieties can be grown. Generally speaking, the Yugoslav peasantry has accepted the varieties of corn which under the existing conditions prove most satisfactory, that is, ecological types. As corn growing has spread throughout the country, it has taken, as a rule, the best land and is a crop to which the peasantry, in areas of subsistence farming, is paying more attention than to any other. A relatively large amount of manure is used for corn. It is cultivated diligently, and in some areas the peasants have developed primitive methods of irrigation for their cornfields. This fact is quite understandable, since life in these areas now largely depends on corn. In these mountain regions corn is more cultivated and its consumption is preferred to that of wheat, apparently for reasons of both taste and economy. Moreover, corn gives more fodder, uses less seed, and, above all, yields more in terms of calories than other grains.

Yugoslavia grows a considerable number of corn types. The type grown in any particular area is adjusted to the soil and climatic conditions of that particular area, to the kind of use, and to the preferences of the population. According to Professor Alois Tavčar of the University of Zagreb, the foremost Yugoslav authority on corn,[8] the distribution of corn types in Yugoslavia in 1950 was as follows: In Montenegro, Macedonia, Dalmatia, and Bosnia and Herzegovina, where most of the corn is grown at higher altitudes, white flint is grown, though in Macedonia and Dalmatia a certain portion of the corn production is yellow flint. In the Vardar Valley in Macedonia some dent corn is produced. In the mountainous and hilly region of the Croatian Zagorje, yellow flint is grown, as a rule, but in some localities in this area people prefer the growing of white flint in order to have "white bread." In Slavonia, Srijem, and Vojvodina, that is, in the flat areas along the Danube, Tisa, Sava, and Drava rivers, the basic corn type grown is yellow dent. Here the feeding of corn to pigs and export of corn, rather than direct consumption, are the rule. Some white dent, but on a minor

[8] Information received in personal conversation on the occasion of his visit to the United States in June 1950.

scale, is produced in Vojvodina. In Serbia white dent is the primary type in low altitudes, but some yellow dent is grown here also, while at higher altitudes white flint predominates, though some yellow flint is grown too. Generally speaking, flint-type corn is grown at higher altitudes and is used for direct human consumption, and the dent-type corn is grown in flat areas and low altitudes, and is generally used either as feed or for export. When corn is grown for direct human consumption and people want a "white bread" type, they grow white flint or white dent. In areas which suffer from droughts, which is especially true of the karst area and Macedonia, the fast-ripening type, the hard white flint corn, often called "one hundred days' corn" is grown. It is short, has small ears, and is planted very thickly.

While this distribution of corn types as grown in various parts of Yugoslavia refers to 1950, it is safe to assume that the situation prevailing during the interwar period was very similar.

STAGNATION OF WHEAT AND GROWTH OF CORN AREA DURING THE 1930's

Table 32 depicted the two most important changes in the grain economy of Yugoslavia during the interwar period: (1) the growth of the area under primary grains, and (2) the increase in the corn area after 1929, while the area under wheat remained practically unchanged during the 1930's (compare, however, footnote 2 on p. 475). The first development was the consequence of the fact that, owing to the overwhelming preponderance of grain growing in Yugoslav agriculture, the increase of the arable land area during the interwar period was bound to be used primarily for the growing of grains, and to the fact that the increase in population forced the agricultural population to grow more grains both for direct consumption in the households and for sale in order to provide income for buying other necessities. The second development, the growth of the corn area and the stagnation of the wheat area during the 1930's, was brought about by a series of factors, partly of an international and partly of purely domestic origin. Little can be added here to what has already been said about the growth of the area under grains during the interwar period. While there was some talk about increasing the cultivation of crops other than cereals, the shifting of land to these crops did not take place. On the contrary, taking 1921 as a base, the increase in the relative area under cereals was much greater than the increase in other crops. This was done partly at the expense of the fallow. The basic reason for this development in cereals was that, under existing conditions, it did not pay to shift from cereals to other crops whether the calculation was made in money or in real terms.

The reasons for the growth of the area under corn during the 1930's are many. Commercially speaking, wheat was a "sick" commodity for more than half of the interwar period. Corn was, apparently, never in such a position. There were several reasons for the respective development of these two commodities. Owing to the great advances in the mechanization of wheat growing, and a seller's market for wheat during World War I and most of the 1920's, the world area under wheat (excluding U.S.S.R. and China) rose from an average of 79.4 million hectares in 1909–13 to 98.7 million hectares in 1924–28, and to 106.3 million hectares in 1934–38, according to the data of the International Institute of Agriculture. There was practically no change in the world's area under wheat from 1929–33 to 1934–38.[9] The increase in the area under wheat in the world (excluding U.S.S.R. and China) between 1909–13 and 1934–38 amounted to 33.2 percent. During the same time the area under wheat in the Yugoslav territory rose from an average of 1,613,000 hectares in 1909–13[10] to 2,182,000 hectares in 1934–38, or 35.2 percent.

On the other hand, the world area under corn (excluding U.S.S.R. and China) rose from an average of 70.7 million hectares in 1909–13 to 76.0 million hectares in 1924–28, and 79.3 million hectares in 1934–38. This represented a rise of only 12.5 percent between 1909–13 and 1934–38. There was a small drop in the world's area under corn from 1929–33 to 1934–38.[9] During the same period the area under corn in the Yugoslav territory rose from an average of 1,938,000 hectares in 1909–13[10] to 2,755,000 hectares in 1934–38, or 42.1 percent. Thus, while the increase in wheat hectarage in Yugoslavia between 1909–13 and 1934–38 was just slightly higher than in the world as a whole, the increase in the hectarage under corn during the same time was almost three and a half times larger.

The larger rise in the world area under wheat between 1909–13 and 1934–38 was partly due to the fact that wheat can be successfully grown under much more varied climatic conditions than corn. Thus wheat

[9] World hectarages under wheat and corn for the period 1909–13 from International Institute of Agriculture, *International Yearbook of Agricultural Statistics 1930–31*, pp. 158, 174; and for the periods 1924–28, 1929–33, and 1934–38 from the Food and Agricultural Organization of the United Nations and International Institute of Agriculture, *op. cit.*, pp. 27, 89.

[10] Data on the hectarages of wheat and corn in the territory which since 1918 forms Yugoslavia for the period 1909–13, as compiled by the U.S. Department of Agriculture. See Vladimir P. Timoshenko, *op. cit.*, pp. 216–17.

area expanded greatly not only in the four chief exporting countries—
that is, the United States, Canada, Argentina, and Australia—but
throughout the world. Increased wheat growing in Germany, Austria,
Czechoslovakia, Italy, and Greece was especially important from the
point of view of the Danubian countries because it was in these markets
that the bulk of the wheat from the Danubian countries was sold. Increased wheat growing in the above European countries was perhaps
the chief expression of the resurgent economic nationalism as applied
to agriculture, and was induced by economic, social, political, and
military reasons. In addition, the greater increase in wheat area was
partly due to the fact that mechanization in wheat growing started
earlier and advanced much further than in corn growing. Both large-
scale mechanization and the introduction of high-yielding hybrid corn
were developments of the late 1930's and the 1940's. Thus, for the
Danubian countries it was relatively much harder to compete against
wheat than against corn from extra-European areas.

Corn, on the other hand, requires special climatic conditions characterized by humid growing periods and hot ripening periods. Because
of this, its cultivation in large quantities is limited to a relatively few
areas: the United States corn belt, Argentina, Brazil, Mexico, and the
Danubian Plain, especially Rumania and Yugoslavia. Moreover, only
the United States, Argentina, and the Danubian countries were corn-
exporting countries. Owing to the fact that in the importing countries
corn was used almost exclusively for feed purposes (a certain amount
for industrial purposes) and that autarky in fats was harder to achieve
in Central European countries than autarky in bread grains, corn had
a more varied and more satisfactory external market. Moreover, a
considerable amount of corn was exported in the form of live pigs, lard,
and pork. Wheat, on the contrary, was used in the importing countries
almost exclusively as bread grain. Above all, corn produced a larger
amount of calories per hectare than wheat or other small grains. It also
produced a somewhat larger amount of fodder than could be obtained
in the form of straw from small grains. Furthermore, the interplanting
of string beans and pumpkins with corn, a practice impossible with
wheat, increased considerably the value of product per hectare of land
under corn.[11] Cornstalks were also used instead of firewood, which, in
forestless areas such as Vojvodina and Srijem, was an additional ad-

[11] It was estimated around 1940 that in Croatia-Slavonia, Bosnia and Herzegovina,
and Dalmatia between 54 and 62 percent of the area under corn was interplanted with
string beans. Božo Turina, *Poljodjelstvo u Nezavisnoj Državi Hrvatskoj* (Agriculture in
the Independent State of Croatia), p. 52 and *passim*.

vantage from corn growing. The fact that corn required a great deal more labor per hectare than wheat and other small grains was of little consequence in most households, as they had a surplus of labor which otherwise would have remained unutilized. In households that had to hire labor, the low wage rates of agricultural workers made that factor relatively less important than in countries with a high agricultural wage level, e.g., in the United States. It should also be pointed out that seed requirements of corn per hectare were only about one-fourth to one-third of those for wheat. This affected the costs of the two grains considerably. Furthermore, a certain amount of the labor cost connected with the cultivation of corn, and of manure applied to corn, should perhaps be added to the cost of wheat, as they had a favorable effect on the yield of wheat in the following year.

Table 33 shows the areas under wheat and corn in 1929 and 1938 by *banovine*, and the percentage change in the areas planted to these crops in the two years. While the area under wheat increased only by 0.3 percent between 1929 and 1938, the area under corn increased by 19.4 percent. But changes in the area under the two crops in various regions differed greatly. There was no *banovina* in which the area under corn decreased during that decade. The region in which the rise in the area under both wheat and corn was the largest, *banovina* Zeta,

TABLE 33.—HECTARAGES UNDER WHEAT AND CORN IN 1929 AND 1938, AND PERCENTAGE CHANGES BETWEEN 1929 AND 1938, BY BANOVINE*

(Thousand hectares)

Banovina	Wheat			Corn		
	1929	1938	Change in percent	1929	1938	Change in percent
Drava	60.1	64.4	+ 7.1	39.4	44.6	+13.2
Drina	286.9	233.5	—18.6	319.2	366.6	+14.8
Dunav	843.1	884.6	+ 4.9	834.0	960.1	+15.1
Morava	203.1	207.8	+ 2.3	318.1	381.1	+19.8
Primorje	43.7	33.6	—23.0	53.5	57.8	+ 7.9
Sava	289.0	320.2	+10.8	366.4	481.4	+31.4
Vardar	226.5	241.6	+ 6.7	171.2	177.4	+ 3.6
Vrbas	148.2	106.1	—28.4	210.6	270.7	+28.6
Zeta	44.0	59.9	+36.2	62.8	97.3	+54.9
Prefecture of Belgrade	4.2	4.5	+ 4.8	5.6	4.6	—18.3
Total	2,148.8	2,156.2	+ 0.3	2,380.8	2,841.6	+19.4

* Source: For 1929 Yugoslavia, *Annuaire statistique 1929* (Belgrade, 1932), pp. 138–39; for 1938 from *Annuaire statistique 1938–1939* (Belgrade, 1939), pp. 166–67.

was insignificant from the point of view of grain production in the country as a whole. The same is true of the two other grain-deficit *banovine*, Primorje and Drava. In the former the area under wheat decreased by 23 percent; that under corn rose by 7.9 percent. In the latter the area under both crops rose, but that under corn rose by almost twice as much as that under wheat. In *banovina* Vardar the areas under both wheat and corn rose, but by a very small percentage. However, it should be noted that in both Vardar and Zeta the combined area under barley and rye rose between 1929 and 1938. In other *banovine* where these secondary grains are used for bread, such as Primorje, Vrbas, Drina, and Morava, their combined areas fell between 1929 and 1938.

In the *banovine* Drina and Vrbas, where the pressure of population growth was most pronounced during the interwar period (see Table 19, p. 300), the hectarages under wheat fell markedly, that is, by 18.6 and 28.4 percent, respectively, while the hectarages under corn rose by 14.8 and 28.6 percent, respectively. This development proves our earlier contention that one of the avenues through which the village adjusted itself to the growing population pressure was the shift to the cultivation of the higher-yielding (in terms of calories) corn at the expense of lower-yielding other grains.

In the most important grain-producing area, *banovina* Dunav, the area under wheat rose by only 4.9 percent, while the area under corn rose by 15.1 percent. In the second most important grain-growing area, *banovina* Sava, wheat area rose by 10.8 and the corn area by 31.4 percent, respectively.

Generally speaking, the increase in rural population was perhaps the most important factor in this greater allocation of land for the growing of corn, because corn produced a larger amount of food in terms of calories, and an equal or larger amount of fodder than small grains produced in the form of straw. Moreover, much of the area under corn was regularly interplanted with string beans and pumpkins. This greater yield, or the more favorable input-output relationship in terms of calories, was no doubt the basic cause for the relative increase in the corn growing in Yugoslavia during the 1930's in the case of the overwhelming number of households. In areas in which corn was marketed either as grain or pigs or both, price relationships and the ability to sell the respective products—that is, wheat on the one hand and corn and/or pigs on the other—undoubtedly played an important role. But here, too, the basic consideration was the input-output relationship between the two crops. The peasants decided for a larger cultivation of corn because its marketing was safer, and, under the circumstances, the revenue from the growing of corn and crops interplanted with corn was higher in relation to cost than the revenue from growing of wheat. It is impossible to prove this contention in monetary terms because the use of farm accounting by Yugoslav peasants was a great rarity. But the decision of many peasants to grow relatively more corn than wheat and the sustained trend of this policy must have been arrived at by the method of trial and error, which was the common method of making shifts in production. The fact is, however, that the ratio between wheat and corn prices in the period 1929–38 in Vojvodina, an area where a large portion of grains was grown for the market and where price influences were important, was, on the average, 1.7 : 1,[12] while at the same time the relationship between the yields of wheat and corn per hectare in *banovina* Dunav was reversed, that is, approximately 1 : 1.7. It should be noted, though, that prices here compared were not prices of wheat and corn on the farms, because such price information does not exist, but rather average prices of these products on the Novi Sad Commodity Exchange at the end of March, June, September, and December of these years. As will be explained in Chapter 26, practically all marketable surpluses of wheat and corn (except corn to be used for feeding of pigs by the producer himself) were marketed within two or three months after the harvest. Thus, with the exception of the first few months after the harvest, prices of grains affected little the money income of the peasants who were producing these commodities.

The total grain area in Yugoslavia during the interwar period hardly reacted to the changes in prices. It kept growing during the 1930's although prices were very much below what they were during the 1920's. But, as was just explained, it did react to the "structural" depression in wheat. The over-all growth of the area under grains was partly due to the subsistence character of the overwhelming portion of Yugoslav agriculture and the need of peasant households for a greater production of cereals resulting from the growth of population. It was also partly due to the fact that there was little possibility of profitably shifting the grain area to other crops. But marketing of cereals will be discussed in Chapter 26.

POTATOES

Among other food crops, potatoes are quite important. An average area of 265,600 hectares was planted with potatoes during the period

[12] Ljubomir S. Dukanac, *Yugoslav Business Cycles (Index Numbers) 1919–1941*, pp. 15–18.

1934–38 with an average production of 1.6 million metric tons per year, of which 75 percent were late varieties. On the whole, potatoes play a much smaller role in the agricultural economy and in nutrition in Yugoslavia than in the Central and Eastern European countries, especially in Poland and Germany. The area under potatoes increased from 214,000 hectares in 1921 to 245,000 in 1930, and to 270,000 in 1938, or 26 percent in 18 years.

In Slovenia and most of Croatia-Slavonia potatoes have been grown since 1778, in Dalmatia since 1809—that is, since the time of the French occupation—and in Bosnia and Herzegovina on a small scale since early in the nineteenth century and on a larger scale since the Austro-Hungarian occupation in 1878.

Potato growing was relatively most important in *banovina* Drava, as here potatoes occupied 18.1 percent of all arable land in the period 1934–38. In this area potatoes serve as an important substitute for cereals. But, in absolute figures, the most important potato-producing area in Yugoslavia was *banovina* Sava, which in the period 1934–38 produced 40 percent of the total crop in the country. Here the production of potatoes had an interesting history, since, prior to 1918, it was helped by a government subsidy on industrial alcohol. This subsidy could be obtained only if certain soil-improvement practices were followed, primarily a higher application of stable manure per unit of land. To produce more manure it was necessary to keep more cattle, and to keep more cattle it was necessary to have more feed. Growing of potatoes, to be used partly for feed and partly for the production of industrial alcohol, was thus encouraged. The bulk of production, of course, was used for human food. Potato growing in this area also helped develop the production of good beef cattle.

It is interesting to note that potato growing is very successful in certain karstic areas, notably in southwestern Croatia (Gorski Kotar) and in parts of Montenegro. This is due to a combination of satisfactory soil and climatic conditions.

VEGETABLES AND LEGUMES

As in all countries of subsistence farming, the area under vegetables for consumption in fresh, dried, or canned form is not as high in Yugoslavia as in countries of industrialized agriculture, modern transportation, modern methods of preservation, modern and large storage facilities, and advanced notions about nutrition. During the period 1934–38 there were in Yugoslavia only 162,100 hectares, or 2.1 percent, of the arable area under vegetables as the chief or only crop. But it was common practice to interplant vegetables with many other crops. Thus, for example, the reported production of dried beans from the area on which beans were interplanted with other crops, chiefly with corn, averaged, in the above period, 103,900 metric tons annually as against an annual average of 31,195 metric tons obtained from the area on which beans were the only crop. Since, as a rule, vegetable growing requires a great deal of water, the fact that Yugoslavia had only a small area of irrigated agriculture was partly responsible for the small area under vegetables.

Among leafy vegetables, cabbage of several varieties is the most important. In certain areas, e.g., in karstic areas, cabbage is essential from a nutritional point of view, because it is the chief leafy vegetable consumed and thus the most important source of vitamins for the population. Other vegetables such as onions, garlic, tomatoes, bell peppers, red beets, lettuce, squash, cucumbers, string beans, peas, broad beans, lentils, eggplant, spinach, Swiss chard, carrots, turnips, asparagus, and cauliflower are also grown, often partly interplanted with other crops. Only around some of the cities and in certain areas of the Pannonian Plain (e.g., around Novi Sad in Vojvodina) are vegetables grown on a larger, commercial scale. In the latter area some vegetables were commercially canned during the interwar period. The vegetable gardeners around some cities were often Bulgarians. But, in fact, the cities and towns had to rely for their requirements of vegetables on the supplies which the surrounding peasants brought to the city markets. Because of this, vegetables were generally of poor and very uneven quality.

Next to cabbage, the most important vegetable is string beans. This crop has a double importance, since it is consumed fresh as well as furnishing dried beans. Dried beans, as in many other European countries, are a basic staple and, with cabbage and potatoes, they represent the main winter dish of a large segment of both the rural and urban populations. This legume is an important source of proteins. In fact, Yugoslavia produced enough dried beans to have a surplus for export during the interwar period. Third among vegetables in terms of area planted as the chief crop are onions. In Yugoslavia onions are eaten not only in the form of seasoning for various other foods but are often eaten with bread only. The area under other vegetables is much smaller than that under the three types mentioned above.

The production of fresh vegetables, as reported in the agricultural statistics, averaged roughly 430,000 metric tons annually in the period 1934–38 and consisted of the following: 247,000 metric tons of cabbage, 79,000 tons of onions and garlic, 31,000 tons of carrots, 25,000 tons of bell peppers, and 48,000 tons of tomatoes. This production came from the area on which vegetables were the only or the chief crop. When account is taken of the fact that the production of fresh string beans, one of the most popular vegetables in the country, fresh peas, fresh broad beans, and many other lesser vegetables was not statistically reported even when grown on a certain area as the chief crop, and the fact that the whole production of fresh vegetables when grown as interplanted crops was not reported, then it becomes quite obvious that the production of vegetables was much larger than indicated in the official statistics. It appears reasonable to assume that the remaining production of vegetables amounted to at least 400,000 metric tons, thus giving a total vegetable production of about 830,000 metric tons during the period 1934–38.

The consumption of vegetables was limited almost exclusively to the season of their harvest. The canning industry was of no consequence, and the prices of the exceedingly small production of canned vegetables were such that they were out of reach even of the medium-income groups. In fact, most people even in towns were unaware of their existence. Of course, certain traditional ways of preserving vegetables were widely practiced. Thus, sauerkraut was made every year in large vats by almost every family in the villages and smaller towns in areas where head cabbage was grown. Sauerkraut was also sold in large quantities. Pickling of bell peppers, tomatoes, and cucumbers in glass containers was also a widespread practice. Some tomato paste was made simply by drying tomato juice in the sun. In some areas turnips were shredded and pickled in the same fashion as sauerkraut. But that was all. The nature of all these preserving practices, with the exception of making sauerkraut and pickled turnips, was such that large quantities could not be put up. The result was that people did not have any leafy vegetables, with the exception of cabbage, except in the harvest season. That was one of the important reasons for the monotony of the diet of the overwhelming portion of the people during much of the year. On the other hand, during the harvest season one ate the vegetable grown in that particular area, e.g., string beans every day for weeks and weeks.

There was considerable talk in Yugoslavia during the 1930's, under the stress of difficulties in cereals and livestock export trade, that the country should pay much more attention to the raising of vegetables, especially of the early varieties, and become a supplier of the Central European market with these specialty crops. But this remained only talk. Those who envisaged Yugoslavia becoming an important producer and exporter of early vegetables were apparently not aware that in a country without irrigated agriculture and with little good soil in areas where climatic conditions were satisfactory for such crops (along the Adriatic coast), such a branch of specialized agriculture had very narrow limits. It is interesting to note, however, that the Bulgarians had considerable success during the 1930's in devoting a larger amount of their agricultural resources to the production of vegetables and fruits for export, though their chief success consisted in increasing greatly their fruit exports.[13] But in regard to the growing of vegetables, the Yugoslavs could not possibly compete with the Bulgarians. The latter are gardeners by tradition, while the Yugoslavs are definitely not, and shifting to the production of vegetable crops on a large scale would have implied acquisition of totally new skills for that part of the population even if the other conditions could be fulfilled. Moreover, it would have been necessary to provide refrigerated transportation and storage facilities, which also involved considerable costs.

The reported production of pulses averaged 148,800 metric tons during the period 1934–38. It consisted of 135,095 metric tons of dried beans, 6,400 tons of dried peas, 2,200 tons of lentils, and 5,100 tons of horse or broad beans. Presumably the total actual production was larger.

In Yugoslav official statistics the area under watermelons and melons is counted as part of the area under vegetables, and we have followed this practice. In Table 39, which gives a consolidated picture of the total Yugoslav food production during the period 1934–38, we show watermelons and melons as a separate item, however. In that period the officially reported crop of watermelons and melons amounted to 172,000 metric tons, but we added another 28,000 metric tons as the assumed production from the area where watermelons and melons were interplanted with other crops, giving a total production of about 200,-000 metric tons.

INDUSTRIAL CROPS

Except for such industrial crops as tobacco, poppies for opium and for oil, cotton, pyrethrum, medicinal herbs, and some oil seeds, which are well suited to the soil and modified Mediterranean climatic conditions of Dalmatia, parts of Herzegovina, and especially Macedonia, the areas of industrial crops are the valleys of the Danube, Tisa, Sava, and Drava rivers. Among the industrial crops in these river valleys the most important are sugar beets, various oil seeds, hemp, flax, and hops.

[13] Milka Deyanowa, "Die staatlichen Massnahmen zur Förderung der Ausfuhr der Agrarprodukte Bulgariens," *Weltwirtschaftliches Archiv*, LI, No. 2 (March 1940), 403–36, esp. 430.

The corn and potatoes that were used for the production of industrial alcohol and starch, and the corn that was used for the production of corn syrup were also produced in these areas. Red bell peppers for the production of paprika powder are also grown in these parts.

As is shown in Table 34, the area under industrial crops more than doubled between 1921 and 1938. In the former year it took only 1.42 percent and in the latter year 2.47 percent of the total arable land area. Growing of industrial crops was, however, relatively more important in the Yugoslav agricultural picture during the interwar period than is indicated by the area under these crops. This was so for several reasons. First, this was a very dynamic part of Yugoslav agriculture, with larger relative changes in hectarage than in the case of any other crop or crop group. Second, industrial crops were exceedingly important as cash crops and as export crops, thus having special importance for agriculture as sources of cash income, and for the Yugoslav economy as sources of foreign exchange. Third, these crops supplied raw materials for some important agricultural industries. Finally, the products of two of these industrial crops, sugar and tobacco, had a very great significance in the Yugoslav taxation system of the interwar period, as they were subject to exceedingly high consumption taxes (see Chapter 28). The area under industrial crops was influenced by many more factors and fluctuated much more widely than, say, the area under cereals. Some of these factors come readily to mind: economic fluctuations at home and abroad, special factors in foreign trade, e.g., greater demand from Germany during the late 1930's, government fiscal and price-guaranty policies, government propaganda in support of these crops, and, in the case of tobacco and poppies for opium, also government regulation of the area to be planted. The area under all industrial crops rose from 1922 to 1924, fell considerably in 1925, and then climbed steadily until 1930. From 1930 to 1933 the area under these crops fell by 35 percent, but thereafter, with the exception of 1937, it rose constantly until 1938. Within this over-all movement of the total area under industrial crops there were very many changes in the area under individual crops, and these changes were caused by a great variety of special factors.

Hemp, like flax, was widely utilized in earlier times for home-produced textiles. But in recent decades it developed primarily into an export crop. While hemp was grown over most of the country, the most important area for its production, especially for export purposes, was Vojvodina, followed by Slavonia. In both of these areas the German minority was the controlling factor both in production and in proc-

TABLE 34.—TOTAL AREA UNDER INDUSTRIAL CROPS AND AREA UNDER PRINCIPAL INDUSTRIAL CROPS, 1921–38*

(*Thousand hectares*)

Year	Total	Hemp	Sugar beets	Tobacco	Flax	Poppies	Cotton	Hops	Rape	Sunflower	Other[a]
1921......	88.8	31.9	17.0	14.4	14.7	3.3	0.7	1.2	4.5	—	1.1
1922......	88.1	30.2	20.0	12.7	13.7	3.6	1.0	1.8	3.3	—	1.8
1923......	99.2	25.5	28.6	21.7	13.8	3.9	0.5	1.1	2.5	—	1.6
1924......	138.7	27.7	49.8	35.9	13.3	3.9	0.8	2.2	2.3	—	2.8
1925......	117.9	39.8	34.1	15.3	13.2	5.4	0.9	2.1	2.8	—	4.3
1926......	118.5	34.4	37.1	15.9	13.0	6.1	0.7	4.3	3.7	—	3.3
1927......	128.0	34.4	42.7	11.7	12.8	6.7	0.6	9.2	4.2	—	5.7
1928......	147.0	31.1	56.5	11.4	13.2	13.2	0.7	9.2	7.4	—	4.3
1929......	153.5	32.7	59.7	15.8	13.9	6.3	1.0	6.3	11.4	—	6.4
1930......	158.4	38.1	53.2	16.0	13.3	14.8	1.4	3.2	12.2	—	6.2
1931......	138.1	27.5	46.2	20.8	12.8	11.7	0.8	2.3	9.3	—	6.7
1932......	122.1	27.1	43.5	22.2	11.8	4.8	1.0	1.5	3.7	—	6.5
1933......	103.0	30.8	30.4	11.5	11.3	6.0	1.1	1.7	3.4	—	6.8
1934......	114.7	37.7	27.9	7.4	11.1	7.7	1.3	2.4	7.9	2.6	8.7
1935......	140.0	44.1	30.0	12.5	12.1	9.0	1.4	2.6	17.6	1.9	8.8
1936......	169.7	53.4	30.2	18.3	13.7	9.8	1.8	2.7	24.6	5.1	10.1
1937......	168.2	56.3	21.5	21.1	13.6	9.1	3.1	3.4	19.0	9.7	11.4
1938[b]...	186.8	57.8	29.4	16.7	14.4	8.1	5.5	3.1	19.0	19.4	13.4

* Source: For 1921–23 from Yugoslavia, *Annuaire statistique 1931* (Belgrade, 1934), pp. 90–93; for 1924–27 from Yugoslavia, Ministry of Agriculture, *Statistique agricole annuelle 1933* (Belgrade, 1934), pp. 14–15; for 1928–37 from Yugoslavia, Ministry of Agriculture, *Statistique agricole annuelle 1937* (Belgrade, 1938), pp. xviii–xix; for 1938 from Yugoslavia, *Annuaire statistique 1938–1939* (Belgrade, 1939), pp. 168–71.

[a] Includes the following crops: anise, castor-oil seed, chicory, pyrethrum, sesame, sorghum, soybean, as well as other industrial crops grown on relatively small area for which no separate data were collected. No data were collected for sesame before 1925, for anise before 1927, and for castor-oil seed, soybean, and sunflower before 1934.

[b] The area for tobacco and for "other" industrial crops in 1938 is only approximate.

essing of hemp. The demand for Yugoslav hemp, especially from Germany, during the second half of the 1930's led to a large increase in the area planted to hemp. Hemp was one of the few export products in which Yugoslavia had a fairly strong competitive position on the European market and for which it could obtain payment in free exchange at a time when the bulk of the Yugoslav export trade was handled under bilateral clearing agreements. Flax was an industrial crop that was practically not affected by the various factors that affected the area planted to other industrial crops. Flax production was concentrated in Croatia-Slavonia and Bosnia, but in smaller quantities it was produced all over the country. The penetration of factory-produced cotton fabrics into the village in South Slav areas reduced the use of linen and therefore the planting of flax, but could not displace it completely. Cotton was grown during the interwar period in Yugoslavia on a very small scale and exclusively in Macedonia, where cotton growing had a long and interesting history.[14] During the interwar period there were two distinct periods in regard to cotton production. From 1921 to 1936 the area under cotton averaged somewhat below 1,000 hectares, and the government paid little attention to the cultivation of this crop. On October 17, 1936, however, the government passed a decree on the purchase of the cotton crop which guaranteed a fixed price for the domestically produced cotton. This price guaranty made the growing of cotton on a larger scale profitable and, during 1937 and 1938, there was a large increase in the area under cotton (see Table 34). The objective of the government subsidy was to increase cotton production and thus to reduce the country's dependence on foreign sources of raw cotton and save on foreign exchange. But even after the increase in hectarage, domestically produced cotton, which the industry considered to be relatively poor in its working and wearing qualities, supplied only a small portion of the Yugoslav cotton requirements. Yugoslavia used to produce small quantities of natural silk during the interwar period. In this case also, the government tried to stimulate silk production by passing a decree which guaranteed a fixed price for the production of silk cocoons (Decree of October 20, 1936).

In terms of area planted, sugar beets equaled on the average the area under hemp. Even more than in the case of hemp, the cultivation of sugar beets was concentrated in Vojvodina, though some were produced in Slavonia and some in central Serbia. While the increase in area under sugar beets in 1924 was not sustained, the area under sugar

[14] Todor Mirović, "Cotton Cultivation in the Vardar Valley and Its Advancement," *Ekonomist*, July–August, 1936, pp. 324–34.

beets rose each year between 1926 and 1929, when it reached its interwar maximum of 59,700 hectares. Since sugar was a luxury for most of the Yugoslav population, the Great Depression had a very unfavorable effect on sugar consumption and production. By 1934 the hectarage in sugar beets had fallen more than 50 percent below its 1929 level. Because of the rather small area, the cultivation of sugar beets was not of any great importance either in the system of crop rotation or as a provider of employment for rural people or in providing large quantities of feed for livestock, as was the case in several Central European states. Interestingly enough, the animal feed obtained from sugar-beet processing in the form of wet and dry pulp was only partially utilized at home. During the period 1933–37 Yugoslavia exported on the average 19,670 metric tons of dried sugar-beet pulp, part of it to the United States. The reason was that, under Yugoslav price conditions, it did not pay to use such feed for livestock. Small quantities of sugar were also exported, but with the exception of the years 1929 and 1930 when the exported quantity amounted to 13,295 and 8,036 metric tons, respectively, these exports were of no consequence.

The area under tobacco showed wider fluctuations from year to year than any other industrial crop during the interwar period, though the area under poppies for opium and under hops also fluctuated very widely. Owing to the fact that tobacco processing and selling were a government monopoly, which during the interwar period served as one of the most important sources of tax revenue, the government was keenly interested in the area planted to tobacco as one of the factors regulating its supply. In fact, the government regulated exactly the area to be planted each year, and even the number of tobacco plants, and the individual peasants could plant tobacco only if they previously had obtained a government license to do so. The government supervised, through special revenue police organs, all the aspects of planting, harvesting, and delivering of tobacco to the authorities of the State Monopoly Administration, which owned and administered all processing, storage, and wholesaling facilities for tobacco products. Three main factors influenced the government's decisions regarding the area to be planted to tobacco: consumption of tobacco products in the country itself, tobacco exports, and the existing tobacco stocks in the hands of the State Monopoly Administration. The largest area planted to tobacco was 35,900 hectares in 1924. In all other years during the interwar period except 1923, 1931, 1932, and 1937 it was below 20,000 hectares, and in 1934 it was only 7,400 hectares. Domestic consumption of tobacco products fluctuated primarily with the fluctuations in income, but also with the changes in the government tax on tobacco products. Yugoslavia exported tobacco every year during the interwar period, but these exports were not large. In the period 1936–38 the tobacco exports (exclusively leaf) averaged 4,715 metric tons annually, representing on the average 2.7 percent of all Yugoslav exports in terms of value in these years. Thus Yugoslav tobacco exports were not nearly so important an item in the country's export trade as were the tobacco exports in the neighboring Greece, Bulgaria, and Turkey where during the period 1936–38 they constituted 47.6, 36.2, and 26.8 percent, respectively, of their total value of exports.[15]

As a rule, somewhat more than one-half of all hectarage under tobacco was in Macedonia. The second most important tobacco-growing region was Herzegovina, but some tobacco was produced also in Vojvodina, Dalmatia, and other parts of the country south of the Sava-Danube rivers. Under the Yugoslav agricultural conditions as they were during the interwar period, the cultivation of tobacco could have been very well used as a crop of constructive assistance to the population in the "passive regions," especially in Herzegovina, Dalmatia, and parts of Montenegro. In these areas, just as in Macedonia, climatic and soil conditions were propitious for the production of high-quality tobacco, but in both its tobacco-buying and its tobacco-selling policies, the government was led exclusively by fiscal considerations.

The cultivation of poppies for opium production was limited to a few counties in Macedonia (*banovina* Vardar). The area under poppies showed great fluctuations during the interwar period; the maximum of 14,800 hectares was reached in 1930.[16] The area under poppies for opium depended basically on two factors: (1) on the possibilities of exports and export prices, and (2) since 1932, on government actions with regard to the area under poppies. The government tried to limit its cultivation by passing a special law in 1931 which was necessitated by Yugoslav participation in international agreements of 1929 on the control of the traffic in drugs. But the government's success in this respect was not satisfactory, because even with lower prices prevailing during the 1930's, the growing of poppies for opium was profitable in some areas of Macedonia, the more so as this crop was regularly grown on low-quality soils and at altitudes up to 800 meters.[17] The reduction

---

[15] League of Nations, *International Trade Statistics 1938*, pp. 55, 123, 256, 276.

[16] In this figure as well as in other figures on the hectarage under poppies in Table 34, a few hundred hectares under poppies in areas outside of Macedonia were included. But these poppies were not used for the production of raw opium.

[17] Blagoje Roganović, "Crop Production," Aleksa Jovanović (ed.), *Spomenica dvadesetpetogodišnjice oslobodjenja Južne Srbije, 1912–1937* (Jubilee Record of the

of the area under poppies in 1932 came primarily as a result of the drop in exports and prices of raw opium. This is best illustrated by the fact that the average value of exported raw opium during the period 1927–30 was 772 dinars per kilogram, while during the period 1931–37 it was only 372 dinars per kilogram. In the period 1927–37 the exports of raw opium from Yugoslavia averaged 51,614 kilograms annually, the maximum quantity of 146,582 kilograms having been exported in 1928 and the minimum of 11,410 kilograms in 1934. The export of raw opium after 1931 was a government monopoly. In addition to raw opium, the cultivation of poppies also yielded seed from which edible oil was obtained.

Yugoslavia also exported considerable quantities of various medicinal and aromatic herbs during the interwar period. The most important among them were pyrethrum, sage, flower of lime tree, flower of camomile, belladonna, and several others of lesser importance. The collection and sale of these herbs became more important during the 1930's than it had been previously. The only exception was pyrethrum, as the sales and prices of this product on foreign markets were unfavorably affected by the competition of similar products from other areas, especially Japan, as well as by the development of synthetic substitutes. In Dalmatia a considerable quantity of oil from rosemary was obtained, and almost all of it was exported.

Hops were also primarily an export product. Hops are grown in Slovenia around Žalec and Celje, and in Vojvodina around Petrovac. The exceedingly high price of hops on foreign markets in 1924 and 1925 led to a great expansion of hops growing, especially in Vojvodina, but it was an expansion of purely speculative nature. Thus, in 1927 and 1928 the area under hops was 9,200 hectares, which was sevenfold the average area planted to hops in 1921–23. The crash in hops prices led to a drastic cut in the area under this crop and, by 1932, it was only slightly larger than in the early 1920's. In the following years the prices improved and the area under hops grew to about one-third of the peak in 1927 and 1928.

The hectarage and production of oilseeds showed an interesting development during the interwar period. During the 1920's rape was the only important oilseed grown for which we have statistical data. The area under rape fell from 4,500 hectares in 1921 to 2,300 hectares in 1923. From 1924 it kept expanding and, in 1930, it reached 12,200 hectares, to fall to 3,400 hectares by 1933. But it seems that by that

Liberation of Southern Serbia, 1912–1937), pp. 547–51; see also "Decree on Opium," *Narodno blagostanje*, January 14, 1939, pp. 21–22.

time a certain area was already under sunflower, for which data are available only from 1934. From 1934 on, a great increase in the area under oilseeds was under way. In 1938 the area under rape reached 19,000 hectares, that under sunflower 19,400 hectares, that under soybeans 3,850 hectares, castor-oil seed 423 hectares, sesame 1,570 hectares, and anise 316 hectares. Thus, in 1938 the area under oilseeds reached 44,610 hectares, or almost four times the area at the time of the pre-Great Depression peak. In addition, sunflower and soybean were newcomers in Yugoslav agriculture.

There were several factors which contributed to this expansion of area under oilseeds during the second half of the 1930's. First, in order to reduce the dependence of the country on imports of oilseeds and save on foreign exchange, the government in 1935 prohibited the import of all edible oilseeds. This prohibition was removed the following year, but meanwhile import duties on all oilseeds were either increased or newly introduced. Second, on June 15, 1936, the government passed a decree on oleaginous seeds, which assured the growers of these crops a profitable price. Finally, as in Rumania and Bulgaria, the Germans tried also to foster the growing of oilseed crops in Yugoslavia. These Balkan countries were supposed, in the case of war, to at least partially replace the Far Eastern and other sources of vegetable oils for Germany. The whole area under sunflower and approximately one-half of the area under soybeans were concentrated in Vojvodina, and the German minority was the most important factor in their production. The increase in oilseed production under German sponsorship was, however, smaller in Yugoslavia than either in Rumania or Bulgaria. In fact, Yugoslavia remained a net importer of oilseeds until the outbreak of World War II.

In addition to oilseeds produced from crops grown as main crops and olive oil, of which more is said below, some oil was also produced from crops where seed was a by-product, such as cottonseed, poppy seed, and especially pumpkin seed. Pumpkins interplanted with corn and other crops gave a yield of approximately 100 metric tons per hectare, from which about 1,600 kilograms of seeds were obtained. It is here assumed that in the period 1934–38 pumpkin seed used for oil extraction averaged 8,000 metric tons annually. Several other minor potential sources of edible oil were at hand in Yugoslavia during the interwar period, but their utilization for oil production was not yet begun or was in the beginning stages.[18] The oil content in various oil-

[18] J. Z. Hamperl, "Our Production of Fats and Oils," *Ekonomist*, October 1940, pp. 384–94.

seeds is assumed to be as follows (in percent): hemp 25, rape 40, poppies 50, sunflower 25, sesame 50, soybeans 15, castor 50, cotton 20, and pumpkin 30. Oil production from domestically produced oilseeds during the period 1934–38 averaged an estimated 11,290 metric tons, distributed as follows among various *banovine* (in metric tons): Drava 140, Drina 1,200, Dunav 5,900, Morava 180, Sava 2,800, Vardar 820, Vrbas 210, and Zeta 40.

One of the important by-products of the edible oil industry was oilseed cake, which was used as concentrated feed for livestock. But, as in the case of sugar-beet pulp and bran, a considerable portion of the oilseed-cake production was exported.

Throughout the interwar period Yugoslavia imported a portion of its oilseed requirements for the production of edible oil. During the period 1934–38 the net importation in terms of edible oil from oilseeds was 4,800 metric tons. Imports consisted mostly of sunflower, peanuts (oil content about 43 percent), and copra (oil content about 60 percent).

During the interwar period Yugoslavia also imported a large part of its requirements of industrial fats and oils. We do not have estimates on domestic production of these, but during the period 1934–38 the imports averaged 3,190 metric tons of industrial oil from oilseeds (mostly in the form of linseed, average oil content 35 percent), 5,210 metric tons of animal fats (mostly tallow), and 1,460 metric tons of fish oil. The chief user of tallow and fish oil was the soap industry.

FEED CROPS AND FEED SUPPLIES

As in all countries characterized by peasant subsistence farming and by agricultural overpopulation, the area of arable land devoted to feed crops in Yugoslavia was and still is very small. It averaged only 341,000 hectares, or 4.6 percent of the total arable area during the period 1934–38. As Table 31, page 474, shows, the area under feed crops rose from 279,000 hectares in 1921 to 356,000 hectares in 1938, but related to the total area of arable land in those two years it was only a rise from 4.5 to 4.7 percent of the total. Almost two-thirds of this area was taken by clover and lucerne, which in 1938 accounted for 33.9 and 29.4 percent, respectively, of the area under feed crops. Other important feed crops were forage beets, vetches, and turnips. The increase in area of all feed crops between 1921 and 1938 was primarily due to the increase in the area under lucerne and forage beets, but especially the former. Lucerne was, and with good reason, the most propagandized feed crop during the interwar period because of its excellence as feed and because of its soil-improving qualities in crop rotation. The area under most other feed crops remained relatively stationary during the whole interwar period.

It would be wrong, however, to judge the feed supplies at the disposal of the Yugoslav economy by the area devoted to these feed crops alone; they represented only a minor, though high-quality, portion of the total supply. Rather, this small area of arable land devoted to feed crops shows clearly that the country is engaged in an extensive type of animal husbandry with very limited stable feeding.

After our earlier discussion of the relationship between the rural population and the area of cultivated land and its generally low productivity, it is easy to understand why the percentage of arable land devoted to the raising of feed crops is small. Production of such foods as milk and other dairy products, meat, animal fats, and eggs through feeding of cereals, potatoes, and special feed crops to animals and poultry is an expensive process of food production which in agriculturally overpopulated areas people cannot afford, except in very limited amounts. It involves too great a sacrifice in terms of calories. Thus, for example, it takes seven to eight kilograms of corn, or approximately 23,000 to 26,500 calories, to produce one kilogram of lard, or roughly 8,000 calories (crude lard) by feeding of corn to the Mangalica, the most important fat-type pig in Yugoslavia. Actually, livestock has been almost completely excluded from competition for the arable land area, with the exception of Vojvodina, Croatia-Slavonia, and Slovenia, where livestock, especially animals destined for export and to a lesser extent also for the domestic market, are partly raised on clover, lucerne, and various root crops and fattened on corn and, to a lesser extent, on potatoes and by-products of various agricultural industries (bran, sugar-beet pulp, oilseed cake). Additional exceptions were dairy cows and draft animals in areas north of the Sava-Danube rivers, which also obtained a certain amount of concentrated feed.

In addition to feed produced on arable land in the form of forage crops, there were several other categories of feed supplies. The combinations of various types of feed and their supply varied greatly from area to area, from season to season, and from year to year under the influence of weather conditions. These types of feed are the following: (1) Green pasture on permanent grazing meadows and on land under green fallow, green pasture in the mountain ranges to which livestock is taken in periodic transhumance, grazing on stubble left after the grain harvest, grazing in orchards which are not cultivated (a considerable part of them), and grazing on meadows after the cutting of hay. Livestock utilizes these feed supplies during the spring, summer, and autumn months, when it derives all or most of its feed by grazing. At this time only working livestock, milking cows, and some of the live-stock in the fattening process are apt to be getting additional feed in the form of green forage, hay, grains, or other concentrates. (2) Hay which is obtained to a small extent from arable land, in the form of dried lucerne, clover, vetches, etc., and hay which is obtained from meadows. (3) Straw from small grain and stover from corn, which in areas north of the Sava-Danube rivers is used to a considerable extent for floor bedding in stables, but here as well as in areas to the south of these rivers is used predominantly or wholly for feed, either alone or mixed with other substances. (4) Grains used for animal feed consist-ing of a portion of corn crop, a portion of barley crop, practically all of the oats crop, most of the millet crop, and a small portion of low-quality wheat crop. (5) A portion of potato crop. (6) A rather large crop of pumpkins which are raised mostly by interplanting with corn, but also with various other crops. (7) By-products and portions of waste obtained in several agricultural industries such as milling, and making of beet sugar, industrial alcohol, and edible oil. (8) Waste after various fruits have been used for the production of brandy. (9) Finally, a whole range of feed of minor importance, such as fruit unfit for human consumption, acorns for pigs in areas with large oak forests, underbrush leaves for sheep and goats, and kitchen swill for pigs.

In parts of Slovenia, parts of Dalmatia, in large portions of Bosnia and Herzegovina, in most of Montenegro and Macedonia, and in parts of Serbia, the livestock economy was based to a considerable extent on periodic transhumance. While it depended on climatic and terrain con-ditions in various areas, it was common to take the herds to the moun-tain pastures late in May or early in June and to return them in Sep-tember. In some cases the same herds are moved to various altitudes in the same mountains several times in order to utilize to the utmost the available grass.[19]

The overwhelming portion of the livestock in Yugoslavia feeds out-side of the stable for about eight months of the year, while during the remaining four winter months it mostly depends on stable feeding. While the feeding of livestock when it depends on grazing is often un-satisfactory because of the poor quality of grasses and, in years of drought or floods,[20] because of insufficiency of feed in many areas, it

---

[19] For a general survey of transhumance areas, chief mountains to which livestock is taken, altitudes at which livestock grazes, and dates of ascent and descent of the herds, as well as for economic patterns pursued in these areas, see Borivoje Ž. Milojević, *Les hautes montagnes dans le Royaume de Yougoslavie*, pp. 185–230.

[20] Floods which occur often in the flat areas of the Pannonian Plain have a negative influence not only on crops but also on livestock. First, they reduce the amount of feed

is the feeding during the winter months that represents the crucial problem in the Yugoslav livestock economy. Needless to say, conditions in this regard differed greatly from area to area.

The basic component of feed supplies raised for the winter feeding in all regions of the country was hay obtained from permanent meadows, which in the period 1934–38 took an average area of 1,837,-700 hectares and gave an annual average hay production of 3,179,800 metric tons. The supplies of hay were also very unevenly distributed, partly owing to the varying area under meadows in different parts of the country and partly owing to great differences in their yield. Furthermore, the quality of hay was poor. It was generally accepted that only approximately one-fourth of this hay was of first quality, while the remaining three-fourths consisted of grasses and weeds of poor nutritive value or without any nutritive value whatsoever.[21] The amount of hay from lucerne and vetches as well as the supplies of forage beets and pumpkins were of importance only in the area north of the Sava-Danube line, but especially in *banovina* Sava. In 1938, a typical year, Sava had one-half of the area under clover, one-fourth of the area under lucerne, one-third under forage beets, one-half under vetches, and more than one-half of the total production of pumpkins in the country. The production of forage crops in areas south of the Sava-Danube line, except in some very limited regions, was negligible.

The second basic component of feed supplies for winter months was straw from small grains and corn stover. In fact, straw and stover provided the chief bulk of the winter feed for livestock in practically all areas of Yugoslavia, but especially in regions south of the Sava-Danube rivers. It was estimated in 1929 by Popović and Mišić that hay from permanent and rotation meadows and feed supplies obtained from forage-crop areas supplied only about 25 percent of the feed amount, while the remainder was straw and stover. The weight of straw and stover from corn is usually taken as twice the weight of harvested grain. During the period 1934–38 that would have given a total amount of approximately 16.4 million metric tons of straw and stover. If one-fourth of this production was used for stable bedding and other nonfeed uses, then somewhat over 12 million metric tons of straw and stover were available for feed purposes. Straw is poor feed, but in many years and many areas there was not enough straw for this purpose.

---

production, and second, they increase the incidence of livestock diseases causing loss of weight and/or death of animals.

[21] Novak Popović and Dušan Mišić, *Naša domaća privreda* (Our National Economy), pp. 239–43.

As a rule, the numbers of livestock kept during the interwar period exceeded the capacity of the peasants to feed them properly during the winter months. In this respect the hopes of the peasants were always in excess of what they could actually do or reasonably expect. Appreciating fully the meaning of the shortage of feed during the winter months, official propaganda and recommendations of the experts during the interwar period tried to induce the peasants to produce more feed, partly by planting more forage crops, partly by paying more attention to the improvement of permanent and rotation meadows, and partly by sowing forage crops immediately following the harvest of small grains. But success in this regard was small.

There is no doubt that the provision of feed for livestock in winter months was one of the most difficult problems of the Yugoslav agriculture during the interwar period. During the winter months when livestock is exposed to short rations, poor feed, and in many cases to outright hunger and starvation, it draws on its bodily reserves in order to live. It was estimated in 1950 that Yugoslav cattle and sheep herds alone lost during the winter months, in this process of living at the expense of their bodily reserves, a total of 154,000 metric tons in weight, and that sheep herds also lost about 1,750 metric tons in wool. To recoup this loss in weight during the spring and summer months, according to the same calculation, 1,834,000 metric tons of feed in terms of hay were needed. It was also estimated that this loss in weight could have been prevented by increasing the necessary feed supplies for the winter period by about 730,000 metric tons in terms of hay.[22]

The situation with feed supplies during the winters following upon years of drought is even more disastrous. The usual consequence is a certain loss in livestock numbers due to starvation, but much more important is a great increase in the sale and slaughter of livestock to prevent their starvation. Obviously, the yield of animals so slaughtered is low and quality of product much poorer than normally. Thus, for example, following upon the droughts of 1921 and 1931 the numbers of selected types of livestock moved as follows:

	Cattle	Buffaloes	Pigs
1921	4,951,339	51,470	3,349,504
1922	4,058,419	31,938	2,887,020
1931	3,871,556	40,563	3,133,164
1932	3,812,208	38,704	2,863,177

[22] Čedomir Obračević, "The Advancement of Animal Husbandry in the People's Republic of Serbia," *Socijalistička poljoprivreda*, May 1951, pp. 33–48, esp. pp. 36–39.

Grains and by-products of various agricultural industries such as bran, oilseed cake, and sugar-beet pulp also formed a part of the winter feed supply for livestock, but the three latter types of feed were of relatively small importance. Except for pigs in the process of fattening, some working animals, milking cows in some parts of the country, and poultry, primarily poultry destined for the market, very little grain was used for the feeding of other animals. There are no official statistics on the amount of grains used for the feeding of livestock during the interwar period. Only some estimates are available. By far the most important type of grain used for livestock feeding was corn, and the issue warrants a closer scrutiny. Corn represented the only important concentrate in the whole supply of feed. It was used primarily for the feeding of pigs, and thus was the chief raw material for the production of animal fats in Yugoslavia during the interwar period, and animal fats, lard in particular, formed the bulk of the supply of fats and oils in the country. Some corn was also used for the feeding of poultry, some small quantities for working oxen and horses, and some for milking cows. The use of grains for animal feeding was practiced on a large scale only in Vojvodina, Srijem, and Slavonia, because here a large portion of peasants produced more grains than they needed for direct human consumption in the family, the animal husbandry was conducted to a considerable extent for the market, and draft animals were larger and were much more utilized than in other areas and thus had to have more and better feed. Here, too, there was a certain amount of commercial hog-finishing in feed lots, and this feeding depended primarily on corn. The feeding of pigs and poultry for the market, especially for export, was concentrated in the fall and early winter months, as these months coincided with the peak of demand for fattened pigs and fattened poultry not only at home but also in the Central European and other markets to which Yugoslavia exported these products.

So far as this writer is aware, there were only two official or semi-official estimates of the amount of corn used in prewar Yugoslavia for feed, and both, though very different, pertain approximately to the same time. The first was contained in a publication of the Ministry of Agriculture and Water Resources dealing with the consumption of bread grains in Yugoslavia. According to this publication, the amount of corn used for animal feeding was arrived at after estimates for other uses were made, and amounted to approximately 770,000 metric tons. In fact, it was stated that in the period 1923–27 "most of this amount of corn was used for feeding of livestock, especially for pigs."[23] The

23 Kingdom of the Serbs, Croats, and Slovenes, Ministry of Agriculture and Water

second estimate, which apparently pertained to 1928 and is identified as "an estimate on the basis of official data," states that the amount of corn utilized for feed, primarily for the feeding of pigs, was between 1.2 and 1.5 million metric tons annually.[24] If the production of corn in the period 1934–38 is taken as the basis and the amounts of corn used for human consumption (see Chapter 24), exports, seed, and waste are deducted, approximately 1 to 1.5 million metric tons remain for use as feed. We assume that 1.5 million metric tons of corn were used for feed. Needless to say, the use of corn for feed fluctuated considerably from year to year under the influence of the crop volume, the changing prices of grains and pigs, and the varying possibilities and prices of exports of both grains and pigs. A portion of the barley crop, most of the oats crop, and a portion of the production of other grains were used for feed, but more about this will be said in Chapter 24.

As pointed out earlier, a portion of the potato crop was used for feed purposes, especially in Croatia-Slavonia and in Slovenia. We assume that in the period 1934–38 approximately 150,000 metric tons of potatoes were thus utilized.

As a rule, feed supplies on the farm determined the manner and intensity of feeding of livestock by the peasants. Buying of feed to finish livestock for the market was exceptional because it implied risks that the peasants did not want to take. Feed was bought in large quantities only in years of droughts and floods, but that was in order to save livestock and not to finish it for the market. Since the manner of feeding livestock depended on the feed produced on the farm, and farms differed in size, and the size influences the pattern of cropping and the types and number of livestock held, it is impossible to talk of any set composition of feed rations or various rates of feeding in the Yugoslav livestock economy. Of course, there were exceptions to this rule among the peasants with large farms in areas of relatively advanced livestock economy. Even in such cases, feed rations were not scientifically devised but rather were arrived at by the trial-and-error method, and in their sufficiency and quality they were greatly influenced by seasonal factors.

This section might well be concluded by repeating that the increase in numbers of livestock and especially in the quality of livestock in Yugoslavia during the interwar period was limited by the narrow feed basis and the poor quality-structure of the existing feed supplies, and

---

Resources, *Potrošnja hlebnih žita u Kraljevini Srba, Hrvata i Slovenaca* (Consumption of Bread Grains in the Kingdom of the Serbs, Croats, and Slovenes), p. vii.

[24] Novak Popović and Dušan Mišić, op. cit., p. 242.

that the principal barrier to an improvement and enlargement of that feed basis was the growing agricultural overpopulation.

The very limited domestic market for animal foodstuffs and the shrinking foreign markets were, doubtless, also basic factors exercising an unfavorabel influence on the livestock economy of Yugoslavia. Had a favorable market at home and abroad existed for these products, a larger share of land and other productive resources in agriculture would have been devoted to the production of animal foodstuffs.

TREE AND BUSH CROPS

In some areas of Yugoslavia, tree crops are of basic economic importance. That is the case with prunes in north central and northwestern Serbia and in northeastern Bosnia; with apples and pears in portions of northeastern Slovenia; and with olive trees in certain sections of Dalmatia and the Montenegrin coast land. The prune is by far the most important fruit tree in Yugoslavia. In the above-mentioned areas of Serbia and Bosnia it is, with grains and livestock, the pillar of economic life. An important feature of the prune orchards in these areas is that they primarily occupy hilly terrain where grains or other field crops could not be grown successfully.

The cultivation of some tree and bush crops in Yugoslav areas, especially of olives and grapevines, goes back to the time of antiquity. Medieval records of Serbia, Bosnia, Dubrovnik (Ragusa), and Croatia are replete with references to wine and olive oil production and trade. The exceptional wealth of Bosnia in orchards was reported by the Turkish travelers in the middle of the seventeenth century and written records referring to dried prunes and dried pears in Bosnia date back to 1668.[25] It might be related, as a matter of historical curiosity, that in some Yugoslav areas the governments of the past centuries showed great interest in fruit growing and took rather strong measures in order to assure the planting of a sufficient number of fruit trees. Thus, for example, the authorities in areas under the Republic of Venice, which controlled for many centuries most of the present Yugoslav Adriatic coast, did not allow young *coloni* to get married before planting a certain number of olive trees. Another factor which favored planting of olive trees in these areas was the fact that under a system of land tenure characterized by the colonate, the *coloni* planted the trees because they were their property and thus increased somewhat their income from and security on the land. In the Croato-Slavonian Military Frontier young

[25] Hamdija Kreševljaković, "Urban Economy and Guilds in Bosnia and Herzegovina from 1463 to 1851," *Godišnjak istoriskog društva Bosne i Hercegovine*, I, 174.

couples could not be married without previously planting a certain number of fruit trees which varied in numbers and types from area to area. This ruling was apparently in force until the demilitarization of the Frontier in the 1870's. Finally, Prince (later King) Nicholas of Montenegro decreed in the 1880's that in the Montenegrin coast land every peasant family had to plant and own a specified number of olive trees.

In 1938 there were in Yugoslavia 71.6 million fruit trees of bearing age, of which 42.7 million were prune trees. Of the remaining 29 million trees there were about 8.5 million apple trees, mostly in Slovenia, Croatia, and Bosnia; 4.5 million pear trees in the same areas; 2.7 million walnut trees mostly in Serbia, Bosnia, and Croatia; 1.6 million peach and 728,900 apricot trees concentrated mostly in Serbia, Vojvodina, and Croatia; 2.1 million cherry trees and 1.1 million sour cherry trees, the former being grown over the whole country while the latter were concentrated primarily in Vojvodina and in Dalmatia. There was also a considerable number of quince and chestnut trees.

Along the Adriatic coast the so-called "Mediterranean" fruits are cultivated. In 1938 there were 4.7 million olive trees; almost one million fig trees; 409,000 almond trees; and something like 50,000 lemon and orange trees in this region.[26]

While it is well known that fruit trees of practically all types suffered from various diseases, their number did not fall in the course of the interwar period as did the number of prune trees (pp. 449–50). In fact, the number of fruit trees, other than prune, rose from 21.5 million in 1921 to 24.5 million in 1930, and to 28.9 million trees of bearing age in 1938. It is very probable, however, that a portion of that increase in the number of fruit trees was due to the improvement in the statistical coverage.

During the period 1934–38 the average, annual, statistically reported production of fresh fruit was as follows (in metric tons): prunes 384,958, apples 120,572, pears 51,358, cherries 24,225, peaches 12,287, figs 10,778, sour cherries 8,194, quinces 5,932, apricots 7,019, oranges 387, and lemons 60 metric tons. This gave an average annual total production of fresh fruit of 625,770 metric tons. Small quantities of such fruits as strawberries and other berries were not statistically reported. To this production of fruit should also be added grapes that were used as fruit, that is, grapes eaten fresh. It is here assumed that only 10 percent of the total grape production was thus used which in the period 1936–38 gave an average of 65,000 metric tons annually (no data on grape production were collected before 1936, only on wine pro-

26 Yugoslavia, *Annuaire statistique 1938–1939*, pp. 176–79.

duction). In some areas the use of fresh grapes as fruit was higher than the average here assumed. For Herzegovina it was estimated in 1938 at about 20 percent. But this was an exception. It is, furthermore, necessary to take into account the reported production of nuts, which amounted to an annual average of 46,954 metric tons, consisting of 32,157 tons of walnuts, 1,615 tons of almonds, and 13,182 metric tons of chestnuts in the period 1934–38.[27]

Most of the fruit production was utilized during the interwar period in what might be called traditional ways. Commercial canning of fruit did not exist, but some marmelade and jam were produced industrially. A considerable amount of a rather simple type of prune marmalade (*pekmez*) without addition of sugar was produced for home and commercial uses by simple implements and in many small establishments, mostly owned by the peasants themselves. Home canning of fruit and jam production was considerable but was practiced almost exclusively in cities and towns. Probably it would have been considerably larger had it not been for an exceedingly high price of sugar and glass containers. Both sugar and glass-container industries were cartelized. And in the case of sugar a high excise tax was paid.

The bulk of the fruit, with the exception of prunes, was marketed and utilized fresh. A relatively small part of the production of apricots, apples, figs, and pears, and almost the whole production of sour cherries were dried. Furthermore, a portion of practically all fruits was used for the production of brandy. There is no doubt that a certain amount of fruit was also fed to pigs, and that a portion of the fruit production, especially in years of bumper crops and low prices, was not utilized at all.

As far as the utilization of the most important fruit crop in Yugoslavia, the prune, was concerned, no official data or estimates are available for the interwar period. It was estimated in 1938 that in Bosnia, which during the 1930's produced about 21 percent of the prune output of the country, 10 percent of the crop was used as fresh fruit, about 20 percent was used for the production of prune marmalade, about 30 percent was dried, and about 40 percent was used for the production of prune brandy.[28] For Serbia, which during the 1930's produced about 66 percent of the total prune crop, it was estimated that about 10 percent was used as fresh fruit (about one-fourth of this was exported),

[27] *Ibid.*

[28] Šerif Bubić, "Fruit Growing in Bosnia and Herzegovina," A. Koen *et al.* (eds.), *Bosna i Hercegovina kao privredno područje* (Bosnia and Herzegovina as an Economic Area), p. 36.

2.5 percent for the production of prune marmalade, 20 percent was dried, and 68 percent of the crop was used for the production of brandy.[29] According to the same writer, who is one of the leading authorities on the prune economy of Yugoslavia, the utilization of the total prune crop in Yugoslavia was approximately as follows; 60 percent was used for distilling into prune brandy, 18 percent was used for drying, 5 percent for the production of marmalade, and 17 percent was utilized fresh, including domestic consumption and exports.[30] These are, thus, the figures which we use in calculating the utilization of the prune crop.

From these figures it is obvious that about three-fifths of the prune crop was and probably still is used for the production of prune brandy (*slivowitz* or *šljivovica*). This is the Yugoslav national drink. The average yield of brandy is approximately 20 liters (roughly 20 kilograms) with an average alcohol content of 25 percent, or 50 proof per 100 kilograms of fresh prunes. There are two types of prune brandy, the mild (*mekana*), having an average alcohol content of about 22.5 to 25 percent (45 to 50 proof), and the strong (*ljuta*), which usually has an alcohol content of 45 percent or 90 proof. But only about 5–10 percent of the prune crop is used for the production of strong brandy.[31] Both are used as occasional drinks, the occasions being many and easily created, as well as with meals. The strong brandy is drunk from small glasses, the mild from wineglasses, often being heated beforehand. The high consumption of prune brandy in many areas of Serbia and Bosnia was considered by some people as a serious health

[29] Milutin J. Niketić, " 'For an Improvement in Our Prune Growing,' " *Socijalistička poljoprivreda*, January 1952, pp. 51–54.

[30] Personal communication from Milutin J. Niketić, Belgrade, of January 1954. It is interesting to compare the utilization of the prune crop in the United States with that in Yugoslavia during the 1930's. The California average annual prune crop of 538,000 tons (fresh basis) during the period 1930–39 was dried, the production of dried prunes being 207,100 tons. In some years a certain amount of prunes remained unharvested owing to unfavorable market conditions. California reported also a production of 64,600 tons of plums. The Yugoslav statistics do not make a distinction between prunes and plums, both being included under the common name *šljive*. During the period 1930–39 the state of Idaho reported a production of 17,570 tons of prunes (fresh basis) and the bulk of it (16,900 tons) was utilized in fresh form. The state of Washington reported a prune crop of 31,450 tons (fresh basis). Of this, 13,860 tons were utilized fresh and 4,710 tons were canned (fresh basis), while 2,890 tons (dry basis) were dried. Oregon reported a crop of 110,400 tons of prunes, of which 16,650 were utilized in fresh form and 15,920 tons were canned (fresh basis), while 21,780 tons (dry basis) were dried. It might also be pointed out that the drying ratio in Washington and Oregon is 3 to 4 pounds of fresh fruit for 1 pound of dried fruit, while in California this ratio is 2.5 to 1. United States, Department of Agriculture, *Agricultural Statistics 1942* (Washington, D.C.), 1942, p. 262.

[31] Personal communication from Milutin J. Niketić.

problem. It is only fair to say, however, that with the exception of some beer, and a considerable production and consumption of wine, and brandy produced from other fruits and from fermented grape mash after wine has been expressed, Yugoslavia was not using any grains or potatoes during the interwar period for the production of strong alcoholic beverages, except for very small quantities of grain, potatoes, or molasses for alcohol which was used for the production of liqueurs.

At the beginning of this century the present Yugoslav territory was an important supplier of the European market with dried prunes. In 1904 the exports of dried prunes from that territory amounted to 108,000 and in 1908 to 85,000 metric tons. But the greatly expanded production of dried prunes in California, especially after World War I, pushed the Yugoslav prune from practically all Western European markets during the interwar period, leaving to Yugoslavia only part of the markets in Central and Eastern Europe. The California prunes are much larger than the Yugoslav (the latter being mostly 90 to 100 per pound), have a higher sugar content, are scientifically prepared, appealingly packed, and expertly sold. The consequence of this competition, as well as of the fact that the chief Yugoslav variety for the production of dried prunes, the požegača, was badly affected by disease, was a switch in Yugoslavia to greater growing of varieties for the production of brandy, and reduction in the production and export of dried prunes. The production of dried prunes in Yugoslavia during the period 1933–37 was estimated at 22,500 metric tons, of which 19,570 metric tons were exported.[32] It appears also that a certain deterioration in the quality of dried prunes produced in Yugoslavia took place during the interwar period, while the competitive situation in the export market would have called for a determined effort to improve and standardize their quality. One reason for the deterioration in the quality of the dried prunes was that fruit had usually been picked too early. Furthermore, it appears that many producers and traders increased the moisture content and added color to dried prunes.[33]

In certain areas of Yugoslavia such as Dalmatia, parts of Herzegovina, Slovenia, Croatia-Slavonia, parts of Banat and of Serbia, the growing of grapes was and is an important branch of agricultural production. As was already stated, around 90 percent of the grape production was used for the production of table wines, the remainder being utilized fresh. No grapevine varieties were cultivated in Yugoslavia

---

[32] Milutin J. Niketić, "The Problems of the Dried Prune Industry," *Socijalistička poljoprivreda*, January 1953, pp. 9–20.

[33] Petar Jekin, "Prune Trade in Bosnia," *Ekonomist*, April 1938, pp. 155–62.

whose grapes were suited for the production of raisins and only small quantities of typical table-grape varieties were produced. As in most other European countries, phylloxera destroyed vineyards in the Yugoslav areas. It reached the peak of destructiveness between 1900 and 1914. In some areas, as for example in Dalmatia where, due to soil and climatic conditions, wine production is of exceptional economic importance, it never recuperated from the consequences of the phylloxera attack. Production of wine in that area averaged, during the period 1935–39, only about 41 percent of the average production in the period 1885–90.[34] The appearance of phylloxera required the planting of the phylloxera-resistant American grapevine stock and its later grafting with European varieties. The area under grapevines increased from 171,635 hectares in 1921, an area greatly reduced by phylloxera in comparison with earlier years, to 218,633 hectares in 1938. Meanwhile, the overhauling of the vineyards on the American grapevine basis was almost completed; in 1938 there remained only 12.3 percent of the vineyard area based on the European grapevine.

During the period 1934–38 Yugoslavia produced an average of 4,145,000 hectoliters of wine annually. This was almost exclusively table wine, as the production of dessert wines was exceedingly small. Such popular types of dessert wine as sherry and port were neither produced nor consumed. A sherry-like wine called *prošek* is produced in Dalmatia but almost exclusively for home consumption. Very small quantities of it enter trade. As could be expected in a country of dwarf and small farms, the production of wine is carried on under very different conditions, and, as a rule, the types of wine differ greatly in alcohol content, color, and aroma. Thus only a small portion of the total wine production was sold under fixed trade names and showed a rather even quality from year to year. From fermented mash obtained after the wine has been expressed, a type of brandy is distilled (called *marc* in France and *grappa* in California). Its alcoholic content varies greatly, but can be as high as 80 to 100 proof.

Finally, there was another tree crop in Yugoslavia, the olive, but it was of importance only in areas along the Adriatic coast. The number of fruit-bearing olive trees rose from 3,250,270 in 1921 to 4,269,711 in 1930, and 4,741,608 in 1938. Here, as in the case of several other tree types, better statistical coverage as the time advanced was probably responsible for a part of the increase in the number reported. During the period 1934–38 the number of olive trees averaged 4,723,641 and

[34] Marin Roje and Vanja Žanko, "Wine Production in Dalmatia," *Ekonomski pregled*, No. 2, 1950, pp. 214–19, esp. p. 215.

the production of olive oil averaged only 49,348 hectoliters annually. Thus, this large number of olive trees gave less than 5,000 metric tons of olive oil per annum. The average yield per tree was only 1.04 kilograms of oil, which was exceedingly low. The reasons for the low yields of the olive trees in most areas were the absence of proper pruning, absence of cultivation of olive groves and of application of manure to olive trees, and the fact that many of the trees were very old. During the period 1934–38 the average annual production of olive oil was distributed as follows, by *banovine*: Primorje 3,200, Sava 280, and Zeta 1,460 metric tons.

CHAPTER 23

ANIMAL HUSBANDRY AND THE OUTPUT OF
ANIMAL FOOD PRODUCTS

IF A WHOLE SERIES of factors are determining the structure of crops and are causing fluctuations in the area under crops, the factors determining the types and numbers of livestock and the methods of its utilization are even more numerous. In addition to climatic and soil conditions, the general cultural level of agricultural population, and the prevailing level of agricultural technology, there are perhaps three basic factors which are among the foremost forces in deciding the types and the numbers of livestock in various areas and on various farms. The first factor is the relationship between the rural population and the amount of cultivated and potentially cultivable land available to this population. As we have seen earlier, the growing agricultural overpopulation was the basic cause preventing the growth in the number of livestock in Yugoslavia during the interwar period. This was especially so in regard to cattle and pigs, and to a lesser extent in regard to horses, that is, species which, unlike sheep and goats, compete with people for the products of arable land. The numbers of sheep and goats rose as fast or faster than the agricultural population. The second factor is the size of farms, which to a large extent is a consequence of the relationship between the rural population and agricultural land. This factor is of extraordinary significance because the size of farms decides what portion of the land can be devoted to the production of feed crops. In turn, this largely determines the types and the number of livestock that can be kept and utilized. One of the basic rules of behavior of the Yugoslav peasants was to adjust the number and types of livestock they held to the available feed basis. The purchase of feed involved such a degree of risk that it could be undertaken by very few people. Purchase of feed was not a rule, but rather a rare exception in the scheme of the livestock economy in Yugoslavia during the interwar period. With regard to the feed basis for livestock, as a rule the Yugoslav peasants tended to keep more livestock than the feed basis allowed. They did not, as a consequence of this fact, regularly buy additional feed but, rather, they produced low-quality livestock. The third factor is the marketability of livestock, which includes both the technical accessibility of the market and the demand for livestock and animal food products and their respective prices. As in regard to crop production, so in regard to animal husbandry, the degree of marketability of production, and thus the influence of the market forces on the structure and volume of production of livestock, was the greatest in the northern areas of the country: Vojvodina, Croatia-Slavonia, and Slovenia. And in these areas we have the most advanced animal husbandry in the country, though animal husbandry there played a relatively smaller role in the total economy of the rural population than it did in the areas south of the Sava-Danube rivers.

There are several ways in which the composition and the number of livestock kept on the farms affect the agriculture and economy of a country as a whole in a profound fashion: (1) Under Yugoslav conditions horses and oxen were practically the only sources of draft power for field work and transportation in rural areas. The supply of draft power affects the way in which such basic operations in agriculture as plowing are performed, and also whether they are performed at the proper time or not. In both cases this affects the quality of agricultural work and, thereby, crop yields. Sometimes it also affects the hectarage planted with certain crops. The number of livestock also affects the supply of manure at the disposal of agriculture, and thus its yields. (2) In addition, the extent of and the way in which animal husbandry is conducted profoundly influences the production of animal food products and, thus, the supply of protective foods. Naturally, the production of food is of foremost importance in any economy, but it is especially so in the underdeveloped countries where most of the energy of the whole population is concentrated on producing the requisites of maintaining life, and where there exists the need for great improvement in nutrition. (3) The agricultural population of Yugoslavia depended to a large extent on the sale of livestock and animal products for cash income and thus for the acquisition of a large part of those products that were bought in the market. (4) Live animals and animal products, especially fat pigs, cattle, horses, lambs, poultry, fresh meat, lard, and eggs, formed a very large part of the export trade of Yugoslavia during the interwar period. (5) By supplying horses and the feed for them, agriculture supplied the main source of draft power for road transport and lumbering, as well as the beasts of burden for pack transport. Moreover, throughout the interwar period both horses and oxen, but especially horses, were considered a basic military resource (for draft purposes). Use of horses for civilian transport work was natural because motor transport was still in its infancy during the interwar period.

516   *Peasants, Politics, and Economic Change in Yugoslavia*

Animal husbandry is thus of basic importance for the whole national economy of Yugoslavia. This is best indicated by the fact that, out of an estimated average national income of 42,672 million dinars in the period 1935–38, the income of agriculture from crops and livestock (not counting such minor agricultural and related activities as bee-keeping, silkworm production, and fisheries) was on the average 18,444 million dinars, of which 7,587 million dinars or 41.1 percent came from livestock. The marketability rate of production of livestock and animal products was somewhat higher than that of crops, although live-stock sales were largely another form of selling crops.

NUMERICAL DEVELOPMENT OF THE HERDS, 1921–38

Table 35 shows the development of all types of livestock and poultry, during the period 1921–38. From 1921 to 1938 the number of horses rose by almost 20 percent. The increase was without interruption and at a rather even rate. The number of donkeys and mules rose by 42 percent during that period, but their importance in the whole livestock economy of Yugoslavia was small. The number of cattle fell by 18 percent from 1921 to 1922, primarily because of the drought of

TABLE 35.—LIVESTOCK HERDS AND POULTRY FLOCKS, 1921–38*

(Livestock in thousands; poultry in millions)

Year	Horses	Donkeys and mules	Cattle	Buffaloes	Pigs	Sheep	Goats	Poultry
1921....	1,062	102	4,951	51	3,350	7,002	1,553	15.1
1922....	1,044	101	4,058	32	2,887	8,462	1,801	13.8
1923....	1,063	110	3,870	32	2,497	7,639	1,730	14.2
1924....	1,054	104	3,784	29	2,518	7,619	1,718	14.9
1925....	1,106	110	3,768	27	2,802	7,907	1,811	16.2
1926....	1,117	111	3,706	32	2,806	7,933	1,721	16.3
1927....	1,120	112	3,729	31	2,770	7,736	1,739	16.3
1928....	1,109	119	3,654	32	2,663	7,722	1,750	16.1
1929....	1,140	122	3,728	37	2,675	7,736	1,804	17.5
1930....	1,161	123	3,812	37	2,924	7,953	1,731	18.8
1931....	1,169	132	3,872	41	3,133	8,426	1,928	19.0
1932....	1,157	131	3,812	39	2,863	8,510	1,872	19.5
1933....	1,187	135	3,876	37	2,656	8,600	1,871	19.8
1934....	1,206	138	3,990	39	2,792	8,868	1,881	20.8
1935....	1,201	139	3,982	37	2,932	9,211	1,896	20.8
1936....	1,216	141	4,074	37	3,126	9,568	1,906	21.5
1937....	1,249	143	4,169	36	3,180	9,909	1,901	22.4
1938....	1,264	142	4,267	38	3,451	10,137	1,890	22.8

* Source: Data for 1921 to 1929 from Yugoslavia, *Annuaire statistique 1929* (Belgrade, 1932), pp. 155–58; for 1930 to 1938 from *Annuaire statistique 1938–1939* (Belgrade, 1939), pp. 180–81.

1921, and it remained markedly below the 1921 level during the entire interwar period. The 1921 crop of hay, potatoes, lucerne, and alfalfa was the lowest of any during the interwar period, and that of corn was among the lowest of the interwar period. Some improvement in the breed composition of cattle has taken place, however, so that the production of beef, veal, and cow's milk probably did not fall as much as the cattle herds. The number of water buffaloes, which are of importance only in Macedonia, fell by two-fifths from 1921 to 1922, recuperated somewhat in later years, but always remained very much under the level of 1921. The number of pigs also fell badly as a consequence of the 1921 drought; in 1938 their number exceeded that of 1921 for the first time. Since the number of pigs can be increased faster than that of any other type of livestock, and since fluctuations in feed production and in market conditions influenced the numbers, and especially the weight at the time of marketing or slaughter, of this type of animal more than any other, this was also reflected in the changes in the number of pigs. The sheep herds increased between 1921 and 1938 by 44.8 percent, that is, by considerably more than the rural population of the country increased during these years. The number of goats also increased but not to the same extent as did the number of sheep. Finally, the number of poultry increased between 1921 and 1938 by 51 percent.

DISTRIBUTION OF LIVESTOCK HERDS BY BANOVINE, 1934–38

Table 36 shows the average livestock population of Yugoslavia by *banovine* during the period 1934–38. This is the numerical and time basis on which all our estimates of the output of animal food products are calculated. This table shows clearly how unevenly livestock was distributed among the various regions, both in numbers and in types. This was obviously connected with the relationship of both rural population and livestock population to the area of productive and cultivated land in various areas, which was shown in Table 23, page 322, but many other factors had some influence on the size and types of livestock in various areas. On the whole, horses, cattle, and pigs are much more numerous in *banovine* Dunav, Sava, and Drava, while sheep and goats predominate in the mountainous areas to the south and west, especially in the center of the country. One thing, however, should always be kept in mind when considering Yugoslav agriculture and animal husbandry: conditions differ basically between the Pannonian Plain and the mountainous areas, especially the karstic areas. In fact, the average figures of livestock in various *banovine* shown in Table 36, especially with

TABLE 36.—AVERAGE NUMBER OF LIVESTOCK BY BANOVINE IN THE PERIOD 1934–38*

(*Thousand head*)

Banovina	Horses	Donkeys and mules	Cattle	Pigs	Sheep	Goats	Poultry	Total in cattle units excluding poultry
Drava	52.8	0.2	371.3	300.2	34.4	10.3	1,185.4	530
Drina	108.4	0.6	524.6	343.8	951.6	164.4	2,249.7	885
Dunav	354.9	2.7	444.1	987.4	902.4	41.4	6,585.8	1,319
Morava	46.7	2.0	331.4	289.8	1,670.8	206.9	2,403.2	663
Primorje	68.7	46.6	193.4	85.9	1,323.2	207.0	851.1	494
Sava	278.6	4.9	848.8	593.0	460.7	54.3	4,079.8	1,469
Vardar	120.8	68.8	545.7	177.2	2,152.6	667.4	1,999.6	1,088
Vrbas	106.8	0.4	433.2	231.4	677.6	130.0	1,520.7	731
Zeta	85.9	14.5	437.8	81.2	1,359.4	413.0	717.7	772
Prefecture of Belgrade	3.6	—	3.7	6.1	5.9	0.3	60.8	11
Total	1,227.2	140.7[a]	4,134.0[b]	3,096.0	9,538.6	1,895.0	21,653.8[c]	7,962[a]
1938	1,264.5	142.3	4,305.0	3,450.9	10,137.4	1,890.4	22,763.2	8,340

* Source: Yugoslavia, Ministry of Agriculture, *Statistique agricole annuelle, 1938* (Belgrade, 1939).
[a] This figure includes approximately 122,000 donkeys and 18,700 mules; the latter are almost exclusively kept in *banovine* Primorje, Vardar, and Zeta. In 1938 there were 123,058 donkeys and 19,265 mules.
[b] This figure includes 37,450 water buffaloes, of which there were 31,600 in *banovina* Vardar, 3,500 in Zeta, 1,700 in Morava, and a few in other *banovine*. In 1938 there were 37,841 water buffaloes.
[c] This figure includes 18,501,700 chickens, 1,044,700 ducks, 1,250,800 geese, and 856,600 turkeys. In 1938 there were 19,418,935 chickens, 1,119,948 ducks, 1,339,218 geese, and 885,063 turkeys.
[d] For coefficients of conversion see footnote *b* Table 12, p. 279.

respect to cattle and pigs, are quite misleading from the production point of view, as are the relative figures on cultivated land. As a hectare of arable land yields on the average almost twice as much wheat, corn, or potatoes in *banovina* Dunav and certain parts of *banovina* Sava as, say, in Primorje, Vardar, and Zeta (see Table 14, p. 281), so a cow in *banovina* Drava and parts of *banovine* Sava and Dunav may yield on the average four or five times as much milk, or a steer two or three times as much meat as elsewhere. The same applies to most pigs and practically all poultry. There are also great differences in respect to the working capacity of horses and cattle in the Pannonian Plain and in areas south of the Sava-Danube rivers. All these differences in yield and working capacity among livestock stem basically from the differences in breeds and in the modes of raising and utilizing the animals. These factors, in turn, are essentially controlled by the amount and type of feed that can be and are devoted to the upkeep of these animals. Of course, the general level of cultural and economic development, the technical accessibility of the market, and the conditions on the market, which in turn influence the technique of production in the field of animal husbandry and the revenue derived from it, play an essential role in all this.

Most species are degenerated in areas south of the Sava-Danube rivers as a result of centuries of inbreeding rather than systematic selection, owing to the insufficiency and poor quality of feed supplies, and the frequent lack of any care of animals whatsoever. The only advantage of this state of livestock degeneration is that livestock has become largely immune to various diseases, to lack of care, to scanty and poor feed, and, in the case of working animals, to hard work. Livestock of good and improved breeds are simply incapable of surviving under such conditions, or if such animals do survive, they soon either dissolve in the sea of the primitive breeds around them or degenerate themselves and then are usually less satisfactory from an economic point of view than the common domestic livestock they were supposed to replace. Such attempts have been made many times and, as a rule, with the same unsatisfactory results. Livestock cannot be improved without a satisfactory feed basis and without giving proper care to the animals.

ON ESTIMATING THE OUTPUT OF ANIMAL FOOD PRODUCTS IN YUGOSLAVIA

On the basis of a search over several years in official Yugoslav publications, digging through literature relating to Yugoslav agriculture published both in Yugoslavia and in other countries, and exchanging letters with a number of experts in Yugoslavia, it can be positively stated that there are no official statistics on the output of animal food products in Yugoslavia for any year or period between the two world wars. Occasionally in reports and speeches of the successive ministers of agriculture, in speeches and articles of officials of the Ministry of Agriculture, in statements of spokesmen for various producers' organizations, and in writings of individual economists, certain statements on the production of meat, lard, milk, cheese, and eggs are found. Statistics on the number and type of animals slaughtered in public abattoirs are available, however, but without indication of the average yield of various animals. Data are also available on the export of live animals and of animal food products. The most complete estimate of the output of animal food products and their value was made by a group of Yugoslav economists who worked on the estimates of the national income of Yugoslavia for the period 1923–25.[1] But neither their estimates nor those of other Yugoslav economists are complete, systematic, or usable as such.

The only systematic efforts aimed at workable estimates of the output of animal food products in Yugoslavia for the late 1930's were made during World War II in London and Washington by various British and United States agencies, Allied committees, and working parties. They were interested in gauging the probable Yugoslav contribution in food to the Axis war machine and, as the war drew to its conclusion, in estimating the relief and rehabilitation requirements for the civilian population when the country was liberated from the enemy. Later, the Food and Agriculture Organization of the United Nations published a consolidated food balance sheet for Yugoslavia for the period 1934–38, including a complete estimate of the output of animal food products.[2] In 1947 the Yugoslav government estimated, while working on the Five Year Plan, the output of animal food products for 1939. This estimate, unfortunately, gives only one over-all figure for meat production, and that greatly reduces its value.[3] Thus, while a considerable number of estimates of the output of animal food products in Yugoslavia for the years immediately preceding World War II exists, none appears acceptable to this writer. In the following pages our own estimates are presented, together with the basic information and assumptions underlying these estimates.

[1] V. M. Djuričić *et al.*, *Naša narodna privreda i nacionalni prihod* (Our National Economy and National Income), pp. 59–101.

[2] Food and Agriculture Organization of the United Nations, *Food Balance Sheets*, pp. 139–44.

[3] Yugoslavia, Office of Information, *Five Year Plan*, pp. 140–41.

The only possible way of proceeding with these estimates was, first, to collect official statistics on the number, types, and distribution of livestock by areas and breeds, then all the information pertaining to reproduction, the rates of natural loss, the rates of slaughter, patterns of utilization in animal husbandry, and all other shreds of information pertinent to the output of animal food products. Unfortunately, it was found on closer inspection that much of the printed matter pertaining to the productivity of animals was very incomplete and, as a rule, greatly overstated the yields. Second, it was necessary to make certain assumptions where no figures whatsoever were available, or when those which were available were inacceptable. That was the case with a whole series of key coefficients, as, for example, with reproduction rates, natural death rates, slaughter rates, and yield rates. Needless to say, the great variety of breeds of practically all types of livestock, their varied productivity, the uneven distribution of these breeds in various parts of the country with great differences in feed supplies called for extreme caution in making these estimates. In some cases, lack of sufficient data or relatively unimportant differences in the productivity of various breeds of animals in different parts of the country, e.g., in regard to sheep, goats, and poultry, made it necessary to disregard these differences and to apply the assumed average productivity rates for all parts of the country.

Undoubtedly, our estimates of animal food products output are more accurate for the country as a whole than for individual *banovine*. There are perhaps some who will see little sense in presenting rather detailed calculations of the output of these products for various regions in a study of this character. But our endeavor throughout this study has been to show and to elaborate the elements of variety in the Yugoslav rural economy, and this picture would remain sadly incomplete if an honest effort were not made to present these differences also in regard to livestock economy and its production. Needless to say, the differences in the crop and animal foods production are one of the most important features in the general economic picture of various areas, and thus one of the basic determinants of the people's welfare.

It is generally agreed that the official statistics understate considerably the numerical strength of livestock herds and poultry flocks. Most understated were probably the herds of sheep and goats, pigs, and poultry. It appears, however, that in the case of pigs the underestimation referred primarily to the number of suckling and young pigs. It is perhaps safe to say that, in the case of sheep and goats also, the number of young animals was more understated than that of older animals.

It is not known whether the livestock numbers were equally understated in all parts of the country. Most probably these numbers were more understated in areas south of the Sava-Danube rivers than in areas north of these rivers. Since data are not available which would permit a reasonably accurate adjustment of the officially reported figures for this underreporting, we have decided to use the official figures as the basis for our calculations of the output of animal food products. But owing to the above facts, our total figures should be considered as underestimates, especially in regard to products obtained from sheep and goats, pigs, and poultry.

CATTLE

If the variety of cattle breeds and their productivity in Yugoslavia were ignored, no sensible regional differences in the estimates of production of beef, veal, or cow's milk would be possible. Since differences in productivity are extremely high, as will presently become clear, it is necessary to take them into consideration. In regard to productivity, a head of cattle in advanced cattle-raising areas such as Slovenia and some areas of Croatia-Slavonia, and a head of cattle in most areas south of the Sava-Danube rivers have nothing but the name in common. Assuming that the distribution of cattle breeds in various *banovine* was the same during the period 1934–38 as in 1933, which is very likely, 45.2 percent of all cattle, or 1,848,600 head, were of the dairy or improved types, consisting primarily of Simmental, and to a lesser degree of Pinzgau, Brown Swiss, Mariahof, Montafon, Murbodner, and their crosses; while 2,074,900, or 50.6 percent, belonged to the domestic breed Buša (*Bos brachyceros europaeus*), and 173,000 or 4.2 percent to the domestic (Pannonian) breed of Podolian cattle.

Table 37 shows the distribution of the average cattle stock during the period 1934–38 by *banovine* on the basis of breed distribution ratios of 1933. The data in this table show the degree of cattle "improvement" that had been achieved by that time in various parts of the country. Thus Drava had not less than 99.6 percent of dairy and improved-type cattle, while Zeta had 97.4, and Vardar 96.5 percent of Buša cattle. The other *banovine* were in an intermediate position, but in two major cattle-raising *banovine*, Dunav and Sava, the percentage of dairy and improved cattle breeds was very high, namely 84.4 and 78.0 percent, respectively.

Buša is the typical cattle breed on all farms in the areas south of the Sava-Danube rivers, and on many dwarf and small farms in Croatia north of the Sava River. It is, furthermore, almost the only breed of

TABLE 37.—DISTRIBUTION OF CATTLE BY BREEDS BY BANOVINE, 1934–38*

(Percent)

Banovina	Total cattle (*Thousand*)	Domestic breeds		Dairy and improved breeds			
		Buša	Podolian	Simmental	Pinzgau	Brown Swiss, Montafon, Murbodner, etc.	Total
Drava	371.3	0.4	—	22.5	21.2	55.9	99.6
Drina	524.6	72.6	9.0	11.0	4.7	2.7	18.4
Dunav	443.6	3.6	12.0	70.1	2.1	12.2	84.4
Morava	329.8	49.0	2.0	33.6	0.5	14.9	49.0
Primorje	193.4	73.4	—	0.2	11.7	14.7	26.6
Sava	848.8	16.0	6.0	56.0	20.1	1.9	78.0
Vardar	513.9	96.5	—	2.1	—	1.4	3.5
Vrbas	433.1	73.5	3.5	0.7	21.3	1.0	23.0
Zeta	434.3	97.4	—	0.5	—	2.1	2.6
Prefecture of Belgrade ..	3.7	—	—	—	—	—	100.0
Total ...	4,096.5	50.6	4.2	26.0	9.9	9.7	45.2

* Based on official data on distribution of cattle breeds in 1933 as published by the Bureau of Animal Husbandry of the Yugoslav Ministry of Agriculture. See Yugoslavia, Ministry of Agriculture, *Glasnik*, Belgrade, XIV (May 1936), 178.

cattle in *banovine* Vardar and Zeta. This is a consequence of the fact that in these areas peasants could not feed larger cattle, most of them would be unwilling or would lack knowledge to properly care for dairy and improved types of cattle, and most of them could not fully utilize the working capacity of large cattle. The Buša is a type of small, primitive cattle accustomed to living under adverse conditions, to poor feed, practically no care, hard work, and is resistant to cattle diseases prevalent in these areas. Differences in weight, milk production, and draft performance between the Buša cattle in the plains and those in the typical mountain areas are considerable because of differences in the supplies and quality of feed. The Podolian is a domestic type of gray, long-horned cattle, exceedingly powerful and admirably suited for draft, but poor both as milk and beef producer. As far as dairy and improved types of cattle are concerned, their names indicate that all of them are the various Central European breeds prevalent in all areas of the Alps. The most numerous and most important among these breeds is the Simmental. Most of the improved breeds, but especially the Simmental, are multipurpose cattle good for milk and beef as well as for draft.

Improvement in cattle breeds, both by importing breeding animals from abroad and by spreading good breeding stock from domestic areas to other domestic areas where an improvement of cattle is necessary, as well as some crossing of improved breeds with domestic cattle, has been going on in a systematic fashion in areas north of the Sava-Danube rivers since the middle of the nineteenth century. In areas south of these rivers it was practiced during the interwar period. In Slovenia, certain sections of Croatia-Slavonia, and parts of Vojvodina this policy has given excellent results. In areas south of the Sava-Danube line where conditions do not allow satisfactory results with dairy and improved types of cattle—and unfortunately this takes a large part of these areas—selection work using good Buša material is considered as a better, cheaper, and safer approach to the improvement of cattle economy. Needless to say, growing agricultural overpopulation, which prevents a marked increase in the area of land available for the raising of feed crops, works against a policy of cattle improvement. Importation of a considerable number of dairy cattle from Germany as reparations during the 1920's was also a welcome addition.[4]

During its operations in Yugoslavia from 1945 to 1947 the United Nations Relief and Rehabilitation Administration supplied that country with several thousand head of cattle of various breeds from the United States, so that at present an even greater variety of cattle breeds exists in Yugoslavia. The UNRRA apparently supplied primarily Holstein cattle. Earlier attempts to raise this type in Yugoslavia were not successful, but the UNRRA-supplied animals are progressing satisfactorily. Holstein bulls are also used for crossing with those types of Simmental cows which come of low milk-producing stock.[5] The technique of artificial insemination of cattle, which was also launched by the UNRRA during its operations in Yugoslavia, may prove to be an effective and cheap way of improving cattle breeds in countries with conditions similar to those of Yugoslavia.

Differences in cattle economy in various areas of Yugoslavia find expression in many factors: breeds, composition of cattle population, utilization, and productivity. Unlike the areas north of the Sava-Dan-

---

[4] Ljudevit Prohaska, "Agriculture and Its Advancement," *Jubilarni zbornik života i rada Srba, Hrvata i Slovenaca, 1918–1928* (Jubilee Record of Life and Work of the Serbs, Croats, and Slovenes, 1918–1928), I, 325–41; "Report of the Conference on the Improvement of Cattle Raising," Yugoslavia, Ministry of Agriculture, *Glasnik*, Belgrade, XIV (May 1936), 176–85.

[5] Ivan Šmalcelj, "Crossbreeding of Cattle," Yugoslavia, Federal Ministry of Agriculture, *Poljoprivreda*, Nos. 3–4 (1950), pp. 56–64. Most of the Holstein cattle imported through the UNRRA has been retained on state farms in the northern and northeastern plains of the country.

ube rivers, where horses are of primary importance as draft power, in areas south of these rivers oxen are primarily kept for draft work in agriculture. While in most parts of Yugoslavia cows are also used for draft, the importance of the oxen as the draft animal was shown earlier (pp. 457–58). This situation in regard to oxen is reflected in the relative number of cows in the cattle population in various areas. The official statistics give 1,911,577 as the average number of cows over two years of age in the period 1934–38. Of these, on the basis of the above percentages of breed distribution by *banovine*, 820,700 were Buša cows, 89,800 Podolian cows, and 1,001,100, dairy and improved-type cows. Generally speaking, the percentage of cows in the total cattle stock was much smaller in areas where domestic breeds predominated than in areas of dairy and improved types of cattle. The percentage of cows in the total stock during 1934–38 by *banovine* was as follows: Sava 60, Dunav 55, and Drava 52, representing the areas of advanced cattle raising; Primorje 40, Vrbas and Zeta 38, Drina 37, Morava 36, and Vardar only 31 percent, representing areas of domestic breeds.

Especially great differences exist in the productivity of cattle in various areas, because cattle raising is quite advanced in some of them, and in others it is still quite primitive. Cows of the domestic breeds mature relatively late (approximately at the age of three) and a large percentage among them remain barren, while cows of dairy and improved breeds mature earlier and a smaller number of them are barren. For the purposes of estimating the calf crop, it was assumed that 55 percent of Buša cows, 50 percent of Podolian cows, and 65 percent of dairy and improved-type cows over two years of age had calves annually, giving an average calf crop of 1,147,000 head during the period 1934–38. Assuming that the annual death loss due to natural causes (disease, accidents, predators) amounted to 2.5 percent of the total cattle stock, and considering that the average annual increase in the stock of cattle during that period was roughly 2 percent of the total stock, the average number of cattle available for slaughter or for export in the period 1934–38 was about 962,600 head annually (358,000 Buša, 37,000 Podolian, and 567,600 dairy and improved-type cattle).[6] It was further assumed that 47 percent of the cattle available for

[6] The Yugoslav experts assume at the present time that the death rate of cattle due to natural causes amounts to between 0.5 and 1 percent of the total stock per annum. This is obviously too low. The contention is that a head of cattle represents a large investment for the peasant and that in the case of sickness or accident the peasant does not wait for the animal to die but rather kills it and tries to utilize most of it. V. M.Djuričić et al. (op. cit., p. 67) assumed in 1927 that the death loss due to natural causes was about 10 percent of the annual calf crop, which, according to their estimates, would

slaughter were slaughtered as calves and 53 percent as mature animals.[7]
Carcass weights assumed for purposes of our calculations of veal and
beef production are as follows: Buša calves 23 kilograms, Buša older
animals 90 kilograms; Podolian, dairy and improved types of cattle,
calves 37 kilograms and older animals 180 kilograms.[8] The figures for
older animals also include tallow (5 to 8 percent of the carcass weight),
which is used partly for food and partly as raw material in soap and
other industries. On the basis of these assumptions, the production of
dressed beef during the period 1934–38 averaged 75,000 metric tons
and that of veal 14,000 metric tons annually. It is further estimated
that the average annual production of buffalo meat during that period
was 600 metric tons, but is here rounded to 1,000 metric tons. The
average annual exports of beef and veal during the period 1934–38
amounted to an estimated 9,500 metric tons, of which 8,000 metric
tons were beef and 1,500 metric tons were veal.[9] The bulk of the veal,
1,100 metric tons, was exported as fresh meat, while in the case of beef
only 250 metric tons were exported as fresh meat and the remainder as
live animals, primarily steers.

There are even greater differences among cows of various breeds
in regard to milk production than among various types of cattle in
regard to meat production. The poorest milk producers are the Podo-

---

represent approximately 3.3 percent of the total cattle stock. This appears to be somewhat too high. According to data of the Bulgarian State Agricultural Bank, which administered a cattle insurance program in Bulgaria—and cattle raising in Bulgaria is
similar to that in a large part of Yugoslavia—the death loss due to natural causes in the
period 1938–42 was on the average 1.79 percent for animals of one year and older and
about 4 percent for calves up to one year. *Narodno Stopanstvo*, Sofia, No. 7 (1947), p. 48.
Our assumption of 2.5 percent as the death loss due to natural causes seems quite
realistic.

[7] During the period 1928–34, for which detailed data on the slaughtered cattle in
slaughterhouses are available (that is, disregarding the slaughter on the farms), 48.6
percent of the total were calves and 51.4 percent older animals. National Bank of the
Kingdom of Yugoslavia, *Bulletin trimestrielle*, January–March, 1935, p. 67. If export
figures of live animals for these years are added to slaughter figures in publicly inspected
slaughterhouses, then the ratio is 44.3 percent for calves and 55.7 percent for older
animals. The 55.7 percent was composed of 3.7 percent bulls, 21.7 percent steers,
17.2 percent cows, and 13.1 percent bullocks and heifers.

[8] The slaughter loss for calves is assumed to be 43 percent and that for older animals
55 percent.

[9] The export of beef and veal, both on the hoof and in slaughtered form, during the
period 1934–38, amounting to an estimated 10.7 percent of the total production, was not
typical of the whole interwar period, but rather of the period of relatively depressed
conditions and of rampant agricultural protectionism in Central European countries and
Italy. During 1934–38 Yugoslav exports of live cattle averaged only 58,540 head, while
during the ten-year period 1922–31 they averaged 135,740 head annually. There was not
much difference in the export of fresh meat in the two periods.

lian cows, partly because they are so wild that it is hard to milk them; then follow Buša cows; and then finally various improved multipurpose and dairy breeds. It is here assumed that 60 percent of Buša and Podolian cows and 80 percent of cows of other breeds which had their young were actually milked and that, on the average, the Podolian cows yielded 200, the Buša cows 300, and the improved and dairy-type cows 1,600 kilograms of milk annually above the needs of their calves. These are estimated country-wide averages, but there is no doubt that the milk productivity of Buša cows in the plains and in the mountains differs considerably, as does the milk productivity of cows of various multipurpose and dairy breeds in various areas, depending on the breed, the feed supplies, the general care accorded to the animals, and the incentive to milk the cows more or less intensively. There are also areas where the Buša breed prevails, such as Macedonia, where these cows are used only occasionally for milking. Their chief function is to produce working oxen. The important sources of milk in Macedonia (*banovina* Vardar) were sheep and goats.[10] The average butterfat content of cow's milk is taken to be a little over 3.5 percent (Buša 4.5, Podolian 4, and other cows 3.5 percent). On the basis of these assumptions the average milk production per cow milked, above the needs of the young, was somewhat above 1,100 kilograms per year, and the total cow's milk production during the period 1934–38 was about 920,000 metric tons annually.

The small production of buffalo cow's milk is disregarded because no data are available which would enable us to undertake a satisfactory estimate.

SHEEP AND GOATS

The Yugoslav sheep herds averaged 9.5 million head during the period 1934–38, of which roughly 9 million were of the domestic or Balkan breed, somewhat less than 500,000 Cigaja sheep, and a few thousand Solčava and Merino sheep.[11] The chief sheep areas of Yugo-

---

[10] Aleksandar Cijuk, "Animal Husbandry," in Aleksa Jovanović (ed.), *Spomenica dvadesetpetogodišnjice oslobodjenja Južne Srbije, 1912–1937* (Jubilee Record of the Liberation of Southern Serbia, 1912–1937) p. 580.

[11] For discussion of the Yugoslav sheep economy see S. Filipović, "Vlašić Mountain and the Production of Milk in Its Area," in Kingdom of the Serbs, Croats, and Slovenes, Ministry of Agriculture and Water Resources, *Glasnik*, Belgrade, V (April–June, 1927), 64–95, and *ibid.*, V (July–September, 1927), 1–49. For the sheep milk production see also Yugoslavia, Ministry of Agriculture, *Arhiv*, II, 148; *ibid.*, IV, 180–83. For material with special reference to wool production see Albert Ogrizek, "Investigations of Wool from our Domestic Sheep Breeds . . . ," in University of Zagreb, *Godišnjak Sveučilišta Kraljevine Jugoslavije u Zagrebu za školske godine 1924/25–1928/29* (Yearbook of the

slavia are those south of the Sava-Danube rivers, but the Cigaja sheep is almost exclusively raised in Vojvodina and Slavonia. The productivity of this sheep is perhaps 50 percent higher than that of the domestic breeds, but because of its limited numbers we are disregarding these differences in our calculations. It is generally agreed that the actual number of sheep in Yugoslavia before World War II was considerably higher, perhaps as much as 20 percent higher, than shown in official statistics.[12] While it is necessary to keep this in mind, we have already explained the reason why we use the official figures as basis of our calculations of the output of animal food products.

Of the above total of 9.5 million head, 6.7 million were ewes, 1.7 million were lambs up to one year of age, and the remainder consisted of breeding rams (393,000) and other rams and ewes (820,000). It is assumed that the lamb crop amounted to 80 percent of the number of breeding ewes, and that 5 percent of the total number of all sheep were lost annually, owing to disease, accidents, and predators. About 3 percent of the lamb crop in the above period were used to increase the herds, while about 48.4 percent of the total stock, or 4,600,000 head, were available for slaughter annually. It is further assumed that 40 percent of this number were slaughtered as lambs, yielding an average of 6 kilograms of meat, and 60 percent as mature animals, yielding an average of 16 kilograms of meat, or an average of 12 kilograms per animal.[13] On the basis of these assumptions the estimated average annual production of lamb and mutton during the 1934–38 period was 55,000 metric tons, of which 11,000 were lamb and 44,000 were mutton. Of this amount, an estimated 4,600 metric tons were exported annually during the period 1934–38, consisting primarily of live animals (annual exports in that period averaged 410,355 lambs, 67,861 rams, and 47,050 ewes) and small quantities of mutton. These export figures are much smaller than during the late 1920's, but sheep exports were not curtailed as drastically as cattle exports during the 1930's.

Except in the case of the Moslem population, which, because of religious rules, does not consume pork products and therefore consumes

---

University of Zagreb for the Academic Years 1924/25–1928/29), pp. 649–74; Tanasije Mitrović, "Production of Wool and the Improvement of Its Quality in Our Country," Yugoslavia, Ministry of Agriculture, *Arhiv*, I, 44–71; Dragiša Nikolić, "Investigations of Wool Quality of Our Sheep Breeds," Yugoslavia, Federal Ministry of Agriculture and Forestry, *Arhiv za poljoprivredne nauke i tehniku*, II, 45–68.

[12] Dragiša Nikolić, *op. cit.*, p. 47.

[13] The bulk of lambs in Yugoslavia are slaughtered when they are 3 to 5 months old and weighing 10 to 20 kilograms. Live weight of adult ewes is about 28 to 30 kilograms, and of rams 40 to 45 kilograms. Slaughter loss amounts to 45 to 55 percent.

mostly mutton, perhaps the larger part of mutton production is not consumed fresh but stored for winter in the form of dried or jerked meat.

Sheep are an important source of milk in Yugoslavia. In areas south of the Sava-Danube rivers they are the basic source of milk and dairy products. In certain parts of Bosnia, central and eastern Serbia, and Macedonia, sheep raising, partly of a quasi-nomadic character, furnishes the basis of livelihood for whole areas. It supplies milk, cheese, a special type of butter called *kajmak*, fresh meat, jerked meat, wool for the production of homespun clothing and bedding, skins for fur-lined clothing, as well as cash income from the sale of various sheep products. The average milk production of sheep of domestic breeds in Bosnia and Serbia is usually taken as being between 40 and 50 kilograms above the needs of the lambs per ewe per lactation period of five to six months; 50 to 60 kilograms for sheep in Macedonia; and about 70 kilograms for sheep of Cigaja breed. It is here assumed that the average milk production per ewe throughout the country is 50 kilograms per lactation period, and that 80 percent of ewes with lambs are milked. The sheep's milk has about 6 percent of butterfat. On the basis of this calculation the production of sheep's milk in the period 1934–38 averaged about 215,000 metric tons annually.

Goat herds were quite important throughout the interwar period, especially in *banovine* Vardar and Zeta, and to a lesser degree also in *banovine* Primorje and Morava. The turnover in goat herds is similar to that of sheep herds, with which they are usually kept. In the period 1934–38 the herds of goats averaged 1,894,955. It is assumed that in the above period about 920,000 goats, or roughly 48.4 percent of the total, were available for slaughter, yielding an average of 12 kilograms of meat per head, or an estimated 11,000 metric tons (9,000 metric tons of meat from mature animals and 2,000 from the young goats). Only 600 tons of goat meat, mostly in the form of mature live animals, were exported annually during the period 1934–38. Goat meat is utilized in the same fashion as mutton and lamb.

Goats are much better milk producers than sheep and are often referred to as the "poor man's cows." It is here assumed that goats yield on the average about 120 kilograms of milk above the needs of the young per lactation period. If it is again assumed that about 80 percent of goats are milked, this calculation gives 97,000 metric tons as the annual production of goat's milk. Some of the improved types of goats, especially the so-called Sana goats, are much higher milk producers, but these goats were not numerous.

It was generally agreed that goats were very destructive of the young trees and thus one of the factors contributing to the deforestation of the karstic areas and Macedonia. Therefore, a reduction in their herds has often been recommended. But apparently no regime prior to 1941 dared to order a severe reduction. Since 1945, however, a policy of drastic reduction of goat herds has been followed, especially in the People's Republic of Macedonia. A special law of 1948 ordered a practical extinction of this species in Macedonia. The goat herds in Yugoslavia numbered 1,890,386 in 1938. At the beginning of 1949 there were 1,319,565 goats in the country, but at the beginning of 1950 only 786,170. In Macedonia their number fell from 648,466 in 1938 (*banovina* Vardar) to 41,671 in 1950.[14] What results this policy will have on reforestation and soil conservation, and, in turn, on the productivity in agriculture in Macedonia and in all karstic areas, remains to be seen.

PIGS

For domestic consumption and export of both meat and animal fats, pigs are the most important source of supply.[15] In the period 1934–38 Yugoslavia had an average of 3,096,055 pigs, rather unevenly distributed by regions. *Banovina* Dunav had approximately one-third of all the pigs in the country and, with *banovina* Sava, more than one-half of the total number. Relatively large numbers of pigs were also kept in *banovine* Drava, Drina, Morava, and Vrbas. The relatively lowest numbers were in *banovine* Zeta, Primorje, and Vardar, which is explainable partly by deficiency in feed supplies in these areas, and partly by their large Moslem populations, which did not raise or utilize pigs.

From the production point of view, in addition to feed, the breed of pigs is essential and, under Yugoslav conditions, also the age at which they are slaughtered. There are two basic types of pigs: the fat-or lard-type of pig raised primarily for the production of lard, and the meat-type pig raised primarily for the production of bacon and hams. Assuming that the distribution of pigs by breeds during 1934–38 was the same as in 1933, the following percentages (in round figures) of the fat-type pigs were kept in various *banovine*: Drava 2, Drina 44, Dunav 67, Morava 24, Primorje 9, Sava 59, Vardar 16, Vrbas 26, Zeta 13, and the Prefecture of Belgrade 67 percent. The country as a whole had 44 percent fat-type and 56 percent meat-type pigs.[16]

[14] Yugoslavia, Federal Bureau of Statistics, *Bulletin statistique*, No. 3 (November 1950), p. 23.

[15] For a review of the Yugoslav hog industry in English see Harry E. Reed, "The Hog Industry in Yugoslavia," United States, Department of Agriculture, *Foreign Agriculture*, I, No. 10, 503–24.

[16] Dragiša Nikolić, "Present Situation in the Yugoslav Pig Raising and Measures for Its Advancement," Yugoslavia, Ministry of Agriculture, *Arhiv*, III, 156–68.

Yugoslavia is known for its domestic breed of fat pigs, the Mangalica, which represented roughly 30 percent of the total stock in the country and, with another fat-type pig, the Šumadinka, not less than 67 percent of all pigs in *banovina* Dunav, the chief pig-raising and pig-exporting area of Yugoslavia. Mangalica is late maturing and of relatively low fertility. It is popular because it is not choosy in regard to feed, requires little care, and is very resistant to disease. Furthermore, it is a top fat producer under the Yugoslav conditions. In *banovina* Sava, the second most important pig-raising area, Mangalica represents 30 percent of the total. Another fat-type pig, the Turopoljka, accounts for 20 percent, and the Bagun for somewhat more than 7 percent. In *banovina* Drina, the Šumadinka is the most numerous species of the fat-type variety, followed by Mangalica. Most numerous among the pure or partially improved meat-type breeds is the Crossed English White (11 percent of the total) and the German Edel (8 percent of the total), the latter type being especially prevalent in *banovina* Drava (62 percent of the total). Experiments with other types of meat pigs imported from abroad proved of little success, apparently the most important reason being various diseases. The most common meat-type pig is the domestic breed Šiška, comprising 23 percent of the total stock in the period 1934–38. Forty-five percent of all hogs in *banovine* Morava and Drina, 55 percent in Vardar and Vrbas, 64 percent in Primorje, and 70 percent in Zeta were Šiška pigs. They are raised on green feed, acorns, kitchen swill, unusable fruits, and the like.

The number of breeding sows averaged 759,000 in the period 1934–38. The average litter of Mangalica sows was five to six, of other breeds somewhat higher. Mangalica sows, generally, had their litters once a year, meat-type sows in northern areas in Croatia-Slavonia and Slovenia had two litters annually, and Mangalica sows on more efficiently managed farms often had two litters a year or three litters in two years. The pig crop, during the period 1934–38, probably amounted to around five million head. The mortality of pigs in Yugoslavia is exceedingly high, however, both in the first month after farrowing as well as throughout their life because of disease, especially hog cholera. It is assumed here that the death rate due to natural causes amounted to 20 percent of the total stock in the above period. During that period the pig stocks increased at an average annual rate of about 5.5 percent. With 3.45 million head in 1938, the total stock was higher than in any year during the interwar period. There is no doubt that in northern areas of the country, namely, in Vojvodina, Slavonia, and in northern Serbia, where pigs are raised in large numbers for the market, the possibilities of sale (including exports) and the level of pig prices as well as the supply and prices of corn, which is fed to pigs for fattening, do exercise a certain influence on the number of pigs produced. But it is absolutely impossible to find a definite correlation between the fluctuations in the number of pigs in these areas and changes in prices of pigs, production or prices of corn, export of pigs, or export of corn. Undoubtedly, the corn crop was related more to the weight of animals marketed and slaughtered on the farms than to the number of pigs raised. It appears, however, that in the period 1935 to 1938 the increase in the number of pigs in the northern areas was favorably influenced by the increasing exports of live pigs, lard, and fresh pork meat, and the large corn crop in Vojvodina between 1936 and 1938.

It was assumed here for the purposes of estimating the production of pork meat and lard that the number of pigs available for slaughter or for export in terms of grown animals during the period 1934–38 amounted to 95 percent of the total average stock, or 2,940,000 head, of which 1,294,000 head were fat-type pigs and 1,646,000 head were meat-type pigs. The size composition of pigs actually slaughtered was very different from that here assumed, owing to customs in nutrition and in the way of celebrating holidays, especially in Serbia and to a lesser degree in Vojvodina, Slavonia, and Bosnia, where a huge number of suckling pigs is slaughtered. Also a considerable portion of both fat-type and meat-type pigs is not completely "finished" before slaughter because of the lack or high cost of feed. The number of pigs actually killed is therefore considerably higher than was here assumed. It was estimated in 1936 that 500,000 fat-type and 100,000 meat-type pigs were slaughtered in the public slaughterhouses, that about one million fat-type pigs and about two million meat-type pigs and suckling pigs were killed on the farms, and that about 250,000 fat-type pigs were exported.[17] Furthermore, it was assumed that the average live weight of fat-type pigs was 110 kilograms and that of meat-type pigs 70 kilograms. It was further assumed that fat-type pigs yielded 43 percent of lard and 40 percent of meat, and the meat-type pigs 20 percent of lard and 60 percent of meat of their respective live weight, thus implying a slaughter loss of 17 percent in the case of the former and 20 percent of the latter. According to this calculation the production of pork meat and lard during the period 1934–38 averaged 210,000 metric tons annually, of which 126,000 metric tons were pork meat and 84,000 metric tons crude lard. These figures also include the exported pork products in live and slaughtered forms amounting to a total of roughly

[17] Dragiša Nikolić, *ibid.*, p. 166.

36,000 metric tons in the above period, of which 19,000 metric tons were lard and 17,000 metric tons pork meat. The composition of these exports was: 244,650 fat-type pigs, 860 meat-type pigs, 5,806 metric tons fresh pork meat, 7,394 metric tons of lard, fresh, salted, and dried fat backs, and approximately 400 metric tons (fresh meat equivalent) of hams, salami, dry pork meat, and canned pork meat.

POULTRY

Poultry was an important source of meat in Yugoslavia in the period between the two world wars. In the period 1934–38 the flocks officially reported averaged 18.5 million chickens, 1 million ducks, 1.2 million geese, and 0.9 million turkeys. The flocks of all types of birds were growing. The breeds of all birds were exceedingly mixed and in most areas degenerated, but at the same time quite hardy. The average production capacity was very low. In the mid-1930's chicken flocks consisted of about 80 percent of domestic and crossed breeds, ducks of 93.2 percent of such breeds, geese 92.5 percent, and turkeys 92 percent of such breeds, while the remainder represented good improved breeds.[18] In most areas of the country poultry production is primitively organized, or, as it used to be said, it was an activity of old women; but there are also areas, such as Vojvodina, Slavonia, and northern Slovenia, where first-class fattened poultry was produced for export, although not on special poultry farms, but on general peasant farms.

Because of the primitive conditions of poultry raising, it is assumed that the annual slaughter averaged approximately the number of poultry reported at the beginning of the year. Assuming that the average drawn weights were one kilogram for chickens (chicken taken in terms of grown units), two kilograms for ducks, four kilograms for geese, and five kilograms for turkeys, the estimated poultry-meat production during the period 1934–38 was 29,000 metric tons, of which the average exports, in both live and slaughtered forms, were 12,800 metric tons.

Regarding egg production, it was assumed that 65 percent of all chickens, or 12,025,000, were laying hens producing on the average 70 eggs of 50 grams each per annum (other species are here disregarded although ducks are quite good egg producers).[19] This calcula-

[18] See the "Report of the Conference on Advancement of Poultry Raising," Yugoslavia, Ministry of Agriculture, *Glasnik*, Belgrade, XIV (January 1936), 12 ff.

[19] *Ibid.* This report estimated that laying hens produced on the average 60 to 80 eggs per annum. The average weight of eggs is about 48 grams in Bosnia, 50–51 grams in Serbia, 52–53 grams in Vojvodina, and about 55 grams in Slovenia. See Velimir Bajkić, "The Organization of and the Rules in the Egg Trade," *Narodno blagostanje*, May 11,

tion gives a total egg production of 840 million eggs (42,000 metric tons), which, after allowing 80 million eggs (4,000 tons) for reproduction, breakage, and spoilage (owing to bad roads, primitive means of transportation and handling, and lack of refrigeration, the rate of breakage and spoilage is high), and 260 million eggs (13,000 metric tons) for export, leaves an estimated 500 million eggs, or 25,000 metric tons, for domestic consumption.

Poultry and eggs were not only important sources of animal proteins in the diet of the Yugoslav population during the interwar period, but they were also important sources of cash for the village economy, and, since a large portion of the output of both poultry and eggs was exported, they were also an outstanding source of foreign exchange. While in areas of advanced poultry raising this activity did entail considerable work and use of grains for feed, in most areas poultry raising required a minimum of work and a minimum of feed that could have been otherwise utilized. And these circumstances made the contribution of the poultry raising to the village economy, both in food and in money income, the more welcome.

CONSOLIDATED BALANCE SHEET OF ANIMAL FOOD PRODUCTS OUTPUT, 1934–38

The preceding discussion and guarded estimates show clearly that animal husbandry was carried on in many parts of Yugoslavia along extensive and primitive lines, and that for the country as a whole the productivity per animal in meat, fats, milk, and eggs was rather low. This production was also very unevenly distributed among various parts of the country (see Table 41, p. 553). This was partly due to natural causes, i.e., different supplies of feed in various areas, and partly to socioeconomic factors such as differences in cultural development of the village, overpopulation, and accessibility of markets.

A consolidated estimate of the animal food products output for the period 1934–38 and the respective exports of these commodities as well as the amounts of these products left for domestic utilization are shown in Table 38. Very little horse meat was produced and consumed in Yugoslavia before World War II, but Yugoslavia exported on the average 13,500 horses for slaughter annually during the 1934–38 period. In the production of animal protein foods, small amounts of meat derived from domesticated rabbits and from game, especially hares, should also be taken into account. On the average, 400 metric

1929, pp. 212–13; and Velimir Bajkić, "The Egg in the Yugoslav and in the World Economy," *ibid.*, May 4, 1929, pp. 193–95.

TABLE 38.—ESTIMATED AVERAGE OUTPUT OF ANIMAL FOOD PRODUCTS, THEIR
AVERAGE EXPORTS, AND DOMESTIC UTILIZATION, 1934–38

(Metric tons)

Commodity	Estimated production	Export Quantity	Percent	Domestic utilization
Meat				
Beef	75,000	8,000	10.7	67,000
Veal	14,000	1,500	10.7	12,500
Buffalo	1,000	200	20.0	800
Mutton	44,000	2,100	4.6	41,900
Lamb	11,000	2,500	22.7	8,500
Goat, mature	9,000	600	6.7	8,400
Goat, young	2,000	—	—	2,000
Pork	126,000	17,000	13.5	109,000
Poultry	29,000	12,800	44.2	16,200
Total	311,000	44,700	14.4	266,300
Lard	84,000	19,000	22.5	65,000
Milk				
Cow	920,000			
Sheep	215,000			
Goat	97,000			
Total	1,232,000	21,800	1.8	1,210,200
Eggs	42,000	13,000	30.8	25,000[a]

[a] After allowing 4,000 tons for reproduction, breakage, and spoilage.

tons of meat from game were exported annually during the 1934–38 period.

It is interesting to note that the share of production of various animal food products which were exported varied greatly from commodity to commodity, the largest being in poultry, 44.2 percent of the total production, and the smallest in milk, amounting to only 1.8 percent of the total estimated production. The reasons why animal food products were exported from Yugoslavia in large quantities during the interwar period have already been given. It is also necessary to add that no animal food products for human consumption worthy of mention were imported during the interwar period as a whole.

Our estimate of meat production for the period 1934–38 of 311,000 metric tons annually is considerably lower than that of the Food and Agriculture Organization of the United Nations for the same period, which amounted (with 22,000 metric tons of offal) to 377,000 metric tons, or that of the Yugoslav government (made in 1947) for 1939, which amounted to 398,500 metric tons, though in the latter case the larger number of animals in 1939 would have to be taken into account. The latter is an aggregate figure and therefore cannot be commented upon. It is not made clear whether either of these two estimates adjusts the officially reported number of livestock herds for the generally assumed underreporting. As explained above, we do not make any allowance in our estimates for underreporting. Our greatest difference with FAO figures lies in the estimate of mutton and lamb, which they give as 84,000 metric tons, and in regard to beef and veal, which they estimate at 98,000 metric tons. Besides, the FAO estimate separately states an estimated tallow production of 13,500 metric tons, which we did not estimate separately, but rather included with beef and mutton. FAO appears to underestimate the export of various types of meat, though in this regard estimates are much easier than in regard to production because full figures on foreign trade are available. The estimates of egg production are almost identical in all three cases, though there are differences with regard to the disposition of production. The FAO estimate apparently fails to provide for reproduction, breakage, and spoilage. The worst disparities, however, appear in regard to the estimates of milk production. According to the FAO estimate, fluid milk production for the period 1934–38 amounted to 2.5 million metric tons above and beyond the need of the young and the waste. And the Yugoslav government estimated (in 1947) the milk production at 2.2 million tons in 1939. Our estimate of 1,232,000 metric tons of milk above the needs of the young lies between two Yugoslav official pre-World War II estimates. One of these estimates gave the total liquid milk production of Yugoslavia as 847,000 metric tons in 1930, of which 672,300 metric tons were cow's milk, 121,400 metric tons sheep's milk, and 53,300 metric tons goat's milk.[20] The other estimate made by the Minister of Agriculture gave the over-all milk production for 1938 as 1.7 million metric tons.[21] Naturally both of these estimates would have to be somewhat adjusted for the differences in the numbers of animals to be strictly comparable with our estimate.

In addition to low average productivity of practically all types of livestock in Yugoslavia, a characteristic of the animal food products was often their low quality. It was stated, for example, that people in

[20] Yugoslavia, *Annuaire statistique 1934–1935*, p. 95.
[21] Yugoslavia, Ministry of Agriculture, *Glasnik*, Belgrade, XVII (February 1939), 135.

few European countries eat lower-quality beef than the Yugoslavs. A large portion of pork meat came from late-maturing fat-type pigs whose meat is not nearly so fine in texture and taste as that of meat-type pigs that mature early. Lard was of lower quality because it was produced by the open-kettle method and did not keep well. A large portion of the exported and domestically sold poultry, especially chicken, was of inferior quality and lacked uniformity. Even large cities like Belgrade and Zagreb did not have milk-supply and milk-distribution organizations to guarantee even a minimum of sanitary requirements. And a large portion of the cheese which was marketed did not meet sanitary requirements.

Needless to say, these factors affected the export chances of Yugoslav products very unfavorably whenever they ran into competition with products from countries using advanced production, packing, storing, and marketing methods. Thus there was a tendency, during the interwar period, toward a reduction of the exports of animals and animal products from Yugoslavia, due not only to the mounting protectionist measures in most of the importing countries, but also to the fact that Yugoslav products did not improve in quality as time advanced as they did in the case of most other competitors.

OTHER PRODUCTS FROM LIVESTOCK

In addition to serving as a source of meat, animal fats, milk and eggs, manure, and, in the case of cattle and horses, serving as draft power in agriculture, animal husbandry and poultry gave a series of other products, all of them being utilized as effectively as the prevailing conditions allowed. Among these products, wool and hides were the most important. Wool production in Yugoslavia prior to World War II was estimated at 1.25 kilograms of unwashed wool per sheep, giving a total production of about 12.5 million kilograms of unwashed wool per annum. This wool was of poor quality. It was estimated that approximately 80 percent of this production was utilized within the peasant household, while about 20 percent was sold for use in industry, and a small amount was exported.[22] The woolen industry actually operated on the basis of imported wool. The high percentage of wool used in the households is a consequence of the fact that the Yugoslav peasant family in areas south of the Sava-Danube rivers—and these are the areas of

---

[22] Dragiša Nikolić, "Investigations of Wool Quality of Our Sheep Breeds," *op. cit.*, pp. 47–48. The chief objective of all efforts in regard to the improvement of sheep raising in Yugoslavia during the interwar period was to increase the production of wool and to improve its quality in order to lessen the need for imports. The success was negligible.

sheep raising—produced the greatest portion of its clothing, bedding, and blankets from home-produced wool. Similarly, mohair was also used, but its production was relatively small.

The bulk of production of cattle and calf hides enters trade, and so does a portion of the sheep-, lamb-, and goatskins. But a large portion of the latter is used in peasant homes. Moreover a large portion of cowhides, simply salted and dried, not tanned, and cut in strips six inches wide and five to seven feet long, is used for the making of soles in the production of *opanci*, the moccasin-like native-type footwear of the peasants. Thin, rolled strips of light skins from sheep and goats are used to weave the upper parts of this footwear. A considerable portion of cowhide, calfskin, sheepskin, goatskin, and lambskin, both in dry and fresh state, was exported. On the other hand, the Yugoslav footwear industry depended largely on imported heavy cowhides, because a large portion of Yugoslav-produced cowhides is light and therefore not fully satisfactory for good footwear. A portion of skins, especially lambskins, is used for the production of fur-lined peasant garments. Some sheep- and goatskins are used as vessels for transportation of wine, oil, and water, and for storing of peasant-made cheese and *kajmak*. While the country supplies a large portion of its needs for tallow for industrial purposes, Yugoslavia used to import some tallow for its industry (see above, p. 500). Use was also found for cattle horns, hog bristles, and animal intestines (for sausage casings). A portion of output of these products was exported. Finally, feathers, especially the down from geese, were collected and used for the making of bed coverings and pillows, and a considerable portion of the feather production was exported.

Beekeeping, which has a long tradition in Yugoslav lands, is also worth mentioning. The average number of beehives in the period 1934–38 was 773,000 and they were rather evenly distributed throughout the country. The average production of honey in this period was 5,000 metric tons annually, and that of beeswax, 540 metric tons. Honey is used to a small extent as a substitute for sugar.

FISHERIES PRODUCTS

To complete the picture on other than vegetable food products, one additional item has to be mentioned—fish. According to the official statistics, Yugoslavia produced on the average 14,500 metric tons of fish (round weight) in the period 1934–38, of which 7,350 metric tons were salt-water fish and 7,150 metric tons were fresh-water fish (3,080 tons from the rivers, 1,410 tons from lakes, and 2,660 metric tons from the fish farms). Fish production as here reported did not include fish caught by the people engaged in fishing for home needs, fish sold to the Italians on the high seas, or fish that was dumped when heavy catches made processing and utilizing impossible. The catch, especially of salt-water fish, was relatively small for the extent of the seacoast in Yugoslavia. There were several reasons for that: the poverty of the Adriatic fishing grounds, poor technical organization of the fishing industry, limited internal market for fresh fish, and lack of adequate storage and transportation facilities for fish from the fishing grounds to the landing ports and from the landing ports to the potential larger markets in the interior. During the period 1934–38 Yugoslavia exported somewhat more than 3,100 metric tons of fish annually, partly fresh, partly in processed form as salted and canned fish; and on the other hand it imported more than 400 metric tons of fish annually, mostly dry cod.

Two-thirds of the salt-water fish catch consisted of pelagic fish, primarily sardines, followed by tuna and mackerel. Of the recorded total catch of salt-water fish in the period 1934–38, 60.4 percent was sold in the fresh form on the domestic market, 11.7 percent was exported fresh, 5.1 percent was canned, and 22.8 percent was salted.[23] Canned fish was preserved almost exclusively in olive oil, which made its price prohibitive, and thus the production very limited. The chief mode of preservation was by salting in barrels and large metal containers, and such fish was consumed almost exclusively by the coastal population. All fresh-water fish was consumed in fresh form. A considerable portion of it, especially from the fish farms, was exported to the large cities of Central Europe.

The 1934–38 average catch of 14,500 metric tons of salt-water and fresh-water fish was distributed among various *banovine* as follows: Drava 40, Drina 100, Dunav 1,870, Morava 90, Primorje 5,120, Sava 4,060, Vardar 1,020, Vrbas 100, and Zeta 2,100 metric tons.

[23] Yugoslavia, *Annuaire statistique 1938–1939*, pp. 185–87.

CHAPTER 24

FOOD UTILIZATION, 1934–38

FOLLOWING the discussion of the characteristics and the level of output of crops and animal foodstuffs during the interwar period, the problem now is to present a consolidated picture of the total production of food in Yugoslavia before World War II, and its utilization. In this chapter we are thus attempting to draw up a rough food balance sheet for Yugoslavia. Obviously it would be very hard, if not impossible, to do this for the entire interwar period. The period 1934–38 was selected for several reasons. These were the last five years before the outbreak of World War II; a considerable amount of statistical and other pertinent information for that period is available in the United States; during that period bumper crops and short crops were relatively well distributed so that the averages can be taken as quite normal; and finally, other attempts of a similar nature have been made for the same or approximately the same period so that comparisons can be made among various estimates.

No systematic efforts were ever undertaken before World War II to ascertain the state of nutrition in either rural or urban areas of the whole of Yugoslavia. The Public Health Service did little in this regard and the Ministry of Agriculture even less, and there was no co-ordination between the two government agencies in the little they did.[1] On the advice of the Committee on Nutrition of the League of Nations, the government established a State Committee for the Study of Nutrition in February 1936; and the Administration for the Study of Agriculture and Nutrition was created in 1939. This writer does not recall ever having seen any information on nutritional conditions in Yugoslavia by either of these two organizations.

The great interest in the problems of nutrition in recent decades had also a certain influence in Yugoslavia. There were a number of physicians in the Public Health Service and in private practice who gave some attention to the problem of nutrition in the South Slav lands prior to 1918 and in Yugoslavia during the interwar period (Drs.

---

[1] Dr. Bogoljub Konstantinović, "The Problem of People's Nutrition," *Socijalno-medicinski pregled*, No. 3 (1938), pp. 255–65, esp. 264–65.

Milan Jovanović-Batut, Stevan Z. Ivanić, Grga Bogić, Josip Rasuhin, Ivo Pirc, Aleksandar Petrović), while the problem of availability and consumption of bread grains was considered by some public and private organizations. But while there were no systematic studies of nutrition covering the whole country, or a region,[2] or an economic group, there were a score of studies of small localities in various parts of the country which dealt with the general sociohygienic situation of these localities and which gave some attention also to the nutrition of the inhabitants of these localities. Thus, Dr. Aleksandar Petrović of the Public Health Service made detailed investigations of sociohygienic conditions in the Serbian villages of Banjane and Rakovica.[3] He also wrote on specific diseases in some villages in various parts of the country and investigated certain specific factors pertaining to the pattern of nutrition in some rural areas, such as the manner of feasting on specific holidays, the consumption of prune brandy in some villages in Bosnia, and the place of paprika in the diet of the rural people in Macedonia.[4] The views of the School of Public Health of Zagreb, an agency of the Public Health Service, on nutrition were presented in a special article by Dr. Rasuhin.[5] In regard to Slovenia an attempt was made in 1937 to cover the problem of housing and nutrition in rural areas.[6] It might be

[2] The study by Dr. Stevan Z. Ivanić, "Nutrition in Rural Areas in Serbia," *Socijalno-medicinski pregled*, No. 1 (1936), pp. 19–40, and No. 2 (1936), pp. 73–85, and that by Dr. Grga Bogić, *Prilozi za istoriju i geografiju ishrane u Jugoslaviji za razdoblje od 1923 do 1925 godine* (Contribution to the History and Geography of Nutrition in Yugoslavia During the Period 1923 to 1925) cannot be taken seriously because of their haphazard, uneven, old, and often obviously unusable material.

[3] Dr. Aleksandar Petrović, *Banjane—Socijalno-zdravstvene i higijenske prilike* (Banjane—Sociohygienic Conditions); Dr. Aleksandar Petrović, *Rakovica—Socijalno-zdravstvene i higijenske prilike* (Rakovica—Sociohygienic Conditions), I, II.

[4] Dr. Aleksandar Petrović, numerous articles in *Socijalno-medicinski pregled*, as follows: "Typhus in Sjeversko," No. 1 (1937), pp. 27–39; "The Symptoms of 'Zličica,'" No. 2 (1939), pp. 111–26; "The Nutrition of Our People: Slava," No. 4 (1939), pp. 378–83; "The Drinking of Prune Brandy in Sitnica," No. 2 (1936), pp. 85–93; "The Nutrition of Our People: Paprika," No. 3 (1940), pp. 353–60. Of a similar character is a short study by Dr. St. Sjelski, "The Village Golubić," *Socijalno-medicinski pregled*, No. 3 (1939), pp. 209–31.

[5] Dr. Josip Rasuhin, "On Proper Nutrition of Our People," *Socijalno-medicinski pregled*, No. 1 (1939), pp. 16–22. Employees of the school trained in home economics tasted dishes in various rural areas in Croatia-Slavonia and tried to encourage the preparation of those dishes that proved most wholesome and healthful and to discourage the preparation of those that proved harmful or unsatisfactory. In this endeavor the school had to contend not only with the scarcity of satisfactory foods, but also with the strong traditionalism of the rural population.

[6] Dr. Ivo Pirc, "The Nutrition of the Peasant Population," in Dr. Ivo Pirc and Franjo Baš, *Socialni problemi slovenske vasi* (Social Problems of the Slovene Village), I, 71–113.

pointed out also that a detailed report on nutrition in the Serbian village Rajković was published in 1951.[7]

Because of their limited coverage and scanty though extremely interesting information, these studies cannot be taken as representative or conclusive in any way. But although they were nothing more than "vignettes of village life," nevertheless they do give some insight into the food-consumption habits not only of individual villages but also of the areas in which these villages are located.

In regard to dietary patterns in Yugoslavia during the interwar period, there is agreement on what the people ate generally and in various seasons, and how they prepared their food, but very little information on the quantitative composition of their diet. The only possible way of estimating the quantities of food consumed and thus the quality of the average diet is to draw up a food balance sheet stating the country's available food supplies in the period under consideration, and draw the national per capita averages. We can then estimate on the basis of other pertinent information how the actual nutrition in various areas and of various groups of people deviated approximately from the national per capita averages.

FOOD BALANCE SHEET, 1934–38

To arrive at an approximate food balance sheet for the period 1934–38, certain preliminary steps have to be taken, i.e., it is necessary to determine what food supplies were available for human consumption within the country. Table 39 shows a consolidated statement of the average annual recorded or estimated food production in Yugoslavia by major commodities or commodity groups during the five-year period 1934–38, net exportation or net importation of individual commodities or commodity groups, estimated quantities used for seed, feed, and industrial purposes, estimated waste, and the total and the average per capita available quantity for human consumption. Such items as coffee, tea, vinegar, salt, and spices, which serve as beverages or seasoning agents but do not add anything, or very little, from a nutritional point of view, have not been taken into account. But it should not be forgotten that the place of some of these items in nutrition is of basic importance, e.g., that of salt, and that the expenditures for these items affect considerably the food budget.

Stocks of food, especially those of cereals, in existence at the beginning of the 1934–38 period and stocks which remained at the end

[7] Aleksandar Giaja, *Ishrana seoske porodice—selo Rajković* (The Nutrition of the Inhabitants of the Village Rajković).

TABLE 39.—AVERAGE ANNUAL FOOD PRODUCTION AND DISPOSITION, 1934–38

(Thousand metric tons)

Commodity	Average crop or estimated production[a]	Net exportation[b] Net importation— in parentheses		Seed, feed, industrial uses, waste	Available for human consumption[c]	Annual per capita availability (Kilograms)[d]
		Quantity	Percent			
Wheat	2,430.0	176.8	7.3	530.0	1,500.0	99.5
Corn	4,690.0	470.2	10.0	1,876.0	2,228.0	147.8
Barley	403.0	7.8	1.9	249.0	102.0	6.8
Rye	206.0	3.2	1.5	60.0	127.0	8.4
Oats	313.0	7.0	2.2	296.0	5.0	0.3
Minor grains	96.0	2.0	2.0	38.0	48.0	3.2
Rice	4.5	(23.8)	528.0	11.0	17.3	1.2
Potatoes	1,630.0	0.3	—	630.0	1,000.0	66.3
Pulses	149.0	30.1	20.2	19.0	100.0	6.6
Vegetables (fresh)	830.0	3.0	0.4	86.0	741.0	49.0
Melons and watermelons	200.0	—	—	20.0	180.0	12.0
Fruits (fresh)	690.0	64.0	9.0	276.0[e]	350.0	23.2
Nuts (in shell)	47.0	1.6	3.4	5.0	40.4	2.7
Sugar[f]	74.6	0.6	0.8	1.5	72.5	4.8
Honey	5.0	—	—	0.2	4.8	0.3
Oilseeds oil	11.3	(4.8)	41.4	0.3	15.8	1.0
Olive oil	4.9	0.2	4.0	0.1	4.6	0.3
Lard	84.0	19.0	22.5	2.0	63.0	4.2
Meat and poultry	311.0	44.7	14.4	6.3	260.0	17.2
Milk (liquid)	1,232.0	21.8	1.8	25.0	1,185.0	78.6
Eggs	42.0	13.0	30.8	4.0	25.0	1.6
Fish	14.5	2.7	18.6	1.5	10.3	0.7
Wine	415.0	1.7	0.4	20.0	393.3	26.0
Beer[g]	23.0	—	—	1.0	22.0	1.4
Prune brandy	41.0	—	—	1.0	40.0	2.6
Brandy (marc)	25.0	—	—	0.5	24.5	1.6

[a] Based on data presented in Chapters 22 and 23. Occasional small discrepancies between figures given in these chapters and those in this column are due to rounding.

[b] Foreign trade figures from Yugoslavia, Ministry of Finance, *Statistique du commerce extérieur* (Belgrade, annually).

[c] Grains in terms of flour on the basis of extraction rates given in text. Rice, milled.

[d] Average estimated population for the period 1934–38 is 15,076,000.

[e] This figure contains only waste and an estimated 207,000 metric tons of prunes used for the production of prune brandy. All other uses of all fruits are accounted for in fresh form.

[f] Sugar, average production for 1932–36.

[g] Beer, average production for 1933–37.

of that period were left out of consideration under the reasonable assumption that they were of a very similar magnitude at the two points of time.

The problems connected with the exports of various foodstuffs and other agricultural products will be discussed more fully in Chapter 26. What is necessary here is simply to state the net exportation or importation, to take each into account in our record of food availability, and to explain briefly the reason behind these food exports.

The following information on the estimated amount of various crops used for seed, feed, and industrial purposes, and on waste of all food products actually complements the data on the production aspects of various foods of vegetable and animal origin furnished in the preceding two chapters.

Official data on the use of seed per hectare are available only for wheat and corn, while seed requirements for secondary and minor grains, potatoes, and pulses are our estimates on the basis of general information. According to this official source, the amount of seed per hectare for wheat in the mid-1920's was 160 and for corn 38 kilograms.[8] All figures on seed requirements are averages for the country as a whole, although considerable differences existed and still exist among various areas, depending on the type of soil, climate, and above all on the level of agricultural technology prevailing in various parts of the country. Seed requirements per hectare during the 1930's were similar to those during the 1920's, and here they are assumed as follows (in kilograms): wheat, rye, and meslin 160, corn and millet 40, barley, oats, spelt, and buckwheat 150, and rice 120. Seed requirements for potatoes are 1,100 kilograms per hectare. Seed requirements for pulses are taken to equal 10 percent of production.

The rate of extraction for cereals is estimated as follows (in percent): wheat, buckwheat, meslin, millet, rye, and spelt 87, corn 95, barley 70, and oats 50. Loss in milling of rice 35 percent. High average extraction rates for all grains, but especially for wheat, are connected with the fact that only a portion of production was milled in commercial mills, primarily in Vojvodina and Slavonia, while the other portion of production was milled in small custom mills where the extraction rate is much higher than in commercial mills. A very small portion of grains was milled in querns owned by individual families in rural areas.

The assumed quantities of grains used for feed are all our estimates on the basis of general information and they are as follows (in metric tons): wheat 60,000 of the lowest quality; corn 1,500,000, used primarily for feeding of pigs in the grain-surplus areas. In the estimate of

[8] Kingdom of the Serbs, Croats, and Slovenes, Ministry of Agriculture and Water Resources, *Potrošnja hlebnih žita u Kraljevini Srba, Hrvata i Slovenaca* (Consumption of Bread Grains in the Kingdom of the Serbs, Croats, and Slovenes), p. 1.

corn used for feed lies the greatest single potential source of error in calculating the per capita availability of cereals for direct human consumption in Yugoslavia during the interwar period. The utilization of secondary and minor grains for feed was estimated as follows (in metric tons): barley 150,000, rye 5,000, oats 220,000, and millet 18,000. It was further assumed that 150,000 metric tons of potatoes were used for feed.

The use of grains and potatoes for industrial purposes was assumed to be as follows (in metric tons): barley, 6,000 for beer; corn, 30,000 for the production of industrial alcohol (mostly spoiled corn), starch, and corn syrup; and potatoes, 30,000 for the production of industrial alcohol and starch. For all grains it was assumed that waste was 5 percent, which might be somewhat too high, and for pulses 3 percent of the total production. For potatoes it was assumed that waste and spoilage amounted to 10 percent.

As stated earlier, the production of vegetables during the period 1934–38 was estimated at 830,000 metric tons. Here it is assumed that about 80,000 metric tons of vegetables fit for human consumption were used for feed or wasted before entering the households. Some vegetables were exported in dried form, but were taken into account in terms of fresh vegetables on the basis of the following conversion rates (dried to fresh): 1 to 10 for paprika, and 1 to 2.5 for mushrooms. Assumed waste for watermelons and melons was 10 percent.

The reported amount of fresh fruit production in Yugoslavia for the period 1934–38 was 625,800 metric tons, to which an estimated 10 percent of the total grape production, or 65,000 metric tons, was added because these grapes were consumed as fruit in fresh form. A considerable portion of actual fruit exports and imports was in the form of dried fruit and small quantities were in the form of marmalade and juices. But all exports and imports are expressed in the form of fresh fruit on the basis of the following conversion rates (dried to fresh): sour cherries, figs, prunes, prune and other marmalade 1 to 2.5; raisins 1 to 3; fruit juices 1 to 4; apples and pears 1 to 5. It was here assumed that 10 percent of the fruit was spoiled or otherwise wasted before it came to the consumer's household. The same percentage of spoilage and waste was assumed for nuts.

The production of sugar of 74,580 metric tons, indicated in Table 39, refers to the annual average for the period 1932–36.[9] Beer

[9] Zvonimir Višnjić, "International Sugar Agreements and the Sugar Economy of Yugoslavia," Yugoslavia, Ministry of Agriculture, *Arhiv*, IV, 148. We assume that 2 percent of sugar and 5 percent of honey production was wasted.

production, as shown in Table 39, represents the annual average for the period 1933–37;[10] average alcoholic content 3.5 percent, waste 3 percent. Assumed waste and spoilage for wine is 5 percent, and average alcoholic content 11 percent. As was indicated while discussing the production of fruit in Yugoslavia (see p. 510), it was estimated that 60 percent of the prune crop was used for distilling prune brandy. This gives a total estimated production of prune brandy of about 41,000 metric tons with an average alcohol content of about 25 percent (50 proof). A portion of the output of other fruits, such as apples, pears, and cherries, was also used for the production of brandy, but no information is available on the output of such brandies during the interwar period.[11] All fruit with the exception of prunes used for distilling of prune brandy is accounted for in fresh form. It is assumed here that the production of brandy (*marc*) from grape mash amounted in the period 1934–38 to 25,000 metric tons with an average alcohol content of 30 percent (60 proof). In the case of beer and brandies it was assumed that the very small exports equaled imports.

Production figures for all animal foodstuffs are our estimates as presented in Chapter 23. Meat figures are on a carcass basis, except for pork. Assumed waste is 2 percent. For milk assumed waste is 2 percent. For lard, olive oil, and all other oils waste and spoilage are assumed to be 2 percent. Eggs needed for reproduction and waste through spoilage and breakage are assumed to amount to 4,000 metric tons. Assumed waste in fish, counted here in round weight, is 10 percent.

As in the case of the estimated output of animal foodstuffs, so with regard to the utilization of most food crops our estimates differ considerably from those of the Food and Agriculture Organization of the United Nations, contained in its food balance sheet for Yugoslavia for the period 1934–38.[12] These differences are many and refer to the assumed amounts of cereals and potatoes used for seed and wasted, the rate of extraction in cereals, and the estimated amounts of various cereals and potatoes used for animal feed and industrial purposes.

[10] S. Djurdjević (ed.), *20 godina kulturnog i privrednog razvitka Kraljevine Jugoslavije* (Twenty Years of Cultural and Economic Development of the Kingdom of Yugoslavia), p. 91.

[11] The magnitude of the production of brandy from other fruits can be judged from the fact that in 1950, when the production of prune brandy amounted to 21,050 metric tons, the output of brandy from other fruit amounted to 10,730 metric tons. Yugoslavia, Federal Bureau of Statistics, *Bulletin statistique*, No. 6 (Belgrade, 1951), p. 49.

[12] Food and Agriculture Organization of the United Nations, *Food Balance Sheets* (April 1949), pp. 139–44.

Moreover, our net exportation figure for wheat and our net importation figure for rice are smaller than those used by the FAO. Space limitation prevents us from discussing these differences. It is, however, because of these and similar differences in various food production and utilization estimates for Yugoslavia for the period immediately preceding World War II that we present in the text detailed information regarding the bases of our estimates.

One important characteristic of the food economy of Yugoslavia during the interwar period was that considerable quantities of cereals, dried legumes, fruits, and especially protective foods of animal origin were exported. This took place in spite of the fact that Yugoslav consumption of protective foods of animal origin was considerably below the per capita average level of Western and Central European countries. Yugoslav exports of these products were thus not the expression of true surpluses over a satisfactory or desired level of consumption of animal foodstuffs, but rather the expression of low purchasing power on the part of the great mass of the Yugoslav population. As the Yugoslav peasants were not able to include these items in their regular daily fare because they were too expensive, so Yugoslavia as a country was unable to afford a larger consumption of these products but exported them. Had the Yugoslav population been able to consume an amount of animal foodstuffs approximately comparable to that of Western and Central European peoples, the country, instead of exporting livestock and animal foodstuffs and feed cereals, would have had to import either additional animal foodstuffs or feedstuffs to produce them.

Table 40 shows the average daily per capita food supply in Yugoslavia during the period 1934–38, expressed in basic nutrients. The supply of food assured the Yugoslav population during that period, on the average, a daily availability of 3,366 calories. Of these, 77 calories came from alcoholic beverages (about 11 grams of alcohol per day), primarily from wine and to a lesser extent from prune and other brandies, and beer. The nutrient supply forming the average daily diet during the 1934–38 period here estimated had approximately 620 grams of carbohydrates, 52 grams of fats from all sources, and 98 grams of protein from all sources.

The Yugoslav diet, which consisted primarily of cereals, was overloaded with carbohydrates. It was relatively well supplied with proteins, but something like 86 percent of all proteins came from vegetable sources (76 percent from cereals, 10 percent from other vegetable sources), and only 14 percent came from animal foodstuffs, which furnish better or more complete proteins. An additional remark is

TABLE 40.—PER CAPITA DAILY AVAILABILITY OF NUTRIENTS, 1934–38

Commodity	Annual per capita availability (Kilograms)[a]	Calories per kilogram[b]	Calories per capita daily	Protein content (Percent)[b]	Protein per capita daily (Grams)	Fat content (Percent)[b]	Fat per capita daily (Grams)
Wheat	99.5	3,500	954	11.7	32	1.5	4
Corn	147.8	3,600	1,458	9.3	37	4.0	16
Barley	6.8	3,320	61	11.0	⎫	1.8	⎫
Rye	8.4	3,410	78	9.0	⎪	1.8	⎪
Oats	0.3	3,850	3	13.0	⎬ 5	7.5	⎬ 1
Minor grains	3.2	3,500	30	11.7	⎪	1.5	⎪
Rice	1.2	3,600	11	6.7	⎭	0.7	⎭
Potatoes ...	66.3	700	127	1.7	3	0.1	⎫
Sugar	4.8	3,870	51	—	—	—	⎪
Pulses	6.6	3,450	62	22.2	4	2.1	⎪
Vegetables (fresh) ..	49.0	220	30	1.4	⎫	0.2	⎪
Melons and watermelons ...	12.0	130	3	0.3	⎪	0.1	⎬ 3
Fruits (fresh) ..	23.2	460	29	0.5	⎬ 3	0.3	⎪
Nuts (in shell) ...	2.7	2,620	20	7.0	⎪	25.0	⎪
Honey	0.3	2,900	2	—	⎭	—	⎭
Oilseeds oil .	1.0	8,840	24	—	—	100.0	⎫
Olive oil ...	0.3	8,840	7	—	—	100.0	⎬ 14
Lard	4.2	8,160	94	3.0	—	89.0	⎭
Meat and poultry ..	17.2	—	96	—	6	—	6
Milk (liquid) .	78.6	660	142	3.5	⎫	3.5	⎫
Eggs	1.6	1,440	6	11.0	⎬ 8	10.4	⎬ 8
Fish	0.7	620	1	8.8	⎭	2.7	⎭
Wine	26.0	—	⎫	—	—	—	—
Beer	1.4	—	⎪	—	—	—	—
Prune brandy ...	2.6	—	⎬ 77	—	—	—	—
Brandy (marc) ..	1.6	—	⎭	—	—	—	—
Total ..			3,366		98		52

[a] From Table 39.

[b] Food and Agriculture Organization of the United Nations, *Food Composition Tables for International Use* (Washington, D.C., October 1949), pp. 9 ff.

pertinent with regard to proteins derived from cereals. It is connected with the position of corn in the Yugoslav diet, whether it was consumed in the form of bread or in the form of cornmeal mush. In the period 1934–38, corn supplied, on the average, 1,458 calories daily, or about 56 percent of all calories derived from cereals, and 43 percent of all caloric availability, including the calories supplied by alcoholic beverages. This reflects on the relative value of proteins derived from cereals, as proteins derived from corn are of lower quality than those from other cereals, primarily from wheat. It is often remarked that the way in which proteins from various sources are combined in a diet plays an important role from the nutritional point of view. Whatever might be the true importance of various combinations of proteins, it is obvious that the large proportion of proteins derived from cereals in general, and from corn in particular, leaves relatively little room for satisfactory protein combinations in the Yugoslav diet.

It is reasonably safe to say that the factor lacking mostly in the Yugoslav diet prior to World War II from the standpoint of wants of the great majority of the population was fats, because the daily availability from all sources during the period 1934–38, according to our estimates, was only 52 grams, supplying about 13 percent of total energy. Considering the occupational and age structure of population, the climatic conditions, and, above all, the prevailing notions among the people in Yugoslavia regarding the place of fats in the dietary pattern, fats should have supplied a higher proportion of total energy, perhaps somewhere between 15 and 22 percent. It is also interesting to note that out of the estimated 52 grams average daily per capita availability of fats, 24 grams, or 46 percent, came from cereals (especially corn), pulses, and nuts, and 28 grams or some 54 percent from oil, animal fats, and other animal foodstuffs. Visible fats and oils, as such, supplied only 14 grams, or 27 percent of the total availability, and most people wanted more of these. The fact, however, that kidney fat of cattle, sheep, and goats was not separately shown, although it was the chief source of fat for some parts of the population, like the Moslems, would slightly increase the per capita availability of fats taken as fats.

Owing to the very low consumption of butter in Yugoslavia, as well as to the low consumption of protective foods of vegetable origin (e.g., green leafy vegetables and fruits) and animal origin (milk, meat), the average intake of vitamins and minerals was probably insufficient.

The average per capita caloric availability in Yugoslavia during the period 1934–38 was higher according to the data published by the

Food and Agriculture Organization of the United Nations than in other
European countries of a similar economic structure, such as Poland,
Hungary, and Greece. Its caloric availability was also higher than in
some Western European countries.[13] But qualitatively the Yugoslav
average diet was far below the average Central and Western European
and United States diets of that time. It was obvious, however, that in
spite of having at their disposal, on the average, enough food to assure
them of a very high average daily caloric intake of well over 3,000
calories, this Yugoslav diet was not well balanced. Actually, considerable segments of the Yugoslav population, especially of its peasantry
in the "passive regions" and of its urban low-income groups, have
suffered from malnutrition and some of them also from undernourishment. Considering the nutrient composition of the Yugoslav diet during the period 1934–38, there could be little doubt that that diet was
in need of improvement.

But as soon as the problem of improvement in diets is raised, the
issue of nutrient requirements comes up. The problem of nutrient requirements necessary to assure a satisfactory and healthful diet for
people of various age groups, for people of various bodily builds and
weights, for people living under different climatic conditions, and
people engaged in various occupations is still a matter of debate. Many
ideas regarding nutrition held by experts only a few years ago have
been discarded and various theoretical dietary standards are repeatedly
undergoing revision. We do not propose, therefore, to establish any
fixed dietary standard for Yugoslavia that would tend to assure the
Yugoslav population a well-balanced healthful diet. Since we just
stated, however, that there was much room for improvement of the
Yugoslav diet as it existed during the 1930's (since the end of World
War II the Yugoslav diet has probably been much less satisfactory than
during the 1930's), we might consider certain modest over-all improvements in that diet. Considering the climatic conditions in Yugoslavia,
the occupational composition and the average build of the Yugoslav
population, it might be reasonably assumed that the people need an
average per capita diet supplying between 2,700 and 3,000 calories
daily. This diet should derive less of its calories from cereals than it
did during the 1930's (say 60 to 65 percent of the total), while the remaining calories should be provided by vegetables, pulses, fruits, meat,

[13] *Ibid., passim.* This report estimates the caloric availability in Yugoslavia during
the period 1934–38 at 3,024 (excluding calories from alcoholic beverages) per day,
that of proteins at 95.1 grams, and that of fat at 60.5 grams per day. The estimated
caloric availability for the same period for Poland was 2,710, Hungary 2,772, and
Greece 2,581 calories (in all cases excluding calories derived from alcoholic beverages).

milk, eggs, and fats. The increase in animal products consumption would result in a better composition of the protein supply though the total supply of proteins need perhaps not be increased. The supply of fats from all sources should be increased to about 70 to 75 grams per day. To assure a more satisfactory supply of vitamins which come from leafy vegetables and fruits, the consumption of these items should be increased. The improvement in the nutrition of the Yugoslav population as here contemplated would require large shifts in hectarage under various crops. It would especially require a much larger portion of agricultural resources for the production of feedstuffs for conversion into protective foods of animal origin.

The assumed improvements in nutrition and the production reorientation which would be required are purely speculative. But in the long run, improvement in nutrition of the majority of the Yugoslav population should be one of the important objectives of the Yugoslav economic policy. The important and as yet unanswerable question in this regard is, of course, When will a considerable improvement in the nutrition of the broad masses of the people of Yugoslavia begin to command a high enough priority among the pressing economic tasks facing the nation? For the time being, large capital investments and expenditures for national defense take first priority, and these outlays are financed primarily at the expense of current consumption, including food consumption, and only to a small extent with foreign aid and foreign loans. One should also not forget that the rapid increase in population and the growing urbanization of the country require a considerable increase in food production just in order to maintain the existing levels of food consumption.

Larger food requirements could, theoretically, be provided by imports. In fact, part of the food requirements during the period 1945–53 was imported, but the reasons for imports of food in these years were of exceptional nature: war damage, droughts, effects of unfavorable food price policies, effects of temporary partial collectivization of agriculture. If large food imports should be considered a permanent policy, then the question arises of how to pay for these imports; and this question cannot be satisfactorily solved. Thus, if any marked improvement in the nutrition of the Yugoslav population should be seriously considered, it would have to be assured essentially by increased and improved domestic production of food.

REGIONAL PRODUCTION OF BASIC FOODS, 1934–38

The preceding food picture, which considers the country as a whole and presents national per capita averages of production and supply of food, is, however, quite misleading without a discussion of regional differences in the production and supply of food. Regional production of food in a country of predominantly subsistence agriculture represents one of the basic problems of food economy, because it is the most important single factor determining the nature and level of nutrition in various regions.

For the sake of simplicity we take into account only the production of basic foods. Table 41 shows the total and the per capita average gross production of basic foods by *banovine* in the period 1934–38. Unfortunately the problem of regional food supply can be discussed only in terms of regional production, because statistical information on internal shipments, the origin of food exports, and the exact areas to which the food imports go is not available, although these factors do affect the food supply picture in various areas. It is well known, however, that *banovina* Dunav and to a much lesser extent *banovina* Sava supplied the bulk of grains and other foodstuffs exported as well as that going into the internal food-deficit areas. Food imports, on the other hand, were practically limited to rice, oilseeds, subtropical fruits, some early vegetables, and small amounts of food specialties, and they were either consumed exclusively by the urban population (subtropical fruits, early vegetables), or were widely distributed over the whole country (rice).

While statistical data on the shipments of cereals from the surplus areas of the northeast to the main deficit areas of the southwest are not available, it is generally assumed that during the second half of the 1930's these shipments amounted to about 600,000 metric tons. More information is available on shipments of cereals from and to various parts of *Banovina* Croatia for the years 1938 and 1939, but *Banovina* Croatia included only a portion, albeit the larger portion, of the cereal-deficit areas, so that there is little point in discussing these data. Moreover, these data pertain to a new administrative division which came into existence in August 1939, while the remainder of our statistical data is based on the administrative division of the country during the period 1929 to August 1939.

Data in Table 41 show the great differences in the production of basic foods among various areas of Yugoslavia. These differences are partly the result of the differences in the available arable land, partly the result of differences in productivity of land and animals, and partly the result of differences in agricultural technology in various areas. The breadbasket of Yugoslavia, as already remarked, was and still is the territory of *banovina* Dunav and the eastern parts of *banovina* Sava,

TABLE 41.—AVERAGE AND PER CAPITA GROSS PRODUCTION OF BASIC FOODS BY BANOVINE, 1934–38*

Banovina	Average population 1934–38 (Thousands)	All grains		Potatoes		Meat and poultry[a]		Fats and oils[b]		Fluid milk		Eggs	
		Thousand metric tons	Kilograms per capita	Thousand metric tons	Kilograms per capita	Thousand metric tons	Kilograms per capita	Thousand metric tons	Kilograms per capita	Thousand metric tons	Kilograms per capita	Millions	Per capita
Drava	1,184	195	165	333	281	26.2	22.1	4.3	3.6	166.1	140	51.7	44
Drina	1,743	802	460	98	56	30.3	17.4	10.6	6.0	75.6	43	88.3	51
Dunav	2,494	3,505	1,405	235	94	71.6	28.7	40.2	16.1	210.1	84	241.7	97
Morava	1,579	734	465	25	16	31.2	19.8	6.2	3.9	109.2	69	96.3	61
Primorje	956	197	206	90	94	16.2	16.9	4.6	4.8	63.1	66	33.7	35
Sava	2,855	1,372	481	649	227	63.7	22.3	22.2	7.8	363.1	127	150.5	53
Vardar	1,725	586	340	40	23	30.4	17.6	4.1	2.4	105.3	61	85.0	49
Vrbas	1,154	500	433	121	105	22.0	19.0	5.2	4.5	66.9	58	60.6	53
Zeta	1,008	234	232	38	37	18.9	18.8	2.9	2.9	70.0	69	31.3	31
Prefecture of Belgrade	378	19	—	1	—	0.5	—	0.2	—	2.4	—	2.5	—
Total	15,076	8,144	540	1,630	108	311.0	20.6	100.5	6.7	1,231.8	82	841.6	56

* Source: For grains and potatoes, Yugoslavia, Ministry of Agriculture, *Statistique agricole annuelle 1938* (Belgrade, 1939); for meat and poultry, fats, fluid milk, and eggs, our own estimates based on data and assumptions presented in Chapter 23.

[a] Meat figure, with the exception of pork, represents the estimated carcass weight, including tallow and kidney fat in the case of beef, mutton, and goat meat. Poultry is taken on the basis of drawn weight. In some areas, e.g., along the Adriatic coast, fish is a relatively important source of protein food. For the distribution of fish catch by *banovine* in the period 1934–38, see page 539.

[b] The fats and oils column contains 84,250 tons of lard, 11,290 tons of oil from oilseeds, and 4,940 tons of olive oil. For distribution of oil production from oilseeds by *banovine*, see page 500, and for olive oil see page 513.

namely, the historical provinces of Vojvodina and Slavonia (including Srijem). These two *banovine* produced the following percentages of Yugoslavia's total production of basic foods during the period 1934–38:

Banovina	Population	Cereals	Potatoes	Meat and poultry	Fats and oils	Liquid milk	Eggs
Dunav	16.5	43.0	14.4	23.0	40.0	17.1	28.7
Sava	18.9	16.8	39.8	20.5	22.1	29.5	17.9
All others	64.6	40.2	45.8	56.5	37.9	53.4	53.4

The share of *banovina* Dunav in the total production is especially impressive. This *banovina* also produced 85 percent of the country's sugar-beet crop. Moreover, practically all of the food produced in this *banovina* was of much better quality than that of other areas, especially that of the areas south of the Sava-Danube line. In *banovina* Sava only the eastern portion was a food-surplus area, while its southwestern and northwestern parts were food-deficit areas.

Taking the estimated Yugoslav national per capita average consumption of food in the period 1934–38 as a base, the following general statement could be made: *banovine* Dunav and Sava were food-surplus areas in all respects; *banovine* Drina, Morava, and Vrbas were self-sufficient in cereals, potatoes, and meat, and Morava in milk, but all were deficit areas in fats and oils, and Drina and Vrbas were deficit areas in milk; *banovine* Drava, Primorje, Zeta, and Vardar were deficit areas in all respects except meat, and Drava in milk. Translating this into the territories of the historical provinces, Vojvodina and Croatia-Slavonia would be in the first group; Serbia and Bosnia would be in the second; while in the third group would be Dalmatia, Herzegovina, Montenegro, Macedonia, and Slovenia.

Although the exports of food and shipments to deficit areas in the country itself came from well-defined regions, namely from *banovina* Dunav and the eastern areas of *banovina* Sava, a certain amount of protective foods, such as meat (mostly on the hoof), poultry, eggs, cheese, and fruit, as well as wine and brandy, were shipped from typical food-deficit areas. Because of their general food deficiency, these areas sold a part of their high-quality foods, which was raised without burdening the arable land (livestock with little or no stable feeding), and wine and brandy, and bought high-calorie foods, chiefly cereals. Thus, e.g., *banovina* Vardar exported considerable numbers of livestock to Greece; *banovine* Vardar, Morava, and Drina supplied cheese; Morava and Drina supplied pigs, poultry, eggs, and fruit; Drava supplied poultry and eggs; and some of the cereal-deficit areas of *banovina* Sava supplied cattle, poultry, and eggs. In some deficit areas, such as parts of Bosnia and Herzegovina, the peasants often sold wheat, barley, and rye and bought corn for their own use. This was also a type of food exchange where quality was sacrificed for quantity.

The supply of food for deficit areas, presenting as it does a problem of internal trade and interregional balance of payments, was one of the most difficult economic problems in Yugoslavia during the interwar period. Its solution remains one of the basic problems of future economic policy of the country. At a later point (see Chapter 26) we discuss the interregional differentials in prices of cereals, a problem of great importance for the cereal-importing areas of the country. Here it might be asked how the food-deficit areas paid for their inshipments of food during the interwar period. The following were the sources from which the food inshipments, consisting primarily of cereals and to a much smaller extent of fats (lard), were paid for:

1. From agricultural export surpluses of these areas, such as tobacco, wine, fruits, medicinal herbs, livestock and livestock products, and, in the case of Adriatic coastal areas, also small quantities of olive oil and fish.

2. From other export surpluses of these areas, consisting of such items as timber, bauxite, cement, artificial fertilizers, and coal. Most of the workers in these industries were actually peasants, but their wages in the above industries represented the chief part of their income.

3. From income derived from seasonal migration into other parts of the country, working in agriculture in seasons of heavy work and especially in the construction industry and lumbering. Actually this seasonal migration was an essential part of the economic pattern in many food-deficit areas of Yugoslavia (Macedonia, Herzegovina, Montenegro, Dalmatia, northeastern parts of Slovenia, northern and southwestern parts of Croatia).[14]

4. From emigrants' remittances, especially from the United States (but also from Canada, Argentina, Chile, Australia, New Zealand, South Africa) and from Western European countries (where the bulk of emigrants went during the 1930's), and to a small extent from people who permanently settled in other parts of Yugoslavia.

5. From earnings from such services as tourist trade and shipping.

6. Small amounts were also derived from pensions.

[14] In this category were also such colorful professions as the Macedonian peddlers of sweet drinks and sweets in the Balkan cities and the traveling peddlers coming from the Dalmatian Zagorje (known there as *galantari*), who, prior to World War I but to a certain extent also during the interwar period, could be found all over Europe.

7. From the financial reserves of families, such as cash, gold coins, and jewelry accumulated from savings and from remittances from overseas and kept for years of famine or other occasions of great stress.

8. Shipments of food, primarily corn, sent into these areas during the interwar period by the government and to a very small extent by voluntary relief organizations. The size of the annual average government cash relief grants and/or shipments of food into the "passive areas" to be distributed either free or through various schemes of "productive relief" (e.g., payment of wages on public works in corn) are not known, but they were small. According to official data, the relief in food granted by the government to all needy areas and not only to "passive areas" for the whole period between 1918 and the end of the fiscal year 1932/33 amounted to only 122 million dinars.[15] This was a pittance for a period of almost 14 years if compared with the tax burden imposed annually on the population of these areas, or with the large revenue from the tax on tobacco, tobacco being an important product of the agriculture of "passive areas" (see Chapter 28).

It should also be mentioned that the "passive regions" did not and could not obtain the needed food inshipments from surplus areas on credit. Thus in each year their food consumption depended on their production, increased by the amount of food that they could pay for from their earnings outside of agriculture and financial reserves that they were willing to use to buy food in that particular year. Relief inshipments were insignificant.

The government undertook no action to relieve the pressure of population and thus the perennial food-deficit problem in these areas, although much could have been done by reclaiming some of the *polja* in the karst area, by changes in the buying price and greater cultivation of tobacco, changes in the excise on wine, a systematic program of public works such as road building and reforestation, and government aid to the fishing industry. The handling of the problem of the "passive regions" was one of the blackest spots in the record of the Yugoslav government during the interwar period, because the whole area, as the saying went, was kept "on a beggar's stick."

VARIATIONS IN DIETS AMONG MAJOR POPULATION GROUPS

Consideration of the average per capita availability of food in Yugoslavia during the period 1934–38 and of the production of basic

[15] Yugoslavia, Ministry of Finance, *Stanje državnih rashoda i prihoda za budžetsku 1932/33 godinu* (Statement of Expenditures and Revenue for the Fiscal Year 1932/33) (Belgrade, 1933), pp. 34–36.

foods in various regions of the country are only two steps, albeit basic steps, in the discussion of the problem of nutrition. The seasonal patterns of food supply and various popular customs which affect considerably nutritional practices will be briefly discussed in the following chapter. Here another problem with regard to nutrition is raised, namely, the effect of various levels of income of individual households and groups of population on their nutrition. This is an issue of basic importance because real income is the controlling factor for the consumption power of individual households and groups of people. Naturally, borrowing can temporarily increase that power, but in the final analysis credit capacity also depends on income. Aid from outside of the household, or region, or nation can also increase the consumption power, but, as a rule, such aid is temporary, except in areas where remittances from outside form a continuous and important portion of the population's income.

Unfortunately, in regard to the relationship between income and nutrition of various groups of people in Yugoslavia we have to be satisfied with a few general remarks, because no statistical data or other acceptable systematic information in this regard is available. It is evident from the food balance sheet that the average Yugoslav diet during the period 1934–38 was one-sided, unpalatable, and extremely bulky because of the overwhelming preponderance of cereals in it. The amount of animal protective foods in the average diet was insufficient and large segments of population would have liked a larger amount of fats in their diet. Shortages probably existed also in regard to various vitamins, both those obtained from animal protective foods and those obtained from vegetables and fruits; and in regard to minerals.

But the general nutritional pattern of the Yugoslav diet was considerably aggravated by the uneven distribution of various nutrients among various groups of population, and this was essentially related to the differences in the level of real income. The basic difference in the level of income in Yugoslavia existed between the rural and the urban population taken as a whole, and this was reflected also in differences between the diet of the rural and the urban population. Partly responsible for the differences in real income between rural and urban populations was the fact that during most of the interwar period the terms of exchange between the village and the city were favorable for the city and also that the city could shift part of its tax load onto the village. Partly responsible for better nutrition of the urban population was the relatively even distribution of their income over the seasons. Furthermore, their higher income enabled them to buy and/or preserve larger quantities of both animal food products and of vegetables and fruits. Besides, low income forced the rural population largely to forego the consumption of protective foods of animal origin in order to buy energy foods or other necessities. The greater know-how and the greater care and time the urban population could devote to food preparation contributed also to its better nutrition. But with the exception of the "passive regions" the per capita caloric intake of food of the rural population was probably not lower during the 1930's than that of the urban population, although from the quality point of view it was much poorer.

As a consequence of the differences in real income there existed great differences in nutrition between the poor and the well-to-do peasant groups, and between the low-income urban groups and the medium- and high-income urban groups. Needless to say, this statement is not made on the basis of any measurements, but rather on the basis of generally accepted opinion which has its roots both in logic and unsystematic but repeated observations of nutritional practices in both rural and urban areas.

Bread, cornmeal mush, and cereal foods of other types such as paste and noodles made the basis of the diet of all population groups in Yugoslavia, supplying the overwhelming bulk of carbohydrates and proteins. The differences in the quality of nutrition among various groups are perhaps most obvious in three aspects: the type of cereal consumed, the consumption of animal protective foodstuffs, and the consumption of fats and oils. The consumption of bread cereals is treated separately in the following section.

In that part of Yugoslav agriculture based on subsistence or predominantly subsistence farming, the bulk of food consumed by peasant households is actually produced on the family farm. Assuming that no outside income is available and that credit is not taken or aid obtained, the smaller the farm the less are the variety and the quantity of food produced per household and the lower the nutrition level of such families. The decreasing size of farms increases the pressure on the household to produce crops yielding the highest possible product in terms of calories, that is, under the Yugoslav conditions, to produce corn. Since most of these households had to buy a portion of their cereal requirements, they were forced to sell most of their meager production of animal foodstuffs. Thus their consumption of meat, milk, and eggs is limited to a few festive days in the year. One could say that, as a general rule, the smaller the farm of a family, the poorer its nutrition. But the size of the farm and the income from farming are definitely not a safe yardstick for the total income and thus for the level of nutrition, especially of dwarf and small peasants, because they are forced to look for additional income through wage work either in agriculture or outside of it. Thus it should be said that, in addition to the farm size, the number of labor units in a peasant household, or more precisely the relationship between the gainfully employed and supported members, is essential in considering their level of nutrition. Owing to the average low income of peasant families, special circumstances, such as sickness, payment of taxes, dowry for a daughter, the need to buy livestock or farm implements, repair of housing, or putting a child through school, may unfavorably affect the nutrition of a peasant family for a considerable length of time, because all these are cash expenditures, which have largely to be financed at the expense of the food budget. Needless to say, natural disasters such as droughts and floods have the same effect. In such years some peasants migrated temporarily in search of food, while others returned to old practices and supplemented their meager food supply by eating various roots, weeds, acorns, limetree bark, etc.[16]

Of course, medium and big peasants in all areas of the country had a much higher level of nutrition than landless, dwarf, and small peasants, because they generally produced a sufficient amount of cereals, had more potatoes and vegetables, had more and better livestock and poultry, and thus produced more animal foodstuffs. But the important factor was that their total income was larger so that it was not necessary to sell most of the better food in order to buy poorer food or other necessities. Their larger income could much better stand the nonfood expenditures without affecting very unfavorably the level of nutrition. Relatively best was the nutrition of medium and big peasants in Vojvodina, Srijem, and Slavonia. This was especially shown in the fact that they did not eat corn bread or cornmeal mush and that they consumed a satisfactory amount of meat, fats, and eggs.

The villages consumed much less than the urban areas of the items which make the diet more palatable, such as sugar, coffee, tea, and alcoholic beverages. The primary reason for this is to be found in the difference in income between urban and rural population. Thus, according to official estimates (see footnote 9, p. 545), the per capita consumption of sugar in the mid-1930's averaged about 13.5 kilograms in urban and only 2.5 kilograms in rural areas.

Of course, in areas in which animal husbandry played a fundamental role in the peasant economy, as in parts of the mountainous areas of

[16] Milenko S. Filipović, "Migrations in Search of Food," *Glasnik Geografskog društva*, XXVII, 76–91.

the country, the peasantry consumed relatively more livestock products, especially milk and cheese, than elsewhere. But the bread of this population was predominantly from corn, and they also consumed much smaller amounts of vegetables and fruits than the peasants in other areas.

Differences in income among various urban groups were pronounced and affected greatly their respective nutrition. Large segments of low-income urban population had a nutritional level near that of the rural population. This is explained by five main reasons: (*a*) these were mostly people who had recently left the village, and they continued to adhere largely to the peasant patterns of nutrition; (*b*) owing to the pressure from the overpopulated rural areas upon the urban labor market and lack of effective labor organizations, wages and salaries were low; (*c*) an unduly high share of income was taken for rent in urban areas (see p. 580); (*d*) high direct and indirect taxes; and (*e*) high middleman margins charged on all food items, as well as the presence of monopoly rents in many prices of industrial products controlled by cartels.

Several attempts were made during the interwar period to obtain information on the nutrition of workers in some cities of Yugoslavia, but the results were not dependable.[17] The most representative diet of the low-income urban groups consisted of bread, potatoes, cabbage (or other vegetables in season), sauerkraut, and dried beans in winter and spring. Like the rural diet, the diet of low-income urban groups was marked by low consumption of animal foodstuffs and fats and oils, as well as sugar and coffee, but their consumption of alcoholic beverages was considerable, especially in areas like Slovenia and Dalmatia.

By far the best-fed group of population in Yugoslavia during the interwar period was the medium- and high-income urban population. They derived a considerably smaller relative portion of their caloric intake from cereals and had a much larger consumption of animal foodstuffs and fats and oils than the national average. Because of their higher income, they were able to buy the protective foods that the peasants had to sell. These people had a predilection for good food and they used a large portion of their income and time to gratify their propensity in this direction. But even their diet was somewhat monotonous in comparison with a well-balanced diet and lacked sufficient leafy vegetables and fruits in winter and spring and dairy products throughout the

---

[17] Arthur Benko Grado, "Bread in Workers' Family Budgets and the Price of Bread in Zagreb During the Past 40 Years," *Indeks*, XII, No. 1, 1–3.

year. This income group could afford a relatively large amount of sugar, coffee, tea, alcoholic beverages, and other items which increase greatly the enjoyment derived from food and drink.

There is little doubt that what a large segment of the people of Yugoslavia missed most in their diet was a larger amount of fats and oils. This was especially true of the people in the "passive regions" and of the low-income groups generally. With the addition of sufficient butter, lard, or oil, even the simplest food, e.g., cornmeal mush, boiled potatoes, any type of paste, boiled cabbage, sauerkraut, or dried beans, acquire a much greater palatability. Some fats, e.g., butter, add valuable nutrients, and all fats and oils add calories in concentrated form. This key position of fats in the dietary pattern in Yugoslavia is seen also from the fact that in peasant families which have to purchase food, fats rank next in priority after cereals. As in other respects in nutrition, the urban medium- and high-income groups had an ample and often an excessive amount of fat in their diet. But even in such households butter was only exceptionally seen on the table—not because they could not afford it but because this was not a habit. There are many sayings among the people regarding the frugal use of fats and oils. This writer recalls well the experiences of a youth in Dalmatia where a great deal of green cabbage (collard greens), usually cooked with potatoes and seasoned with olive oil, is eaten as the main dish, with bread and a glass of wine (diluted with water) most often the only accompaniment. A proper dose of oil to a plateful of cabbage would have required making one or preferably two signs of a cross with the oil decanter over the plate. But his mother, watching the application of oil to food, would almost invariably say: "My son, only 'In the name of the Father . . . !' " When people wanted to say that a family ate well they often said that their food "swims in oil."

Finally, economic fluctuations had an important influence on nutrition in both rural and urban areas. The index of real wages (without taking into account rents and taxes) rose from 100 in 1926 to 133.6 in 1932 and stayed at a level of between 120 and 130 up to 1938. Undoubtedly this enabled those people who worked (the index of insured workers rose from 100 in 1926 to 134.9 in 1930, fell to 109.8 in 1933, and rose gradually to reach 150.7 in 1938) to have better nutrition as their wage dinar went considerably farther during the 1930's than it did during the 1920's.[18] But the Great Depression had an opposite effect on the nutrition of the peasants because it decreased their real

[18] Ljubomir Dukanac, *Yugoslav Business Cycles (Index Numbers) 1919–1941*, p. 27.

income by moving the terms of exchange with the city to their disadvantage. Besides forcing the peasants to sell more of their products to achieve the necessary minimum of cash income and affecting unfavorably the level of peasant nutrition, the Great Depression caused a drop in the real income of the peasantry from wages in urban economy and from emigrants' remittances, having the same unfavorable effect on their nutrition. Furthermore, after 1932 it was almost impossible for the peasants to obtain any credit, which was also reflected in poorer nutrition.

BREAD—THE STAFF OF LIFE

The food balance sheet for 1934–38, the repeated observations of diets throughout Yugoslavia, and the earlier mentioned "vignettes of village life" show that bread was and still is the basis of the Yugoslav diet, the staff of life in the true Biblical sense. This fact makes the almost religious reverence for bread by all peoples in Yugoslavia easily understandable.

For an overwhelming portion of the Yugoslav rural population the question of nutrition is essentially reduced to the question of cereals. This being the case, it is quite understandable that the supply of cereals in the village was a matter of government and scientific interest during the interwar period. The simple, but at the same time most important, questions which were considered were the following: what types of bread or cereals in other forms are consumed, how much of various types of bread grains are consumed, what percentage of peasant households had to buy a part of their bread-grain requirements, and what was the quality of the bread consumed by the population in various parts of the country.

There is no publication which even tried to answer all these questions for the country as a whole. We are, therefore, forced to present a picture which is pieced together from scattered and incomplete information. Needless to say, all of the following figures, like all figures relating to food availability, have to be understood as indicating the order of magnitude rather than as figures obtained by unimpeachable statistical procedures.

The most ambitious attempt to answer the questions, what and how much of different bread cereals are consumed annually per capita in various parts of the country, was made in 1927 by the Ministry of Agriculture and Water Resources. In the same survey the answer was obtained on the quantity of potatoes used in various areas as an admixture in breadmaking. This survey estimated the average per capita annual consumption of bread grains (and of potatoes for breadmaking) in 1927 as follows:[19]

	Rural communes		Urban communes	
	Kilograms	Percent	Kilograms	Percent
Wheat	97	30.1	145	46.5
Corn	157	48.8	121	38.8
Barley	30	9.3	21	6.7
Rye	26	8.1	19	6.1
Oats	2	0.6	1	0.3
Potatoes	10	3.1	5	1.6
Total	322	100.0	312	100.0

In the rural communes of various regions (in 1927 the country was still divided administratively into 33 regions or *oblasti*), the estimated per capita consumption of bread grains, including potatoes for bread-making, ranged from an average of 271 kilograms in the Sarajevo region in central Bosnia to 355 kilograms in the Vrbas region in north-western Bosnia. In the 390-odd urban communes (including here also a great number of very small towns) which were not grouped by regions, the average estimated consumption of bread grains in the same year ranged from 150 kilograms for the Dalmatian city of Dubrovnik to 450 kilograms for the city of Darda in Vojvodina.[20] Some minor grains such as meslin and spelt were taken into account with the other grains, and millet, buckwheat, and rice were, apparently, not taken into account, although small quantities of millet and buckwheat were consumed either as bread or mush, and rice was consumed in small quantities throughout the country.

According to this survey, and also according to other less systematic observations, wheat bread was exclusively or predominantly (more than 50 percent) consumed in the rural areas of Vojvodina, Slavonia, Slovenia, and along the Adriatic coast. On the average, wheat bread predominated in all urban communes in the country, though many of them in areas south of the Sava-Danube line, with the exception of urban communes along the Adriatic coast and Macedonia, consumed more corn than wheat. In many rural and urban areas, mixed wheat-corn bread was consumed. In the majority of rural areas, however, corn bread predominated. In areas in which conditions are best suited for the growing of barley and rye, these grains were used for bread-

---

[19] Kingdom of the Serbs, Croats, and Slovenes, Ministry of Agriculture and Water Resources, *Potrošnja hlebnih žita* . . . , p. vi.

[20] *Ibid.*, pp. 1–2, 131–39.

making. In very limited areas in which minor grains such as meslin, spelt, and millet are grown, all or a portion of their production was used for breadmaking. The same applied to oats in a few counties of Bosnia and Serbia. Potatoes were used as admixture in breadmaking in some areas where otherwise predominantly wheat or predominantly corn was used for breadmaking.

The estimates in the above survey of the Ministry of Agriculture and Water Resources were collected in 1927, but by and large these data applied throughout the interwar period. However, there is little doubt that during the 1930's the portion of corn in the cereal consumption in Yugoslavia had increased, as is indicated by data in Table 33, page 486.

This structure of the consumption of bread grains is one indicator of the quality of nutrition in various areas of the country. To a very large extent the type of bread consumed is indicative of the economic position of geographic areas, income groups, and individual households. But there are many exceptions to this general rule. There are areas where people actually prefer corn to wheat, for example, in many mountainous parts of the country. The people along the Adriatic coast, although they are in a typical "passive region" and relatively poor, consume predominantly wheat bread. And in other areas, such as Macedonia, people eat more barley and rye bread than elsewhere because their soil and climatic conditions favor the production of these grains.

Some additional data were collected on the type of bread grains used in specific areas of the country toward the end of the 1930's. Thus, the survey of the Chamber of Agriculture for *banovina* Drina showed that only 7.36 percent of the peasant households consumed wheat bread, 41.58 percent only corn bread, 42.94 percent used mixed wheat-corn bread, and 8.12 percent of the households used bread from other cereals, especially from barley. But considerable differences existed between the population in mountainous areas and that in the plains in regard to the type of bread consumed.[21]

Type of bread consumed	*Banovina* Drina	Mountainous areas	Plains
	(*Percent of households*)		
Wheat	7.36	1.20	16.92
Corn	41.58	48.75	29.03
Mixed wheat-corn	42.94	38.35	53.41
Other cereals	8.12	11.70	0.64

[21] Milan M. Obradović, *Selo Drinske banovine u brojevima* (The Village of *Banovina* Drina in Figures), p. 22.

This survey did not try to ascertain, however, the estimated average annual per capita consumption of bread grains by the rural population.

The Gospodarska Sloga of the Croatian Peasant party surveyed the "most pressing needs" of the rural population in *Banovina* Croatia in October 1939. Bread grain requirements of the rural population, locally available supplies, and surpluses or shortages of bread grains in various areas were the chief problem of the whole survey. According to the statements of the peasants the per capita average annual requirements of cereals in *Banovina* Croatia by areas were as follows (in kilograms): [22]

	Wheat	Corn
Agricultural area (surplus or self-sufficient)	280	130
Livestock-raising area	160	270
"Passive regions"	140	190
Average for *Banovina* Croatia...............	190	200

The type and quantity of bread and of other foods consumed in rural areas of Slovenia were the subject of a special study by the Public Health Service of *banovina* Drava in 1937. In this survey figures are supplied only for the rural area around the city of Ljubljana, and they showed that the average annual per capita requirements of bread grains were only 182 kilograms (68 kilograms of wheat, 30 of barley, 15 of rye, 68 of corn, and 1 of oats). But in this area the average annual per capita consumption of potatoes was 180 kilograms, which is about three times the national average, and of other roots 70 kilograms, which is also much above the national average. Detailed data on two individual rural households from other parts of Slovenia showed an average per capita bread-grain consumption of 254 and 297 kilograms, respectively. [23]

The available information regarding the percentage of rural households which had normally to buy a certain amount of bread grains to carry them from one harvest to another does not indicate the portion of rural families that had to provide for bread from other than agricultural income or the percentage of annual grain requirements that had to be bought (there is one exception in this regard). But in a country in which during the interwar period 82 percent of all arable

---

[22] Gospodarska Sloga, *Anketa Gospodarske Sloge: Najnužnije narodne potrebe* (Survey by Gospodarska Sloga: The Most Pressing Needs of the People), p. 32. For the extent of various areas, which were divided into subareas for the purpose of this survey, see *ibid.*, Map 1, p. 4.

[23] Dr. Ivo Pirc, *op. cit.*, pp. 86–92.

land was under cereals and in which the overwhelming portion of all peasants who could do so tried to produce sufficient grains for their own needs, even this limited piece of information is of great interest. The amount of cereals that individual rural households had to buy depended on a number of factors, among which the most important were the type of farm production, the size of farms, the grain harvest, and the number of people in the family. The first data which showed the percentage of rural households that had to buy cereals were obtained in the survey of peasant debts made by the Chartered Agricultural Bank in 1932. These data showed that in the entire country 51.3 percent of all rural households had to buy a portion of their grain requirements. According to *banovine* these percentages were as follows:[24]

Banovina	Percent of all rural households	Banovina	Percent of all rural households
Drava	47.6	Sava	49.1
Drina	56.0	Vardar	46.6
Dunav	29.8	Vrbas	61.2
Morava	48.1	Zeta	78.3
Primorje	94.6		

The 1939 survey by the Chamber of Agriculture for *banovina* Drina established an almost identical percentage of rural households in that area that had to buy grains annually—56.8 percent.[25] This, however, should be ascribed to coincidence rather than to the statistical precision of either of the two surveys. In addition, they were made seven years apart.

The survey of *Banovina* Croatia by the Gospodarska Sloga estimated that in the crop year 1939/40 about 2,050,000 of its rural people (out of a total of approximately 3 million) had to buy grains. The respective per capita shortages were estimated to average about 210 kilograms in the agricultural area, 125 kilograms in the livestock-raising area, and 166 kilograms in the "passive regions."[26] While these figures are only approximations, we have no means of judging how good the approximations are.

In addition to the fact that much of the grains from which bread was made was not well suited for breadmaking, such as corn, or was of poor quality, there were several other factors which were responsible for the proverbially poor quality of bread consumed in many rural

---

[24] Milan J. Komadinić, *Problem seljačkih dugova* (The Problem of Peasant Debts) p. 58.

[25] Milan M. Obradović, *op. cit.*, p. 23.

[26] Gospodarska Sloga, *op. cit.*, p. 31.

areas of Yugoslavia. The overwhelming portion of bread grains consumed in rural areas did not go through trade channels and was not
milled in commercial mills. It was grown on the farms of the people
who consumed it, and it was not properly cleaned before milling. The
overwhelming portion of grain consumed in areas south of the Sava-
Danube rivers was milled in primitive, small custom mills, thousands
of which dotted the rivers and creeks in these parts of the country.
Some grain was milled in very crude querns, and occasionally peasants
used mortars to crush the grain instead of milling it. Flour was often
not properly sifted before use.

The making of bread itself is in many areas poor. Bread is often
made with cold instead of warm water, using no yeast at all or only
poor yeast (leavened dough from previous baking), sometimes no salt
is added, and the dough is not sufficiently kneaded. Often not enough
time is allowed for leavening or no leavening is sought, and the baking
itself is often incomplete. When poor baking is added to poor flour and
poor preparation of dough, the resulting product can only be poor.

Inferior quality of Yugoslav peasant bread was also discussed in
literature outside of Yugoslavia. Adam Maurizio analyzed samples of
bread of pre-1914 years from Dalmatia and from southwestern Croatia
(area of the Velebit mountain range), made out of mixed corn and
barley flour, mixed rye and barley flour, Russian millet, Italian millet,
rye, corn, spelt, barley, and wheat, and found them all of poor quality.[27]
On the basis of this information Naum Jasny said in 1950 that these
"breads certainly were uneatable according to our most unpretentious
habits" and that the "daily bread and other cereal food eaten by most
of the population in classical antiquity has to be visualized much like
that described by Maurizio for Yugoslavian peasants."[28]

Data by Maurizio and the inferences by Jasny have to be qualified,
however, lest they be taken as representative of bread generally consumed by the peasants of Yugoslavia. First, barley, rye, and especially
millet and spelt are used very little as bread cereals in Yugoslavia.
After all, the production of millet during the period 1934–38 averaged

[27] A. Maurizio, *Die Geschichte unserer Pflanzennahrung von den Urzeiten bis zur Gegenwart*, pp. 386–89, especially the table on p. 386.

[28] Naum Jasny, "The Daily Bread of the Ancient Greeks and Romans," *Osiris*, IX, 227–53, esp. 229–30. The only figure that Jasny adduces from Maurizio's figures, the average percentage of sand in bread, amounting to 1.75 percent on a dry basis (p. 230), is wrong. On the basis of figures supplied by Maurizio, the amount of sand in bread is 1.33 percent. But if his explanation with regard to bread made from millet is taken into account, the average amount of sand in bread, resulting from outside impurities, amounted to only 0.98 percent.

only 26,000 metric tons and that of spelt only 12,000 metric tons. Second, the poor quality of peasant bread does not obtain in the whole country. The breads analyzed by Maurizio and referred to by Jasny come from some of the poorest and culturally and economically most backward areas of Yugoslavia. In Vojvodina, Slavonia, parts of Slovenia, and along parts of the Adriatic coast, where exclusively or predominantly wheat bread is eaten, it is most often prepared quite satisfactorily. Third, it was generally agreed that the technique of breadmaking in rural areas had somewhat improved during the interwar period although no systematic educational effort was undertaken in that direction. The meager data used by Maurizio were collected 40 years ago. Fourth, breads investigated by Maurizio were made of flour milled in querns and baked under a "pot." Neither of these procedures was representative of the country as a whole. Besides, baking of bread under a pot (in most Yugoslav areas this pot is not like the earthen pot used in Rumania and described by Maurizio, but rather, it is a utensil of about 18 to 24 inches in diameter and about 6 to 8 inches high, made of sheet steel or wrought iron) is not necessarily responsible for its bad quality. Such bread can be excellent. In addition to the type and quality of flour used and the technique of preparing the dough, the most important factor in regard to bread so made is whether the base on which the bread is baked is of brick, stone, or earth. Bread baked on stone or earth is much poorer because it retains much water.

There are many factors which influenced the manner of breadmaking in different areas and among various families. This writer's mother occasionally baked bread under the pot, but since such bread was fresh, of excellent quality, and different from the bread normally consumed, it disappeared as if it were cake. The rule in the family was, therefore, to make bread in the bread oven only once every week. (In that part of Yugoslavia, but definitely not in all parts, there was a bread oven in the kitchen of almost every family, and as a rule it was large enough to bake enough bread for an average family for the whole week.) The decision whether to bake bread in the oven or under the pot often depended on the availability of woman labor in the family, the number of people in the family, whether any hired hands were employed, and finally on the sense of thriftiness of the housewife.

It is also necessary to point out that poor quality bread was often made purposely. Thus grain was often not properly cleaned nor flour sifted in order to have "more" bread. Bread was often insufficiently baked because people thought that such bread was more filling. Bread was often made only once a week because stale bread lasted longer. And the basic, although not the only, reason behind all this was poverty.

It might be mentioned that there is no set seasonal pattern in the consumption of various types of bread in rural areas where several kinds are eaten. That was repeatedly established by the physicians of the Public Health Service who, by inspecting bread brought for lunch by school children, found all possible types of bread at the same time. This suggests that peasants alternate bread of various grains within a very short time, perhaps in order to have some variety and possibly to relieve the strain on their digestive organs caused by poorer quality breads. Some of the "vignettes of village life" showed that wheat bread in areas in which relatively little wheat bread is consumed was saved for holidays, for fasting days, for pregnant women, and for the sick.

In conclusion it should be repeated that bread was and remains the staff of life for the Yugoslav peasantry, and that having sufficient bread remains the central problem in their food economy.

CHAPTER 25

HEALTH IN RURAL AREAS

EARLIER DISCUSSIONS of the estimated average life expectancy in Yugoslavia (p. 296) and of the rates of infant mortality (p. 293) indicated
generally bad health conditions in the country as a whole. In this chapter we propose to take a closer look at the state of health in the rural
areas, at the factors determining health conditions, and at policies and
facilities developed during the interwar period to improve health conditions of the rural population.

The state of health of a population is an economic factor of basic
importance, to say nothing of the purely psychological satisfaction
and fullness of life that is incident to satisfactory health, or of the
mental anguish and bodily suffering that goes with disease. As an economic factor, the state of health influences the potential labor force
at the disposal of a population. Sick people are incapable of work, or
at best have only a reduced work capacity, and, moreover, they require
the time and labor of others who could be otherwise employed. Furthermore, sick persons are usually preferential food consumers in their
respective households. Illness in a household leads to reduced production and income and to greater but less uniform consumption among
its members, and thus causes unfavorable effects from two directions.

Considering the specific Yugoslav rural conditions of agricultural
overpopulation, one might say that the high disease incidence did not
affect too unfavorably the amount of work performed: agricultural
overpopulation was such that in spite of sickness in rural areas there
was plenty of labor power for the available jobs. A part of the preventable loss of labor due to disease should perhaps not be considered
a loss since the labor would not have been used anyway. While there
is some validity in that point of view, the fact is that the peak in the
incidence of some diseases, e.g., malaria, coincides with the peak of
farm work, thus causing a greater strain on the remaining population.
Moreover, owing to the seasonality of farm work and primitive techniques, the relative supply of labor in times of peak labor requirements
is insufficient, in spite of the absolute overabundance of labor, and
farm work is often done late, reflecting unfavorably on the level of
yields. It is also well known that labor power is very unevenly divided

570

among rural households and that disease affects households with both surplus and insufficient labor. Be that as it may, the fact remains that the high incidence of illness imposed a large, though largely preventable, burden on the working rural population, since they had to provide the necessary means of living and care not only for those who were unemployable, such as children and the old, but also for the sick. High mortality, which removed a large number of people before they could start producing and a large number of those who were in the best productive age, resulted obviously in the loss of a large amount of potential labor power, which incurred costs of raising and maintaining but failed to repay them in full or in part. Good health is an asset to the individual and to his family; high productive capacity, which is obtainable only from healthy people, is an asset to both the individual and his family and to the nation.

FURTHER CONSIDERATION OF NUTRITION

The character and amount of nutrition are perhaps the most important single factor influencing the level of health in a population. Deficient nutrition is not only responsible for the greater incidence of typical nutritional deficiency diseases, but by weakening the bodily strength it makes people less resistant to practically all diseases, especially such diseases as tuberculosis and malaria.

In the preceding chapter we have discussed the availability of food and various nutrients in Yugoslavia during the period 1934–38. The general conclusion was that the average level of nutrition which was allowed by domestic food production plus imports minus exports was qualitatively unsatisfactory, although it supplied an ample amount of energy food. In addition, there were such aggravating factors as seasonal maldistribution, wasteful holiday consumption, and improper cooking techniques, all of which bear directly upon the dietary patterns. These problems will be our principal concern in this section.

A general characteristic of the dietary pattern of the rural population in Yugoslavia is that its adequacy and variety are basically influenced by the seasonal factors in the local production of food. As a rule, nutrition is at its best in the fall and early winter months. Cereals, potatoes, onions, and in some areas turnips, from the current harvest, last into these months in most families; some types of cabbage are available in fresh form, as are some types of fruit. Legumes and some fruits are available in dried form, and some vegetables are pickled. Among the preserved vegetables, by far the most important is sauerkraut. The supply of fresh and dried meat, animal fats and oils, and cheese is most plentiful at that time. These foods of vegetable and animal origin are the "winter reserves" (*zimnica*) that every family tries to secure for the months when there is little or nothing in the fields.

On the other hand, the nature and amount of work to be performed in the months when food is best and most plentiful are limited, the days are short, and the length of time available for sleeping and leisure is much longer. That is also the period of most frequent feasting because of many holidays, while the number of fasting days is limited.

But in the spring, in some households beginning in January or February, nutrition in the villages suffers. A large portion of rural families have by that time used up their home-produced cereals and practically all other winter reserves of food, and have to start buying much of what they need for subsistence. Of course, the medium and wealthier peasants have sufficient cereals to last them the whole crop year, and their winter reserves of other foods last usually well into the spring. The very fact that many peasants have to start buying food contributes to quantitative and qualitative worsening of the diet. Generally speaking, the peasant diet during the spring months is limited to cereals, home-produced or bought, dried beans, some potatoes, and what the family is able to afford of such products as rice and pastes (both cereal foods), and such vegetables as onions. The intake of meats, dairy products, and fats and oils is reduced much below that of the previous months, and so is the intake of wine in areas in which wine is produced. Until the late spring there are no vegetables and fruits in the fields and gardens. The supply of milk and eggs begins at this time to be larger, but practically all of such products have to be sold in order to buy the high-calory foods.

On the other hand, field work becomes progressively heavier with the advance of spring and summer, the days become longer, and the time available for sleeping and leisure is drastically cut. It is in these months that, owing to poorer nutrition and greatly intensified physical exertion, a great portion of the peasants become dangerously less resistant to the ravages of disease. It is during these months that most of them lose weight, their faces become drawn, their skin acquires a parchment-like color, their eyes become dull. In these months the appearance of most of the rural people is in profound contrast to the budding spring around them. Only when the summer finally arrives is there bread from the fields and a more plentiful and more varied supply of vegetables and fruits. Moreover, as the autumn approaches, the rhythm of farm work becomes slower. During the fall months the body actually has to spend a considerable amount of time and nutrients to replace the loss of weight and recoup the strength lost in the previous months.[1] Now, while this rhythm in nutrition in rural areas could be called a natural one because it reminds us of a similar pattern (though at other seasons) in the case of wild animals and also of most of the livestock herds in Yugoslavia, it is certainly nothing in which one could find any comfort when it applies either to people or to domestic animals. Was not one of the foremost objectives of mankind from the dawn of civilization to secure life against the vagaries of nature, including the rhythm in nature's production? Abundance and variety of production of food, high income, well-organized trade, development of storage facilities and food-preservation technology have almost completely eliminated the influence of seasonality of food production on the pattern of nutrition in advanced countries. Underdeveloped areas, on the contrary, are very far indeed from this goal.

Needless to say, the diet of the urban population was also basically affected by seasonality in food production. Medium- and higher-income groups were able, however, to afford a relatively varied diet throughout the year, although, in their case too, the consumption of vegetables and fruits off season was very limited. Their consumption of animal foodstuffs and fats and oils throughout the year tended to be adequate. Moreover, their requirements in energy were considerably smaller than those of industrial workers and peasants. Low-income urban groups, as already stated, subsisted on a qualitatively unsatisfactory diet with little variation.

In addition to the seasonality in food production, there were some other factors which aggravated the discrepancies in food consumption over time. In most areas the peasants consumed an altogether disproportionate amount of the available high-quality food on a few festive occasions, such as Christmas, Slava (family saint's day of the people belonging to the Serbian Orthodox Church), weddings, baptisms, and the like, by indulging unreasonably in food and drink themselves and by treating all their neighbors, relatives, and friends. Since, according to the popular conception of this mistaken form of hospitality, the honor and pride of the family would be irreparably impaired if it would not go to great lengths in treating friends and neighbors, the families not only exhausted a large part of their best food on these occasions,

---

[1] Aleksandar Giaja, *Ishrana seoske porodice—selo Rajković* (The Nutrition of the Inhabitants of the Village Rajković), pp. 70–80. This study of the "vignette type" of a small village in Serbia investigated among other problems of nutrition also the issue of changes in weight. It would be wrong, however, to take the results of this survey as representative of all rural areas of Yugoslavia.

but often went into debt in order to comply with this social usage. Psychologically, this behavior is easily understandable. Such rare festive occasions gave people license to indulge (at their own homes and at the homes of their friends, who are under the same social obligation) in good food and drink and to forget that most of the year they actually subsisted on a simple and poor fare and that many of them suffered not only from malnourishment but often also from undernourishment. Although such customs have been ridiculed and fought to a certain extent by many popular educators, they persisted throughout the entire interwar period and probably still exist. It might be interesting to note that such customs do not disappear even when Yugoslav families move out of the country, as can be seen from the following example. A Serbian family from Herzegovina that has been living in a rural community in California for over 40 years had on its table on the day of its Slava in the winter of 1945, according to a letter of the daughter of the hostess, the following foods and drinks:

Roast of beef, roast stuffed turkey, roast pork, roast lamb, spiced ham, meat balls in sauerkraut leaves (*sarma*), sauerkraut and frankfurters, macaroni with meat sauce, salami, several types of cheese, potato salad, green salad, all kinds of pickles and relishes, olives, cranberry sauce, anchovies, several kinds of bread, fruits, cakes, puddings, wine, beer, whisky, tea, and coffee—all of this in heaping platters.

Certain religious observances, especially the prolonged fasting of the population of the Serbian Orthodox denomination during the spring months (other denominations fasted less), put a great strain on the physical endurance of the peasant people at a time when they were least able to stand it.

Besides being deficient in nutritive content and very unevenly distributed over the seasons, food of the rural population of Yugoslavia was often poorly and/or uneconomically prepared. As already explained, this was especially true of bread in some areas, which is the more important since it is the foremost component of the Yugoslav diet in both rural and urban areas. Vegetables are in some areas prepared by boiling excessively, with a resultant loss of a portion of nutrients. Because of the poverty and crude simplicity of the diet, scarcity of fuel for cooking in some parts of the country, lack of time in seasons of heavy field work, and lack of health education, peasant families in some areas go without hot meals for many days. In other areas, as a rule, three hot meals are prepared in winter and two in summer. Poor quality, lack of variety, and poor preparation of food are especially detrimental to small children after they are weaned, so that enteric diseases account for a large percentage of deaths among infants and children.

In many cold meals, bread not only forms the basis of the meal but is practically identical with the meal itself. People use small amounts of cheese, jerked meat, bacon, occasionally an egg, or salted fish (e.g., along the Adriatic coast), fresh vegetables, oil, dried fruits and nuts, as "companion" food (*smok*) in order to make bread more palatable or even literally more "swallowable." But in peasant families with dwarf and small farms, to say nothing of the landless families, the supply of such foods of animal origin is very limited indeed. Among vegetables used as companion foods are onions, popular in all parts of Yugoslavia, and in season bell peppers and tomatoes. Depending on the companion used and its quantity, this practice is advantageous from a nutritional point of view. A considerable amount of nutrients is found in whey and in the saltish juice which forms in vats of pickled sauerkraut, both of which are generally used for bread dipping or with cornmeal mush. But little nutritional besides seasoning is found in crushed dried pepper, black pepper mixed with salt, or in vinegar mixed with water, which are used for bread dipping in some parts of the country, especially Macedonia. While some of these companion foods are highly nutritive (animal foodstuffs and oil), their portion in the meal in comparison with bread is exceedingly small, so that an element of deception is common to most such meals. When crushed dried red pepper or vinegar with water is used for bread dipping, companion foods furnish nothing but pure illusion.

In areas in which the production of milk is large and when it cannot be sold because of the distance to the market, most of it is used for the production of cheese, but a portion is used in fresh form. It is mostly consumed with bread or cornmeal mush. Where animal husbandry is based primarily on sheep raising, the supply of milk is concentrated in the late spring and summer months.

The consumption of alcoholic beverages, particularly wine, in certain rural areas of Dalmatia, Slovenia, Croatia-Slavonia, Serbia, and Vojvodina, and prune brandy (Slivowitz) in parts of Bosnia and Serbia, was relatively high. The consumption of prune brandy was occasionally criticized as injurious to the health of the people. Considering the dietary patterns and also the fact that in some areas drinking water was of poor quality, the drinking of alcoholic beverages was understandable. In many areas wine is diluted with water to make it go further. Wine and prune brandy were consumed by peasant households, as a rule, only if produced at home, and in many areas only the poorer qualities, while the good-quality product was sold in order to buy other food. If not produced at home, alcoholic beverages were bought by peasant families only for festive days. Male members of the family would occasionally go into the local tavern and drink there. In some areas women drank no alcoholic beverages. Proposals to utilize more of the grapes and prunes in fresh and preserved form rather than for the production of fermented or distilled beverages were not successful. In fact, the types of grapes and most of the prunes produced were adjusted for the latter utilization because demand for other products was very limited. The point to remember is that in areas in which considerable amounts of wine and brandy are consumed they are important sources of energy and make the otherwise poor diet more palatable.

But while the peasantry did not spend much money on alcoholic beverages, there was one item in their consumption which took money that could have been used for the buying of food. That item was tobacco. As will be shown in Chapter 28, the price of tobacco included an exceedingly high tax. Thus, by consuming tobacco the peasants not only did not obtain anything useful for their money (although smoking is pleasurable), but opened themselves to the tax arm of the government, which they could have avoided. This problem can be somewhat better visualized only by comparison of some figures. Thus, the cost to the rural population for tobacco, cigarette paper, and matches amounted, according to our estimates, to about 950 million dinars in the fiscal year 1931/32, of which about 670 million dinars was tax. On the other hand, the total wheat crop in 1931 was worth about 5,000 million dinars at the average annual wholesale price of 186 dinars per 100 kilograms, and the total corn crop in that year was worth about 2,820 million dinars at the average annual wholesale price of 88 dinars per 100 kilograms. Needless to say, the prices for these products paid on the farm were considerably lower, and only a portion of these crops was sold.

HOUSING

The types of rural settlements and rural houses in the South Slav lands have been one of the favored themes of Jovan Cvijić[2] and his school of human geographers. But other geographers also have paid considerable attention to this problem.[3] With regard to location, Cvijić

[2] Jovan Cvijić, *La Péninsule Balkanique*, pp. 207–51. On the problem of rural housing in Serbia and Macedonia, see Olive Lodge, *Peasant Life in Jugoslavia*, pp. 51–91.

[3] Anton Melik, *Slovenija* (Slovenia), I, Pt. 2, 530–98; Zvonimir Dugački and Milan

divided the villages into (*a*) those in higher altitudes (up to 1,600 meters elevation), where houses are built on the edges of the valleys, on hillsides, and on plateaus, (*b*) villages situated at the bottom of valleys, and (*c*) villages in the plains. According to their pattern he divided all villages in the Balkans into (*a*) the dispersed village, of which several separate types exist, depending on the topography, the density of population, and the chief foundation of the village economy (pastoral as against crop raising), and (*b*) the compact village, of which there are also several types, depending on various factors. While the location of villages can by itself be of great importance from the point of view of health—e.g., proximity of marshes as a factor in malaria, greater abundance of agricultural resources in the plains, nearness to urban areas and lines of communication—we need not go into any details in discussing these factors. Nor could we do justice to the variety of village types in Yugoslavia by describing more fully one or several villages. Thus we have to be satisfied with merely mentioning the above classification of rural settlements.

Peasant houses in Yugoslavia range from the most primitive, dry stone-wall lean-tos to rather spacious, relatively comfortable and well-built units. The overwhelming majority are between these extremes. Certain well-developed styles of rural houses are characteristic of certain regions, depending on the climatic conditions prevailing there, on the type of the readily available building material, and on cultural influences affecting these areas. Individual houses within these styles depend, naturally, on the economic and cultural level of the population, the climate, and occasionally on the size of the family. Needless to say, there are also many rural houses of a nondescript type, as well as those which are copies of houses in other areas without much regard to how well they fit the conditions in areas in which they are located. Very often houses in rural areas have artistic embellishments. And also very often they look better from the outside than they actually are on the inside.[4]

One could say as a rule that housing conditions in the rural areas of Yugoslavia are as bad and as primitive as is nutrition. In some areas, especially in areas south of the Sava-Danube rivers, many people

---

Šenoa, "The Settlements," Zvonimir Dugački (ed.), *Zemljopis Hrvatske* (Geography of Croatia), Pt. 2, pp. 592–608.

[4] A good pictorial presentation of the Croatian village and peasants, including their houses, peasant costumes, and agricultural implements and tools, is found in Josip Predavec, *Selo i seljaci* (The Village and the Peasants), pictorial appendix. See also Olive Lodge, *op. cit.*, pp. 51–91, 267–92.

live in primitive huts and sleep under the same roof with cattle and sheep, either separated only by a wooden or stone partition, or with livestock taking the first floor and people the second floor in the structure. When peasant houses are of the one-story type—and a large percentage of all peasant houses in the country are so built—the floors are often of packed earth. Generally, such dwellings are damp and drafty. In such areas as Vojvodina the high water table and poor insulation make almost all houses damp. Even when houses are built of strong material such as stone, brick, unburned brick, or timber and are of the two-story type, proper lighting, airing, and heating are often impossible. There are areas in which only a small percentage of peasant homes have latrines of any kind.

Assuring a supply of water for drinking and other household uses is a very difficult problem in some parts of the country. In the karstic areas the chief source of water for household use is rain water, which is caught and stored in cisterns. In summer months, especially in years of more than common droughts, this source of water is exhausted by a large portion of households. Thereupon, fetching of water becomes a difficult and time-consuming household task, which often requires traveling for hours to the infrequent wells or to people who can spare some water from their cisterns. In other parts of the country water is commonly supplied by wells, but since wells are seldom built in a contamination-proof fashion, pollution from the surface finds its way into the water. According to the opinion of Yugoslav public health engineers during the interwar period, provision of healthful drinking water in amounts sufficient to cover the needs at all times and to supply other household needs, including those of the livestock, was one of the primary tasks of sanitary improvement in all rural areas of Yugoslavia.

Housing conditions in rural areas of Yugoslavia have never been systematically investigated for their adequacy from the point of view of healthful living. But some data pertaining to housing conditions, contained in certain surveys of special areas obtained with other general information, can serve as indicators of the situation prevailing in much of the country. According to the already quoted survey made by the Chamber of Agriculture of *banovina* Drina in 1939, the rural population of 1,256,717 people lived in 219,279 separate households. Of the recorded 192,811 separate houses, 31,039 were built of brick, 60,249 of unburned brick, and 101,523 of other building material, including many of mud and reed. Out of 219,279 households only 106,-085, or 48.4 percent, had rooms with wood or other hard flooring, and only 100,381 households, or 45.7 percent, had a latrine of some sort.

Of all households, 101,776, or 46.4 percent, had no beds to sleep in. All these rural households had only 605 manure pits built of concrete and only 25,085 stables which met sanitary requirements. This survey showed that rural housing conditions were relatively much better in the Serbian than in the Bosnian counties and that the mountainous villages were generally worse off than those situated in the plains.[5] People lacking beds slept on the floor on straw, mats of some sort, or wooden planks, and a certain number slept in stables, or those parts of houses serving as stables, in hay. In winter many people slept around an open fire which was kept going most of the time. While this survey pertains exclusively to the territory of *banovina* Drina, its data on housing might well be taken as representative for most of the territory south of the Sava-Danube rivers.

Another example refers to ten representative villages from ten counties in *banovina* Sava which were closely surveyed for tuberculosis incidence during the 1930's by the School of Public Health in Zagreb. Here it was found in 1938 that 73.2 percent of all peasant houses had only one room for living and sleeping, that in 63.4 percent of all households there were five or more persons living and sleeping in one room, and, finally, that 48.7 percent of all houses lacked latrines of any kind.[6]

A considerable amount of haphazard information and good insight into the problems of rural housing, including such things as the type of house construction, house furnishings, provision of water, and supply of beds in the "passive areas" south of the Sava river inhabited by Croats, has been collected by Rudolf Bićanić and his co-workers in their field trips through these parts in 1935. According to Bićanić, the absence of beds in an overwhelming portion of homes in these areas is not only a matter of lack of purchasing power, but is also connected with the lack of room for beds in these small houses, and above all with the fact that people had not yet learned to appreciate the comforts of sleeping in a bed since most of them never had done it.[7] A discussion of the problem of sanitation in the Slovene village, beginning with the provision of drinking water, construction and interior arrangement of rural houses, construction of stables, manure pits, and latrines, has been presented in a special study by the Public Health Service. Here,

[5] Milan M. Obradović, *Selo Drinske banovine u brojevima* (The Village of *Banovina* Drina in Figures), pp. 4–9, 23.

[6] Dr. Miron Malojčić, "The Results of the Survey of the Prevalence of Tuberculosis in the Village," *Socijalno-medicinski pregled* (1940), No. 4, p. 437.

[7] Rudolf Bićanić, *Kako živi narod* (How the People Live), I, 12–16, 89–98.

rural housing conditions are generally better than in most other areas of Yugoslavia.[8]

A word might be said also about housing in urban areas. Housing conditions in cities and towns were relatively satisfactory from a sanitary point of view for the higher- and medium-income groups, but for the low-income groups they were as poor or even poorer than the housing conditions in rural areas, or at least more dangerous to health. Often families numbering four to six members lived in one basement room, which was used for living, cooking, and sleeping. The great majority of workers' dwellings in cities and towns were damp, without proper heating, without proper ventilation and water, and with crudely made toilets serving many families. One of the most appalling facts established by a survey in 1934 was that 86 percent of all people suffering from tuberculosis in Belgrade were sleeping in the same rooms with noninfected people and that 42.6 percent of them slept in the same bed with noninfected people.[9]

An additional factor worth mentioning with regard to urban housing, affecting especially the laboring class, is that the rent took a disproportionately high share of their income, leaving less for food, clothing and footwear, and other essential expenditures, to say nothing of making it impossible for them to save part of their income for emergencies or for old age. According to a survey made by the Chamber of Labor in Belgrade, workers in Belgrade spent 30 to 50 percent of their earnings for rent, while white-collar workers, e.g., lower government and business employees, spent 40 to 60 percent of their income for rent during the early 1930's.[10]

Three further points should be made. First, large growth of rural households during the interwar period made it imperative for about 400,000 to 450,000 new households to provide some kind of housing facilities for their people and livestock, and to appoint their living quarters with a certain amount of furnishings, kitchen and eating utensils, and other necessities. Owing especially to the fact that during the 1930's the prices of products bought were relatively high in terms

[8] Dr. Ivo Pirc, "The Improvement of Sanitation in the Village," Dr. Ivo Pirc and Franjo Baš, *Socialni problemi slovenske vasi* (Social Problems of the Slovene Village), I, 7–69.

[9] S. Vidakovitch, "Influence des conditions économiques et sociales sur la natalité, la morbidité et la mortalité des enfants dans les villes de Yougoslavie," *Bulletin Mensuel de l'Office International d'Hygiène Publique*, XXX, 350.

[10] Quoted in Ahmed Kemura, "Ownership by Floors in Urban Housing," *Spomenica I. Kongresa ekonomista Kraljevine Jugoslavije* (Proceedings of the First Convention of the Economists of the Kingdom of Yugoslavia), p. 269.

of those sold, the provision of housing imposed a tremendous financial burden on the rural population. Even the upkeep of the existing housing involved high cost. What this meant was simply that the provision of housing absorbed a large share of the savings that the peasant population had or was forced to make and that it forced many of them into debt, thus leaving less capital for investment in production processes on the farm. Second, the house, or rather, the outside shell of the house, was considered in some rural areas a matter of conspicuous display. Because of that, many people who never left home, as well as thousands of returning émigrés, sank a large portion of their savings into building their houses. But very often these savings were exhausted before the houses were finished inside. And there remained nothing for improving production on the farm. Third, in other areas people with savings were interested primarily and almost exclusively in buying more land, keeping at a minimum all other expenditures including those connected with the provision of fairly acceptable housing.

CLOTHING AND FOOTWEAR

The bulk of rural population in all areas of Yugoslavia during the interwar period wore clothing and footwear made according to special regional or local customs, thus showing a tremendous variety in forms, patterns, and color combinations. The styles of peasant clothing have been handed down from one generation to the other since the time of the closed household economy when all clothing and footwear that the peasant family needed were made at home from home-produced raw materials. In some rural areas, simplified rural clothing styles and sometimes old but adapted and frozen styles of urban clothing have taken the place of pure peasant types. This process of change is continuing.

As long as the peasants lived under conditions of a closed household economy, especially in large families (zadrugas), producing at home all the raw materials and observing an appropriate family division of labor, production of clothing and footwear at home was the general rule. But with the penetration of market and money economy, with partial production for the market, the dissolution of large families, and much smaller per capita production of textile raw materials and hides, the peasants have lost the technical and economic ability to produce all their clothing at home. In fact, factory-made textiles and footwear made by cobblers were among the first important consumers' goods that the market economy brought into the village.

During the interwar period a large portion, perhaps 60 to 70 percent, of the clothing and footwear consumed by the rural population was made at home either from home-produced wool, flax, and untanned hides and skins, or from cotton and wool yarn and cotton and wool yard goods and leather bought in the market. Only the remainder was bought ready-made. Thus spinning, weaving, and clothmaking and mending are very important household chores of the women in all South Slav rural areas.

Whether clothing and footwear were made out of bought yarn, yard goods, and leather, or were ready-made, the expenditures for clothing and footwear became in most rural families the single most important cash outlay. There are no data on the average per capita amount of clothing and footwear that was consumed annually during the interwar period in Yugoslavia. But even if we had such figures, it would be always necessary to distinguish between the urban areas, which consumed much more than the national average, and the rural areas, which consumed less than that average.[11] One of the extremely expensive customs in some rural areas, e.g., Slavonia and Vojvodina, was excessive spending on clothing, footwear, and jewelry for young girls, which began in their twelfth or thirteenth year and lasted until their marriage. Such expenditures were by far the highest cash item in peasant families with young girls and were several times as high as the expenditures for clothing for all other members of the family.[12]

In many areas, such as Macedonia, Slavonia, Slovenia, Montenegro, and parts of Dalmatia, peasant costumes are often elaborate and artistic.[13] But their suitability from the point of view of comfort, health, and cost is altogether another matter. Often of very heavy homespun wool or other coarse material (linen), occasionally with rich and elab-

---

[11] Some notion about the total consumption of clothing can be obtained from data on the use of textile raw materials and semifinished textile products. But the great variety of clothing from the point of view of quality and weight precludes any possibility of expressing these figures in terms of yardage or poundage of cotton fabrics and woolens. During the period 1936–39 the peoples of Yugoslavia consumed annually, on the average, about 300 metric tons of raw cotton of domestic origin, 19,025 metric tons of imported raw cotton, 14,113 tons of imported cotton yarn, and 2,920 tons of imported cotton fabrics; about 15,000 tons of raw wool of domestic production (greasy basis), 4,000 tons of imported wool (greasy basis), 1,630 tons of imported woolen yarn, and 1,315 tons of imported woolen fabrics; 2,720 metric tons of imported rayon yarn, 33 tons of imported rayon fabrics; and, finally, about 20 tons of domestic raw silk.

[12] Nada Sremec, "Extravagance in the Village," Rudolf Bićanić and Željko Macan (eds.), *Kako živi narod* (How the People Live), II, 168–72.

[13] An impression of the variety of folk costumes in various areas of Yugoslavia can be obtained from a number of articles in the *National Geographic Magazine*. Compare the following issues: January 1928, pp. 47–90; September 1930, pp. 257–310; June 1939, pp. 691–730.

orate embroidery, they are difficult to keep clean, and often are un-
comfortable while working. Moreover, because of their high cost in
terms of working hours or in terms of products which the peasants sell,
many peasants, especially those with large families and small farms can
afford little more than one set of clothing and footwear. Under such
conditions it is impossible to keep clothing and footwear clean and in
good repair.

The typical footwear of a large segment of the Yugoslav peasants
during the interwar period was the various types of moccasin-like *opanci*
with soling of untanned leather and uppers of woven rolled strips of
sheep or goat skins. This footwear is unsuitable in wet weather. In
other areas, again, both men and women like to wear high boots. As
boots cost dearly, a great many people went barefoot whenever weather
conditions allowed, saving footwear for bad weather or festive occas-
sions. A veritable revolution in the footwear habits of the Yugoslav
peasants was created during the 1930's when the Yugoslav factory of
the Czechoslovak shoe concern Bata began to produce on a mass basis
and at low price a simple rubber-soled shoe for the peasants.

As a rule, it could be said that during the interwar period the bulk
of the Yugoslav peasants were poorly clad and shod. Needless to say,
in such relatively rich areas as Slavonia and Vojvodina, wealthier peasant families were well provided with clothing and footwear, but, as
pointed out above, clothing for young girls claimed an unduly high
share of the family's expenditures for clothing. But generally poor
clothing conditions, which, among other things, prevented proper cleaning of clothing, were an important contributing factor to the unsatisfactory conditions in regard to personal and home cleanliness. Poor
clothing and footwear had therefore an unfavorable influence on
people's health.

The Great Depression contributed greatly to the worsening of the
clothing and footwear conditions in rural areas because it impaired
the terms of exchange between agricultural and industrial products.
There was some propaganda on the part of the Croatian Peasant party
to induce the peasants to grow more flax and to install more weaving
facilities in their homes in order to reduce their cash expenditures for
clothing. The results of these propaganda efforts were apparently very
limited. Needless to say, the supply of clothing and footwear of the
rural population was and remains a matter closely connected with their
real income. Spreading of education and bringing of the village into
closer touch with the urban areas will gradually result in reducing the
number of people who wear folk costumes, which from the point of

view of health and comfort would in most cases be a salutary development.

Home and personal cleanliness leave much to be desired in both rural and urban areas. This is understandable if one has in mind various factors with regard to housing conditions and the supplying of people with clothing and footwear, which were just discussed, as well as the low educational level of large segments of the rural population. But there were several other factors which have to be mentioned. Most important were perhaps the lack of water and the lack of wood for heating of water—or both, in many places—and the inability of many people to buy sufficient quantities of soap. During the interwar period the average per capita consumption of soap of all kinds in Yugoslavia, both factory-made and homemade, was about five pounds per year. As in the case of protective foods, sugar, coffee, clothing, and footwear, the average per capita consumption of soap in the towns, especially among the medium- and high-income groups, was much above the national average and in the village much below it.

Surveys in some villages in eastern Bosnia showed that in most cases no soap at all was used in the washing of clothes and little if any in body washing. Clothing was mostly washed with the help of a detergent derived from wood ashes when warm water was passed through them, which is a poor substitute for soap. After letting clothing soak in this water for several hours—the length of soaking depending primarily on whether the members of the family had another change of clothing—they were rinsed and beaten in creeks or rivers. When peasants in this area said that they changed their underclothing "often," that meant actually every two weeks. Considering the fact that the same clothing was used for work and for sleep and that neither work nor sleeping accommodations were clean, clothing was dirty most of the time. There was no definite pattern to the bathing practices of rural population in these areas. Younger people, especially men who were in the armed services, bathed more often, while many other people "only from Christmas to Christmas."[14]

Lack of personal and home cleanliness invites and makes possible the existence of pests such as lice, bedbugs, and flies. Some of these, such as lice, are carriers of important infectious diseases (typhus). And the spread of most other diseases, but especially of tuberculosis,

---

[14] Dr. Aleksandar Petrović, "Typhus in the Village Sjeversko," *Socijalno-medicinski pregled* (1937), No. 1, pp. 27–39.

is greatly facilitated by filth. While uncleanliness and pests which thrive upon it contribute to the spread of diseases under regular conditions, they make the suppression of epidemics much more difficult when they break out.

Of course, these rather drastic conditions were not characteristic of the whole rural population, but there is little doubt that a considerable portion of the rural people in Yugoslavia during the interwar period lived under such or similar conditions. There are rural areas in Yugoslavia in which people pay much attention to personal and home cleanliness and where even poverty cannot prevent people from being clean. Thorough body washing, if not bathing, is regular, clothing is kept clean even if it has many patches, underclothing is regularly changed every Sunday. Houses are regularly whitewashed, outside and inside, with lime.

Dirtiness is not only injurious to health, but is also a sign of ignorance, and detracts greatly from human dignity. But it should not be forgotten that poverty is its most important cause. Among all aspects of living already discussed, education is perhaps as important for the improvement of personal and home cleanliness as an increase in real income. But without the latter there is no possibility of improving the supply of clothing and footwear of rural population, improving housing conditions, or supplying sufficient water, wood, and soap.

PREVALENCE OF DISEASES IN YUGOSLAVIA

Bad nutrition, poor housing, unsatisfactory clothing and footwear, lack of home and personal cleanliness, limited preventive medical services, scarcity and high cost of curative medical services, adverse climatic and geographic conditions in some areas (e.g., marshy land in connection with malaria), long hours and difficult conditions of work, many health-impairing popular customs, and great ignorance and widespread superstition, all contributed to the high disease incidence and to a generally low resistance against disease on the part of the broad masses of the peoples of Yugoslavia during the interwar period. Nevertheless this did not imply the diverting of an unduly high proportion of money income for medical expenses. Because of the inadequacy of income such expenses were kept at a minimum. Lack of education and lack of medical services within reach of the great majority of rural peoples reduced still further the propensity to seek medical aid. Economically, the main result of this situation was the impairment of the working and producing capacity of a large segment of people and their living exclusively or largely as consumers, often priority consumers within the household, thus affecting unfavorably both the total real income of the family and its distribution to various uses. Furthermore, the great disease incidence meant physical suffering of hundreds of thousands of people and their protracted or permanent living under a cloud of despair.

Not only was the prevalence of disease extremely great, but also the chances of survival or recovery from illness requiring intensive medical attention, prolonged treatment, and wholesome food were extremely poor. It cost too much to get well and few people could afford it. Moreover, under the housing and living conditions prevailing in Yugoslav rural and urban areas where proper segregation of the sick was impossible, a sick person was always a direct and immediate danger to his family and his neighbors, especially in the case of tuberculosis, venereal diseases, and the acute contagious diseases. Also since the family tried to save its sick member he became a priority consumer in regard to protective foods, and that meant that such food had usually to be taken away from the mouths of other family members, thus making them more ready victims of disease.

In both rural and urban areas, pulmonary tuberculosis was the greatest menace to the health of the peoples of Yugoslavia. The exact number of people suffering from tuberculosis in any year during the interwar period was not known, but it was generally agreed that it caused considerably more deaths than any other single ailment. In 1924, out of a total number of deaths of 254,527, the reported deaths from pulmonary tuberculosis, according to official statistics, amounted to 38,082, or 15.0 percent. In the following years the relative number of tuberculosis deaths was lower. In 1937 it amounted to 12.5 percent of the total.[15] The falling trend of tuberculosis mortality was revealed also by intensive area studies of some mixed urban-rural and of some purely urban areas.[16] Some experts thought, however, that tuberculosis incidence and mortality did not diminish materially during the interwar period.

Judging from statistics of reported tuberculosis deaths, its incidence was quite unevenly distributed in the country, although a part of the difference was probably caused by differing accuracy in reporting. The rates of tuberculosis deaths during the period 1934–37 averaged by

[15] Yugoslavia, *Annuaire statistique 1938–1939*, p. 124.

[16] Dr. Stjepan Mecger, "The Movement of Tuberculosis Incidence in the City and County of Vinkovci," *Socijalno-medicinski pregled* (1940), No. 4, pp. 422–32; Dr. Sergije Ramzin, "Deaths from Tuberculosis in Belgrade," *ibid.* (1936), No. 3, pp. 158–70.

banovine as follows: Drava 9.5, Vardar 9.7, Primorje 11.1, Zeta 11.3, Dunav 12.4, Drina 13.1, Sava 13.2, Morava 13.9, Vrbas 17.1, and the Prefecture of Belgrade (a purely urban district) 17.5 percent of all deaths.[17] It was generally agreed, however, that the mortality from tuberculosis was higher. The basic reason for this contention was that the statistics on the causes of death were poor. Thus, for example, in ten counties in *banovina* Sava (economically and culturally a relatively advanced area of Yugoslavia) which were closely surveyed for tuberculosis in 1935, causes of death were attested by a physician in only 15.3 percent of the cases, and only in 40 percent was sufficient information on the cause of death supplied.[18] The cause of death in the great majority of cases, especially in rural areas, was recorded in the way indicated by the relatives of the deceased to the keepers of records of deaths and births, namely, to the parish priests or commune scribes.

The 1937 death rate from pulmonary tuberculosis, when related to 10,000 people, was higher in Yugoslavia than in any other European country. In Yugoslavia it amounted to 19.9 persons per 10,000, followed by Rumania with 17.8, Hungary with 15.2 (for 1936), etc.[19] It is important to point out that the relatively highest percentage of deaths from tuberculosis occurs among people between the ages of 15 and 25, which makes the loss greater from an economic point of view. It was thought for quite some time that mortality from tuberculosis, and thus most probably its incidence, was higher in urban than in rural areas, as is the case in most other countries. Apparently this was the case until and including 1932. From 1933 onward mortality from pulmonary tuberculosis, related to 10,000 people, was apparently slightly higher in rural than in urban areas. The Great Depression and growing agricultural overpopulation come readily to mind as factors which might have contributed to that change.

Being the number one problem of public health in the country, tuberculosis was studied relatively intensively, and several small areas have been closely surveyed. The most ambitious of these surveys was made in 1935 in *banovina* Sava. Intensive surveys for tuberculosis were carried on in ten villages in ten widely separated representative counties of the *banovina*, while extensive surveys in the same program—that is, the study of social and economic conditions affecting the health of the

---

[17] Yugoslavia, *Annuaire statistique 1938–1939*, pp. 412–19.

[18] Dr. Miron Malojčić, *op. cit.*, p. 436.

[19] Dr. Eduard Mosbacher, "The Problem of Social Medicine in an Agricultural Country in the Balkans," *Socijalno-medicinski pregled* (1940), No. 2, p. 101.

population—covered the whole population of the ten counties. The survey was carried out under the auspices of the School of Public Health in Zagreb. Dr. M. Malojčić, who conducted the survey, expressed the opinion that the results of the survey could be taken as representative of the whole *banovina*. On the basis of this survey it was found that for every 100 rural people 3.84 suffered from tuberculosis of various types, with somewhat higher morbidity in the case of women (4.11 as against 3.54 percent in the case of men surveyed). Second, it was found that for every death from tuberculosis there were about 15 sick.[20] If we assume that tuberculosis incidence and deaths in *banovina* Sava represented approximately the average for the country as a whole—and that is not an unreasonable assumption—then the total number of those suffering from tuberculosis in Yugoslavia in the mid-1930's was somewhere between 400,000 and 500,000 people. This figure was divided between the rural and urban population in approximately direct relation to their share in the total population of the country.

Tuberculosis is primarily a disease of the poor and the uneducated, who, if left to themselves, have little chance against it. It is also a disease against which neither preventive measures in the narrower sense nor curative measures can be fully effective if certain other basic preconditions are not fulfilled. The basic precondition is the raising of the plane of living and of the educational level of the population as a whole. The raising of the plane of living was the chief reason that the incidence of and mortality from tuberculosis have been so much reduced in the countries of Western Europe and in the United States during the past 100 years. Since economic conditions of large segments of the Yugoslav population, especially in rural areas, actually worsened during the 1930's, it is not surprising that the struggle against tuberculosis showed relatively little success. Data on mortality from tuberculosis by *banovine* suggest strongly that it is not only the average general level of consumption which controls tuberculosis incidence, because mortality from tuberculosis was considerably higher in relatively rich *banovina* Dunav than in poor *banovina* Zeta. This simply indicates that other factors, such as climate, nature and conditions of work, and nature and frequency of gatherings of people which facilitate transmission of infection, have also to be taken into account in the study of tuberculosis.

Malaria was during the interwar period the second greatest menace

[20] Dr. Miron Malojčić, *op. cit.*, pp. 440–45.

to health in Yugoslavia. It was spread practically all over the country, although the northern Dalmatian mainland, the Neretva River Delta, Macedonia, and the plains along the Danube, Sava, and Drava rivers were the most severely affected. According to the estimates of the malaria investigating commissions which reported in 1921, the number of people suffering from malaria immediately after World War I was 1.2 to 1.5 million, or 10 to 12 percent of the total population of the country.

Following various antimalaria measures, its incidence was reduced. In 1938 it was estimated that during the 1930's there were between 500,000 and 600,000 malaria cases in the country, or that between 4 and 5 percent of the total population was infected, of which the largest number was in *banovina* Vardar.[21] From microscopic tests in the anti-malaria work of the public health organizations, which showed, between 1929 and 1938, an annual average of 76,750 positive reactions (annual examinations during the same period averaged 253,560 persons), there were found 66.9 percent of benign tertian type, 26.8 percent tropical malignant tertian, 5.3 percent quartan, and 1 percent mixed-type malaria.[22]

The prevelence of malaria in Yugoslavia was due to several factors, of which the most important were the existence of large stretches of marshy and swampy land serving as breeding grounds of the malaria-carrying mosquitoes, and the poverty of the people, which resulted in bad nutrition, bad housing, and inability to take advantage of medical services. Some land reclamation work has been undertaken which has reduced the extent of mosquito breeding grounds and, together with other preventive and curative measures carried on primarily by the special organizations of the public health service, has resulted in reducing considerably the malaria incidence. But as in many other diseases, the basic cure consists of improvement of the economic and educational status of the people, which then would make the various specific preventive and curative measures fully effective.

Third in importance as a disease in rural areas of Yugoslavia during the interwar period was endemic syphilis. It was limited to a few counties in northeastern Serbia where it was brought by the Russian soldiers in the 1870's and to a score of counties in Bosnia and Herzegovina where it was imported from Asia Minor by the Turkish troops around 1780. The Bosnian variety has been studied for decades, partly

[21] Dr. Stevan Z. Ivanić, "Malaria in Yugoslavia and Its Suppression," *Socijalno-medicinski pregled* (1938), No. 4, pp. 350–59.

[22] Yugoslavia, *Annuaire statistique 1938–1939*, p. 409.

because of its specific, rather benign, characteristics, partly in order to ascertain the scope of infection and to devise means and ways of fighting it. The Asia Minor origin of syphilis in Bosnia bears on its age, namely, makes it more recent than it would be had it been imported from Western Europe, and this in turn, according to most investigators, seems to be one of the reasons making the Bosnian variety rather benign.[23]

Systematic surveys of syphilis infection in Bosnia during the 1930's have shown great differences in its incidence among various communes and counties affected. The study which was based on obligatory examinations in 44 communes belonging to 14 different counties of *banovina* Drina between 1936 and the end of 1939, and which included 136,116 serological examinations out of a total population of these communes of 257,267, discovered 19,611 cases of syphilis, or 14.4 percent of the total number of people examined. But the rate of incidence ranged in various communes from a low of 0.9 to a high of 37.2 percent of the number of people examined.[24] While the exact number of people suffering from endemic syphilis in Bosnia was not known, and it was especially impossible on the basis of the existing data to say whether the disease had been reduced or further spread in comparison with pre-1914 years, experts estimated that the number of people affected by that disease in Bosnia in 1939 was about 100,000.[25]

Most affected was the Moslem population, followed by Roman Catholics, and then members of the Serbian Orthodox Church. The spreading of the disease does not regularly take place by sexual contact, but primarily by living together, by use of the same eating and drinking utensils by all members of the family, and by other bodily contact. The largest number of cases is outwardly identified by infection of the lips and mouth. Because of this process of spreading infection, a large percentage of the infected are children. An improvement in housing conditions and the raising of the economic and educational status of the population, which would improve the living patterns from a hygienic point of view, would be the most important means of reducing the incidence of this disease and eradicating it.

To further the eradication of endemic syphilis a special law was passed in 1931 which, among other things, provided also for free

[23] Dr. Sima Ilić, "Endemic Syphilis in Yugoslavia and Its Suppression," *Socijalno-medicinski pregled* (1940), No. 2, pp. 128–32.

[24] Dr. Ernest I. Grin, "Study and Incidence of Endemic Syphilis in *Banovina* Drina," *Socijalno-medicinski pregled* (1940), No. 1, pp. 48–54.

[25] *Ibid.* (1939), No. 3, pp. 298–300.

treatment of the people affected by that disease. A more ambitious program for combating venereal diseases in general was contemplated by the Law on the Suppression of Venereal Diseases of 1934. Among its regulations this law provided also for obligatory examination of all males planning to marry and prohibited the marriage of those who were unable to show a medical affidavit that they are free from venereal ailment (syphilis, gonorrhea, soft chancre). This particular provision of the law was on the statute books only from the end of July 1934 to the end of April 1935, when it was repealed under the pressure of conservative forces. Furthermore, organized prostitution was prohibited by law. And the government maintained a considerable number of stationary and mobile units for the combat of all venereal diseases.

Trachoma is endemic in certain counties of Slovenia, Croatia-Slavonia, and Vojvodina (*banovine* Drava, Sava, and Dunav), but its prevalence has been greatly reduced through control measures during the past 70 years. During the 1930's about 15,000 cases of trachoma were reported and treated in the government trachoma-control stations. These cases were fairly evenly divided among the above three regions.[26] The actual number of cases was probably higher. From published data no tendency during the 1930's can be found for the lowering of trachoma incidence.

Among the acute infectious diseases, the louse-borne typhus was perhaps the most dreaded. Considering the ravages of the typhus epidemic in Serbia in 1915 (pp. 222–23), this fear was quite natural. In some sections of eastern Bosnia and parts of Serbia typhus is endemic. Through preventive measures, reported typhus cases were reduced to less than 200 by 1932, but they rose to 825 in 1933 and 2,210 in 1934, to fall again to about 700 cases in 1938. The fatality rate also declined. But the disease remained a potential threat because in some areas louse infestation, lack of personal and home cleanliness, impossibility of segregation of the sick, and lack of medical aid continued. During World War II typhus epidemics reached large proportions in both Bosnia and Serbia.

In terms of reported cases and fatalities, typhus was much less costly during the interwar period than typhoid fever. Between 1931 and 1938 the number of officially reported cases of typhoid fever averaged 5,770 annually with a fatality rate of about 10 percent. This had become primarily a disease of rural areas and was apparently closely related to contaminated water.

[26] Yugoslavia, *Annuaire statistique 1938–1939*, p. 408.

Many other acute infectious diseases such as bacillary dysentery, scarlet fever, diphtheria, epidemic meningitis, chickenpox, and whooping cough were common during the interwar period. No cases of relapsing fever or smallpox had been reported since 1929 and 1930, respectively.

The number of cases of acute infectious diseases, and deaths from them, as reported in special statistics on infectious diseases, however, was much smaller than the number of deaths ascribed to them in the statistics on the causes of death. To give only one example: the number of cases of typhoid fever in 1936 and deaths from it, according to the special statistics on infectious diseases, was 7,017 and 667, respectively, while the statistics on the causes of death for the same year ascribe 4,168 deaths to the same ailment.[27]

There is no doubt that poor nutrition was one of the important reasons for the generally poor health conditions in rural areas and among the low-income urban groups in Yugoslavia, for their low resistence to disease, and for high morbidity and mortality among children. As nutritional research of somewhat more systematic nature was only beginning in Yugoslavia during the late 1930's, the prevalence and nature of nutritional deficiency diseases in the country were not known.

PUBLIC HEALTH POLICIES AND FACILITIES

The Yugoslav public health organization and programs for rural areas during the interwar period were much more advanced than in most other countries of a similar socioeconomic structure, in terms of the thinking of the leaders of the public health service, in terms of the number, variety, and scope of health organizations and programs, and in terms of the thinking of a very large part of the medical profession. The progressive philosophy of public health, especially regarding the improvement of health and sanitary conditions, spread of health education, and practice of preventive medicine in rural areas, has a relatively long tradition in the South Slav lands. The great man in social medicine in Serbia between about 1885 and 1914 was Dr. Milan Jovanović-Batut. (Between 1918 and 1940, when he died at the age of 93, he had the position of an elder statesman in public health.) As a medical scientist, university professor, writer, popular educator, government adviser, and promoter of progressive ideas of health policy and organizations interested in that field, he was a man of vision, determination, and international renown. The most important and interna-

[27] *Ibid.*, pp. 404–5; 124.

tionally best-known promoter and organizer of public health services in Yugoslavia during the interwar period was Dr. Andrija Štampar, who headed the public health service of the country from the early 1920's to 1930, and who is still active.

The philosophy of the public health service as formulated by Dr. Štampar can be roughly summarized as follows: educating the people and creating among them a correct attitude toward matters of public health is of basic importance; promotion of public health is not a monopoly of the physicians, it is a task of the whole population; social therapy is essential because a physician cannot go far with individual therapy; the physicians should not be economically dependent on their patients; in matters of public health no distinction should be made between the rich and the poor; a health organization should be created in which the physician seeks the patients and not the patients the physician; the problem of public health is primarily an economic issue; the place of the physician is not in the laboratory or consulting room but in the dwellings and working places of the people; the physician must be the teacher of the people.[28] These ideas were developed on the basis of conditions existing in Yugoslavia, primarily in its rural areas, and designed primarily to serve the people in rural areas. Here the position was taken that it is fundamentally the business of the state to care for the health of the nation. This function was considered to be essentially in the same category as the maintenance of law and order or the provision of free basic education. In a country in which 76 percent of the total population is engaged in agriculture, where poverty, lack of education, superstition, and sparse communications were the rule rather than the exception, rural people if left to themselves in matters of health would have had little chance of improvement.

The epidemics of typhus and smallpox after World War I were the first urgent health problems of the newly created state. They were brought under control and new epidemics were prevented. A systematic campaign against malaria, and campaigns on a smaller scale against tuberculosis, venereal diseases, and trachoma were undertaken. A number of state institutions were established to combat various diseases through preventive and curative medical work and through education. A whole system of public health service has been developed and staffed. Three medical schools have been established where there was none before. Numerous surveys of the "vignette type" were made of

[28] Dr. A. Štampar, *Public Health in Jugoslavia*, p. 9. For a general discussion of the health issues in the Yugoslav village, see also Dr. Božidar Milosavljević-Čampar, *Život i zdravstveno stanje sela* (Life and Health Conditions in the Village).

general health conditions, of special diseases or special health problems in various parts of the country. The public health service also made some contribution toward improving the water supply in rural areas and in spreading health education, including information and advice on nutritional practices, to the rural population. All that the public health authorities achieved was done despite severe handicaps, of which the most important were the magnitude of the tasks, the lack of funds, technical facilities, and trained personnel, and the political conditions in which the work in and for rural areas had an exceedingly low priority.

As in many other countries, medical services in Yugoslavia during the interwar period were provided by three separate types of organizations. First, some medical service was provided by private physicians on a fee basis. Second, workers, miners, and many white-collar workers were members of various social insurance organizations which had their own medical and hospital services. Third, there was the state medical organization, which on the basis of special laws provided for free treatment of patients suffering from quite a number of diseases. Since practically all hospitals were in the hands of the state, regional, or local governments, their services, if not free, were provided on the basis of fees which were related to the property and tax capacity of the patient. The chief functions of the public health service were administration of public health and sanitary laws, study and combat of mass diseases through special organizations, practice of preventive medicine, and spreading of health education.

A system of special health co-operatives was in operation in Yugoslavia during the interwar period.[29] In 1938 there were 93 (134 officially registered) active rural health co-operatives with 65,436 members.[30] While these co-operatives first began to be established in the early 1920's in Serbia, they became most successful later among the German minority in Vojvodina. They also engaged in general public health work and in educational activities, and they were subsidized by the state.

The supreme organ dealing with the problems of social welfare and public health in Yugoslavia during the interwar period was the Ministry of Social Policy and Public Health (up to 1929 these were two separate ministries). Its Division of Public Health administered public health and sanitation organizations and activities, including the operation of

[29] M. Colombain, "Rural Hygiene and Health Co-operative Societies in Yugoslavia," *International Labour Review*, XXXII, 19–38.

[30] Yugoslavia, *Annuaire statistique 1938–1939*, p. 420.

government hospitals and supervision of the few private hospitals. It worked through the banovinal and county administrations and special public health organizations. The Central Institute of Hygiene in Belgrade and the School of Public Health in Zagreb were under the control of the Ministry and operated as technical bureaus in the fields of applied hygiene, sociomedical research, and health education. Each of the nine *banovine* had an Institute of Hygiene, responsible to the Central Institute. Under the direction of the banovinal institutes of hygiene in 1938 there were 50 health centers engaged in field activities in larger communities and the surrounding areas. The health centers supervised 149 health stations operating in rural areas which were not served by the centers. Furthermore, over one hundred special stationary and/or mobile units for public health work were in operation.

According to a special law of 1930, rural communes with more than 6,000 inhabitants had to constitute themselves as autonomous health districts, and communes with smaller populations had to be consolidated for that particular purpose, but their combined population could not exceed 15,000.

Hospital facilities in Yugoslavia were scant. In 1938 there were only 201 hospitals, including 7 mental hospitals and 22 university clinics. Of these 140 were owned by *banovine* and municipalities, and the remainder by the central government, social insurance organizations, and religious orders. Only 4 hospitals were owned by private interests.

Table 42 shows the distribution of physicians, public health institutions, and hospital beds in Yugoslavia in 1938, by *banovine*. These data show great differences in the supply of health personnel and health facilities per 10,000 persons in various areas. For the country as a whole, there was one physician (counting also those engaged in administration and research) for every 3,240 persons and one hospital bed for every 530 persons. Small as was the number of physicians in relation to the whole population, the geographical maldistribution of physicians made the conditions very much worse. It was estimated that in 1938 only slightly more than 800 physicians were working in rural areas, serving roughly 11.5 million people, while the remaining 4,000 physicians were in the cities, serving the urban population of roughly 3.5 million. Of course, the physicians from urban areas served also some rural people, and hospital facilities, located almost exclusively in urban areas, were at the disposal of both urban and rural population, but were not easily accessible to the latter. Nevertheless, it is interesting to note that the Prefecture of Belgrade with slightly

TABLE 42.—MEDICAL PERSONNEL, PUBLIC HEALTH INSTITUTIONS, AND HOSPITAL
FACILITIES IN 1938, BY BANOVINE*

Banovina	Population in 1938	Number of physicians[a]	Public health institutions[b] Health centers	Health stations	Hospital beds[c]	Per 10,000 people Physicians	Hospital beds
Drava	1,195,000	556	2	21	4,293	4.6	35.9
Drina	1,801,000	396	5	7	2,723	2.2	15.1
Dunav	2,522,000	990	6	19	3,730	3.9	14.8
Morava	1,617,000	238	5	6	2,217	1.5	13.7
Primorje	969,000	229	3	19	1,433	2.4	14.8
Sava	2,897,000	939	7	22	7,498	5.2	25.9
Vardar	1,766,000	275	11	30	1,242	1.6	7.0
Vrbas	1,187,000	91	4	7	520	0.8	4.4
Zeta	1,032,000	206	7	16	967	2.0	9.4
Prefecture of Belgrade	401,000	827	—	2	4,390	20.7	109.5
Total	15,387,000	4,747	50	149	29,013	3.1	18.9

* Source: Yugoslavia, *Annuaire statistique 1938–1939* (Belgrade, 1939), pp. 402–3.

[a] In 1938 there were in Yugoslavia 353 dentists and 373 dental technicians. Practically none of them were in rural areas. In the same year there were in that country 2,846 trained nurses and 1,425 male trained nurses. Almost all of them were employed in hospitals and sanatoriums. In addition, there were 2,199 trained midwives.

[b] Not including the Central Institute of Hygiene in Belgrade, the School of Public Health in Zagreb, the nine banovinal institutes of hygiene, and about 100 other public health organizations of which the most important were 32 school polyclinics, 7 tuberculosis dispensaries, 22 auxiliary antimalaria stations, and 26 sanatoriums and convalescent homes.

[c] Of the 201 hospitals of all kinds, 12 belonged to the central government, 140 to *banovine* and municipalities, 16 to social insurance organizations, 4 to private interests, 22 were university clinics, and 7 were hospitals for mental diseases, all of which belonged to the state except one.

over 400,000 people in 1938 had more physicians than the entire peasant population of the country. It should be mentioned, however, that this maldistribution of physicians was characteristic of all countries in the world. It is a natural consequence of the system of commercial medicine under which medical services for sale are concentrated in areas of effective demand, namely, in cities and towns.

The great differences among various *banovine* in regard to available medical personnel and facilities were essentially an indication of their relative economic and educational development as well as of their relative urbanization. Poorest both in terms of available physicians and available hospital beds was *banovina* Vrbas, where there was only one physician for every 13,000 people and only 4.4 hospital beds were available for every 10,000 people. Somewhat better off were *banovine*

Morava, Vardar, and Zeta. Disregarding the completely urban area of the Prefecture of Belgrade, *banovina* Sava was best off in regard to physicians, as there were 5.2 physicians per 10,000 people. *Banovina* Drava was best supplied with hospital beds, as it had 35.9 hospital beds per 10,000 people. These favorable relationships were obviously related to the fact that these two *banovine* included the cities of Zagreb and Ljubljana, respectively, and that these two areas were among the most industrialized and urbanized parts of the country.

Not only were almost all hospitals in the country owned by the public authorities, but also an overwhelming number of physicians were employed by public agencies, although a large portion among them had also private practices. Of a total of 4,747 physicians in Yugoslavia in 1938, 1,918 were on the payroll of the state and the *banovine*, 530 on the payroll of the communes, 667 were working for social insurance organizations, and 381 for other institutions dispensing medical services. Of the remaining 1,251 physicians only about 900 were exclusively in private practice. This dependence of physicians on public service shows that in spite of great need for medical services and the absolutely small number of physicians in the country, the effective demand for their services was able to maintain only a relatively small number of physicians. To make sure of a minimum income and of a pension in old age, a great number of physicians sought and received government employment. Others did this in order better to fulfill their professional task. At the end of 1938, public health service in Yugoslavia had 485 physicians (of whom 118 were part time), 372 graduate nurses, and 1,483 other technical and auxiliary personnel.

The maldistribution of physicians between urban and rural areas was keenly felt throughout the interwar period, and the government attempted to remedy the situation. According to a Decree of August 25, 1939, every physician who wanted to enter government service, social insurance service, or licensed private hospitals was required to have two years of practical work in villages or in townships of a rural character with less than 4,000 people. This time was to be credited to them in regard to retirement. The provincial government of *Banovina* Croatia, controlled by the Croatian Peasant party, intended in 1940 to go even further and to be guided in all promotions and appointments of physicians in public service by their respective contribution to the promotion of health in rural areas.

The Public Health Service was active during the interwar period also in the field of sanitary engineering. Its specialists considered two problems as most important: improvement in rural housing and the provision in rural areas of sufficient pure water for drinking and other domestic uses, including the needs of livestock. The provision of drinking water was especially difficult to solve in karstic areas because of the nature of the soil, while in most other areas the chief problem was to ensure water against contamination. Up to 1938 the School of Public Health in Zagreb built for the rural population 78 kilometers of water pipes, 60 cisterns, 320 wells, and improved another 310 existing wells.[31] But a much larger effort in this regard was made by the Ministry of Public Works, which during the interwar period had built 980 wells, 610 cisterns, installed considerable water piping, and assisted in the improvement of the existing facilities for the provision of drinking water, in both rural and urban areas.[32]

HEALTH EDUCATION AND PROPAGANDA

The raising of the health level in rural areas through health education and propaganda has been a matter of public interest in the South Slav lands since about 1880. But during the interwar period the efforts in this direction were greatly enlarged and improved. The task was neither a simple nor an easy one. The level of health in a country, as is obvious from the preceding pages, is determined by many factors, and improvement can result only through modification of these underlying factors. Without improvement in the economic bases, better health education is a barren proposition.

The chief organization that worked during the interwar period on health education in both rural and urban areas was the Public Health Service. A special Decree on Popular Health Education was issued in March 1928. Active in the field of health education in some rural areas were also the health co-operatives, and to a lesser extent regular schools, organizations for adult education, and to a small extent some of the general co-operative organizations.

Health education and propaganda had to deal with many aspects of rural health. These weapons were used, first of all, to combat ailments of mass character such as tuberculosis, malaria, venereal diseases, and to combat diseases which were endemic in various parts of Yugoslavia, such as typhus and typhoid fever, and required constant vigilance to prevent potential outbreaks of epidemics. One of the important fields of health education and propaganda in rural areas re-

[31] Dr. Josip Rasuhin, "On Proper Nutrition of Our People," *Socijalno-medicinski pregled* (1939), No. 1, p. 21.

[32] League of Nations, *European Conference on Rural Life—Yugoslavia*, p. 76.

ferred to the building of sanitary facilities for the provision of drinking water, construction of more sanitary dwellings, stables, latrines, and manure pits. In regard to personal and home cleanliness, health education and propaganda tried to impress upon the people the need for regular washing of hands and body, for washing and changing of clothing, and for fighting lice. Some effort in health education was directed also against popular ways of treating various ailments and popular medicines, which, in a country where human urine and cattle excretions were apparently often used as popular medicines, was sorely needed.[33] Throughout the interwar period some attention in health education was paid to the care and nutrition of infants and small children in order to reduce the high infant and child mortality rates.

As stated earlier, there are rural areas in Yugoslavia where birth control is practiced by repeated abortions. Nothing was done during the interwar period to instruct people in practicing birth control by means which are not harmful to the health. It must be kept in mind, though, that with the low educational level of the peasantry, their low income, the scarcity and high cost of medical services and supplies, and most difficult housing conditions, it was hardly possible to follow birth control practices which were satisfactory from a hygienic point of view.

Need for mass education was felt also with regard to feasting and use of excessive food on a few festive occasions. But the eradication of such deep-rooted, though harmful, customs is a long-range proposition and progress up to World War II was not encouraging.

If a marked improvement in nutrition in rural areas of Yugoslavia is to take place in the future, it would be necessary not only to increase greatly the domestic agricultural production and to change considerably its structure, but people will have to learn much more about the preservation, utilization, and preparation of food. A certain amount of work of the public health education organs during the interwar period was directed toward teaching the peasants better food preparation techniques. This effort was carried on by special stationary and mobile schools and through courses on home economics in rural areas, by issuing and spreading of booklets on preparation of healthy meals, and by lectures.

The agencies and organizations engaged in health education and propaganda used, in addition to special schools and short lecture courses in home economics, other methods suited for reaching large

[33] Dr. Aleksandar Petrović, "A Contribution to the Study of Our Popular Medicines," *Socijalno-medicinski pregled* (1939), No. 3, pp. 263–74.

masses of population, such as books, pamphlets, posters, and films.[34] But in a country with high illiteracy and semiliteracy, education and propaganda with the help of the printed word had narrow limitations. From its establishment in 1926 to 1938 the School of Public Health in Zagreb organized 308 courses on home economics in various villages of its area of activity, which were attended by 4,869 women.[35] These four-week courses were intended not only to teach the direct participants, but to reach a much wider number of people through the participants—either as teachers or simply as examples worth following. For the training of leaders in the village in practically all socioeconomic and educational matters and on the principle of serving as spearheads of progress in the village, the same school organized in Zagreb the Peasant University (Seljačko sveučilište), to which young peasants from its area came. From 1926 to 1938 several hundred young men attended that educational program.

As stated above, health education is a barren proposition if the economic bases of health are not improved. Its success in rural areas as elsewhere is therefore conditioned by a general improvement in the plane of living of the population. On the other hand, satisfactory health conditions of the rural population would tend to increase its economic welfare. Needless to say, the proverbial peasant conservatism is a mighty barrier with which health education is confronted, and it might take several generations to fully overcome this problem.

[34] Dr. Bojan Pirc, "Hygienic Education and Propaganda in Yugoslavia," *ibid.* (1936), No. 3, pp. 179–87.

[35] Dr. Josip Rasuhin, *op. cit.*, pp. 19–21.

CHAPTER 26

AGRICULTURE AND THE MARKET

IN THIS chapter we discuss the relationship between agriculture and the market (including the foreign markets), i.e., the conditions under which Yugoslav agriculture sold its products and bought its necessities during the interwar period. In other words, we are here interested in the forces and institutional arrangements that determined the degree of marketability for agricultural products in Yugoslavia and in the terms of exchange between agriculture and other branches of national economy.

MARKETING OF AGRICULTURAL PRODUCTS

Owing to the predominantly subsistence character of the overwhelming portion of Yugoslav farm units, the portion of the agricultural production that was marketed was much smaller than in the Western European countries. In the latter, it varied between 70 and 80 percent during the 1930's, while in Yugoslavia and most of the other countries of Southeastern and Eastern Europe it was estimated for the late 1930's to be below 50 percent.[1]

The Avramović Survey, conducted in Serbia between 1910 and 1912, showed great variations in the rate of marketability of agricultural production depending on the size of peasant farms. This survey, however, referred exclusively to the marketing of cereals, while such products as fruits, livestock, and animal foodstuffs were not taken into account.[2] In Serbia, fruits (prunes and prune products) and livestock were important products of agriculture, and a considerable part of the production was marketed. The estimates of the Avramović Survey in this respect, therefore, cannot be accepted, although they have entered into general literature as if they were referring to the total agricultural production. In its statement accompanying the proposed budget for 1937/38 the Yugoslav Ministry of Finance estimated that the monetary portion of the total income of agriculture, including income from cottage industries—that is, the rate of marketability in agriculture—was about 55 percent. Maksim Goranović, who has written a series of good

[1] Royal Institute of International Affairs, *Agrarian Problems from the Baltic to the Aegean*, p. 46.

[2] Mihailo Avramović, *Naše seljačko gazdinstvo* (Our Peasant Farming), pp. 21–23.

602   *Peasants, Politics, and Economic Change in Yugoslavia*

articles on Yugoslav agriculture of the interwar period and who quotes
the above figures of the Ministry of Finance, considers that these estimates are too high, although he does not venture an estimate of his
own.[3] In 1939 Djordje Puljo estimated that approximately one-third
of the production of wheat and corn was marketed in the period
1928–37.[4] Puljo took into account only that portion of the corn crop
which was marketed as grain and disregarded the large portion of the
crop that was used for feed and marketed in the form of livestock and
livestock products, especially in the form of fat pigs. In 1944 Rudolf
Bićanić repeated on the basis of estimates of the Ministry of Finance
that in 1938, 55 percent of the income of agriculture, including that
part resulting from cottage industries, was derived from products sold
in the market, while the remainder represented the value of products
utilized by households of the producers themselves.[5]

The estimates of Avramović and Puljo are unacceptable because
they obviously cover only a portion of agricultural production—the
cereals. We consider also that the estimates of the Ministry of Finance
and thus also those of Bićanić are too high. In our opinion the rate of
marketability in Yugoslav agriculture, including the cottage industries,
during the depression years of the early 1930's was somewhere between
35 and 45 percent and during the later 1930's perhaps somewhere between 40 and 50 percent of the total. It is interesting to note that in
neighboring Bulgaria, a country that had much better organized statistical services than any other country of Southeastern Europe during the
interwar period, the rate of marketability in agriculture was estimated
at only 30 to 40 percent for the first half of the 1930's.[6]

As we have said in Chapter 24, a considerable part of the marketed
food products of both vegetable and animal origin would never have
seen the market place if the capacity of the masses of the Yugoslav
rural population to consume had been greater. The portion of agricultural production, except in the case of industrial crops, that was
actually marketed did not therefore represent genuine surplus over a
satisfactory consumption level, but a relative surplus over the actually
possible low level of food consumption due to the low level of income.

[3] Maksim Goranović, "Poljoprivredni dohodak Jugoslavije" (Agricultural Income
of Yugoslavia), reprint from Yugoslavia, Ministry of Agriculture, *Arhiv*, IV, 10–11.
[4] Djordje Puljo, "The Trade in Grains and Grain Elevators," *Pravna misao*, May-
June, 1939, pp. 234–51.
[5] Rudolf Bićanić, "The Effects of War on Rural Yugoslavia," *Geographical Journal*, CIII, Nos. 1 and 2, 30–49.
[6] Oskar N. Anderson, "Some Theoretical Aspects of the Business Cycle Movements in the Southeast European Agricultural Countries," *Publications of the Statistical Institute for Economic Research, State University of Sofia*, No. 1, 1936, p. 15.

A basic factor which influenced the part of production that the peasants had to sell was the degree of need of the rural population for a certain amount of cash to pay direct taxes, interest and debts, doctors' and lawyers' bills, and to buy small amounts of such essential items as textiles and footwear, salt, kerosene, matches, roofing tiles, agricultural implements, pesticides, a little sugar and coffee, and in some areas timber. In cereal-deficit areas, the buying of cereals has, naturally, the first priority. Needless to say, the part of agricultural production which was marketed varied very much from region to region, from the outcome of the harvest, from the nature of production on the farm and its volume in relation to the needs of the producers' households, from the size of farms, from the distance of the farm to the market, and from the relative purchasing power of the products that the peasants sell in terms of products that they buy.

There were some purely technical factors that exercised a great influence on the rate of marketability of agricultural production. First of all, there was the paramount problem of internal communications, which influenced the ability of the peasants to avail themselves of the market. The availability of communications also determined the costs in time and waste connected with marketing, and thus influenced the returns of agriculture. The effect of bad communications was well expressed in great differences in prices of agricultural commodities among various regions or even localities of the same region, and in the impossibility of speedy price adjustment through adjustment of supply and demand on an interregional or even intraregional basis. One of the basic characteristics of the organization of the market for agricultural and livestock products was its subdivision into a great number of local markets without a unifying regional or national market. These local markets were usually larger localities which were both marketing and administrative centers of their respective areas.[7] Lack of communica-

---

[7] The survey conducted by Gospodarska Sloga in *Banovina* Croatia in 1939 showed that the active area of these local trading centers depended greatly on topographic conditions and on the available communications and transportation facilities. As a rule, the diameter of these local trading areas extended from 20 to a maximum of 50 kilometers. In other words, the peasants wanted to be able to go to the market, do their marketing, and return home in one day, though the day might begin much before dawn and end late in the evening. Significantly enough, it was also found that the peasants in selling their products depended almost completely on their respective local markets, while in buying their necessities they often went farther afield, namely, to the larger regional marketing centers. The development of the motor road transport during the 1930's was beginning to change the established patterns of the trading organization in rural areas. Gospodarska Sloga, *Anketa Gospodarske Sloge: Najnužnije narodne potrebe* (Survey by Gospodarska Sloga: The Most Pressing Needs of the People), pp. 40–45.

tions made it virtually impossible for many peasants to attend to the marketing of their products, so that a considerable portion of production of perishable goods was utilized less effectively than it would have been if it could have been marketed. In other cases production was so managed that the same basic product was sold in the form in which it could stand the long storage and the long trip to market. Thus, hard cheese or cheese in large primitive containers such as barrels or sheepskins was sold instead of milk and butter, dried fruits or brandy instead of fresh fruit, wine instead of fresh grapes, and the like.

Closely connected with the lack of communications, causing great losses and inconveniences to agriculture, was the lack of proper storage facilities even in areas where large marketable surpluses of various commodities, such as grains, fruits, vegetables, milk, and eggs, existed. Lack of proper storage facilities on the individual farm was, of course, a result of the small size of the overwhelming portion of all farms which made it impossible and unnecessary for the individual peasant to invest in such facilities. Agricultural co-operatives which could have contributed to the development of a system of storage facilities on a co-operative basis never considered this problem seriously. And lack of storage facilities in principal markets was a result of the crude organization of such markets. Discussion about a program of grain warehouse-building by the government began in the early 1930's but it was only in 1938 that a government-financed corporation was organized for this purpose. In early 1939 plans were made to build a net of 45 grain elevators with a total capacity of 150,000 metric tons or about 8 percent of the estimated marketed amount of wheat and corn in an average crop year.[8] It was also planned to build a series of small grain elevators in cereal-deficit areas so that unfavorable weather conditions in winter months would not, as often happened, endanger the supply of cereals to these areas. Only a small part of this construction program was completed when World War II broke out. The lack of proper storage facilities also resulted in a failure to develop agricultural credit forms which use stored commodities as collateral.

Another factor which influenced the marketing of agricultural and animal products in an unfavorable way was the low quality, unevenness, and poor consumer appeal of most products. Of course, one could argue that such appearance of agricultural and livestock products on the market corresponded to the lack of discrimination on the part of the consumers. Actually, the consumer in the country itself was not a great problem even though he often was the victim of such conditions. As

[8] Djordje Puljo, *op. cit.*, p. 245.

an illustration, one could take the example of milk supply in the capital city of Belgrade. In the early 1930's only about 20 percent of the milk consumed in Belgrade was bought from milk stores while the remainder was purchased from peasants and traders who brought milk to Belgrade directly from the villages in small quantities and more often than not in improper and unclean containers. Laboratory tests discovered that a large percentage of samples of milk thus peddled was unfit for consumption.[9] But when it came to exports, poor and uneven quality and inferior preparation and packaging of products was a distinct drawback because Yugoslav products were compared with similar products from competing countries. In most countries of advanced agriculture the quality and preparation of products for the market improved greatly during the interwar period, but not in Yugoslavia. One example of the lack of standardization in agricultural production in Yugoslavia may illustrate the difficulties of the exporters. It was reported in 1929 that Yugoslavia, which in the period 1927–29 exported on the average 20,500 metric tons of dried beans annually, raised not less than 186 different varieties of beans.[10] It is interesting to note, therefore, that during the interwar period in Yugoslavia the chief pressure for improvement in the quality of agricultural production, for standardization of agricultural products, and generally for a shift toward more labor- and capital-intensive crops which had better prospects for exports did not come from "the federations of agricultural co-operatives, from representatives of peasant political parties, or from the representatives of agricultural sciences, but rather from the exporters, that is, from the representatives of the trading capital."[11] Lack of standardization of agricultural products was a natural result of the multitude of producing units of small and medium size, of the primitive character of agricultural production in general, and of the low level of education among the peasant population.

The institutional structure of the markets in which the peasants sold their products and bought their necessities was not such as to favor the interests of the peasants. Between the peasants as producers and as consumers and other people who consumed agricultural products or produced commodities for the peasants, there existed a whole series of middlemen. The biggest among them were specialized as buyers of

[9] Sima Miljuš, "Lard or Milk?" *Narodno blagostanje*, January 1, 1934, pp. 5–6.
[10] Mijo Mirković, *Ekonomska struktura Jugoslavije, 1918–1941* (Economic Structure of Yugoslavia, 1918–1941), p. 87.
[11] *Ibid.*, p. 88. See also in this regard Velimir Bajkić, "The Conflict Between Agriculture and Trade at the Seventh Convention of Businessmen," *Narodno blagostanje*, September 28, 1929, pp. 549–51.

grains, wine, livestock, fruits, poultry, eggs, and the like, or as sellers to agricultural areas of textiles, footwear, household utensils, farm equipment, and other commodities. Large trading firms which were buying agricultural commodities usually had many buyers who came into direct contact with the producers and worked either for a commission or as independent small operators. Livestock was usually bought at local fairs, but also by buyers in villages.

In many areas the most important type of middlemen was the general country storekeepers in villages and in local trading places. They were both buyers of agricultural products produced by the peasants and sellers of practically all commodities and some services needed by the peasant population. The country storekeepers often controlled small flour mills, transportation facilities to the larger trading and administrative centers, and trade in building materials; they held licenses for the sale of government monopoly products and often operated village taverns. Moreover, in all areas of the country the rural storekeepers were, with professional usurers, up to 1932 the most important source of credit for the peasants (see Table 46, p. 673). This was primarily credit in the form of supplies. Thus a complicated relationship existed between the merchants and the peasants which covered not only the trading function, but also often the crediting function.

One of the important factors which worked against the interests of the peasants was the fact that the number of buyers of their products was small and they often acted in collusion, while the peasants as sellers were many, they had small quantities to sell, were unorganized, and, as a rule, were incapable of postponing the selling of their products. On the other hand, when the peasants were buying various commodities, they were again many, unorganized, and above all could not delay their purchases because their needs were pressing. The merchants were few, they could wait with their sales, and also in selling they often acted in collusion. In both cases the merchants were in a strong position and the peasants in a weak one. In both cases also, prices were established to the advantage of the former and to the disadvantage of the latter. The worst part in this whole system of trading was that the great majority of the peasants, either as sellers or as buyers, were not in a position either to wait or to bargain, while the merchants could indulge in both. Thus price formation in rural areas was marked by widespread oligopolistic and oligopsonistic practices and the peasants resented strongly such conditions. But the economic power of the country merchants and usurers could not have been curbed without large-scale development of co-operative trading and the establishment of credit institutions which would make sufficient credit available to all categories of peasants at reasonable interest rates.

While speaking of monopolistic practices in trade in the rural areas, one should also mention that many industrial prices were regulated by cartels and therefore included, in addition to normal profits, also a monopoly rent. In 1939 there were 80 cartels and cartel-like organizations in operation in Yugoslavia which under the rules of the Decree on Cartels of August 18, 1934, were registered with the Ministry of Trade and Industry.[12] The basic factor making possible their existence, as in other countries, was the presence of a highly protective industrial tariff. According to Stevan M. Kukoleča, who had access to unpublished official data, cartels controlled only 5.76 percent of the existing factories (a factory is defined here as a manufacturing enterprise employing 16 or more workers) at the beginning of 1939, but as a rule the cartelized enterprises owned the biggest and most modern factories and at that time accounted for 22.36 percent of all industrial investments in the country. In addition there were many "wild cartels" which were active but not registered as required by law. In many instances the Yugoslav cartels were branches of international cartels, and because of the small size of the Yugoslav component in such cartels, they were completely dominated by foreign interests.

The effect of monopolistic factors in an economy depends on the share of the market so controlled. About four-fifths of all Yugoslav cartels in 1939 affected the country's agriculture directly. Among such cartels were those controlling the production, marketing, and prices of sugar, calcium carbide, calcium cyanamide, tanning extracts, kerosene, glue, superphosphate, glassware, pesticides, paints, socks and stockings, denim, cement, bricks, roofing tiles, screws, locksmith's wares, wire, nails, chains, table utensils, currycombs, and matches. Effects of many other cartels were probably felt in an indirect fashion also in agriculture. In the case of some of the above articles, as for example sugar, kerosene, and matches, the high excise tax was a much bigger burden than the private monopoly rent. All of these market controls of products bought by the peasants had one essential consequence: they reduced their purchasing and consumption power and some of them reduced their productive power.

One of the great difficulties under which Yugoslav agriculture

---

[12] Stevan M. Kukoleča, "Cartels and Their Significance for the Yugoslav Economy," in Yugoslavia, Ministry of Social Welfare, *Socijalni arhiv*, V (July–August, 1939), 203–37; Stevan M. Kukoleča, *Industrija Jugoslavije, 1918–1938* (The Industry of Yugoslavia, 1918–1938), pp. 422–54.

labored during the interwar period was the absence of orderly marketing. That means that no branch of Yugoslav agriculture developed a system of marketing that would supply the market at a rate it was capable of absorbing and that would tend to eliminate excessive price fluctuations by preventing the periods of glut and shortage which are inherent in the seasonal character of agricultural production. The overwhelming portion of Yugoslav peasants were forced to sell almost the whole marketable portion of their production immediately after it became available. This was so because of the small size of the farms, lack of financial reserves, and permanent indebtedness of a large segment of peasant households. The market was swamped with supplies and an unduly great postharvest fall in prices was inevitable. Thus agriculture as a whole was unable to avoid losses induced by seasonal factors in supply. On the other hand, when the peasants were buying agricultural products, primarily cereals, as were those in food-deficit areas and most landless and dwarf peasants all over the country, the seasonal factor in price formation was against them, because they bought cereals in the later part of the crop year after they had exhausted their home-produced supplies (see p. 566).

Information on seasonal price fluctuations of agricultural products in Yugoslavia during the interwar period is relatively scanty. By far the greatest amount of such information is available for wheat which was traded on commodity exchanges and in practically every market place in the country. Considerable information is available also in regard to corn.

The prices of wheat were influenced by a great number of factors: the current wheat harvest at home, the carry-over from the preceding crop, the total export surplus, the harvest of wheat abroad and export surpluses in export countries, the need for wheat imports in the Central European countries to which the bulk of the Yugoslav wheat exports always went, the trade policies of these countries with respect to agricultural products, and to wheat in particular, and, after 1931, the buying policy of the government wheat export organization (see pp. 629–35). Furthermore, they were influenced by the domestic crop of corn and corn prices, which affected the use of corn as a substitute for wheat and vice versa.

It was agreed by all students of the Yugoslav wheat problem during the interwar period that the overwhelming bulk of wheat that was marketed by the Yugoslav peasants was sold during the first two or three months after the harvest. The selling of corn by the peasants required a longer time because it took longer to prepare for the market, and unfavorable weather conditions during the winter months usually slowed the rate of corn sales. The prices paid for grain in the months the peasants had grain to sell were the only prices that affected their income in that crop year. As will be explained below, the demand for exports for all agricultural products with exportable surpluses at the time when their bulk was brought to the market played a basic role in the formation of their prices.

While there was, as a rule, a postharvest slump in wheat prices, its extent and timing varied greatly from year to year, depending on the combination of the above-mentioned factors affecting the wheat market in each particular crop year. Thus, for example, Vojvodina wheat that sold at prices between 242 and 250 dinars per 100 kilograms in the period February–April, 1929, was quoted at 205 to 210 dinars in June of the same year, 190 to 195 dinars in September 1929, and 215 to 220 dinars in February 1930.[13] On the other hand, Vojvodina wheat that sold at 238.75 dinars per 100 kilograms in June 1938 was sold at only 148 dinars per 100 kilograms the following August. But during the next 14 months, until November 1939, it never rose (monthly averages) above 159.50 dinars per 100 kilograms.[14] It should be noted also that in 1929 and 1930 there was no government intervention on the wheat market, while in 1938 and 1939 there was such intervention.

There were three main reasons for the absence of orderly marketing for agricultural products in Yugoslavia during the interwar period. First, agriculture was not in possession of the necessary financial means and storage facilities to engage in orderly marketing with success, either through its co-operative organizations alone or with government help. Second, complete absence of standardization of agricultural products and animal foodstuffs also precluded effective use of the technique of orderly marketing. Third, there was very little dependable information, statistical or otherwise, on the structure and dynamics of the market for various agricultural and livestock products. And without satisfactory information it would be impossible to supply the market properly. Some market regulations did exist during the 1930's, especially in regard to wheat, and they will be discussed in later sections.

In addition to the great seasonal fluctuations in prices of cereals (as well as other agricultural products), two other conditions were deeply felt and much discussed. First, there was the problem of local disparities between the prices paid to the peasants and prices charged to

---

[13] *Narodno blagostanje*, for 1929 and 1930, *passim*.
[14] National Bank of the Kingdom of Yugoslavia, *L'activité économique en Yougoslavie en 1939*, Supplement to No. 12 of 1939, p. 5.

the peasants when they bought these products. Second, and much more important, there was the great disparity in prices of cereals between the grain-surplus and grain-deficit areas. Although the amount of statistical data in this regard is very limited, the information which was collected by the Gospodarska Sloga in its survey of about 2,000 villages in *Banovina* Croatia in the fall of 1939 covered the typical grain-surplus areas of Slavonia and Srijem and the typical grain-deficit areas of the Croatian Zagorje, southwestern Croatia, Dalmatia, and parts of Bosnia and Herzegovina, and therefore can serve as a good illustration of the problems here under consideration. This survey found that in the period between October 1 and October 15, 1939, there were (1) great disparities in selling prices of wheat and corn in various villages of the same counties. These differences were explainable perhaps partly by the differences in quality, partly by transportation factors, and partly by the nature of trading organization in various places. (2) In the chief wheat-surplus areas surveyed (Slavonia and Srijem) the disparity between the prices paid the peasants and the prices charged to peasants and other people when they bought wheat was only about 7 to 15 percent, but in some subsidiary surplus areas (northeastern Bosnia) as well as in the wheat-deficit areas these differences rose to 50 percent. As a rule, these differentials were much higher in wheat-deficit areas than in wheat-surplus areas and, according to general experience, became higher as the crop year advanced. (3) Differentials between prices paid to the producers and charged to the consumers for corn in the same localities at the same time were, generally, somewhat higher than the differentials in wheat prices. (4) The most important and economically far-reaching problem under Yugoslav conditions was, however, the differentials between the prices at which peasants were selling wheat and corn in grain-surplus areas and those at which peasants were buying wheat and corn in grain-deficit areas. These differentials ranged from about 50 to more than 150 percent. These high price differentials, of course after the deduction of the transportation costs and carrying charges, were pocketed by the middlemen. They were the highest in grain-deficit "passive areas," that is, in areas in which population was least able to stand them. Naturally, trade was entitled to a reasonable profit margin, but it was generally felt that these profits were out of proportion to the service performed and the risk carried by the trade.[15]

---

[15] In October 1939 the peasants in the wheat-surplus areas surveyed by the Gospodarska Sloga were selling wheat, on the average, for 130 dinars per 100 kilograms, with the lowest recorded price of 110 and the highest of 150 dinars. The price of wheat of the quality here considered on the commodity exchanges was 152 dinars per 100 kilograms (actually this was the government guaranteed price) at that time. At the same

AGRICULTURAL INDUSTRIES

Successful marketing of many crops and livestock produced in an area depends greatly on the level of development and the variety of industries which process these materials into final products. Highly developed agricultural industries in an area or country indicate high and relatively steady demand for their products whether this demand originates in the domestic market or from abroad. There was a whole series of agricultural industries in Yugoslavia of the interwar period. Moreover, a large percentage of all handicraft enterprises, which in 1938 numbered about 156,000, used agricultural raw or semifinished materials for processing into final products.[16]

The most important in terms of the number of industrial establishments, purchases of raw materials from agriculture, and the value of gross production was the food-processing industry. Very important also was the tobacco industry. The leather industry depended only partly on domestically produced raw materials, the textile industry only slightly, so they are not taken into account here. Out of the total number of factories (regarding the definition of a factory in the official Yugoslav statistics, see footnote 14, p. 171) in Yugoslavia of 4,257 in 1938 and a total gross production estimated at 15,755.5 million dinars, food and agricultural industries accounted for 1,374 units (32.28 percent) and a gross value of 3,830.6 million dinars (24.32 percent). There were also five factories of tobacco products with a total gross value of production in 1939 of 929.5 million dinars.[17]

In terms of gross value of production the most important branches of agricultural industry were flour milling with a gross value of production in 1938 of 2,022.8 million dinars (766 factories), the sugar industry with 344.2 million, meat packing (only smoked and similarly prepared meat products) with 287.5 million, the edible oil industry

---

time, in the grain-deficit areas the peasants were paying over 200 dinars for wheat, with the lowest recorded price of 175 and the highest of 300 dinars per 100 kilograms. The average transportation costs from surplus to deficit areas were about 30 dinars per 100 kilograms. The price of corn in the corn-surplus areas was at that time 110 to 115 dinars, while the peasants in the corn-deficit areas were paying 160 and even as high as 200 dinars per 100 kilograms. Gospodarska Sloga, *op. cit.*, pp. 46–53.

[16] Stevan M. Kukoleča, *Industrija Jugoslavije, 1918–1938*, pp. 57–62.

[17] Yugoslavia, Ministry of Trade and Industry, *Statistika industrije Kraljevine Jugoslavije* (Industrial Statistics of the Kingdom of Yugoslavia), pp. 10, 30. The number of factories as of 1938 in this official publication and in the above-quoted book by Kukoleča, which was also based on official information of the Ministry of Trade and Industry whose official he was, differ slightly owing to somewhat different criteria used in the two publications. Data in neither of these publications include the armament factories.

with 203.0 million, beer brewing with 93.6 million, and the production of industrial alcohol with 87.0 million dinars. The total gross value of production of more than two scores of other food and agricultural industries (465 factories) amounted in 1938 to only 792.4 million dinars, or 20.6 percent of the total value. Some branches of food industry such as the canning of fruits and vegetables, the canning of meat products, and the industrial production of dairy products were of small consequence in Yugoslavia. The value of production of canned meat in 1938 was only 10.3 million dinars, while the production of canned fruits and vegetables was only 6.7 million dinars. The value of the industrial production of dairy products was only 4.1 million dinars,[18] but the output of dairy products in enterprises which qualified as handicrafts and in the cottage industry was incomparably larger.

In spite of the fact that the number of factories in the food-processing and agricultural industries in Yugoslavia was relatively large, these industries were actually poorly developed. That is especially true if the agricultural industries of Vojvodina are left out of consideration. This situation is easily understandable. First, in a country in which a large portion of its agriculture is of a subsistence character and the remainder which largely produces for the market is not very specialized, there is little possibility for a greatly diversified and successful agricultural industry. Second, in a national economy in which the per capita income is low and in which nutrition is based on a few staples, there is no need for a large development of such industry because there is no sufficient demand for its products at home. The foreign market had a tendancy to shrink during the interwar period.

Agricultural industries were best developed, had the longest tradition, and were most diversified in *banovina* Dunav (especially in Vojvodina), followed by *banovine* Sava and Drava, and the Prefecture of Belgrade. *Banovina* Dunav had in 1938 not less than 45.7 percent of the total number of factories in the food-processing industries; there were 22.1 percent in Sava, 10.0 percent in Drava, and 3.9 percent in the Prefecture of Belgrade. The relatively great development of food and agricultural industries in Vojvodina goes back largely to the pre-1918 period when this area was an important section of the territory which formed the food basket of the Austro-Hungarian Monarchy. Moreover, during the interwar period, and especially during the first five years after World War I, most of the new factories in this field were established in Vojvodina and other areas north of the Sava–Danube

[18] Yugoslavia, Ministry of Trade and Industry, *op. cit.*, pp. 28–29.

rivers. This development was connected with the fact that Vojvodina had an abundance of agricultural raw materials and that a large portion of its agriculture was specialized and commercialized. In the six *banovine* south of the Sava-Danube line only 18.3 percent of the total number of factories in this field were located in 1938,[19] and most of them were established after 1918.

In addition to relatively poor development of the food and agricultural industries there was another characteristic typical of these industries during much of the interwar period, and that was low utilization of their production capacity. Throughout the 1930's, and also during the 1920's in the case of flour milling, beer brewing, and sugar and industrial alcohol production, only a portion of the total capacity was utilized. According to private estimates, flour-milling and sugar industries utilized in 1938 only about half of their capacity, beer brewing only about one-seventh of its capacity, and industrial alcohol only about one-fourth of its capacity.[20] In order to help the industry of industrial alcohol and to save foreign exchange, the government decreed in October 1937 that all motor fuel, except that used for the needs of the military services, had to contain 20 percent of industrial alcohol.

Low utilization of a great number of leading food-processing and agricultural industries during the 1930's was connected with three principal factors. First, Central European countries which were the chief buyers of Yugoslav agricultural and livestock products preferred to import these products in their crude form or as live animals, thus saving for themselves the employment and benefits connected with the processing of these products. Moreover, their imports were reduced, owing to a vigorous agricultural protectionism. Second, some of the products of food and agricultural industries, such as sugar, beer, and industrial alcohol, were subject to exceedingly high excise taxes, which reduced their consumption at home. The same situation applied to tobacco. Third, the Great Depression was also responsible for reduced demand, both at home and abroad, for the products of these industries during the first half of the 1930's.

There is no doubt that an expansion of the food-processing and agricultural industries in Yugoslavia would have helped in improving the marketing conditions for crops and livestock. But such an expansion could not take place without an increase in effective demand for the

[19] Stevan M. Kukoleča, *op. cit.*, p. 65.
[20] S. Djurdjević (ed.), *20 godina kulturnog i privrednog razvitka Kraljevine Jugoslavije* (Twenty Years of Cultural and Economic Development of the Kingdom of Yugoslavia), pp. 90–92.

products of such industries either from the domestic or from foreign markets. Under the conditions existing in Yugoslavia during the 1930's the prospects for a sizable increase in such demand were poor and thus also the prospects were poor for a marked increase in the food-processing and agricultural industries.

AGRICULTURAL CO-OPERATIVES AND MARKETING OF AGRICULTURAL PRODUCTS

A pertinent question in discussing marketing problems of Yugoslav agriculture during the interwar period is that of the role of agricultural co-operatives. At the end of 1938 there were in Yugoslavia a total of 10,832 co-operative societies organized in 37 federations with a total of 1,414,876 members.[21] These numbers included all types of co-operatives, and not only those active in agriculture. Furthermore, many people were members of more than one co-operative society, so that the membership was higher than the number of households participating in co-operatives. A considerable number of co-operatives, estimated by some people at 20 to 30 percent, were inactive.

The largest number, 4,909 societies, were credit co-operatives, though some of these in rural areas also engaged in buying necessities for their members and selling commodities produced by them. Next in order of numerical strength were the consumers co-operatives with a total of 2,521 at the end of 1938. The most important group in marketing was producers and marketing co-operatives, with only 1,165, or slightly more than 10 percent of all co-operative societies in 1938. These co-operatives were divided as follows: 237 dairy and cheese, 169 grain, 162 wine, 125 apiculture, 93 fruit, 36 olive oil, 16 rosemary oil, 168 unclassified marketing co-operatives, and 159 marketing co-operatives of artisans and workers (the latter group, of course, did not belong to agricultural co-operatives). But there was a large group in the miscellaneous co-operatives (which in 1938 numbered 2,237 societies) which was actually producers and marketing co-operatives. Most important among them were 747 livestock-breeding co-operatives and 18 poultry-breeding co-operatives. There were also 490 multipurpose agricultural co-operatives in 1938, a certain portion of which also engaged in marketing operations.

Generally speaking, agricultural co-operatives played a much smaller role in interwar Yugoslavia than in such countries as Denmark, Czechoslovakia, or even Bulgaria. By far the best-developed, best-led, most

---

[21] Yugoslavia, *Annuaire statistique 1938–1939*, pp. 340–41.

diversified, best-co-ordinated, and most effective agricultural co-operatives existed in Slovenia. But there were some powerful co-operative organizations in Croatia-Slavonia, in Serbia, and during the 1930's also among the German minority in Vojvodina and Slavonia. There were many shortcomings in the organization and functioning of the agricultural co-operatives in Yugoslavia. Individual co-operative societies were often small units and therefore quite weak. Most of the co-operatives were organized along political or nationality lines and thus were open to outside pressures to further nonbusiness purposes which often proved greatly disadvantageous for co-operatives as business enterprises. The co-operatives often lacked a truly co-operative spirit, so that while there were, on the one hand, many members of co-operatives who participated only halfheartedly, other people, often in positions of leadership, abused the co-operatives for their personal gain. Though co-operatives according to their special line of business and organizational pattern had their special central organizations or federations for auditing and financing purposes, these central organizations were often weak in both leadership and financial power.

Agricultural producers and marketing co-operatives exerted a certain influence on the improvement of agricultural and livestock products and affected to a small extent the timing of marketing of some of these products. Working as larger units which could often supply sizable amounts of products of relatively uniform quality, some agricultural co-operatives were able to establish and maintain intensive contacts for selling their products in foreign markets. Many producers and marketing co-operatives with impressive names, such as co-operatives for cattle or pig breeding, or co-operatives of wine producers, actually consisted of a few big and medium operators who by organizing into co-operatives were entitled to various privileges such as exemption from certain fees, occasionally preferential treatment in obtaining export licenses, and the like. The producers and marketing co-operatives in Yugoslavia in the interwar period were thus not of basic importance either for the marketing of agricultural products or for their price formation. Agricultural co-operatives lacked both storage and financial facilities to be of any significance in organizing orderly marketing procedures for agricultural and livestock products, although in most other countries that was one of the principal functions of agricultural marketing co-operatives.

It is necessary to stress that agricultural producers and marketing co-operatives (as well as credit co-operatives) were primarily of help to big and medium peasants who had sizable amounts of goods to sell, who could buy their necessities in larger quantities, who could pay in cash for most of their purchases, or, when they needed credit, could furnish satisfactory security. Even to join many of these co-operatives one had to have a certain amount of assets, and a large segment of peasant households could not pass that test.

There is no need to describe in any detail either the organization or the business development of various types or groups of agricultural co-operatives. A few figures on the business volume of the producers and marketing co-operatives will suffice to indicate their limited scope. According to published data, the value of products sold in 1935 by the federations of producers and marketing co-operatives, and of other co-operatives which handled the selling of products of their member organizations, amounted to only 37.1 million dinars. The amount sold by the central organizations of the producers and marketing co-operatives (the intermediary level of the co-operative organization) was 102.2 million dinars. The value of products sold by local producers and marketing co-operative societies is not known. According to partial data their sales amounted to about 120 million dinars in 1935, but a large number of local co-operatives failed to report the volume of their business. If one compares these figures with the value of commodities (also only partially reported) handled by all consumers and purchasing co-operatives which was in excess of 600 million dinars in 1935, the limited scope of agricultural producers and marketing co-operatives becomes very obvious.[22]

One of the most interesting and most versatile co-operative organizations in Yugoslavia during the second half of the 1930's was the Gospodarska Sloga, the economic co-operative arm of the Croatian Peasant party. It was established in July 1935. Its membership rose from 6,186 at the end of 1935 to 116,011 at the end of 1936, to 144,951 at the end of 1937, to 172,352 at the end of 1938, and to 201,190 at the end of 1939. In April 1940 the membership reached 227,456. It was organized at that time in 4,570 local committees and covered 5,258 villages. The membership represented at that time perhaps one-third of all peasant households in *Banovina* Croatia. In one county (Samobor near Zagreb) 92 percent of all households were included and in a number of other counties well over 50 percent of all peasant households were members.[23]

[22] Yugoslavia, *Annuaire statistique 1936*, pp. 330–33.

[23] *Gospodarska Sloga*, No. 11-12, June 1, 1940, pp. 3–9. This issue contains the annual report of the organization for 1939, which in fact represents the most complete published report on the growth, principles, and activities of this organization known to this writer.

Early in its life the Gospodarska Sloga came to the attention of the peasantry and the general public, as well as to traders on livestock markets, by its dramatic intervention on the cattle market in order to increase the prices of cattle and, generally, to improve marketing rules to the advantage of the cattle raisers. This action began in mid-February 1936 in Zagreb and soon spread over all Croatia-Slavonia. Low prices were answered by setting minimum prices for cattle by special market committees created by and consisting of peasants themselves, below which nobody was allowed to sell. Furthermore, these committees classified the cattle into the prevailing market categories and saw to it that their classification prevailed. They insisted upon and controlled the weighing of animals, and insisted on shortening the market hours. For some time the peasants even abstained from taking their cattle to market, thus engaging in a sellers' strike. In cases when peasants lacked feed and were forced to sell their cattle in spite of the strike, the village either took the cattle off their hands or made arrangements to supply feed. Since the buyers in the cattle market were few and usually acted in agreement on what prices to pay, the concerted action of the peasants who had both the political party organization and popular sympathy on their side was definitely the most effective measure that could be used to check the power of traders and middlemen. It was generally agreed that this "livestock market action" to raise cattle prices and to improve conditions on livestock markets was successful. Later the Gospodarska Sloga tried to accomplish an even larger aim by sponsoring the organization of special co-operatives for the export of livestock which intended to exclude the middlemen altogether.

Gradually the Gospodarska Sloga spread its activity into practically every aspect of economic life of the Croatian peasants as producers and sellers, as consumers, and also as workers when they were working for wages in agriculture or forestry. To mention just a few of these activities: livestock breeding and inoculations against disease, establishment of dairy co-operatives, improvement in quality and better marketing of wool, better marketing of poultry and eggs, honey, wine, and salt-water fish. It established an outlet and warehouses in Zagreb for vegetables and fruits supplied by its members.

To help the peasants as buyers it acted in two fields. First, it served as a purchasing agent for agricultural implements, copper sulphate, and seed. By guaranteeing relatively large purchases and eliminating the middlemen it was able to acquire these products considerably below the prevailing prices. It also sponsored the establishment of seed reserve funds, especially in grain-deficit areas, from which each member peasant could borrow seed with the obligation of repaying both the principal and interest in kind. Second, it bought considerable quantities of grain in surplus areas (within and without *Banovina* Croatia) and sold it in food-deficit areas.[24]

By promoting special collective wage agreements between peasant agricultural workers and their employers, Gospodarska Sloga tried also to raise the wages of agricultural workers. The first such agreement was concluded in 1936 and was later followed by several others. The final objective, which was not achieved, was to establish minimum wages in agriculture by law. Through special committees Gospodarska Sloga also tried to increase the interest of the peasants in health education and was sponsoring the extension of electrification into rural areas.

Generally speaking, Gospodarska Sloga was quite successful in its operations. This success has to be ascribed not only to the feasibility of co-operative action in most of its undertakings and to satisfactory leadership, but especially to the fact that it was the creation and instrument of a political party at a time when this party enjoyed tremendous popularity and was the undisputed party-political authority among the Croats generally, and among the Croatian peasants in particular. One of the factors that undoubtedly was helpful was that the Yugoslav economy after 1935 was experiencing a general revival. Because of its specific political character the organization could use in its actions not only rational persuasion but also economic propaganda throughout the party press and organizations, political and social pressure, and in some cases near-coercive methods in support of its activities. After the entry of the Croatian Peasant party into the government (August 1939) and the establishment of *Banovina* Croatia under complete control of the Peasant party, Gospodarska Sloga became almost a quasi-governmental agency of the banovinal government for all questions of food policy and administration.

It would be useless to speculate what would have become of Gospodarska Sloga had there been no World War II. It disintegrated, together with the cessation of the rule of the Peasant party after the Axis invasion of Yugoslavia in April 1941. It was not re-established after World War II. Its example showed, however, that a politically well-organized peasantry can use the co-operative arm most effectively and, among other things, exert a considerable influence on the market for agricultural products.

Another case of very successful producers and marketing co-opera-

[24] *Ibid.*, p. 26.

tives in interwar Yugoslavia was the co-operative organizations of the German minority in Vojvodina. The most important organization of this kind was Agraria. Its counterpart in the field of co-operative agricultural credit was the Bauernhilfe (Farmers' Aid). The Agraria was established in 1922 by transforming the economic department of the Schwäbisch-Deutschen Kulturbund into a central co-operative, to which many newly formed, local co-operatives were later attached. The Agraria engaged in the bulk-purchasing of supplies needed by its members (artificial fertilizers, agricultural machinery), in selling their products (grains, hemp, etc.), and in giving technical advice regarding agricultural and marketing problems facing the farmers of the German minority in Yugoslavia. For some important special purposes, like pig raising and marketing, it sponsored the establishment of separate co-operatives.[25]

It is interesting to note that the Agraria, like the Gospodarska Sloga, was the creation and instrument of a tightly organized political grouping, the political party of the German minority. The activity and strength of the Agraria grew by leaps and bounds during the 1930's. Its leadership was taken over by people of Nazi inclination, and even before the German invasion of Yugoslavia it became an important instrument of German economic penetration in Yugoslavia. After the German invasion, the Agraria became even more of a cog in the German program of utilizing the food and agricultural raw material supplies of Vojvodina and Slavonia for both their armed forces and their civilian population. The defeat of the Germans and the exodus of the German minority from Yugoslavia spelled the end of the Agraria.

While in the above two cases political parties were able to organize and utilize large agricultural co-operative organizations to great advantage, a reversed procedure where an old-established and relatively successful co-operative organization was used as basis for a political party did not prove successful. This was the case with the Federation of Serbian Agricultural Co-operatives, which in the early 1920's and to a lesser extent in later years served as the basis of the Serbian Peasant party, the "Union of Peasants." This party had a certain number of adherents throughout the interwar period but it never developed into a strong political force. Its various factions continued to have political ambitions. The Federation of Serbian Agricultural Co-operatives, comprising all types of agricultural co-operatives, remained, however, the

[25] For the history, development, and activity of the Agraria and other co-operative organizations of the German minority in Yugoslavia up to 1930, see Andreas Dammang, *Die deutsche Landwirtschaft in Banat und in der Batschka*, pp. 165–88.

strongest and most vocal co-operative group in Serbia throughout the interwar period.

As already pointed out, co-operative organizations were best developed in Slovenia and the bulk of them were associated with the Slovene People's party. As such, they were used to carry its economic program in the village.

EXPORTS OF AGRICULTURAL AND LIVESTOCK PRODUCTS

Owing to the predominantly agricultural character of the Yugoslav economy, between 50 and 60 percent of the country's exports in terms of value during the interwar period consisted of agricultural and livestock products.[26] Table 43 shows the exports of principal agricultural and livestock products between 1921 and 1939 in five-year averages both in absolute value and as percentages of total exports. But Yugo-

TABLE 43. — EXPORTS OF PRINCIPAL AGRICULTURAL AND LIVESTOCK PRODUCTS DURING THE INTERWAR PERIOD IN FIVE-YEAR AVERAGES*

(Million dinars; percent of total exports)

Commodity	1921–25 Million dinars	Percent	1926–30 Million dinars	Percent	1931–35 Million dinars	Percent	1936–39[a] Million dinars	Percent
Wheat and wheat flour	573.8	8.8	687.3	9.7	170.9	4.5	409.7	7.7
Corn	668.7	10.2	501.5	7.1	329.6	8.6	342.6	6.4
Fresh and dried prunes	227.4	3.5	170.6	2.4	120.4	3.1	118.2	2.2
Hemp	106.3	1.6	95.1	1.3	70.2	1.8	199.4	3.8
Cattle	516.2	7.9	322.6	4.6	100.6	2.6	107.7	2.0
Pigs	254.6	3.9	359.9	5.1	238.3	6.2	427.2	8.1
Fresh meat	405.6	6.2	275.2	3.9	182.6	4.8	300.2	5.7
Eggs	445.3	6.8	510.6	7.2	193.4	5.1	140.9	2.7
Total	3,197.9	48.9	2,922.8	41.3	1,406.0	36.7	2,045.9	38.6
Total exports	6,528.8	100.0	7,072.9	100.0	3,828.6	100.0	5,304.3	100.0

* Source: Yugoslavia, Ministry of Finance, *Statistique du commerce extérieur*, Belgrade, annually, 1921–39.
[a] Four-year average.

[26] For a more detailed discussion of Yugoslav foreign economic relations during the interwar period, a more complete presentation of the commodity composition of exports and imports and directional orientation of foreign trade, and the main lines of the Yugoslav foreign trade policies, see Jozo Tomasevich, "Foreign Economic Relations, 1918–1941," in Robert J. Kerner (ed.), *Yugoslavia*, pp. 169–214. In regard to the Yugoslav foreign trade policy of that period see especially Sava D. Obradović, *La politique commerciale de la Yougoslavie*.

slavia exported a considerable number of other products of agricultural and animal origin, such as dried beans, grapes, fresh apples, sour cherries, hops, tobacco, oilseeds, wine, medicinal herbs, raw opium, horses, lambs, poultry, lard, hides, and feathers. This listing of agricultural exports indicates that Yugoslavia did not depend only on one or a few agricultural export products, as is often the case with underdeveloped countries. Nevertheless, products listed in Table 43 represented the bulk of all agricultural exports of the country and, on the average, over 40 percent of the total value of exports during the interwar period.[27]

The chief markets for Yugoslav agricultural exports during the interwar period were the industrial countries of Central Europe—Austria, Czechoslovakia, and Germany—and Italy. Yugoslav exports to these four countries in selected years were as follows (in percent of total value):[28]

	1925	1930	1935	1937
Austria	18.6	17.7	14.3	13.5
Czechoslovakia	9.4	8.2	13.4	7.9
Germany	7.2	11.7	18.7	21.7
Italy	25.3	28.3	16.7	9.4
Total	60.5	65.9	63.1	52.5

In most years Greece and Switzerland were important customers for Yugoslav agricultural and livestock products, and during the second half of the 1930's Great Britain was also an important buyer of these products. Since Austria, Czechoslovakia, Germany, and Italy were not only the chief customers of Yugoslavia, but also the principal suppliers of its imports, trade relations with these four countries were the most important problem of Yugoslav foreign trade policy throughout the interwar period from the standpoint of both agriculture and the remainder of the country's economy. As shown above, the relative shares in exports going to the four principal customer countries between 1925 and 1937 (the last year before Germany began to absorb various countries in Central Europe) have changed considerably. The two outstanding changes were the decreased exports to Italy during the 1930's and the increased exports to Germany. In both cases these changes were

[27] The average exports of foods of both vegetable and animal origin during the period 1934–38 as percentages of the estimated domestic production have been shown in Tables 38 and 39 (pp. 535 and 543). These figures are net export figures, but since imports, except in the case of rice and oilseeds, were naught or negligible, the figures indicated in these tables can be taken as exports.

[28] Yugoslavia, Ministry of Finance, *Statistique du commerce extérieur*, annually, 1925–38.

induced to a large extent by political factors. As far as Italy was concerned, it favored, for political reasons, the imports from Hungary and Austria at the expense of those from Yugoslavia. Moreover, economic sanctions against Italy during the Ethiopian war affected Yugoslav exports to Italy and thus the Yugoslav economy most severely. On the other hand, Germany's trade drive into Southeastern Europe after 1934 and its gradual emergence as the principal customer and supplier of all small states in that area, including Yugoslavia, were a part of the German preparation for the coming war.

Data in Table 43 indicate that the value of the principal agricultural exports and the share of these exports in the total value of exports were considerably lower during the 1930's than they were during the 1920's. The fall in the total value of exports was caused by a reduction in the quantities exported and especially by a fall in prices (see Table 44, p. 637). The reduction in the volume of exports of agricultural commodities was caused by these principal factors: the fall in the demand for these commodities in the importing industrial countries due to the Great Depression and its aftereffects, the difficulties in the balance of payments of the importing countries which tended to reduce imports and often to shift their origin, the reduced import requirements of food by these countries as a result of their agricultural protectionism, and the relatively low competitive power of many of the Yugoslav products on the foreign markets.

From Table 43 one sees also that a certain shift in the structure of agricultural exports has taken place during the interwar period. Most pronounced was the reduction in the exports of wheat and wheat flour, cattle, and eggs during the 1930's, while the greatest relative increase was in the exports of fat pigs and hemp. If exports of additional products during the 1930's are taken into account, then one sees that increases in the exports of tobacco, lard, fresh fruits other than prunes, and several less important products were such that the share of all agricultural and livestock products in the total value of exports remained relatively stable after 1925.

The exports of agricultural and livestock products were of basic importance not only for Yugoslav agriculture but for the entire Yugoslav economy. This key significance of agricultural exports resulted from their influence on the price formation for agricultural and livestock products on the Yugoslav market and thus on the aggregate income of agriculture. This strong influence of the demand for exports on prices of agricultural products was related to the fact that Yugoslavia had exportable surpluses in practically all of its crop and livestock products.

Since the bulk of all marketable surpluses, including the exportable surpluses, tended to appear on the market immediately after the harvest or after livestock was ready for sale, this increased supply had the tendency of strongly depressing the prices. If the demand for exports was satisfactory at that strategic point of time, prices were formed under the influence of this higher demand and, after the export surpluses had been cleared, had the tendency of keeping on a higher level. If, however, the demand for exports was lacking at that time, exportable surpluses usually depressed the prices more than proportionately to their size and resulted in a lower aggregate income for agriculture.[29]

By favorably influencing the prices of commodities with exportable surpluses and the income of their producers, the effect of satisfactory exports was translated through a higher demand of the agricultural population for the products of industry, handicrafts, and service industries to the income of the remainder of the private economy. Furthermore, the higher level of agricultural income tended to raise the income of the government from taxes, especially from excise taxes on products of mass consumption, and the revenue of government-owned enterprises, and thus also their expenditures. While this transfer of income from agriculture to the government had a deflationary influence on the spending of the agricultural population, the government was by far the most important employer in the urban economy and basically influenced the level of its income. In turn this affected the demand of the urban sector for the products of agriculture, and thus the income of agriculture.

Each additional amount spent by the agricultural population as a consequence of agricultural exports had the tendency, on the basis of the multiplier principle, of raising the aggregate income of the national economy by a multiple of the amount so spent. On the contrary, in years of low demand for exports in comparison with the supplies for exports, the exportable surpluses pressed heavily on the market and had the tendency of lowering prices of all agricultural products in which exportable surpluses existed, thus reducing the income of the agricultural sector as a whole. This situation in agricultural income influenced in turn all other branches of the national economy by reducing the

---

[29] As will be shown in the following section, the primary objective of the wheat intervention policy in Yugoslavia after the unsatisfactory experiences with the external and internal government wheat trade monopoly of 1931/32 was to remove immediately after the harvest all exportable surpluses from the wheat market at a government-decreed price, which was usually considerably above the export parity level. Thus the connection between the domestic and the world market price was broken and a higher price maintained with relative ease.

demand and prices of their products and, in turn, their income. Lower exports thus resulted in the lowering of the national income. Moreover, changes in agricultural exports and prices tended to influence the price-cost relations in the whole economy by influencing the demand for the products of the remainder of the economy and the cost of that economy by influencing the prices of food and raw materials produced in agriculture. Needless to say, wages were also affected.

The same reasoning that applied here to the inflow of funds in payment of agricultural exports should be applied to the inflow of funds for other exports and the inflow of funds generally. The two basic additional sources of foreign funds were the inflow of foreign capital and emigrants' remittances, which next to international merchandise trade were the principal links between the Yugoslav and the European and world economy. These were the channels through which the expansion and contraction movements in European and world business cycles transmitted themselves to Yugoslavia. The inflow of foreign capital was an exceedingly volatile factor, limited almost exclusively to the years of business expansion and prosperity. Emigrants' remittances were throughout the interwar period an important source of income for the "passive regions" from which most of the emigrants originated and an important credit item in the Yugoslav balance of payments, although much more so during the 1920's than during the 1930's. The importance of this item can perhaps best be judged by comparing it with the import surplus on the merchandise account during the interwar period. The import surplus between 1919 and 1939 amounted to 6,852 million dinars while the inflow of emigrants' remittances during the same period was estimated at about 15 billion dinars.[30]

The increased inflow of funds resulted also in enlarging the foreign exchange reserves of the central bank and in increasing deposits with private and government banks, which then raised the capacity of the banking system to grant more and cheaper credit and made possible greater spending on investment and consumption. Reduced exports and reduced inflow of foreign capital and emigrants' remittances tended

---

[30] J. N. Dunda, "The Role of Emigrants' Remittances in the Yugoslav Balance of Payments," *Ekonomist*, April-May, 1940, pp. 142–54. A certain amount of money was sent abroad each year by foreigners living and working in Yugoslavia, but these outward remittances were of relatively small significance in comparison with the incoming amounts. An additional remark should be made in regard to emigrants' remittances. Since most of the emigrants lived in the United States and their remittances were greatly influenced by their earnings, which in turn depended on the level of employment and income in the United States, there existed also a special link between United States business cycles and business cycles in Yugoslavia.

also through this mechanism to reduce the total amount of spending, and thus the national income. Moreover, all these changes affected the terms of trade, the exchange rates, and the methods of international payments, which, in turn, influenced the development of both external and internal economic conditions of the country.

Of course payments for imports and the outflow of funds for other reasons had an opposite effect from that just described for the inflow of funds from abroad. But under Yugoslav conditions a considerable portion of new investment, especially in industry, was impossible without importing of machinery and various tools and appliances, various raw materials, and fuel, so that spending on new investment partly counteracted the contracting influence of imports on national income.

Unfortunately, it is impossible on the basis of the existing Yugoslav data to corroborate the interrelationships between the value of exports and other inflow of funds from abroad, minus the outflow of funds for imports and other reasons, on the one hand, and the level of income in agriculture and the remainder of the economy, on the other. Generally speaking, however, one is quite right in saying that most of the periods of economic revival and prosperity in Yugoslav economy during the interwar period were associated with a growing or high level of exports and a large inflow of funds, while the periods of contraction and depression were characterized by falling or low exports and low inflow of other funds from abroad. Characteristic of the first situation was the period between 1927 and 1929, while the years of the Great Depression furnish an excellent example of the second situation.

In the course of these years a great change in the terms of trade took place. During the period 1927 to 1930 the terms of trade were quite favorable to Yugoslavia (this apparently was the case also during most of the years from 1919 to 1926); by 1931 they were only slightly favorable, while in the period 1932 to 1937 the terms of trade turned sharply against Yugoslavia. A similar situation applied in these years to all countries exporting food and raw materials. Thus, according to the price indexes of the National Bank of Yugoslavia (1926 = 100), the index of export products stood in 1929 at 114.3 as against the index of import products at 91.4, while in 1933 the price index of export products stood at 58.4 and that of import products at 74.1. In 1938 the terms of trade turned again in favor of Yugoslavia, but in the following two years they were again slightly against Yugoslavia.

Having an extremely important influence on prices of export commodities and thus on the income of their producers, the conditions in the export trade exercised a great influence on the production of export

commodities. This can well be seen from the stagnation of the wheat
hectarage during the 1930's and especially from the changes in the
hectarage under various industrial crops grown primarily for export,
such as hemp, hops, and poppies for opium (see Table 34, p. 494). The
difficulties with exports undoubtedly were also one of the reasons which
in the early 1930's led to a stagnation in the herds of cattle and especially to a reduction in the number of pigs. When conditions in the
export market improved in the second half of the 1930's, especially in
regard to pigs, the number of animals grew.

Although the export possibilities for some industrial crops (hemp,
oilseeds) and such specialty crops as early vegetables and fine-quality
fruits were relatively more favorable than those for grains, especially
wheat, there was little determined effort to shift to the production of
these crops on a larger scale. Such a shift would have required greater
application of labor and of capital. Higher requirements of labor for
such crops would have been welcome in an agriculturally overpopulated
country like Yugoslavia, but larger capital investments, needed, for
example, in the building of irrigation facilities for growing of vegetables, were difficult or impossible to obtain. The shifts in production
which were made during the interwar period were relatively small and
did not change the traditional patterns of the Yugoslav agricultural and
livestock production. Two most important difficulties regarding the
shifts in production were perhaps the impossibility for the overwhelming number of peasant households, because of their small farms, to
assume the risk involved in the change of the production pattern, and
the traditionalism of the Yugoslav peasantry.

Since the key significance of the export trade, and of agricultural
exports in particular, for the whole national economy was generally
recognized, the government paid considerable attention to the promotion of exports. Actually most of the government actions which affected
the marketing of agricultural and livestock products during the interwar
period were connected with exports or imports of these commodities.

Immediately after World War I the government introduced a system
of licensing of exports of practically all foods and feedstuffs. This
policy was intended to mitigate the shortages of these products resulting from the war. The Yugoslav agricultural production became relatively normalized within a few years after that war and licensing of
exports almost completely disappeared by 1922. Since the government
desired to profit, in a fiscal sense, from the favorable export conditions,
export duties were introduced in 1920 on almost all agricultural and
livestock products. As agriculture gradually recuperated in the prin-

cipal importing countries of Central Europe, the export conditions for Yugoslav products deteriorated and by 1924 all export duties on agricultural products were removed.

On the other hand, the government fully protected the domestic market for home agriculture by high import duties on agricultural and livestock products and products of food industries of any consequence.[31] Thus throughout the interwar period the import of food, with the exception of such products as rice, oilseeds for the production of edible oils, tropical and subtropical fruits, dried fish, and small quantities of specialty food products, was almost completely excluded. But from the point of view of agriculture much more important was the high level of tariff protection accorded to domestic industries both prior to and in the Tariff Act of 1925, because this markedly raised the domestic prices of all industrial products. The whole interwar tariff policy of Yugoslavia, defended on economic, political, and military grounds, served primarily the interests of the industry and much of its burden was carried by the agricultural population.[32]

In order to further the export of agricultural and livestock products (including, of course, other export products), the Yugoslav authorities spent a great deal of energy in trying to negotiate favorable trade agreements with importing countries and in exchange were granting tariff concessions on some industrial products. The problem of tariff negotiation remained of basic importance throughout the interwar period, although after 1930 it was essential to negotiate for preferential tariff rates, export quotas, and for satisfactory payment arrangements with foreign countries. The nature of the Yugoslav problem in this regard may be judged from the fact that from 1934 to 1939 an average of 75.6 percent of all exports and 73.3 percent of all imports were made under bilateral clearing agreements.

A turning point in the Yugoslav trade policies of the 1930's occurred in June 1936 when the government decreed that certain commodities, representing roughly 35 percent of the total value of imports, could not be imported from nonclearing countries except under special license from the central bank. The country was forced to this step, on the one hand, by large import surpluses in trade with hard currency countries which had to be paid in free exchange and, on the other, by large export surpluses in trade with some clearing countries, particularly with Germany, the proceeds of which were blocked for a considerable length of time. The objective of the new policy was to cut

[31] Stevan M. Kukoleča, *op. cit.*, p. 492.
[32] *Ibid.*, pp. 457–522; Sava D. Obradović, *op. cit.*, p. 11 and *passim*.

the imports from the former and increase those from the latter group of countries. In practice that increased the Yugoslav dependence on trade with Germany. But under the existing conditions there was no other alternative.[33]

To promote exports the government established in 1929 a special agency—the Office for the Promotion of Foreign Trade—which studied foreign markets and engaged in various promotional activities. The consular service was also considerably enlarged. In 1932 a special Agency for the Export of Livestock was established within the above office. The principal function of this agency was to issue export licenses for pigs and cattle exported to Austria and Czechoslovakia in fulfillment of export quotas at preferential tariff rates.

Like many other countries Yugoslavia used subsidies to promote exports of a few agricultural products. This was the case with industrial alcohol and wine and brandy. This export subsidization was introduced in 1929 and lasted only for a few months; it could not be sustained because of the resulting high cost. The most elaborate scheme of subsidized exporting applied to wheat after 1930, but this problem will be dealt with in the next section.

Another type of government intervention inaugurated in 1936 was the establishment of government-guaranteed prices for oilseeds, cotton, and silk cocoons, but here, too, the foreign economic factor was the principal cause of action. The objective was to increase the domestic production of these commodities in order to reduce (cotton) or completely eliminate (oilseeds, silk) the imports and thus to reduce the requirements for foreign exchange.

Between September 1939, when World War II broke out, and the invasion of Yugoslavia in April 1941, the position of the Yugoslav economy steadily deteriorated. The pressure from the Axis powers, especially Germany, for foods and raw materials greatly increased, while at the same time the power and the willingness of the Axis area to supply vital imports decreased. During 1940 approximately three-fourths of all exports went to the Axis-controlled area and approximately the same share of imports came from that area. The remainder of trade was carried on with Western Europe and the overseas countries. A growing number of articles was subject to government export monopoly. Price controls and rationing of certain foods and other products were introduced and laws against speculation were passed. But inflation continued to advance rapidly, primarily as a result of greatly enlarged

[33] Jozo Tomašević, "The Yugoslav Trade Policy at the Turning Point," *Privreda,* XI, Nos. 7–8, pp. 110–19.

defense expenditures. New government organizations—the Director-
ate for Foreign Trade, the Administration for the Study of Agriculture
and Nutrition, and the Ministry of Supply—were established to deal
with new problems. But the external and internal pressures on the
Yugoslav economy during that period were such that all these measures
were of practically no avail. When the invasion came, the Yugoslav
economy was in a weak and quite disorganized position and with the
war, occupation, and dismemberment of the country it ceased to function as a unit altogether.

GOVERNMENT INTERVENTION ON THE WHEAT MARKET

In the preceding section we discussed the importance of foreign
trade for Yugoslav agriculture during the interwar period, the composition of agricultural exports, and some of the measures undertaken by
the government to further the export of agricultural and livestock products. As long as the export outlets for these products were sufficient and
the relationship between the prices of agricultural and industrial products was favorable for the former—and that was the case throughout
the 1920's—there was no pressure on the government to intervene
directly in the market for agricultural products. But after the precipitous drop in the prices of agricultural and livestock products and the
great reduction in the exports of these products which followed after
the onset of the Great Depression, the Yugoslav government followed
the example of many other countries by intervening on the wheat
market.

Government intenvention on the Yugoslav wheat market began on
the basis of a law of April 15, 1930. This law provided for the establishment of a Chartered Company for the Export of Agricultural Products (later renamed Chartered Company for Export), commonly known
under its initials as PRIZAD, and for a special government credit to
finance the operations of this organization on the cereals market. By
engaging in the export of wheat and corn through PRIZAD, the government intended, first, to circumvent foreign companies which were
exporting cereals from Yugoslavia and tended to retain abroad a large
portion of the foreign exchange proceeds from these exports, and thus
to increase the inflow of foreign exchange. Second, the government
tried through PRIZAD to get into closer contact with the producers of
cereals and to limit, if not fully to exclude, the middlemen's margin,
and thus to increase the revenue of wheat and corn producers. PRIZAD
exported 44 percent of wheat and 52 percent of corn during the 1930/31
crop year, but total exports of both were relatively low. In addition

PRIZAD paid a small subsidy on privately exported cereals during that crop year.

Great changes took place in the objectives and in the methods of operation of PRIZAD during the following decade, but it remained throughout the 1930's the most important factor on the Yugoslav wheat market, and its operations as the executor of the government wheat policy represent the Yugoslav version of the interventionist wheat policy practiced in most wheat-exporting countries during the 1930's.[34]

During the crop year 1930/31 wheat prices in Yugoslavia and abroad continued to fall, and further fall in prices was expected. This fact and the expected bumper wheat crop in 1931 induced the Yugoslav government to overhaul completely its wheat policy in mid-1931. On the basis of a law of June 27, 1931, the government introduced an export monopoly of wheat, rye, and wheat and rye flour and PRIZAD was put in charge of this operation. The main objection of the whole policy was now to maintain the domestic price of wheat at a level completely detached from and considerably above the export parity. The price for the producer was put at 160 dinars per 100 kilograms, loaded on railroad car or barge, with an additional 3 dinars per 100 kilograms for the middleman's margin. This basic minimum price was to be increased as the crop year advanced.

To finance the difference between the minimum guaranteed price and the much lower prices at which wheat was exported, as well as to cover the handling and storage charges, the government put at the disposal of PRIZAD a large initial credit. But the government wanted immediately to open a special source of revenue to finance its wheat policy in a permanent fashion on the principle of self-financing. Thus on July 10, 1931, a law was passed which introduced a domestic wheat trade monopoly and also put this task in the hands of PRIZAD. From then on PRIZAD was buying not only wheat intended for export but also wheat entering commercial channels for home consumption. The idea was to sell wheat at home at such a price that the margin between the buying and the selling price at home would cover the losses connected with the wheat exports. In other words, the losses connected

---

[34] An excellent review of the Yugoslav wheat policies from 1930/31 to 1935/36 is to be found in a study by Vladimir Pertot, "Die Weizenregulierungen in Jugoslawien," *Weltwirtschaftliches Archiv*, XLV, No. 3 (May 1937), 628–59. A running and usually excellent commentary of the Yugoslav wheat policies and the activities of PRIZAD throughout the 1930's by Professor Velimir Bajkić is to be found in the Belgrade weekly economic review, *Narodno blagostánje*. The analysis of the balance sheets and thus of the activities of PRIZAD was given annually in the supplement to *Narodno blagostanje—Analiza bilansa*. For a brief discussion of the Yugoslav wheat policies during the 1930's see Antonin Basch, *The Danube Basin and the German Economic Sphere*, pp. 96–98.

with wheat exports were to be borne by the domestic wheat consumers. The internal wheat trade monopoly covered only wheat going through commercial mills, leaving aside wheat milled in the small custom mills. Thus, in practice, only urban consumers of wheat and those wheat consumers in rural areas who did not produce wheat were supposed to carry the losses connected with the wheat exports. The existence of the domestic wheat trade monopoly and of a fixed wheat price made it necessary to introduce temporarily price control for bread.

Although PRIZAD was the sole exporter and the sole seller of wheat to domestic commercial mills during most of the 1931/32 crop year, it did not develop its own organization for the buying of wheat directly from the wheat producers. It bought wheat of specified quality and at specified points of delivery only in lots of 50 metric tons or more. This last specification made it necessary to buy wheat primarily from the established grain merchants and to a much smaller extent from the agricultural co-operatives. Only very small quantities were bought from the producers directly because only few of them had such quantities to sell. This pattern of sales to PRIZAD prevailed throughout the 1930's, although the share of the co-operatives increased somewhat, as time advanced.[35]

The wheat policy developed in mid-1931 ran into great difficulties from the very beginning. Owing to the record harvest and the high minimum price paid by PRIZAD, the deliveries of wheat immediately after the harvest greatly exceeded both its financial and its storage capacities. Because of the lack of storage facilities at home, a large portion of wheat destined for export had to be stored in Hungary, Austria, and Czechoslovakia, greatly increasing the costs of the whole operation. The internal wheat trade monopoly was characterized from the beginning by corruption, contraband, and unsurmountable difficulties in proper enforcement. The rules regulating that trade were changed several times, and even before the expiration of the 1931/32 crop year the internal wheat trade monopoly was abolished. In order to finance the losses on wheat exports, additional taxes were introduced on flour and bread. Since PRIZAD was paying a very high minimum price and the harvest was large, its funds were exhausted rapidly, and after its first two months of operations it began to pay approximately half of the value of new wheat deliveries in government-guaranteed

[35] During the crop year 1938/39 PRIZAD bought 73 percent of its wheat purchases from the merchants, 21.7 percent from the co-operative organizations, and only 5.3 percent directly from the producers. But part of the quantity bought from the co-operative organizations was actually merchants' wheat because it was sold to the co-operatives not directly by the producers but by grain merchants.

bonds, which immediately and sharply depreciated in price. PRIZAD also obtained credit from Swiss banks, using wheat stored abroad as collateral.

The wheat regime of 1931/32 was a complete failure in every respect. There were many reasons which contributed to that outcome: PRIZAD had a very large export surplus to deal with, it tried to maintain a high differential between the domestic buying price and the world market price at which it was exporting wheat, it had only limited financial means at its disposal and the government was forced to undertake unpopular and difficult financial measures, it had practically no storage facilities, and, finally, only a portion of the Yugoslav wheat consumers were to carry most of the financial burden of the whole operation. The loss sustained by the government during the crop year 1931/32 was 344 million dinars. But in addition to that financial loss, the handling of the wheat regime impaired greatly the confidence of the public in the capacity of the government to operate an intricate scheme of intervention on the market of agricultural products.[36] In later years the government never tried to repeat most of the features of the 1931/32 policy. As was stated earlier, the internal wheat trade monopoly was abolished before the expiration of that crop year, and from the beginning of the 1932/33 crop year the export monopoly for wheat was also abolished. In later years private exporters could engage in wheat export, but only with government permission, and were allowed to export exclusively to those countries with which Yugoslavia did not have wheat export quota agreements at preferential tariff rates.

The chief function of PRIZAD after 1931/32 was to fulfill the export quotas of wheat and other products[37] to those countries which granted preferential treatment to Yugoslav products, especially to Czechoslovakia, Germany, and Austria. Only in periods when the existing exportable surpluses of wheat were just sufficient to meet the preferential quotas was the export monopoly of wheat by PRIZAD re-established for the necessary length of time.

The operations of PRIZAD from the 1932/33 to the 1935/36 crop

---

[36] The inauguration of the wheat subsidization policy had apparently also a political objective, that is, mollifying of the peasantry in the wheat-surplus areas in these early stages of the Great Depression and of securing their support for the royal dictatorship.

[37] In addition to fulfilling the preferential export quotas for wheat, PRIZAD also filled the preferential quotas for corn, dried beans, hides and furs, apples, grapes, oilseeds, wine, and prunes. These quotas were relatively small in comparison with wheat export quotas. It also handled the government export monopoly of raw opium. It did not attempt to maintain prices of any of these products (with the exception of raw opium) as it maintained the price of wheat. Of course, these purchases for export under preferential conditions exerted a favorable influence on the domestic prices of these products.

year were very limited because of the relatively small export surpluses of wheat. In 1936/37 when the Yugoslav wheat crop reached its record size up to that time, Yugoslavia had no difficulties in disposing of the large export surplus because of the short crop in most other wheat-exporting countries and in most European wheat-importing countries. A large portion of all exports went to nonquota countries and the bulk of this export was carried out by various Central European grain firms. PRIZAD's export monopoly was re-established when the exportable surpluses shrank to the approximate amount required to cover the remaining preferential export quotas.

PRIZAD's operations were regulated from year to year either by special regulations issued by the Ministry of Trade and Industry or by special decrees covering the current crop year. There were considerable changes from year to year in its policies, depending on the exportable surpluses, on the conditions in the international wheat market, and on the success of Yugoslav efforts to secure outlets for wheat through bilateral agreements with various European countries.

The chief objective of the government wheat policy was to detach the Yugoslav wheat price from the export parity and to maintain it at a considerably higher level above that parity. In order to do this it endeavored to purchase the bulk of the estimated wheat export surplus within the first two or three months after the harvest at a decreed minimum price in order to remove the pressure of this surplus from the market. The PRIZAD price, which in some crop years changed several times up or down under the influence of changes on the domestic and foreign wheat markets, served as a floor for the domestic wheat price. In some years the domestic price rose above the PRIZAD price, indicating that all export surpluses had been removed and that the wheat price was being formed exclusively under the influence of domestic market factors. The development of the average annual world market parity and the domestic price for wheat in Yugoslavia between 1932/33 and 1937/38 was as follows:

Crop year	Average export parity	Average domestic price	Domestic price above export parity
	(Dinars per 100 kilograms)		*(Percent)*
1932/33............	84.76	182.47	115.3
1933/34............	62.00	114.36	84.4
1934/35............	68.24	132.35	93.9
1935/36............	98.90	152.58	54.3
1936/37............	151.25	160.56	6.1
1937/38............	138.50	190.00	37.2

Source: *Narodno blagostanje*, Belgrade, November 12, 1938, p. 724. Up to 1935/36 the export parity was based on the Rotterdam price and thereafter on the Liverpool price.

The principal question in regard to PRIZAD's operations is how it succeeded in maintaining the domestic wheat price so much above the export parity, thus subsidizing those wheat producers who had surpluses for the market. As already explained, the complicated wheat regime of 1931/32 was a failure and resulted in large losses for the government, which were borne partly by the general taxpayer and partly by a portion of the wheat consumers. Had the subsidization of wheat exports depended principally on funds from government general revenue, it is most probable that it could not have been maintained. Successful PRIZAD operations in the time between 1932/33 and 1935/36 were made possible primarily by the short wheat crops and the absence of sizable wheat export surpluses. A considerable portion of wheat purchases by PRIZAD was turned over to the armed forces to cover their needs. During the 1936/37 bumper crop year the average Yugoslav domestic price was very near the export parity, owing to the special conditions already explained. But there was one specific factor which after 1932/33 facilitated the operations of PRIZAD from a financial point of view. Yugoslavia was successful in concluding a series of agreements with Czechoslovakia, Austria, and especially Germany, which accepted certain quotas of wheat from Yugoslavia under preferential conditions. Thus Austria and Czechoslovakia were buying Yugoslav wheat at the world market price, but restituted a part of their duty on wheat to Yugoslavia. In some years Germany was paying the domestic Yugoslav price for wheat and in addition restituted to Yugoslavia part of the German wheat duty on the agreed quota. Not all of the preferential wheat export quotas could be fully utilized. Some such agreements remained only good intentions. But enough concessions were utilized to provide considerable revenue for PRIZAD. The revenue from the duty restitution was not distributed to the wheat growers but was used by PRIZAD for three main purposes: to finance the losses sustained in the export of wheat, to finance some actions of the government to improve the quality of agricultural products, and particularly to develop the so-called "intervention fund" which was used by PRIZAD to finance its operations on the wheat market. Needless to say, the government put at the disposal of PRIZAD at the beginning of each export season sufficient operating funds. But since the government was fully reimbursed for these funds, PRIZAD actually developed as time went on a system of self-financing of its operations on the wheat market.

PRIZAD operations after 1932/33 were generally considered as successful. Its main objective was to absorb immediately after the harvest the annual export surplus at a price above the export parity.

Once that was achieved, it was possible without much effort or financial means to maintain the domestic price considerably above the export parity by using the PRIZAD price as a floor. Transport costs and the import duty of about 55 dinars per 100 kilograms prevented this higher domestic price from attracting wheat imports. It was also generally agreed that PRIZAD operated in a businesslike manner and that it was free from graft. Considering the fact that a considerable portion of Yugoslav agricultural exports during the 1930's took place under preferential quota agreements, an organization like PRIZAD was indispensable for the proper fulfillment of Yugoslav obligations under these agreements.[38]

The principal beneficiaries of the wheat subsidization program were those peasants who had marketable surpluses of wheat and the grain traders who were buying wheat from the producers for resale to PRIZAD. The latter avoided the risk of large domestic price fluctuations and especially the risk of price and foreign exchange fluctuations in export business. The subsidization of wheat prices helped to maintain at a higher level the income and thus the expenditures of those peasants who had wheat surpluses for the market. But, on the other hand, this policy tended to increase the costs of living of that part of the rural population that had to purchase cereals and of the low-income urban groups who spent a large portion of their income on cereal foods. The wheat subsidization undoubtedly affected the hectarage under wheat during the 1930's, but its effect could hardly be isolated. Without it the wheat hectarage would probably have been reduced during the 1930's instead of remaining relatively stationary. Considering the fact that Yugoslavia's prospects of continuing as an exporter of wheat under free market conditions were poor, the subsidization of wheat was preventing a more rational allocation of land resources and thus in the long run was an unrealistic proposition.

AGRICULTURE AND BUSINESS CYCLES

In order to complete the discussion of the relationship between agriculture and the market, it is necessary also to raise the issue of the development of business cycles in Yugoslavia during the interwar period

---

[38] There were several proposals after 1937 that PRIZAD should accumulate a wheat reserve which could be used in the case of war, but also in time of peace, as a buffer which could release wheat in years of short crops and thus serve as an instrument for stabilizing the domestic wheat price over longer periods of time. Two important factors made the practical implementation of this proposal impossible: lack of funds and lack of wheat storage facilities in the country.

and of the position of agriculture in these cycles. Unfortunately, no systematic investigation of this important problem has ever been undertaken (the publication by Dukanac referred to in footnote 39 is not a study of the business cycles in Yugoslavia, but a valuable collection of time series for such a study). In this section we intend simply to convey some of the available data indicating the course of the business cycles in Yugoslavia in order to show the cyclical framework within which the Yugoslav agriculture operated during the interwar period.[39]

Business cycles in Yugoslavia during the interwar period were caused and controlled by a combination of international and domestic economic factors. The international forces operated through the mechanism of international trade and other factors, causing transfer of funds to and from the Yugoslav economy and inducing income changes within it, as briefly sketched in the section on the export of agricultural products. Among the most important domestic factors were the variations in harvests (which in turn had important influences on the international economic relations of the country), changes in the investment activity financed by domestic capital, changes in government monetary and fiscal policies undertaken independently of foreign factors, and psychological factors of purely domestic origin.

Table 44 shows the principal indicators of cyclical fluctuations in Yugoslavia between 1921 and 1939. On the basis of these data we can tentatively distinguish several cycles during that time.

1. The first cycle covered the period from the end of World War I until 1926. Practically no statistical data are available on the movement of various economic factors until 1923, but this was a period of expansion characterized by postwar inflation, by large investments in

---

[39] The only available and commonly used indexes of wholesale prices and of some financial operations during the interwar period were those published by the National Bank of Yugoslavia, with 1926 as the base year, and available only for years after 1926. The general wholesale price index of the National Bank was based on prices of only 55 products. For years prior to 1926 the price indexes of the Belgrade general trade newspaper *Privredni pregled* were often used (1913 = 100). Shortly before the outbreak of World War II, the National Bank was preparing a revision of its price indexes— among other things, more than doubling the number of commodities included in the general index. Knowing the materials assembled by the National Bank, and using the indexes and price quotations of *Privredni pregled* for years prior to 1926, and a great deal of additional material, Ljubomir S. Dukanac developed and published in 1946 the most complete set of indexes pertaining to the development of the Yugoslav economy during the interwar period (again using 1926 as the base year), and we use his indexes most of the time. Ljubomir S. Dukanac, *Yugoslav Business Cycles (Index Numbers) 1919–1941*. Two remarks are necessary, however: first, Dukanac's series are annual series, and without quarterly and/or monthly figures no detailed analysis of the business cycles is possible; and second, his figures, as most of the Yugoslav statistical figures, have to be considered with caution.

TABLE 44.—PRINCIPAL INDICATORS OF BUSINESS CYCLES IN YUGOSLAVIA, 1921–39

(1926 = 100)

Year	Wholesale price indexes[a]				Production indexes		Financial indexes			Foreign trade indexes	
	General	Crop products	Livestock products	Industrial products	Grain production[b]	Insured workers[c]	Banknote circulation[d]	Private bank loans[d]	Government expenditures[e]	Export value[d]	Import value[d]
1921	...	...	...	...	63.9	...	80.7	42.4	...	31.5	54.0
1922	...	...	...	...	65.7	...	86.7	64.2	...	47.2	84.4
1923	143.2	153.0	143.7	135.5	73.2	92.7	99.6	71.5	...	103.0	108.9
1924	135.8	146.5	142.8	125.5	97.1	95.0	103.3	83.5	90.8	122.0	107.7
1925	115.3	123.6	113.9	110.1	109.3	99.1	104.3	98.8	102.2	113.9	114.7
1926	100.0	100.0	100.0	100.0	100.0	100.0	100.0	100.0	100.0	100.0	100.0
1927	105.5	118.4	105.2	102.4	71.1	107.4	98.8	100.5	99.4	81.9	95.5
1928	113.3	141.6	105.9	102.4	88.8	119.2	95.1	114.5	104.0	82.4	102.7
1929	101.8	110.2	105.4	93.2	122.5	128.6	100.1	116.7	118.3	101.3	99.5
1930	83.7	72.5	91.3	84.8	104.1	134.9	92.9	128.3	118.5	86.7	91.2
1931	78.1	71.4	73.6	87.9	107.0	128.3	89.0	111.9	118.3	61.4	62.9
1932	70.2	63.5	60.0	81.4	113.3	113.2	82.1	94.7	92.4	39.1	37.5
1933	66.9	53.7	57.4	81.3	115.9	109.8	74.5	77.3	88.5	43.2	37.8
1934	63.3	51.6	55.8	73.5	126.6	114.5	75.4	75.8	86.1	49.6	46.8
1935	66.7	62.9	55.6	75.8	93.5	118.9	84.1	71.4	90.3	51.6	48.5
1936	66.8	60.9	60.0	75.5	143.9	129.8	93.1	72.7	99.6	56.0	53.4
1937	72.7	65.8	60.6	83.9	136.2	143.3	100.4	67.3	105.4	80.2	68.6
1938	76.6	79.0	62.5	83.1	139.3	150.7	119.1	60.3	...	64.6	65.2
1939	79.0	76.2	68.4	84.2	...	151.9	166.9	...	...	70.6	62.3

[a] Price indexes from Ljubomir S. Dukanac, *Yugoslav Business Cycles (Index Numbers) 1919–1941*, Belgrade, 1946, p. 12.

[b] Based on Table 32, p. 476. For changes in the production of various grains see Table 32. Another indicator of production in agricultural economy is the index of livestock herds (in terms of cattle). This index (1926 = 100) fell sharply from 1921 to 1924, changed very little from 1925 to 1929, and rose slowly but steadily from 1930 to 1938. For changes in the numbers of various types of livestock see Table 35, p. 516.

[c] From Ljubomir S. Dukanac, *op. cit.*, p. 27. The index of insured workers is taken as an indicator of the activity of the urban economy. The figures on which this index is based do not include railroad employees and miners who had their separate insurance plans. They include, however, besides industrial workers (about 68 percent of the total), also employees of municipalities, tradeand banking, and house servants.

[d] Ljubomir S. Dukanac, *op. cit.*, pp. 51, 61, and 63.

[e] Based on figures given in Yugoslavia, Ministry of Finance, *Ministarstvo Finansija Kraljevine Jugoslavije, 1918–1938* (Ministry of Finance of the Kingdom of Yugoslavia, 1918–1938) (Belgrade, 1939), pp. 28–32. Comparable data for years prior to 1924 are not available. The figures refer to fiscal years 1924/25 to 1937/38 (April 1 to March 31). The original figures include not only expenditures foreseen in budget estimates, but also expenditures made through the Account of Working Capital of the Central State Treasury (for more information about this account see below, p. 693).

industry,[40] transportation, agriculture, and residential and other construction.[41] This large investment was undertaken partly in order to make
up for the damages and lack of replacements during the war years and
partly to take advantage of the rising prices. From the monetary point
of view the following were the chief marks of this period: inflationary
policy of the government because insufficient tax revenue forced it to
banknote printing to cover a part of its expenditures, the expansion of
bank loans and loans by other sources (usurers, country storekeepers),
great inflow of emigrants' remittances, and some inflow of foreign
capital in the form of public loans. The price level rose markedly, but
did not reach hyperinflationary proportions as in many neighboring
countries. The international value of the Yugoslav currency kept falling until 1923. Foreign trade in this period was marked by large import
surpluses, but exports were growing rapidly. The gap in the balance of
payments was filled by emigrants' remittances, reparations receipts, and
some import of foreign capital.

[40] A good indication of the growth of industrial activity in Yugoslavia during the
interwar period is supplied in the following tabulation of indexes of the number of
existing factories, the number of working places, the capacity of installed machinery in
terms of horsepower, and the value of investment in the processing industries in selected
years (1918 = 100). Unfortunately, these data are not available on an annual basis.
They also do not include such important segments of the Yugoslav industrial activity
as extractive industries and the construction industry. The index of value of investment
represents the value of real estate and installed machinery of industrial enterprises.

Year	Number of factories	Number of working places	Installed machinery (*horsepower*)	Value of investment
1918..............	100.0	100.0	100.0	100.0
1923..............	135.1	137.9	119.3	125.5
1928..............	163.7	159.2	126.5	135.9
1933..............	191.7	176.9	147.5	149.5
1938..............	213.1	188.6	151.7	154.9

Source: Based on Stevan M. Kukoleča, *Industrija Jugoslavije, 1918–1938* (The Industry of Yugoslavia, 1918–1938) (Belgrade, 1941), pp. 73–233.

Data in this tabulation indicate that the rate of industrial growth was higher during the first five-year period after World War I than in any of the succeeding three
periods. These data also show that after 1918 the newly established factories were
smaller in size than those existing in that year and also that the relative capital intensity
per worker decreased during the interwar period. This last development was obviously
related to the low cost of labor and high cost of capital in the country.

[41] In the Yugoslav investment and employment picture in the urban economy
during the interwar period a basic role was played by the construction industry. The
most important segment in that activity was undoubtedly the construction of private
urban residential housing and business buildings. Very large also was the investment
of the central government and local governments in highways, office buildings, and
public buildings for other purposes. We have stated earlier that the rapid growth of
population necessitated also considerable investment in housing in rural areas. Un-

The position of agriculture in this period was rapidly recovering from the effects of the war. The area under crops, especially that under cereals, was increasing and the production of crops was growing. Prices of crop and livestock products were rising. Demand for these products for export was very favorable and so was the domestic demand. The terms of trade between agricultural and industrial products favored agriculture.

In regard to prices the downturn occurred in the latter part of 1923 and their downward movement lasted until 1926, but the movement of other factors in the country's economy, as indicated in Table 44, continued to rise, although at greatly reduced rates. The developments during the period 1924–26 are rather mixed. While this period is generally referred to as the period of deflation, and the sharp and general decline in prices clearly indicates a deflationary process, the banknote circulation actually rose somewhat in 1924 and 1925 and fell only slightly in 1926, and the amount of bank loans, as shown in Table 44, kept growing without interruption. As far as the banknote circulation was concerned, the rate of its growth was greatly reduced during these years, and the rise in bank loans was most probably simply an accounting phenomenon. In a country where at that time industrial enterprises financed by domestic banks paid between 20 and 30 percent interest, nonpayment of interest for one or two years greatly increased the debts to the banks. There was most probably also some hoarding of income

fortunately no data are available on the extent of private investment in construction activity. But data on the outlay of the central government on construction are available and so are the data on the housing construction in the seventeen principal cities of Yugoslavia in 1938, and these allow us to form an impression of the order of magnitude of investment in construction activity. Thus in 1938 the central government spent an amount of 572 million dinars on construction, of which 58 percent was for the repair and construction of roads, 14 percent for buildings, and 28 percent for other purposes. In the same year the estimated value of housing construction in the seventeen principal cities of Yugoslavia amounted to 1,018 million dinars, of which 667.4 million dinars were in the two main cities, Belgrade and Zagreb. In the same year private investment in the real estate and machinery of new factories in processing industries was only 41.6 million dinars. The average spending by the central government for construction purposes (without railroads) between 1929 and 1938 averaged 457.4 million dinars, while investment in processing industries during the same period averaged 143.6 million dinars. The investment in processing industries in 1929 was 338.3 million dinars and in 1930 it amounted to 409.6 million dinars, because in these years some important plants, including the huge shoe factory of the Bata concern, were built. Investment in processing industries between 1931 and 1938 averaged 86.1 million dinars (all current dinars). Stevan M. Kukoleča, *op. cit.*, pp. 182–92. As will be shown later, housing construction in urban areas enjoyed concessions in tax and interest rates, but there were also other factors which favored heavy investment in that field. We guess that perhaps between 50 and 60 percent of the current capital formation in Yugoslavia during the interwar period was invested in housing construction (see p. 687).

because both the internal and the external values of the dinar were rising. Moreover, effective demand, in spite of record exports, was unable to absorb the greatly increased agricultural production (see Table 32, p. 476) at earlier prices. A considerable number of failures among banks and industrial and commercial enterprises suggests also that considerable malinvestments occurred in the period of inflation, for whose products and services there was now no sufficient demand.

Agricultural production rose sharply in 1924 and 1925 and was high also in 1926, which explains partly the decline in agricultural prices. But the interesting point is that the employment in urban economy, as indicated by the index of insured workers, rose between 1924 and 1926 in spite of declining industrial prices. The rise proceeded, however, at a low rate. Owing in large part to the big harvests of 1924, 1925, and 1926, exports and export surpluses reached in the first two years a level never equaled during the remaining years of the interwar period. Emigrants' remittances reached their maximum in 1924 and receipts from reparations were large. In spite of the severe drop in agricultural prices, the position of agriculture in these years was quite satisfactory because grain production was very high, exports were large, and the terms of trade favored agricultural products.

Considering the development of most economic factors, the years 1924–26 appear as a period of adjustment following upon the years of postwar inflation and not as a period of depression, although the price decline was severe and there was a considerable number of failures in banking, industry, and trade.

2. What appears to be the second cycle lasted from 1927 to 1934. But during the upward phase of this cycle, until 1929, and during 1930 when the downward movement gathered force, there prevailed a definite lack of homogeneity in the movement of various economic factors. The upward movement was most pronounced in prices of crop products, largely because of poor grain harvests of 1927 and 1928 (especially strong was the rise in the price of corn which affected the whole index). In 1929, partly owing to large wheat and corn crops, there occurred a precipitous fall in agricultural prices. In contrast, livestock prices remained almost stable throughout the period 1927–29. The prices of industrial products rose slightly in 1927 and 1928 and fell in 1929.

In spite of the fact that the banknote circulation fell in 1927 and 1928 and rose only slightly in 1929, this period showed a genuine expansion of bank loans and other credit. And the rise of government expenditures, which basically influenced the volume of income in the urban economy, was large. One of the important marks of this period was a great rise in savings deposits with commercial and savings banks and a substantial decline in the interest rates. Moreover, this was the period of the greatest inflow of foreign capital, which controlled the overwhelming portion of the Yugoslav extractive industries and industries requiring large capital outlays, as well as a large portion of consumers goods industries such as textiles and footwear.[42] All of these factors influenced favorably industrial investment activity and employment as reflected in the rising number of insured workers.

The value of exports fell much during 1927 and 1928, primarily owing to the low exports of wheat and corn, but wheat exports in 1929 were at their maximum and corn exports were also large. In 1929 there was a general increase in exports of most other commodities. Large inflow of foreign capital and emigrants' remittances during 1927 and 1928 neutralized the deflationary influence of lowered exports.

The important point with regard to agriculture which has to be stressed is that by 1929 a condition of general overproduction of practically all staples had appeared in almost all exporting countries. Furthermore, in importing countries economic nationalism as applied to agriculture became more widespread. Agriculture entered into a profound depression on a world-wide basis.

In certain aspects, as for example in regard to price movements, the downward turn had already started during 1929, but the movement of some other important economic factors was still in an upward direction. Thus the index of insured workers and the index of bank loans continued to rise during 1930, and the level of government expenditures remained unchanged between 1929 and 1931, although during 1930 and 1931 part of government expenditures was covered by deficit financing. Closely related to the price decline both as cause and effect was a considerable drop in the value of exports during 1930. A further basic development which occurred during 1930 was the weakening of the international position of the Yugoslav economy, shown primarily in the reduction of gold and foreign exchange reserves of the National Bank (see p. 668). This was the combined result of a sizable import surplus in 1930, somewhat reduced emigrants' remittances, complete cessation of import of foreign capital, withdrawal of foreign credits, and some flight of domestic capital. Thus, as far as agriculture and the foreign economic factors were concerned—and both of them were of primary importance for the development of the Yugoslav business cycles —the downward process was in full swing during 1930. To the de-

---

[42] Jozo Tomasevich, "Foreign Economic Relations, 1918–1941," pp. 186–95.

flationary pressures from these quarters were soon added many others.

A series of developments in Central and Western Europe in the spring and summer of 1931 (the crash of the Vienna Creditanstalt, the Hoover moratorium for German reparations, the German banking crisis, and the abandonment of the gold standard by Great Britain), which showed that all of the European economy was engulfed by the depression, helped to complete the process of business demoralization and financial disorganization in Yugoslavia by leading to a prolonged run on the banks and a complete breakdown of the banking system. The growing disequilibruim in the balance of payments, which was only partially alleviated by the stabilization loan of 1931, soon led to the depreciation of the currency and severe foreign exchange controls. The whole of the Yugoslav economy entered in the second half of 1931 into a profound depression.

With the exception of grain production, which kept rising throughout the 1930's, all economic factors, as indicated in Table 44, showed a downward movement. The severity of the Great Depression in Yugoslavia was especially indicated by the great fall in prices and foreign trade, and in the complete breakdown of private banking. The downward movement, as shown by various indicators, continued in some cases until 1933 (insured workers), or more commonly until 1934 when the depression in Yugoslavia reached its bottom.

The position of agriculture during the Great Depression was undoubtedly much more difficult than that of the urban economy. This is well indicated by the much greater fall in agricultural than in industrial prices and by the unfavorable relationship in terms of trade between agricultural and livestock products, on the one hand, and industrial products, on the other. Owing to the fall in agricultural prices and reduced sales of agricultural products abroad and perhaps also at home (especially as far as sales of agricultural products to peasants themselves was concerned), and owing to reduced earnings of the agricultural population in the urban economy and the greatly reduced emigrants' remittances, the spending by the rural population was correspondingly reduced. This spending was further curtailed after the declaration of the moratorium for peasant debts in April 1932 (pp. 667–75), because thereafter the peasants could not obtain any credit whatsoever. While there are no data on the consumption of textiles, which would be the best indicator of the consumption of industrial products by the peasant population, the consumption of kerosene, tobacco, matches, and cigarette paper, perhaps half of which was accounted for by the peasant population, showed a large decrease. Thus between the fiscal years

1929/30 and 1933/34, although the population rose in the meanwhile by about 7 percent, the consumption of kerosene fell by 24.4 percent, matches by 32.6, tobacco by 28.0, and cigarette paper by 58.6 percent.[43] Undoubtedly the consumption of these items fell more severely in the rural than in the urban areas, because income in rural areas fell relatively much more than income in urban areas. The extraordinary decrease in the investment activity in agriculture is well indicated by the fall of imports of agricultural machinery, tools, and implements, and the use of artificial fertilizers, as shown in Tables 29 and 30 (pp. 441 and 447). Actually, a widespread process of disinvestment took place in agriculture in these years by failing to provide for the necessary replacements of used capital resources.

The contraction of income in urban areas was much smaller than in rural areas. This is well indicated by the relatively small drop in the number of insured workers and in the index of government expenditures. This meant that the urban economy was producing primarily for its own needs. Moreover, since the agricultural population paid much more in taxes than it received in benefits from the government, it subsidized the relatively higher level of employment and income in urban economy. Actually it was doing this throughout the interwar period. The real wage in urban areas increased considerably in comparison with the pre-1929 years (see p. 561).

3. The third cycle began in 1935. Its expansion phase was later fused with the inflationary period shortly preceding and following the outbreak of World War II.[44] The upward turn in 1935 and the extent of general economic recovery in the following years are shown by practically all indicators: the price level, insured workers, government expenditures, banknote circulation, and the rise of foreign trade.

From the monetary point of view the most important factors were the expansion of banknote circulation, the great rise in the loans by the government-owned banks (pp. 678–79), and the rise in government expenditures. The latter was necessary partly for the financing of increased military expenditures and partly for the financing of govern-

---

[43] Yugoslavia, Ministry of Finance, *Ministarstvo Finansija Kraljevine Jugoslavije, 1918–1938* (Ministry of Finance of the Kingdom of Yugoslavia, 1918–1938), pp. 195–202. All of these products were sold as government monopoly articles and that is the reason that data are available on their consumption. Of course no data are available on the amount of these products sold in contraband, which in the case of tobacco and especially cigarette paper was considerable and tended to be larger during the depression years.

[44] For the influence of war on the Yugoslav economy from September 1939 to October 1940 see Mirko Lamer, "Kriegswirtschaftliche Einflüsse in Jugoslawien," *Weltwirtschaftliches Archiv*, LIII (January 1941), No. 1, 112–38.

ment industrial investments and public works. The volume of loans granted by private banks kept going downward, however, because private banking never recuperated from the disastrous breakdown during the Great Depression. The peasants remained incapable of obtaining credit because the moratorium for old debts continued in effect.

The rise in the index of insured workers testifies to the great increase in the activity of the urban economy after 1935. Several important agricultural industries continued, however, to utilize only a portion of their capacity (see p. 613). In certain fields, as, for example, in the mining of nonferrous ores and their smelting, foreign capital was the principal factor responsible for growth, but this expansion was fostered also by government policies. The construction activity financed by the government increased during these years partly as a result of public works. Investment in new factories in processing industries (footnote 40, p. 638) continued to be low, but the utilization of the existing capacities in the processing industries (with the exception of agricultural industries) most probably increased considerably during the second half of the 1930's. As was indicated earlier (footnote 41, p. 638) private investment in urban housing was very high in these years.

The rise in the exports of agricultural products was undoubtedly one of the principal causes of the rise of their prices and, together with the very large grain crops during the period 1936–38, contributed to the rise of agricultural income. Increased industrial activity at home contributed also to a rise in the demand for agricultural products, and vice versa. Data in Tables 29 and 30 (pp. 441 and 447), indicate that there was also some increase in the investment activity in agriculture, but as yet definitely not enough even to balance the lack of replacements in earlier years. The increase in livestock herds, especially of pigs and cattle (Table 35, p. 516), was another form of increased investments in agriculture.

This is a rough and tentative picture of the development of business cycles in Yugoslavia during the interwar period and of the specific position of agriculture in these fluctuations. But, even so, the discussion showed the great variety and complexity of forces of both foreign and domestic character, including the great variations in the harvests, which caused and affected these fluctuations. A full elaboration of the problem of business cycles in Yugoslavia during the interwar period would require much work. Owing to the lack of sufficient and good data, satisfactory completion of this task may prove altogether impossible. But this rough picture suffices for our purposes. In conclusion it should be stressed that the structural situation of the Yugoslav economy during the interwar period, characterized as it was by backward and costly agricultural production, growing agricultural overpopulation, dearth of capital, and a difficult international position, was an unenviable one and that under such conditions profound and long depressions were even more deeply felt than in other countries which were free of such structural impediments. Needless to say, a country that is so much affected by its international economic relations, but because of its small size and low economic capacity cannot influence these relations in a positive manner, is incapable of conducting independent countercyclical policies.

CHAPTER 27

AGRICULTURAL CREDIT

ONE of the essential aspects in which agriculture is connected with the market and with the other parts of national economy is through credit operations. Yugoslav agriculture's demand for credit during the inter-war period far exceeded its ability to make savings deposits with the private and government banks and co-operative organizations even in years of most favorable economic conditions. The problem of agricultural credit was never solved in Yugoslavia as a whole. It was only in Slovenia that the agricultural credit system was satisfactorily organized and functioned efficiently. The reason is simple. The structural dearth of capital which was characteristic of the Yugoslav economy and the resulting high rates of interest led the capital flow into channels of high and secure profits and of relatively satisfactory liquidity. These were the fields of trade, various branches of highly protected mass consumer-goods industries such as textiles, shoes, various metal products, and, above all, real estate investment in urban areas which, in addition, enjoyed substantial tax subsidies. Thus little capital was left to be put at the disposal of agriculture. As was explained earlier, a considerable share of wealth that was formed by doing business with and by granting loans to agriculture was constantly pulled out of rural areas and invested in the urban economy.

ORGANIZATION OF AGRICULTURAL CREDIT BEFORE WORLD WAR I

As interwar Yugoslavia was composed of former states and provinces of varied economic structure and of varied political and socio-economic background, the organization and patterns of agricultural credit in the years before World War I differed very much from area to area. These differences related to the organization of agricultural credit, its sources, the role of the state in providing agricultural credit or in controlling the conditions under which it was given, limitations imposed upon the peasants to use agricultural credit, interest rates, and political factors in agricultural credit.[1]

---

[1] For a review of the development and organization of agricultural credit by provinces prior to World War I, see Momir Glomazić, *Istorija Državne hipotekarne banke, 1862–1932* (History of the State Mortgage Bank, 1862–1932), pp. 21–108; Milan J. Komadinić,

The problem of peasant credit, and especially of usury, was for a long time one of the important economic and political questions in the South Slav lands, and as such it was an issue of party politics. But in no other area was agricultural credit so much abused politically and at the same time less satisfactorily solved from an economic point of view than in Serbia. The problems of peasant credit and usury were economic and political issues in Serbia since the early 1830's. To protect the peasantry to a certain extent against the dangers involved in using credit, the institution of a protected minimum homestead was introduced in 1836. After a lapse in the 1840's and the 1850's, it was revived in 1860 and greatly enlarged in 1873 by the enactment of the famous Section 4(a) of Article 471 of the Civil Procedure Act. The Serbian government had already begun in 1836 to use trust funds administered by the state to grant loans to the peasants. That scheme was enlarged in 1839 on the basis of a special law, and this practice continued during the 1840's and 1850's. It was finally stopped in 1860 because of many abuses. The minimum sum for loans under the scheme of 1839 was 300 ducats. Together with innumerable formalities connected with the obtaining of loans, this excluded all but the wealthiest and the craftiest among the peasants from using that credit source. The bulk of these funds was actually taken by wealthy peasants, merchants, and high government officials and was used primarily for making further loans at usurious rates of interest and not for purposes of advancing agricultural production.

The second measure of the Serbian government for the use of state funds in the field of agricultural credit was the establishment of the Funds Management Administration (Uprava fondova) in 1862. Instead of medium and small peasants, the chief beneficiaries of credit through this organization were again wealthy peasants, merchants, politicians, and government officials, and again a large portion of these funds was not used for production purposes but rather for further loaning at usurious rates. These practices continued after the so-called district savings banks began to be established after 1871 as branches of the Funds Management Administration. Later the Administration became the central agency in Serbia for urban real estate credit, and one of the chief creditors of the central government, local government bodies, and government enterprises. This was also its main function during the interwar period.

Problem seljačkih dugova (The Problem of Peasant Debts), pp. 5–20. For the role of agricultural credit co-operatives in this regard, see Ivan M. Varga, "Our Co-operativism," in *Jubilarni zbornik života i rada Srba, Hrvata i Slovenaca, 1918–1928* (Jubilee Record of Life and Work of the Serbs, Croats, and Slovenes, 1918–1928), I, 262–98.

There was another institution that was organized in Serbia with the primary intention of serving as a protection for the peasants in years of poor crops, by granting them grain loans. This was the institution of communal granaries. According to a Decree of 1839, every tax head in rural areas was required to deposit in the communal granary (*opštinski koš*) about 70 kilograms of grain. In case of need each depositor, and under certain circumstances also other people, could obtain loans from these granaries in kind and sometimes even in money. This institution was abolished in 1842 because of irregularities in administration, but re-established in 1854, and fully reorganized on the basis of a law of 1889. This law was still on the statute books during the interwar period but it was not enforced.[2]

Government actions in organizing and financing agricultural credit were insufficient to satisfy the need for credit in the rural areas of Serbia. The cry of practically an entire nation to clear up peasant debts and to control and suppress the usurers arose periodically, the periods coinciding with economic depressions induced from abroad or caused by failure of crops, such as, for example, in 1836, 1856, 1859, and 1873, when the burden of debts was felt more heavily than otherwise and when the interest rates tended to reach their peaks. But this was in vain, because the wealthier people and those who profited from usury controlled or were the political pillars of those who controlled the state.

The activity of agricultural credit co-operatives in Serbia, which began to be established in 1894, was not a very important factor in providing credit for the village. Moreover, the co-operative movement in Serbia was always a target even of groups who should have been among its main supporters, such as rural priests, and political parties which professed to be peasant parties.[3]

Thus the chief source of peasant credit in Serbia prior to 1914 was the individual country lenders, country storekeepers, tavernkeepers, and country banks. There was, however, one very interesting organizational change which took place in Serbia toward the close of the nineteenth century. Since "usurers" (*zelenaši, lihvari*) were in disrepute and were constantly a political target, many usurers and merchants organized small country banks and thus hid behind a respectable

[2] B. D. Milošević, "The Production and Consumption of Bread Grains in Our Kingdom," Kingdom of the Serbs, Croats, and Slovenes, Ministry of Agriculture and Water Resources, *Glasnik*, Belgrade, VI (April–June, 1928), 140–41.

[3] Milan J. Komadinić, *Skice i ogledi za jednu istoriju zadrugarstva u Srbiji* (Sketches and Examples for a History of Co-operativism in Serbia), pp. 27–37.

façade. But that had little effect on the interest rates they charged. The politicians of Serbia also established banks to promote their personal and political ambitions, because it was felt, as pointed out earlier, that "the peasant in debt is the safest voter."

Agricultural credit organization in Yugoslav Macedonia prior to its liberation and incorporation into Serbia in 1913 was a part of the Ottoman organization for agricultural credit. The main institutional source of this credit was the Agricultural Bank in Istanbul, which was established in 1903. It had one regional branch and about 20 agencies in the territory now belonging to Yugoslavia. It may be mentioned that prior to the establishment of the Ottoman Agricultural Bank in 1903, in most parts of the Ottoman Empire there existed a half-businesslike half-charity type of organization in rural areas which granted small loans at low rates of interest to peasants in need, especially in years of bad crops, on the basis of simple promisory notes. These organizations, called the *menafi sanduks*, were financed by special government surtaxes. But in Macedonia, too, the chief source of credit to the peasants was the usurers.

In Montenegro a special State Mortgage Bank on the model of the Serbian Funds Management Administration was established with government funds in 1911. Its purpose was to supply mortgage credit both for agriculture and for urban real estate, and especially to help the peasants already indebted at usurious interest rates to repay their old debts with funds obtained from the Bank at reasonable interest. The Montenegrin State Mortgage Bank developed soon, as did its Serbian counterpart, into an organization primarily for granting mortgage credit to urban real estate. Both before 1914 and during the interwar period, usury was as rampant in Montenegro as in Serbia, and the chief source of credit to the peasants was individual moneylenders and country storekeepers.

In Dalmatia a special Mortgage Administration was established by the provincial government in 1898. It granted long-term loans, at 5½ percent interest, both to agriculture and to the urban real estate owners. Its funds came from issuing mortgage bonds and selling them through banks in Vienna and Trieste on the basis of special agreements. Some private banks and some agricultural credit co-operatives were organized, but here, too, individual moneylenders and country storekeepers were the most important sources of credit for the peasants. The bulk of the heavy indebtedness in the Dalmatian village prior to 1914 was incurred for purely consumption purposes and for the purchase of ship tickets by emigrants going overseas.

In Bosnia and Herzegovina the Turks began in 1867 to establish the *menafi sanduks* which made small loans to needy peasants without great formalities and at reasonable interest rates. Their funds were provided by a special surtax on the basic government tax, the tenth. These organizations granted most of their small loans in winter and spring for the buying of food and feed, and they were repaid after the harvest. After the Austro-Hungarian occupation of 1878 these institutions were preserved, but they were somewhat reorganized in 1886 and renamed "county assistance endowments." They continued in operation until the end of the interwar period. To grant somewhat larger loans for the purchase of quality seed, livestock, and agricultural machinery, the government began to establish government-supported "county agricultural co-operatives." Most writers appraised favorably the activity of these organizations. The organization of banks for long-term agricultural mortgage credit began in 1889 at the initiative of the Austrian and Hungarian banks. In the beginning they made only mortgage loans to free peasants. The attempts of several banks, all of them established and owned by Vienna and Budapest banks and enjoying many special privileges, to finance long-term agricultural credit by issuing mortgage bonds proved unsuccessful. The private banks and various groups of free co-operatives that were established in Bosnia and Herzegovina prior to 1914 could fill only a part of the need for credit in the village. Here too, therefore, a large portion of the demand for credit in rural areas was met by private lenders and country storekeepers.

Agricultural credit in the other South Slav provinces that until 1918 formed parts of the Austro-Hungarian Monarchy, that is, in Croatia-Slavonia, Vojvodina, and Slovenia, as far as it was supplied by banking organizations, was supplied by two sources: first, directly by banks in Vienna and Budapest, and second, by local banks whether they were established by local capitalists or simply creations of Vienna and Budapest banks. Most mortgage bonds issued for the financing of mortgage credit in Austria-Hungary prior to 1914, and most of the shares of stock of many banks engaged in mortgage credit, were sold in France and other Western European countries. One of the basic reasons that effective demand for mortgage credit existed and that mortgage credit could be obtained at satisfactory rates of interest in the territory of the Austro-Hungarian Monarchy was the existence of many large estates and large peasant farms. Such farm units also existed in Croatia-Slavonia, Slovenia, and especially in Vojvodina.

In Croatia-Slavonia the oldest (established in 1846), and during the 1920's the most powerful, bank of domestic capital, the First Croatian Savings Bank, was one of the two important banks supplying agricultural and urban real estate mortgage credit in Croatia prior to 1914. It began these operations in 1903 and financed them by issuing mortgage bonds. More important in terms of business was the Croato-Slavonian Mortgage Bank which was established in 1892 by Vienna and Budapest banks. Beginning with 1904, this bank started to give special long-term loans for purposes of subdivision of large estates and for land reclamation work.

In pre-1914 Croatia-Slavonia there were three important co-operative systems engaged in granting loans to the village. First, there was a system of agricultural credit co-operatives with its center in Budapest, which was nothing but a part of the Hungarian state-wide agricultural credit co-operatives system. It was established on the basis of a law of 1898. This was a powerful co-operative organization enjoying not only many privileges from the state but also large financial subsidies. In the early 1900's there were already more than 200 such co-operatives in Croatia-Slavonia. Here, however, these co-operatives had two political objectives among their aims: financial support of the Magyar element which was already settled or was in process of settling in Croatia-Slavonia, and second, to bring the Croatian peasantry into a greater political and economic dependence on Hungarian economic institutions and thereby also on pro-Hungarian political parties. It was, therefore, quite understandable that Croatian nationalist politicians would launch as early as 1901 a separate, Croatian system of agricultural credit co-operatives, whose economic aim was to help the village with credit and to foster thrift among the peasants, but whose political task was to counteract the activity of the Hungarian-sponsored and financed credit co-operatives. The Croatian co-operatives also had their special central financial and auditing organization, the Croatian Agricultural Bank. This bank engaged in most other regular banking operations, including the financing of the subdivision and colonization of large estates. This system comprised 238 co-operatives in 1910. Finally, the Serbian population in Croatia-Slavonia had its own system of agricultural credit co-operatives, which by 1914 was well launched. Its financial center was the Serbian Bank in Zagreb, which was the foremost banking corporation owned by the Serbs of Croatia-Slavonia.

As in most other areas already mentioned, banks and co-operatives could satisfy the demand for only a part of the credit needed in the village, so that in Croatia-Slavonia too the individual moneylenders and the country storekeepers had a wide scope for their activity. It must be remembered, though, that the interest rates in Croatia-Slavonia prior to 1914 on all types of loans to agriculture, including those by the latter group, were much below the rates in Serbia and other already mentioned areas. It was rare to pay more than 12 to 14 percent interest even on credit from individual lenders and rural storekeepers. One factor that was partly responsible for lower interest rates was that during the two decades prior to World War I the bill of exchange found wide application as a credit instrument in the village of Croatia-Slavonia, but its strictness was not at all pleasing to the peasants and gave reason for much complaining.

There is little specific to say about agricultural credit organization in Vojvodina prior to 1914. Vojvodina was an integral part of Hungary up to 1918. Long-term mortgage loans in this area, especially to the large estates, were made available to some extent by the Austro-Hungarian Bank, but mostly by a number of Budapest banks specializing in mortgage credit operations. Loans to peasants were granted by commercial and savings banks, and after 1898 by the already mentioned Hungarian system of agricultural credit co-operatives. Some savings banks and credit co-operatives were formed by the Serbs of Vojvodina but they were not of any particular consequence. There were no credit or other co-operatives among the German minority in the Vojvodina territory prior to 1914.

The development of agricultural credit in what became the province of Slovenia after 1918 was greatly influenced by political factors. Up to the middle of the nineteenth century, the Germans as the middle class and the ruling nation in the Slovene areas were in full control politically and economically. Banks and savings banks were first established by the Germans in this area and these institutions promoted primarily German interests. The national awakening of the Slovenes led inevitably to attempts to advance in the economic and financial fields and to shake off the economic tutelage of the local Germans. The first Slovene organization in the spirit of economic emancipation was established in 1855. In 1883 the first federation of Slovene co-operatives was formed. Up to 1895 the activity of the co-operative societies was concentrated in urban areas. From 1895, when a second co-operative federation was established as the economic arm of the Slovene People's party, the activity of the co-operatives shifted to rural areas. This second system of co-operatives had full support of the Catholic priests in rural areas, and the co-operatives were instrumental in acquiring and maintaining an almost complete control of the Slovene People's party over the Slovene village until the end of the interwar period. Finally, the liberal political forces in the Slovene lands established their own co-operative federation in 1907, because co-operative organizations in both urban and rural areas were used as tools of political struggle. All these federations included not only credit co-operatives, but also production and marketing co-operatives, though the first type was the most numerous.

In addition to credit co-operatives that supplied a large portion of credit needs of the Slovene village, there was also a well-developed system of savings banks that was active in that field. Commercial banks, though there were only a few of them in Slovenia prior to 1918 except as branches of Vienna banks, also engaged in financing agriculture. Finally, there was in Carniola a special Mortgage Administration which in its structure and operations was similar to the already mentioned provincial mortgage credit institution in Dalmatia. While in Slovenia prior to 1914 the issue of agricultural credit was quite satisfactorily solved through the organization of agricultural credit co-operatives, there was still enough room left for the activity of the individual moneylenders and country storekeepers as creditors of agriculture.

This brief review of the agricultural credit organization in South Slav lands prior to 1914 has shown the great differences from an organizational point of view, the various political forces interested in agricultural credit, and the variety of sources of credit for agriculture and the conditions under which this credit was obtained. In this, as in most other economic aspects, the interwar period brought about many changes.

USES OF CREDIT AND THE INTEREST RATES

As explained earlier, the peasants in the South Slav provinces have been forced to use credit since the days when peasant agriculture began to be more intensively integrated with the market and money economy. The more the market economy advanced in these areas, the greater became the need for credit. In principle two broad categories of agricultural credit can be distinguished: credit for production purposes and credit for consumption purposes. There are a great number of factors which contribute to the need of the agricultural household for a specific type of credit, ranging from the wish to make the agricultural enterprise economically more efficient to the dire need for credit to enable the farm family to acquire seed for planting its crops or food to feed its members until the new harvest.

All typical production credit in agriculture, such as credit for buying of land and its long-range improvements, and the credit for the payment of shares in the farm to outgoing family members, credit to buy machinery, implements, and livestock, and credit for the construction of farm buildings, is actually medium- and long-term credit and, as such, ought to be available at relatively low interest rates. But for such credit to be obtainable at relatively low interest rates, there must exist the appropriate organizations, and agricultural households have to be able to furnish satisfactory security for the credit they utilize. Such credit organizations during the interwar period existed only in Slovenia, and only medium and big peasants were able to give the necessary guaranties for loans either by mortgaging their land or supplying other satisfactory collateral.

In addition to this typical long- and medium-term agricultural credit, the Yugoslav peasants, especially those with farms up to five hectares, needed a special type of short-term credit to tide them over in bad crop years and in late months of practically every crop year. This was partly consumer and partly production credit because it kept alive one of the basic production factors in peasant farming, the family labor. In addition to the perennial need for this type of credit, the peasants also often needed credit for a variety of other purposes, such as the buying of clothing and footwear and proper celebration of various expensive folk customs, for the giving of dowry, for court expenditures, for medical services, for travel expenses incurred in search of seasonal work or for long-term emigration, for the schooling of children, and for the payment of taxes.

The structure of peasant debts as ascertained by the survey of 1932, according to their use and related to the size of farms, is shown in Table 45. This table shows clearly that in the case of landless, or until recently landless, peasant households, and of dwarf farms, more credit was used to buy food than for any other purpose. This was also true in the case of farms of two to five hectares. But in all larger categories of farms, the buying of land was the foremost reason for incurring debt. This is a rather natural consequence of the proverbial hunger for land among the Yugoslav peasants. Another reason for using credit that was especially important in farms between 5 and 50 hectares was in order to consolidate old debts. The construction of buildings was also among the important reasons for getting into debt. It is quite interesting to note that in smaller farms the payment of the shares of members leaving the family's fold has been an important reason for incurring debt. On the other hand, buying livestock and the financing

TABLE 45.—PEASANT DEBTS ACCORDING TO THEIR USE BY VARIOUS SIZES OF FARMS IN 1932*

(Percent of total)

Use	Landless	Farms in hectares					
		0–2	2–5	5–10	10–20	20–50	Over 50
Buying of land	8.82	16.11	21.22	32.36	28.19	49.36	71.86
Buying of livestock	1.87	3.67	6.66	5.81	3.57	2.09	0.32
Buildings	7.75	14.97	16.53	13.34	14.52	8.98	12.38
Production purposes	10.49	5.91	6.85	3.44	9.21	7.44	11.45
Paying of shares to outgoing family members and similar expenses	26.78	15.28	16.15	9.50	5.87	4.60	0.33
Paying of debts	2.87	12.42	12.00	26.84	25.88	25.69	3.62
Buying of food	41.42	31.64	20.59	8.71	12.76	1.84	0.04
	100.00	100.00	100.00	100.00	100.00	100.00	100.00

* Source: Milan J. Komadinić, *Problem seljačkih dugova* (The Problem of Peasant Debts) (Belgrade, 1934), p. 51.

Note: Data in this table and in Table 46, p. 673, are either taken from or calculated on the basis of statistical material in the above book by Komadinić. While this book is a private publication, it was actually based upon and contains all pertinent statistical material collected in the survey of peasant debts that the Chartered Agricultural Bank undertook for the Ministry of Trade and Industry in 1932, which was otherwise not made public. Thus data in these tables can be taken as official.

of purely production expenditures in farming played a relatively subsidiary role as reasons for borrowing.

The survey of peasant debts of 1932 showed that 31.12 percent of
all debts was secured by bills of exchange, 26.32 percent by mortgages,
25.83 percent by promisory notes, while 16.73 percent was obtained
on a purely personal basis.

The plight of the Yugoslav peasants and their need for credit is
best shown by the fact that in many areas, but especially in Serbia, the
interest rates charged were exceedingly high. Thus, for example, there
was the well-known practice of crediting peasants with grain for food
or seed in winter or spring with the promise that repayment be made
in at least double quantity after the harvest, which meant a rate of
100 to more than 200 percent per annum. The small Serbian provincial
banks "with a better reputation" usually charged 24 percent interest
per annum, excluding the so-called "commission and costs," while
banks with a "bad reputation" charged 36 to 50 percent, excluding
"commission and costs." This "commission and costs" increased the
effective rate of interest markedly in all cases. But very often the
famous rate of "one dinar per ten-dinar banknote per month" (*"dinar
na banku"*) was charged which, when not compounded, amounted to
120 percent per annum.[4] These were the rates charged by the country
banks. The rates that the individual country usurers charged were
usually higher.

The consumer credit for peasants in Yugoslavia was in all areas
closely connected with the purchasing of food, clothing, footwear,
tools and utensils, and other goods from rural storekeepers and with
the sale of agricultural products to the storekeepers. Needless to say,
in the case of landless, dwarf, and small peasants the need for credit
to obtain food was of primary importance. Since the choice for the
peasant was often either starvation or payment of these exorbitant interest rates for what he bought on credit, it is understandable that he
chose the latter. As a matter of fact, many a peasant debtor was not
able, because of illiteracy, to control his accounts with the storekeeper
or creditor, and was completely at his mercy. This was a type of bondage
that the Yugoslav peasant hated and feared as much as the old, formalized bondage under serfdom. Other debtors were afraid to antagonize
their creditors, knowing well that their services would be needed year
in, year out. They paid, without questioning, whatever the storekeepers charged for goods sold to them and accepted practically any

[4] Miloš Radosavljević, "Usury and Our Village," in Miloslav Stojadinović (ed.),
Naše selo (Our Village), p. 553.

price offered to them for their produce. As the small and dwarf peasant had no other collateral to give, there was either a written or a verbal (but equally binding) obligation on the part of the debtor to sell his crop to the creditor. Use of the crop on the stubble or "on the green" as collateral, and especially selling of the crop "on the green," was another source of abuse of the debtor. It was bitter irony that the peasant often bought in winter or spring at much higher prices from the storekeeper the very same grain that he had sold him after the preceding harvest in payment of debt, and naturally at a much lower price.

The varying relation between the demand for and the supply of credit to agriculture in various areas of Yugoslavia, and different sources from which this credit was available, were responsible for great differences in the rates of interest charged. As the survey of peasant debts of 1932 has shown, the following sources supplied loans to agriculture: the State Mortgage Bank, the Chartered Agricultural Bank, commercial and savings banks including the savings banks established by various local governments, agricultural co-operatives, and other private lenders (including here country moneylenders), and especially the country storekeepers. The interest rates differed among the various provinces and according to the source of the credit. The above examples have shown us the interest rates that were charged by commercial banks in Serbia. The State Mortgage Bank and the Chartered Agricultural Bank charged 8 percent on loans to co-operative organizations, which of course had to charge more to their members, and 9 or 10 percent on mortgage credit. Commercial banks in Croatia-Slavonia and Bosnia and Herzegovina charged between 20 and 50 percent interest per annum during the early 1920's. The Slovene agricultural co-operatives, which were the best-organized and most powerful credit organizations of the kind in Yugoslavia, charged the lowest interest rate on their loans, namely between 6 and 9 percent. The "county agricultural endowments" in Bosnia and Herzegovina charged 10 percent for their small loans. But for the whole remainder of credit, especially the credit from individual moneylenders and from country storekeepers, the peasants paid exorbitant rates of interest.

This problem of the extremely high rates of interest was not an issue facing the peasants alone, but was one of the most difficult problems of the Yugoslav economy as a whole. Up to 1925 even the best and safest industrial enterprises paid 20 to 30 percent interest per annum. In 1922 and 1923 the Yugoslav central bank was of the opinion that an interest rate of 18 to 20 percent to be charged by the commercial banks and an interest rate of 10 percent paid by the banks for savings deposits were appropriate.[5] By 1929 the prevailing interest rates for first-class commercial and industrial enterprises sank to 10 to 14 percent, but there were always special charges for "commission and costs." In 1933 the interest rates to be charged by commercial banks were limited to 4.5 to 5 percent above the discount rate of the central bank, which fluctuated around 6 percent, and in January 1935 the government decreed that the interest rate charged by private banks could not exceed 10 percent. But after 1932 it was difficult or impossible to obtain any credit at all.

The basic reason that interest rates charged in various parts of the country differed so much is to be found in the varying supply of and demand for credit in different areas. Furthermore, due to the poor organization of banking, there was no tendency for an interregional equalization of supply and demand for credit, and thus of the interest rates. All credits given by government financial institutions, such as the State Mortgage Bank, the Postal Savings System, the National Bank, and since 1929 the Chartered Agricultural Bank, were granted at much lower rates of interest than similar credits given by other sources. Thus, such credits represented a subsidy to the individuals and firms who were able to obtain them. Needless to say, the interest rate was not the regulator of supply of credit on the part of these organizations. The amount of credit was limited as a matter of policy and this amount distributed at these lower interest rates.[6]

SOURCES OF AGRICULTURAL CREDIT DURING THE INTERWAR PERIOD AND GOVERNMENT ORGANIZATIONS FOR AGRICULTURAL CREDIT

The pre-1914 agricultural-credit organization in various South Slav lands was completely destroyed or badly shaken during World War I. The new frontiers of 1918 severed some of the organizations from their only or their chief sources of supply of funds. No system of agricultural credit was in existence which could be easily extended over the whole country, and some of the old organizations simply could not make the transition to new conditions. Political conditions in the new state were not conducive to constructive work in the field of agricultural credit, or in any field of political or socioeconomic endeavor. On the other hand,

[5] National Bank of the Kingdom of Yugoslavia, *Narodna banka, 1884–1934* (National Bank, 1884–1934), p. 181.

[6] Jozo Tomašević, *Novac i kredit* (Money and Credit), pp. 227–47.

the need for reconstruction of agriculture and animal husbandry following the ravages caused by the war and later unfavorable developments put Yugoslav agriculture in dire need of credit.[7]

It was a formidable task even to disentangle the myriad of pre-1914 and wartime credit contracts in agriculture, which were expressed in half a dozen different currencies and made according to legal requirements of more than half a dozen legal systems, and to reduce all these contracts to a common denominator. In fact, it took several years to unravel the tangle. In regard to the new institutional setup that emerged in the early 1920's, which was of interest from the point of view of serving agriculture with credit, a few general remarks must suffice. More will be said about certain specific organizations and problems which arose in regard to agricultural credit during the interwar period.

As far as government banking was concerned, the two old Serbian institutions, the National Bank and the Funds Management Administration, renamed in 1922 as the State Mortgage Bank (Državna hipotekarna banka), served after their return from exile as nuclei for the organization of central banking and mortgage credit in the new state. The Postal Savings System was added to this pair of government banks in the early 1920's. The important fact to be pointed out with regard to the old mortgage credit operations carried out by government institutions is that the State Mortgage Bank took over the old accounts of the Ottoman Agricultural Bank which operated in Macedonia until 1912, of the Montenegrin State Mortgage Bank, of the Dalmatian Mortgage Credit Administration, and the mortgage credit accounts of the former Austro-Hungarian Bank in Yugoslav territory. Only the Carniola Mortgage Credit Administration was reorganized into a corporation and taken over by the savings banks of Slovenia. Thus, with the exception of the State Mortgage Bank, which long before had become primarily an organization for financing of urban real estate and government needs, there was no other government credit institution for agricultural credit in the early 1920's.

A great number of commercial and savings banks came into being in the inflationary years of the early 1920's. A great majority were small, local units. Old banking institutions of domestic capital grew

---

[7] In addition to the already quoted works by Momir Glomazić, Milan J. Komadinić, and Ivan M. Varga, there are a considerable number of other studies dealing with the problems of agricultural credit in Yugoslavia during the interwar period. Among these the most important are Velimir Bajkić, *Seljački kredit* (Peasant Credit) and Blagoje Nikosavić, *Die Agrarverfassung und der landwirtschaftliche Kredit Jugoslawiens* (Germany, Ministry for Food and Agriculture, *Berichte über Landwirtschaft*, N.F., Sonderheft No. 112).

fast and big. The former branches of the Vienna and Budapest banks in Yugoslav territory were transformed into Yugoslav banks, but they were so only in name and in the area of their activity. The overwhelming portion of their stock was held partly by their former central offices, partly directly by the Western European banking houses which of old were large-scale financiers of the Vienna and Budapest banks. In one regard, and of great interest from the point of view of agricultural credit, a basic change took place in comparison with the pre-1914 days. Private banks in South Slav lands, which had formerly financed their mortgage credit operations by issuing mortgage bonds and selling them mostly through their Vienna and Budapest contacts, completely stopped this type of operations. Foreign loans were not available for such purposes, and some attempts to place such securities on the domestic market failed, though they carried more than double the pre-1914 interest rate. While both commercial and savings banks made considerable amounts of loans available to agriculture throughout the 1920's, their chief interest lay in the financing of industry and trade. In April 1932, as shown in Table 46, page 673, peasants owed commercial and savings banks of all types 32.43 percent of all their indebtedness. Lacking long-term funds, commercial and savings banks financed a large portion of their formally short-term, but actually long-term engagements in agriculture and industry with funds deposited with them in the form of savings and demand deposits.

Agricultural credit co-operatives and agricultural co-operatives in general, which prior to 1914 had to struggle in many South Slav areas against great odds, were expected to grow and develop greatly in the new state and to be of great assistance to the agricultural population. But with the exception of Slovenia, they performed disappointingly in most areas. As a rule they were tools of politics. Business could not be kept separate from politics, and the result was not favorable. Moreover, co-operatives and co-operative federations were often managed by people who had little or no understanding of the business in which they were engaged, and the co-operatives were occasionally used by unscrupulous businessmen for the promotion of their personal business ventures. In both cases the results were disastrous for the co-operatives. The difference between the co-operatives in Slovenia and elsewhere is clearly shown by the fact that while the Slovene co-operative federations charged their member co-operatives between 8 and 9 percent interest for loans in 1927 (and these interest rates regulated the interest rates charged by the individual co-operatives on loans to their members), the Croatian and the Serbian federations charged between 12 and 20 percent per annum.[8] Except in Slovenia agricultural credit co-operatives were definitely a subsidiary source of credit for agriculture. Of the total peasant indebtedness in 1932 only 12.08 percent was owed to the co-operatives (see Table 46, p. 673). In Slovenia (*banovina* Drava) that proportion was 33 percent while in the remainder of the country it was only 7.7 percent.

The most important source of credit for agricultural population during the interwar period in Yugoslavia was the individual lenders and country storekeepers. According to the survey of peasant debts of 1932 (Table 46, p. 673), not less than 45.27 percent of all peasant debts at that time was owed to this category of creditors. Prior to 1929, the year in which the Chartered Agricultural Bank was established, this share was probably even higher.

Since commercial and savings banks and credit co-operatives did not supply agriculture with sufficient credit and charged usurious interest rates (except in Slovenia) for the credit they supplied, and since individual moneylenders and country storekeepers, who charged usurious rates, were the chief sources of credit for the village, it was quite natural that the demand for the suppression of usury would arise and become an issue of party politics. Thus all political parties interested in the peasant vote, and that meant all parties, promised to combat usury and to work for an effective system of agricultural credit at reasonable rates of interest. Under conditions prevailing in most of Yugoslavia during the interwar period, there was only one way of combating usury effectively, that is, by a substantial increase in the supply of credit to agriculture, and, with the exception of Slovenia, this could only have been achieved by state action.

There were, under the conditions existing in Yugoslavia in the 1920's, two ways in which this state action in furnishing sufficient credit to agriculture could be accomplished: (*a*) by creating a special system of government banks, "funds," or "co-operatives" with their own representatives or branches all over the country in direct touch with the peasants and granting credit directly to the peasants, and (*b*) by making ample credit available to the peasants through the already existing co-operative organizations by discounting their paper with a special government central agricultural bank, which could be partly financially supported by the central bank or other government financial organizations.

The first proposal to create a state organization for agricultural credit was made in November 1920. It was proposed to create a Cen-

[8] Ivan M. Varga, *op. cit.*, p. 293.

tral Agricultural Credit Co-operative, which would be financed in the beginning with government funds without interest and would itself engage exclusively in the financing of the already existing federations of agricultural co-operatives which functioned as financial centers for their member co-operatives. This proposal never materialized. Such an organization would have been largely run by the representatives of organizations which it served, i.e., the organizations of free co-operatives. Since most of the free co-operatives were at that time under the influence of opposition parties and in areas outside of Serbia, the government parties (essentially Serbian) looked with disfavor on their activity and power and, naturally, refused to increase that power still more. On the other hand, the following of the first alternative had for them two political advantages. First, it was a weapon for combating the opposition-controlled free co-operatives and thus the hold of the opposition parties on the village, and second, it gave the government parties the political advantage of control over the granting of agricultural credit out of government funds.

It was in this spirit of enmity against the existing free credit co-operatives and with an eye on the political abuse of a state organization for agricultural credit that the Law on Agricultural Credit of June 12, 1925, was passed. On the basis of this law the government organized an Administration for Agricultural Credit within the Ministry of Agriculture and Water Resources with a capital of 500 million dinars that was to be subscribed by annual appropriations in the government's budget. It was also supposed to receive the administration and investment of some government trust funds and to obtain a share in the profits of the state lottery. This Administration started its operations in 1927 by organizing its "village credit co-operatives," but since these co-operatives never succeeded in obtaining any deposits from their members, the amount of credit available to their members and thus to agriculture from the Administration for Agricultural Credit equaled the actual budget allocations for its capital, which, until April 1929, amounted to only 115.5 million dinars instead of the 500 million dinars with which it was supposed to be organized. Until the end of 1928, 952 such co-operatives with 40,713 members[9] were established, approximately two-thirds of which were in the territory of pre-1912 Serbia. Needless to say, the granting of loans through these co-operatives was guided largely by political considerations. At the same time the Administration for Agricultural Credit and the government-run banks refused any financial

[9] *The Chartered Agricultural Bank, 1930*, p. 15.

assistance to the already existing co-operative organizations. They also refused assistance to the "county assistance endowments" in Bosnia, considering them as remainders of the former enemy rule without judging their actual achievements or potential services. These endowments obtained some loans from the Agricultural Bank after 1932 and, during the 1930's, somewhat increased the scope of their activity.

The experiment with the Administration for Agricultural Credit, which was the first large-scale government assistance program in favor of agriculture during the interwar period (disregarding the agrarian reform and the internal colonization), proved to be a dismal failure. There were two basic reasons for this failure. First, the principle of its whole organization, namely, the creation of a whole system of state "co-operatives," was faulty, and second, the financial means that the government appropriated in its budgets for the formation of the capital of the Administration, on which its capacity to grant credit to agriculture depended, were pitifully small. At the time when this government program of agricultural credit was getting under way in 1927 and 1928, three plans for the regulation of peasant debts, coming from various politicians in Serbia, acquired considerable popularity. Some of the basic common features of these projects were: temporary moratorium for the existing peasant debts, reduction of interest rates on the existing debts, suppression of usury in the future, government shouldering of the burden resulting from the regulation of the existing peasant debts, and a better organization of peasant credit in the future with government help.[10] Nothing came of these proposals at that time, but the idea of a moratorium for agricultural debts was not forgotten.

In spite of the fact that the Administration for Agricultural Credit proved a failure, or perhaps because of it, and because of the fact that the issue of peasant debts and agricultural credit was a subject of political speculation, it is quite understandable that the dictatorship regime of King Alexander (established January 6, 1929), which was as much interested in acquiring the confidence and support of the peasants as any other previous government or political party, would also try to "solve" the problem of agricultural credit. This task appeared even more pressing and politically popular as many signs of an impending agricultural depression were gathering and Yugoslav agriculture with the remainder of the economy suffered from the heavy burden of debts. Thus, on April 16, 1929, the government issued a law on the establishment of a Chartered Agricultural Bank with a share capital of 300 million dinars.

[10] Velimir Bajkić, *op. cit.*, pp. 47–95.

Its principal function was to supply agriculture with credit, to reduce the interest rates on credit to agriculture by increasing the supply of credit, and generally to bring more order in the country's organization of agricultural credit. The oversubscription of the capital caused an increase in the share capital to 700 million dinars. The Bank began its operations in October 1929. It had the form of a private corporation, but its whole organization was such that it was actually a government financial institution. By the end of 1933 practically the whole share capital was paid up. Of the total capital of 700 million dinars, the government subscribed 120 million dinars directly by turning over to the Bank the predominantly frozen assets of the now defunct Administration for Agricultural Credit;[11] another 120 million dinars was subscribed by government financial institutions—the National Bank, the State Mortgage Bank, the Postal Savings System, and the State Lottery; the remainder of the capital was subscribed by private banks, co-operatives, local government bodies, and to some extent also by private investors. According to the law the Bank could issue mortgage bonds in order to acquire additional funds for its operations. The Chartered Agricultural Bank worked with both the government system of "co-operatives" and with the existing free co-operatives. As explained in Chapter 20, one of the novelties that the law on the Agricultural Bank brought about was making the peasants in Serbia and Montenegro free to be parties to contracts in the form of bills of exchange. This was an important departure from the previous legislation in these areas, but much less so from the previous practice.

According to law, the Agricultural Bank was empowered to grant long-term mortgage loans with the duration of 5 to 25 years, never in excess of 50 percent of the current market value of the land; medium-term loans of one to three years through the participating co-operatives, mostly for the buying of agricultural machinery and livestock; short-term loans up to one year in duration for the needs connected with planting, harvesting, and marketing of crops, again through the co-operatives; and finally, loans for the financing of export trade in agricultural products. A large portion of the mortgage loans as well as of the medium-term loans was actually used for the consolidation of existing debts.

The organization of the Agricultural Bank seemed to be an important step toward improvement of the agricultural credit situation in the

[11] The state-sponsored "co-operatives" established under this scheme of agricultural credit continued to exist after the liquidation of the Administration for Agricultural Credit.

country. The Bank obtained promises for considerable loans (200 million dinars each) from the National Bank, the State Mortgage Bank, and the Postal Savings System, but because of the banking and general economic crisis that broke out in Yugoslavia in mid-1931, these loans could be used only to a very limited extent. And without strong backing from the government credit institutions, which had an abundance of funds, the new Bank could not succeed. It was, so to speak, financially anemic. Furthermore, it did not succeed in attracting savings deposits in any quantity, to say nothing of increasing them to a substantial amount during the 1930's, as was the case with the State Mortgage Bank and the Postal Savings System. Thus it did not have at its disposal this all-important source of funds to increase the volume of its operations. In spite of the fact that this Bank was the most ambitious undertaking in regard to agricultural credit ever tried in the South Slav lands, it proved a great disappointment to both agriculture and to those people in the country who were genuinely interested in a solution of the perennial issue of agricultural credit.

From the day of its establishment until the end of 1937 the Bank made loans amounting to 1,498.7 million dinars available to agriculture. Of this amount, 609.4 million dinars were mortgage loans, 850.7 million dinars were loaned to individual farmers through and with the guaranty of the co-operative organizations, and 38.6 million dinars were loaned on the basis of bills of exchange and similar collateral. Mortgage loans were given to only 20,576 peasants, of whom roughly 18,500 had less than 20 hectares of land. But these obtained only 50 percent of the total sum loaned on mortgages. At the end of 1937 the balance of all outstanding loans was 742.5 million dinars, of which 424.7 million dinars were mortgage loans, 304.4 million dinars were loans through co-operatives, and 13.4 million dinars were loans to the "water co-operatives."[12]

The sum of the outstanding loans of 742.5 million dinars at the end of 1937 was almost identical with the Bank's share capital and surplus (738.2 million). A certain amount of its loans was written off, however, on the basis of the Decree of September 1936, which regulated the peasant debts. The Bank acquired no funds by issuing mortgage bonds, which it was authorized to do, because there was no market for such securities. Owing to the nature of a large portion of its loans and to the generally unfavorable development of the Yugoslav economy, its investments became largely frozen during the first three years of its opera-

[12] Yugoslavia, *Annuaire statistique 1938–1939*, pp. 300–301.

tions. Taken as a whole, the lending operations of the Chartered Agricultural Bank were not of great importance. From 1936 on, its main function was to administer a part of the Decree of September 25, 1936, on the settlement of peasant debts, of which more will be said presently.

It is important to note two additional facts. First, the area in which the Agricultural Bank granted most loans was Vojvodina, an area of quasi-commercialized and specialized farming in which dealing with banks and mortgage credit had a long tradition. In other areas, except parts of Serbia and Bosnia, its loans were rather limited, and in Slovenia its loans were not utilized at all because they were more expensive than those granted by the co-operatives. Second, the Bank gave the bulk of its loans, both mortgage and other, to big and medium peasants. Small and dwarf peasants were again ignored and were forced to seek credit in other less formal, but more expensive sources.

There were three additional government financial institutions from which a greater supply of agricultural credit was expected than was forthcoming: the National Bank (the central bank), the State Mortgage Bank, and the Postal Savings System. The State Mortgage Bank, as explained earlier, was established with an idea of increasing and improving agricultural credit in Serbia, but from its earliest beginnings there was a growing tendency for it to become primarily or exclusively an organization for the financing of urban real estate and of the government. Still it always continued to grant some loans to agriculture. It had no capital stock. Its funds came from three sources: it administered all government trust funds; it accepted savings and business deposits from the general public; and it acquired funds through the sale of bonds abroad (in Switzerland and the United States). After the establishment of the Agricultural Bank in 1929 the State Mortgage Bank gave few if any new loans to agriculture, though it continued to hold its old mortgages on agricultural real estate. The survey of peasant debts of 1932 showed that agriculture owed only 203.9 million dinars to the State Mortgage Bank (Table 46, p. 673), while at the end of 1931 mortgage loans and loans on the current account granted by the Bank to private economy including agriculture amounted to 2,769.0 million dinars (2,445.5 million dinars in mortgage loans and 323.5 million dinars in other loans). In addition, 77.6 million dinars were loaned to the "water co-operatives," which also benefited agriculture.

Traditionally, central banks are not organizations which engage much in financing agriculture (though there were and are exceptions, as the case of the former Austro-Hungarian Bank showed), but in practically all countries the laws and statutes pertaining to central banks stipulate that they can rediscount a certain amount of paper originating in agriculture and with somewhat longer tenor, e.g., nine months instead of the customary 90 days with the typical commercial paper. According to Article 10 of the Law on the National Bank of June 17, 1931, the Yugoslav central bank was permitted to rediscount nine-months bills of exchange originating in agriculture "with at least three safe signatures," up to 25 percent of the amount of its rediscount loans outstanding. But at the end of 1937 only 59 million dinars in paper from agricultural co-operatives were in the hands of the National Bank, or 4.12 percent of the total amount of rediscount loans of 1,432.6 million dinars.

The third government financial organization, the Postal Savings System, did not engage in financing agriculture either directly or through the co-operative organizations. But in 1937 it began, by agreement with the Chartered Agricultural Bank, to grant loans to some agricultural co-operative organizations in order to help them re-establish their liquidity, which had been impaired since 1932. At the end of 1937 these loans amounted to about 100 million dinars, while the total amount of its loans at that time, mostly to the Ministry of Finance and to various government enterprises, amounted to 1,437.1 million dinars. At the same time, it held another 756.3 million dinars in government securities.

THE MORATORIUM FOR PEASANT DEBTS OF APRIL 1932 AND THE BANKING CRISIS

The problems of peasant debts and the banking crisis in Yugoslavia were treated by the same legislation during the 1930's. The problem of peasant debts and of debts in general in Yugoslavia had its origin in the inflationary period after World War I, which lasted until 1923 (but was not of a hyperinflationary character), and in the ensuing period of deflation. During the deflation many trade, industrial, and banking enterprises went bankrupt. But the bulk of the high-interest indebtedness remained and weighed heavily on the shoulders of the Yugoslav economy in the following years. Peasant debts were one of the most important items in this whole picture.

Considering the exorbitant interest rates on loans to the peasants, the money (nominal) value of peasant debts would have grown at a terrific speed even if no new loans were made after 1928, because agriculture became less and less capable of meeting either the interest payments or the payments on the principal. And the decline in prices of agricultural products after 1928 reduced still further the ability of agriculture to repay its debts by increasing greatly the real content of the debts. More-over, agriculture was less able to sell its products even at these lower prices than before. Thus, when the Great Depression came in its full force, agriculture, as well as other branches of the economy, simply could not meet its obligations.

Three factors precipitated the run on the banks in Yugoslavia, which ushered in the breakdown of the whole credit system of the country: the downfall of the Creditanstalt of Vienna, an international bank with large holdings in Yugoslavia and in Central and Southeastern Europe in general, in May 1931; the German banking crisis of July 1931; and the departure of Great Britain from the gold standard in September 1931. The pressure on the international monetary position of Yugo-slavia could be best judged from the development of its gold and foreign exchange reserves. First, these reserves fell from 2,879.6 million dinars at the end of 1929 to 1,812.1 million dinars at the end of 1930. This in fact shows that in its international relations the Yugoslav economy was already in crisis in 1930, although domestically the banking and other branches of the economy, except agriculture, still appeared to be sound. Second, in May 1931 Yugoslavia obtained an international stabiliza-tion loan which netted 1,869.6 million dinars in foreign exchange, but in spite of that the gold and foreign exchange reserves at the end of June 1931 were only 2,291.5 million dinars. The rate of loss of foreign exchange during the first half of 1931 was therefore much higher than during 1930. Third, these reserves fell to 2,096.8 million dinars at the end of 1931 (in spite of a loan of 660 million dinars from France in October 1931), and to 1,906.2 million dinars at the end of 1933. This loss in international currency during 1930 and 1931 was primarily caused by the withdrawal of foreign capital from Yugoslavia and, to a much smaller extent, by the flight of domestic capital, and a surplus of imports in 1930. The internal pressure on commercial and savings banks can be seen from the development of the savings deposits held with them, because savings deposits had key significance in Yugoslav banking during the interwar period. The savings deposits in commercial banks fell from their peak of 10,294.1 million dinars at the end of 1930 to 8,804.1 million dinars at the end of 1931 and to only 5,314.4 million dinars at the end of 1937.

The Yugoslav government and the National Bank were during the Great Depression very much under the influence of France and French thinking in financial matters, and thus followed, like the French, a strong deflationary policy. It was hard to do otherwise, as France was the chief diplomatic supporter of the country (from 1918 to about 1934), the chief subscriber of the Yugoslav 7 Percent International Stabilization Loan of May 1931, and the grantor of a loan in October 1931, both of which had the nature of a diplomatic subsidy. Furthermore, it should be remembered that the policy of deflation was not as yet in the disrepute in which it was held later. The Yugoslav leaders were therefore determined to "save" the currency even if it required a sacrifice of both the national credit system and the national economy, which in fact it did. The currency could not be saved and the credit system was crippled to such an extent that it could not recuperate. The banks could not increase their rediscounts with the central bank. Not even government securities were acceptable as collateral for loans, as their prices were decreasing daily. To be able to respond to their obligations to their depositors, the banks pressed their debtors, thus strengthening the deflation. But most of their loans, although formally short-term, were actually medium- and long-term investments and could not be easily liquidated. The lax investment policy of the banks in times of prosperity proved to be largely responsible for their doom. Of course, lack of proper liquidity safeguards within the Yugoslav banking structure and the shortsighted policy of the government and of the central bank were important factors causing the severity and the long duration of the banking crisis. The process of "loan cancellation" reached the peasants rather early, but because of reduced prices of agricultural and livestock products and because of the diminished ability to sell these products, the peasants were now less able to pay their debts than ever before.

The only "solution" of the problem of peasant debts and of the banking crisis under the existing conditions was to declare a moratorium. Thus a Law on the Protection of Peasants was issued on April 19, 1932. Article 1 of this law provided for a general moratorium for all peasant debts as of that date for six months and a suspension of all foreclosures in process, and forbade new foreclosures until a final regulation of peasant debts had been achieved. Article 5 of this law gave the permission to commercial banks and other credit organizations to ask for a "postponement" of payment (moratorium) of their liabilities in case of financial difficulties. The reaction of the indebted peasants to this law was naturally favorable. But the answer of the depositors was an intensified run on the already greatly weakened banks. And the request for a moratorium by a number of the leading commercial banks of the country followed shortly thereafter. In 1933 a special decree temporarily allowed the merchants and the artisans to ask, individually, for a moratorium for their debts, if they were in difficulties, instead of going into bankruptcy.

The above-mentioned Law of April 19, 1932, was followed by a veritable flood of new laws and decrees dealing with peasant debts and the banks. The first to follow, promulgated December 19, 1932, was characteristically entitled a Law on the Prolongation of Protection of Peasants. It was obvious that the moratorium for both peasant debts and the banks was here to stay and that the government did not know what to do about either of the two problems, except to keep postponing their solution. An ingenious pattern was devised. Before certain actions foreseen in the current decree were to take place, a new decree was promulgated. And so the decrees followed each other on December 27, 1932, November 22, 1933, August 3, 1934, November 23, 1934, September 30, 1935, and finally September 25, 1936. Three possible ways stood open to the banks. They could ask, on the basis of the Decree of November 22, 1933, for (*a*) a six-year moratorium, (*b*) reorganization, or (*c*) liquidation by a nonbankruptcy procedure. As a rule, the banks chose the first alternative. In either case a government commissioner was placed in charge of the bank as a general supervisor, and a strict division between the "old" and the "new" business was instituted, prescribing, among other things, special investment rules for funds obtained in the "new" business. Very small amounts for special purposes were exempted from the moratorium.

By the end of 1937, 303 out of about 670 commercial banks and savings banks were formally under moratorium and 36 were in the process of liquidation. This represented banks with about 48 percent of all share capital invested in commercial and savings banks and with more than 50 percent of all savings deposits in commercial and savings banks. Actually, a considerable number of other banks were *de facto* although not *de jure* under moratorium on that date.

The Yugoslav government and the central bank showed during the early 1930's an unbelievable lack of understanding of what was happening in the Yugoslav banking and national economy and of measures that would have been appropriate under the existing conditions. As in purely political matters, the leading principle of policy was to delay the honest facing and settlement of any problem, while at the same time trying desperately to make political capital out of the national economic disaster. The conception about handling some problems of the banking crisis that one of the leading politicians of Yugoslavia had is shown by the following. When asked by a written memorandum for advice on how to treat the depositors who wanted to withdraw their savings deposits, the then Minister of Trade and Industry, Kosta Kumanudi, whose ministry had the jurisdiction over the chartering and supervision of banks, counseled the representatives of the Vojvodina Bankers Association of Novi Sad that "the banks should throw out by force from their premises all the depositors asking for their money, and if that proves of no avail, should report them to the police authorities as anti-state elements."[13] This "statesmanlike" utterance of the Minister of Trade was not the only one of its kind regarding the handling of financial and monetary matters during the early 1930's but it was one of the more choice ones.[14]

The Yugoslav banking crisis meant two things for the peasants: (1) almost all savings deposits that they had in the banks, however small, were now frozen, the more so as some of the oldest and most popular large banks with huge savings deposits (e.g., the First Croatian Savings Bank, the Serbian Bank, the Yugoslav Bank, and the Yugoslav Union Bank, all of Zagreb, but with many branches in the country) were among the first to apply for a moratorium, and (2) banks could not and would not serve any more as a source of credit to agriculture. In fact, the lending function of the commercial and savings banks for new loans ceased almost completely after 1932 and the banks became essentially treasurers and agents for foreign exchange operations of their clients. Actually, a large portion of the Yugoslav commercial banking was in the process of piecemeal liquidation after 1932.

The legislation on the moratorium for peasant debts of April 1932 was preceded by and led to further investigations of agricultural indebtedness in the country. These investigations showed some very interesting facts. First of all, it was found that only 35.7 percent of all rural households (census of 1931) were in debt. This showed not that the remaining households did not need credit, but rather that many peasant households were not capable of obtaining credit. Second, the total amount of debt was 6,880 million dinars. This equaled about 46 percent of the estimated gross income of agriculture from crops and

---

[13] Vojvodina Bankers Association, "Referat Udruženja Vojvodjanskih banaka" (Report of the Vodjvodina Bankers Association), April 23, 1933, p. 3 (mimeographed). In the political vernacular of the interwar period in Yugoslavia, "antistate element" was a very popular term used by state ministers, government officials, police organs, and supporters of the succeeding regimes. It applied especially to the outlawed Communists, to the temporarily outlawed members of the Croatian Peasant party, and in a larger sense to all those who disagreed with the government and its officials.

[14] Lest it be thought that a man with Mr. Kumanudi's ideas had become a minister by political accident, it should be said that as a member of the Democratic party (overwhelmingly Serbian) he was minister in both the parliamentarian governments prior to January 1929 and in dictatorship governments thereafter. At one time or another he headed the ministries of Finance, Constitutional Affairs, Education, Forests and Mines, Public Works, Posts and Telegraphs, Trade and Industry, and he was also a minister without portfolio.

livestock in 1931, and perhaps between 80 and 90 percent of the total cash income of agriculture in the same year. In addition to this debt, agriculture also owed a considerable amount of money to the state and local governments for tax arrears, but neither the exact amount of these tax arrears nor the exact portion that was owed by agriculture is known. The amount of tax arrears owed to the central and local governments at the end of 1932 was estimated at 3.5 billion dinars, of which a large share was owed by agriculture. Third, it was established that as of April 19, 1932, the feared and hated class of private moneylenders and country storekeepers as a group was the most important source of agricultural credit in the country.

There existed great differences among various *banovine* with regard to the sources of loans made to agriculture, the percentage of rural households indebted, the percentage of cultivated land that the indebted households held, the average burden of debt in dinars per hectare of indebted cultivated land, and the average amount owed by indebted households. All these data are presented in Table 46. The story locked in this table is extremely interesting and could be told at considerable length. But if one keeps in mind our earlier discussions in the course of this chapter, the table is self-explanatory and a few additional remarks will suffice. It is very interesting, for example, that even in Slovenia, the area with the best-developed agricultural credit organization, 48.3 percent of all debt in agriculture was owed to private moneylenders and country storekeepers. On the other hand, the lowest percentage of debt owed to private moneylenders was in the *banovine* Dunav and Morava. There is little doubt that in regard to *banovina* Morava, which was a purely Serbian region, this was largely a consequence of the fact that, quite some time before, many country usurers, merchants, and politicians had banded together and formed small provincial banks. Thus the portion of peasant debt to commercial and savings banks in *banovina* Morava (52.6 percent) was, after *banovina* Dunav (52.9 percent), higher than in any other area. Since *banovina* Dunav included also the north-central portion of Serbia, the percentage of debt owed to private moneylenders and to commercial and savings banks in this *banovina* has also been affected by this specific organizational pattern of rural credit in Serbia. On the other hand, in the two most overpopulated and poorest *banovine*, Primorje and Zeta, the private moneylender and country storekeeper were by far the most important source of credit, supplying in the first *banovina* 71.3 and in the latter 66.8 percent of the total reported.

The percentage of indebted households showed great differences

TABLE 46.—PEASANT DEBTS BY BANOVINE, ACCORDING TO THE SURVEY OF 1932*

(Million dinars; percent; dinars)

Banovina	Total debt	Owed to					Percent owed to private lenders	Percent of rural households in debt	Percent of cultivated land in debt	Debt in Dinars	
		State Mortgage Bank	Agricultural Bank	Commercial and savings banks	Agricultural co-operatives	Private money-lenders				Per hectare of indebted land	Per household indebted
Drava	1,192.1	6.0	—	216.8	393.7	575.6	48.3	45.9	59.9	5,493	19,387
Drina	625.3	21.7	104.5	190.7	53.8	254.6	40.7	44.4	51.3	1,489	6,718
Dunav	1,683.7	45.7	244.2	891.6	137.6	364.6	21.6	22.3	24.5	3,106	18,968
Morava	320.2	5.5	34.8	168.4	35.3	76.2	23.8	26.4	25.0	1,625	5,592
Primorje	839.0	45.3	20.9	136.2	38.6	598.0	71.3	51.9	34.7	7,558	12,979
Sava	1,185.1	19.4	37.4	357.8	98.7	671.8	56.7	39.6	37.7	2,333	7,396
Vardar	209.4	10.5	13.4	78.3	20.1	87.1	41.6	16.6	16.5	1,485	6,372
Vrbas	328.9	11.7	21.7	109.6	31.3	154.6	47.0	58.9	57.7	937	3,853
Zeta	496.3	38.1	22.3	82.1	22.1	331.7	66.8	44.5	53.9	2,954	8,638
Total	6,880.0	203.9	499.2	2,231.5	831.2	3,114.2	45.3	35.7	34.8	2,591	9,812
Percent of Total	100.00	2.96	7.26	32.43	12.08	45.27					

* Based on Milan J. Komadinić, *Problem seljačkih dugova* (The Problem of Peasant Debts) (Belgrade, 1934), pp. 60–64. Our banovinal percentages of indebted rural households differ from those in Komadinić's book, because we use as basis for our calculation the 1931 census data on rural households which were not available when he published his book. Cf. Yugoslavia, *Annuaire statistique 1936* (Belgrade, 1937), pp. 48–53. The percentage of cultivated land belonging to indebted households in various *banovine* is based on Komadinić's figures of indebted land related to figures of cultivated land in 1931, as shown in Table 23, p. 322. The average indebtedness per hectare of indebted land and the average indebtedness per indebted household were calculated on the basis of figures supplied by Komadinić's book.

from area to area. It was the highest, 58.9 percent, in *banovina* Vrbas. That was probably partly connected with the fact that here the "county assistance endowments" were active and that more rural households were "eligible" for credit, because loans were often very small in amount. The lowest percentage of rural households indebted was in *banovina* Vardar (Macedonia). The population of this area is known as extremely thrifty, and the patterns of its consumption are less diversified and thus less dependent on products bought in the market than perhaps in any other part of the country. The percentage of cultivated land in the hands of indebted households was the highest in *banovina* Drava, and the lowest in *banovina* Vardar.

The last two columns in the table give the average debt in dinars per hectare of cultivated land of indebted peasant households and the average debt in dinars per indebted household. Here again the differences among *banovine* are extremely great. The indebtedness per hectare of indebted land was the highest in *banovina* Primorje, which is partly understandable because of the fact that high-value vineyards comprise a considerable portion of cultivated land in this area. The lowest per hectare indebtedness was in *banovina* Vrbas. The highest average indebtedness per indebted household was in *banovina* Drava, followed closely by *banovina* Dunav, and then by *banovina* Primorje; and the lowest in *banovina* Vrbas. To some extent the order of these averages follows the order of averages of indebtedness per hectare of indebted land. It would appear that the availability of credit at satisfactory interest rates, especially when agriculture in an area was quasi-commercialized and specialized, led to a larger average indebtedness. At least the figures for *banovina* Drava and also to a considerable extent for *banovina* Dunav would suggest this conclusion.

Unfortunately, data on peasant debts, as collected in 1932 and published by Komadinić, do not show the relationship between the size of farms and the amount of debt. His sampling of this relationship in certain counties of the country does not seem to be sufficient.

To see the full significance of the absolute amounts of indebtedness and of the respective differences among *banovine*, as given in Table 46 (p. 673), it would be necessary to relate these figures to the productivity of land in various areas, the crop structure, the ratio of rural population to cultivated land, the prices of land, and finally to the sources of credit which influenced the rate of interest and thus largely also the real burden of the debt. Space limitations prevent us from discussing these issues. But for the purpose of illustration one point is raised, the relationship between the average indebtedness per indebted household and the estimated average income per household. The income of agriculture from crops and livestock was estimated in 1931 at 15,007 million dinars. The income from apiculture, silk-cocoon raising, fisheries, and hunting was estimated at 149 million dinars, and income from cottage industries at 3,628 million dinars. This gave a total of 18,784 million dinars, or roughly 9,500 dinars per household. On the basis of our assumptions of the marketability rate of agricultural production (see p. 602), cash income of Yugoslav agriculture in 1931 amounted to between 7,500 and 8,500 million dinars. Divided among 1,963,400 rural households, which were in existence in 1931, that gave an average cash income per rural family of 3,800 to 4,300 dinars. But these are averages for the country as a whole, while it is quite obvious from what was said about Yugoslav agriculture of the interwar period that agricultural income varied very much from region to region, and that it had been considerably higher in areas north of the Sava-Danube rivers than in areas south of these rivers. Thus, relating of the average indebtedness per indebted peasant household in 1932 in various *banovine* to the estimated average total or cash income per rural household in 1931 for the country as a whole has to be taken with great caution. Actually, it is here indicated only to give an impression of the magnitudes involved.

CONSOLIDATION OF PEASANT DEBTS AS OF SEPTEMBER 1936

Let us now look at the fate of peasant debts after the flood of obviously temporary legislation had subsided, and at the development in Yugoslav banking and agricultural credit in the second half of the 1930's. The peasant debts were consolidated on the basis of the Decree on the Settlement of Peasant Debts of September 25, 1936, which remained in operation until the outbreak of World War II, and to a certain extent until the final disposition of this problem after World War II. This decree covered only debts incurred up to April 20, 1932, and ordered the following: Debts to commercial and savings banks and credit co-operatives were reduced by 50 percent if they did not exceed 25,000 dinars, and larger debts could be reduced from 30 to 50 percent, depending on the amount of the debt and its relation to peasants' property; the remainder had to be repaid in 12 years with 4.5 percent interest. Debts to storekeepers and artisans for goods and services bought from them remained intact and had to be repaid in 12 years, but without any interest. Debts to private moneylenders were reduced by 50 percent and were to be repaid in 12 years with 3 percent interest. This concession did not apply to debtors who were in a better financial situation than their respective creditors. Debts to the Chartered Agricultural Bank were reduced by 25 percent. The period of repayment of peasant debts to the State Mortgage Bank was extended to 32 years and the interest rate reduced to 4.5 percent. And, finally, debts to the insurance companies and various trust funds had to be repaid in their entirety in 12 years with 3 percent interest.

Besides aiming at a solution of the problem of peasant debts from the peasant's point of view, the decree also intended to be a major step in the mobilization of banks. With that aspect in mind the decree concentrated its attention upon peasant debts to credit establishments. The Agricultural Bank, acting for the state, took over all peasant debts, reduced by 25 percent, to commercial and savings banks and credit co-operatives. The remaining 25 percent had to be covered by the banks and co-operatives out of their surplus and, if need be, up to 50 percent of their share capital. If these two sources were not sufficient, the deficiency was to be borne by the state, paying the credit establishments in government bonds. Of the peasants' original debts, 50 percent was credited by the Agricultural Bank to the individual credit establishments in current account and was to be repaid with 3 percent interest as a government debt to the banks over a period of 14 years, beginning January 1, 1938. The service of this debt to the banks was to be financed by the payment of annuities by the indebted peasants to the Agricultural Bank during 12 years with 4.5 percent interest, and by straight government contributions to cover any differences. The remaining 25 percent of the original debt, which was transferred to the Agricultural Bank, was to be paid to the banks by the state in 3 percent government bonds, payable in 20 years and issued for the state account by the Agricultural Bank. These bonds could be used by the banks for the payment of tax arrears until 1932, and also for the payment of deposits to "old" (prior to April 20, 1932) depositors and other creditors of the banks under moratorium, but only at the request of the former and in proportion to their respective claims.

To contribute to the mobilization of banks by mobilizing peasant debts transferred to the Agricultural Bank, it was decreed that the Bank might make cash advances to the banks on the basis of these assets or issue them bonds which could serve as collateral for loans. It was also decreed that peasants might use these bonds for repayment of their debts to the Agricultural Bank, but only if they became its debtors through legislation on peasant debts.

After the Decree of September 25, 1936, the Agricultural Bank was the only creditor of the peasants whose debts it took over from the commercial and savings banks and credit co-operatives, and its claims against the peasants were collected by tax collectors on the basis of special lists in the same manner as government taxes.

The Agricultural Bank took over from the commercial and savings banks and credit co-operatives a total of 2,997 million dinars of peasant debts representing 764,910 various credit contracts. Liability for 25 percent of this debt, or 750 million dinars, was assumed by the state automatically, as it had to bear 25 percent of the original debt. Since the commercial banks had exhausted a considerable portion of their reserve funds (surplus) and share capital by 1935, the state in all probability had to assume a part of their share. Thus the state's share in the settlement of peasant debts was perhaps between 900 million and 1 billion dinars, or about one-third of the original amount of peasant debts to commercial and savings banks and credit co-operatives.

In the appraisal of the peasant-debts legislation the most important problems are how various measures influenced the economic position of the peasantry and the functioning of the nation's credit system and, through these two channels, the whole of the national economy. There is no doubt that the moratorium introduced by the Law of April 19, 1932, meant a great relief for the indebted peasants from both psychological and economic points of view. Considering the extent of the fall of prices of agricultural products, lessened ability to sell them, and the cancellation of outstanding loans on the part of creditors, scores of thousands of peasants would probably have lost their properties to creditors without the protective legislation. But there is even less doubt that the protective legislation on peasant debts was used by the dictatorial regime of Yugoslavia as a measure of pacifying the peasants and securing their support for the regime. Of course, the government did not want to antagonize the creditor groups which had to be affected by this legislation, and therefore delayed as long as possible the scaling down of the debts, reducing the interest rates, and extending the schedules of repayment as finally incorporated in the Decree of September 25, 1936. As far as commercial and savings banks and credit co-operatives were concerned, the possibility of invoking a six-year moratorium for their liabilities, granted to them by the legislation on peasant debts and banking, saved about one-half of the banks and a considerable number of co-operatives from bankruptcy. Because of this, it was often stated in Yugoslavia during the 1930's that the whole legislation on peasant debts was much more a scheme to assist the banks, or at least to avoid the bankruptcy of many of them, than to help the peasants. Even if this legislation saved the banks which invoked moratorium from bankruptcy, a large number of these banks entered under the provisions of the protective legislation into virtual liquidation.

But the legislation on peasant debts also had grave consequences for the peasants both before 1936 and after. After 1932 the peasants were not able to obtain any credit either from the banks or from private moneylenders, as everybody was afraid that subsequent politically conditioned government measures might unfavorably affect these credit contracts. In addition, greatly reduced interest rates (by decree) made all credit operations by financial institutions much less attractive, especially in view of the added risks. Needless to say, during the 1930's the need of the peasants for credit was as great as before. Thus, in the final analysis the peasants' former financial obligations were reduced nominally, though in real terms much less so because of the fall in prices, and repayment was postponed, but at the price of their complete inability to obtain new credit either to finance consumption in times of stress or to finance new investments on the farms.

Furthermore, there were now few groups of creditors who could afford to give them credit even if safety existed. Not only were the private moneylenders afraid of the new legislation, but also a large portion of their resources was frozen in the hands of the peasants. Commercial and savings banks, weakened by the withdrawal of savings deposits and by losses in their investments in industry, trade, and shipping, and leading an inactive existence under the actual or threatened moratorium, were both unwilling to and incapable of extending new credit either to peasants or to anyone else. The rules pertaining to the investment of "new" funds of banks under moratorium were so stringent that most of these funds had to be invested either in government securities or kept in cash. The chief source of funds for investment of all commercial and savings banks, the savings and business deposits, was steadily falling. A great number of credit co-operatives were also in serious difficulties because a large part of their funds was frozen in the hands of the peasants and because their savings deposits were also reduced. The Chartered Agricultural Bank, as already pointed out, lacked any means for the financing of agriculture once it had invested the funds obtained from the subscription of its share capital.

But while practically all private financial institutions and some of the specialized government financial institutions (Agricultural Bank, Artisans Bank) were becoming financially more and more anemic and a large number of commercial and savings banks were slowly liquidating their affairs, the two government banks, the State Mortgage Bank and the Postal Savings System, were attracting practically all new savings deposits in the economy as well as a large part of those savings deposits that could be withdrawn from private banks. The basic reason was that deposits in these two financial institutions enjoyed government guaranty and were presumed not to be exposed to freezing. This whole development of the weakening of commercial and savings banks and of credit co-operatives, on the one hand, and of greatly strengthening the two government banks, on the other, is clearly indicated in Table 47. But the basic point in connection with this development was

TABLE 47.—SAVINGS DEPOSITS BY CATEGORIES OF FINANCIAL INSTITUTIONS
AT THE END OF 1930 AND 1937*

(Million dinars)

Category	1930	1937
State Mortgage Bank	528.9	1,383.9
Postal Savings System	203.4	1,249.0
Artisans Bank	32.5	44.7
Chartered Agricultural Bank	9.8	48.0
Commercial and savings banks	10,294.1	5,314.4
Savings banks of autonomous bodies	1,415.0	2,028.1
Co-operatives	2,400.3	1,985.2[a]
Total	14,884.0	12,053.3

* Source: Yugoslavia, *Annuaire statistique 1931* (Belgrade, 1934), pp. 227–41, 292–99, for 1930, and *Annuaire statistique 1938–1939* (Belgrade, 1939), pp. 292–304, for 1937.
[a] This figure refers to the end of 1935, *Annuaire statistique 1936* (Belgrade, 1937), pp. 334–35.

that the funds which flowed into the two government banks during the 1930's were used almost exclusively for the financing of government deficits and for the needs of numerous and growing government-owned industries, a part of them intended to strengthen the defensive power of the country. Private industry and trade saw little and agriculture almost no direct benefit from the greatly increased capacity of these government banks to make loans. There was no segment in the Yugoslav credit system that was capable of supplying or willing after 1932 to supply any credit to agriculture.

The measures incorporated in the Decree of September 25, 1936, did not alter this picture at all, except that a basic step was made in the direction of cleaning up the complex of peasant debts. By the end of 1939 the Agricultural Bank collected from the peasants 338 million dinars as annuities on their debts toward the Bank according to the Decree of September 25, 1936. On the other hand, the Bank paid to commercial and savings banks and credit co-operatives until the end of 1939 a total of 199 million dinars in cash and delivered to them 411 million dinars in 3 percent government bonds. Thus, while nominally the commercial and savings banks and credit co-operatives until the end of 1939 received from the Agricultural Bank somewhat over one-fifth of the original debts transferred to that Bank, they actually got only one-fifteenth in cash and the remainder in another type of "heavy asset," the 3 percent government bonds. Thus the operations of the Agricultural Bank from 1936 to 1939 contributed little toward the mobilization of banks under moratorium. Nor did they restore the ability of the peasants to obtain credit. Yet a proper solution of the problem of old peasant debts should have striven exactly toward these two aims.

CHAPTER 28

AGRICULTURE AND TAXATION

A STUDY of Yugoslav peasantry and agriculture during the interwar period would not be complete without discussion of the burden of taxation imposed upon the peasantry and of the benefits accruing to the peasantry from the activity of the state. This discussion will be brief, partly because of the limitations of space, and partly because of the lack of data on the distribution of the tax burden.

When Yugoslavia was established in 1918, each one of the provinces and portions of provinces included in the new state had its special system of taxation and its special fiscal administration. These differences existed with regard to central and regional and local government taxes. The approach to the problem of central government taxes, immediately after World War I, was very different with regard to direct and indirect taxes. In the field of regional and local government taxation, great differences continued to exist throughout the interwar period. Until the beginning of 1929 the existing direct taxes in the various provinces were maintained, but high surtaxes were introduced to account for the greatly increased fiscal needs of the state and for the depreciation of the currency. This situation caused great differences in the tax burden of various areas. As a rule, taxes were higher in areas outside of Serbia. Taxation thus was an important political issue during the 1920's. A unified system of direct taxes was introduced by the Law on Direct Taxes of February 8, 1928, which became effective as of January 1, 1929. Indirect taxes levied by the central government were gradually unified in the early 1920's. As a rule, the unification was effected by extending the pre-1914 Serbian laws on various forms of indirect taxes to the whole country. At the same time tax rates were raised to meet the new fiscal needs of the government.

In the first two years after World War I, Yugoslavia was faced with the problem of currency unification, because at the close of the war six different currencies circulated in its territory. The problem was successfully solved, but it involved somewhat higher burdens for the part of the population outside of Serbia. Furthermore, in the early postwar years a large portion of government expenditures was financed by the issue of paper money, which resulted in inflation and its usual conse-

681

quences. The newly established state inherited a large public debt, partly composed of obligations contracted in pre-1914 years and partly of loans obtained from the Allied powers and the United States during and immediately after World War I. It took several years before the main issues connected with that indebtedness were cleared up. The service of these debts greatly increased the tax burden in the country and complicated the problem of the balance of payments throughout the interwar period. Financial settlement of the domestic damages caused by the war and of claims of landlords affected by the agrarian reform were also carried out by payment with government bonds. On the other hand, Yugoslavia received large amounts from former enemy countries, especially from Germany, in the form of reparations. This type of revenue, mostly in kind, was important until 1930.

The nature of the Yugoslav taxation system during the interwar period is best seen in the structure of the tax revenue. As there was not much change in the basic composition of tax revenue from year to year, any particular fiscal year can serve as an example. Thus, in the fiscal year 1931/32 (April 1, 1931–March 31, 1932) the total tax revenue of the central government of 6,205.4 million dinars was derived from the following sources:

Direct taxes		1,471.0 million dinars
Indirect taxes		
Consumption excise taxes	703.7	
Stamp duties	1,044.7	
Custom duties	1,053.7	
Monopoly taxes[1]	1,618.2	
Turnover tax	314.1	4,734.4 million dinars

Direct taxes accounted for only 23.7 percent and indirect taxes for 76.3 percent of the total revenue from taxes.

In addition, in that fiscal year the government had a surplus in the revenue of government enterprises of 224.4 million dinars, it received 146.9 million dinars as the cash portion of its receipts from reparations, and finally there was a sundry revenue of 180.9 million dinars.

Over the years there was a small increase in the proportion of revenue derived from direct taxes as compared with revenue from indirect taxes. Official statistics in this regard are misleading and show a much larger shift toward direct taxes. The explanation lies in the fact that the general turnover tax, a typical general tax on consumption, is taken

---

[1] Monopoly taxes are consumption excise taxes imposed on articles whose production and/or trade was a government monopoly (see p. 690).

as a direct tax in official statistics. This tax increased continually during the interwar period. Moreover, in years of depression the relative share of revenue from indirect taxes, where the taxpayer has some latitude in avoiding them, has usually fallen more, in spite of increased rates, than the revenue from direct taxes whose payment was enforced with harshness.

It is, however, only through a closer look at both the direct and indirect taxes levied by the central, regional, and local governments that one can see the many ways in which the peasants were subjected to taxation and the approximate extent of the burden imposed on the agricultural population by taxes.

DIRECT TAXES

Table 48 gives the recenue from direct taxes in the fiscal year 1930/31, the estimated revenue for the fiscal year 1931/32, and the actual revenue for that fiscal year. There was no general income tax in Yugoslavia during the interwar period. Specific types of income were subject to special basic taxes and surtaxes without regard to income from other sources. The gross income of the taxpayer was not taken into account for taxation purposes, although, under considera-

TABLE 48.—REVENUE FROM DIRECT TAXES IN FISCAL YEARS
1930/31 AND 1931/32*

(*Million dinars*)

Type of tax	Actual revenue in 1930/31	Estimated revenue in 1931/32	Actual revenue in 1931/32
Land tax	662.0	610.0	479.6
Tax on income from houses	171.6	258.0	191.3
Tax on income from non-corporate business	296.6	220.0	214.8
Tax on interest and dividends ..	55.7	62.0	60.2
Corporation tax	301.8	160.0	126.3
Payroll tax	274.6	260.0	278.4
Tax on bachelors	—	1.0	3.3
Military exemption tax	4.5	5.0	5.4
Tax arrears	150.4	50.0	87.8
Interest on due taxes	33.9	30.0	23.9
Total	1,951.1	1,656.0	1,471.0

* Source: As computed on the basis of official data from Jozo Tomašević, *Financijska politika Jugoslavije, 1929–1934* (Fiscal Policy of Yugoslavia, 1929–1934) (Zagreb, 1935), p. 87.

tion of dependents and other legitimate deductions, it alone is the true expression of his capacity to pay taxes. Thus, through the variation of the basic and surtax rates applying to income from various sources, it was possible to grant special tax exemptions or subsidies to specific groups of the population, of which more will be said presently.

The most important single type of direct tax was the tax on the income from land. With the exception of two minor direct taxes (the tax on bachelors and the military exemption tax, which was imposed on some peasants), the land tax was the only type of tax levied by the central government that every peasant clearly "saw" and felt. The peasants tried to reduce this tax by underdeclaration of land property, tried to postpone its payment by eluding the tax collector, and cursed it when finally forced to pay it. As we shall see later, they paid, together with this tax, also the surtaxes imposed by the regional and local governments. From the other direct tax to which the peasants could most logically be subjected, the tax on houses, they were fully exempted according to the law of 1928. Of course, in so far as the peasants had other income that was subject to other special direct taxes, they had to pay them, but, with the exception of payroll tax, which was deducted by the employer each time he paid the wages, that was a rare occasion.

The tax on income from land consisted of a basic tax and of a progressive surtax. The basic tax was originally (in 1928) set at 12 percent, and the surtax started with 2 percent for incomes from land between 1,000 and 2,000 dinars and rose up to 17 percent for incomes in excess of 150,000 dinars. Both the tax and the surtax were based on the cadastral net income. The cadastral net income or income from land used as basis for tax assessment was defined by the Tax Law of 1928 as "the money value of the average yield of land which can be achieved with prevailing methods of farm operation after the deduction of the average amount of regular production costs." As the basis for the calculation of the average income from land, the government took the average prices of agricultural products and the costs in the period July 1925 to June 1926. Toward the end of 1929 the surtax rates were reduced to a maximum of 12 percent for incomes above 25,000 dinars, and by a law of May 30, 1930, these surtax rates were reduced to a maximum of 8 percent. Under the influence of the Great Depression, the parliament (created in 1931 by King Alexander) enacted reductions of the land tax on several occasions during the early 1930's. First, the land tax assessments for 1931 were reduced by 20 percent; second, the basic tax on the income from land was reduced from 12 to 10 percent; and in 1933 additional temporary reductions were written into the law. It was revealed in the budget debate in the beginning of 1936, however, that the tax collectors in rural areas, on orders from the Ministry of Finance, completely disregarded these temporary reductions of the land tax enacted by the parliament. Further, and this time genuine, reductions in the land tax were enacted in 1936 by reducing the cadastral net income, and continued to be observed until the end of the interwar period. Land tax assessments in these years were substantially below those of the early 1930's.

Temporarily freed from the land tax was income from reclaimed land, from newly planted vineyards for a varying length of time depending on the type of soil on which they were planted, from newly planted olive groves, from newly planted prune orchards (only from varieties used for production of dried prunes), from reforested land, and from land affected by natural disasters.

During the early 1930's there were increases in all other direct taxes in order to increase the tax revenue and thereby to reduce the deficit in the budget. Moreover, the procedure in the collection of all direct taxes became much more severe. It was especially severe in the villages where the depression greatly reduced the income of the population and thereby its capacity to pay taxes. Writing early in 1935 about the development of tax policies in Yugoslavia, this writer said: "During the past three years the chief concern [of the government] was to increase direct taxes and to collect them by methods which truly mark this period as a time of taxation terror."[2] Needless to say, the existing indirect taxes were also increased and new commodities and services subjected to taxes.

The tax burden imposed on income from noncorporate businesses, on income of corporations, and on wages and salaries was also quite heavy, but the first two could largely be shifted onto other people. On the other hand, there were two types of income, as a rule both of them received by people in high income brackets, which were either fully freed from direct taxes or subjected to a relatively low tax burden. In the first group was income from holdings of most government securities which was fully exempted from tax. This was one means of attracting investors. But the most important case of taxation of income at exceptionally low rates, which amounted to tax subsidization, was applied

---

[2] Jozo Tomašević, *Financijska politika Jugoslavije, 1929–1934* (Fiscal Policy of Yugoslavia, 1929–1934), p. 200. For a general review of the development of taxation and government finances during the interwar period see Yugoslavia, Ministry of Finance, *Ministarstvo Finansija Kraljevine Jugoslavije, 1918–1938* (Ministry of Finance of the Kingdom of Yugoslavia, 1918–1938), pp. 19–213.

to income from new housing in urban centers. According to the original provision of the Tax Law of 1928 (similar conditions existed also before the enactment of that law), owners of housing in urban areas built after World War I paid only a flat tax rate of 3 percent on their net income from such housing. This virtual tax exemption was granted for cities of 50,000 or more people, and also for all newly built hotels, for a period of 20 years, and for other towns for a period of ten years. In December 1932 this rate was raised to 6 percent for buildings which were subject to tax payment prior to December 31, 1931, and to 12 percent for buildings which became subject to taxes after that date. Moreover, the income from old urban housing was taxed at considerably lower rates than corresponding income from other sources.

The worst economic consequence of this tax subsidization of urban rental housing was the fact that a large portion of the current domestic capital formation went into the investment of this type of durable consumer goods. The pretext on which this tax subsidization was defended was the rapid growth of urban population and the need for additional housing facilities. There is little doubt, however, that it was partly enacted to favor the interests of the upper income groups in urban centers who represented the main support for the regime. In addition to favorable tax legislation there were, however, some other factors which attracted capital into urban housing. First, in interwar Yugoslavia this type of investment was considered not only among the most profitable but also one of the safest investments. Second, it required little if any managing skill, which was an important consideration in a country where lack of truly entrepreneurial ability was a serious bottleneck. Third, housing construction in urban areas, especially in Belgrade, enjoyed not only this tax subsidization but the interest rate subsidization also. A large portion of mortgage credit for the financing of urban housing was granted by the State Mortgage Bank at interest rates which were considerably below the prevailing free market rates for similar credit. The high rents for urban housing, which were mentioned above, resulted not only from high demand for housing, but also from high cost of housing construction. These had several causes, the most important being that prices of building materials were cartelized, labor methods in the construction industry were primitive, safety rules were quite extravagant, and most of the electrical and plumbing appliances had to be imported from abroad.

It was, however, not only individuals who were eager to invest in urban housing. Various organizations which administered trust funds, such as associations of professional groups, educational foundations, and churches, invested practically all of their funds in urban housing. Moreover, insurance companies which lacked sufficient suitable opportunities of investment for their funds in other fields were forced to invest even more in urban housing than prescribed by law. Finally, the government itself conducted throughout the interwar period a policy of investing large sums in buildings for the needs of the government, many of which were conceived more for representation than to serve their function at the least cost.

To complete the picture with regard to investment in housing during the interwar period, it is necessary to remember what was said earlier about the housing in rural areas (see pp. 580–81). The fact that between 400,000 and 450,000 new peasant households were established during the interwar period necessitated large investment of capital of the rural population in housing. This, naturally, reduced their ability to invest in the production processes of agriculture.

There were, thus, many reasons for the fact that throughout the interwar period a large portion of current capital formation was put into housing, especially urban housing. While there are no statistical data to prove this point exactly, one may not be too wrong in saying that perhaps 50 to 60 percent of the current domestic capital formation went into housing and government buildings. This situation, however, was not limited to Yugoslavia, but apparently was a general pattern characteristic of other economically underdeveloped areas of Southeastern and Eastern Europe and Latin America. In countries in which the lack of capital was the chief bottleneck preventing economic development, investment of an unduly high proportion of domestic capital in residential and public buildings was obviously harmful. In Yugoslavia at least, the tax policy was an important factor which contributed to that development.

INDIRECT TAXES

As shown above, the proportion of indirect taxes in the total tax revenue of the central government of Yugoslavia in the fiscal year 1931/32 amounted to 76.3 percent of the total. Under the existing socioeconomic circumstances, that was quite understandable. Indirect taxes were easy, simple, and cheap to administer, while direct taxes, which involved the filing of tax declarations and individual payments to tax collectors, were quite cumbersome in a country of small agricultural proprietors, where a large portion of output was not marketed, widespread illiteracy prevailed, and where the administration was generally inefficient. Indirect taxes are very effective from a fiscal point of view, because they catch the taxpayer as consumer on every occasion that he makes use of his income to purchase taxed commodities or services. Indirect taxes are paid much more easily by the uninitiated public as they are included in the price of goods and services and thus, so to speak, are concealed. Moreover, here the principle "pay as you go" is perfectly realized, a fact which is important in regard to people with low incomes. The basic consideration was that the government needed a certain amount of public revenue, and without the accent on indirect taxes it would never have been able to collect it. In view of this overriding consideration in its fiscal policy, the government followed a policy of charging its citizens as often as possible and as heavily as possible; taking the money where it could find it, and getting it from those who made the least outcry rather than according to the principle of ability to pay.

Indirect taxes in Yugoslavia during the interwar period consisted of five categories: consumption excise taxes, stamp duties, monopoly taxes, customs duties, and general turnover tax. Table 49 shows the

TABLE 49.—REVENUE FROM INDIRECT TAXES IN FISCAL YEARS
1930/31 AND 1931/32*

(Million dinars)

Type of tax	Actual revenue in 1930/31	Estimated revenue in 1931/32	Actual revenue in 1931/32
Consumption excise taxes	910.5	803.0	703.7
Stamp duties	1,196.5	1,245.2	1,044.7
Monopoly taxes (net)	1,779.5	1,839.2	1,618.2
Customs duties	1,479.7	1,488.2	1,053.7
General turnover tax	143.0	450.0	314.2
Total	5,509.2	5,825.6	4,734.5

* Source: As computed on the basis of official data from Jozo Tomašević, *Financijska politika Jugoslavije, 1929–1934* (Fiscal Policy of Yugoslavia, 1929–1934) (Zagreb, 1935), p. 86.

actual revenue from indirect taxes in the fiscal year 1930/31, the estimated revenue for the fiscal year 1931/32, and the actual revenue for that year.

A large number of products of mass consumption that were not subject to either the monopoly tax or the import duty (except coffee, which was subject to the latter) were subject to the consumption excise tax. The backbone of central government consumption excise taxes was the excise on sugar which, in the period 1931 to 1935, annually yielded an average of 548.2 million dinars. The tax amounted to approximately 200 percent of the value of sugar at the factory. Other products which were subject to consumption excise tax in 1931 were coffee, wine, brandies and liqueurs, beer, industrial alcohol, yeast, gas for lighting, electric bulbs, acetic acid, and gasoline. In the following years some other products were subjected to excise tax, while others, such as wine and brandy, were transferred to the tax jurisdiction of the regional and local governments. It is obvious that most of these articles were consumed primarily by the city population. But in the case of sugar and coffee a considerable portion was consumed in the village. In the case of wine and brandy the excise was supposed to be fully carried by the consumer, but in fact it was largely borne by the producer.

The stamp duty was an important source of tax revenue, but was paid only by those who engaged in certain activities or asked the state for certain services, e.g., the issue of a birth certificate, a school certificate, or a license of some kind. To be legally valid, all these documents had to be provided with revenue stamps. It might be said that, except for purposes of information, a citizen could not approach the government in any but written form by submitting a "request" (*molba*), and, to be acceptable for consideration, the written request had to be taxed. The peasants did not pay a great deal of this tax directly, but a portion of it was shifted to them in the trading process.

Customs duties were an important type of indirect taxation of great interest to the peasant population. It is true that import duties on most agricultural products, such as grains, wine, eggs, and livestock, protected the agricultural producers from imports of such commodities from abroad. But there were also export duties on some products of agriculture needed for domestic industries which tended to depress the prices of these products, because if they could have been freely exported, they perhaps could have been sold at higher prices. The great burden for agriculture resulted, however, from import duties which it had to pay on products which it needed, whether they were imported from abroad or produced at home behind the wall of tariff protection. In this category there was a large number of products used by the peasants such as agricultural implements and machinery, artificial fertilizers, pesticides, textiles, footwear, coffee, glassware, and kitchen utensils. Moreover, various other classes of people who were paying customs duties and who traded with the peasants were able to shift at least a part of that burden to the peasants.

A turnover tax existed in Yugoslavia from 1920 onward. Only goods which were subject to heavy monopoly taxes and products of agriculture and animal husbandry when sold by the producer for the first time were exempt from it. The products of the cottage industry were also exempt provided that no wage labor was used in their production. It is necessary to stress, however, that agricultural and livestock products were subject to this tax if they were objects of trade after the initial sale by the producer. The rates of this tax were steadily increased, its coverage was enlarged to include commodities, services, and claims, and its collection was greatly improved, especially after the reform of 1930. This can be seen best from the fact that in 1930/31 the revenue from this tax was 143.0 million dinars, in 1931/32 it rose to 314.2 million dinars, and, after further increases in rates and improvements in administration, it yielded not less than 834.0 million dinars in 1937/38.

In no other group of indirect taxes was the extortionist character of the Yugoslav taxation system of the interwar period so obvious as in the case of the state monopoly taxes. The articles included in government monopolies and the respective gross revenue from each in the calendar year 1931 were as follows (in million dinars): tobacco 1,710.4; matches 119.4; cigarette paper 85.0; salt 316.1; and kerosene 126.9. Even if the peasants smoked the low-quality cigarettes or the lower-priced cut tobacco, they carried a large portion of the burden of the tobacco monopoly tax because of their great numbers. The same can be said for the companion monopoly articles, cigarette paper and matches (pipe smoking was very limited in Yugoslavia). Some of the smokers were able to acquire contraband tobacco and cigarette paper. To protect match consumption, lighters were prohibitively taxed. The peasants were hit not only as consumers of tobacco products but in areas where tobacco was produced the interests of the peasants were unfavorably affected by the production and price policies of the Monopoly Administration regarding raw tobacco. As a rule, the price for raw tobacco was only a small fraction of the price (including tax) that the government charged the consumers. But even more appalling than the situation with regard to tobacco monopoly was the fact that salt, both for human and for livestock consumption, was a monopoly article paying a high tax. In that case, the tax was virtually taken from the mouths of even the poorest people in the country. Kerosene was primarily an article used in rural areas for lighting and it was also subject to a heavy monopoly tax.

The tax element in the gross revenue of the Monopoly Administration in the fiscal years 1924/25 to 1926/27 was, on the average (in percent): tobacco 68.3, salt 63.4, cigarette paper 82.8, matches 89.6, and kerosene 97.9. In the case of kerosene, gross revenue apparently represented only the monopoly tax, and the difference of 2.1 percent, the cost of collecting it from the producers. The same relationships most probably obtained also in the fiscal year 1931/32.

GOVERNMENT-OWNED ENTERPRISES

One of the important characteristics of the Yugoslav economy during the interwar period, which was also common to its neighboring countries, was that the central and local governments owned and operated a great number of business enterprises. Shortly before World War II the central government owned and operated all railroads (some small lines which were privately owned were leased to the government), all telegraph and telephone lines and radio stations, most of river shipping and harbor storage facilities, the canals, large areas of forests, some large lumber mills, a score of coal mines, some iron ore mines and steel plants, all processing facilities for tobacco and salt, and several sugar factories. The central government owned some hotels, a large number of hospitals, several large publishing enterprises, practically all stage theaters and opera companies, and a large portion of the country's banking. It had also part interests in other enterprises. Local governments, especially municipalities, owned urban transport and other public utilities, hospitals, slaughterhouses, and savings banks. The chief reasons for this were the lack of capital and the fact that only the state, with its taxing power, was capable of contracting large loans needed to finance many of these enterprises. Lack of entrepreneurial talent was a contributing factor in this whole development. Moreover, a large number of these enterprises were in the nature of public services, which often lacked profit prospects and therefore did not attract private capital. It should be pointed out that Yugoslavia acquired some business enterprises, e.g., large timber mills, and some forests and farms, by taking over former enemy property in accordance with the treaties of peace after World War I or in accordance with the legislation on the agrarian reform.

The imposing extent of business enterprises owned by the central government during the interwar period can be seen from the fact that in the fiscal year 1931/32, when the total government expenditures for administrative purposes amounted to 7,384.3 million dinars, the expenditures of government-owned enterprises amounted to 4,145.4 million dinars. The bulk of these expenditures was made by the enterprises managed by the Ministry of Transportation (railroads, river shipping, postal, telegraph, and telephone services) which amounted to 2,904.9

million dinars. Second largest, 665.1 million dinars, were the expenditures of enterprises in the Ministry of Finance, followed by those in the Ministry of Forests and Mines, which were 410.7 million dinars. Expenditures of enterprises managed by other ministries were small.

By owning such enterprises as railroads and river shipping, the government had at its disposal facilities to affect the private economy in general, and agriculture in particular, by properly adjusting its rates for services. Generally speaking, government enterprises did not show any special consideration for the interests of the agricultural population. It is also very important to stress that the government failed to develop enterprises which could have been used for systematic assistance to agriculture. Here two types of enterprise come readily to mind. On the one hand, the government failed to engage in large-scale land reclamation and irrigation programs, which could have been combined with the development of electric power. On the other hand, it even failed, until 1939, to start building storage facilities for agricultural products, primarily grains, although this would have improved the marketing of cereals and most probably would have contributed to the increase in the income of agriculture. The activity of government enterprises in the marketing of agricultural products and in providing loans to agriculture has already been discussed.

While prices of goods and rates for services charged by government enterprises might have contained an element of tax, perennial deficits (with occasional surpluses) of these enterprises suggest that this was not a general practice. Thus, when considering the cost of government and the tax load in Yugoslavia during the interwar period, it is in order to leave the revenue and expenditures of government-owned enterprises out of consideration.

GOVERNMENT EXPENDITURES

The problem of public finances from the point of view of the agricultural population was not only that taxes represented a tremendous burden on their income, but also that they saw little good from government expenditures. Government expenditures in the fiscal year 1931/32 (except the expenditures of government-owned enterprises and of another category mentioned below) are shown in Table 50. The relationships of actual expenditures for various branches of government administration as shown in the fiscal year 1931/32 can be taken as typical of the whole interwar period.

It would be wrong, however, to think that the figures on government revenue and expenditures, as published for wide circulation,

TABLE 50.—APPROPRIATIONS AND ACTUAL EXPENDITURES FOR GOVERNMENT
ADMINISTRATION IN THE FISCAL YEAR 1931/32*

(*Million dinars*)

	Appropriations	Actual expenditures
Crown and the supreme government administration	259.9	170.8
Pensions	1,168.1	1,088.8
Public Debt Service	1,220.3	918.6
Ministry of Justice	435.9	397.2
Ministry of Education	1,001.1	914.3
Ministry of Foreign Affairs	156.0	143.8
Ministry of the Interior	644.0	590.4
Ministry of Finance	400.9	366.0
Ministry of Army and Navy	2,598.9	2,187.8
Ministry of Public Works	279.3	192.2
Ministry of Transportation	177.9	117.1
Ministry of Agriculture	97.0	56.4
Ministry of Trade and Industry	71.0	55.0
Ministry of Social Policy and Public Health	230.5	177.7
Reserve credits	40.7	8.2
Total	8,781.5	7,384.3

* Source: Yugoslavia, *Annuaire statistique 1931* (Belgrade, 1934), p. 457.

actually included all government revenues and expenditures in the respective fiscal years. A considerable amount of revenue, that is, revenue other than that from taxes and government enterprises—e.g., reparations receipts up to 1931, short-term and long-term borrowing, revenue from the revaluation of gold stock, and revenue from coining token money, as well as a great number of expenditures of various kinds—was shown only in the so-called Account of Working Capital of the Central State Treasury. In the course of the fiscal years 1929/30 to 1933/34 the expenditures of this account averaged 1,307 million dinars and the revenue averaged 1,183 million dinars annually. In the fiscal year 1931/32 its expenditures amounted to 1,450 million dinars and its revenues were 2,946 million dinars, the bulk coming from the proceeds of the foreign stabilization loan of 1931. In this cursory review of Yugoslav public finances, which is primarily interested in showing the tax burden imposed upon agriculture and the services and benefits agriculture received from the government, the financial operations conducted through the Account of Working Capital of the Central State Treasury can be left out of consideration. It should be pointed out, however, that Yugoslavia did not engage in systematic deficit financing as a means of combating depression during the 1930's. Deficits were an annual occurrence between the 1930/31 and 1934/35 fiscal years, but were considered a financial sin, and all ministers of finance took great pains in trying to show that they were smaller than they actually were. But even if the deficits were held in such low esteem, they had the salutary tendency of raising the national income at a time when this was especially needed.

The most outstanding fact about government expenditures for administration throughout the interwar period was that between about 28 and 35 percent was openly spent for military purposes. Certain military expenditures were also probably financed through the Ministry of the Interior and the Ministry of Transportation. Needless to say, military expenditures imposed a terrific burden upon the nation's economy. It is interesting to note that during the entire interwar period there was not a voice raised against so high a level of military expenditures, even by the otherwise very vocal members of the opposition parties. The armed forces were above any criticism. The tragedy of the situation, in retrospect, was that when the Yugoslav interwar military establishment was put to the test following the invasion in April 1941, it collapsed overnight, both morally and militarily. There is little doubt, however, that during the interwar period these large military expenditures sapped the economic and financial strength of the country, retarded its economic development, and were one of the causes contributing to the low level of living.

The large expenditures of the Ministry of the Interior, which was in charge of the police forces, were quite understandable for a police state. These expenditures were considerably increased after 1929, namely, after the introduction of King Alexander's dictatorship. The expenditures for the payment of retirement pensions for government employees were also interesting because of their large size. This figure also included the pensions of invalids of the earlier wars. In the 1931/32 fiscal year this item took 14.7 percent of all expenditures for government administration.

It is quite understandable that every state tries to provide for its security against outside as well as inside enemies. But it is also clear that the protection of national security in the case of a small country at the crossroads of international power politics might have perhaps been better served by such conduct of national affairs that the mass of people would acquire a genuine interest in the state as a promoter of their welfare. No such feeling was present in the Yugoslav state during the interwar period.

The best proof of how little the government thought of promoting the economic and social interest of its population is to be found in the pitifully low expenditures for government functions and services to further economic development in the fields of agriculture, industry, and trade. Also expenditures on education and public health were very inadequate compared with the existing needs. Government activities for the promotion of agriculture were discussed in Chapter 21. In the fiscal year 1929/30, the most prosperous year in Yugoslavia during the interwar period, the total expenditures of the central government for administration were 7,386 million dinars, in which the Ministry of Agriculture participated with 78.5 million dinars, or 1.06 percent. In the fiscal year 1931/32 the share of the Ministry of Agriculture in total expenditures of the central government for administrative purposes was reduced to 56.4 million dinars, or 0.76 percent. As we shall see below, local governments, especially the *banovine*, spent additional money for the purposes of "advancement of agriculture," but these expenditures were also very small. The reason for this situation was quite simple. The task of improving the economic situation of the population at large, and especially of the peasantry, was at the bottom of the scale of priorities as established by the interwar governments.

REGIONAL AND LOCAL GOVERNMENT FINANCES

In a centralistically organized state such as Yugoslavia during the interwar period, a large portion of the activities of regional and local governments consisted in serving as organs of central government. This situation was reflected both in their delegated and in their autonomous functions, as well as in the nature, sources, and amount of their revenue. Of the three layers of such government which existed in Yugoslavia during the interwar period, only *banovine* (and former *oblasti*) and the communes had independent budgets and a special system of revenues and expenditures. The counties—which were interposed between the *banovine* and the communes—were operated exclusively as organs of the banovinal and central governments and were financed solely through their respective budgets.

The rural and urban communes and *banovine* were financed by five types of regular revenue: surtaxes on direct taxes imposed by the central government, consumption excise taxes, stamp duties and fees, payment in cash in lieu of the personal work obligation, and the grants-in-

aid from the central government. In 1931 the tax revenue of regional
and local governments, including the grants-in-aid from the central government, were as follows (in millions of dinars):[3]

	Rural communes	Munici- palities	*Banovine*
Surtaxes	361.6	235.7	172.9
Consumption excise taxes	37.8	306.9	154.3
Stamp duties and fees	23.3	203.4	72.4
Payments in lieu of personal work	4.5	30.3	41.2
Grants-in-aid from the central government	8.0	27.3	101.3
Total	435.2	803.6	542.1

But in addition to the revenue from taxes and grants-in-aid, regional
and local governments also had other sources of revenue. Disregarding
the cash position at the beginning and at the end of 1931, which did
not differ much, total revenue of these governments was as follows:
rural communes 604.2; municipalities 1,814.1; and *banovine* 907.3
million dinars. The difference between the revenue from taxes and
grants-in-aid and the total revenue came from arrears of earlier years
(partly tax), business enterprises and landed property, from interest on
holdings of securities, from borrowing, and from other unforeseen
sources. The revenues of municipalities from business enterprises and
land property were especially large (558 million dinars). There is
little doubt, however, that a portion of profits made by business enterprises of regional and local governments, especially of municipalities,
was actually a tax charged in the form of higher prices for services rendered (such as profits from slaughterhouses, city market places, and
city transportation).

The tax revenue of rural communes depended essentially (83.1
percent) on surtaxes upon the basic portion of direct tax on the income
from land levied by the central government. Municipalities, on the
other hand, derived only 29.3 percent and *banovine* 31.9 percent of
their tax revenue from surtaxes. There existed tremendous differences
in surtax rates imposed by various communes and municipalities. In
1930 approximately one-half of all communes imposed surtaxes ranging from 100 to 300 percent, and about 230 communes had surtaxes
ranging from 500 to 2,000 percent of the basic tax.[4] Surtaxes upon the
basic tax of the central government imposed by the *banovine* at that
time ranged only from 15 to 35 percent.

[3] Yugoslavia, *Annuaire statistique 1931*, pp. 468–69.
[4] Milorad B. Tošić, "Local Government Finances in 1930," *Narodno blagostanje*,
February 20, 1932, pp. 118–19.

While the consumption excise taxes and stamp duties were only a minor source of tax revenue, including grants-in-aid, of rural communes (14 percent), the municipalities derived from these two sources 63.5 and the *banovine* 41.8 percent of all their revenue from taxes and grants-in-aid. The excise taxes were imposed by municipalities and *banovine* not only upon some of the products that also paid an excise tax to the central government, e.g., alcoholic beverages and coffee, but upon practically all products that entered their territory for purposes of trade or consumption. These charges were also imposed on practically all products that the peasants brought into the cities for sale. The leading position in this regard was held by the capital city of Belgrade, which in 1935 charged consumption excise tax on 231 different commodities.[5] Most of the stamp duties imposed by rural communes, municipalities, and *banovine* were also in the form of surcharges on or parallel to central government stamp duties. A certain amount of income was derived by regional and local governments from cash payments in lieu of personal work that, according to law, all taxpayers were obliged to render, essentially in repairing of roads.

The excise taxes and various fees imposed on agricultural and livestock products brought into the towns and cities for sale were especially hard on the peasantry. Needless to say, in years when the terms of exchange between the village and the city were unfavorable for the former, the excise taxes and various fees connected with marketing of agricultural products, which in principle were supposed to be paid by the producer but finally carried by the city consumers, were actually paid and carried by the producer in the form of lower prices that he received for his products. Since the municipalities gave nothing in exchange to the peasantry for this heavy burden in taxes, it was especially resented. The main "service" that the towns and cities provided for the surrounding peasants was to serve as trading places. But that gave the cities and towns the opportunity, first, to profit by that commerce, second, to shift a portion of their tax burden onto the shoulders of the peasants—at least in proportion to the purchases by the rural population of the products and services sold in these urban areas—and third, to derive a great deal of tax revenue from peasants as sellers, thus taxing their own constituents less.

What were the benefits that the peasantry derived from the services of the regional and local governments? From municipalities they received nothing except the facilities for trading, for which they paid dearly, as explained above. Out of their total expenditures of 1,814.1

[5] Ljubomir S. Dukanac, *Prevaljivanje poreza* (The Shifting of Taxation), pp. 125–26.

million dinars in 1931, municipalities spent only 10.8 million dinars on the "advancement of agriculture and animal husbandry." Rural communes, which in the same year spent a total of 604.2 million dinars, used only 19.1 million dinars for the "advancement of agriculture and animal husbandry." Of their other expenditures which benefited agricultural population directly, there were 47.6 million dinars for the repair of buildings and roads, 96.5 million dinars for education, 19.1 million dinars for sanitary purposes, and 18.2 million dinars for policing purposes. It is interesting to note that in rural communes the "advancement of agriculture and animal husbandry" was given the same amount of money as policing. Close to one-third of all their expenditures was used for personnel salaries, and the remainder was spent for other purposes, of which only a part benefited the agricultural population. Of the total amount of 907.3 million dinars spent by *banovine* in 1931, 99.6 million dinars was spent for "advancement of agriculture and animal husbandry," 56.4 million for education, 135.6 million for sanitary purposes, and 285.5 million dinars for the construction and repair of roads and buildings. But only a part of the three last categories of expenditures benefited the peasantry.

TAX BURDEN OF AGRICULTURE

According to the official estimates, the total income of the agricultural population amounted in 1931 to 18,784 million dinars, and, according to our estimates of the rate of marketability of agricultural production, its cash income in 1931 amounted to between 7,500 and 8,500 million dinars. The remainder was the value of products utilized by the agricultural households that produced them.

We repeat our earlier warning that all these figures on national income and on the portion of crop, livestock, and cottage-industries production that was marketed are only estimates and that they have to be considered with caution. Needless to say, some of the following figures with regard to the portion of various taxes carried ultimately by the agricultural population also have to be taken with caution, because they are nothing more than approximations. But if one tries to obtain an approximate picture of the position of agriculture vis-à-vis the other parts of the national economy and of its economic conditions during the interwar period, the burden imposed on it by taxation cannot be left out of consideration. This picture would be much more distorted by leaving the problem of taxation out of consideration than it possibly could be by a considerable margin of error in the estimates of burdens caused to agriculture by various forms of taxation. It bears stressing, however, that our aim here is not to present exactly the load of taxation carried by agriculture, but rather to indicate the order of magnitude of that burden.

In the fiscal year 1931/32 agriculture paid 479.6 million dinars in land tax. Assuming that the relative number of bachelors and of men who paid the military exemption tax was the same as the relationship between the rural and the urban population (three fourths as against one fourth), the burden caused to agricultural population by these two minor direct taxes was 6.6 million dinars. Disregarding the tax arrears and the interest on unpaid taxes, these were the only direct taxes levied by the central government upon the rural population. But, together with these taxes, they also paid the surtax imposed by rural communes, which in 1931 amounted to 361.6 million dinars, and a part of the surtax imposed by the *banovine*, which, we assume, amounted to one-third of that tax, or about 58 million dinars in 1931. It is here assumed that agriculture was unable at that time to shift any of these taxes through higher prices of its products onto their consumers or through forcing down the prices of products that it bought from the urban economy. Thus the outright load of direct taxes imposed on agriculture in 1931/32 was about 900 million dinars, or approximately 10 to 12 percent of its cash income.

There is little doubt, however, that in addition to these direct taxes, the peasants also carried a portion of some other direct taxes, through tax shifting. Since the elasticity of supply of products which the peasants sold and their elasticity of demand for products they were buying were low, and since the terms of trade between agriculture and the urban economy shifted more and more to the disadvantage of agriculture after 1929, agriculture was less able to resist the shifting of other taxes to it. This was especially true in the case of direct taxes imposed upon the income from noncorporate and corporate businesses. It is here assumed that the noncorporate and the corporate businesses were able in 1931 to shift one-half of the amount of the direct tax imposed upon them onto the shoulders of the final buyers of their goods and services, and that one-half of their total sales was made to the rural population. The estimated tax burden shifted upon agriculture on that account amounted thus to about 90 million dinars. It is here assumed that the taxes on income from urban housing, on income from interest and dividends, and on income from salaries and wages, totaling 530 million dinars in the 1931/32 fiscal year, were not further shifted and that no part of them was carried by agriculture. We are aware, however, that this assumption is somewhat unrealistic.

An additional direct tax burden which was partly shifted to the agricultural population was the surtax imposed by municipalities upon direct taxes levied by the central government, because a large portion of people who were paying these taxes did a portion of their business with the peasantry in the surrounding areas. It is here assumed that approximately one-third of that tax load, or about 80 million dinars, was thus shifted upon the peasants. We also assume that one-third of the tax payment in lieu of personal work collected by the municipalities and the *banovine*, or about 20 million dinars, was shifted onto the peasants. Thus, on balance, the shifting of direct taxes levied by the central government, *banovine*, and municipalities resulted, according to our estimate, in a total charge for agriculture of about 190 million dinars.

But the bulk of tax revenue of both central, regional, and local governments consisted of indirect taxes imposed on consumption of commodities and services. Here, as in the case of direct taxes, the problem of shifting the tax by the taxpayer forward toward the consumer of goods and services that he sells, or backward toward the seller of commodities and services that he buys, is involved. The peasants were hit by both the forward and backward tax shifting.

In the case of indirect taxes it is also necessary to distinguish between that part that the rural population paid directly and was supposed to bear and that part that was shifted to them by other people through the market operations. We have already assumed that, owing to the unfavorable position of agriculture in the marketing process, especially after 1929, agriculture itself was unable to shift any of its taxes either onto the consumers of its products or onto the suppliers of its necessities. There is no possibility of tracking down with any certainty either one of the above two components of indirect taxes carried by the peasantry, because there are no data on the consumption of various taxed commodities and services by the rural and the urban populations, and because there are no empirical studies on tax shifting in Yugoslavia during the interwar period.

Estimates of consumption of some taxed commodities and general knowledge about the interwar patterns of consumption of others are helpful, however, in estimating the approximate tax load imposed on the rural population by indirect taxes. In the case of most indirect taxes, however, a rather arbitrary approach is the only possible one. In the case of the sugar excise, the burden imposed on the peasant population in 1931 was about 40 percent of the total revenue from this tax form, or about 190 million dinars, because, according to official estimates of sugar consumption, the peasantry consumed about 40 percent of the total (see p. 559). The same ratio probably applied to coffee, resulting in a tax load for the rural population of about 20 million dinars (disregarding here the high customs duty on coffee). In regard to salt it could be readily assumed that, because of the inelastic character of demand for this product, the consumption was divided between the urban and rural areas in the same ratio as the respective populations, which would give a salt monopoly tax load for the rural population of about 150 million dinars. While perhaps between 80 and 90 percent of electric power production, which paid an excise tax, and 100 percent of gas production, which was also taxed, was consumed by the urban population, possibly about 80 percent of the heavily taxed kerosene was used by the rural population, resulting in a kerosene monopoly tax charge of about 90 million dinars. It is interesting to point out that for consumption taxes on salt and kerosene alone the rural population paid a great deal more than the whole urban population on the income from housing or the business community on the income from noncorporate business, and twice as much as corporate business paid on corporate income in direct taxes (disregarding the shifting of these taxes).

As for monopoly taxes imposed on tobacco, cigarette paper, and matches, it is here arbitrarily assumed that one-half was carried by the rural and the other half by the urban population. This, then, represented a tax charge for the rural population of about 670 million dinars.

For other excise duties imposed by the central government, amounting in 1931 to 300 million dinars (this figure included 131 million dinars collected from excise tax on beer, wine, and brandy), and for stamp duties, it is assumed that only one-fourth was carried by the rural population, resulting in a charge for the peasant population of about 330 million dinars. As for custom duties and the general turnover tax, it is here assumed that 40 percent of their amounts was carried (disregarding the shifted portion) by the rural and 60 percent by the urban population. The bill on this account for the rural population was thus about 550 million dinars.

Thus, of the total amount of indirect taxes of 4,734.5 million dinars levied by the central government in the fiscal year 1931/32, an estimated 2,000 million dinars, or 42 percent of the total, was paid outright and carried by the peasant population. Of the remainder of the indirect taxes, it is assumed quite arbitrarily that about one-fifth, or 550 million dinars, was successfully shifted upon them by the urban population through higher prices of what the peasants bought or through lower prices for commodities that the peasants sold to them.

Finally, there were also the indirect taxes imposed by the regional and local governments. Obviously, the indirect taxes imposed by rural communes were carried by the peasantry, resulting in a total charge of about 60 million dinars. Of the excise duties imposed by the municipalities and *banovine*, it is assumed that 40 percent was carried by the peasantry, and of the stamp duties imposed by the municipalities and *banovine*, it is assumed that one-fourth was carried by the peasantry, both groups totaling about 250 million dinars. Of the remaining excise taxes and stamp duties of 483 million dinars, it is assumed that one-fifth, or 100 million dinars, the urban people shifted onto the shoulders of the peasants. These indirect taxes resulted in 1931/32 in a tax burden for the rural population totaling about 410 million dinars.

In recapitulation, it appears that the total tax load of Yugoslav agriculture, paid both directly and through tax shifting, in the fiscal year 1931/32 amounted to approximately 4,000 million dinars, or about 50 percent of its total estimated cash income.[6] Even granting that our estimate erred by 20 percent on the high side, which is improbable though not impossible, that would still leave a tremendous tax burden of about 3,200 million dinars, or about 40 percent of the total cash income of agriculture. Considering the very low aggregate income of the agricultural population, this tax burden was extremely high.

When this tremendous tax burden is compared with the mentioned outlays of the central and the local governments, which directly or indirectly were of assistance to the rural population, the comparison is disastrous from the point of view of the peasantry. But only if this essentially unrequited tax burden is added to other unfavorable factors under which the agricultural population of Yugoslavia labored during the interwar period, can one properly appraise its uneviable economic position. This situation would have been somewhat mitigated had a sizable portion of the revenue from taxes that the agricultural population paid to the central, regional, and local governments been used for a systematic development of nonagricultural productive resources, which in the long run could have reduced the pressure of population in agriculture. But this was not the case, because the tax revenue was used almost exclusively for the financing of government administration and national defense.

[6] According to the investigations of the Statistical Institute for Economic Research at the State University of Sofia, Bulgaria, it appears that direct and indirect taxes in the mid-1930's represented roughly one-half of the money value of goods marketed by Bulgarian agriculture. O. N. Anderson, "Some Theoretical Aspects of the Business Cycle Movements in the Southeast European Agricultural Countries," *Publications of the Statistical Institute for Economic Research, State University of Sofia*, No. 1 (1936), p. 17.

BIBLIOGRAPHY

SELECTED WORKS

Books and Pamphlets

Agrarna reforma u Hrvatskoj, Sloveniji i Vojvodini (Agrarian Reform in Croatia, Slovenia, and Vojvodina). Opinion of the professors of the Department of Agriculture and Forestry, University of Zagreb. Zagreb, 1923.

Austria-Hungary, Gemeinsames Finanzministerium. *Bericht über die Verwaltung von Bosnien und der Herzegowina, 1906.* Vienna, 1906.

Avramović, Mihailo. *Naše seljačko gazdinstvo* (Our Peasant Farming). Belgrade, 1928.

Bajkić, Velimir. *Seljački kredit* (Peasant Credit). Belgrade, 1928.

Balen, Josip. *Naš goli krš* (Our Bare Karst). Zagreb, 1931.

Bićanić, Rudolf. *Ekonomska podloga hrvatskog pitanja* (The Economic Basis of the Croatian Question). 2d ed. Zagreb, 1938.

———. *Kako živi narod* (How the People Live). I. Zagreb, 1936.

Bösendorfer, Josip. *Agrarni odnosi u Slavoniji* (Agrarian Relations in Slavonia). Zagreb, 1950.

Busch-Zantner, Richard. *Agrarverfassung, Gesellschaft und Siedlung in Südosteuropa.* Leipzig, 1938.

Ćorović, Vladimir. *Historija Bosne* (History of Bosnia). I. Belgrade, 1940.

———. *Istorija Jugoslavije* (History of Yugoslavia). Belgrade, 1933.

Croatian Peasant party. *Temeljni nauk ili program hrvatske republikanske seljačke stranke* (Basic Principles or the Program of the Croatian Republican Peasant Party). As adopted and proclaimed in 1921.

Čulinović, Ferdo. *Seljačke bune u Hrvatskoj* (Peasant Rebellions in Croatia). Zagreb, 1951.

Cvijić, Jovan. *La Péninsule Balkanique.* Paris, 1918.

Dammang, Andreas. *Die deutsche Landwirtschaft in Banat und in der Batschka.* Munich, n.d. [1930 or 1931].

Djuričić, V. M., *et al. Naša narodna privreda i nacionalni prihod* (Our National Economy and National Income). Sarajevo, 1927.

Dubić, Slavoljub. *Prilog istraživanju seljačkoga gospodarstva* (A Contribution to the Study of Peasant Farming in Yugoslavia). Križevci, Croatia, 1933.

Dukanac, Ljubomir S. *Yugoslav Business Cycles (Index Numbers) 1919–1941.* Belgrade, 1946.

Frangeš, Otto von (Frangeš, Oto). *Die sozialökonomische Struktur der jugoslawischen Landwirtschaft.* Berlin, 1937.

Giaja, Aleksandar. *Ishrana seoske porodice—selo Rajković* (The Nutrition of the Inhabitants of the Village of Rajković). Belgrade, 1951.

Gibb, H. A. R., and Bowen, Harold. *Islamic Society and the West.* I. London and New York, 1950.

Glomazić, Momir. *Istorija Državne hipotekarne banke, 1862–1932* (History of the State Mortgage Bank, 1862–1932). Belgrade, 1933.

Goranović, Maksim. *Položaj seljaka u Jugoslaviji.* (The Situation of the Peasants in Yugoslavia). Belgrade, 1938.
Gospodarska Sloga. *Anketa Gospodarske Sloge: Najnužnije narodne potrebe* (Survey by Gospodarska Sloga: The Most Pressing Needs of the People). Zagreb, 1940.
Grafenauer, Bogo, et al. (eds.). *Istorija naroda Jugoslavije* (History of the Peoples of Yugoslavia). I. Belgrade, 1953.
Gratz, Gustav, and Schüller, Richard. *Der wirtschaftliche Zusammenbruch Österreich-Ungarns.* Vienna and New Haven, 1930.
Grünberg, Karl. *Die Agrarverfassung und das Grundentlastungsproblem in Bosnien und der Herzegowina.* Leipzig, 1911.
Hollmann, A. H. *Agrarverfassung und Landwirtschaft Jugoslawiens.* Germany, Ministry for Food and Agriculture, *Berichte über Landwirtschaft*, N.F., Sonderheft No. 30. Berlin, 1931.
Ilić, Ananije V. *Sistem prava o kućnoj zajednici u Crnoj Gori* (The System of Law on the Zadruga in Montenegro). Belgrade, 1936.
Ivšić, Milan. *Les problèmes agraires en Yougoslavie.* Paris, 1926.
Jászi, Oscar. *The Dissolution of the Habsburg Monarchy.* Chicago, 1929.
Jireček, Konstantin. *Istorija Srba* (History of the Serbs). 4 vols. Translated from the German by Jovan Radonić. Belgrade, 1922–24.
Jovanović, Aleksa (ed.). *Spomenica dvadesetpetogodišnjice oslobodjenja Južne Srbije, 1912–1937* (Jubilee Record of the Liberation of Southern Serbia, 1912–1937). Skoplje, 1937.
Jovanović, Dragoljub. *Agrarna politika* (Agrarian Policy). Belgrade, 1930.
Jovanović, Jagoš. *Stvaranje crnogorske države i razvoj crnogorske nacionalnosti* (Formation of the Montenegrin State and Development of the Montenegrin Nationality). Cetinje, 1948.
Jovanović, Slobodan. *Političke i pravne rasprave* (Political and Legal Studies). Collected Works. II and III. Belgrade, 1932.
———. *Ustavobranitelji i njihova vlada* (The Defenders of the Constitution and Their Rule). Collected Works. V. Belgrade, 1933.
Jubilarni zbornik života i rada Srba, Hrvata i Slovenaca, 1918–1928 (Jubilee Record of Life and Work of the Serbs, Croats, and Slovenes, 1918–1928). 2 vols. Belgrade, 1928–29.
Kann, Robert A. *The Multinational Empire.* 2 vols. New York, 1950.
Kerchnawe, Hugo, et al. *Die Militärverwaltung in den von den österreichisch-ungarischen Truppen besetzten Gebieten.* Vienna and New Haven, 1928.
Kingdom of the Serbs, Croats, and Slovenes, Ministry of Agrarian Reform. *Agrarna reforma—uredbe, naredbe i raspisi* (Agrarian Reform—Decrees, Orders, and Circulars). 2 vols. Zagreb, 1920–25.
———, Ministry of Agriculture and Water Resources. *Potrošnja hlebnih žita u Kraljevini Srba, Hrvata i Slovenaca* (Consumption of Bread Grains in the Kingdom of the Serbs, Croats, and Slovenes). Belgrade, 1928.
Kirk, Dudley. *Europe's Population in the Interwar Years.* League of Nations. Princeton, 1946.
Koen, A., et al. (eds.). *Bosna i Hercegovina kao privredno područje* (Bosnia and Herzegovina as an Economic Area). Sarajevo, 1938.
Komadinić, Milan J. *Problem seljačkih dugova* (The Problem of Peasant Debts). Belgrade, 1934.

Krišković, Vinko. *Hrvatsko pravo kućnih zadruga* (Croatian Zadruga Law). Zagreb, 1925.

Kukoleča, Stevan M. *Industrija Jugoslavije, 1918–1938* (Industry of Yugoslavia, 1918–1938). Belgrade, 1941.

Lopašić, Radoslav. *Urbari na hrvatskom jeziku* (*Urbars* in Croatian Language). Yugoslav Academy of Science and Art, *Monumenta historico-juridica Slavorum meridionalium.* V. Zagreb, 1894.

Lybyer, Albert H. *The Government of the Ottoman Empire in the Time of Suleiman the Magnificent.* Cambridge, Mass., 1913.

Melik, Anton. *Jugoslavija—Zemljopisni pregled* (Yugoslavia—A Geographic Survey). Ljubljana, 1949.

———. *Slovenija* (Slovenia). 2 pts. Ljubljana, 1936.

Mirković, Mijo. *Agrarna politika* (Agrarian Policy). Belgrade, 1940.

———. *Održanje seljačkog posjeda* (The Preservation of Peasant Property). Zagreb, 1937.

Mitrany, David. *The Land & the Peasant in Rumania.* London and New Haven, 1930.

———. *Marx Against the Peasant.* Chapel Hill, 1951.

Moore, Wilbert E. *Economic Demography of Eastern and Southern Europe.* League of Nations. Geneva, 1945.

Neugebauer, Viktor. *Vojvodjanski černozem, njegova veza sa černozemom istočne i jugoistočne Evrope i pravac njegove degradacije* (Vojvodina's Chernozem, Its Relation to the Chernozem of Eastern and Southeastern Europe and the Direction of Its Degradation). Novi Sad, 1951.

Nikosavić, Blagoje. *Die Agrarverfassung und der landwirtschaftliche Kredit Jugoslawiens.* Germany, Ministry for Food and Agriculture, *Berichte über Landwirtschaft,* N.F., Sonderheft 112. Berlin, 1935.

Notestein, Frank W., *et al. The Future Population of Europe and the Soviet Union—Population Projections 1940-1970.* League of Nations. Geneva, 1944.

Novak, Viktor, and Skok, Petar. *Supetarski kartular* (Cartulary of St. Peter). Zagreb, 1952.

Novaković, Stojan. *Selo* (The Village). Belgrade, 1891.

Obradović, Milan M. *Selo Drinske banovine u brojevima* (The Village of *Banovina* Drina in Figures). Sarajevo, 1939.

Obradović, Sava D. *La politique commerciale de la Yougoslavie.* Belgrade, 1939.

Ostrogorsky, Georg. *Pronija—Prilog istoriji feudalizma u Vizantiji i u južno-slovenskim zemljama* (Pronoia—A Contribution to the History of Feudalism in Byzantium and in the South Slav Lands). Belgrade, 1951.

Petričević, Jure. *Untersuchungen über die Betriebsformen der Bauernbetriebe Kroatiens.* Aarau, Switzerland, 1942.

Petrović, Dr. Aleksandar. *Banjane—Socijalno-zdravstvene i higijenske prilike* (Banjane—Sociohygienic Conditions). Belgrade, 1932.

———. *Rakovica—Socijalno-zdravstvene i higijenske prilike* (Rakovica—Sociohygienic Conditions). 2 vols. Belgrade, 1935–39.

Petrović, Jelenko. *Okućje ili zaštita zemljoradničkog minimuma* (The Protected Minimum Homestead). Belgrade, 1930.

Popović, Novak, and Mišić, Dušan. *Naša domaća privreda* (Our National Economy). Belgrade, 1929.

Popović, Vasilj. *Agrarno pitanje u Bosni i turski neredi za vreme reformnog režima Abdul-Medžida (1839–1861)* (The Agrarian Question in Bosnia and Turkish Disorders During the Period of the Reform Rule of Abdul-Medjid, 1839–1861). Belgrade, 1949.
Predavec, Josip. *Selo i seljaci* (The Village and the Peasants). Zagreb, 1934.
Schultze Jena, L. *Makedonien.* Jena, 1927.
Schumacher, Rupert von. *Des Reiches Hofzaun.* 4th ed. Darmstadt, 1943.
Seton-Watson, Hugh. *Eastern Europe Between the Wars, 1918–1941.* Cambridge, England, 1946.
Seton-Watson, R. W. *Sarajevo—A Study in the Origins of the Great War.* London, 1926.
Sicard, Émile. *La Zadruga Sud-slave dans l'évolution du groupe domestique.* Paris, 1943.
Šišić, Ferdo (Šišić, Ferdinand von). *Dokumenti o postanku Kraljevine Srba, Hrvata i Slovenaca, 1914–1919* (Documents on the Establishment of the Kingdom of the Serbs, Croats, and Slovenes, 1914–1919). Zagreb, 1920.
———. *Geschichte der Kroaten.* Zagreb, 1917.
———. *Povijest Hrvata u vrijeme narodnih vladara* (History of the Croats in the Period of Domestic Rulers). Zagreb, 1925.
Skerlić, Jovan. *Svetozar Marković, njegov život, rad i ideje* (Svetozar Marković, His Life, Work, and Ideas). Belgrade, 1910.
Stamenkovitch, Christa. *L'émigration yougoslave.* Paris, 1929.
Stanojević, Stanoje (ed.). *Narodna enciklopedija srpsko-hrvatsko-slovenačka* (National Encyclopedia of the Serbs, Croats, and Slovenes). 4 vols. Belgrade, 1929.
Stebut, Aleksandar. *Naši glavni poljoprivredni reoni* (Our Main Agricultural Regions). Belgrade, 1926.
Taranovsky, Teodor. *Istorija srpskog prava u Nemanjićkoj državi* (History of Serbian Law in the Nemanid State). 3 vols. Belgrade, 1931–35.
Tomašević, Jozo (Tomasevich, Jozo). *Financijska politika Jugoslavije, 1929–1934* (Fiscal Policy of Yugoslavia, 1929–1934). Zagreb, 1935.
Tončić, Dragutin. *Vrhovne upravne i sudske rješidbe k zakonu od 9.V.1889 o zadrugama i zadružnoj noveli od 30.IV.1902* (Supreme Administrative and Court Decisions Regarding the Law on the Zadrugas of May 9, 1889, and Its Amendments of April 30, 1902). Zagreb, 1925.
Trouton, Ruth. *Peasant Renaissance in Yugoslavia, 1900–1950.* London, 1952.
Turina, Božo. *Poljodjelstvo u Nezavisnoj Državi Hrvatskoj* (Agriculture in the Independent State of Croatia). Zagreb, 1943.
Utiešenović, Og. M. *Die Hauskommunionen der Südslaven.* Vienna, 1859.
Vasiliev, A. A. *History of the Byzantine Empire, 324–1453.* Madison, Wis., 1953.
Vežić, Milivoj. *Urbar hrvatsko-slavonski* (The Croato-Slavonian *Urbar*). Zagreb, 1882.
Vlajinac, Milan Z. *Moba i pozajmica, narodni običaji udruženoga rada* (The Bee and the Labor Loan—Folk Customs of Communal Labor). Belgrade, 1929.
———. *Zgon ili kulučenje van mesta stanovanja od srednjega veka do naših dana* (The *Corvée* Outside of the Place of Living from the Middle Ages to the Present). Belgrade, 1932.

Vucinich, Wayne S. *Serbia Between East and West.* Stanford, Calif., 1954.

Vučo, Nikola. *Privredna istorija naroda FNRJ* (Economic History of the Peoples of the Federal People's Republic of Yugoslavia). Belgrade, 1948.

Warriner, Doreen. *Economics of Peasant Farming.* London, 1939.

Wendel, Hermann. *Der Kampf der Südslawen um Freiheit und Einheit.* Frankfurt a/M., 1925.

Wlainatz, Milan (Vlajinac, Milan Z.). *Die agrarrechtlichen Verhältnisse des mittelalterlichen Serbiens.* Jena, 1903.

Yovanovitch, Dragolioub (Jovanović, Dragoljub). *Les effets économiques et sociaux de la guerre en Serbie.* Paris and New Haven, 1930.

Yugoslavia. *Annuaire statistique 1929.* Belgrade, 1932.

———. *Annuaire statistique 1931.* Belgrade, 1934.

———. *Annuaire statistique 1936.* Belgrade, 1937.

———. *Annuaire statistique 1938–1939.* Belgrade, 1939.

———. *Annuaire statistique 1940.* Belgrade, 1941.

Yugoslavia, Federal Bureau of Statistics. *Bulletin statistique.* Belgrade, beginning July 1950.

Yugoslavia, Ministry of Agriculture. *Statistique agricole annuelle 1933.* Belgrade, 1934.

———. *Statistique agricole annuelle 1937.* Belgrade, 1938.

———. *Statistique agricole annuelle 1938.* Belgrade, 1939.

Yugoslavia, Ministry of Finance. *Ministarstvo Finansija Kraljevine Jugoslavije, 1918–1938* (Ministry of Finance of the Kingdom of Yugoslavia, 1918–1938). Belgrade, 1939.

———. *Statistique du commerce extérieur.* Belgrade, annually 1921–39.

Yugoslavia, Ministry of Trade and Industry. *Statistika industrije Kraljevine Jugoslavije* (Industrial Statistics of the Kingdom of Yugoslavia). Belgrade, 1941.

Yugoslavia, Office of Information. *Five Year Plan.* Belgrade, 1947.

Zakon o agrarnoj reformi i kolonizaciji (The Law on the Agrarian Reform and Internal Colonization). 2d ed. Belgrade, 1948.

Živanović, Ž. *Politička istorija Srbije u drugoj polovini devetnaestog veka* (Political History of Serbia During the Second Half of the Nineteenth Century). 4 vols. Belgrade, 1923–25.

Articles

Anderson, O. N. "Some Theoretical Aspects of the Business Cycle Movements in the Southeast European Agricultural Countries," *Publications of the Statistical Institute for Economic Research, State University of Sofia* (Sofia), 1936, No. 1, pp. 5–21.

Barkan, Omer Lutfi. *"Čiftlik,"* Serbo-Croatian translation by Hamid Hadžibegić of an article published in the Turkish edition of *The Encyclopaedia of Islam* in 1945, *Godišnjak Istoriskog društva Bosne i Hercegovine* (Sarajevo), II (1950), 286–98.

Bićanić, Rudolf. "The Agricultural Crisis of 1873 to 1895 and Its Effect on the Economic and Social Structure of Croatia," *Ekonomist* (Zagreb), issues for March, April, and May, 1937, pp. 97–108, 151–59, and 199–207.

Bićanić, Rudolf. "The Effects of War on Rural Yugoslavia," *Geographical Journal* (London), CIII (January–February, 1944), Nos. 1 and 2, 30–49.

———. "Industrial Revolution in Croatia and the Year 1848," *Historijski zbornik* (Zagreb), I (1948), 67–101.

———. "The Liberation of the Serfs in Croatia in 1848," *Djelo* (Zagreb), I (March 1948), 190–200.

Bogićević, Vojislav. "The Abolition of *Corvée* and the Introduction of the *Trećina* in 1848," *Istorisko-pravni zbornik* (Sarajevo), III-IV (1950), 181–99.

Bogojević, Djoko. "The Agrarian Reform," *Jubilarni zbornik života i rada Srba, Hrvata i Slovenaca, 1918–1928* (Jubilee Record of Life and Work of the Serbs, Croats, and Slovenes, 1918–1928) (Belgrade), I (1928), 299–316.

Bösendorfer, Josip. "How It Came to the Slavonian *Urbar* of 1756," Yugoslav Academy of Science and Art, *Rad* (Zagreb), CCXL (1931), 220–56; CCXLII (1931), 1–92.

Čubrilović, Vaso. "The Origin of Moslem Nobility in Bosnia and Herzegovina," *Jugoslovenski istoriski časopis* (Ljubljana-Zagreb-Belgrade), I (1935), 368–403.

Dabinović, Antun. "The Relationship of the Croats to the Byzantine Empire from the Point of View of Public Law," Yugoslav Academy of Science and Art, *Rad* (Zagreb), CCLXX (1941), 49–148.

Deny, J. "Timar." *The Encyclopaedia of Islam* (Leyden and London), IV (1934), 767–76.

Dimitrijević, Relja. "Problems of Crop Production in Macedonia," University of Belgrade, *Godišnjak Poljoprivrednog fakulteta* (Yearbook of the Faculty of Agriculture) (Belgrade), II (1949), 277–311.

Djurdjev, Branislav. "A Contribution to the Problem of the Development and Nature of the Timar Organization in Turkish Feudalism," *Godišnjak Istoriskog društva Bosne i Hercegovine* (Sarajevo), I (1949), 101–67.

———. "The Influence of Turkish Rule on the Development of Our Peoples," *Godišnjak Istoriskog društva Bosne i Hercegovine* (Sarajevo), II (1950), 19–82.

———. "Investigations of the *Voynuks*, with Special Reference to the Development of Turkish Feudalism and the Question of Bosnian *Agalik*," *Glasnik Zemaljskog muzeja u Bosni i Hercegovini* (Sarajevo), New Series, II (1947), 75–137.

Dugački, Zvonimir. "The Settlements and the Density of Population in the Croatian Zagorje," *Geografski vestnik* (Ljubljana), XVI (1940), 41–67.

Egoroff, Pawel P. "Die Arbeit in der Landwirtschaft," in Janaki St. Molloff (ed.), *Die sozialökonomische Struktur der bulgarischen Landwirtschaft.* (Berlin, 1936), 131–59.

Fellner, Friedrich von. "Die Verteilung des Volksvermögens und Volkseinkommens der Länder der ungarischen heiligen Krone zwischen dem heutigen Ungarn und den Successions-Staaten," *Metron* (Ferrara), III (1923), No. 2, 226–307.

Frangeš, Otto von. "The Agrarian Reform in Yugoslavia," International Institute of Agriculture, *Bulletin of Agricultural Economics and Sociology* (Rome), 1934, pp. E 89–100, 125–36, 174–98, 209–30, 269–87, 311–27.

———. "The Problem of Relative Overpopulation in Yugoslavia," Yugoslavia, Ministry of Agriculture, *Arhiv* (Belgrade), V (1938), reprint.

Goranović, Maksim. "Agricultural Income of Yugoslavia," Yugoslavia, Ministry of Agriculture, *Arhiv* (Belgrade), IV (1937), reprint.

Grafenauer, Bogo. "Some Problems Regarding the Settlement of the South Slavs in the Balkans," *Zgodovinski časopis* (Ljubljana), IV (1950), 23–126.

Hadžibegić, Hamid. "A Treatise by Ali Čauš of Sofia About the Timar Organization in the Seventeenth Century," *Glasnik Zemaljskog muzeja u Bosni i Hercegovini* (Sarajevo), New Series, II (1947), 139–205.

Hamperl, J. Z. "Our Production of Fats and Oils," *Ekonomist* (Zagreb), October 1940, pp. 384–94.

Hauptmann, Ljudmil. "The Arrival of the Croats," Yugoslav Academy of Science and Art, *Zbornik kralja Tomislava* (Symposium of King Tomislav) (Zagreb), 1925, pp. 86–127.

———. "The Origin of the Croatian Nobility," Yugoslav Academy of Science and Art, *Rad* (Zagreb), CCLXXIII (1942), 79–112.

Hersch, L. "La mortalité causée par la guerre mondiale," *Metron* (Padova), Pt. 1, V (1925), No. 1, 89–133; Pt. 2, VII (1927), No. 1, 3–82.

Ilešič, Svetozar. "The Increase in Population in the Territory of Yugoslavia, 1880–1931," *Geografski vestnik* (Ljubljana), XVI (1940), 3–25.

Jovanović, Slobodan. "Prince Miloš and the Peasant Problem," *Sociološki pregled* (Belgrade), I (1938), 13–26.

Karanović, Milan. "Some of the Large Zadrugas in Bosnia and Herzegovina," *Glasnik Zemaljskog muzeja u Bosni i Hercegovini* (Sarajevo), XLI (1929), 63–77; XLII (1930), 133–56.

Klaić, Nada. "Regarding Some Problems of Feudal Organization in Medieval Slavonia," *Historijski zbornik* (Zagreb), IV (1951), 107–31.

Klaić, Vjekoslav. "Croatian Tribes from the Twelfth to the Sixteenth Centuries," Yugoslav Academy of Science and Art, *Rad* (Zagreb), CXXX (1897), 1–85.

———. "*Marturina*—The Slavonian Tax in the Middle Ages," Yugoslav Academy of Science and Art, *Rad* (Zagreb), CLVII (1904), 114–213.

Kniewald, Dragutin. "The Veracity of the Latin Sources Regarding the Bosnian Christians," Yugoslav Academy of Science and Art, *Rad* (Zagreb), CCLXX (1949), 115–276.

Kos, Milko, "Colonization and Germanization of the Slovene Land," *Historijski zbornik* (Zagreb), IV (1951), 9–19.

Kos, Milko; Šišić, Ferdo; and Stanojević, Stanoje. "The Periodization of Yugoslav History," *Jugoslovenski istoriski časopis* (Ljubljana-Zagreb-Belgrade), I (1935), Nos. 2 and 3, 313–35.

Kostić, Borislav. "Equipment of Serbian Agriculture with Machinery, Implements, and Tools," *Socijalistička poljoprivreda* (Belgrade), April 1951, pp. 31–53.

Kostrenčić, Marko. "The Vinodol Law," *Historijski zbornik* (Zagreb), II (1949), 131–52.

———. "The Vinodol Law," Yugoslav Academy of Science and Art, *Rad* (Zagreb), CCXXVII (1923), 110–226.

Krbek, Ivo. "The Nationalization of Land Associations and Property Communes," Yugoslav Academy of Science and Art, *Rad* (Zagreb), CCLXX (1949), 41–66.

Kreševljaković, Hamdija. "Captainships and Captains in Bosnia and Herzegovina," *Godišnjak Istoriskog društva Bosne i Hercegovine* (Sarajevo), II (1950), 89–141.

Krstić, Djordjo. "Agrarian Policy in Bosnia and Herzegovina," in A. Koen et al. (eds.), *Bosna i Hercegovina kao privredno područje* (Bosnia and Herzegovina as an Economic Area) (Sarajevo, 1938), pp. 69–162.

Kukoleča, Stevan M. "Cartels and Their Significance for the Yugoslav Economy," Yugoslavia, Ministry of Social Welfare, *Socijalni arhiv* (Belgrade), V (1939), 203–37.

Lah, Ivo. "L'Âge moyen et la vie moyenne de la population en R.P.F. de Yougoslavie," *Statistička revija* (Belgrade), I (March 1951), No. 1, 86–112.

Lamer, Mirko. "Kriegswirtschaftliche Einflüsse in Jugoslawien," *Weltwirtschaftliches Archiv* (Jena), LIII (January 1941), No. 1, 112–38.

Lutovac, Milisav V. "Geographic Spreading of Corn Cultivation in Yugoslavia," *Glasnik Geografskog društva* (Belgrade), XXII (1936), 59–67.

Maister, Hrvoj. "The Employment of Peasant Population," in Hrvoj Maister and Filip Uratnik, *Socialni problemi slovenske vasi* (Social Problems of the Slovene Village) (Ljubljana, 1938), II, 91–116.

Malojčić, Dr. Miron. "The Results of the Survey of the Prevalence of Tuberculosis in the Village," *Socijalno-medicinski pregled* (Belgrade), 1940, No. 4, pp. 433–45.

Melik, Anton. "The Development of Railroads in the Territory of Yugoslavia," *Geografski vestnik* (Ljubljana), XIV (1938), 118–34.

Mirković, Mijo. "On the Twentieth Anniversary of Our Agrarian Reform," Yugoslavia, Ministry of Social Welfare, *Socijalni arhiv* (Belgrade), March–April, 1939, pp. 65–72.

Mosely, Philip E. "Adaptation for Survival: The Varžić Zadruga," *The Slavonic and East European Review* (New York), XXI (1943), 147–73.

————. "The Peasant Family: The Zadruga, or Communal Joint-Family in the Balkans, and Its Recent Evolution," in Caroline F. Ware (ed.), *The Cultural Approach to History* (New York, 1940), pp. 95–108.

Moskovljević, Miloš S. "The Peasant Movement Among the Serbs," *Pregled* (Sarajevo), XIII (July–August, 1937), 418–27.

Müller. "Die Landwirtschaft in der europäischen Türkei," Germany, Reichsamt des Innern, *Berichte über Handel und Industrie* (Berlin), XIX (June 21, 1913), Pt. 13, 701–35.

Niketić, Milutin J. "The Problems of the Dried Prune Industry," *Socijalistička poljoprivreda* (Belgrade), January 1953, pp. 9–20.

Nikolić, Dragiša. "The Present Situation in Yugoslav Pig Raising and Measures for Its Advancement," Yugoslavia, Ministry of Agriculture, *Arhiv* (Belgrade), III (1936), 156–68.

Obračević, Čedomir. "The Advancement of Animal Husbandry in the People's Republic of Serbia," *Socijalistička poljoprivreda* (Belgrade), May 1951, pp. 33–48.

Ostrogorsky, Georg. "Agrarian Conditions in the Byzantine Empire in the Middle Ages," in J. H. Clapham and Eileen Power (eds.), *The Cambridge Economic History of Europe* (Cambridge, 1941), I, 194–223.

Perić, Živojin M. "The Institution of the Protected Minimum Homestead with Regard to Division in the Serbian Law," *Ekonomist* (Zagreb), July–August, 1939, pp. 304–12.

Pertot, Vladimir. "Die Weizenregulierungen in Jugoslawien," *Weltwirtschaftliches Archiv* (Jena), XLV (May 1937), No. 3, 628–59.

Pirc, Dr. Ivo. "The Improvement of Sanitation in the Village," in Dr. Ivo Pirc and Franjo Baš, *Socialni problemi slovenske vasi* (Social Problems of the Slovene Village) (Ljubljana, 1938), I, 7–69.

———. "The Nutrition of the Peasant Population," in Dr. Ivo Pirc and Franjo Baš, *Socialni problemi slovenske vasi* (Social Problems of the Slovene Village) (Ljubljana, 1938), I, 71–113.

Popović, Jovo. "Agricultural Production," in A. Koen *et al.* (eds.), *Bosna i Hercegovina kao privredno područje* (Bosnia and Herzegovina as an Economic Area) (Sarajevo, 1938), pp. 7–34.

Popović, Vasilj. "The Zadruga—Theories and Literature," *Glasnik Zemaljskog muzeja u Bosni i Hercegovini* (Sarajevo), XXXIII-XXXIV (1921–22), 73–114.

Prohaska, Ljudevit. "Agriculture and Its Advancement," *Jubilarni zbornik života i rada Srba, Hrvata i Slovenaca, 1918–1928* (Jubilee Record of Life and Work of the Serbs, Croats, and Slovenes, 1918–1928) (Belgrade), I (1928), 317–45.

Rački, Franjo. "The Bogomils and Patarini," Yugoslav Academy of Science and Art, *Rad* (Zagreb), VII (1869), 84–179; VIII (1869), 121–87; X (1870), 160–263.

———. "The Internal Conditions in Croatia Before the Twelfth Century. Pt. V: Property and Economic Relations," Yugoslav Academy of Science and Art, *Rad* (Zagreb), CV (1891), 202–38.

Reed, Harry E. "The Hog Industry in Yugoslavia," United States, Department of Agriculture, *Foreign Agriculture* (Washington, D.C.), I, No. 10, 503–24.

Robertson, C. J. "Population and Agriculture, with Special Reference to Agricultural Overpopulation," in International Institute of Agriculture, *Documentation for the European Conference on Rural Life 1939* (Rome, 1939), pp. 9–67.

Seraphim, Hans Jürgen. "Die statistische Erfassung der landwirtschaftlichen Übervölkerung und Untervölkerung." Germany, Ministry for Food and Agriculture, *Berichte über Landwirtschaft* (Berlin), N.F. XIII (1930), 193–244.

Šidak, Jaroslav. "The Problem of the 'Bosnian Church' in our Historiography from Petranović to Glušac," Yugoslav Academy of Science and Art, *Rad* (Zagreb), CCLIX (1937), 37–182.

Solovjev, Aleksandar. "The Disappearance of Bogomilism and the Islamization of Bosnia," *Godišnjak Istoriskog društva Bosne i Hercegovine* (Sarajevo), I (1949), 42–79.

Šoštarić-Pisačić, Karlo. "Consumption of Artificial Fertilizers in Yugoslavia and Abroad," *Ekonomist* (Zagreb), January 1940, pp. 1–11; February–March 1940, pp. 100–110.

Starc, Artur. "Some Problems of Land Fertility and Land Utilization," *Socijalistička poljoprivreda* (Belgrade), July–August, 1951, pp. 1–21.

Stojković, Lazar. "Crop Rotation in the Grain-Producing Areas," *Socijalistička poljoprivreda* (Belgrade), April 1951, pp. 12–30.

Švob, Držislav, and Petrić, Franko. "Zadruga Domladovac." Yugoslav Academy of Science and Art, *Zbornik za narodni život i običaje Južnih Slavena* (Zagreb), XXVII (1929), Pt. 1, 92–110.

Timoshenko, Vladimir P. "The Danubian Basin as a Producer and Exporter of Wheat," *Wheat Studies*, Food Research Institute, Stanford University, Calif., VI, No. 5 (March 1930).

Tomasevich, Jozo. "Foreign Economic Relations [of Yugoslavia], 1918–1941," in Robert J. Kerner (ed.), *Yugoslavia* (Berkeley and Los Angeles, 1949), pp. 169–214.

———. "The Yugoslav Trade Policy at the Turning Point," *Privreda* (Zagreb), XI (July 1936), Nos. 7-8, 110–19.

Truhelka, Ćiro. "The Historical Foundations of the Agrarian Problem in Bosnia," *Glasnik Zemaljskog muzeja u Bosni i Hercegovini* (Sarajevo), XXVII (1915), 109–218.

Uratnik, Filip. "Agricultural Workers in Slovenia," in Hrvoj Maister and Filip Uratnik, *Socialni problemi slovenske vasi* (Social Problems of the Slovene Village) (Ljubljana, 1938), II, 3–90.

Urošević, A. "The Agrarian Reform and Colonization," in Aleksa Jovanović (ed.), *Spomenica dvadesetpetogodišnjice oslobodjenja Južne Srbije, 1912–1937* (Jubilee Record of the Liberation of Southern Serbia, 1912–1937) (Skoplje, 1937), pp. 819–33.

Varga, Ivan M. "Our Co-operativism," *Jubilarni zbornik života i rada Srba, Hrvata i Slovenaca 1918–1928* (Jubilee Record of Life and Work of the Serbs, Croats, and Slovenes, 1918–1928) (Belgrade), I (1928), 262–98.

Vrbanić, Fran. "Studies in the Economic Development of the Croato-Slavonian Military Frontier During the Nineteenth Century," Yugoslav Academy of Science and Art, *Rad* (Zagreb), CXLIV (1900), 40–131.

———. "One Hundred Years of the Development of Population of Croatia-Slavonia," Yugoslav Academy of Science and Art, *Rad* (Zagreb), CXL (1899), 17–58.

Vukosavljević, Sreten V. "About the Land Property in the Village," *Istorisko-pravni zbornik* (Sarajevo), 1949, No. 1, pp. 37–77.

Waizner, Ernst. "Das Volkseinkommen Alt-Österreichs und seine Verteilung auf die Nachfolgestaaten," *Metron* (Rome), VII (1928), No. 4, 97–183.

Žontar, Josef. "Hauptprobleme der jugoslavischen Sozial- und Wirtschaftsgeschichte," *Vierteljahrschrift für Sozial- und Wirtschaftsgeschichte* (Stuttgart), XXVII (1934), 347–73.

Zoričić, Milovan. "Population of the Kingdoms of Croatia and Slavonia by Profession and Occupation," Yugoslav Academy of Science and Art, *Rad* (Zagreb), CXXV (1896), 50–197.

OTHER WORKS CITED

Books and Pamphlets

Adamović, L. *Pflanzenwelt der Adrialänder.* Jena, 1929.

Adams, John C. *Flight in Winter.* Princeton, 1942.

Agricultural Bank. *The Chartered Agricultural Bank, 1930.* Belgrade, 1931.

Babić, Anto. *Istorija naroda Jugoslavije* (History of the Peoples of Yugoslavia). Sarajevo, 1948.

Barada, Miho. *Hrvatski vlasteoski feudalizam po Vinodolskom zakonu* (Croatian Feudalism According to the Vinodol Law). Zagreb, 1952.

Basch, Antonin. *The Danube Basin and the German Economic Sphere.* New York, 1943.

Bićanić, Rudolf. *Agrarna prenapučenost* (Agricultural Overpopulation). Zagreb, 1941.

———. *Doba manufakture u Hrvatskoj i Slavoniji (1750–1860)* (The Period of Manufacture in Croatia-Slavonia, 1750–1860). Zagreb, 1951.

———. *Pogled iz svjetske perspektive i naša ekonomska orijentacija* (Our Economic Orientation in International Perspective). Zagreb, 1939.

Bogdanov, Vaso. *Društvene i političke borbe u Hrvatskoj 1848/49* (Social and Political Struggles in Croatia in 1848/49). Zagreb, 1949.

Bogić, Dr. Grga. *Prilozi za istoriju i geografiju ishrane u Jugoslaviji za razdoblje od 1923 do 1925 godine* (Contribution to the History and Geography of Nutrition in Yugoslavia During the Period 1923 to 1925). Belgrade, 1939.

Bogišić, Valtazar. *Pravni članci i rasprave* (Legal Articles and Studies). I. Belgrade, 1927.

Božić, Ivan. *Dubrovnik i Turska u XIV i XV veku* (Dubrovnik and Turkey in the Fourteenth and Fifteenth Centuries). Belgrade, 1952.

Brailsford, H. N. *Macedonia.* London, 1906.

Braudel, Fernand. *La Méditerranée et le Monde méditerranéen à l'époque de Philippe II.* Paris, 1949.

Carnegie Endowment for International Peace. *Enquête dans les Balkans.* Paris, 1914.

Clark, K. G., and Sherman, Mildred S. *Prewar World Production and Consumption of Plant Foods in Fertilizers.* U.S. Department of Agriculture, Misc. Publ. No. 593. Washington, D.C., April 1946.

Cresin, Roman. *Recensământul agricol al României din 1941* (Agricultural Census in Rumania in 1941). Bucharest, 1945.

Cvijić, Jovan. *Balkansko poluostrvo i južnoslovenske zemlje* (The Balkan Peninsula and the South Slav Lands). Belgrade, 1922.

Decaris, A. *Die Agrarfrage Dalmatiens.* Split, 1928.

Djordjević, Tihomir R. *Iz Srbije Kneza Miloša—Stanovništvo, Naselja* (From Serbia of Prince Miloš—Population, Settlements). Belgrade, 1924.

Djurdjević, S. (ed.). *20 godina kulturnog i privrednog razvitka Kraljevine Jugoslavije* (Twenty Years of Cultural and Economic Development of the Kingdom of Yugoslavia). Belgrade, 1938.

Draganof. *La Macédoine et les Réformes.* Paris, 1906.

Dubić, Slavoljub. *Sociologija sela* (Rural Sociology). Split, 1941.

Dukanac, Ljubomir S. *Prevaljivanje poreza* (The Shifting of Taxation). Belgrade, 1935.

Durham, M. E. *Some Tribal Origins, Laws and Customs of the Balkans.* New York, 1929.

Durman, Milan. *Hrvatska seljačka buna 1573* (The Croatian Peasant Rebellion of 1573). Zagreb, 1936.

Dvornik, Francis. *The Making of Central and Eastern Europe.* London, 1949.

Dvorniković, Vladimir. *Karakterologija Jugoslovena* (The Yugoslav National Character). Belgrade, 1939.

Eichler, Eduard. *Das Justizwesen Bosniens und der Herzegowina.* Vienna, 1889.

Engelhardt, Ed. *La Turquie et le Tanzimat.* 2 vols. Paris, 1882–84.

Erdeljanović, Jovan. *Kuči, pleme u Crnoj Gori* (Kuči, A Tribe in Montenegro). Belgrade, 1907.

——. *Stara Crna Gora* (Old Montenegro). Belgrade, 1926.

Filipović, Milenko S. *Nesrodnička i predvojena zadruga* (The Zadruga of Non-relatives and the Split Zadruga). Belgrade, 1945.

Food and Agriculture Organization of the United Nations. *Food Balance Sheets.* Washington, D.C., April 1949.

Food and Agriculture Organization of the United Nations and International Institute of Agriculture. *Les grands produits agricoles—Compendium international de statistique 1924–1938.* Rome, 1948.

Galić, Ivan Z. *Problem agrarne politike u Hrvatskoj i Slavoniji* (The Problem of Agrarian Policy in Croatia-Slavonia). Zagreb, 1921.

Gavrilović, M. *Miloš Obrenović* (Miloš Obrenović). 3 vols. Belgrade, 1909.

Geller, Karl. *Die Strukturänderung der ungarischen Volkswirtschaft nach dem Kriege und die Stellung Ungarns im mitteleuropäischen Wirtschaftsraum.* Münster in Westphalia, 1938.

Gesemann, Gerhard. *Heroische Lebensform—Zur Literatur und Wesenskunde der balkanischen Patriarchalität.* Berlin, 1943.

Gjonović, Nikola. *Crna Gora pre i posle ujedinjenja* (Montenegro Before and After the Unification). Belgrade, 1939.

Glušac, Vaso. *Istina o bogomilima* (The Truth About the Bogomils). Belgrade, 1945.

Goodwin, A. (ed.). *The European Nobility in the Eighteenth Century.* London, 1953.

Gračanin, Mihovil. *Pedološka istraživanja Ličkog polja* (Pedological Investigations of the Lika *polje*). Zagreb, 1931.

Graham, Malbone W., Jr. *New Governments of Central Europe.* New York, 1924.

Grekov, B. D. *Vinodolskii statut ob obshchestvenom i politicheskom stroye Vinodola.* Moscow-Leningrad, 1948.

Hadrovics, Ladislas. *Le peuple serbe et son église sous la domination turque.* Budapest and Paris, 1947.

Handwörterbuch des Grenz- und Auslanddeutschtums. 3 vols. Breslau, 1933–40.

Helmreich, Ernst C. *The Diplomacy of the Balkan Wars, 1912–1913.* Cambridge, Mass., 1938.

Horvat, Josip. *Politička povijest Hrvatske, 1918–1929* (Political History of Croatia, 1918–1929). Zagreb, 1938.

——. *Stranke kod Hrvata i njihova ideologija* (Political Parties in Croatia and Their Ideology). Belgrade, 1939.

Horvat, Rudolf. *Najnovije doba hrvatske povijesti* (The Latest Period of Croatian History). Zagreb, 1906.

Hungary. *Ungarisches statistisches Jahrbuch.* New Series, XXIII. Budapest, 1921.

Iaranoff, D. *La Macédoine économique.* Sofia, 1931.

Ilančić, Dragan. *Brojčani razvitak stočarstva u hrvatskim zemljama* (The Numerical Development of Livestock Herds in Croatian Lands). Zagreb, 1942.

Illés, Aladár Edvi, and Halász, Albert. *Hungary Before and After the War in Economic-Statistical Maps.* Budapest, 1926.

International Institute of Agriculture. *International Yearbook of Agricultural Statistics 1930–31.* Rome, 1931.

Ivić, Aleksa. *Istorija Srba u Vojvodini* (History of the Serbs in Vojvodina). Novi Sad, 1929.

———. *Migracije Srba u Hrvatsku tokom 16, 17 i 18 stoleća* (Migrations of Serbs into Croatia in the Course of the 16th, 17th, and 18th Centuries). Subotica, 1923.

———. *Migracije Srba u Slavoniju tokom 16, 17 i 18 stoleća* (Migrations of Serbs into Slavonia in the Course of the 16th, 17th, and 18th Centuries). Subotica, 1926.

Ivšić, Milan. *Temelji seljačkoga zakonika* (The Principles of the Peasant Code). Zagreb, 1933.

Jelačić, Aleksije. *Seljački pokret u Hrvatskoj i Slavoniji god. 1848–49* (Peasant Movement in Croatia-Slavonia in 1948–49). Zagreb, 1925.

Jelenić, Djurdje. *Nova Srbija i Jugoslavija* (New Serbia and Yugoslavia). Belgrade, 1923.

Jovanović, Jovan M. *Južna Srbija od kraja XVIII veka do oslobodjenja* (Southern Serbia from the End of the Eighteenth Century to the Liberation). Vol. XVI of the collection *Srpski narod u XIX veku* (The Serbian People in the Nineteenth Century). Belgrade, n.d. [around 1938].

Jovanović, Slobodan. *Vlada Aleksandra Obrenovića* (The Reign of Alexander Obrenović). Collected Works, X–XII. Belgrade, 1934–36.

Kayser, Kurt. *Westmontenegro.* Stuttgart, 1931.

Kingdom of the Serbs, Croats, and Slovenes. *Résultats préliminaires du recensement de la population dans le Royaume des Serbes, Croates et Slovènes.* Sarajevo, 1924.

Klaić, Vjekoslav. *Povjest Hrvata* (History of the Croats). III. Zagreb, 1911.

Kleinwaechter, Friedrich F. G. *Der Untergang der österreichisch-ungarischen Monarchie.* Leipzig, 1920.

Kolarz, Walter. *Myths and Realities in Eastern Europe.* London, 1946.

Komadinić, Milan J. *Skice i ogledi za jednu istoriju zadrugarstva u Srbiji* (Sketches and Examples for a History of Co-operativism in Serbia). Belgrade, 1934.

Konstandinović, Nikola. *Agrarna politika* (Agrarian Policy). 3 pts. Belgrade, 1947.

———. *Seljačko gazdinstvo u Jugoslaviji* (Peasant Farming in Yugoslavia). Belgrade, 1939.

Kos, Milko. *Srednjeveški urbarji za Slovenijo. II: Urbarji Slovenskega Primorja* (Medieval *Urbars* for Slovenia. II: The *Urbars* of the Slovene Littoral). Ljubljana, 1948.

Kosić, Mirko M. *Osnovi ekonomne politike* (Principles of Economic Policy). Belgrade, 1925.

Krekić, Bogdan. *Radnička nadnica kao privredni, socijalni i kulturni faktor* (The Worker's Wage as an Economic, Social, and Cultural Factor). Belgrade, 1934.

Krische, Paul. *Bodenkarten und andere kartographische Darstellungen der Faktoren der landwirtschaftlichen Produktion verschiedener Länder.* Berlin, 1928.

Kukla, Stanislav. *Razvitak kreditne organizacije u Srbiji* (The Development of the Credit Organization in Serbia). Belgrade, 1924.

Lakatoš, Josip. *Narodna statistika* (Nationality Statistics). Zagreb, 1914.

Lanović, Mihajlo. *Zapadno-evropski feudalizam i ugarsko-hrvatski donacionalni sustav* (Western European Feudalism and the Hungaro-Croatian Donational System). Zagreb, 1928.

Laveleye, Émile de. *The Balkan Peninsula.* London, 1887.

League of Nations. *European Conference on Rural Life—Yugoslavia.* Geneva, 1939.

——. *International Trade Statistics 1938.* Geneva, 1939.

——. *Statistical Year Book of the League of Nations 1932/33.* Geneva, 1933.

——. *Statistical Year Book of the League of Nations 1940/41.* Geneva, 1941.

——. *Statistical Year Book of the League of Nations 1942/44.* Geneva, 1945.

Lodge, Olive. *Peasant Life in Jugoslavia.* New York, 1942.

Lončar, Dragotin. *The Slovenes: A Social History.* Translated from the Slovenian by Anthony J. Klančar. Cleveland, Ohio, 1939.

Lončarević, Dušan A. *Jugoslaviens Entstehung.* Vienna and Zurich, 1929.

Lorković, Mladen. *Narod i zemlja Hrvata* (The People and the Land of the Croats). Zagreb, 1939.

Marjanović, Čedomir. *Agrarni udar i zadužbinska, crkvena i manastirska imanja* (The Agrarian Reform and the Endowment, Church, and Monastic Properties). Belgrade, 1927.

Marković, Milan. *Die serbische Hauskommunion.* Leipzig, 1903.

Marković, Svetozar. *Celokupna dela—Srbija na istoku* (Collected Works—Serbia in the Orient). VI. Belgrade, 1892.

Masleša, Veselin. *Svetozar Marković* (Svetozar Marković). Belgrade, 1945.

Maurizio, A. *Die Geschichte unserer Pflanzennahrung von den Urzeiten bis zur Gegenwart.* Berlin, 1927.

May, Arthur J. *The Hapsburg Monarchy, 1867–1914.* Cambridge, Mass., 1951.

Mazour, Anatole G. *The First Russian Revolution 1825.* Berkeley, Calif., 1937.

Milojević, Borivoje Ž. *Glavne doline u Jugoslaviji* (The Main River Valleys in Yugoslavia). Belgrade, 1951.

——. *Les hautes montagnes dans le Royaume de Yougoslavie.* Belgrade, 1939.

Milosavljević-Čampar, Dr. Božidar. *Život i zdravstveno stanje sela* (Life and Health Conditions in the Village). Belgrade, 1932.

Mirković, Mijo. *Ekonomska struktura Jugoslavije, 1918–1941* (Economic Structure of Yugoslavia, 1918–1941). Zagreb, 1950.

Mitrinović, Čedomil, and Brašić, Miloš. *Les Skoupchtinas et les Diètes Yougoslaves.* Belgrade, 1937.

Munro, Robert. *Rambles and Studies in Bosnia-Herzegovina and Dalmatia.* Edinburg and London, 1895.

National Bank of the Kingdom of Yugoslavia. *Narodna banka, 1884–1934* (National Bank, 1884–1934). Belgrade, 1935.

——. *L'activité économique en Yougoslavie en 1939,* Supp. to No. 12 of 1939. Belgrade, 1940.

Nedeljković, Milorad. *Istorija srpskih državnih dugova* (History of the Serbian Public Debts). Belgrade, 1909.

Nintchitch, Momtchilo. *La crise bosniaque, 1908, et les puissances européennes.* 2 vols. Paris, 1937.

Novak, Grga. *Prošlost Dalmacije* (Dalmatia's Past). 2 pts. Zagreb, 1944.

Novak, Viktor. *Antologija jugoslovenske misli i narodnog jedinstva* (Anthology of the Yugoslav Idea and National Unity). Belgrade, 1930.

Nuttonson, M. Y. *Agricultural Climatology of Yugoslavia and Its Agroclimatic Analogues in North America.* International Agro-Climatological Series, No. 4. Washington, D.C., 1947.

Obolensky, Dmitri. *The Bogomils.* Cambridge, England, 1948.

Ostović, P. D. *Truth About Yugoslavia.* New York, 1952.

Ostrogorsky, Georg. *Istorija Vizantije* (History of Byzantium). Translated from German. Belgrade, 1947.

Paulová, Milada. *Jugoslavesnki Odbor* (The Yugoslav Committee). Zagreb, 1925.

Perić, Živojin M. *Porodično zadružno pravo u Crnoj Gori* (Zadruga Law in Montenegro). Belgrade, 1925.

Petranović, Božidar. *Bogomili. Crkva bosanska i krstjani* (The Bogomils. The Bosnian Church and the Bosnian Christians). Zadar, 1867.

Pfeffer, Leo. *Istraga u sarajevskom atentatu* (The Investigation of the Sarajevo Assassination). 2d ed. Zagreb, 1938.

Popovics, Alexander. *Das Geldwesen im Kriege.* Vienna and New Haven, 1925.

Pribićević, Adam. *Seljak* (The Peasant). Zagreb, 1936.

Radić, Stjepan. *Savremena Evropa* (Contemporary Europe). Zagreb, 1905.

Ristić, Teofan. *Borba za zemlju i naša agrarna reforma* (The Struggle for Land and Our Agrarian Reform). Belgrade, 1938.

Royal Institute of International Affairs. *Agrarian Problems from the Baltic to the Aegean.* London, 1944.

Rus, Jože. *Glavni statistički podaci o državi Srba, Hrvata i Slovenaca* (The Main Statistical Data on the State of the Serbs, Croats, and Slovenes). Ljubljana, 1920.

Sanders, Irwin T. *Balkan Village.* Lexington, Ky., 1949.

Sax, Carl Ritter von. *Geschichte des Machtverfalls der Türkei.* 2d ed. Vienna, 1913.

Schmitt, Bernadotte E. *The Annexation of Bosnia, 1908–1909.* Cambridge, England, 1937.

———. *The Coming of the War 1914.* 2 vols. New York, 1930.

Šećerov, Slavko. *Iz naše agrarne politike, 1919–1929* (On Agricultural Policy, 1919–1929). Belgrade, 1930.

Seton-Watson, R. W. "The Role of Bosnia in International Politics (1875–1914)." Reprint from the *Proceedings of the British Academy,* XVII. London, 1931.

———. *The Southern Slav Question and the Habsburg Monarchy.* London, 1911.

Sicard, Émile. *Problèmes familiaux chez les Slaves du Sud.* Paris, 1947.

———. *La Zadruga dans la littérature serbe (1850–1912).* Paris, 1943.

Šišić, Ferdo. *Povijest Hrvata za kraljeva iz doma Arpadovića (1102–1301)* (History of the Croats During the Reign of the Árpád Dynasty, 1102–1301), Pt. I (1102–1205). Zagreb, 1944.

———. *Pregled povijesti hrvatskoga naroda* (A Survey of the History of the Croatian People). Zagreb, 1916.

Štampar, Dr. Andrija. *Public Health in Jugoslavia.* London, 1938.

Stanojević, St. *Srpsko-turski rat 1912 godine* (The Serbo-Turkish War of 1912). Belgrade, 1928.

Stebut, Aleksandar. *Zemljišta Drino-Savo-Moravske oblasti* (The Soils of the Drina-Sava-Morava Region). Belgrade, 1924.

Stoyanovitch, Costa. *Economic Problems of Serbia.* Paris, 1919.

Südland, L. v. (Pilar, Ivo). *Die südslawische Frage und der Weltkrieg.* Vienna, 1918.

Thompson, James W. *Feudal Germany.* Chicago, 1928.

Tomašević, Jozo. *Novac i kredit* (Money and Credit). Zagreb, 1938.

———. *Die Staatsschulden Jugoslaviens.* Zagreb, 1934.

Tomašić, Dinko (Tomasic, Dinko). *Društveni razvitak Hrvata* (Social Development of the Croats). Zagreb, 1937.

Tomasic, Dinko. *Personality and Culture in Eastern European Politics.* New York, 1948.

Tončić, Dragutin. *Zakon od 9. svibnja 1889. o zadrugama i Zakon od 30. travnja 1902. o promjeni odnosno nadopunjenju nekih ustanova zak. od 9. svibnja 1889. o zadrugama* (The Law on the Zadrugas of May 9, 1889, and the Law of April 30, 1902, on the Amendments to the Law of May 9, 1889). Zagreb, 1902.

Turk, Dragan. *Osnovi naše agrarne politike* (Principles of Our Agrarian Policy). Zagreb, 1922.

Vargha, Julius von. *Die wirtschaftlichen und kulturellen Verhältnisse Ungarns.* Budapest, 1908.

Vinski, Zdenko. *Die südslavische Grossfamilie in ihrer Beziehung zum asiatischen Grossraum.* Zagreb, 1938.

Vojnović, Lujo. *Dubrovnik i Osmansko carstvo* (Dubrovnik and the Ottoman Empire). Belgrade, 1898.

Vojvodina Bankers Association. "Referat Udruženja Vojvodjanskih banaka" (Report of the Vojvodina Bankers Association). Mimeo. Novi Sad, April 23, 1933.

Vukosavljević, Sreten V. *Istorija seljačkog društva,* I, *Organizovanje seljačke zemljišne svojine* (History of the Peasant Society, I, Organization of the Peasant Land Property). Belgrade, 1953.

Wilkinson, H. R. *Maps and Politics: A Review of the Ethnographic Cartography of Macedonia.* Liverpool, 1951.

Yates, P. Lamartine, and Warriner, Doreen. *Food and Farming in Post-War Europe.* London, 1943.

Yugoslavia, Central Press Bureau. *La Yougoslavie par les chiffres.* Belgrade, 1937.

Yugoslavia, Federal Bureau of Statistics. "Poljoprivredna gazdinstva predratne Jugoslavije prema popisu od 1931 g." (Farms in Prewar Yugoslavia on the Basis of the 1931 Census). Mimeo. Belgrade, 1945.

———. *Preliminary Results of the Population Census of March 15, 1948.* Belgrade, 1948.

Yugoslavia, Ministry of Finance. *Stanje državnih rashoda i prihoda za budžetsku 1932/33 godinu* (Statement of Expenditures and Revenue for the Fiscal Year 1932/33). Belgrade, 1933.

Zbornik uredaba za novooslobodjene i prisajedinjene oblasti (A Collection of Decrees for Newly Liberated and Annexed Areas). Belgrade, 1915.
Zloković, Djordje. *Prilog poznavanju zemljišta Metohije* (A Contribution to the Study of Soil of Metohija). Belgrade, 1951.
Zografski, D., *et al. Egejska Makedonija vo našata istorija* (Aegean Macedonia and Our History). Skopje, 1951.
Zoričić, Milovan. *Statistika ratarske produkcije god. 1888–1892 u kraljevinah Hrvatskoj i Slavoniji* (Statistics of Agricultural Production 1888–1892 in the Kingdoms of Croatia and Slavonia). Zagreb, 1894.

Articles

A. V. P. "Our Agricultural Machinery and the Problem of Its Standardization," *Socijalistička poljoprivreda* (Belgrade), February 1951, pp. 47–51.
Avramović, Mihailo. "The Agrarian Reform and the Peasant Movement," *Nova Evropa* (Zagreb), II (May 21, 1921), 244–49.
Bajkić, Velimir. "The Conflict Between Agriculture and Trade at the Seventh Convention of Businessmen," *Narodno blagostanje* (Belgrade), September 28, 1929, pp. 549–51.
———. "The Egg in the Yugoslav and in the World Economy," *Narodno blagostanje* (Belgrade), May 4, 1929, pp. 193–95.
———. "The Organization of and the Rules in the Egg Trade," *Narodno blagostanje* (Belgrade), May 11, 1929, pp. 212–13.
Benko Grado, Arthur. "Bread in Workers' Family Budgets and the Price of Bread in Zagreb During the Past 40 Years," *Indeks* (Zagreb), XII (1940), No. 1, 1–3.
Bićanić, Rudolf. "The Land to the Peasant," *Gospodarska Sloga* (Zagreb), February 15, 1940, pp. 1–2.
Bogdanov, Vaso. "The Beginning of Party-Political Life in Croatia," *Hrvatsko kolo* (Zagreb), 1951, Nos. 1–2, pp. 112–33.
Bogićević, Vojislav. "The Situation of the *Reaya* in Bosnia and Herzegovina on the Eve of the Revolt of 1875–1878," *Godišnjak Istoriskog društva Bosne i Hercegovine* (Sarajevo), II (1950), 143–84.
Božić, Ivan. "Economic and Social Development of Dubrovnik in the Fourteenth and Fifteenth Centuries," *Istoriski glasnik* (Belgrade), 1949, No. 1, pp. 21–61.
Bubić, Šerif. "Fruit Growing in Bosnia and Herzegovina" in A. Koen, *et al.* (eds.), *Bosna i Hercegovina kao privredno pudučje* (Bosnia and Herzegovina as an Economic Area) (Sarajevo, 1938), pp. 35–48.
Čemerikić, Milan. "Trade, Handicrafts, Industry, and Credit Establishments from 1875 to 1937," in Aleksa Jovanović (ed.), *Spomenica dvadesetpetogodišnjice oslobodjenja Južne Srbije, 1912–1937* (Jubilee Record of the Liberation of Southern Serbia, 1912–1937) (Skoplje, 1937), pp. 685–732.
Cijuk, Aleksandar. "Animal Husbandry," in Aleksa Jovanović (ed.), *Spomenica dvadesetpetogodišnjice oslobodjenja Južne Srbije, 1912–1937* (Jubilee Record of the Liberation of Southern Serbia, 1912–1937) (Skoplje, 1937), pp. 573–87.
Colombain, M. "Rural Hygiene and Health Co-operative Societies in Yugoslavia," *International Labour Review* (Geneva), XXXII (1935), 19–38.

Crist, Raymond E. "The Peasant Problem in Yugoslavia," *The Scientific Monthly*, May 1940, pp. 385–402.

Deny, J. "Ziamet," *The Encyclopaedia of Islam* (Leyden and London), IV (1934), 1221–22.

Deyanowa, Milka. "Die staatlichen Massnahmen zur Förderung der Ausfuhr der Agrarprodukte Bulgariens," *Weltwirtschaftliches Archiv* (Jena), LI (March 1940), No. 2, pp. 403–36.

Djurdjev, Branislav. "The *Kanun-name* for Bosnia of 1530," *Glasnik Zemaljskog muzeja u Bosni i Hercegovini* (Sarajevo), New Series, III (1948), 189–200.

————. "The *Kanun-name* of the Požega Sandjak of 1545," *Glasnik Zemaljskog muzeja u Bosni i Hercegovini* (Sarajevo), New Series, I (1946), 129–38.

————. "The *Kanun-name* of the Srijem Sandjak of 1588/89," *Glasnik Zemaljskog muzeja u Bosni i Hercegovini* (Sarajevo), New Series, IV–V (1950), 269–84.

Dobovšek, Marijan. "The Movement of Population in Carniola . . .," *Geografski vestnik* (Ljubljana), X (1934), 104–16.

Dolenc, Metod. "Slovene People's Courts in the Period from the Sixteenth to the Eighteenth Centuries," Yugoslav Academy of Science and Art, *Rad* (Zagreb), CCXXXIX (1930), 1–55.

Dugački, Zvonimir, and Šenoa, Milan, "The Settlements," in Zvonimir Dugački (ed.), *Zempljopis Hrvatske* (Geography of Croatia) (Zagreb, 1942), Pt. 2, pp. 592–608.

Dunda, J. N. "The Role of Emigrants' Remittances in the Yugoslav Balance of Payments," *Ekonomist* (Zagreb), April–May, 1940, pp. 142–54.

Ehrlich-Stein, Vera. "The Southern Slav Patriarchal Family," *The Sociological Review* (London), XXXII (July–October, 1940), Nos. 3 and 4, 224–41.

Fiamengo, Ante. "The Peasant Rebellion of 1573," *Djelo* (Zagreb), I (February 1948), 94–103.

Filipović, Milenko S. "Migrations in Search of Food," *Glasnik Geografskog društva* (Belgrade), XXVII (1947), 76–91.

Filipović, Nedim. "A *Kanun-name* of the Zvornik Sandjak," *Glasnik Zemaljskog muzeja u Bosni i Hercegovini* (Sarajevo), New Series, III (1948), 223–34.

Filipović, S. "Vlašić Mountain and the Production of Milk in Its Area," Kingdom of the Serbs, Croats, and Slovenes, Ministry of Agriculture and Water Resources, *Glasnik* (Belgrade), V (April–June, 1927), 64–95; (July–September, 1927), 1–49.

Frangeš, Otto von. "The Agrarian Reform in the Northern Areas of Yugoslavia," *Ekonomist* (Zagreb), November 1935, pp. 343–53.

Gračanin, Mihovil. "A Contribution to the Geography of Podzol Soils in Croatia," *Hrvatski geografski glasnik* (Zagreb), 1939, Nos. 8-9-10, pp. 59–61.

Grafenauer, Bogo. "A Contribution to the Critic of Constantine Porphyrogenitus on the Arrival of the Croats," *Historijski zbornik* (Zagreb), V (1952), 1–56.

Grin, Dr. Ernest I. "Study and Incidence of Endemic Syphilis in *Banovina* Drina," *Socijalno-medicinski pregled* (Belgrade), 1940, No. 1, pp. 48–54.

Gujić, Kasim. "Ali Pasha Rizvanbegović," *Nova Evropa* (Zagreb), XXIX (1936), Nos. 7–8, 244–53.

Gušić, Dr. Branimir. "Today's Herzegovina," *Nova Evropa* (Zagreb), XXIX (1936), Nos. 7–8, 202–7.

Hadžibegić, Hamid. "The *Kanun-name* for Bosnia of 1565," *Glasnik Zemaljskog muzeja u Bosni i Hercegovini* (Sarajevo), New Series, III (1948), 201–22.

Hauptmann, Ljudmil. "The Migrations of the Croats and Serbs," *Jugoslovenski istoriski časopis* (Ljubljana-Zagreb-Belgrade), III (1937), 30–61.

Heffening, W. "*Wakf*," *The Encyclopaedia of Islam* (Leyden and London), IV (1934), 1096–1103.

Hollmann, A. H. "Kolonisation und Entwicklung der Landwirtschaft in Süd-serbien (Makedonien)," Germany, Ministry for Food and Agriculture, *Berichte über Landwirtschaft* (Berlin), N.F., VIII (1928), 269–94.

Ilešič, Svetozar. "The Agrarian Overpopulation in Slovenia," *Tehnika in gos-podarstvo* (Ljubljana), VI (1940), 60–70.

Ilić, Dr. Sima. "Endemic Syphilis in Yugoslavia and Its Suppression," *Soci-jalno-medicinski pregled* (Belgrade), 1940, No. 2, pp. 128–32.

Ivanić, Dr. Stevan Z. "Malaria in Yugoslavia and Its Suppression," *Socijalno-medicinski pregled* (Belgrade), 1938, No. 4, pp. 350–59.

————. "Nutrition in Rural Areas in Serbia," *Socijalno-medicinski pregled* (Belgrade), 1936, No. 1, pp. 19–40; No. 2, pp. 73–85.

Janković, Milan, and Džuverović, Josip. "Animal Husbandry and Livestock Production in Bosnia and Herzegovina," in A. Koen, *et al.* (eds.), *Bosna i Hercegovina kao privredno područje* (Bosnia and Herzegovina as an Eco-nomic Area) (Sarajevo, 1938), pp. 49–63.

Jasny, Naum. "The Daily Bread of the Ancient Greeks and Romans," *Osiris* (Bruges, Belgium), IX (1950), 227–53.

Jovanović, Aleksa. "The Guerrilla Movement in Southern Serbia During the Turkish Rule," in Aleksa Jovanović (ed.), *Spomenica dvadesetpetogodiš-njice oslobodjenja Južne Srbije, 1912–1937* (Jubilee Record of the Libera-tion of Southern Serbia, 1912–1937) (Skoplje, 1937), pp. 271–307.

Jovanović, Dragoljub. "The Unity of the Peasant Movement," *Pregled* (Sara-jevo), XIII (July–August 1937), pp. 440–48.

Jekin, Petar. "Prune Trade in Bosnia," *Ekonomist* (Zagreb), April 1938, pp. 155–62.

Kemura, Ahmed. "Ownership by Floors in Urban Housing," *Spomenica I. Kongresa ekonomista Kraljevine Jugoslavije* (Proceedings of the First Con-vention of the Economists of the Kingdom of Yugoslavia) (Zagreb), 1937, pp. 261–71.

Konstantinović, Dr. Bogoljub. "The Problem of People's Nutrition," *Socijalno-medicinski pregled* (Belgrade), 1938, No. 3, pp. 255–65.

Konstantinović, Mihailo. "The Ideas of Valtazar Bogišić About the Customary and the Statutory Law," *Sociološki pregled* (Belgrade), I (1938), 272–82.

Kos, Milko. "History [of Slovenia]," in Anton Melik and Milko Kos, *Slovenačka* (Slovenia) (Belgrade, 1927), pp. 33–85.

Kostić, L. M. "The Population of Montenegro," in Danilo Vulović (ed.), *Cetinje i Crna Gora* (Cetinje and Montenegro) (Belgrade, 1927), pp. 278–90.

————. "The Village and the Law," Miloslav Stojadinović (ed.), *Naše selo* (Our Village) (Belgrade, 1929), pp. 250–54.

Kreševljaković, Hamdija. "Urban Economy and Guilds in Bosnia and Herze-govina from 1463 to 1851," *Godišnjak Istoriskog društva Bosne i Hercegovine* (Sarajevo), I (1949), 168–209.

Lanović, Mihajlo. "The Constitutional Law of the Croatian State Under Domestic Rulers," Yugoslav Academy of Science and Art, *Rad* (Zagreb), CCLXV (1938), 167–242; CCLXVI (1939), 1–92.

Lebl, Arpad. "Land Enclosure in Vojvodina," *Naučni zbornik Matice Srpske* (Novi Sad), I (1950), 48–71.

Lipoglavšek, Slava. "Cultivated Land in Yugoslavia," *Geografski vestnik* (Ljubljana), XVI (1940), 76–88.

Ljubić, Djuro. "Leagues and Fraternities in the Old Croatian Law and Their Relation to the Statute of Poljica," Yugoslav Academy of Science and Art, *Rad* (Zagreb), CCXL (1931), 1–104.

Mandić, Oleg. "The Class Character of the Bourgeois Theories on the Origin of the Zadruga," *Istorisko-pravni zbornik* (Sarajevo), 1950, Nos. 3–4, pp. 131–55.

Mecger, Dr. Stjepan. "The Movement of Tuberculosis Incidence in the City and County of Vinkovci," *Socijalno-medicinski pregled* (Belgrade), 1940, No. 4, pp. 422–32.

Melik, Anton. "The Density of Population in Yugoslavia," *Geografski vestnik* (Ljubljana), XVI (1940), 88–104.

———. "The Village in Slovenia," in Miloslav Stojadinović (ed.), *Naše selo* (Our Village) (Belgrade, 1929), pp. 66–68.

Miljuš, Sima. "Lard or Milk?" *Narodno blagostanje* (Belgrade), January 1, 1934, pp. 5–6.

Milošević, B. D. "The Production and Consumption of Bread Grains in Our Kingdom," Kingdom of the Serbs, Croats, and Slovenes, Ministry of Agriculture and Water Resources, *Glasnik* (Belgrade), VI (April–June 1928), 120–45.

Mirković, Mijo. "The Agricultural Proletariat in Vojvodina," *Ekonomist* (Zagreb), March 1937, pp. 114–17.

———. "Contemporary Problems of Yugoslav Agriculture," *Spomenica I. Kongresa ekonomista Kraljevine Jugoslavije* (Proceedings of the First Convention of Economists of the Kingdom of Yugoslavia) (Zagreb), 1937, pp. 123–37.

———. "Economic Relations in Trogir in the Thirteenth Century," *Historijski zbornik* (Zagreb), IV (1951), 21–54.

Mirkowich, Nicholas. "Die Bevölkerungsentwicklung Jugoslawiens und das Problem der agrarischen Übervölkerung," *Weltwirtschaftliches Archiv* (Jena), L (July 1939), No. 1, 98–144.

Mirović, Todor. "Cotton Cultivation in the Vardar Valley and Its Advancement," *Ekonomist* (Zagreb), July–August 1936, pp. 324–34.

Mitrović, Tanasije. "Production of Wool and the Improvement of Its Quality in Our Country," Yugoslavia, Ministry of Agriculture, *Arhiv* (Belgrade), I (1934), 44–71.

Mosbacher, Dr. Eduard. "The Problem of Social Medicine in an Agricultural Country in the Balkans," *Socijalno-medicinski pregled* (Belgrade), 1940, No. 2, pp. 97–114.

Mrvaljević, Milutin. "The Question of War Invalids," *Jubilarni zbornik života i rada Srba, Hrvata i Slovenaca, 1918–1928* (Jubilee Record of Life and Work of the Serbs, Croats, and Slovenes, 1918–1928) (Belgrade), II (1929), 672–81.

Niketić, Milutin J. " 'For an Improvement in Our Prune Growing,' " *Socijalistička poljoprivreda* (Belgrade), January 1952, pp. 51–54.

Nikolić, Dragiša. "Investigations of Wool Quality of Our Sheep Breeds," Yugoslavia, Federal Ministry of Agriculture and Forestry, *Arhiv za poljoprivredne nauke i tehniku* (Belgrade), II (1947), 45–68.

Novak, Viktor. "The Slavonic-Latin Symbiosis in Dalmatia During the Middle Ages," *The Slavonic and East European Review* (London), XXXII (December 1953), 1–28.

Ogrizek, Albert. "Investigations of Wool from Our Domestic Sheep Breeds . . .," University of Zagreb, *Godišnjak Sveučilišta Kraljevine Jugoslavije u Zagrebu za školske godine 1924/25–1928/29* (Yearbook of the University of Zagreb for the Academic Years 1924/25–1928/29) (Zagreb), 1929, pp. 649–74.

Ostojić, Tihomir. "Peasant Democracy," *Nova Evropa* (Zagreb), I (September 1920), 14–19.

Pejanović, Djordje. "Population of Bosnia and Herzegovina for the Past One Hundred Years, 1840–1940," *Pregled* (Sarajevo), March 1948, pp. 186–94.

Perić, Živojin M. "Obituary for Dragutin Tončić," *Arhiv za pravne i društvene nauke* (Belgrade), February 1937, pp. 198–205.

Petričević, Jure. "The Importance of Consolidation," *Gospodarska Sloga* (Zagreb), December 24, 1939, p. 5.

Petrović, Dr. Aleksandar. "A Contribution to the Study of Our Popular Medicines," *Socijalno-medicinski pregled* (Belgrade), 1939, No. 3, pp. 263–74.

———. "The Drinking of Prune Brandy in Sitnica," *Socijalno-medicinski pregled* (Belgrade), 1936, No. 2, pp. 85–93.

———. "The Nutrition of Our People: Paprika," *Socijalno-medicinski pregled* (Belgrade), 1940, No. 3, pp. 353–60.

———. "The Nutrition of Our People: Slava," *Socijalno-medicinski pregled* (Belgrade), 1939, No. 4, pp. 378–83.

———. "The Symptoms of 'Zličica,' " *Socijalno-medicinski pregled* (Belgrade), 1939, No. 2, pp. 111–26.

———. "Typhus in the Village Sjeversko," *Socijalno-medicinski pregled* (Belgrade), 1937, No. 1, pp. 27–39.

Pirc, Dr. Bojan. "Hygienic Education and Propaganda in Yugoslavia," *Socijalno-medicinski pregled* (Belgrade), 1936, No. 3, pp. 179–87.

Popović, D. J. "Vojvodina During the Turkish Rule," in D. J. Popović (ed.), *Vojvodina* (Vojvodina) (Novi Sad), 1939, pp. 145–300.

Poštić, Stjepan. "The Influence of the Distance of Parcels on the Profitability of Individual Crops and Crop Rotations on Peasant Farms in the Neighborhood of Osijek," University of Zagreb, *Godišnjak Sveučilišta Kraljevine Jugoslavije u Zagrebu za školske godine 1924/25–1928/29* (Yearbook of the University of Zagreb for the Academic Years 1924/25–1928/29) (Zagreb), 1929, pp. 577–97.

Puljo, Djordje. "The Trade in Grains and Grain Elevators," *Pravna misao* (Belgrade), May–June, 1939, pp. 234–51.

Radosavljević, Miloš. "Usury and Our Village," in Miloslav Stojadinović (ed.), *Naše selo* (Our Village) (Belgrade, 1929), pp. 553–54.

Ramzin, Dr. Sergije. "Deaths from Tuberculosis in Belgrade," *Socijalno-medicinski pregled* (Belgrade), 1936, No. 3, pp. 158–70.

Rasuhin, Dr. Josip. "On Proper Nutrition of Our People," *Socijalno-medicinski pregled* (Belgrade), 1939, No. 1, pp. 16–22.

"Report of the Conference on the Improvement of Cattle Raising," Yugoslavia, Ministry of Agriculture, *Glasnik* (Belgrade), XIV (May 1936), 176–85.

"Report of the Federal Conference on Agricultural Research," Yugoslavia, Ministry of Agriculture and Forestry, *Arhiv za poljoprivredne nauke i tehniku* (Belgrade), II (1947), No. 2, Supp.

Roganović, Blagoje. "Crop Production," in Aleksa Jovanović (ed.), *Spomenica dvadesetpetogodišnjice oslobodjenja Južne Srbije, 1912–1937* (Jubilee Record of the Liberation of Southern Serbia, 1912–1937) (Skoplje, 1937), pp. 533–59.

Roje, Marin, and Žanko, Vanja. "Wine Production in Dalmatia," *Ekonomski pregled* (Zagreb), 1950, No. 2, pp. 214–19.

Ružić, Ante. "Small Private Forest Property in Slovenia," in Aleksandar Ugrenović (ed.), *Pola stoljeća šumarstva, 1876–1926* (One-Half Century of Forest Economy, 1876–1926) (Zagreb, 1926), pp. 279–99.

Sagadin, Stevan. "Our Local Governments," *Jubilarni zbornik života i rada Srba, Hrvata i Slovenaca, 1918–1928* (Jubilee Record of Life and Work of the Serbs, Croats, and Slovenes, 1918–1928) (Belgrade), II (1929), 612–21.

———. "State Government," *Jubilarni zbornik života i rada Srba, Hrvata i Slovenaca, 1918–1928* (Jubilee Record of Life and Work of the Serbs, Croats, and Slovenes, 1918–1928) (Belgrade), I (1928), 97–110.

Schmid, Heinrich Felix. "Die Grundzüge und Grundlagen der Entwicklung des kirchlichen Zehnrechts auf kroatischem Boden während des Mittelalters," in Grga Novak (ed.), *Zbornik naučnih radova posvećen Ferdi Šišiću (Mélanges Šišić)* (Zagreb, 1929), pp. 423–54.

Schmitt, Bernadotte E. "Serbia, Yugoslavia, and the Habsburg Empire," in Robert J. Kerner (ed.), *Yugoslavia* (Berkeley and Los Angeles, 1949), pp. 41–65.

Seifert, Josef Leo. "Von Bogomil über Huss zu Lenin," *Zeitschrift für Völkerpsychologie und Soziologie* (Leipzig), III (1927), 129–58.

Šerko, Alfred. "The Karst Phenomena in Yugoslavia," *Geografski vestnik* (Ljubljana), XIX (1947), 43–66.

Setinski, Viktor. "The Meaning and Importance of Land Improvements," *Gospodarska Sloga* (Zagreb), November 15, 1939, p. 4.

Šidak, Jaroslav. "Bosnia Under Turkish Rule," *Encyclopaedia Croatica* (Zagreb), III (1942), 151–54.

———. "Revolution of 1848–49," *Historijski zbornik* (Zagreb), I (1948), 25–41.

Simić, V. T. "Popular Education," *Jubilarni zbornik života i rada Srba, Hrvata i Slovenaca, 1918–1928* (Jubilee Record of Life and Work of the Serbs, Croats, and Slovenes, 1918–1928) (Belgrade), I (1928), 410–17.

Sjelski, Dr. St. "The Village Golubić," *Socijalno-medicinski pregled* (Belgrade), 1939, No. 3, pp. 209–31.

Skarić, Vladislav. "The Census of the Bosnian Spahis of 1123 (1711)," *Glasnik Zemaljskog muzeja u Bosni i Hercegovini* (Sarajevo), XLII (1930), 1–99.

———. "The Formation and Development of Serfdom in Bosnia and Herzegovina," *Pregled* (Sarajevo), 1937, pp. 481–89.

———. "The Influence of the Turkish Rule on Social Life," *Knjiga o Balkanu* (Book on the Balkans) (Belgrade, 1937), II, 134–42.

Šmalcelj, Ivan. "Crossbreeding of Cattle," Yugoslavia, Federal Ministry of Agriculture, *Poljoprivreda* (Belgrade), 1950, Nos. 3–4, pp. 56–64.

Šobajić, Petar. "The Montenegrin Village," in Miloslav Stojadinović (ed.), *Naše selo* (Our Village) (Belgrade, 1929), pp. 69–73.

Solovjev, Aleksandar. "Grant Charters Issued by the Bosnian Rulers," *Istorisko-pravni zbornik* (Sarajevo), I (1949), 79–105.

Šoštarić-Pisačić, Karlo. "The Qualities of Our Wheats," University of Zagreb, *Godišnjak Sveučilišta Kraljevine Jugoslavije u Zagrebu za školske godine 1924/25–1928/29* (Yearbook of the University of Zagreb for the Academic Years 1924/25–1928/29) (Zagreb), 1929, pp. 513–31.

Spaić, Vojislav. "The Land Property System in Medieval Bosnia," *Istorisko-pravni zbornik* (Sarajevo), I (1949), 107–15.

Sremec, Nada. "The Dowry in Land," in Rudolf Bićanić and Željko Macan (eds.), *Kako živi narod* (How the People Live) (Zagreb, 1939), II, 173–81.

———. "Extravagance in the Village," in Rudolf Bićanić and Željko Macan (eds.), *Kako živi narod* (How the People Live) (Zagreb, 1939), II, 168–72.

Strong, Dr. Richard P. "The Anti-Typhus Campaign in 1915 in Serbia Considered in Connexion with the Present Typhus Epidemic in Poland," *International Journal of Public Health* (Geneva), I (July 1920), No. 1, 7–33.

Šusta, Josef. "Zur Geschichte und Kritik der Urbarialaufzeichnungen," Study No. 8, *Sitzungsberichte der philosophisch-historischen Classe der kaiser-lichen Akademie der Wissenschaften* (Vienna, 1898).

Taylor, Charles H. "Note on the Origin of the Polyptychs," *Mélanges d'histoire offerts à Henri Pirenne* (Brussels), II (1926), 475–81.

Tkalčić, Ivan K. "Resistance to the Church Tithe and Rebellion Against It in the Diocese of Zagreb in the Fourteenth Century," Yugoslav Academy of Science and Art, *Rad* (Zagreb), XLIX (1879), 165–230.

Todorović, Dobroslav B. "The Mechanical Analysis of the Principal Soil Types of Serbia," University of Belgrade, *Yearbook of the Faculty of Agriculture and Forestry* (Belgrade), II (1949), 7–30.

———. "The Principal Agricultural Characteristics of the Skoplje *kotlina*," University of Belgrade, *Yearbook of the Faculty of Agriculture and Forestry* (Belgrade), I (1948), 5–29.

Tošić, Milorad B. "Local Government Finances in 1930," *Narodno blagostanje* (Belgrade), February 20, 1932, pp. 118–19.

Vidakovitch, S. "Influence des conditions économiques et sociales sur la natal-ité, la morbidité et la mortalité des enfants dans les villes de Yougoslavie," *Bulletin Mensuel de l'Office International d'Hygiène Publique* (Paris), XXX (February 1938), 339–62.

Višnjić, Zvonimir. "International Sugar Agreements and the Sugar Economy of Yugoslavia," Yugoslavia, Ministry of Agriculture, *Arhiv* (Belgrade), IV (1937), 144–55.

Vrbanić, Fran. "Demographic Conditions of the South Slavs," Yugoslav Academy of Science and Art, *Rad* (Zagreb), CXXIX (1896), 172–254.

Vucinich, Alexander. "The Soviet Theory of Social Development in the Early Middle Ages," *Speculum* (Boston), XXVI (April 1951), 243–54.

Vujević, Pavle. "The Climate of the Kingdom of the Serbs, Croats, and Slovenes," in Pavle Vujević (ed.), *Recueil de travaux offert à M. Jovan Cvijić* (Belgrade, 1924), pp. 625–46.

Vukičević, Janko. "Agriculture," in Aleksa Jovanović (ed.), *Spomenica dva-desetpetogodišnjice oslobodjenja Južne Srbije, 1912–1937* (Jubilee Record of the Liberation of Southern Serbia, 1912–1937) (Skoplje, 1937), pp. 523–31.

Vukosavljević, Sreten V. "The Development of Certain Forms of Feudal Order During the Eighteenth and Nineteenth Centuries," *Letopis Matice Srpske* (Novi Sad), January–February, 1946, pp. 100–109.

Wilkinson, H. R. "Jugoslav Macedonia in Transition," *Geographical Journal* (London), CXVIII (December 1952), Pt. 4, 389–405.

INDEX

Accounting, farm, 314 n., 432–33

Adamović, L., 264 n.

Adams, J. C., 222 n.

Administrative divisions, 238–40; Map, 239

Adriatic coastal towns, 21, 53, 113–15, 119

Advancement of agriculture: barriers to, 434, 471–72; chambers of agriculture, 471; education, 460–64; government expenditures for, 695, 698; research, 464–68; societies for, 470. *See also* Technology

Agaliks, 99–101, 103, 105–6, 352–54

Agas, Bosnian. *See* Nobility

Agrarian reform, after 1918: appraisal of, 369–81; basic decree, 347–50; "elective purchases," 362–63, 366; general objectives, 381–82; indemnity for expropriated land, 347–49, 353–55, 357, 359–60, 363, 365–66, 380–81; "land belongs to those who till it," 38–42, 344, 423; land involved by provinces, 355–56, 361, 366–69; large estates defined, 348, 364; party politics and, 345, 350–51, 379; political climate surrounding it, 230–32, 344–49; proclamations regarding, 345–47; and volunteers' bonus, 346, 348–49, 380

Agrarian reforms, before 1918: Bosnia, 101, 104–7; Croatia-Slavonia, 82, 84–87; Dalmatia, 118; Macedonia, 124–25; Serbia, 38–41; Slovenia, 131; Vojvodina, 136, 169

Agricultural credit, 42–46, 165–67, 186–87, 248–49, 648–49; consolidation of peasant debts, 675–79; credit co-operatives, 614, 648, 650–53, 660–61, 673; government organizations for small, cheap credits, 648–50; interest rates, 656–58; moratorium for peasant debts, 669–71; organization of, before 1918, 646–53; peasant debts in 1932, 655, 671–75; and protected minimum homestead, 414–20; sources of, 658–67, 673; uses of, 653–56; usury, 43–44, 406, 409–10, 648–49, 661

Agricultural households: approximate annual growth of, 397; increase in number during interwar period, 306–7, 333; and need for housing, 580–81, 654–55, 687

Agricultural industries, 138, 611–14, 627

Agricultural overpopulation: beginnings of, 158, 211, 213, 433; in Bulgaria, Rumania, and Yugoslavia compared, 316–18; compared by *banovine*, 321–26; indicated "surplus" population, 312–19, 321–26; indicators of, 310–15, 318–19; Moore's studies of, 280 n., 312–14; population–cultivated land standard ratio accepted in this study, 315; remedies for, 327–43; socioeconomic and political consequences of, 319–21, 433–34; underutilization of farm labor, 312–19, 321–26, 450–57. *See also* Agricultural population, Cultivated land

Agricultural policy, 425–27

Agricultural population: growth during interwar period, 303–7; infant mortality in rural areas, 293; landless in Vojvodina and Slovenia, 386, 393; related to cultivated land and livestock by *banovine*, 321–26; and in selected European countries, 308–10, 316–18. *See also* Agricultural overpopulation, Land resources

Agricultural regions, 284–86, 351–52, 431, 552–55

Agricultural research, 464–68

Agriculture and business cycles, 176–77, 635–45, 667–71, 677–81, 684–85. *See also* Business cycles

Agronomists, 462–63, 470

Alcohol, industrial: admixture to motor fuel, 613; excise tax, 689; export subsidy, 628; production, 489, 545, 612

Alcoholic beverages. *See* Wine, Grapes, Vineyards

Alexander, King of Yugoslavia, 219, 240, 243, 244 n., 347, 663, 684, 694

Ali Čauš of Sofia, 23 n.

Alluvial soil, 272

Alod land, 13–18, 60–62, 85–86, 91–92

Alps, in Yugoslavia, 262

Anderson, Oskar N., 602 n., 702 n.

Andrássy, Count Julius, 107 n.

Animal draft power in agriculture, 191, 430, 457–60, 515, 524–25. *See also* Tractors

Animal food products: consumption, 543, 548–51, 558; exports, 286, 535, 620–21;